Lecture Notes in Computer Science 11845

More information about this series at http://www.springer.com/series/7412

George Bebis · Richard Boyle ·
Bahram Parvin · Darko Koracin ·
Daniela Ushizima · Sek Chai ·
Shinjiro Sueda · Xin Lin ·
Aidong Lu · Daniel Thalmann ·
Chaoli Wang · Panpan Xu (Eds.)

Advances in
Visual Computing

14th International Symposium on Visual Computing, ISVC 2019
Lake Tahoe, NV, USA, October 7–9, 2019
Proceedings, Part II

 Springer

Editors
George Bebis
University of Nevada
Reno, NV, USA

Bahram Parvin
University of Nevada
Reno, NV, USA

Daniela Ushizima
Lawrence Berkeley
National Laboratory
Berkeley, CA, USA

Shinjiro Sueda
Texas A&M University
College Station, TX, USA

Aidong Lu
University of North Carolina
at Charlotte
Charlotte, NC, USA

Chaoli Wang
Notre Dame University
Notre Dame, IN, USA

Richard Boyle
NASA Ames Research Center
Moffett Field, CA, USA

Darko Koracin
Desert Research Institute
Reno, NV, USA

Sek Chai
Latent AI
Palo Alto, CA, USA

Xin Lin
Louisiana State University
Baton Rouge, LA, USA

Daniel Thalmann
École Polytechnique Fédérale
de Lausanne
Lausanne, Switzerland

Panpan Xu
Bosch Research North America
Palo Alto, CA, USA

ISSN 0302-9743   ISSN 1611-3349 (electronic)
Lecture Notes in Computer Science
ISBN 978-3-030-33722-3   ISBN 978-3-030-33723-0 (eBook)
https://doi.org/10.1007/978-3-030-33723-0

LNCS Sublibrary: SL6 – Image Processing, Computer Vision, Pattern Recognition, and Graphics

This Springer imprint is published by the registered company Springer Nature Switzerland AG
The registered company address is: Gewerbestrasse 11, 6330 Cham, Switzerland

Preface

It is with great pleasure that we welcome you to the proceedings of the 14th International Symposium on Visual Computing (ISVC 2019), which was held in Lake Tahoe, Nevada, USA, during October 7–9, 2019. ISVC provides a common umbrella for the four main areas of visual computing including vision, graphics, visualization, and virtual reality. The goal is to provide a forum for researchers, scientists, engineers, and practitioners throughout the world to present their latest research findings, ideas, developments, and applications in the broader area of visual computing.

This year, the program consisted of 13 oral sessions, 2 special tracks, 3 tutorials, and 6 keynote presentations. We received 163 submissions from which we accepted 62 papers for oral presentation and 29 papers for poster presentation. Special track papers were solicited separately through the Organizing and Program Committees of each track. A total of 9 papers were accepted for oral presentation in the special tracks.

All papers were reviewed with an emphasis on the potential to contribute to the state of the art in the field. Selection criteria included accuracy and originality of ideas, clarity and significance of results, and presentation quality. The review process was quite rigorous, involving three independent blind reviews followed by several days of discussion. During the discussion period we tried to correct anomalies and errors that might have existed in the initial reviews. Despite our efforts, we recognize that some papers worthy of inclusion may have not been included in the program. We offer our sincere apologies to authors whose contributions might have been overlooked.

We wish to thank everybody who submitted their work to ISVC 2019 for review. It was because of their contributions that we succeeded in having a technical program of high scientific quality. In particular, we would like to thank the ISVC 2019 area chairs, the organizing institutions, the industrial sponsors, the international Program Committee, the special track organizers and their Program Committees, the keynote speakers, the reviewers, and especially the authors who contributed their work to the symposium. In particular, we would like to express our appreciation to Springer for sponsoring the Best Paper Award this year.

We sincerely hope that ISVC 2019 offered participants opportunities for professional growth.

September 2019

George Bebis
Richard Boyle
Darko Koracin
Bahram Parvin
Daniela Ushizima
Sek Chai
Shinjiro Sueda
Xin Li
Aidong Lu
Daniel Thalmann
Chaoli Wang
Panpan Xu

Organization

Steering Committee

George Bebis   University of Nevada, Reno, USA
Richard Boyle   NASA Ames Research Center, USA
Bahram Parvin   University of Nevada, Reno, USA
Darko Koracin   Desert Research Institute, USA,
                                 and University of Zagreb, Croatia

Area Chairs

Computer Vision

Daniela Ushizima   Lawrence Berkeley National Lab, USA
Sek Chai   Latent AI, USA

Computer Graphics

Shinjiro Sueda   Texas A&M University, USA
Xin Li   Louisiana State University, USA

Virtual Reality

Aidong Lu   UNC Charlotte, USA
Daniel Thalmann   École Polytechnique Fédérale de Lausanne,
                                 Switzerland

Visualization

Chaoli Wang   Notre Dame University, USA
Panpan Xu   Bosch Research North America, USA

Publicity Chair

Ali Erol   Eksperta Software, Turkey

Local Arrangements Chair

Alireza Tavakkoli   University of Nevada, Reno, USA

Special Tracks Chairs

Gholamreza Amayeh   Arraiy, USA
Zehang Sun   Apple, USA

Tutorials Chairs

Fabien Scalzo	UCLA, USA
Emily Hand	University of Nevada, Reno, USA

Awards Chairs

Amol Ambardekar	Microsoft, USA
Leandro Loss	Quantaverse, USA

Web Master

Isayas Berhe Adhanom	University of Nevada, Reno, USA

Program Committee

Emmanuel Agu	Worcester Polytechnic Institute, USA
Touqeer Ahmad	LUMS, Pakistan
Kostas Alexis	University of Nevada, Reno, USA
Amol Ambardekar	Microsoft, USA
Mehdi Ammi	University of Paris 8, France
Mark Apperley	University of Waikato, New Zealand
Antonis Argyros	Foundation for Research and Technology – Hellas, Greece
Vijayan K. Asari	University of Dayton, USA
Vassilis Athitsos	University of Texas at Arlington, USA
Melinos Averkiou	University of Cyprus, Cyprus
George Baciu	The Hong Kong Polytechnic University, Hong Kong, China
Selim Balcisoy	Sabanci University, Turkey
Reneta Barneva	SUNY Fredonia, USA
Ronen Barzel	Independent, UK
George Bebis	University of Nevada, Reno, USA
Michael Behrisch	Tufts University, USA
Alexander Belyaev	Heriot-Watt University, UK
Jan Bender	RWTH Aachen University, Germany
Bedrich Benes	Purdue University, USA
Ayush Bhargava	Clemson University, USA
Harsh Bhatia	Lawrence Livermore National Laboratory, USA
Sanjiv Bhatia	University of Missouri–St. Louis, USA
Ankur Bist	Govind Ballabh Pant University of Agriculture and Technology, India
Ayan Biswas	Los Alamos National Laboratory, USA
Dibio Borges	Universidade de Brasília, Brazil
Alexandra Branzan Albu	University of Victoria, Canada
Jose Braz Pereira	EST Setúbal/IPS, Portugal

Valentin Brimkov	Buffalo State College, USA
Gerd Bruder	University of Central Florida, USA
Tolga Capin	TED University, Turkey
Sek Chai	SRI International, USA
Jian Chang	Bournemouth University, UK
Sotirios Chatzis	Cyprus University of Technology, Cyprus
Aashish Chaudhary	Kitware Inc., USA
Abon Chaudhuri	WalmartLabs, USA
Rama Chellappa	University of Maryland, USA
Jie Chen	University of Oulu, Finland
Yang Chen	HRL Laboratories, LLC, USA
Zhonggui Chen	Xiamen University, China
Yi-Jen Chiang	New York University, USA
Isaac Cho	UNC Charlotte, USA
Min Choi	University of Colorado Denver, USA
Amit Chourasia	San Diego Supercomputer Center, UCSD, USA
Kichung Chung	Oracle Corporation
Sabine Coquillart	Inria, France
Adam Czajka	Warsaw University of Technology, Poland
Aritra Dasgupta	NYU, USA
Jeremie Dequidt	University of Lille, France
Sotirios Diamantas	Tarleton State University, USA
Alexandra Diehl	University of Konstanz, Germany
Cosimo Distante	CNR, Italy
Choukri Djellali	UQÀM- UQAR LATECE, Canada
Ralf Doerner	RheinMain University of Applied Sciences, Germany
Gianfranco Doretto	West Virginia University, USA
Anastasios Doulamis	Technical University of Crete, Greece
Ye Duan	University of Missouri at Columbia, USA
Soumya Dutta	Los Alamos National Laboratory, USA
Achim Ebert	University of Kaiserslautern, Germany
Mohamed El Ansari	University of Ibn Zohr, Morocco
Mark Elendt	Side Effects Software Inc., Canada
Luis Miguel Encarnacao	Innovation by Design Intl. Consulting, USA
Barrett Ens	Monash University, Australia
Alireza Entezari	University of Florida, USA
Ali Erol	Sigun Information Technologies, UK
Thomas Ertl	University of Stuttgart, Germany
Mohammad Eslami	Technical University of Munich, Germany
Mona Fathollahi	University of South Florida, USA
Matteo Ferrara	University of Bologna, Italy
Nivan Ferreira	Universidade Federal de Pernambuco, Brazil
Francesco Ferrise	Politecnico di Milano, Italy
Rony Ferzli	Intel, USA
Julian Fierrez	Universidad Autonoma de Madrid, Spain
Gian Luca Foresti	University of Udine, Italy

Steffen Frey	Visualisierunsginstitut der Universität Stuttgart, Germany
Ioannis Fudos	University of Ioannina, Greece
Issei Fujishiro	Keio University, Japan
Xifeng Gao	Florida State University, USA
M. Gavrilova	University of Calgary, Canada
Krzysztof Gdawiec	University of Silesia, Poland
Robert Geist	Clemson University, USA
Gurman Gill	Sonoma State University, USA
Daniela Giorgi	ISTI – CNR, Italy
Randy Goebel	University of Alberta, Canada
Wooi-Boon Goh	Nanyang Technological University, Singapore
Roberto Grosso	Friedrich-Alexander-Universität Erlangen-Nürnberg, Germany
Miguel Angel Guevara Lopez	Computer Graphics Center, Portugal
Hanqi Guo	Argonne National Laboratory, USA
Rongkai Guo	Kennesaw State University, USA
David Gustafson	Kansas State University, USA
Riad Hammoud	Delphi, UK
Felix Hamza-Lup	Georgia Southern University, USA
Emily Hand	University of Nevada, Reno, USA
Xuejun Hao	Columbia University, USA
Mohammad Ahsanul Haque	Aalborg University, Denmark
Brandon Haworth	York University, UK
Harry Hochheiser	University of Pittsburgh, USA
Ludovic Hoyet	Inria Rennes - Centre Bretagne Atlantique, France
Muhammad Hussain	King Saud University, Saudi Arabia
José A. Iglesias Guitián	Universitat Autònoma de Barcelona, Spain
Atsushi Imiya	IMIT Chiba University, Japan
Kei Iwasaki	Wakayama University, Japan
Yun Jang	Sejong University, South Korea
Michael Jenkin	York University, UK
Stefan Jeschke	NVIDIA, USA
Ming Jiang	LLNL, USA
Anshul Joshi	University of Utah, USA
Stefan Jänicke	Leipzig University, Germany
Rossi Kamal	IROBIX
Chandra Kambhamettu	University of Delaware, USA
Martin Kampel	Vienna University of Technology, Austria
Takashi Kanai	The University of Tokyo, Japan
Kenichi Kanatani	Okayama University, Japan
David Kao	NASA, USA
Edward Kim	Drexel University, USA
Hyungseok Kim	Konkuk University, South Korea

Min H. Kim	Korea Advanced Institute of Science and Technology, South Korea
Benjamin Kimia	Brown University, USA
James Klosowski	AT&T Labs Research, USA
Steffen Koch	University of Stuttgart, Germany
Elena Kokkinara	Inflight VR, Spain
Stefanos Kollias	National Technical University of Athens, Greece
Dimitris Kosmopoulos	University of Patras, Greece
Igor Kozintsev	Facebook, USA
Jens Krueger	SCI Institute, USA
Arjan Kuijper	TU Darmstadt, Germany
Yoshinori Kuno	Saitama University, Japan
Tsz Ho Kwok	Concordia University, Canada
Hung La	University of Nevada, Reno, USA
Yu-Kun Lai	Cardiff University, UK
Robert S. Laramee	Swansea University, UK
D. J. Lee	Brigham Young University, UK
Robert R. Lewis	Washington State University, USA
Frederick Li	University of Durham, UK
Xin Li	Louisiana State University, USA
Jie Liang	Sydney University of Technology, Australia
Kuo-Chin Lien	XMotors.ai, USA
Chun-Cheng Lin	National Chiao Tung University, Taiwan
Stephen Lin	Microsoft
Peter Lindstrom	LLNL, USA
Lars Linsen	Westfälische Wilhelms-Universität Münster, Germany
Zhanping Liu	Old Dominion University, USA
Manuel Loaiza	Universidad Católica San Pablo, Peru
Benjamin Lok	University of Florida, USA
Leandro Loss	QuantaVerse, ITU, ESSCA
Joern Loviscach	University of Applied Sciences, Germany
Aidong Lu	UNC Charlotte, USA
Xun Luo	Tianjin University of Technology, China
Brendan Macdonald	NIOSH, USA
Anthony Maeder	Flinders University, Australia
Sokratis Makrogiannis	Delaware State University, USA
Luigi Malomo	ISTI – CNR, Italy
Rafael M. Martins	Linnaeus University, Sweden
Yoshitaka Masutani	Hiroshima City University, Japan
Kresimir Matkovic	VRVis Research Center, Austria
Stephen Maybank	Birkbeck, UK
Tim Mcgraw	Purdue University, USA
Qurban Memon	UAE University, UAE
Daniel Mestre	Aix-Marseille University, France
Xikui Miao	Brigham Young University, UK
Gabriel Mistelbauer	Otto-von-Guericke University, Germany

Filip Sadlo	Heidelberg University, Germany
Punam Saha	University of Iowa, USA
Naohisa Sakamoto	Kobe University, Japan
Kristian Sandberg	Computational Solutions, Inc., USA
Allen Sanderson	SCI Institute, USA
Alberto Santamaría-Pang	General Electric Research, USA
Nickolas S. Sapidis	University of Western Macedonia, Greece
Muhammad Sarfraz	Kuwait University, Kuwait
Andreas Savakis	Rochester Institute of Technology, USA
Jacob Scharcanski	UFRGS, Brazil
Thomas Schultz	University of Bonn, Germany
Mohamed Shehata	Memorial University, USA
Yun Sheng	East China Normal University, China
Gurjot Singh	Fairleigh Dickinson University, USA
Sandra Skaff	NVIDIA, USA
Alexei Skurikhin	Los Alamos National Laboratory, USA
Pavel Slavik	Czech Technical University in Prague, Czech Republic
Dmitry Sokolov	Université de Lorraine, France
Fabio Solari	University of Genoa – DIBRIS, Italy
Paolo Spagnolo	National Research Council, Italy
Jaya Sreevalsan-Nair	IIIT Bangalore, India
Diane Staheli	Massachusetts Institute of Technology, USA
Chung-Yen Su	National Taiwan Normal University, Taiwan
Shinjiro Sueda	Texas A&M University, USA
Changming Sun	CSIRO, Australia
Guodao Sun	Zhejiang University of Technology, China
Zehang Sun	Apple inc., USA
Tanveer Syeda-Mahmood	IBM, USA
Carlo H. Séquin	University of California, Berkeley, USA
Ahmad Tafti	Mayo Clinic, USA
Alireza Tavakkoli	University of Nevada, Reno, USA
João Manuel R. S. Tavares	INEGI, University of Porto, Portugal
Daniel Thalmann	École Polytechnique Fédérale de Lausanne, Switzerland
Holger Theisel	Otto-von-Guericke University, Germany
Yan Tong	University of South Carolina, USA
Thomas Torsney-Weir	Swansea University, UK
Stefano Tubaro	Politecnico di Milano, Italy
Georg Umlauf	HTWG Konstanz, Germany
Daniela Ushizima	Lawrence Berkeley National Laboratory, USA
Dimitar Valkov	University of Muenster, Germany
Jonathan Ventura	California Polytechnic State University San Luis Obispo, USA
Athanasios VouVoulodimos	National Technical University of Athens, Greece
Chaoli Wang	University of Notre Dame, USA
Michel Westenberg	Eindhoven University of Technology, The Netherlands

Benjamin Weyers	Trier University, Germany
Alexander Wiebel	Worms University of Applied Sciences, Germany
Thomas Wischgoll	Wright State University, USA
Kin Hong Wong	The Chinese University of Hong Kong, Hong Kong, China
Panpan Xu	Bosch Research North America, USA
Wei Xu	Brookhaven National Lab, USA
Goshiro Yamamoto	Kyoto University, Japan
Xiaosong Yang	Bournemouth University, UK
Yueming Yang	Baldwin Wallace University, USA
Hsu-Chun Yen	National Taiwan University, Taiwan
Lijun Yin	State University of New York at Binghamton, USA
Zeyun Yu	University of Wisconsin-Milwaukee, USA
Chunrong Yuan	Technische Hochschule Köln, Germany
Xiaoru Yuan	Peking University, China
Xenophon Zabulis	FORTH-ICS, Greece
Jiri Zara	Czech Technical University in Prague, Czech Republic
Wei Zeng	Florida International University, USA
Dong Zhang	NVIDIA, USA
Zhao Zhang	Hefei University of Technology, China
Ye Zhao	Kent State University, USA
Yuanjie Zheng	Shandong Normal University, China
Changqing Zou	University of Maryland, USA

Special Tracks

ST1: Vision for Remote Sensing and Infrastructure Inspection

Hung M. La	University of Nevada, Reno, USA
Alireza Tavakkoli	University of Nevada, Reno, USA
Trung-Dung Ngo	University of Prince Edward Island, Canada
Trung H. Duong	Colorado State University-Pueblo, USA

ST2: Computational Vision, AI and Mathematical Methods for Biomedical and Biological Image Analysis

| Sokratis Makrogiannis | Delaware State University, USA |
| Alberto Santamaria-Pang | General Electric Global Research, USA |

Tutorials

T1: Analysis and Visualization of 3D Data in Python

Daniela Ushizima	Berkeley Institute for Data Science, UC Berkeley, USA
Alexandre de Siqueira	Berkeley Institute for Data Science, UC Berkeley, USA
Stéfan van der Walt	Berkeley Institute for Data Science, UC Berkeley, USA

T2: Computer Vision for Underwater Environmental Monitoring

Alexandra Branzan Albu   Electrical and Computer Engineering,
                            University of Victoria, Canada

Maia Hoeberechts   Ocean Networks Canada, Canada

T3: Visual Object Tracking Using Deep Learning

Mohamed H. Abdelpakey   Memorial University of Newfoundland,
                            St. John's, Canada

Mohamed S. Shehata   Memorial University of Newfoundland,
                            St. John's, Canada

Additional Reviewers

Ahmed, Habib
Alderighi, Thomas
Grießer, Dennis
Han, Jun
Hazarika, Subhashis
Heinemann, Moritz
Helm, Daniel
Hermann, Matthias
Hong, Seokpyo
Huang, Jida
Li, Yan Ran
Loizou, Marios
Mera Trujillo, Marcela

Muralidharan, Lakshmi Priya
Nayeem, Raihan
Nefian, Ara
Oagaz, Hawkar
Parakkat, Amal Dev
Penk, Dominik
Pulido, Jesus
Sabri, Sinan
Schoun, Breawn
Shead, Timothy
Vrigkas, Michalis
Wang, Li

Sponsors

 MITSUBISHI ELECTRIC RESEARCH LABORATORIES

Contents – Part II

Virtual Reality II

Object Recognition/Detection/Categorization

Posters

Contents – Part I

xxiv   Contents – Part I

Segmentation/Recognition

Video Analysis and Event Recognition

Visualization

Virtual Reality I

Applications I

Applications II

Dual Snapshot Hyperspectral Imaging System for 41-Band Spectral Analysis and Stereo Reconstruction

Fatih Tanriverdi[(⊠)], Dennis Schuldt[(⊠)], and Jörg Thiem[(⊠)]

University of Applied Sciences and Arts Dortmund, Dortmund, Germany
{fatih.tanriverdi,dennis.schuldt,joerg.thiem}@fh-dortmund.de

Abstract. This paper deals with a novel hyperspectral imaging system based on a stereo camera arrangement. The spectral specifications of both cameras are complement to each other. Therefore, a total of 41 bands are available for the visual and near infrared range. The combined usage of different HSI cameras allow 3D reconstruction as well as the spectral analysis. For each pixel, there are 41 features that describe the location with spectral information. A geometrical alignment, radiometric calibration and normalization is needed to perform accurate measurements. Furthermore, the developed system will be evaluated with regard to its applicability for medical assistance functions.

Keywords: Hyperspectral imaging · Band alignment · Stereo reconstruction · Spectral analysis · Snapshot

1 Introduction

In modern medicine, spatial and spectral analysis methods are often used separately from each other. Today stereo camera systems have been used for 3D reconstruction in e.g. robotic and automotive applications. In pathology spectral analysis methods have even been established much earlier and are an important part of the diagnosis. The importance of these two topics underline the current research in this field [1–4]. The combination of these two technologies is a novel way to apply them in the field of medical image analysis. Prior research work [5–8] about this topic deals with the field of autonomous vehicle guidance, phenotyping of plants or large-area environment detection. All of them are using hyperspectral imaging (HSI) to obtain the spectrum for each pixel in the image. The used hyperspectral camera systems are considerably larger, not capable of real-time processing and therefore unsuitable for most medical applications. Only the published work of the Fraunhofer Institute [5] uses a camera comparable to the one used in this paper. However, Heide et al. apply this technology in the context of autonomous driving and concentrate on the implementation of a stereo matching algorithm on a GPU. Our work is focusing on the design of a hyperspectral stereo camera system with a broad spectral range. The aim of this

© Springer Nature Switzerland AG 2019
G. Bebis et al. (Eds.): ISVC 2019, LNCS 11845, pp. 3–13, 2019.
https://doi.org/10.1007/978-3-030-33723-0_1

work is to align the bands of two different sensors, to calibrate the system using the different spectral bands and to evaluate the accuracy based on measurements of Euclidean distances in order to derive conclusions for applicability in medical applications.

The content of this paper covers the description of the used hardware and the required experimental setup, followed by the methodological aspects for the correct interpretation of the considered data and finally the results, which are first presented, then discussed and closed by an outlook about the next challenges in future work.

2 Materials

In this section, the hardware and the required experimental setup is described.

2.1 Reference Target

One preprocessing step requires the use of a white reference board, see Sect. 3.2 for details. We used a white balance target from X-Rite [9] to obtain an accurate white level reproduction. This is an important step for further calculations and cross sensor comparisons. The target reflectance is near-constant between 470 nm and 1000 nm at around $46\% \pm 2\%$, which provides a neutral reference point across different lighting conditions that could be encountered during image acquisition.

2.2 Illumination

When using a hyperspectral camera the light source on the target has a high influence on the captured data, which in turn has to be considered when interpreting the data. First of all the spectral response of the camera is a key property. Secondly, it is important to choose an illumination type, which can stimulate the given spectral wavelengths. In this work, we focused on two different spectral ranges. This requires a light source, which is nearly constant and homogeneous over the complete spectral range of both cameras. Besides daylight, appropriate lighting is also a halogen light source.

2.3 Hyperspectral Camera System

This section introduces our camera hardware, the SSM4 × 4 and SSM5 × 5. The SSM4 × 4 hyperspectral imaging camera systems is based on the intelligent camera platform D3 by VRmagic [10]. This platform is an industrial type camera solution with high computing power on board. The DaVinci processor by Texas Instruments combines a 1 GHz 32-bit ARM Cortex-A8 processor and a C674x DSP core running at 700 MHz. The ARM core runs a custom headless Ubuntu operation system. Complex image processing tasks can be solved efficiently on board.

The second key feature of SSM4 × 4 and SSM5 × 5 are the hyperspectral sensors manufactured by imec. The base of these sensors are common CMOS sensors, CMV2000 by CMOSIS, with a resolution of 2048 × 1088. On top of the sensor array are interference based optical filters, which are added at the wafer level. The used interferometer design are Fabry-Pérot etalon filters, which are monolithically integrated, for each pixel, on the imager. The resulting wavelength sensitivity for the SSM4 × 4 is between 470 nm and 635 nm and 670 nm up to 950 nm for the SSM5 × 5. Two parallel mirror surfaces are reflecting the light several times [11]. If the mirror distance L is firmly defined (etalon), the incoming light rays λ are transmitted upon fulfilment of the resonance condition (1).

$$k\lambda = 2L; k \in \mathbb{N} \tag{1}$$

The 16 different spectral bands are the result of the Fabry-Pérot etalon filters, which are arranged in a 4 × 4 mosaic pattern on the sensor. Each element of the mosaic pattern corresponds to one specific spectral band. To cover the whole sensor surface, the mosaic pattern is repeated 256 times for the height and 512 times for the width of the sensor. The rest of the sensor is not used. Hence, the usable area is smaller than the sensor area. The SSM4 × 4 is able to capture spectral and spatial information in one shot with up to 340 hyperspectral cubes per second. This method is also referred to as a snapshot sensor. In this work, all measurements were performed with the integration time set to 30 ms with a bit depth of 8-bit. The integration time is adjusted when taking the reference image for the radiometric calibration in Sect. 3.2 to keep the magnitude of the spectral response of the hyperspectral camera within the maximum range. Further components used are lenses and filters according to the spectral specifications. The composition of the final spectral response R of SSM4 × 4 can be computed by Eq. (2). The same basic structure applies to the SSM5 × 5, only adapted to a 5 × 5 pattern. This leads to 25 different spectral bands, which are repeated 216 times over the height and 409 times over the width of the sensor.

$$R(\lambda) = R_{\text{SSM4}\times4}(\lambda) \cdot R_{\text{filters}}(\lambda) \tag{2}$$

2.4 Hyperspectral Stereo Setting

For the dual snapshot system we set up our two single HSI cameras as a horizontal stereo system as shown in Fig. 1. We used well-established methods to calibrate the stereo rig based on [12,13]. Our calibration target is a 9 × 6 checkerboard which can be captured by both HSI cameras in the VIS and NIR spectra under normal daylight, therefore eliminating the need for a controlled illumination method. The necessary intrinsic and extrinsic camera parameters that are needed for the characterization of the stereo camera system are estimated. The baseline is fixed at about 70 mm, which leads to a working range of about 20 cm to 50 cm while the disparity range is between 130 px–200 px. This is highly specific to the test objects, which will be analyzed by such a system. Our calibrated system achieves a re-projection error of about 0.08 px, this extremely low value is explained by the low image resolutions of the images (per band) and the distance to the calibration target. Our current research is focused on static test scenes but nonetheless, another important topic is the synchronization of both cameras. In our case, this is ensured by the use of trigger signals (I/O ports).

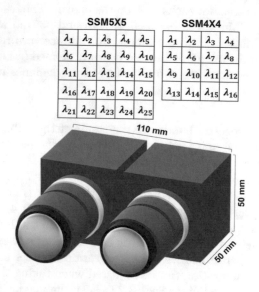

Fig. 1. Setup of HSI stereo camera system

3   Method

This section deals with the used methods that are important for the correct interpretation of the data.

3.1   Geometrical Alignment

RGB cameras are using various variants of a Bayer filter, which is a color filter array for arranging RGB color filters on an image sensor. In its original form the Bayer filter is covered with a color filter, which usually consists of 50% green and 25% red and 25% blue. One color pixel consists of four subpixels, two green, one red and one blue pixel. This mosaic pattern has the size of a 2×2 grid. Each subpixel provides information for a single color component, so that for a complete image with the same dimensions, the adjacent pixels of the same color must be used for color interpolation. This is based on the assumption that there are only minor color differences in the image between two adjacent pixels of the same color and that the gray values of the pixels are stochastically dependent of each other. Of course, this does not have to apply to every object in an image.

The process of color interpolation is also known as demosaicing. Sub-sampling, despite subsequent interpolation, can cause interferences at edges or thin lines in an image, which can be noticeable by Moiré patterns in the image [14]. Various interpolation methods were tested in [15]. As already described in Sect. 2.3 to sample more than three wavelength bands our image sensors use a hyperspectral filter array. Therefore, the demosaicing algorithm has to be adapted. In [16] a review, over several demosaicing methods for image sensors, with more than three bands, is given. As well as a new method called pseudo-panchromatic image difference (PPID). The work of Mihoubi et al. is using multispectral images of a simulated acquisition process based on an imec sensor with the goal to compare the demosaicing performance between a simulated snapshot camera and an ideal camera with no inter-band overlapping. The demosaicing methods, which are compared are evaluated by peak signal-to-noise ratio (PSNR) and computation time. The results show that the proposed PPID outperforms the established algorithms in terms of PSNR and in visual assessment. However, the computational time is approximately eight times higher than the simple well-known approach of interpolation. Due to the higher computation time, we are focusing on established interpolation methods.

3.2 Preprocessing

Hyperspectral imaging systems consist of many different highly sensitive optical and electronic components. Generally, such systems require corrections by spectral preprocessing and calibration before being able to perform reliable data analysis. In [17] the main goals for calibration are wavelength alignment and assignment, converting from radiance values received at the sensor to reflectance values of the target surface, and the reduction of random sensor noise. The calibration of the wavelength is done by imec themselves and is provided with every sensor. By using the corresponding calibration file, the assignment of a discrete wavelength to the hyperspectral image band is not necessary. Consequently, the extraction of information from hyperspectral images to associate the correct wavelengths to the observed target is ensured.

Radiometric Calibration. The radiometric calibration is one of the most important preprocessing steps that are necessary. Before preprocessing the radiance, it is called uncorrected radiance. The uncorrected radiance is not even the same when capturing the same target under the same imaging conditions with different hyperspectral imaging systems. A radiometric calibration of hyperspectral image data is required to perform a comparison with other sensors. This also ensures that radiometric calibration facilitates the transfer of results and findings from one study to other similar studies. Additionally, the radiometric calibration process reduces errors due to uncorrected data. Finally, this preprocessing step leads to the ability of spectra comparison with other spectra measurements of known materials, to isolate absorption characteristics and to link them to chemical compounds and physical attributes of materials. The most common process for radiometric calibration encompass a pixel-by-pixel calibration of hyperspectral image data to percentage of reflectance. Usually in earth remote sensing, which is one of the origins of hyperspectral camera technology, the solar radiation is the only target illumination that exists. This leads to an inevitable influence of the atmosphere. Therefore, in earth remote sensing one of the major parts is the calibration of hyperspectral data by space hyperspectral imagery systems. In lab-based environments, such a correction is usually not necessary. The main goal of radiometric calibration in this case is to reduce the inherent spatial non-uniform artificial light intensity on the target. Moreover, the compensation of non-constant artificial light intensity is a part of the radiometric calibration [17]. The approach consists of recording the reference image $I_{\text{reference}}$ of a white balance target, followed by a dark current image I_{dark} and finally the target image I_{target}. Thereafter, the Eq. (3) can be applied [18].

$$I_{\text{corrected},i\lambda} = \frac{I_{\text{target},i\lambda} - I_{\text{dark},i\lambda}}{I_{\text{reference},i\lambda} - I_{\text{dark},i\lambda}} \cdot c_{i\lambda} \tag{3}$$

Here c is the correction factor for the reference image, which depends on the reflectance characteristic of the white balance target. The pixel position on the image is indexed by i and λ specifies the wavelengths.

Radiometric Normalization. An additional preprocessing step is applied to standardize input data and to offset light variations in the reflectance data. In the work of Cheng et al. [19] it is shown that apples with different intensity of dark-colored surface lead to detection errors. Especially bright-colored defective apples could be easily confused with dark-colored good apples. To solve this issue data normalization was applied to the original images I_{original}. Several normalization implementations are mentioned in [17] like [20] and [21]. Here we used the normalization approach (4) of Cheng et al. in [19], where $I_{\text{max},\lambda}$ is the maximum value in the image and c_0 is equal to the highest gray value in 8-bit images (here: 255).

$$I_{\text{norm},i\lambda} = \frac{I_{\text{original},i\lambda}}{I_{\text{max},\lambda}} \cdot c_0 \tag{4}$$

3.3   Dual Hyperspectral Imaging System

This section discusses the technical basis for the evaluation of the system in Sect. 4. For the stereo calibration, it is sufficient to do the calibration only once, if the above-mentioned geometric alignment has been performed successfully. It is therefore an essential step for further processing. It reduces the total effort to a single stereo calibration instead of calibrating each band of each camera in all combinations. It also reduces complexity, time, and the number of stereo parameters to be considered. The investigations have shown that the first bands of both cameras are used for stereo calibration. By aligning all other bands with the first band, it is ensured that the stereo parameters are also valid for the other bands. This also extends the validity of the stereo parameters for any combination of the bands of both cameras. This will be proven in the following section with evaluated data.

4   Results

Primarily, both cameras must be interpolated individually and aligned by itself. This creates the basis for the stereo system. The geometric alignment described in Sect. 3.1 is applied. In the following, the functionality of this alignment will be shown by the detection of the checkerboard pattern. For this, the checkerboard pattern of the calibration target from Sect. 2 is used. Every single corner of the checkerboard pattern is automatically detected by a subpixel accurate algorithm. This step is performed for each λ, beginning with the uncorrected image. Figure Fig. 2a shows the detected corner across all bands. Here the 4×4 pattern is clearly visible. For the figure Fig. 2b, the spline interpolation method was chosen. Comparing both figures it can be seen that the distance between the detected points is reduced by factor four, which clearly shows an improvement to the uncorrected images.

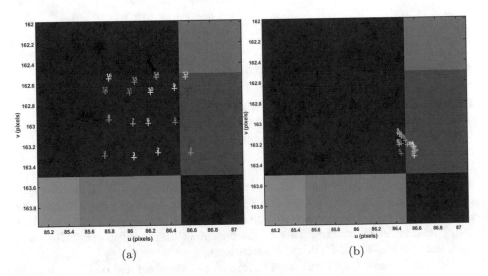

(a)   (b)

Fig. 2. Checkerboard detection with (a) and without (b) geometrical alignment

The next step, the measurement accuracy of the stereo system is analyzed. For this purpose, the length of a checkerboard field in the stereo image pair is measured. The exact length is known as 6.1875 mm. The measurement of an edge length is done by calculating the Euclidean distance between two adjacent detected corners. To get an overall impression of the measurement accuracy, all vertical and horizontal edges of the checkerboard pattern are taken into account and the mean error is calculated. In Table 1, it can be seen that our system is able to measure three-dimensional spatial information. It is important to highlight that the largest Euclidean distance between two bands was selected here - i.e. for the left camera band 1 and for the right camera band 25. This leads to the largest possible error of all band combinations. Furthermore, the table depicts that the error is reduced by applying geometrical alignment. For demonstration purposes, a fresh green leaf and a brown autumn leaf have been compared. In the Fig. 3, you can see the scene, the corresponding depth map and the spectrum of the objects measured at the marked positions. As can be seen, the developed system provides detailed information about spatial as well as spectral information, which is available for further processing and will be analyzed with medical test objects in the future.

Table 1. Error of Euclidean distance measurement (Band 1 of SSM4 × 4 and Band 25 of SSM5 × 5)

Geometrical alignment	Error	
	mean [mm]	std [mm]
Yes	−0.16602	0.10883
No	−0.19327	0.10797

5   Discussion and Future Work

In this paper, we showed that it is possible to develop a dual snapshot hyperspectral imaging system, which enables us to get spatial and spectral information from 41 bands for each pixel in an image with a single shot camera system. This setup will undoubtedly lead to more robustness for the spectral analysis. We still have to solve an error, which occurs when generating the spectral curves at 850 nm, which might be due to a spectral calibration problem. One issue that quickly became apparent is if the test objects are not visible in both images due their spectral properties. There will be challenges to match both images, which could lead to worse results. This might be something to overcome with more complex and controlled illumination solutions.

One of the most important steps to improve our system will be the validation of the spectral curves so that we can reliable perform spectral and geometrical measurements of medical test objects. We are looking into generating 3D models from the images, improved by matching in multiple bands and combining the results. Furthermore, we will be integrating and improving the research on RGB reconstruction [22] and combine it with overlaying spectral information to easily distinguish and asses different materials, conditions and communicate them to the end-user. In order to get the best out of the hardware, we are also looking into implementations for PSNR-optimized methods for the band adjustment [16].

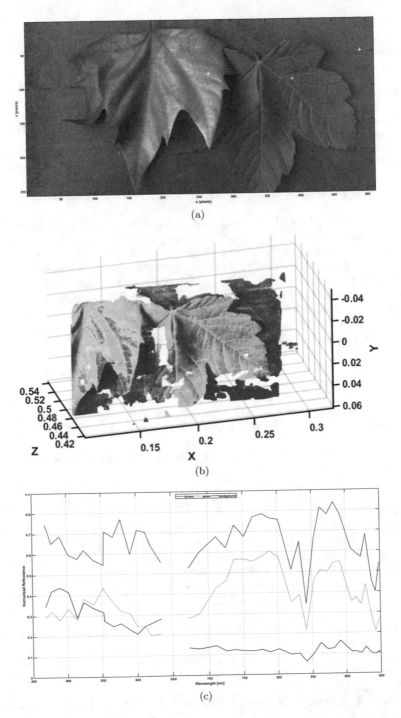

Fig. 3. (a) Green and brown leaf with green marks, (b) Depth map, (c) Spectral Reflectance of the marked points (Color figure online)

Acknowledgement. The authors gratefully acknowledge the financial support of Avicenna-Studienwerk e.V. and University of Applied Sciences and Arts Dortmund for the PhD scholarships.

References

1. Mahmoud, N., et al.: Live tracking and dense reconstruction for hand-held monocular endoscopy. IEEE Trans. Med. Imaging **38**, 79–89 (2018)
2. Schuldt, D., Tanriverdi, F., Thiem, J.: Performance of stereo matching algorithms in 3D endoscopy. Biomed. Eng./Biomedizinische Technik **63**(s1), 50 (2018)
3. Kumar, N., et al.: Hyperspectral tissue image segmentation using semi-supervised NMF and hierarchical clustering. IEEE Trans. Med. Imaging **38**(5), 1304–1313 (2019)
4. Zheng, C., Wang, N., Cui, J.: Hyperspectral image classification with small training sample size using superpixel-guided training sample enlargement. IEEE Trans. Geosci. Remote Sens. **57**(10), 1–10 (2019)
5. Heide, N., Frese, C., Emter, T., Petereit, J.: Real- time hyperspectral stereo processing for the generation of 3D depth information. In: 2018 IEEE International Conference on Image Processing, Proceedings, 7–10 October 2018, pp. 3299–3303. Megaron Athens International Conference Centre, Athens, Greece (2018)
6. Zhao, H., Xu, L., Shi, S., Jiang, H., Chen, D.: A high throughput integrated hyperspectral imaging and 3D measurement system. Sens. (Basel, Switz.) **18**(4), 1068 (2018)
7. Zhu, K., et al.: Hyperspectral light field stereo matching. IEEE Trans. Pattern Anal. Mach. Intell. **41**(5), 1131–1143 (2019)
8. Karaca, A.C., Erturk, A., Gullu, M.K., Erturk, S.: A novel panoramic stereo hyperspectral imaging system. In: 6th International Symposium on Communications, Control and Signal Processing (ISCCSP), Proceedings, Athens, Greece, 21–23 May 2014, pp. 145–148 (2014)
9. X-Rite: ColorChecker White Balance. https://xritephoto.com/colorchecker-white-balance. Accessed 27 Jun 2019
10. VRmagic: D3 Intelligent Camera Platform. https://www.vrmagic.com/fileadmin/downloads/imaging/Brochures/141201_D3_platform_WEB_DP.pdf. Accessed 27 Jun 2019
11. IMEC: Hyperspectral Imaging: Dezember 2015 Activity Update (2015)
12. Heikkila, J., Silven, O.: A four-step camera calibration procedure with implicit image correction. In: IEEE Computer Society Conference on Computer Vision and Pattern Recognition, pp. 1106–1112 (1997)
13. Zhang, Z.: A flexible new technique for camera calibration. IEEE Trans. Pattern Anal. Mach. Intell. **22**(11), 1330–1334 (2000)
14. Erhardt, A.: Einführung in die Digitale Bildverarbeitung: Grundlagen, Systeme und Anwendungen. Vieweg+Teubner/GWV Fachverlage GmbH Wiesbaden, Wiesbaden (2008)
15. Sakamoto, T., Nakanishi, C., Hase, T.: Software pixel interpolation for digital still cameras suitable for a 32-bit MCU. IEEE Trans. Consumer Electron. **44**(4), 1342–1352 (1998)
16. Mihoubi, S., Losson, O., Mathon, B., Macaire, L.: Multispectral demosaicing using pseudo-panchromatic image. IEEE Trans. Comput. Imaging **3**(4), 982–995 (2017)
17. Sun, D.-W.: Hyperspectral Imaging for Food Quality Analysis and Control, 1st edn. Academic Press, Amsterdam (2010)

18. Delwiche, S.R., Kim, M.S.: Hyperspectral imaging for detection of scab in wheat. In: Biological Quality and Precision Agriculture II, Boston, MA, pp. 13–20 (2000)
19. Cheng, X., Tao, Y., Chen, Y.R., Luo, Y.: NIR/MIR dual sensor machine vision system for online apple stem-end/calyx recognition. Trans. ASAE **46**(2), 551–558 (2003)
20. Polder, G., van der Heijden, G.W.A.M., Young, I.T.: Spectral image analysis for measuring ripeness of tomatoes. Trans. ASAE **45**(4), 1155–1161 (2002)
21. Lu, R.: Detection of bruises on apples using near-infrared hyperspectral imaging. Trans. ASAE **46**(2), 523 (2003)
22. Tanriverdi, F., Schuldt, D., Thiem, J.: Hyperspectral imaging: color reconstruction based on medical data. In: IEEE EMBS Conference on Biomedical Engineering and Sciences (2018)

Joint Optimization of Convolutional Neural Network and Image Preprocessing Selection for Embryo Grade Prediction in *In Vitro* Fertilization

Kento Uchida[1]([✉]), Shota Saito[1,3], Panca Dewi Pamungkasari[1,2], Yusei Kawai[1], Ita Fauzia Hanoum[4], Filbert H. Juwono[5], and Shinichi Shirakawa[1]

[1] Graduate School of Environment and Information Sciences, Yokohama National University, Yokohama, Japan
`uchida-kento-nc@ynu.jp`
[2] Department of Information and Communication Technology, Universitas Nasional, Jakarta, Indonesia
[3] SkillUp AI Co., Ltd., Tokyo, Japan
[4] Infertility Laboratory of Permata Hati Program, RSUP DR Sardjito, Yogyakarta, Indonesia
[5] Department of Electrical and Computer Engineering, Curtin University Malaysia, Miri, Sarawak, Malaysia

Abstract. The convolutional neural network (CNN) is a standard tool for image recognition. To improve the performance of CNNs, it is important to design not only the network architecture but also the preprocessing of the input image. Extracting or enhancing the meaningful features of the input image in the preprocessing stage can help to improve the CNN performance. In this paper, we focus on the use of the well-known image processing filters, such as the edge extraction and denoising, and add the preprocessed images to the input of CNNs. As the optimal filter selection depends on dataset, we develop a joint optimization method of CNN and image processing filter selection. We represent the image processing filter selection by a binary vector and introduce the probability distribution of the vector. To derive the gradient-based optimization algorithm, we compute the gradients of weight and distribution parameters on the expected loss under the distribution. The proposed method is applied to an embryo grading task for *in vitro* fertilization, where the embryo grade is assigned based on the morphological criterion. The experimental result shows that the proposed method succeeds to reduce the test error by more than 8% compared with the naive CNN models.

Keywords: Convolutional neural network · Image processing filter · Embryo grading · *In vitro* fertilization

---

K. Uchida, S. Saito and P. D. Pamungkasari—Equal contribution.

© Springer Nature Switzerland AG 2019
G. Bebis et al. (Eds.): ISVC 2019, LNCS 11845, pp. 14–24, 2019.
https://doi.org/10.1007/978-3-030-33723-0_2

1   Introduction

Convolutional neural networks (CNNs) continue to update the state-of-the-art performance of image classification and detection. The performance improvement of CNNs is not only caused by the architecture design but also preprocessing of input images. Traditional image processing filters, such as denoising and edge enhancement filters, help to remove unuseful noise or extract important features in input images. For instance, Calderon et al. [4] analyze the impact of denoising, contrast, and edge enhancement as a preprocessing for CNN, and show that such preprocessing has the potential to improve the performance of CNN in X-ray image dataset.

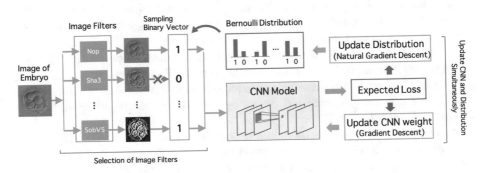

Fig. 1. Conceptual illustration of the proposed method.

Adequate preprocessing should be selected depending on the datasets to exploit the potential of image preprocessing for CNNs. We focus on the problem to select the adequate image processing filters as preprocessing from candidates prepared in advance. In this paper, we develop a method for optimizing the image processing filter selection during a single CNN training. In our method, a binary vector represents the selection of image processing filters, i.e., each bit indicates that the corresponding filter is selected or not. It is difficult to optimize the binary vector by gradient method because it is discrete. To handle this difficulty, we consider the multivariate Bernoulli distribution as the underlying distribution of the binary vector and introduce an alternative differentiable objective function parameterized by the distribution parameters and the weights of a neural network. This relaxation technique is called *stochastic relaxation*, which is used in the one-shot neural architecture search [1,13] and embedded feature selection [14]. Instead of directly optimizing the binary vector, we optimize the distribution parameters jointly with the weights. Figure 1 shows the conceptual image of the proposed method. Since the proposed method requires the model training only once, the increase of computational time is not significant.

We believe that the image processing filters, such as edge detection and denoising, are useful for medical images rather than for general object images, because a small difference in the edge or shape may be important in medical images. To verify the effect of our selection scheme of image processing filters, we apply the proposed method to the prediction of embryo grade for *in vitro* fertilization (IVF) using day 3 embryo images. The experimental result shows that the proposed method can reduce the test error by more than 8% compared with the naive CNN model without image processing filters.

2   Joint Optimization of CNN and Image Preprocessing Filter Selection

We consider the general problem setting on supervised learning with a given training image dataset $\mathcal{D} = \{X, Y\}$. Let $X = \{x_1, \ldots, x_N\}$ be the set of input images, and $Y = \{y_1, \ldots, y_N\}$ be the set of corresponding target variables. The goal of a machine learning algorithm is to find a better-generalized model $\phi : x \mapsto y$ that works well on unseen (test) data (x, y).

In this paper, we consider a CNN model with image preprocessing denoted by $\phi(W, M)$ parameterized by the weight vector W and binary vector $M \in \mathcal{M} = \{0, 1\}^d$, where M represents the filter selection. Each bit in M determines whether or not the preprocessed image by the corresponding filter appears in the input images for CNN.

Specifically, we prepare the image processing filters, $\psi_1, \ldots, \psi_d$, that transform an original image x into the filtered images $\bar{x} = \{\psi_1(x), \ldots, \psi_d(x)\}$. These filters are expected to extract or enhance the useful features of the original image. The filtered images are concatenated to the channel direction and used as the input of CNN. We determine whether each filtered image is included in the input of CNN by the binary vector. Therefore, the input of CNN can be obtained by $\{m_1\psi_1(x), \ldots, m_d\psi_d(x)\}$, where $m_i \in \{0, 1\}$ indicates i-th element of M. As the useful image processing filters depend on datasets and the unmeaningful filters may lead the performance deterioration, we develop the algorithm that finds the better binary vector in a single CNN training.

Given a loss function $\mathcal{L}(W, M)$ to be minimized, such as the cross-entropy, the gradient with respect to (w.r.t.) M cannot be obtained because M is discrete variable. We transform the original objective into the differentiable one by using the probability distribution of M. Let us consider the multivariate Bernoulli distribution $p_\theta(M) = \prod_{i=1}^{d} \theta_i^{m_i}(1 - \theta_i)^{1-m_i}$, where $\theta \in \Theta \subseteq [0, 1]^d$ is the distribution parameter. The value θ_i is the probability that m_i becomes 1 and can be regarded as the selection probability of the i-th filter. By taking the expectation of $\mathcal{L}(W, M)$ under the distribution, we get an alternative objective function for W and θ: $\mathcal{G}(W, \theta) = \mathbb{E}_{p_\theta}[\mathcal{L}(W, M)]$. This transformation of objective function is called *stochastic relaxation*. Different from the original objective function $\mathcal{L}$, the transformed objective function $\mathcal{G}$ is differentiable w.r.t. both W and θ.

We adopt the optimization algorithm proposed in [13, 14] to minimize the expected loss $\mathcal{G}(W, \theta)$. The vanilla (Euclidean) gradient w.r.t. W and the natural gradient w.r.t. θ are given by $\nabla_W \mathcal{G}(W, \theta) = \sum_{M \in \mathcal{M}} \nabla_W \mathcal{L}(W, M) p_\theta(M)$ and $\tilde{\nabla}_\theta \mathcal{G}(W, \theta) = \sum_{M \in \mathcal{M}} \mathcal{L}(W, M) \tilde{\nabla}_\theta \ln p_\theta(M) p_\theta(M)$, respectively, where $\tilde{\nabla}_\theta = F(\theta)^{-1} \nabla_\theta$ is the so-called natural gradient [3] that is the steepest direction of θ

Algorithm 1. The training procedure of the proposed method.

Input: Training data $\mathcal{D}$ and hyperparameters $\{\lambda, \eta_\theta\}$
Output: Optimized parameter of W and θ

1   **begin**
2   Initialize the connection weights of CNN and Bernoulli distribution parameter as $W^{(0)}$ and $\theta^{(0)}$
3     $t \leftarrow 0$
4   **while** *not stopping criterion is satisfied* **do**
5   Get N mini-batch samples from $\mathcal{D}$
6   Sample $M_1, \ldots, M_\lambda$ from $p_{\theta^{(t)}}$
7   Compute the loss $\bar{\mathcal{L}}(W, M_i)$ for each sample
8   Update the distribution parameter to $\theta^{(t+1)}$ using (2)
9   Force $\theta^{(t+1)} \in [1/d, 1 - 1/d]^d$
10   Update the connection weights to $W^{(t+1)}$ using (1) by any SGD
11      $t \leftarrow t + 1$

---

w.r.t. the Kullback-Leibler divergence, and $F(\theta)$ is the Fisher information matrix of p_θ. The training of the model ϕ is done by iteratively updating both W and θ to the above gradient direction.

In practice, these gradients are approximated by Monte-Carlo using λ samples, $M_1, \ldots, M_\lambda$, drawn from p_θ. Also, the loss function is approximated using N mini-batch data samples $\mathcal{Z}$ as $\mathcal{L}(W, M) \approx \bar{\mathcal{L}}(W, M; \mathcal{Z}) = \frac{1}{N} \sum_{z \in \mathcal{Z}} l(z, W, M)$, where $l(z, W, M)$ represents the loss of a datum. Consequently, the gradient w.r.t. W is given by

$$\nabla_W \mathcal{G}(W, \theta) \approx \frac{1}{\lambda} \sum_{i=1}^{\lambda} \nabla_W \bar{\mathcal{L}}(W, M_i; \mathcal{Z}) \ . \tag{1}$$

The gradient $\nabla_W \bar{\mathcal{L}}(W, M_i; \mathcal{Z})$ can be computed using back-propagation and we can use any stochastic gradient descent (SGD) method for optimizing W.

Since we consider the Bernoulli distribution as p_θ, the natural gradient of the log-likelihood can be analytically obtained as $\tilde{\nabla} \ln p_\theta(M) = M - \theta$. Then, we can get the approximation of the natural gradient w.r.t. θ as $\tilde{\nabla}_\theta \mathcal{G}(W, \theta) \approx \frac{1}{\lambda} \sum_{i=1}^{\lambda} \bar{\mathcal{L}}(W, M_i; \mathcal{Z})(M_i - \theta)$. For the natural gradient estimate, we transform the loss value into the ranking-based utility as was done in [13,14] as follows: $u_i = 1$ for best $\lceil \lambda/4 \rceil$ samples, $u_i = -1$ for worst $\lceil \lambda/4 \rceil$ samples, otherwise $u_i = 0$. The ranking-based utility transformation makes the algorithm invariant to the order preserving transformation of $\mathcal{L}$. With this utility transformation, the θ update becomes

$$\theta^{(t+1)} = \theta^{(t)} + \frac{\eta_\theta}{\lambda} \sum_{i=1}^{\lambda} u_i (M_i - \theta^{(t)}) \ , \tag{2}$$

where η_θ is the learning rate for θ. We note that the minimization problem is turned into the maximization problem due to the utility transforms. In the algorithm implementation, we restrict the range of θ_i within $[1/d, 1 - 1/d]$ to keep the possibility of generating any binary vector. The training procedure is summarized in Algorithm 1.

After the model training, we choose the most likely binary vector to predict a new data as $\hat{M} = \mathrm{argmin}_M \, p_\theta(M)$ such that $m_i = 1$ if $\theta_i \geq 0.5$, otherwise $m_i = 0$. Then, we predict new data using the image processing filters decided by $\hat{M}$.

3   Embryo Grading Task and Dataset

IVF is the most common fertility treatment which assists a woman for getting pregnancy with genetic technology. The low success rate of IVF has become a major issue to date. According to [6], embryo grading is responsible for around one-third of implantation failures. Hence, the determination of the morphological embryo grading for the base of the selection is very important. Currently, the embryo selection is done through a manual grading by embryologist using a microscope. The manual selection makes the process dependent on the embryologist's skills and experiences. Therefore, embryo grading is subjective and the fate of an embryo is determined only based on restricted information and observation. The machine learning techniques have been applied to embryo images to automate and improve the embryo grading process. For instance, the number of cells in day 3 embryo, one of the important criterion to determine the embryo grade, was predicted using features extracted from embryo image by conditional random fields [11] or Adaboost [19]. Khan et al. [8] showed that CNN could improve the performance of cell counting in embryo image. Also, CNN was used to predict the embryo grading from the fifth day's embryo image directly [5,9].

In this paper, we use the day 3 embryo images that were collected from 2016 to 2018 at the Infertility Clinic in Indonesia. The day 3 embryo grading is more crucial than the day 5 embryo grading since it makes the decision whether the embryo will be transferred to uterus or cultured until the blastocyst phase [2,12]. The grade of the embryo was categorized by an embryologist based on the standard morphological criterion introduced by [18]. Due to the limitation of the dataset, the grades for embryos were adjusted to be 3 groups; they could be either excellent, moderate, or poor. Table 1 shows the correspondence of our grading scheme with the grading of [18] and the morphological criterion. The dataset consisted of 254, 599, and 533 images for excellent embryos, moderate embryos, and poor embryos, respectively. The total number of images was 1386, which was collected from 238 patients, and each patient had about 4 embryos on the 3rd day. Figure 2 shows the examples of the embryo for each grade. The task is to classify the embryo images into three categories (grades). In the experiment, the images were resized to 128×128 and converted to grayscale. Then, we randomly assigned 80% of all images as the training dataset, and 20% as the test dataset.

4   Experiment and Result

4.1   Experimental Setting

The CNN architecture used in the experiment is based on the VGG-Net [15] consisting of 16 convolutional layers with 3×3 kernel. Different from the original VGG-Net, we add the batch normalization in the convolutional and fully-connected layers and remove the dropout [16] in the fully-connected layers. In addition, we insert the global average pooling [10] before the first fully-connected layer. As our embryo grading task is classification, the loss function is the softmax cross-entropy.

Table 1. Correspondence of the modified grading applied to our dataset with the grade introduced by [18] and morphological criterion for the embryo on the 3rd day.

Grade [18]	Modified grade	Number of cells	Blastomere	Fragmentation
1	Excellent	7–8 cells	Similar	Less than 5%
2	Moderate	7–8 cells	Similar	5–15%
3	Poor	6–8 cells	Fairly similar	15–25%
4	Poor	4–6 cells	Fairly similar	25–30%
5	Poor	4–5 cells	Not similar	More than 30%

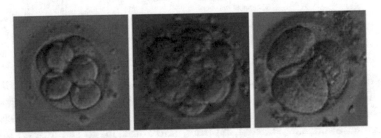

Fig. 2. Examples of embryo image in excellent (left), moderate (center), and poor (right) grades.

We set the mini-batch size to 64 and the maximum number of epochs to 3,000 (about 54,000 training iterations). The weight parameters are initialized by He's initialization [7] and optimized by using Nesterov's accelerated stochastic gradient method [17] with a momentum of 0.9. We also use the weight decay of 10^{-4} for the training of the weight parameters. The learning rate for the weights is initialized by 0.1 and divided by 10 at 1/2 and 3/4 of the maximum number of epochs. These parameter settings are based on [13]. We prepare 15 image processing filters including no operation (Nop) listed in Table 2. The sample size of the binary vector in each iteration is $\lambda = 2$, and the learning rate for distribution parameters is set to $\eta_\theta = 1/15$. The distribution

Table 2. Image processing filters used in the experiment.

Filter	Abbreviation		
	–	$(3 \times 3$ kernel)	$(5 \times 5$ kernel)
Original image	Nop	–	–
Blur filter	–	Blur3	Blur5
Gaussian filter	–	Gau3	Gau5
Sharpening filter	–	Sha3	Sha5
Laplacian filter	–	Lap3	Lap5
Vertical-Sobel filter	–	SobV3	SobV5
Horizontal-Sobel filter	–	SobH3	SobH5
Median filter	–	Med3	Med5

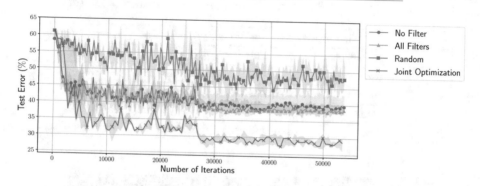

Fig. 3. Transitions of test error for each model.

parameters θ are initialized by 0.5. Each preprocessed image by the image processing filters is standardized, i.e., each pixel value is subtracted by the mean pixel value and divided by the standard deviation. Also, we apply the standard data augmentation, i.e., shifting, flipping, and rotation, to the filtered images.

To investigate the effect of the proposed method, we compare the following four models:

1. **No Filter:** the model without image preprocessing filters (naive CNN)
2. **All Filters:** the model using all preprocessed images as inputs
3. **Random:** the model with fixed filter selection probability of 0.5 (i.e., our method without θ optimization)
4. **Joint Optimization (ours):** the model that are jointly optimized CNN and the image preprocessing filter selection

We report the experimental results based on five trials with different random seeds. For the compared models, No Filter, All Filters, and Random, we set the mini-batch size to 128. The numbers of data samples used to the parameters update become equal among all models by setting such batch size because our method uses the doubled number of data samples ($\lambda = 2$) in each iteration.

4.2 Result and Discussion

Figure 3 shows the transitions of the median value and the inter-quartile range of test error for each model. Our method can reduce the test error than the other models after about 5000 iterations. The values of median (lower and upper quartile) of the test error at the final iteration are as follows; No Filter: 39.57% (37.05%, 39.93%), All Filters: 38.13% (38.13%, 42.45%), Random: 46.04% (44.24%, 50.72%), and Joint Optimization (ours): 28.78% (26.62%, 28.78%). We observe that our method significantly reduces the test error at the final iteration by more than 8% compared to No Filter and All Filters. This result implies that the redundant image preprocessing has the potential to lead a adverse effect, but selecting appropriate filters can improve the performance of CNN. The result of Random significantly worse than other models, suggesting that the optimization algorithm of our method can work well. We note that the total training time of all models is more or less the same. Thus, the proposed method can improve the prediction accuracy without additional computational cost.

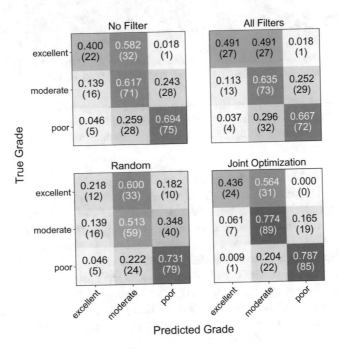

Fig. 4. Confusion matrices of test data for each model. The values in each cell indicate the ratio of data samples classified into each category, and the values in parentheses indicate the number of data samples. We report the confusion matrix of the trial that recorded the median of test error for each model.

Figure 4 depicts the confusion matrices of test data for each model. We can see that the recall obtained by our method is higher than others for moderate and poor grades. For the excellent grade, the accuracy of all models is not so high and the excellent embryo tends to be predicted incorrectly as the moderate grade.

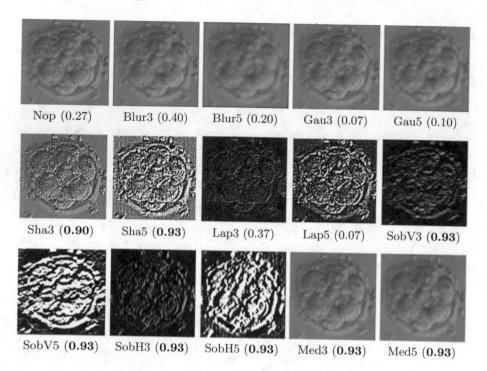

Fig. 5. Preprocessed images of the embryo by the image processing filters. The values in the parentheses are the selection probability of each filter, where the bold font means the selection probability is higher than 0.8. The result is the trial that recorded the median of test error.

According to Table 1, the difference between the excellent grade and moderate grade is only the amount of fragmentation. We believe that this poor accuracy for excellent embryo data is because the number of data graded as excellent is not sufficient for learning such differences. We emphasize that the ratio of the worst misclassification, where the excellent embryo is predicted as poor, or the inverse case, is very low in our method. From the viewpoint of IVF, this result is encouraging as both of the excellent and moderate embryos can be transferred to the uterus. Moreover, distinguishing poor embryo is the most important task because the worst situation is transferring the poor embryo to the uterus. This improvement suggests that the selected image processing filters can extract useful features for accurate grade prediction.

Figure 5 shows the preprocessed images and their selection probabilities at the final iteration. We observe that the selection probability of Nop is not high, implying that the preprocessed images are useful in embryo grade prediction rather than the original image. The filters whose selection probability is more than 0.8 are Sha3, Sha5, SobV3, SobV5, SobH3, SobH5, Med3, and Med5. Regarding the criterion of embryologist in Table 1, Med3 and Med5 contribute to eliminating the fragmentation, and Sha3 and Sha5 conversely emphasize them. The edge detection filters (SobV3, SobV5, SobH3, and SobH5) are expected to help to count the embryo and to determine the similarity of blastomere.

5   Conclusion

We have proposed the method that jointly optimizes CNN and the image processing filter selection. We introduced the Bernoulli distribution as a law of binary vector for filter selection. The distribution parameter and the connection weight of CNN were jointly updated to the gradient directions. We applied the proposed method to the embryo grading prediction for IVF, where the labels of the dataset were given by an embryologist based on the morphological criteria. We have shown that the test error of the proposed method can be reduced by more than 8% compared to naive CNN.

The different types of image processing filters are often applied several times to extract and enhance meaningful features. In our method, each image processing filter is employed only once to the original image. Optimizing the combination of image processing filter sequences is one of the future works. In the embryo image dataset, we consider that the prediction of the excellent grade directly is difficult because its criteria are similar to those of moderate grade. Therefore, constructing the CNN that predicts the criteria for embryo grading, i.e., cell number, the similarity of blastomere and amount of fragmentation, may contribute to the improvement of the prediction accuracy for embryo grading.

In the experiment of this paper, most of the prepared filters were linear filters and can be represented by a convolution operation in CNNs. Nevertheless, we confirmed that the proposed method is useful in our embryo dataset. Although the evaluation of our method on other datasets, such as large scale dataset, is another important future work. In addition, as our method can adopt non-linear and non-differentiable image preprocessing, adding such non-linear filters is promising future work.

References

1. Akimoto, Y., Shirakawa, S., Yoshinari, N., Uchida, K., Saito, S., Nishida, K.: Adaptive stochastic natural gradient method for one-shot neural architecture search. In: Proceedings of the 36th International Conference on Machine Learning (ICML), vol. 97, pp. 171–180 (2019)
2. Alfaraj, S., Alzaher, F., Alshwaiaer, S., Ahmed, A.: Pregnancy outcome of day 3 versus day 5 embryo transfer: a retrospective analysis. Asian Pac. J. Reprod. **6**(2), 89–92 (2017). https://doi.org/10.12980/apjr.6.20170208
3. Amari, S.: Natural gradient works efficiently in learning. Neural Comput. **10**(2), 251–276 (1998)
4. Calderon, S., et al.: Assessing the impact of the deceived non local means filter as a preprocessing stage in a convolutional neural network based approach for age estimation using digital hand X-ray images. In: 25th IEEE International Conference on Image Processing (ICIP), pp. 1752–1756 (2018). https://doi.org/10.1109/ICIP.2018.8451191
5. Chen, T.J., Zheng, W.L., Liu, C.H., Huang, I., Lai, H.H., Liu, M.: Using deep learning with large dataset of microscope images to develop an automated embryo grading system. Fertil. Reprod. **01**(01), 51–56 (2019). https://doi.org/10.1142/S2661318219500051

6. Craciunas, L., et al.: Conventional and modern markers of endometrial receptivity: a systematic review and meta-analysis. Hum. Reprod. Update **25**(2), 202–223 (2019). https://doi.org/10.1093/humupd/dmy044

7. He, K., Zhang, X., Ren, S., Sun, J.: Delving deep into rectifiers: surpassing human-level performance on ImageNet classification. In: IEEE International Conference on Computer Vision (ICCV), pp. 1026–1034 (2015). https://doi.org/10.1109/ICCV.2015.123

8. Khan, A., Gould, S., Salzmann, M.: Deep convolutional neural networks for human embryonic cell counting. In: Hua, G., Jégou, H. (eds.) ECCV 2016. LNCS, vol. 9913, pp. 339–348. Springer, Cham (2016). https://doi.org/10.1007/978-3-319-46604-0_25

9. Khosravi, P., et al.: Deep learning enables robust assessment and selection of human Blastocysts after in vitro fertilization. Nat. Partner J. Digit. Med. **02**, 21 (2019). https://doi.org/10.1038/s41746-019-0096-y

10. Lin, M., Chen, Q., Yan, S.: Network in network. In: International Conference on Learning Representations (ICLR) (2014)

11. Moussavi, F., Wang, Y., Lorenzen, P., Oakley, J., Russakoff, D., Gould, S.: A unified graphical models framework for automated human embryo tracking in time lapse microscopy. In: IEEE 11th International Symposium on Biomedical Imaging, pp. 314–320 (2014)

12. Racowsky, C., Jackson, K.V., Cekleniak, N.A., Fox, J.H., Hornstein, M.D., Ginsburg, E.S.: The number of eight-cell embryos is a key determinant for selecting day 3 or day 5 transfer. Fertil. Steril. **73**(3), 558–564 (2000). https://doi.org/10.1016/S0015-0282(99)00565-8

13. Shirakawa, S., Iwata, Y., Akimoto, Y.: Dynamic optimization of neural network structures using probabilistic modeling. In: Thirty-Second AAAI Conference on Artificial Intelligence (AAAI), pp. 4074–4082 (2018)

14. Shota, S., Shirakawa, S., Akimoto, Y.: Embedded feature selection using probabilistic model-based optimization. In: Proceedings of the Genetic and Evolutionary Computation Conference Companion (GECCO), pp. 1922–1925 (2018). https://doi.org/10.1145/3205651.3208227

15. Simonyan, K., Zisserman, A.: Very deep convolutional networks for large-scale image recognition. In: International Conference on Learning Representations (ICLR) (2015)

16. Srivastava, N., Hinton, G., Krizhevsky, A., Sutskever, I., Salakhutdinov, R.: Dropout: a simple way to prevent neural networks from overfitting. J. Mach. Learn. Res. **15**, 1929–1958 (2014)

17. Sutskever, I., Martens, J., Dahl, G., Hinton, G.: On the importance of initialization and momentum in deep learning. In: Proceedings of the 30th International Conference on Machine Learning (ICML), vol. 28, pp. 1139–1147 (2013)

18. Veeck, L.: An Atlas of Human Gametes and Conceptuses: An Illustrated Reference for Assisted Reproductive Technology. The Parthenon Publishing Group, New York (1999)

19. Wang, Y., Moussavi, F., Lorenzen, P.: Automated embryo stage classification in time-lapse microscopy video of early human embryo development. In: Mori, K., Sakuma, I., Sato, Y., Barillot, C., Navab, N. (eds.) MICCAI 2013. LNCS, vol. 8150, pp. 460–467. Springer, Heidelberg (2013). https://doi.org/10.1007/978-3-642-40763-5_57

Enhanced Approach for Classification of Ulcerative Colitis Severity in Colonoscopy Videos Using CNN

Sure Venkata Leela Lakshmi Tejaswini[1], Bhuvan Mittal[1],
JungHwan Oh[1(✉)], Wallapak Tavanapong[2], Johnny Wong[2],
and Piet C. de Groen[3]

[1] Department of Computer Science and Engineering,
University of North Texas, Denton, TX 76203, USA
Junghwan.Oh@unt.edu
[2] Computer Science Department, Iowa State University, Ames, IA 50011, USA
{tavanapo,wong}@iastate.edu
[3] Department of Medicine, University of Minnesota, Minneapolis, MN, USA

Abstract. Ulcerative Colitis (UC) is an inflammatory bowel disease that causes inflammation, ulcers and bleeding of the colon affecting more than 500,000 people in the United States. To achieve the therapeutic objectives for UC, which are to first induce and then maintain disease remission, physicians need to evaluate the severity of UC. However, objective assessment of US is difficult because of the non-uniform nature of symptoms and large variations in disease presentation. To address this, in our previous work, we developed two different approaches in which one uses the image textures, and the other uses CNN (Convolutional Neural Network) to measure and objectively classify the severity of UC as seen on optical colonoscopy video frames. However, we found that the image texture based approach could not handle large numbers of variations in patterns, and the CNN based approach could not achieve very high accuracy. In this paper, we improve our CNN based approach in two ways to provide better accuracy for UC severity classification. We add more thorough and essential preprocessing, subdivide each class of UC severity and generate more classes for the classification to accommodate large variations in patterns. The experimental results show that the proposed preprocessing and generation of more classes can improve the overall accuracy of automated classification of the severity of UC.

Keywords: Medical image classification · Convolutional Neural Network · Medical video processing · Ulcerative Colitis Severity

1 Introduction

Ulcerative colitis (UC) is a chronic inflammatory disease of the colon characterized by periods of relapses and remissions affecting more than 500,000 people in the United States [1]. Endoscopic disease severity may better predict future outcomes in UC than

© Springer Nature Switzerland AG 2019
G. Bebis et al. (Eds.): ISVC 2019, LNCS 11845, pp. 25–37, 2019.
https://doi.org/10.1007/978-3-030-33723-0_3

symptoms. Therefore, UC severity measurement is very important. It is very difficult to evaluate the severity of UC objectively because of non-uniform nature of symptoms associated with UC, and large variations in their patterns [2]. In our previous work [3], we measured and classified the severity of UC presented in optical colonoscopy video frames based on the image textures. However, we found that it could not handle larger numbers of variations in their patterns. To address this, we proposed a different approach using CNN (Convolutional Neural Network) to measure and classify the severity of UC presented in optical colonoscopy video frames objectively [4]. It utilizes endoscopic domain knowledge and CNN to classify different UC severity of colonoscopy images. The experimental results showed that the proposed method could evaluate the severity of UC reasonably at the video level, but its frame level accuracy was still very low (44.8%). It needs to be improved to provide better results.

In this paper, we improve our previous CNN based approach [4] in two ways to provide better accuracy for the classification. First, we add more thorough and essential preprocessing which includes three steps. The first step is to distinguish frames that cannot be classified correctly due to their contents. These frames consist of blurry frames which are out-of-focus frames, and water and bubble frames which contain large amounts of water or bubbles. The second step is to discard frames with excessive specular reflection areas which do not provide much information for severity classification. The third step is to discard frames with very high uneven illumination, which may provide incorrect characteristics of severity. By discarding these frames from further processing, we can provide more accurate analysis. More details will be discussed in Sect. 3.1. The remaining frames after these three steps of pre-processing will be used for further processing.

Second, we subdivide each class of UC severity, and generate more classes for the classification to accommodate large variations in their severity patterns. For the evaluation of the severity of UC, one 'Normal' class and three UC classes such as 'Mild', 'Moderate' and 'Severe' are used typically [5] as seen in Fig. 1. As seen in Fig. 1, the frames within a single class can appear very different, which indicates that there can be large variations in visual appearance within one class. To accommodate these large variations, we subdivide each class of UC severity, and generate more classes systematically based on their visual appearance. More details will be discussed in Sect. 3.2. Using the frames filtered by the preprocessing steps and classified to more detailed classes, we implement CNNs using AlexNet [6], GoogLeNet [7], and Google's TensorFlow library [8], and compare the results in terms of accuracy and speed. In Sect. 3.3 we discuss the actual implementations.

Contributions: To provide better accuracy, (1) we add more thorough and essential preprocessing; and (2) we subdivide each class of UC severity and generate more classes systematically based on their visual appearance. (3) We propose a new CNN-based UC severity classification using Google's TensorFlow library [8].

The remainder of this paper is organized as follows. Related work is presented in Sect. 2. The proposed technique is described in Sect. 3. In Sect. 4, we discuss our experimental setup and results. Finally, Sect. 5 presents some concluding remarks.

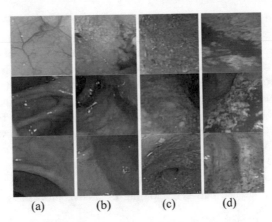

(a)   (b)   (c)   (d)

Fig. 1. Frames in class of (a) Normal, (b) Mild, (c) Moderate, and (d) Severe.

2   Related Work

In our previous work [3], we measured and classified the severity of UC based on image texture. We introduced a novel feature extraction algorithm based on accumulation of pixel value differences, which provided better accuracy for 'severe' and 'moderate' classes, and faster speed than the existing methods did. Since there is no one type of texture feature providing reasonable accuracies for all the classes, we proposed a hybrid approach in which a new proposed feature mentioned above is combined with an existing feature such as LBP (Local Binary Pattern). But, our results showed that this method could not handle a great variety in within class patterns.

To address this, we proposed a different approach using Convolutional Neural Network (CNN) methodology to classify objectively the severity of UC presented in optical colonoscopy video frames [4]. The proposed approach using CNN utilizes endoscopic domain knowledge and CNN to classify different UC severity of colonoscopy images. The experimental results showed that the proposed method could evaluate the severity of UC reasonably at the video level, but its frame level accuracy was very low (44.8%). Clearly, we need to improve results at the frame level.

3   Methodology

In this section, we discuss image preprocessing, how to subdivide each class of UC severity and generate more classes, and how to implement CNNs using AlexNet [6], GoogLeNet [7], and Google's TensorFlow library [8].

3.1   Image Preprocessing

The colonoscopy videos that we are using were captured at 30 frames per second with 720×480-pixel resolution. The captured videos were labeled by domain experts into four UC classes being 'Normal' 'Mild', 'Moderate', and 'Severe'. For convenience, we put a number value for each class being 0 for Normal, 1 for Mild, 2 for Moderate, and 3 for Severe. From each captured video, we extract a sequence of frames at the rate of three frames per second. The number of frames per second was chosen as a balance between having frames that are too similar to each other (sampled from the same second in the video) and having frames that do not capture enough information about the video (if colonoscopy tip with camera was moving fast). Then, we crop an area (224 × 224 pixels) centered on the center pixel of the original frame (720 × 480 pixels). This will ensure that we get most information from a frame while removing all black border areas that surround all frames and do not include any useful information. A larger frame size requires more processing time for training various CNNs, but does not guarantee better performance. This cropped size of 224 × 224 pixels was chosen experimentally as a balance between avoiding excessive processing time and limiting loss of image details.

The first step is to distinguish the frames that we cannot classify correctly due to their contents. These frames consist of blurry frames which are out-of-focus frames (Fig. 2(a) and (b)), and water and bubble frames which are show water and bubbles covering colonic mucosa (Fig. 2(c), (d), (e), and (f)). To distinguish these frames, we already developed CNN-based methods in our previous work [9]. Among them, we use Blurry-AlexNet, Water-AlexNet, and Bubble-AlexNet to distinguish blurry, water, and bubble frames respectively. These are CNN-based methods using the pre-trained network, AlexNet [6]. We refine these methods by retraining them with a larger number of blurry, water and bubble frames in this paper. Table 1 shows how many frames are used for retraining Blurry-AlexNet, Water-AlexNet, and Bubble-AlexNet. Using these refined CNN-based methods, we discard those frames from further processing to provide more accurate analysis

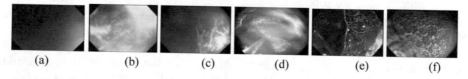

(a)   (b)   (c)   (d)   (e)   (f)

Fig. 2. Blurry frames: (a) and (b), water frames: (c) and (d), and bubble frames: (e) and (f)

Table 1. Dataset details for retraining Blurry-AlexNet, Water-AlexNet, and Bubble-AlexNet

Frame types	Blurry	Non-blurry	Water	Non-water	Bubble	Non-bubble	Total
Frames	6,759	5,327	1,215	1,567	705	1,136	**16,709**

The second step is to discard frames with specular reflection (Fig. 3), which do not provide much information for severity classification. To remove these frames, specular reflection pixels are detected by the light reflection detection algorithm in [10], which uses three threshold values for value (V > 0.5), saturation (S < 0.2) and probability saturation (P_s = 0.5) in HSV (Hue, Saturation and Value) color space. Once all specular pixels are found, we calculate their percentage over the entire frame. If this percentage is greater than a threshold ($SR_{Thld} = 20\%$), we discard the frame.

The third step of the preprocessing is to distinguish frames with very high uneven illumination as seen in Fig. 4, which provide incorrect characteristics of UC severity. The uneven illumination is characterized by calculating the standard deviation of the gray scale values of all the pixels in a frame. If a standard deviation is greater than a threshold ($SD_{Thld} = 0.3$), we discard the frame. The actual values of the thresholds discussed above were determined experimentally.

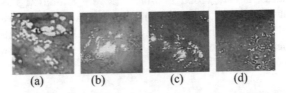

(a)   (b)   (c)   (d)

Fig. 3. Examples of frames with specular reflection

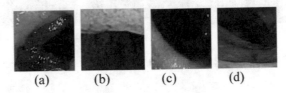

(a)   (b)   (c)   (d)

Fig. 4. Examples of frames with uneven illuminations

3.2   Refinement of UC Severity Classes

As seen in Fig. 1, frames within a single class can appear very different, which indicates that there can be large variations in visual appearance within a given class. To accommodate these large variations, we subdivide each class of UC severity and generate more classes systematically based on their visual appearance.

First, each of three classes such as 'Mild', 'Moderate', and 'Severe' will be subdivided to 'blood' and 'non-blood' classes based on the amount of blood appearing in a frame. 'Normal' class is not divided to 'blood' and 'non-blood' classes since it is not 'Normal' if it includes any amount of blood. Now, we have a total seven classes such as 'Normal', 'Mild_blood', 'Mild_nonblood', 'Moderate_blood', 'Moderate_nonblood', 'Severe_blood', and 'Severe_nonblood'. To generate these seven classes, we need to distinguish the non-blood frames from the blood frames. To do this, we use the method described in [10]. It uses three threshold values for saturation ($S < 0.9$), value ($V > 0.08$) and probability saturation ($P_s = 0.5$) in HSV (Hue, Saturation and value) color space. Once all blood pixels are found, we calculate their percentage over the entire frame. If this percentage is greater than a threshold ($BL_{Thld} = 2\%$), we consider it as blood frame as seen in Fig. 5. Figure 5(a), (b), (c) and (d) have 19.7%, 11.3%, 0.0%, and 0.7% of blood pixels, respectively, based the above calculations. The actual values of the thresholds were determined experimentally.

In the next step, each of these seven classes generated above are subdivided to 'flat' and 'nonflat' classes based on the visual contents from different viewing directions (Fig. 6). 'Flat' frames have the very even mucosa surface as seen in Fig. 6(a) and (b). 'Nonflat means the opposite cases as seen in Fig. 6(c) and (d). Therefore, we now have a total of 14 classes: 'Normal_flat', 'Normal_nonflat', 'Mild_blood_flat', 'Mild_blood_nonflat', 'Mild_nonblood_flat', 'Mild_nonblood_nonflat', 'Moderate_blood_flat', 'Moderate_blood_nonflat', 'Moderate_nonblood_flat', 'Moderate_nonblood_nonflat', 'Severe_blood_flat', 'Severe_blood_nonflat' 'Severe_nonblood_flat', and 'Severe_nonblood_nonflat'. To divide the frames into flat and non-flat classes, we train a CNN using AlexNet [6] with properly picked flat and non-flat frames. We call this CNN Flat-AlexNet for convenience. For training Flat-AlexNet, manually selected 359 flat and 370 non-flat frames were used.

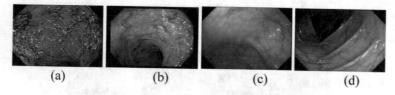

(a)   (b)   (c)   (d)

Fig. 5. Blood frames: (a) and (b), and non-blood frames (c) and (d)

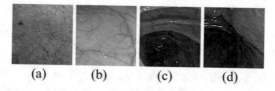

(a)   (b)   (c)   (d)

Fig. 6. Examples of flat frames: (a) and (b), and non-flat frames: (c) and (d)

3.3   Implementation of CNN

All the preprocessing steps discussed above remove frames depicting false characteristics and create within main classes up to two sub-classifications. Frames in each of the 14 classes have similar characteristics. Using these frames, we implement CNNs using AlexNet [6], GoogLeNet [7], and TensorFlow library [8]. Next we will discuss how we did this.

3.3.1   Implementation of AlexNet

In this section we discuss how to use AlexNet [6] to implement various CNNs such as Blurry-AlexNet, Water-AlexNet, Bubble-AlexNet, and Flat-AlexNet, which are discussed above. Also, AlexNet is used to implement a CNN to classify the video frames into one of 14 classes discussed above. We call it UCS-AlexNet (Ulcerative Colitis

Severity CNN using AlexNet). A pre-trained network such as AlexNet can be trained to learn a new task using fine tuning which is a concept of transfer learning [11]. Transfer learning is commonly used in deep learning applications. Fine-tuning a network with transfer learning is usually much faster and easier than training a network with randomly initialized weights from scratch. As mentioned in [11], the learned kernels from the pre-trained CNNs on ImageNet are useful for medical image classification tasks even though they were trained on a completely different image domain. Since we have a relatively small number of training images, we use the pre-trained networks and modify them accordingly to fit our purpose of fine tuning.

As mentioned above, AlexNet [6] is used for five different CNNs (Blurry-AlexNet, Water-AlexNet, Bubble-AlexNet, Flat-AlexNet, and UCS-AlexNet). The following discussion is based on UCS-AlexNet since the other four can be implemented similarly. AlexNet has a pre-trained network which was trained on more than one million images, and capable of classifying 1,000 classes [6]. It has a total of 8 layers. Among them the last three layers are configured for 1,000 classes. So these three layers need to be modified (fine-tuned) for our classification purposes. First, we change the number of classes from 1,000 to 14. The last three layers are replaced with three fully connected layers initialized with random numbers, and a softmax layer with 14 class outputs. To learn faster in the new modified layers compared with the existing layers, WeightLearnRateFactor and BiasLearnRateFactor values need to be increased. WeightLearnRateFactor is a learning rate factor for the weights. This factor is multiplied by the global learning rate to get a learning rate for the weights in the layer. We set this WeightLearnRateFactor to 20. BiasLearnRateFactor is a learning rate factor for the biases. It is also set to 20. InitialLearningRateFactor is set to a small value, 0.001, to slow down learning in the transferred layers. The learning rate factors for fully connected layers are increased to speed up the learning in the final layers.

These combinations ensure fast learning in the new modified layers, and slow learning in the other layers. A pre-trained network does not need to be trained with a large number of epochs compared with a network designed from scratch. Besides that, the minimal batch size and the validation data are defined. We keep the minimal batch size to 100 images and the number of epoch to 30. The training data and validation data are split to 80% and 20% respectively. The validation loss is computed after five iterations. The training automatically stops if validation loss does not improve.

3.3.2 Implementation of GoogLeNet

In this section we discuss how to use GoogLeNet [7] to implement a CNN to classify the video frames into one of 14 classes discussed above. We call it UCS-GoogLeNet (Ulcerative Colitis Severity CNN using GoogLeNet). GoogLeNet is a convolutional neural network that is trained on more than a million images from the ImageNet database. This network has 22 layers and can classify images into 1,000 object categories. Similar to UCS-AlexNet mentioned in the previous section, the last three layers of GoogLeNet are modified. These layers contain the information features (unique characteristics of input image), class probabilities and labels. The last layer of the remaining network is connected with the newly designed layers. To ensure fair comparisons among all the CNNs discussed, minimal batch size, initial learning rate and number of epochs are kept the same as in UCS-AlexNet.

3.3.3   TensorFlow CNN

In this section we discuss our implementation of UCS-TensorFlow (Ulcerative Colitis Severity CNN using TensorFlow) using Google's TensorFlow library [8] to classify the video frames into one of 14 classes discussed above. The UCS-TensorFlow consists of nine layers. As seen in Fig. 7, it has four convolution layers, four pooling layers, and one fully-connected layer. All four convolutional layers have the kernel of size 3 × 3, but use different number of kernels at 16, 32, 64 and 128. All the pooling layers take a 2 × 2 sliding window, and subsample the resulting image with a stride of 2. For activation function, Sigmoid, Tanh, or ReLU functions are typically used [8]. We use ReLU function. To speed up training of CNN and reduce the sensitivity to network initialization, we use batch normalization layers between convolutional layers and activation (ReLU) layers (We do not show these layers in Fig. 7 due to the space limitation). In addition to these, we use a fully connected layer between the final pooling layer and the softmax layer to flatten the feature vector into one dimensional array. Finally, the output layer is a softmax layer which outputs a class along with the class probability of the input image. To ensure fair comparisons among all the CNNs discussed, minimal batch size and the learning rate are kept the same as in UCS-AlexNet, but the number of epochs for the UCS-TensorFlow is increased to 50. Adam Optimizer is used as the optimization algorithm. The parameters are set to Batch size of 100, 50 epochs, and validation split of 0.2 (i.e., 80% of the input dataset is used for training, and 20% for validation).

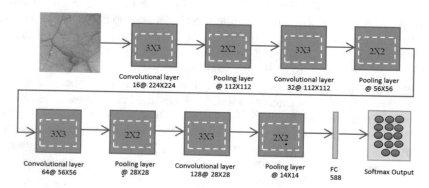

Fig. 7. Architecture of UCS-TensorFlow

3.4   Assigning Severity Score

Until now we have discussed how to assign a class label for each frame. The next step is to assign a severity score for a whole video clip of a patient. We follow the same method that we proposed in our previous work [4]. Typically, physicians manually assign a severity score, 0 for normal, 1 for mild, 2 for moderate, and 3 for severe for a given video clip using her/his own subjective evaluations. Here, we assign a severity score for a whole video clip automatically based on the class label assigned to each frame. We calculate severity score, S_v for a given video clip as an average of class labels of all frames as follows, $S_V = \frac{\sum_{i=1}^{n} C_i}{n}$, where n is a total number of frames, and C_i is a label assigned to frame i of a given video clip.

4 Experiments and Results

In this section, we assess the effectiveness of the proposed UCS-AlexNet, UCS-GoogLeNet, and UCS-TensorFlow. The final goal is to determine the severity in terms of four classes (Normal – 0, Mild – 1, Moderate – 2, and Severe – 3). Therefore, after classifying the frames into 14 classes, the final results are mapped to four classes.

4.1 Dataset

In our dataset, we have 316 colonoscopy video clips. We extracted **185,724** frames from these videos using the sampling rate of three frames per second. The details of the dataset are shown in Table 2. The frames were then divided at the clip level into training and testing sets. After all the preprocessing steps mentioned in Sect. 3.1 on the dataset in Table 2, we obtained 85,034 frames. From these 85,034 frames, we used 44,766 frames for training (29,841 frames), and testing (14,925 frames) as seen in Tables 3 and 4, respectively. These training and testing datasets are mutually exclusive. To ensure fair comparisons, we used the same video clips used in our previous work [4] for training and testing.

Table 2. Details of the initial dataset

Classes	Video clips	Frames	Length (h:mm:ss)
Normal	115	50,820	4:42:20
Mild	92	62,544	5:47:28
Moderate	60	40,221	3:43:27
Severe	49	32,139	2:58:33
Total	**316**	**185,724**	**17:11:48**

Table 3. Details of training dataset

Classes	Normal	Mild	Moderate	Severe	Total
Video clips	99	77	41	37	**254**
Frames	10,448	6,288	5,868	7,237	**29,841**

Table 4. Details of test dataset

Classes	Normal	Mild	Moderate	Severe	Total
Video clips	16	15	19	12	**62**
Frames	3,496	4,175	3,686	3,568	**14,925**

4.2   Comparison of UCS-AlexNet, UCS-GoogLeNet, and UCS-TensorFlow

Based on the discussion in Sect. 3, we trained each of UCS-AlexNet, UCS-GoogLeNet, and UCS-TensorFlow using a sample training dataset in Table 5, which is a subset of the dataset in Table 3. The sample training set was not a random selection but best examples, in which the selected frames are indicating very clear and distinguishable characteristics of each class. It has 6,347 frames from 129 video clips. Since the training takes very long time, we used a reduced size training dataset.

Table 5. Details of sample training dataset

Classes	Normal	Mild	Moderate	Severe	Total
Video clips	43	32	26	28	**129**
Frames	1,615	1,476	1,520	1,736	**6,347**

To compare the performance of UCS-AlexNet, UCS-GoogLeNet, and UCS-TensorFlow, we chose a sample testing dataset in Table 6, which is a subset of the dataset in Table 4, and was not used for any training. When we selected these sample testing frames, we considered frames that had clearly distinguishable characteristics for each class.

Table 6. Details of sample test set

Classes	Normal	Mild	Moderate	Severe	Total
Video clips	8	11	12	9	**40**
Frames	616	657	307	902	**2,482**

We ran UCS-AlexNet, UCS-GoogLeNet, and UCS-TensorFlow using the testing dataset in Table 6. Table 7 shows the comparison of frame level accuracies. The frame level accuracy is defined as the number of correctly classified frames divided by the total number of frames with label values. Overall, UCS-AlexNet was better than UCS-GoogLeNet and UCS-TensorFlow in terms of frame level accuracy.

Table 7. Comparison of frame level accuracies for test set in Table 6 (unit:%)

Methods	Normal	Mild	Moderate	Severe	Total
UCS-AlexNet	96.3	85.5	81.4	97.0	**91.9**
UCS-GoogLeNet	77.9	63.8	59.6	80.0	**72.7**
UCS-TensorFlow	89.0	27.4	38.1	81.5	**63.7**

UCS-AlexNet outperforms UCS-GoogLeNet and UCS-TensorFlow. Therefore, we trained UCS-AlexNet using a larger training dataset in Table 3, and tested with a larger testing dataset in Table 4. Table 8 shows the comparison of frame level accuracy of UCS-AlexNet. Note that results are – as expected – much lower compared to using best examples of each class as shown in Table 7. The same test with the same test set using our best previous classifier showed an accuracy of 44.8% [4]. Our current result, 60.6% accuracy, is a 15% improvement, which is a significant. However, as expected the accuracies of 'Mild' and 'Moderate' classes are a little worse than those of 'Normal' and 'Severe'. To improve accuracy in these classes will be difficult as human annotators have difficulty scoring these classes as well.

Table 8. Comparison of frame level accuracies for test set in Table 4 (unit:%)

Methods	Normal	Mild	Moderate	Severe	Average
UCS-AlexNet	64.1	60.5	44.8	73.4	**60.6**

4.3 Comparison of Severity Scores

We calculated the severity scores for the test datasets in Table 4 using the equation in Sect. 3.4. We used UCS-AlexNet for severity score computation since it provided a better performance compared to the others. The results are shown in Table 9. To compare the proposed calculations of severity scores with those from our domain experts, we calculated Pearson correlation coefficients in the last column of Table 9, which shows a highly linear relationship between the proposed calculations of severity scores and those from our domain experts. When we did the same Pearson correlation calculation with the same test set in our previous work [4], the best coefficient was 0.71. The increase to 0.94 is a significant improvement.

Table 9. Average severity scores for test dataset in Table 4

UCS-AlexNet	Normal	Mild	Moderate	Severe	Pearson coefficient
Severity score	0.24 (0)	0.94 (1)	2.04 (2)	2.72 (3)	**0.94**

(a number in () is our domain expert's manual evaluation)

4.4 Time Analysis

The experiments were run on 3.4 GHz machine with 32 GB of memory. They were implemented using MatLab and the MatConvNet library. The proposed UCS-AlexNet CNN could classify a single frame in 14.13 ms on average.

5 Concluding Remarks

In this paper, we improve in two ways our previous CNN-based endoscopic UC classification [4]. First, we add more thorough and essential preprocessing. Second, we subdivide each class of UC severity and generate sub-classes for the classification to accommodate large in class variations. The experimental results show that the proposed method provides a greatly improved accuracy to evaluate the severity of UC. As expected the accuracies of 'Mild' and 'Moderate' classes are a little worse than those of 'Normal' and 'Severe'. Given that inter-annotator agreement for these subclasses is challenging as well, we may not need to improve this further as the current results may be sufficient for use in clinical practice. However, when used in clinical practice, we will have to calculate segmental as well as whole colon UC scores in order to distinguish a mostly normal colon with severe proctitis from mild pan-colitis which both may have a similar whole colon UC score. Clearly, our current CNN-based application needs formal evaluation in clinical practice.

Acknowledgements. This research was supported in part by a grant from the NIH (Grant #1R01DK106130-01A1). Tavanapong, Wong, and Oh have an equity interest and management role in EndoMetric Corporation, Ames, IA50014, USA, a for profit company that markets endoscopy-related software. De Groen has a financial interest in EndoMetric. The terms of this arrangement have been reviewed and approved by Iowa State University and University of Minnesota in accordance with its conflict of interest policies.

References

1. Kappelman, M.D., Rifas-Shiman, S.L., Kleinman, K., Ollendorf, D., Bousvaros, A., Grand, R.J., et al.: The prevalence and geographic distribution of Crohn's disease and ulcerative colitis in the United State. Clin. Gastroenterol. Hepatol. **5**, 1424–1429 (2007)
2. Nosato, H., Sakanashi, H., Takahashi, E., Murakawa, M.: An objective evaluation method of ulcerative colitis with optical colonoscopy images based on higher order local auto-correlation features. In: IEEE 11th International Symposium on Biomedical Imaging ISBI, pp. 89–92 (2014)
3. Dahal, A., Oh, J., Tavanapong, W., Wong, J., de Groen, P.C.: Detection of ulcerative colitis severity in colonoscopy video frames. In: IEEE/ACM International Workshop on Content-Based Multimedia Indexing - CBMI 2015, Prague, Czech Republic, 10–12 June 2015, pp. 1–6 (2015). http://doi.org/10.1109/CBMI.2015.7153617
4. Alammari, A., Rezbaul Islam, A.B.M., Oh, J., Tavanapong, W., Wong, J., De Groen, P.C.: Classification of ulcerative colitis severity in colonoscopy videos using CNN. In: 9th International Conference on Information Management and Engineering (ICIME 2017), Barcelona, Spain, 9–11 October 2017, pp. 232–237 (2017)
5. De Chambrun, G.I.P., Peyrin-Biroulet, L., Lémann, M., Colombel, J.F.: Clinical implications of mucosal healing for the management of IBD. Nat. Rev. Gastroenterol. Hepatol. **7**(1), 15–29 (2010)
6. Krizhevsky, A., Sutskever, I., Hinton, G.: Imagenet classification with deep convolutional neural networks. In: Proceedings of Neural Information Processing Systems 2012 (NIPS), pp. 1106–1114 (2012)

7. Szegedy, C., et al.: Going deeper with convolutions. In: Proceedings of the IEEE Conference on Computer Vision and Pattern Recognition, pp. 1–9 (2015)
8. Abadi, M., Agarwal, A., Barham, P., et al.: TensorFlow: large-scale machine learning on heterogeneous distributed systems (2016). https://arxiv.org/abs/1603.04467
9. Alammari, A., Rezbaul Islam, A.B.M., Oh, J., Tavanapong, W., Wong, J., de Groen, P.C.: Non-informative frame classification in colonoscopy videos using CNNs. In: 3rd International Conference on Biomedical Imaging, Signal Processing (ICBSP 2018), Bari, Italy, 11–13 October 2018, pp. 35–42, (2018)
10. Wang, Y., Tavanapong, W., Wong, J., Oh, J., de Groen P.C.: Light reflection detection for colonoscopy images. Technical report, Department of Computer Science, Iowa State University (2009)
11. Tajbakhsh, N., et al.: Convolutional neural networks for medical image analysis: full training or fine tuning? IEEE Trans. Med. Imaging **35**(5), 1299–1312 (2016)

Infinite Gaussian Fisher Vector to Support Video-Based Human Action Recognition

Jorge L. Fernández-Ramírez[1](✉), Andrés M. Álvarez-Meza[2],
Álvaro A. Orozco-Gutiérrez[1], and Julian David Echeverry-Correa[1]

[1] Automatics Research Group, Universidad Tecnológica de Pereira, Pereira, Colombia
jorgeferram17@utp.edu.co
[2] Signal Processing and Recognition Group,
Universidad Nacional de Colombia - Sede Manizales, Manizales, Colombia

Abstract. Human Action Recognition (HAR) is a computer vision task that attempts to monitor, understand, and characterize humans in videos. Here, we introduce an extension to the conventional Fisher Vector encoding technique to support this task. The methodology, based on the Infinite Gaussian Mixture Model (IGMM) seeks to reveal a set of discriminant local spatio-temporal features for enabling the precise codification of visual information. Specifically, it is much simpler to handle the infinite limit from the IGMM, than working with traditional Gaussian Mixture Models (GMMs) with unknown sizes, that will require extensive cross-validation. Under this premise, we developed a fully automatic encoding methodology that avoids heuristically specifying the number of components in the mixture model. This parameter is known to greatly affect the recognition performance, and its inference with conventional methods implies a high computational burden. Moreover, the Markov Chain Monte Carlo implementation of the hierarchical IGMM effectively avoids local minima, which tend to plague mixtures trained by optimization-based methods. Attained results on the UCF50 and HMDB51 databases demonstrate that our proposal outperforms state of the art encoding approaches concerning the trade-off between recognition performance and computational complexity, as it drastically reduces both number of operations and memory requirements.

Keywords: Human Action Recognition · Infinite Gaussian Mixture Model · Fisher Vector · Video processing

1 Introduction

Human action recognition (HAR) is a computer vision task that seeks to monitor, understand, and characterize humans in videos [7]. This task has a wide pool of applications that include automatic surveillance, video indexing and retrieval, and virtual reality [5]. The conventional pipeline for action recognition can be

© Springer Nature Switzerland AG 2019
G. Bebis et al. (Eds.): ISVC 2019, LNCS 11845, pp. 38–49, 2019.
https://doi.org/10.1007/978-3-030-33723-0_4

divided into three stages: (i) feature extraction from raw videos, (ii) data representation, (iii) and classification into predefined categories [20].

In regard to feature extraction, the literature exhibits two trends, hand-crafted and Convolutional Neural Networks (CNNs) features. Both intend to describe the local space, codify the motion information, and then combine these sources for allowing the proper transcription of human activity [15]. To the date, Two-stream CNNs is the most effective framework for action recognition, employing two deep networks and fusion techniques to take advantage of both appearance and motion clues [13]. However, CNN-based methods hamper in-depth action analysis and understanding as there is not visual interpretability [22]. Moreover, deep learning requires large amounts of training data, which in many applications is not available [1]. On the contrary, The most popular hand-crafted feature estimation technique is known as Improved Dense Trajectories (iDT) [20]. The method, describes the local space of trajectories generated by tracking a dense grid of points. Employing descriptors such as Histograms of Oriented Gradients (HOG) for codifying appearance through color gradients, Histograms of Optical Flow (HOF) for describing movement, and Motion Boundary Histograms (MBH) for codifying changes in motion [3].

For data representation, authors proposed feature encoding and relevance analysis for highlighting salient patterns and enabling codification of visual information [12]. Super-vector based methods such as Fisher Vector (FV) and Vector of Locally Aggregated Descriptors (VLAD) are presented as the most well-known approaches for feature encoding in action recognition tasks [19]. On the other hand, non-linear relevance analysis using kernel methods have shown promising results in recent research [7]. Nevertheless, their kernel evaluation requires computing and storing large distance matrices, while also tuning parameters which increases computational complexity [7]. Lastly, it is convention to employ Support Vector Machines (SVM) for classification [17].

Both FV and VLAD methods are supported by the Gaussian Mixture Model (GMM) to generate a codebook of visual words [21]. These methods quantify the similarity between a video sample and previously computed codebook for encoding visual information through calculating Gaussian responsibilities [6]. However, GMMs trained by optimization-based methods, e.g. Expectation Maximization (EM), require extensive cross-validation for selecting the number of visual words in the codebook [8]. Moreover, the initialization required by these training methods makes models fall into local minima [2]. Therefore, using conventional GMM implies large number of operations and memory requirements, which increases the computational burden of conventional recognition systems.

In this paper, we introduce a novel data encoding framework using Bayesian inference and Dirichlet processes to support video-based HAR. Our approach is fully automatic, allowing every parameter in the model to be updated hierarchically through the Markov Chain Monte Carlo (MCMC) algorithm Gibbs sampling. Specifically, our approach includes a Infinite Gaussian Mixture model (IGMM) for revealing a set of discriminant visual words, trained through a MCMC-based optimization that evades local minima. In Fact, the infinite limit on the number components avoids estimating this parameter through extensive cross-validation. Attained results on both UCF50 and HMDB51 databases demonstrate that our proposal obtained promising recognition performance and computational savings, favoring HAR tasks.

The rest of the paper is organized as follows: Sect. 2 presents the main theoretical background. Section 3 describes the experimental setup. Section 4 introduces results and discussions. Finally, Sect. 5 presents conclusions and future work.

2   Infinite Gaussian Model for Fisher Vector Encoding

Let $\{Z_n \in \mathbb{R}^{T_n \times D}, y_n \in \mathbb{N}\}_{n=1}^N$ be an input-output pair set holding N human action videos. Each sample Z_n, is represented by T_n observations. The local space of every observation is characterized by a D-dimensional descriptor, as in [20]. The output label y_n denotes the specific human action of video n. From $Z \in \mathbb{R}^{T \times D}$, where $T = \sum_{n=1}^N T_n$, we aim to train a generative model using IGMM. The procedure is as follows [4]:

The likelihood from observation $z_t \in \mathbb{R}^D$ to a GMM with k_{rep} components is:

$$p(z_t | \{\mu_j, S_j, \pi_j\}_{j=1}^k) = \sum_{j=1}^{k_{\text{rep}}} \pi_j \mathcal{N}(\mu_j, S_j^{-1}) \tag{1}$$

where $\mu_j \in \mathbb{R}^D$ are mean vectors, $S_j \in \mathbb{R}^{D \times D}$ are precision matrices, and π_j are the mixing proportions. Variable k_{rep} denotes the number of Gaussian components that have associated data, named represented classes [14].

2.1   Component Parameters

The component means μ_j and precisions S_j are given by Gaussian and Wishart priors, respectively:

$$p(\mu_j | \lambda, R) \sim \mathcal{N}(\lambda, R^{-1}) \qquad p(S_j | \beta, W) \sim \mathcal{W}(\beta, W^{-1}) \tag{2}$$

where $\lambda \in \mathbb{R}^D$ is a mean vector, $R \in \mathbb{R}^{D \times D}$ and $W \in \mathbb{R}^{D \times D}$ are precision matrices, and β is the degrees of freedom. These hyper-parameters are common to all components. The conditional posterior on μ_j is obtained by conjugating its prior:

$$p(\mu_j | \lambda, R, \{z_t : c_{t,j} = 1\}, S_j) \propto \prod_{t: c_{t,j}=1} p(z_t | \mu_j, S_j) \times p(\mu_j | \lambda, R)$$
$$\sim \mathcal{N}\left((T_j \bar{z}_j S_j + \lambda R)(T_j S_j + R)^{-1}, (T_j S_j + R)^{-1}\right) \tag{3}$$

$c_t \in \mathbb{R}^k$ is a latent variable, with notation 1 of k, where k include both represented and unrepresented classes. Unrepresented classes are virtually infinite [18]. T_j is the number of observations belonging to class j. likewise, $\overline{z}_j$ is the average vector of these observations.

$$\overline{z}_j = \frac{1}{T_j} \sum_{t:c_{t,j}=1} z_t, \quad T_j = \sum_{t=1}^{T} c_{t,j} \tag{4}$$

The conditional posterior on S_j is obtained by conjugating its prior:

$$p(S_j|\beta, W, \{z_t : c_{t,j}=1\}, \mu_j) \propto \prod_{t:c_{t,j}=1} p(z_t|\mu_j, S_j) \times p(S_j|\beta, W)$$

$$\sim \mathcal{W}(\beta + T_j, [\frac{1}{\beta + T_j}(\beta W + \sum_{t:c_{t,j}=1} (z_t - \mu_j)^\top (z_t - \mu_j))]^{-1}) \tag{5}$$

2.2   Hyper-parameters

For hyper-parameters λ, R, and W the priors are defined as follows:

$$p(\lambda) \sim \mathcal{N}(\mu_Z, \mathbf{cov}_Z) \quad p(R) \sim \mathcal{W}(1, \mathbf{cov}_Z^{-1}) \quad p(W) \sim \mathcal{W}(1, \mathbf{cov}_Z) \tag{6}$$

variables $\mu_Z \in \mathbb{R}^D$ and $\mathbf{cov}_Z \in \mathbb{R}^{D \times D}$, are respectively the mean and covariance of Z. Following the procedure exposed in Sect. 2.1, the posterior distributions on hyper-parameters are obtained straight forward using the mean and precision priors, Eq. 2, as likelihoods in each case:

$$p(\lambda|\{\mu_j\}_{j=1}^{k_{\text{rep}}}, R) \propto \prod_{j=1}^{k_{\text{rep}}} p(\mu_j|\lambda, R) \times p(\lambda)$$

$$\sim \mathcal{N}\left((\mu_Z \mathbf{cov}_Z^{-1} + R \sum_{j=1}^{k_{\text{rep}}} \mu_j)(\mathbf{cov}_Z^{-1} + k_{\text{rep}} R)^{-1}, (\mathbf{cov}_Z^{-1} + k_{\text{rep}} R)^{-1} \right) \tag{7}$$

$$p(R|\{\mu_j\}_{j=1}^{k_{\text{rep}}}, \lambda) \propto \prod_{j=1}^{k_{\text{rep}}} p(\mu_j|\lambda, R) \times p(R)$$

$$\sim \mathcal{W}\left(k_{\text{rep}} + 1, \left[\frac{\mathbf{cov}_Z + \sum_{j=1}^{k_{\text{rep}}}(\mu_j - \lambda)^\top(\mu_j - \lambda)}{k_{\text{rep}} + 1}\right]^{-1} \right) \tag{8}$$

$$p(W|\{S_j\}_{j=1}^{k_{\text{rep}}}, \beta) \propto \prod_{j=1}^{k_{\text{rep}}} p(S_j|\beta, W) \times p(W)$$

$$\sim \mathcal{W}\left(k_{\text{rep}}\beta + 1, \left[\frac{\mathbf{cov}_Z^{-1} + \sum_{j=1}^{k_{\text{rep}}} S_j}{k_{\text{rep}}\beta + 1}\right]^{-1} \right) \tag{9}$$

Parameter β remains scalar after conjugacy. According to Rasmussen [16], it has gamma prior of the form:

$$g = \beta - D + 1 \tag{10}$$

$$p(g^{-1}) \sim \mathcal{G}(1, \frac{1}{D}) \quad \rightarrow \quad p(g) \propto g^{-\frac{3}{2}} \exp\{-\frac{D}{2\,g}\} \tag{11}$$

For this parameter the posterior distribution takes the following form:

$$p(g|\{\boldsymbol{S}_j\}_{j=1}^{k_{\mathrm{rep}}}, \boldsymbol{W}) \propto \prod_{j=1}^{k_{\mathrm{rep}}} p(\boldsymbol{S}_j|\beta, \boldsymbol{W}) \times p(g)$$

$$\propto (\frac{\beta}{2})^{\frac{k_{\mathrm{rep}}\,\beta\,D}{2}} g^{-\frac{3}{2}} \Gamma_D(\frac{\beta}{2})^{-k_{\mathrm{rep}}} \exp\{-\frac{D}{2g}\} \prod_{j=1}^{k_{\mathrm{rep}}} |\boldsymbol{W}\,\boldsymbol{S}_j|^{\frac{\beta}{2}} \exp\{-\frac{1}{2}\beta\,\mathrm{tr}(\boldsymbol{W}\,\boldsymbol{S}_j)\} \tag{12}$$

The later density is not standard form. However, $p(\log(g)|\{\boldsymbol{S}_j\}_{j=1}^{k_{\mathrm{rep}}}, \boldsymbol{W})$ is log-concave, so we may generate independent samples using the Adaptive Rejection Sampling technique (ARS), and transform these samples to get values of β.

2.3   Mixing Proportions and Latent Variables

In this section k is not limited to represented classes. For the mixing proportions π_j, the prior is a symmetric Dirichlet distribution with concentration α/k.

$$p(\{\pi_j\}_{j=1}^{k}|\alpha) \sim \mathrm{Dir}(\{\alpha/k\}_{j=1}^{k}) = \frac{\Gamma(\alpha)}{\Gamma(\alpha/k)^k} \prod_{j=1}^{k} \pi_j^{\alpha/k-1}, \tag{13}$$

where $\Gamma(\cdot)$ is the gamma function. Likewise, the joint distribution for the latent variable $\boldsymbol{c}_t$ has the following form:

$$p(\{c_{t,j}\}_{j=1}^{k}|\{\pi\}_{j=1}^{k}) = \prod_{j=1}^{k} \pi_j^{c_{t,j}}, \quad \{\forall t : \prod_{j=1}^{k} \pi_j^{T_j}\}, \tag{14}$$

Using the Dirichlet integral type I, the prior is directly written in terms of the latent variable:

$$p(\{c_j\}_{j=1}^{k}|\alpha) = \int p(\{c_j\}_{j=1}^{k}|\{\pi_j\}_{j=1}^{k})\, p(\{\pi_j\}_{j=1}^{k})d\pi_1 \cdots d\pi_k$$

$$= \frac{\Gamma(\alpha)}{\Gamma(\alpha/k)^k} \prod_{j=1}^{k} \frac{\Gamma(T_j + \alpha/k)}{\Gamma(\alpha/k)}. \tag{15}$$

For estimating variable $\boldsymbol{c}_t$, it is required the prior for a single indicator given all others. This is obtained from Eq. 15, keeping all but a single indicator fixed:

$$p(c_{t,j}=1|\boldsymbol{c}_{-t}, \alpha) = \frac{T_{-t,j} + \alpha/k}{T - 1 + \alpha}. \tag{16}$$

where the subscript $-t$ indicates all the indexes except t and $T_{-t,j}$ is the number of observations, excluding z_t, that are associated with component j.
Lastly, an inverse Gamma prior is chosen for parameter α:

$$p(\alpha^{-1}) \sim \mathcal{G}(1,1) \rightarrow p(\alpha) \propto \alpha^{-3/2} \exp\{-1/2\alpha\}. \tag{17}$$

The likelihood for α is derived from Eq. 15, its posterior distribution takes the following form:

$$p(\alpha|\{T_j\}_{j=1}^k, k) = p(\{T_j\}_{j=1}^k|\alpha) \times p(\alpha)$$
$$\propto \frac{\alpha^{k-3/2} \exp\{-1/2\alpha\}\Gamma(\alpha)}{\Gamma(T+\alpha)} \tag{18}$$

Sampling from the later density requires employing ARS. In the limit where $k \rightarrow \infty$, the conditional prior for c_t, Eq. 16, becomes:

Components where $T_{-t,j} > 0 :$ $\quad p(c_{t,j} = 1|c_{-i}, \alpha) \quad = \quad \dfrac{T_{-i,j}}{T-1+\alpha},$

else: $\quad p(c_t \neq c_{t'}, \{\forall t \neq t'\}|c_{-t}, \alpha) \quad = \quad \dfrac{\alpha}{T-1+\alpha}. \tag{19}$

The posterior is obtained by multiplying the complete likelihood, Eq. 1, and the latent variables prior, Eq. 19:

Components where $T_{-t,j} > 0 :$ $\quad p(c_{t,j} = 1|c_{-i}, \boldsymbol{\mu}_j, \boldsymbol{S}_j, \alpha)$

$$\propto \frac{T_{-i,j}}{T-1+\alpha} |\boldsymbol{S}_j|^{\frac{1}{2}} \exp\{-\frac{1}{2}(z_t - \boldsymbol{\mu}_j)\, \boldsymbol{S}\,(z_t - \boldsymbol{\mu}_j)^\top\}, \tag{20}$$

else: $\quad p(c_t \neq c_{t'}, \{\forall t \neq t'\}|c_{-t}, \boldsymbol{\lambda}, \boldsymbol{R}, \beta, \boldsymbol{W}, \alpha)$

$$\propto \frac{\alpha}{T-1+\alpha} \int p(z_t|\boldsymbol{\mu}_j, \boldsymbol{S}_j)\, p(\boldsymbol{\mu}_j, \boldsymbol{S}_j|\boldsymbol{\lambda}, \boldsymbol{R}, \beta, \boldsymbol{W})\, d\boldsymbol{\mu}_j\, d\boldsymbol{S}_j. \tag{21}$$

The likelihood for components with observations other than z_t is Gaussian with parameters $\boldsymbol{\mu}_j$ and $\boldsymbol{S}_j$. On the other hand, for unrepresented classes the likelihood parameters are obtained by sampling from the components priors, as the marginalization of existing parameters is not analytically tractable [16]. When an unrepresented class is chosen, a new class is introduced to the model. Likewise, when a class becomes empty, the class is removed from the model.

3   Experimental Setup

Database. To test our *Infinite Gaussian Fisher Vector* encoding approach (IGFV), we employ both the UCF50 [17] and HMDB51 [11] databases. The

UCF50 database contains realistic videos taken from Youtube, with substantial variation in-camera motion, object appearance, and illumination changes. For concrete testing, we use $N = 5967$ videos concerning 46 human action categories. Following the standard procedure, we perform a leave-one-group-out cross-validation scheme and report the average accuracy over 25 predefined groups [17]. On the other hand, the HMDB51 database is collected from a variety of sources. For the sake of simplicity, we use $N = 6510$ video sequences concerning 51 action categories. Following the proposed protocol, we perform 3-fold cross-validation and report the average accuracy over three predefined train-test splits [11].

Settings. For each video sample, we employ the hand-crafted Improved Dense Trajectory feature estimation technique (iDT), with the code provided by the authors in [20]. Using the default settings, we extract the following trajectory aligned descriptors: Histogram of Oriented Gradients (HOG), Histogram of Optical Flow (HOF), and Motion Boundary Histogram (MBHx, and MBHy). All descriptors are extracted along all valid trajectories and the resulting dimensionality D is 96 for HOG, MBHx, and MBHy, and 108 for HOF.

In practice, using the standard Wishart distribution for sampling model precisions S_j, R, and W may generate matrices that are not symmetric positive semidefinite (SPD). To avoid this inconvenient, we employ the Frobenius norm positive approximation from [10], that is: For an arbitrary matrix $A \in \mathbb{R}^{N \times N}$, its nearest SPD Frobenius approximation is set to be $\widehat{A}_F = (B + H)/2$, where H is the symmetric polar factor of $B = (A + A^\top)/2$.

We use the ARS algorithm for sampling scalar parameters β and α. In brief, the algorithm employs piecewise exponential functions for approximating any univariate log-concave density $h(x)$ through an envelope (upper hull) and squeezing function (lower hull). Both touch the density function at m sampled points, known as abscissae $(x_1, \ldots, x_m)$. Conventionally, the starting point x_1 is chosen such that $h'(x_1) > 0$, and the final point x_m is chosen such that $h'(x_m) < 0$, where $h'(x) = h(x)/dx$. Even though the method is adaptive and approximated curves will converge to the density function. An erroneous initialization generates ill-posed samples that hamper the proper operation of the algorithm. We solve this issue through a trial-and-error iterative solution. Finally, the samples are obtained as stated in [9].

Training. Initially, we randomly select a subsample of 5000 trajectories per category from the training set. Then, using PCA we select the most relevant attributes until 90% of input variability is preserved. Later, we employ the spatio-temporal pyramid technique for distributing the training partition into cells. For each spatio-temporal cell, we estimate an IGMM codebook using the procedure exposed in Sect. 2. The model starts with a single component, then 1000 iterations of Gibbs sampling are performed for updating all parameters and hyper-parameters iteratively from their posterior distribution, with 800 "burn in iterations". From the remaining 200 repetitions, we use Bayesian Information Criterion (BIC) for choosing the best available mixture model. Afterward, the conventional FV encoding technique is employed for representing locally described samples as super-vectors [7]. In short, the method quantifies the similarity between a video sample and trained IGMM model, named codebook. To the resulting super-vector, we apply a Power Normalization (PN) followed by the L2-Normalization. The above procedure is performed per descriptor. Ultimately, all four IGFV representations are concatenated together.

For the classification step, we use a one-vs-all Linear SVM with regularization parameter equal to 100. Figure 1 summarizes the IGFV training pipeline. It is worth noting that the feature extraction was performed in C++ and the remaining experiments in MATLAB.

4   Results and Discussions

ARS Correction. Figure 2 shows the proposed correction for ARS initialization, when sampling parameter α. In Fig. 2a, we see that abscissae x_1 and x_3 are chosen according to the conventional criteria (i.e., $h'(x_1) > 0$ and $h'(x_3) < 0$). Though $x_3 = 2.38$ satisfy the restriction, $m_3 = -0.002$. This value creates wide upper hull that may generate ill-posed samples. In this case, $\widehat{\alpha} = 3019$ when the abscissae range (most probable values) is around $[1.5, 2.4]$. To solve this problem, we iteratively increase x_3 by 50% until the upper hull is relatively constrained. Figure 2b is obtained through this procedure. Here, $x_3 = 3.6$, $m_3 = -2.18$, and the sampled parameter is $\widehat{\alpha} = 2.05$.

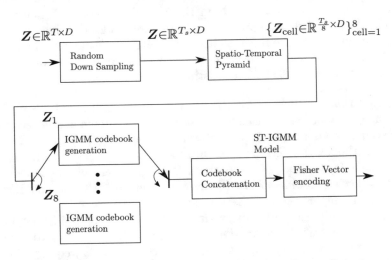

Fig. 1. Sketch of the proposed IGFV data encoding technique.

Confusion Matrices. Figure 3 shows the obtained confusion matrices using linear SVM for both employed databases. The proposal achieves $88.5 \pm 4.07\%$ and 57.6 ± 1.93 of mean accuracy, within the cross-validation scheme for each

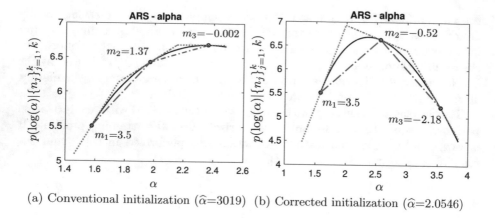

(a) Conventional initialization ($\widehat{\alpha}$=3019) (b) Corrected initialization ($\widehat{\alpha}$=2.0546)

Fig. 2. Adaptive Rejection Sampling with initialization correction. ——concave log-density, —·— lower hull, and · · · upper hull. Circular points indicate the initial three abscissae (x_1, x_2, x_3).

database. From a visual inspection on Fig. 3a, the system demonstrates the ability to discriminate among human actions, with slight errors in a few categories. On the other hand, the visual inspection on Fig. 3b shows how difficult it is for the system to classify actions from the HMDB51 dataset. When reviewed in detail, the provided bounding boxes from some videos do not correspond, partially or entirely, to the reported activity. Thus, the bad performance of the system may be explained by this issue, considering the importance of an effective human detection within iDT feature estimation.

Comparison with the State of the Art. In turn, Table 1 presents a comparative study among similar feature encoding approaches for human action recognition. In this study, we are analyzing properties and comparing characteristics among encoding methodologies. Thus, for feature extraction and classification we standard methods for the sake of comparison. Employed benchmarks have in common the following considerations: (i) are tested in both UCF50 and HMDB51 databases, (ii) employ the iDT feature estimation technique, (iii) perform classification through linear SVM. In particular, ST-VLAD [5] and SFV-STP [20], follow all requirements. However, they require extensive cross-validation for estimating the number of components k in their codebook. Moreover, ST-VLAD also needs searching the number of Spatio-temporal groups, which for both SFV-STP [20] and our IGFV are fixed to 8 cells, one division for each spatial and temporal axis.

Our main contribution is the automation of a methodology that conventionally requires extensive cross-validation. Thus, the slight drop in accuracy from our method, when compared to benchmarks, is compensated with computational savings, because it both reduces number of operations and memory requirements.

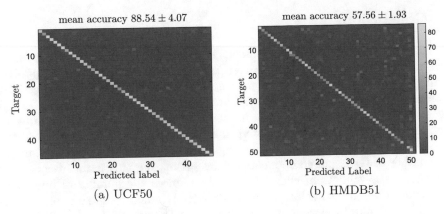

Fig. 3. Confusion matrices from Human Action Recognition in UCF50 and HMDB51 databases.

In particular, conventional GMM codebooks perform maximum likelihood estimation, through EM, of model parameters. Such optimization, performs a large number of iterations (in our case 500), and its convergence depends on initialization. Furthermore, this method needs fixing the number of components k before optimizing all other parameters (means, precision, and priors). Authors in [20], proposed searching k in a set comprising 10 different values and then selecting the best value according to classification performance. This approach requires cross-validating k in an operation that increases the number of iterations by 10 times the number of folds in the cross-validation. In terms of memory requirements, it requires storing all parameters 10 times, until the best k is chosen.

The drop in accuracy from our method could be attributed to the precisions sampled by the IGMM. In our case, IGMM samples complete precision matrices that are considering the correlation between attributes. For us, this is a disadvantage as the IGMM codebook suffers from low resolution, i.e., complete Gaussians can explain massive data clusters. Meanwhile, benchmarks approaches constrain covariances to diagonal or spherical matrices. Thus, the estimated number of components from IGMM is in the order of tens, whereas the exhaustive search from benchmarks converges to hundreds of components. This is an interesting result that demonstrates the quality of IGMM estimated codebooks, as fewer components allows the codification of discriminant visual information.

Table 1. Comparison with similar approaches on UCF50 and HMDB51 datasets.

Methods	Components	UCF50 [%]	HMDB51 [%]
ST-VLAD [5]	$k=256$ (exhaustive search)	90.7	59.0
SFV+STP [20]	$k=256$ (exhaustive search)	91.7	60.1
IGFV (proposal)	Automatic	88.5	57.6

5　Conclusions

We introduced a novel Infinite Gaussian Fisher Vector feature encoding framework to support video-based Human Action Recognition (IGFV). Our approach is fully automatic, allowing every parameter in the model to be updated hierarchically through the MCMC algorithm Gibbs sampling. The IGFV encoding allows revealing a set of discriminant local spatio-temporal features for enabling the precise codification of visual information, with competitive recognition results and computational savings. In particular, the infinite limit on the number of Gaussian components evades estimating this parameter through extensive cross-validation, which drastically reduces the number of operations and memory requirements for performing HAR. Attained results on both UCF50 and HMDB51 database showed that our proposal correctly classified 88.5% and 57.6% of human actions under the specific cross-validation of each dataset. Our IGFV obtained promising results that are comparable with state-of-art encoding approaches. Furthermore, it outperforms those approaches considering the trade-off between accuracy and computational complexity, as our proposal reduces both number of operations and memory requirements.

As future work, authors will evaluate alternatives for enhancing the resolution from IGMM codebooks, such as placing diagonal or spherical constrains to the sampled precision. We are convinced that all the already mentioned benefits from Bayesian inference and Dirichlet processes, combined with an enhanced model resolution, will yield better performance in human action recognition tasks.

Acknowledgments. Under grants provided by the project: "Prototipo de un sistema de recuperación de información por contenido orientado a la localización y clasificación de grupos de microcalcificaciones en mamografías - PROTOCAM", CV E6-19-1, from the VIIE-UTP. Also, J. Fernández is partially funded by the Colciencias program: *Jóvenes investigadores e innovadores-Convocatoria 812 de 2018*, and by the project "Sitema de clasificación de videos basado en técnicas de representación utilizando métodos núcleo e inferencia bayesiana", CV E6-19-2, from the VIIE-UTP.

References

1. Bloom, V., Argyriou, V., Makris, D.: Linear latent low dimensional space for online early action recognition and prediction. Pattern Recogn. **72**, 532–547 (2017)
2. Borges, P.V.K., Conci, N., Cavallaro, A.: Video-based human behavior understanding: a survey. IEEE Trans. Circuits Syst. Video Technol. **23**(11), 1993–2008 (2013)
3. Carmona, J., Climent, J.: Human action recognition by means of subtensor projections and dense trajectories. Pattern Recogn. **81**, 443–455 (2018)
4. Chen, T., Morris, J., Martin, E.: Probability density estimation via an infinite Gaussian mixture model: application to statistical process monitoring. J. R. Stat. Soc. Ser. C Appl. Stat. **55**(5), 699–715 (2006)
5. Duta, I.C., Ionescu, B., Aizawa, K., Sebe, N.: Spatio-temporal VLAD encoding for human action recognition in videos. In: Amsaleg, L., Guðmundsson, G., Gurrin, C., Jónsson, B., Satoh, S. (eds.) MMM 2017. LNCS, vol. 10132, pp. 365–378. Springer, Cham (2017). https://doi.org/10.1007/978-3-319-51811-4_30

6. Fan, W., Bouguila, N., Liu, X.: A nonparametric Bayesian learning model using accelerated variational inference and feature selection. Pattern Anal. Appl. **22**(1), 63–74 (2019)
7. Fernández-Ramírez, J., Álvarez-Meza, A., Orozco-Gutiérrez, Á.: Video-based human action recognition using kernel relevance analysis. In: Bebis, G., et al. (eds.) ISVC 2018. LNCS, vol. 11241, pp. 116–125. Springer, Cham (2018). https://doi.org/10.1007/978-3-030-03801-4_11
8. Field, M., Stirling, D., Pan, Z., Ros, M., Naghdy, F.: Recognizing human motions through mixture modeling of inertial data. Pattern Recogn. **48**(8), 2394–2406 (2015)
9. Gilks, W.R., Wild, P.: Adaptive rejection sampling for Gibbs sampling. J. R. Stat. Soc. Ser. C (Appl. Stat.) **41**(2), 337–348 (1992)
10. Higham, N.: Computing a nearest symmetric positive semidefinite matrix. Linear Algebra Appl. **103**(C), 103–118 (1988)
11. Kuehne, H., Jhuang, H., Garrote, E., Poggio, T., Serre, T.: HMDB: a large video database for human motion recognition. In: Proceedings of the International Conference on Computer Vision (ICCV) (2011)
12. Li, Q., Cheng, H., Zhou, Y., Huo, G.: Human action recognition using improved salient dense trajectories. Comput. Intell. Neurosci. **2016**, 1–11 (2016)
13. Ma, C.Y., Chen, M.H., Kira, Z., AlRegib, G.: TS-LSTM and temporal-inception: exploiting spatiotemporal dynamics for activity recognition. Sig. Process. Image Commun. **71**, 76–87 (2019)
14. Priya, T., Prasad, S., Wu, H.: Superpixels for spatially reinforced Bayesian classification of hyperspectral images. IEEE Geosci. Remote Sens. Lett. **12**(5), 1071–1075 (2015)
15. Qian, Y., Sengupta, B.: Pillar networks: combining parametric with non-parametric methods for action recognition. Robot. Autonomous Syst. **118**, 47–54 (2019)
16. Rasmussen, C.: The infinite Gaussian mixture model, pp. 554–559 (2000)
17. Reddy, K.K., Shah, M.: Recognizing 50 human action categories of web videos. Mach. Vis. Appl. **24**(5), 971–981 (2013)
18. Sicre, R., Nicolas, H.: Improved Gaussian mixture model for the task of object tracking. In: Real, P., Diaz-Pernil, D., Molina-Abril, H., Berciano, A., Kropatsch, W. (eds.) CAIP 2011. LNCS, vol. 6855, pp. 389–396. Springer, Heidelberg (2011). https://doi.org/10.1007/978-3-642-23678-5_46
19. Uijlings, J., Duta, I.C., Sangineto, E., Sebe, N.: Video classification with densely extracted HOG/HOF/MBH features: an evaluation of the accuracy/computational efficiency trade-off. Int. J. Multimedia Inf. Retrieval **4**(1), 33–44 (2015)
20. Wang, H., Oneata, D., Verbeek, J., Schmid, C.: A robust and efficient video representation for action recognition. Int. J. Comput. Vis. **119**(3), 219–238 (2016)
21. Wang, S., Hou, Y., Li, Z., Dong, J., Tang, C.: Combining convnets with hand-crafted features for action recognition based on an HMM-SVM classifier. Multimedia Tools Appl. **77**(15), 18983–18998 (2018)
22. Weng, J., Weng, C., Yuan, J., Liu, Z.: Discriminative spatio-temporal pattern discovery for 3D action recognition. IEEE Trans. Circuits Syst. Video Technol. **29**(4), 1077–1089 (2019)

Deep Learning II

Do Humans Look Where Deep Convolutional Neural Networks "Attend"?

Mohammad K. Ebrahimpour[1]([✉]), J. Ben Falandays[2], Samuel Spevack[2], and David C. Noelle[1,2]

[1] EECS, University of California, Merced, USA
{mebrahimpour,dnoelle}@ucmerced.edu
[2] Cognitive and Information Sciences, University of California, Merced, USA
{bfalandays,sspevack}@ucmerced.edu

Abstract. Deep Convolutional Neural Networks (CNNs) have recently begun to exhibit human level performance on some visual perception tasks. Performance remains relatively poor, however, on some vision tasks, such as *object detection*: specifying the location and object class for all objects in a still image. We hypothesized that this gap in performance may be largely due to the fact that humans exhibit *selective attention*, while most object detection CNNs have no corresponding mechanism. In examining this question, we investigated some well-known attention mechanisms in the deep learning literature, identifying their weaknesses and leading us to propose a novel attention algorithm called the *Densely Connected Attention Model*. We then measured human spatial attention, in the form of eye tracking data, during the performance of an analogous object detection task. By comparing the learned representations produced by various CNN architectures with that exhibited by human viewers, we identified some relative strengths and weaknesses of the examined computational attention mechanisms. Some CNNs produced attentional patterns somewhat similar to those of humans. Others focused processing on objects in the foreground. Still other CNN attentional mechanisms produced usefully interpretable internal representations. The resulting comparisons provide insights into the relationship between CNN attention algorithms and the human visual system.

Keywords: Visual spatial attention · Computer vision · Convolutional Neural Networks · Densely connected attention maps · Class Activation Maps · Sensitivity analysis

1 Introduction

Recent years have seen huge advances in the use of artificial neural networks (ANNs) in a wide variety of machine learning applications. One particularly

© Springer Nature Switzerland AG 2019
G. Bebis et al. (Eds.): ISVC 2019, LNCS 11845, pp. 53–65, 2019.
https://doi.org/10.1007/978-3-030-33723-0_5

promising domain is computer vision, for which deep Convolutional Neural Networks (CNNs) have been proven successful in tasks such as classification, semantic segmentation, image captioning, and object detection. The impressive capabilities of such networks, which have met or even surpassed human performance in some vision tasks [5], are somewhat surprising given how little is actually understood about their internal operations. Due to the large number of nonlinear interactions inside these networks, ANNs have long been treated as "black boxes", with their inner workings opaque to even their creators.

However, just as the "black box" perspective on the human mind gave way to the development of new methods and theoretical tools, researchers in computer science have recently begun finding new ways of understanding the intermediate representations produced by ANNs [14]. For example, methods of "deep visualization" examine the representations learned by individual artificial neurons by iteratively generating a synthetic input image that maximally activates each neuron. The images produced in this process are often surprisingly interpretable by the human eye [5], suggesting that these networks may learn feature representations that are perhaps similar to those of the human visual system.

Of course, ANNs have been at the heart of powerful models of human cognitive processes for over three decades [8]. In the field of computational cognitive neuroscience, ANNs have served a crucial role in discriminating between various proposed models of the structure and dynamics of cognitive and brain systems [6]. By comparing the performance of human participants to ANNs of various designs, researchers can investigate the feasibility of specific network models for explaining aspects of brain and behavior. For example, while most CNNs designed for object recognition are purely feedforward, Rajaei and colleagues recently argued, based on neuroimaging data and computational models, that recurrent connections are crucial for performance under cases of degraded input, such as partial object occlusion [7]. This serves to illustrate that, by examining where humans succeed and ANNs fail, we can improve both our understanding of the brain and create more effective computer vision systems.

In this spirit, computer scientists have been taking inspiration from the human visual system to improve the speed and accuracy of CNNs for object detection. In particular, visual selective attention has been proposed as one mechanism that is crucial for human object detection performance, but such a mechanism is absent from most algorithms designed for the same purpose. Several CNN techniques have now been proposed that implement some form of selective attention [2,9,16], but it is unknown how these attention algorithms compare to human selective attention. Examining the differences and similarities between human overt visual attention and the attentional representations produced in these CNNs will help to hone our understanding of specifically which features of the human visual system may most fruitfully be modeled by CNNs (and for which tasks), or, indeed, whether deep networks offer a promising approach to understanding human vision, at all. Given the relative power of human vision in comparison to state-of-the-art object detection CNNs, comparisons of

Fig. 1. Results of the human eye tracking study on some of our test images. The heatmaps reveal the distribution of attention.

this kind might also suggest new and better biologically-inspired approaches to selective attention in computer vision.

For the sake of comparison, we took human behavior to be approximately normative with regard to the allocation of attention. We recorded the eye motions of humans as they detected objects in still images, and we took these data as indicating the image regions most worthy of overt selective attention. We then examined a variety of CNN approaches to attention, including a new architecture, proposed here, called the *Densely Connected Attention Model*. We assessed the approaches with regard to their correspondence to human performance. The resulting analyses have produced insights into both human selective attention and the design of computer vision object detection systems. By identifying the layers within the Densely Connected Attention Model that best capture human selective attention, we were able to identify the sort of visual features that best predict the distribution of human eye fixations. By comparing various CNN methods, we were able to characterize their relative strengths and weaknesses for attention-guided object detection.

2 Eye Tracking Study

Participants. Our participants were 15 healthy undergraduate students (12 female, 3 male; age: mean ± s.d. = 20.06 ± 1.62) at University of California, Merced. Participants received one hour of course credit for their participation. Participants provided informed consent in accordance with IRB protocols. Participation was restricted to individuals with normal vision, as reported on a pre-screen survey.

Materials. The stimuli were a subset of 200 images drawn from the PASCAL Visual Object Classes 2007 database [4]. Each image was scaled up to twice its original size for display on a 1920 × 1080 screen. The display width of images was between 636–1000 pixels, subtending 23.83–34.76° of visual angle. The display height of images was between 350–1000 pixels, subtending 13.68–34.76° of visual angle. Images were centered on a black background.

Fig. 2. Results of the CAM attention algorithm. The heatmaps reveal the attention of the CNN.

Procedure. Participants completed an object detection task individually in the lab. Participants were seated at a desk in front of a computer screen and wore a head-mounted Eyelink II eye tracker. The eye tracker was set to pupil/corneal reflection recording mode and sampled at a rate of 250 Hz. A microphone was placed near participants to record their speech. Before beginning the task, the eye tracker was calibrated with a nine-point grid. Participants were also shown how to perform a drift correction, which occurred prior to each trial. Eye movement data was collected with the Eyelink software and custom Matlab scripts, implemented with the Psychophysics toolbox Matlab package [1].

Each trial started with a drift correction in which participants had to fixate a center dot and press the space bar to initiate the trial. Participants were allowed to pause on the drift correction screen for as long as they wished before initiating a trial. Then, a randomly selected image was displayed on the screen for 5000 ms. Participants were instructed to name out loud as many unique objects as they could detect within the time limit. This was repeated until participants had viewed all 200 images, once each. The experiment took about 30 min to complete, with ∼10 min dedicated to setup and calibration and ∼20 spent on the task itself.

Data Processing. The raw eye tracking data was first converted into a Matlab-compatible data structure using the `Edf2Mat` package. Then, custom scripts were used to generate fixation heatmaps for each image. Recorded fixations contributed to the heatmaps only if they fell entirely within the period of display. Fixations were first pooled from all participants. Then, for each image a zero matrix was generated with the same dimensions as the pixel dimensions of the original (before scaling for display) image. Fixation coordinates from the display images were then scaled down to map onto the coordinates of the original sizes. Each possible fixation position then corresponded to a position within the zero matrix for that image. For each recorded fixation at a given location, the value of the corresponding cell in the zero matrix was increased by the duration of the fixation in milliseconds. Then, all values were divided by the maximum value in the matrix such that possible values ranged between zero and one. Finally, we performed a convolution over the matrix with a Gaussian kernel ($\sigma = 20$, size $= 80 \times 80$). This process generated a fixation heatmap showing the relative likelihood of fixations occurring at each region of each image. Examples of the human eye tracking overt visual attention maps are illustrated in Fig. 1.

3   Attention Models

In recent years, deep CNNs have demonstrated human level performance on image classification tasks when given large amounts of supervised training data. This impressive performance has led to a growing interest in understanding the internal representations learned by the networks [3,10,14,15]. Of particular interest, here, are the mechanisms of "selective attention" in these networks that allow them to focus on relevant portions of input images. In this section, we review several previously published approaches and then propose a novel CNN architecture: the *Densely Connected Attention Model.*

3.1   Class Activation Maps

Zhou et al. proposed a technique called *Class Activation Maps (CAM)* [16]. These were predicated on the observation that deep CNN architectures for computer vision lose spatial information close to the network output due to the use of fully connected layers after the convolutional layers. The authors proposed "chopping off" the fully connected layers and calculating the *Global Average Pooling (GAP)* of activation at the last convolutional layer, aggregating the spatial information in each channel. For a given image, let $f_k(x,y)$ represent the activation of filter k in the last convolutional layer at spatial location (x,y). Then, for filter k, the result of performing GAP is $F^k = \sum_{x,y} f_k(x,y)$. A linear regression can be conducted between the F^k values and each output score, S_c, for each object class, c, producing regression weights, w_k^c. Given these weights, the CAM for a given image, with regard to object class, c, is:

$$M_c(x,y) = \sum_k w_k^c f_k(x,y) \tag{1}$$

The authors argued that using this approach would preserve more spatial location information for the main objects in the image. Examples of CAMs are depicted in Fig. 2. This method has a number of drawbacks. Specifically, determining the regression weights takes time, and using the attention information in the suggested manner can noticeably decrease classification performance.

Gradient Based Class Activation Maps. With the goal of improving on the CAM method, Selvaraju and colleagues proposed a different approach [9]. They argued that the weights for each channel that are used in CAMs are implicit in the CNN, itself, so there is no need to perform additional regressions [9]. They

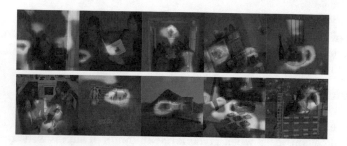

Fig. 3. Results of the Grad-CAM attention algorithm. The heatmaps show attended regions.

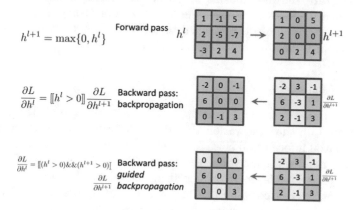

Fig. 4. An illustration of the training process used in guided-backpropagation.

suggested taking the derivative of the winning (i.e., greatest) object class output with regard to the activation in the last convolutional layer of the network:

$$A = \frac{\partial y_c}{\partial f} \tag{2}$$

where y_c is the output activation for object class, c, and $f \in \mathbb{R}^{W \times H \times K}$ is the last convolutional layer. The derivative values are aggregated channel-wise into a matrix, A, and the weights for each channel are computed as:

$$a_k^c = \frac{1}{W \times H} \sum_{x \in W} \sum_{y \in H} A(x, y) \tag{3}$$

This weight, a_k^c, is intended to capture the "importance" of channel k for a target class c. The corresponding attention maps are calculated similarly to CAMs, though values are rectified (ReLU) to be positive:

$$L_{Grad-CAM}^c = ReLU(\sum_k a_k^c f_k) \tag{4}$$

Notice that this results in a coarse heatmap of the same size as the convolutional feature maps (14 × 14 in the case of the last convolutional layers of the VGG network). Since this method made use of gradient information, it is called *Grad-CAM*. Example Grad-CAM attention maps are illustrated in Fig. 3.

Guided-Backpropagation. The *Guided-Backpropagation* technique was proposed as a way to train CNNs so as to make activation in convolutional feature maps easier to interpret [12]. The goal was to encourage units to only become active if they are contributing to the activation of the appropriate object class output. This would make the spatial location of active units indicative of where objects were. The method involved modifying the standard *backpropagation of error* algorithm [8] by suppressing negative gradients. Unit error (delta) values were rectified, hindering the formation of strong negative connection weights. The bias toward positive weights made the "meaning" of learned features easier to interpret. A very simple example of this learning process is illustrated in Fig. 4. Figure 5 shows the resulting attention maps (where activation is high) for some example images.

Guided-Gradient Based Class Activation Maps. In order to obtain information about both relevant image regions and relevant pixels within regions, Selvaraju and colleagues fused Guided-Backpropagation with Gradient Based Class Activation Maps, producing the *Guided Grad-CAM* method [9]. The merging of the previous algorithms was done in a simple manner. The attention maps resulting from the two algorithms were combined using point-wise multiplication. Some example results are displayed in Fig. 6.

The reviewed attention algorithms so far are using the last convolutional layer as their main source for attention. The encapsulated information in the last convolution layer is mostly abstract and it has lost lots of spatial information due to the pooling under sampling layers. To overcome this issue, we suggest using the hidden information in all layers, the early ones as well as the deepest ones, to maximize the sophisticated information as well as the spatial information of the input image.

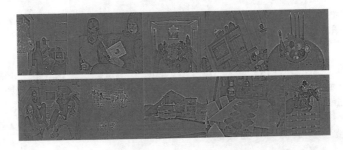

Fig. 5. Results of the Guided-Backpropagation attention algorithm. The color-coded maps show attended pixels.

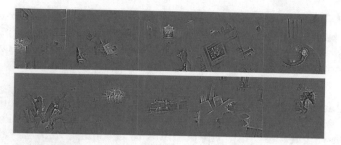

Fig. 6. Results of the Guided-Grad-CAM attention algorithm. The color-coded maps show attended pixels.

3.2   The Densely Connected Attention Model

All of these CNN attentional mechanisms rely on activation in the last convolutional layer. Information in earlier layers of the networks is ignored. It is possible, however, that useful guidance for attention might be found in the earlier convolutional layers, where spatial resolution tends to be higher and detected visual features tend to be more simple and smaller. Our proposed *Densely Connected Attention Model* assembles information from each channel and each spatial location across all of the layers in the CNN image classifier. Our method is fast and efficient, and it does not require any additional training of the CNN. A schematic of our approach is shown in Fig. 7.

Spatial Attention. Generally speaking, objects occupy only portions of images, leaving background regions that can distract and misinform object detection systems. Instead of considering all parts of an image equally, spatial attention can focus processing on foreground regions, supporting the extraction of features most relevant for determining object class and object extent.

Formally, the annotation that we use to represent the activation of convolutional feature layer n is $f_n \in \mathbb{R}^{W \times H \times C}$, where W and H are the spatial dimensions of the rectangular layer and C is the number of feature channels in the layer. Spatial positions are specified by coordinate pairs: $\mathbb{L} = \{(x, y) | x = 1, 2, \ldots, W; y = 1, 2, \ldots, H\}$.

For layer n in a pretrained image classification network, the layer-specific spatial attention map is . . .

$$A_n^s = W_n^s \odot f_n \tag{5}$$

. . . where W_n^s are weights that indicate the importance of each spatial location, across all of the convolutional channels. We initially calculate these weights based on the sensitivity of the *Gestalt Total (GT)* activation of the network to the feature [2]. The Gestalt Total is calculated from the activation of the last convolutional layer, A_{last}, as follows:

$$GT = \frac{1}{H \times W \times C} \sum_{i,j,k} A_{last}^s(i, j, k) \tag{6}$$

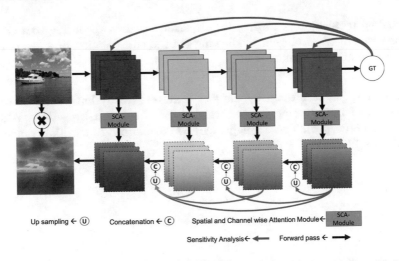

Fig. 7. The network architecture of the *Densely Connected Attention Model.*

The sensitivity of GT to a feature at layer n is ...

$$G_n = \frac{\partial GT}{\partial f_n} \tag{7}$$

$$\hat{W}_n^s(x,y) = \sum_c^C G_n(x,y,c), \tag{8}$$

... where $\hat{W}_n^s$ is not normalized (i.e., the weights are not in the $[0,1]$ range). To normalize the weights for each location, we apply a softmax operation to the weights spatially ...

$$W_n^s(x,y) = \frac{\exp(\hat{W}_n^s(x,y))}{\sum_{i\in W, j\in H} \exp(\hat{W}_n^s(i,j))}, \tag{9}$$

... where $W_n^s(x,y)$ denotes the weight for location (x,y) in layer n.

Channel-Wise Attention. The spatial attention calculation assigns weights to spatial locations, which addresses the problem of distractions from background regions. There is another way in which distractions can arise, however. Specific channels at a given layer can be distracting. When dealing with convolutional features, most of the existing methods treat all channels without distinction. However, different channels often have different degrees of relevance for objects of specific classes. Here, we introduce a channel-wise attention mechanism that assigns larger weights to channels for which the GT is sensitive, given the currently presented image. Incorporating these channel-wise attentional weights are intended to reduce this kind of distracting interference.

For channel-wise attention, we unfold f_n as $f = [f_n^1, f_n^2, \ldots, f_n^C]$, where $f_n^i \in \mathbb{R}^{W\times H}$ is the ith channel slice of f_n, and C is the total number of channels.

The goal is to calculate a weight, W_n^c, to scale features according to a channel-specific assessment of relevance, allowing for the construction of a layer-specific channel-wise attention map:

$$A_n^c = W_n^c \cdot f_n \tag{10}$$

Computing W_n^c is facilitated by the fact that we already have the sensitivities, G_n. Thus, an initial value for the weights can be found by setting $\hat{W}_n^c(c) = \sum_{x \in W, y \in H} G_n(x, y, c)$. These weights can be normalized to the $[0, 1]$ range using the softmax function:

$$W_n^c(c) = \frac{\exp(\hat{W}_n^c(c))}{\sum_{i \in C} \exp(\hat{W}_n^c(i))}, \tag{11}$$

These are the final channel-wise weights for layer n.

Dense Attention Maps. Given the spatial attention weights and the channel-wise attention weights, an attention weighted feature for layer n is calculated as
...

$$f_n^{SCA} = A_n^c \cdot f_n + A_n^s \odot f_n, \tag{12}$$

...with $f_n^{SCA} \in \mathbb{R}^{W \times H \times C}$. (In Fig. 7, this computation is done in the *Spatial and Channel wise Attention Module – SCA-Module*.) For the last convolutional layer, m, the attention map is simply the weighted features: $A_m = f_m^{SCA}$. For earlier layers, the weighted features are concatenated across layers, incrementally from the last layer to the first, but this is done after up-scaling lower spatial resolution (later) convolutional layers:

$$A_i^{SCA} = [UP(f_m^{SCA}), UP(f_{m-1}^{SCA}), \ldots, f_i^{SCA}]$$
$$i = \{1, \ldots, m-1\} \tag{13}$$

This process generates dense combination maps that are intended to incorporate both semantic information from the late layers and higher resolution spatial information from the early layers. The maps are aggregated to produce a single attention map for the whole image. Since each layer can have a different number of channels, we simplify this aggregation by averaging each layer's attention map across channels, transforming each A_i^{SCA} into a $W \times H$ matrix. The aggregated attention maps at each layer are then computed as:

$$A_i = A_m^{SCA} + A_{m-1}^{SCA} + \ldots + A_i^{SCA}. \tag{14}$$

It is important to note that the attention weights (W_n^s and W_n^c) are not learned as part of a training process. We begin with a pretrained image classification network (VGG16 [11]), and the attention weights are efficiently calculated for each layer when a given image is presented to that network. Some resulting attention maps from our model are shown in Fig. 8.

4 Comparing CNN and Human Attention Maps

We have reviewed several existing CNN attention algorithms, and we have proposed a novel Densely Connected Attention Model which incorporates spatial attention as well as channel-wise attention in each layer. We compared the attention maps of the various CNNs with overt visual attention maps produced from our eye tracking data, using exactly the same images in all cases. Our summary comparison statistic was the mean absolute error (MAE) between attention maps ...

$$MAE = \frac{1}{W \times H} \sum_{x=1}^{W} \sum_{y=1}^{H} |S(x,y) - G(x,y)| \qquad (15)$$

...where W and H are the width and height of the image, $S(.)$ is the attention map from a network, and $G(.)$ is the "ground truth" (human performance) attention map. We compared different CNN attention methods, but we also examined the fit of various attention maps at individual internal layers of the Densely Connected Attention Model. The resulting error values are summarized in Fig. 9.

These results reveal that the CAM algorithm provides the closest match to overt visual human attention on our test images, while the second layer in our proposed attention mechanism comes in second place. The fact that layer 2 of our network is much closer to the attentional patterns of human participants than later layers is quite surprising, given the total reliance on the final convolutional layer seen in other mechanisms. However, the combination of layers in our attention mechanism makes the attentional pattern somewhat dissimilar to that of humans.

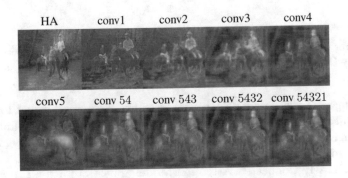

Fig. 8. Results of the Densely Connected Attention Model for each convolutional layer, as well as for combinations of layers. The numbers following the "conv" label indicate layer number. For instance, "conv 54" refers to the combination of layers 5 and 4. Human eye tracking results for this example image are also shown (HA).

5   Discussion

We investigated various deep CNN visual attention mechanisms and compared their attentional patterns to that of human participants. We also proposed a novel attention algorithm which integrates more kinds of information, at multiple scales, than the other approaches. We found that the CAM algorithm provides the best match to human performance, with the second convolutional layer of our Densely Connected Attention Model ranking second. In general, none of the CNN algorithms provided a particularly good match to overt visual human attention, however. Thus, while deep CNNs may learn a hierarchy of visual features similar to the response properties of neurons in the human visual system [13], current attentional mechanisms in CNNs do not seem to align with human overt attention.

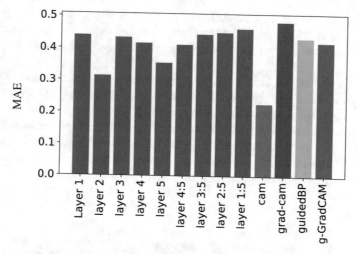

Fig. 9. Error between human attention maps and those produced at various layers of the Densely Connected Attention Model. Also shown are errors for other algorithms.

This suggests that human attention may not be a good guide for improving the object detection performance of deep CNNs. We have found that the attention maps produced by CAM, Grad-CAM, Guided-Backpropagation, and Guided Grad-CAM tend to focus on a single salient object in the image. In contrast, the Densely Connected Attention Model appears to attend to all objects in the image, ignoring background distractions. Despite these benefits, the CNN attention maps in our model were quite different than those of humans, with the greatest similarity appearing in layers that encode fairly low-level features. Interestingly, the results suggest that the distribution of human spatial attention is largely driven by low level visual features, as evidenced by the better performance of layer 2. We are left with interesting questions concerning the nature of the differences between CNN object detection and human vision that give rise to this mismatch of attentional patterns.

References

1. Brainard, D.H., Vision, S.: The psychophysics toolbox. Spat. Vis. **10**, 433–436 (1997)
2. Ebrahimpour, M.K., et al.: Ventral-dorsal neural networks: object detection via selective attention. In: WACV (2019)
3. Erhan, D., Bengio, Y., Courville, A., Vincent, P.: Visualizing higher-layer features of a deep network. Univ. Montreal **1341**(3), 1 (2009)
4. Everingham, M., Van Gool, L., Williams, C.K.I., Winn, J., Zisserman, A.: The PASCAL visual object classes (VOC) challenge. Int. J. Comput. Vis. **88**(2), 303–338 (2010)
5. Nguyen, A., Yosinski, J., Clune, J.: Multifaceted feature visualization: uncovering the different types of features learned by each neuron in deep neural networks. arXiv preprint arXiv:1602.03616 (2016)
6. O'Reilly, R.C., Munakata, Y.: Computational Explorations in Cognitive Neuroscience: Understanding the Mind by Simulating the Brain. MIT Press, Cambridge (2000)
7. Rajaei, K., Mohsenzadeh, Y., Ebrahimpour, R., Khaligh-Razavi, S.M.: Beyond core object recognition: Recurrent processes account for object recognition under occlusion, p. 302034 (2018). bioRxiv
8. Rumelhart, D.E., McClelland, J.L.: Parallel Distributed Processing: Explorations in the Microstructure of Cognition. Volume 1: Foundations. MIT Press, Cambridge (1986)
9. Selvaraju, R.R., Cogswell, M., Das, A., Vedantam, R., Parikh, D., Batra, D.: Grad-CAM: visual explanations from deep networks via gradient-based localization. In: ICCV (2017)
10. Simonyan, K., Vedaldi, A., Zisserman, A.: Deep inside convolutional networks: visualising image classification models and saliency maps. arXiv preprint arXiv:1312.6034 (2013)
11. Simonyan, K., Zisserman, A.: Very deep convolutional networks for large-scale image recognition. arXiv preprint arXiv:1409.1556 (2014)
12. Springenberg, J.T., Dosovitskiy, A., Brox, T., Riedmiller, M.: Striving for simplicity: the all convolutional net. arXiv preprint arXiv:1412.6806 (2014)
13. Yamins, D.L.K., Hong, H., Cadieu, C.F., Solomon, E.A., Seibert, D., DiCarlo, J.J.: Performance-optimized hierarchical models predict neural responses in higher visual cortex. Proc. Natl. Acad. Sci. **111**(23), 8619–8624 (2014)
14. Yosinski, J., Clune, J., Nguyen, A., Fuchs, T., Lipson, H.: Understanding neural networks through deep visualization. arXiv preprint arXiv:1506.06579 (2015)
15. Zeiler, M.D., Fergus, R.: Visualizing and understanding convolutional networks. In: ECCV (2014)
16. Zhou, B., Khosla, A., Lapedriza, A., Oliva, A., Torralba, A.: Learning deep features for discriminative localization. In: CVPR (2016)

Point Auto-Encoder and Its Application to 2D-3D Transformation

Wencan Cheng and Sukhan Lee[✉]

SungKyunKwan University, Suwon 16419, South Korea
{cwcl260,lshl}@skku.edu

Abstract. PointNet has been shown to be an efficient way to encode the global geometric features of a point cloud representation of 3D objects based on supervised learning. Although it is quite interesting to have a decoder integrated into PointNet for possible unsupervised end-to-end learning, similar to conventional auto-encoders, only a few methods have been proposed to date. The proposed methods are shown to be able to reconstruct the given input point cloud from the corresponding global features through decoders, however, further improvements not only in their performance of training in terms of accuracy but also in their power of generalization in decoding testing samples. This paper presents a Point Auto-Encoder, or Point AE, which is implemented based on the novel semi-convolutional and semi-fully-connected layers proposed that can handle the problem of mapping from single global feature vector to massive numbers of 3D points. The proposed Point AE is not only simpler in its architecture but also more powerful in terms of training performance and generalization capability than state-of-the-art methods. The effectiveness of Point AE is well verified based on the ShapeNet and ModelNet40 dataset. Furthermore, in order to demonstrate the extended capability of Point AE, we apply Point AE to the automatic transformation of images from 2D to 3D and 3D to 2D.

Keywords: Deep learning · Point cloud · 3D auto-encoder · 3D reconstruction · Single image reconstruction

1 Introduction

In three-dimensional object recognition, 3D point cloud representation has been widely used as a powerful tool in autonomous driving, machine vision, virtual reality, etc., and many excellent methods for such representation have emerged. However, the processing of 3D point cloud is very difficult because of its disorder, which contradicts the structure of the traditional convolutional neural network (CNN), because CNN requires data input that is ordered and related to adjacent elements. In order to solve this problem, voxelization is proposed to fit for the structure of CNN, but voxelization sacrifices the details of the point cloud, while ordering adds a large number of redundant voxels, which unnecessarily increases the computational overhead and reduces the accuracy. The emergence of PointNet [1] completely solves this problem. With its lightweight and efficient symmetrical structure, state-of-art results can be

© Springer Nature Switzerland AG 2019
G. Bebis et al. (Eds.): ISVC 2019, LNCS 11845, pp. 66–78, 2019.
https://doi.org/10.1007/978-3-030-33723-0_6

obtained in the direct processing of disordered point clouds. However, the symmetrical structure in which max-pooling operation generates global features poses a challenge to unsupervised reconstruction, because it retains part of the global information and discards a large amount of structural information, making it more difficult to reconstruct the three-dimensional structure using the global features.

Most of the existing unsupervised reconstruction methods use the fully-connected layer after the global feature, trying to store the structural information that lost in the previous learning through a massive structure, but this requires very large storage and calculation. Later, the proposal of the FoldingNet [2] showed that the performance of the original fully-connected structure can be achieved even with a very lightweight structure.

In this work, we proposed a novel semi-convolution semi-fully-connection layer, by which we can avoid a large amount of storage and calculation of the original fully connected structure. Base on this new operation, we proposed a novel Auto-Encoder structure. the Auto-Encoder uses the basic structure of PointNet [1] to extract the global information of the disordered point cloud. The encoder output is a global feature that can be used as high-dimensional information of the corresponding 3D point cloud. In addition, in the decoder, we will recover the original 3D structure directly from the high-dimensional global feature by using multiple proposed semi-convolution semi-fully-connection layers.

At the same time, using the above-mentioned global feature-based decoder reconstruction network, we cannot only restore the original point cloud through the global feature of the point cloud obtained by the point encoder. Moreover, we also proposed a method for combining and training a global feature with a two-dimensional image auto-encoder so as to enable the extraction of a global feature corresponding to a 3-dimensional point cloud from a 2-dimensional image. In addition, through the reconstruction network, the transformation from a 2D image to a 3D point cloud can be achieved. On the other hand, through this concept, we can also extract 2D images generated from a projection that is relative to a surface from a 3D point cloud.

The contribution of this work can be summarized as follows:

We proposed novel semi-convolutional and semi-fully-connected layers for implementing the decoder of PointNet. The proposed Point AE is not only simpler in its architecture but also more powerful in terms of training performance and generalization capability than state-of-the-art methods.

We also show a transformation network that achieves transformation from 2D to 3D and from 3D to 2D using the global feature of the autoencoder.

2 Related Work

Auto-Encoder for 3D Point Cloud. The Auto-Encoder (AE) is an unsupervised learning algorithm typically used for dimension reduction [7, 8] and network pretraining [10]. Especially in the unsupervised learning of two-dimensional images, AE can extract useful features from images and filter out useless information, allowing for the extracted features to then be reconstructed by a decoder [7, 9, 11, 12, 18]. Based on

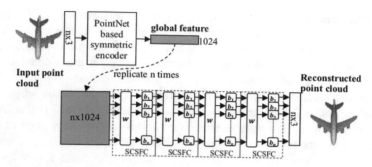

Fig. 1. Point Auto-Encoder Architecture. The encoder that contains the max-pooling layer has the same structure as PointNet [1]. The decoder first replicates global feature n times, then use our proposed semi-convolutional and semi-fully-connected layer to handle the mapping problem from single global feature to different points.

these a priori experiments, some autoencoders based on 3D objects have been proposed and have achieved good results in different fields. These include [4, 13, 14] based on the 3D voxel CNN structure. These methods are mainly obtained by voxelating the input point cloud or CAD model so as to obtain the serialized input and input to the network with the similar structure of the original 2D AE (Fig. 1).

The emergence of [1] provided the network with the ability to directly deal with disordered point clouds, which led to the creation of AE based on this network [2, 3, 16, 17, 19]. The previous study that is most relevant to our work is [2]. They proposed a folding operation network that solves the problem of it being difficult to recover the three-dimensional structure after extracting the global feature by max-pooling by fetching a two-dimensional grid to fit the three-dimensional point cloud. The two key differences between our network and [2] are: (1) We proposed using a semi-convolution semi-fully-connection operation to directly map the high dimensional global feature to three-dimensional points instead of folding two-dimensional grids. (2) The size of our reconstruction point cloud can be the size of the original input point cloud, or any other number, not the size specified by the two-dimensional grid.

2D-3D Transformation from a Single Image. Reconstructing 3D objects based on 2D images is a very important field in computer graphics. Many mature research applications have shown that the three-dimensional structures of objects can be geometrically reconstructed from 2D images. The representative research has achieved reconstruction based on stereo vision [24, 25] and monocular vision reconstruction [21–23, 26]. However, these reconstruction methods required a large amount of 2D images to reconstruct objects or scenes, which is not in line with the thinking habits of the human brain. The human brain is good at imagining the three-dimensional structure in which objects may exist from a single two-dimensional image. In some cases, not even the image is necessary, and only the global description of the object, such as the basic shape and category, can be given to roughly restore the possible structure of the object. In order to achieve this, it is necessary to be able to extract the global information of an object from a single 2D image and use this information for 3D reconstruction. The approaches based on this methodology include [4, 6, 15], which are based on ShapeNet, and [3, 5, 20], which are based on PointNet. The method we proposed is also in line with this idea. We first use 2D AE to extract the global information of a single image, then map the information to the global feature space of PointAE and reconstruct it by Point AE.

3   Method

3.1   Semi-Convolution Semi-Fully-Connected Layer

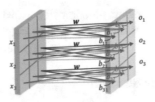

Fig. 2. Semi-convolutional and Semi-fully-connected layer. Every filter from same column are consist of sharing weights and dependent bias.

Semi-convolutional and semi-fully-connected (SCSFC) layer is a structure similar to a fully connected layer, but unlike the fully connected layer, the filters in each column share the same weights w, and their bias b remains independence. Then the output of the j-th column of the layer (Fig. 2)

$$o_j = f\left(wx_j + b_j\right) \tag{1}$$

Obviously, in the case where the input is the same for each row (assuming that the vector for each row is a copy of the global feature), the equal value can be easily mapped to a different point due to the existence of various biases. And the output dimensions can be adjusted at any layer, which means that it can be mapped map to different dimensional space. Here the interaction between x and b determines which bias will be activated and sent to the next processing layer. So in essence, the structure can be regarded as the features of different dimensional spaces are stored in the biases. When different global features are input, different features are activated, and the combination of the activated features forms the final reconstruction result.

But this design also determines that the single-layer SCSFC structure does not have a strong learning ability. And through the superposition of multiple layers, it has similar performance to the fully connected layer. If the number of input vectors is N, the number of parameters is 1/N of the fully connected layer.

3.2   PointNet-Based Encoder Structure

The encoder side has the same architecture as the PointNet [1] classification network, which is used for generating global features from unordered point cloud, then for classification. The encoder uses a set of 1-by-k (k is the dimension size of the current point) of the convolutional filter with 1-by-1 stride in order to ensure that each point will be mapped to the high-dimensional space by the same mapping function, and to ensure that the results are not affected by the order of the point cloud. The output of the convolutional layer uses the symmetric operator max-pooling to extract the global feature of the point cloud.

Formally, suppose the input point cloud contains point set S, and so the global feature vector is

$$\theta = \underset{x_i \in S}{MAX}\{h(x_i)\} \tag{2}$$

where $h(\cdot)$ is a symmetric mapping function that consists of a set of convolutional operations and *MAX* is a vector max-pooling that obtains n equal length vectors as input, then computes the element-wise maximum to generate a new equal length vector.

3.3 SCSFC-Based Decoder Structure

The basic idea of Decoder is to solve the one-to-many mapping problem, and the proposed SCSFC structure can solve this problem well. Thus, prior to the mapping operation, we first need to obtain the same number of samples as the reconstruction point cloud points. Here we use the replication operation, copy the global feature n times, and obtain n high-dimensional samples to form an n-by-k matrix, where k is the length of the global feature vector, and n is the size of the point cloud that needs to be recovered; in this paper, k is 1024, and n is 2048, which is the same size as the input point cloud. Because the global feature is extracted from the input point cloud, it necessarily carries the information of the original input point cloud. However, it is worth noting that the value of each row in this matrix is the same, which means that if the subsequent operations are symmetrical, each row will be mapped to the exact same point, so it cannot recover the original 3D structure. So the subsequent structure we used to complete the one-to-many mapping by superimposing multiple SCSFC layers. Here we use a four-layer SCSFC layer, the output dimensions of each layer are 512, 512, 512, 3. The 3 dimensional output of the last layer is the point cloud reconstructed by the decoder.

The entire decoder is essentially a mapping operation from high-dimensional to three-dimensional with many independent mapping functions of the global feature.

It is clear that, when the order of the input point cloud changes, since the encoder is symmetric, the global feature remains constant. And the biases are also fixed once the training is done, so the mapping function of each point is also fixed. Finally, the point that is mapped from each row in the replicated matrix to the three-dimensional space must remain consistent. Thus, the final output point cloud will be determined by the global feature vector.

3.4 Chamfer Loss Function for Point AE

Since the output point cloud is related to the bias, which is sequential while the input point cloud is unordered, the element-wise distance between input and output matrix cannot be simply used to measure the difference between the output point cloud and the input point cloud.

Here we define the *chamfer distance* [4] as the loss function of the network, because the *chamfer distance* is measured as the distance between each point and its closest target point, so it is independent of the order of the point cloud.

Assuming that the input point cloud is a point set S and the reconstructed output point set is S_o, the chamfer distance of this two-point set is

$$L_{CH} = \frac{1}{|S|} \sum_{x \in S} \underset{o \in S_o}{\text{MIN}} \|x - o\|_2 + \frac{1}{|S_o|} \sum_{o \in S_o} \underset{x \in S}{\text{MIN}} \|o - x\|_2 \tag{3}$$

In our proposed Auto-Encoder network, the definition of S_o is

$$S_o = [o_1, o_2, \ldots o_j, \ldots, o_n] \tag{4}$$

where,

$$o_j = h'\left(\underset{x_i \in S}{\text{MAX}} \{h(x_i, w_e)\}, w_d, b_j \right) \tag{5}$$

where w_e and w_d are the parameters of the encoder and decoder, respectively, and b_j is set of all the bias connect to the j-th row.

Thus, the target function of our network is expressed as follows,

$$T = \underset{w_e, w_d, b}{\text{argmin}} \left\{ \frac{1}{|S|} \sum_{x_i \in S} \underset{o_j \in S_o}{MIN} \|x_i - o_j\|_2 + \frac{1}{|S_o|} \sum_{o_j \in S_o} \underset{x_i \in S}{MIN} \|o_j - x_i\|_2 \right\} \tag{6}$$

3.5   Combine with 2D Auto-Encoder

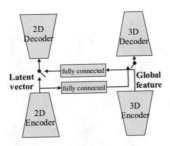

Fig. 3. Dual Auto-Encoder Architecture for generating the 2D-to-3D and 3D-to-2D transformations. The left -side network is a standard 2D auto-encoder structure which can extract the latent vector of each 2D image. The right-side network is our proposed Point AE. The two associated fully-connected networks in the center are used to transform 2D latent vector to 3D global feature and 3D global feature to 2D latent vector, respectively.

The significant advantage of our proposed Point AE is that it can reconstruct a complete 3D point cloud based on a single global feature vector. Therefore, we propose the use of a dual auto-encoder network [32] and its training method to extract the global feature from the 2D image, and complete the transformation from 2D to 3D by using the reconstruction ability of Point AE. Its network structure is shown in Fig. 3.

The 2D image encoder consists of six convolutional layers, the output channels of which are 64, 128, 384, 512, 512, and 1024, and three fully connected layers, the output channels of which are 400, 200, 50. The filter shapes of all of the convolutional layers are 3-by-3, except for the last two layers, which are 2-by-2. In addition, the stride of each layer is 2-by-2, and the input images are reshaped to 128-by-128, while the size of the channel is 3. The latent vector is extracted by the last layer of the fully-connected part. The 2D image decoder has the exact opposite structure, consisting of three fully-connected layers, first with 50, 200, and 500 output channels, respectively, and six deconvolutional layers, the output channels of which are 512, 512, 384, 128, 64, and 3. The filter shapes of all of the convolutional layers are also 3-by-3, except for the first two layers, which are 2-by-2. In addition, the stride of each layer is also the same as the encoder. Moreover, the decoder can choose to use the global feature generated by the encoder as the input source or output of the fully-connected network.

4   Experiments

4.1   Training Process of Point AE

Table 1. Training process of point AE

0 iters	5K iters	10K iters	20K iters	50K iters	300K iters	1.5M iters

We implemented this network based on TensorFlow. The training of our Point AE is based on the ShapeNet [14] dataset, which contains 16 categories, and the input point cloud of this dataset that we used is generated by [1]. We trained our network using an ADAM optimizer [28] with a learning rate of 0.0001, batch size of 32, beta1 of 0.9, and beta2 of 0.999. In addition, the initializer for initial weights is Xavier Initialization [27]. A part of the reconstruction result is shown in Table 1. It can clearly be seen that the reconstruction point cloud gradually fits from a randomly distributed point to the specified structure.

And the training loss is shown in Fig. 4, which means the difference between reconstructed point cloud and input. So it is clear that the training loss is lower, the reconstructed result is more accurate. We compared our result with original FoldingNet and PointNet using the same folding operation as FoldingNet because our network is based on PointNet. Obviously, the loss of our network is lower than folding operation, and it can produce more accurate reconstructed point cloud (Table 2).

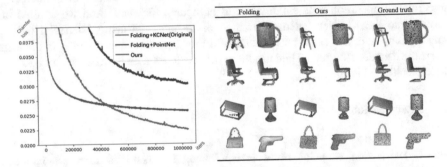

Fig. 4. Efficiency comparison with Folding Operation. Left: The training loss of KCNet + Folding (original FoldingNet), PointNet + folding operation based decoder and our PointAE, respectively. Right: The reconstructed 3D point clouds generated by PointNet + folding operation and our PointAE after 1.5M iters training.

Table 2. Generalization in decoding testing samples. This experiment shows our method is more accuracy on testing dataset. This test is evaluated after 1.5M iters training.

Folding	Ours	Ground Truth

Loss:0.052   Loss:0.042

4.2 Classification Accuracy

Table 3. The comparison on classification accuracy. We firstly trained our network by ShapeNet then through this trained model generated high-dimensional representations based on ModelNet40 dataset. Finally applied the SVM to test representations.

LFD [30]	VConv-DAE [13]	3D-GAN [31]	PointNet + Folding	PointNet + Ours	KC-Net + Folding	KC-Net + Ours
75.5%	75.5%	83.3%	85.5%	86.0%	88.4%	**88.5%**

For more clearly comparing the efficiency with FoldingNet [1] and other unsupervised learning for point cloud, we trained a linear SVM classifier using the global feature that is extracted from our PointAE by following the same routine that [2, 32], [33]. Since our network is based on original PointNet but the FoldingNet is based on a new network called KC-Net [29], so we add another network that is consist of PointNet and same folding operation with FoldingNet to compare efficiency. And we applied our decoder into the KC-Net. Then we trained these networks using ShapeNet dataset, same learning rate, and same loss function. In this experiment, everything is the same expect the decoder structure. Then use these models to train an SVM classifier based on ModelNet40 (Table 3).

4.3 Interpolation

Table 4. Illustration of point cloud interpolation. The first two rows are intra-class interpolations. The last two rows are inter-class interpolations. The model used here is trained after 1.5M iters.

Source	Interpolations	Target

We also implemented a point cloud interpolation experiment to show the ability of our proposed Point AE. The illustrations are shown in Table 4.

4.4   2D-3D Transformation

The structure of the Dual Auto-encoder is complex and contains four sub-networks, so the training process of this network is divided into four steps as well:

(1) **Training of the original 2D AE.** In order to ensure that the input of 2D AE and the point cloud data of Point AE are one-to-one, we first conduct the expansion process for the points in the point cloud of the ModelNet40 dataset and project these expanded points into a specified plane in the three-dimensional space so as to form a 2D data set. Based on this generated training set, we completed the training of 2D AE. For the loss function of this network, we used the Mean Squared Error (MSE) between input images and reconstructed images. Except for the learning rate of 0.00001, the remaining training parameters are consistent with Point AE.

(2) **Training of Point AE.** See Sect. 4.1.

(3) **Training of the 2D-to-3D association network.** The training target of the 2D-3D association network is to make the output of the association network fit to the global feature vector extracted by the Point AE as well as possible. Based on this, we first input the corresponding 2D image and 3D point cloud into the two encoders in order to obtain the global feature and latent vector, respectively. The latent vector is then used as the input to the association network to calculate the latent vector-based global feature. Finally, the ADAM optimizer is used to optimize the MSE between the latent vector-based global feature and the global feature extracted by point AE (Tables 5 and 6).

Table 5. 2D-to-3D transformation. The input is the 2D image that captured by a virtual camera in 3D space from a specific 3D testing object point cloud. The output is the transformation output of corresponding 2D projection image. The output size is chosen as same as target.

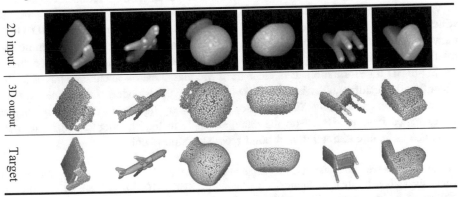

76   W. Cheng and S. Lee

Table 6. 3D-to-2D transformation. The input is the raw 3D point cloud data from testing dataset. The output is the transformation output in 2D space.

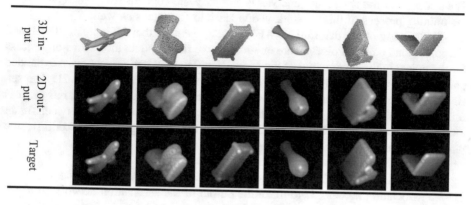

(4) **Training of the 3D-to-2D association network.** Basically, this training process is similar to the training of 2D-to-3D, except that the input of the association network is replaced by the global feature. The network is also trained by optimizing the MSE error between the input of the association network and the latent vector.

5 Conclusion

The proposed 3D point cloud decoding network based on a novel semi-convolutional and semi-fully-connected network performs better than folding operation in terms of reconstruction loss and classification accuracy. The use of SCSFC reduces the number of variables significantly which helps in achieving faster training and lowers reconstruction errors. It can be easily applied to the single-view reconstruction, 3D GAN network, and occlusion restoration. This method also has the potential to handle the rotation regression. Based on this, we proposed a dual-auto-encoder that can achieve the 2D-to-3D transformation. It is clear from the classification accuracy shown in the paper that the feature quality is essentially affected by the encoder. If the same network is applied as an encoder, the SCSFC based decoder can slightly improve the quality of the extracted features. Based on the changes made in the encoder structure, its performance of feature extraction and point reconstruction is enhanced.

Acknowledgement. This research was supported, in part, by the "3D Recognition Project" of Korea Evaluation Institute of Industrial Technology (KEIT) (10060160) and, in part, by the Institute of Information and Communication Technology Planning & Evaluation (IITP) grant sponsored by the Korean Ministry of Science and Information Technology (MSIT): No. 2019-0-00421, AI Graduate School Program and, in part, by "Robocarechair: A Smart Transformable Robot for Multi-Functional Assistive Personal Care" Project, KEIT P0006886, of the Korea Evaluation Institute of Industrial Technology (KEIT).

References

1. Qi, C.R., Su, H., Mo, K., Guibas, L.J.: Pointnet: deep learning on point sets for 3D classification and segmentation. In: CVPR (2017)
2. Yang, Y., Feng, C., Shen, Y., Tian, D.: Foldingnet: point cloud auto-encoder via deep grid deformation. In: CVPR (2018)
3. Girdhar, R., Fouhey, D.F., Rodriguez, M., Gupta, A.: Learning a predictable and generative vector representation for objects. In: Leibe, B., Matas, J., Sebe, N., Welling, M. (eds.) ECCV 2016. LNCS, vol. 9910, pp. 484–499. Springer, Cham (2016). https://doi.org/10.1007/978-3-319-46466-4_29
4. Fan, H., Su, H., Guibas, L.J.: A point set generation network for 3D object reconstruction from a single image. In: Proceedings of the IEEE Conference on Computer Vision and Pattern Recognition, pp. 605–613 (2017)
5. Choy, C.B., Xu, D., Gwak, J., Chen, K., Savarese, S.: 3D-R2N2: a unified approach for single and multi-view 3D object reconstruction. In: Leibe, B., Matas, J., Sebe, N., Welling, M. (eds.) ECCV 2016. LNCS, vol. 9912, pp. 628–644. Springer, Cham (2016). https://doi.org/10.1007/978-3-319-46484-8_38
6. Hinton, G.E., Salakhutdinov, R.R.: Reducing the dimensionality of data with neural networks. Science **313**(5786), 504–507 (2006)
7. Liu, W., Wang, Z., Liu, X., et al.: A survey of deep neural network architectures and their applications. Neurocomputing **234**, 11–26 (2017)
8. Vincent, P., Larochelle, H., Bengio, Y., et al.: Extracting and composing robust features with denoising autoencoders. In: Proceedings of the 25th International Conference on Machine Learning, ACM, pp. 1096–1103 (2008)
9. Bengio, Y., et al.: Greedy layer-wise training of deep networks. In: Advances in Neural Information Processing Systems (2007)
10. Vincent, P., Larochelle, H., Lajoie, I., et al.: Stacked denoising autoencoders: learning useful representations in a deep network with a local denoising criterion. J. Mach. Learn. Res. **11**, 3371–3408 (2010)
11. Kingma, D.P., Welling, M.: Auto-encoding variational bayes. arXiv preprint arXiv:1312. 6114 (2013)
12. Sharma, A., Grau, O., Fritz, M.: VConv-DAE: deep volumetric shape learning without object labels. In: Hua, G., Jégou, H. (eds.) ECCV 2016. LNCS, vol. 9915, pp. 236–250. Springer, Cham (2016). https://doi.org/10.1007/978-3-319-49409-8_20
13. Wu, Z., Song, S., Khosla, A., et al.: 3D shapenets: a deep representation for volumetric shapes. In: Proceedings of the IEEE Conference on Computer Vision and Pattern Recognition, pp. 1912–1920 (2015)
14. Smith, E., Meger, D.: Improved adversarial systems for 3D object generation and reconstruction. arXiv preprint arXiv:1707.09557 (2017)
15. Zamorski, M., Zięba, M., Nowak, R., et al.: Adversarial Autoencoders for Generating 3D Point Clouds. arXiv preprint arXiv:1811.07605 (2018)
16. Shoef, M., Fogel, S., Cohen-Or, D.: PointWise: An Unsupervised Point-wise Feature Learning Network. arXiv preprint arXiv:1901.04544 (2019)
17. Makhzani, A., Shlens, J., Jaitly, N., et al.: Adversarial autoencoders. arXiv preprint arXiv: 1511.05644 (2015)
18. Achlioptas. P., Diamanti, O., Mitliagkas, I., et al.: Learning representations and generative models for 3D point clouds. arXiv preprint arXiv:1707.02392 (2017)

19. Zhu, R., Kiani Galoogahi, H., Wang, C., et al.: Rethinking reprojection: closing the loop for pose-aware shape reconstruction from a single image. In: Proceedings of the IEEE International Conference on Computer Vision, pp. 57–65 (2017)
20. Durrant-Whyte, H., Bailey, T.: Simultaneous localization and mapping: Part I. IEEE Robot. Autom. Mag. **13**(2), 99–110 (2006)
21. Montemerlo, M., Thrun, S., Koller, D., et al.: FastSLAM: a factored solution to the simultaneous localization and mapping problem. In: AAAI/IAAI, pp. 593–598 (2002)
22. Bailey, T., Durrant-Whyte, H.: Simultaneous localization and mapping (SLAM): Part II. IEEE Robot. Autom. Mag. **13**(3), 108–117 (2006)
23. Woodham, R.J.: Photometric method for determining surface orientation from multiple images. Opt. Eng. **19**(1), 191139 (1980)
24. Geiger, A., Roser, M., Urtasun, R.: Efficient large-scale stereo matching. In: Kimmel, R., Klette, R., Sugimoto, A. (eds.) ACCV 2010. LNCS, vol. 6492, pp. 25–38. Springer, Heidelberg (2011). https://doi.org/10.1007/978-3-642-19315-6_3
25. Mur-Artal, R., Tardós, J.D.: ORB-SLAM2: an open-source slam system for monocular, stereo, and RGB-D cameras. IEEE Trans. Robot. **33**(5), 1255–1262 (2017)
26. Glorot, X., Bengio, Y.: Understanding the difficulty of training deep feedforward neural networks. In: Proceedings of the Thirteenth International Conference on Artificial Intelligence and Statistics, pp. 249–256 (2010)
27. Kingma, D.P., Ba, J.: Adam: a method for stochastic optimization. arXiv preprint arXiv: 1412.6980 (2014)
28. Shen, Y., Feng, C., Yang, Y., et al.: Mining point cloud local structures by kernel correlation and graph pooling. In: Proceedings of the IEEE Conference on Computer Vision and Pattern Recognition, pp. 4548–4557 (2018)
29. Kazhdan, M., Funkhouser, T., Rusinkiewicz, S.: Rotation invariant spherical harmonic representation of 3D shape descriptors. In: Symposium on Geometry Processing, vol. 6, pp. 156–164 (2003)
30. Wu, J., Zhang, C., Xue, T., et al.: Learning a probabilistic latent space of object shapes via 3D generative-adversarial modeling. In: Advances in Neural Information Processing Systems, pp. 82–90 (2016)
31. Achlioptas, P., Diamanti, O., Mitliagkas, I., et al.: Representation learning and adversarial generation of 3D point clouds. **2**(3), 4 (2017). arXiv preprint arXiv:1707.02392
32. Ul Islam, N., Lee, S.: Learning typical 3D representation from a single 2D correspondence using 2D-3D transformation network. In: Lee, S., Ismail, R., Choo, H. (eds.) IMCOM 2019. AISC, vol. 935, pp. 440–455. Springer, Cham (2019). https://doi.org/10.1007/978-3-030-19063-7_35

U-Net Based Architectures for Document Text Detection and Binarization

Filipp Nikitin$^{(\boxtimes)}$ [iD], Vladimir Dokholyan [iD], Ilia Zharikov [iD],
and Vadim Strijov [iD]

Moscow Institute of Physics and Technology, Dolgoprudny, Russia
filipp.nikitin@phystech.edu

Abstract. With the increasing popularity of document analysis and recognition systems, text detection (TD) and text binarization (TB) in document images remain challenging tasks. In the paper, we introduced a two-step architecture for the TD task. Firstly, a U-net based model is used to get a text mask in terms of word-level bounding boxes. Secondly, we approximate the mask of the bounding boxes with rectangles using a classic computer vision method. The model achieves state-of-the-art result on document images and outperforms other popular approaches. Moreover, we introduce the Hybrid U-net architecture, which helps to solve the TB and TD problems at the same time. The model demonstrates high results on both problems. The shared convolution encoder allows to reduce the number of parameters and consumed memory compared to separate models without reducing the model performance.

Keywords: Document processing · Document recognition · Pattern recognition · Semantic segmentation · Text detection · Text binarization · U-net

1 Introduction

Extraction and understanding textual information from a large range of document types have attracted recent attention in the computer vision community. In this paper, we focus on the document text detection problem. The key difference between classic object detection and the text detection problem statements is that the acceptable overlap of the original and predicted box is much higher in text detection tasks, because losing a part of a letter can make it impossible to determine it clearly. On the contrary, non-text objects have extra features which help to recognise them by its part.

In general, the research field devoted to the text detection problem can be divided into two categories. The first category is represented by SWT [3,11], MSER [10,25], HoG [23] and similar methods based on classic computer vision that allow to extract low-level character features. These approaches have a serious disadvantage: in some cases, it is impossible to correctly recognise a character

© Springer Nature Switzerland AG 2019
G. Bebis et al. (Eds.): ISVC 2019, LNCS 11845, pp. 79–88, 2019.
https://doi.org/10.1007/978-3-030-33723-0_7

or word placed in isolation. At the same time, recognition can be easily done by analysing contextual information. Methods from the second category use deep neural networks for efficient feature extraction. Deep learning has recently advanced general object detection [7,17] and image segmentation [18]. The approach was successfully applied to solve the text detection problem. Recent studies aim at solving scene text detection problem [2,12,23,24,26]. As opposed to document images, images of natural scenes contain little text. Main properties of documents includes dense text, various tables, graphics, diagrams. In our work, we want to focus on improving results on documents with complex structure.

Despite the great interest of the scientific community in the problem of scene text detection and recognition, there is a lack of open-source solutions for document text detection problem. The most popular tools, Tesseract [20] and EAST [26], do not demonstrate high results on dense text, tables, and other common structures that can be in documents. In the paper, we want to demonstrate the advantage of a U-net model for text detection in documents images over state-of-the-art object detection models. One of the advantages that come from U-net based model is the ability to solve both text detection and text binarization problems. The modified U-net architecture is capable of solving both problems with shared parameters simultaneously. It allows to reduce the number of parameters by a third in comparison with two separate models.

The rest of this paper is organised as follows. In the following section, we consider related works and discuss their advantages and disadvantages. In the third section, we give information about used datasets. The third section provides a detailed description of the proposed architectures. The fifth section is devoted to experimental results. The last section concludes the results and discusses the contribution of this paper.

2   Related Works

Nowadays deep learning approaches outperform other methods in the field of document analysis and recognition. According to our best knowledge, many machine learning engineers use state-of-the-art scene text detection models while creating a document analyses pipeline. In the following, we will look through popular models in more detail.

EAST. An Efficient and Accurate Scene Text Detector (EAST) is a common solution to detect text on images. It was implemented into OpenCV library [1]. Authors used FCN [15] to produce word or text-line level predictions without any intermediate steps. The model output is represented by rotated rectangles or quadrangles. To yield the final results authors of the model use Non-Maximum Suppression [16].

CTPN. Connectionist Text Proposal Network (CTPN) accurately localises text lines in natural scene image. The general pipeline is the following. The convolutional feature maps are created using VGG16 [19]. The feature maps are used to generate proposals with a particular architecture. The prediction is obtained by the merging of fine-scale text proposals. One of the features of the described is a vertical anchor mechanism that predicts location and text/non-text score of each fixed-width proposal. The obtained proposals become the input of a recurrent neural network, that leads to overall quality improvement of the model.

Faster R-CNN. The model is one of the most widely used models in the object detection field. Faster R-CNN [5] composes two main parts: Regional Proposals Network (RPN) and detection network. The parts share full-image convolutional features resulting in the model computational efficiency. RPN is a fully convolutional network that simultaneously predicts object bounds and object detection scores at each position. RPN is trained end-to-end to generate high-quality region proposals, which are used for detection.

3 Using Datasets

DDI-100. The synthetic dataset was produced using 7 000 real unique document pages. The pages were augmented with various distortions and geometric transformations. As a result, DDI-100 dataset consists of more than 100 000 images. Ground truth includes text masks, word-level and character-level bounding boxes with annotations for each page (see Fig. 1).

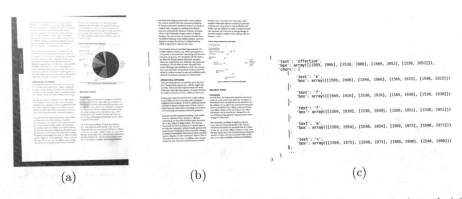

(a)   (b)   (c)

Fig. 1. Example of an image (a), its text mask (b) and the image ground truth (c) from the DDI-100 dataset.

Real-DDI. The dataset was created from DDI-100 documents. It consist of 100 photos of documents from DDI-100 (see Fig. 2). The photos were collected using different smartphones on a flat surface under different lighting condition. Ground truth for the photos includes word-level bounding boxes and text annotations.

FUNSD [13]. The dataset is based on a subset of the RVL-CDIP dataset [6] that contains grayscale images of various documents from 80's-90's. The introduced dataset consists of randomly sampled 200 images with more than 30000 word-level annotations. The structure of a document one can see in the Fig. 2. Part of the documents contains handwriting.

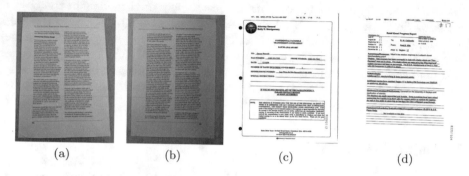

(a)   (b)   (c)   (d)

Fig. 2. Examples of images from Real-DDI (a), (b) and FUNSD (c), (d) datasets.

4   Models

4.1   U-Net Architecture

The U-net is an architecture of a neural network which originally solves semantic segmentation problem. The neural network architecture is symmetric and includes an encoder and decoder (see Fig. 3).

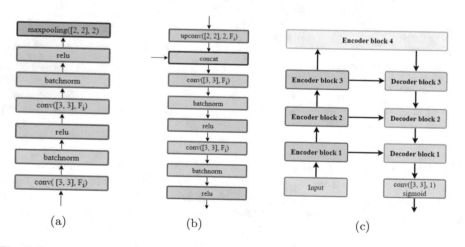

(a)   (b)   (c)

Fig. 3. Structure of encoder block (a), decoder block (b) and U-net neural network (c). F_i is a number of convolutional feature channels in the block.

The encoder is a sequence of convolution blocks. The first block comprises two convolution layers with batch normalization and ReLU activation function. Number of filters in the convolution layers is equal to 2. Next blocks have the same structure with the doubled number of filters and reduced dimension due to the max-pooling operation.

In contrast to encoder, in the decoder resolution of the blocks grows. The feature map from the previous block is up-sampled using transposed convolution operations. In the process number of feature, channels reduce by half. Then outputs of the encoder block with the same size are concatenated. Similar to encoder, convolution operations and nonlinearity are applied to the maps. Finally, convolution operations and Sigmoid activation function are applied to get the segmentation map.

Main property of the described network is a skip connections between encoder and decoder blocks. The links allow to keep information which can be lost due to pooling operation.

4.2   Hybrid U-Net Architecture

We use U-net based architecture for solving the text detection and binarization problem simultaneously (see Fig. 4) that we called Hybrid U-net. The approach was inspired by Mask-RCNN [7]. Authors trained one model for object detection and instance segmentation task with shared convolutional encoder. As a result, solving described two problems simultaneously improves overall model performance. Hybrid U-net model has a shared encoder and two separate decoders. The encoder and decoder structure is the same as in U-net architecture Sect. 4.1.

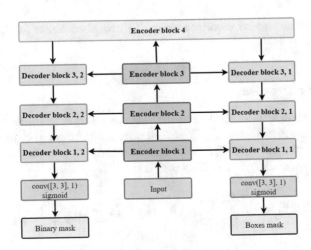

Fig. 4. Hybrid U-net architecture.

4.3 Post Processing

U-net model predicts segmentation map from which we can obtain mask using threshold (see Fig. 5(a)). To get bounding boxes from the map we use classic computer vision methods. Firstly, we apply erosion and dilation operators [8] with a small kernel to remove noise (Fig. 5(b)). On the last post-processing stage, each connected area is approximated by a rotated rectangle [4] (Fig. 5(c)).

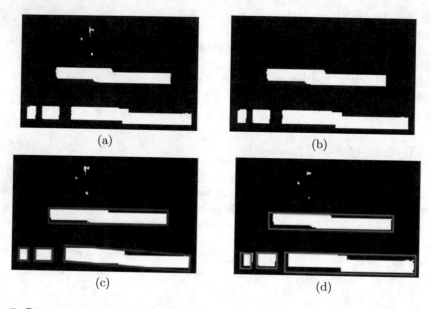

(a)   (b)

(c)   (d)

Fig. 5. Post processing: (a) predicted mask; (b) processed mask; (c) found boxes on the mask; (d) true boxes.

4.4 Training Process

We used either binarization or detection masks as a target in the training process. During the process we minimise loss function with Adam [14] modification of stochastic gradient descent. The total loss function (1) is a convex combination of pixel-wise cross-entropy and Dice loss [21].

$$\mathcal{L}(o,p) = -\lambda \sum_{i=1}^{W} \sum_{j=1}^{H} o_{i,j} \log p_{i,j} - (1-\lambda) \frac{2\langle o,p \rangle}{|o| + |p| + \varepsilon}, \tag{1}$$

where o denotes an original mask, p—predicted, $\langle \cdot, \cdot \rangle$ is a Euclidean scalar product, and $|\cdot|$ defines sum of elements.

We employ multi-task learning to jointly optimize parameters in the Hybrid U-net model. The loss on binarization and detection heads is given by formula (1). Final loss function is a convex combination of losses on each heads.

5   Experimental Results

5.1   Metrics

We consider that a word is successfully detected if the Intersection over Union (IoU) is above a threshold. IoU is an evaluation metric that equals to the area of overlap between the ground-truth and predicted bounding boxes divided by the area of union. As discussed above in the text detection problem the IoU threshold is very important. We chose it equal to 0.8 because a larger threshold value rejects a considerable number of recognizable boxes. The disadvantage of this metric comes from small punishment for losing parts of the letters which is important in text recognition problems (see Fig. 6). After for evaluation of predicted boxes we use common metrics: precision, recall, and F-score. To evaluate binarization models we use pixel-wise analogues.

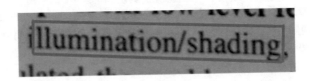

Fig. 6. An example of incorrectly predicted bounding box with a large IoU value.

5.2   Text Detection

The first experiment demonstrates the advantage of the U-net model for the text detection problem. Other popular approaches were compared to the U-net based method on FUNSD, Real-DDI, DDI-100 datasets. First of all, we assessed the quality of the EAST model without any re-training. We chose an implementation from the OpenCV [1] library. The model was chosen to show the performance of the most popular open-source product for TD problem. Faster-RCNN model was built with Tensorflow Object Detection API [9]. The model remains a state-of-the-art solution for many object detection problems. We used ResNet50 [22] as convolution encoder for this architecture. We wanted to include CTPN model in the list, however, the model ignores the text line delimiters between words and we could not modify it for word detection in case of dense text.

Table 1. Result of the text detection models on FUNSD, Real-DDI, DDI-100 datasets (**P**recision, **R**ecall, **F**-score).

	FUNSD			Real-DDI			DDI-100		
	P	R	F	P	R	F	P	R	F
EAST	0.96	0.59	0.73	0.98	0.89	0.93	0.96	0.85	0.91
U-net	0.89	0.79	0.84	0.99	0.95	**0.97**	0.93	0.96	**0.95**
Faster-RCNN	0.95	0.89	**0.92**	0.96	0.78	0.86	0.93	0.91	0.92

The experiment results are presented in Table 1. It can be seen that U-net demonstrates the best quality on Real-DDI, DDI-100. However, Faster-RCNN model demonstrates the best results on FUNSD dataset. We believe that it can be explained by properties of the dataset. FUNSD consists of scanned documents with horizontally oriented text. It worth noting that our version of Faster-RCNN shows better results than the model from the original paper described FUNSD [13].

Results of the conducted experiment shows that the proposed segmentation model demonstrates strong quality on document photos with dense text, tables, diagrams.

5.3 Hybrid U-Net

Table 2 demonstrates the performance of the Hybrid U-net model on both text detection and text binarization problems. We can see that on DDI-100 Hybrid U-net demonstrate the same quality compared to separate models with the same structure for each task. Due to shared convolutional encoder, the proposed model takes less memory without reducing the overall model quality.

Table 2. Result of Hybrid U-net for text detection and text binarization problems compared to separate U-net models for each task (**P**recision, **R**ecall, **F**-score).

	Text detection			Text binarization		
	P	R	F	P	R	F
Hybrid U-net	0.93	0.96	0.95	0.87	0.75	0.81
U-net (for detection)	0.93	0.96	0.95	–		
U-net (for binarization)	–			0.87	0.76	0.81

6   Discussion

In the paper, we propose a new approach to solve the text detection problem. The methods consist of two steps. On the first step, word boxes are semantically segmented with U-net based architecture. Next, the segmented areas are approximated with rectangles. The proposed method solves the semantic segmentation problem as opposed to most of the modern methods that imply regression problem statement to obtain bounding boxes.

The U-net based architecture demonstrates high-quality results on DDI-100 and Real-DDI datasets. We also display that the method helps to solve the binarization problem and effectively solve both problems by sharing encoder part. However, Faster-RCNN model works better on the FUNSD dataset. According to the experiments results, the proposed model suits better for images with oblique, dense text.

Future promising research directions might include: applying multi-task learning for the text detection problem, finding better loss function. To enhance the text detection model we want to solve additional problems: segmentation of delimiters between words and text lines. All of the problems may be solved using U-net model with shared parameters by multi-task learning approach. In the current paper, we focused on choosing the best neural network architecture not paying attention to finding the best loss function for the problem. Further research in those directions might yield significant results.

References

1. Bradski, G.: The OpenCV library. Dr. Dobb's J. Softw. Tools **25**, 120–125 (2000)
2. Busta, M., Neumann, L., Matas, J.: Fastext: efficient unconstrained scene text detector. In: Proceedings of the IEEE International Conference on Computer Vision, pp. 1206–1214 (2015)
3. Epshtein, B., Ofek, E., Wexler, Y.: Detecting text in natural scenes with stroke width transform. In: 2010 IEEE Computer Society Conference on Computer Vision and Pattern Recognition, pp. 2963–2970. IEEE (2010)
4. Freeman, H., Shapira, R.: Determining the minimum-area encasing rectangle for an arbitrary closed curve. Commun. ACM **18**(7), 409–413 (1975)
5. Girshick, R.: Fast R-CNN. In: Proceedings of the IEEE International Conference on Computer Vision, pp. 1440–1448 (2015)
6. Harley, A.W., Ufkes, A., Derpanis, K.G.: Evaluation of deep convolutional nets for document image classification and retrieval. In: 2015 13th International Conference on Document Analysis and Recognition (ICDAR), pp. 991–995. IEEE (2015)
7. He, K., Gkioxari, G., Dollár, P., Girshick, R.: Mask R-CNN. In: Proceedings of the IEEE International Conference on Computer Vision, pp. 2961–2969 (2017)
8. Heijmans, H.J.: Morphological Image Operators, vol. 4. Academic Press, Boston (1994)
9. Huang, J., et al.: Speed/accuracy trade-offs for modern convolutional object detectors. In: Proceedings of the IEEE Conference on Computer Vision and Pattern Recognition, pp. 7310–7311 (2017)
10. Huang, W., Qiao, Y., Tang, X.: Robust scene text detection with convolution neural network induced MSER trees. In: Fleet, D., Pajdla, T., Schiele, B., Tuytelaars, T. (eds.) ECCV 2014. LNCS, vol. 8692, pp. 497–511. Springer, Cham (2014). https://doi.org/10.1007/978-3-319-10593-2_33
11. Huang, W., Lin, Z., Yang, J., Wang, J.: Text localization in natural images using stroke feature transform and text covariance descriptors. In: Proceedings of the IEEE International Conference on Computer Vision, pp. 1241–1248 (2013)
12. Jaderberg, M., Simonyan, K., Vedaldi, A., Zisserman, A.: Reading text in the wild with convolutional neural networks. Int. J. Comput. Vis. **116**(1), 1–20 (2016)
13. Jaume, G., Ekenel, H.K., Thiran, J.P.: FUNSD: a dataset for form understanding in noisy scanned documents. arXiv preprint arXiv:1905.13538 (2019)
14. Kingma, D.P., Ba, J.: Adam: a method for stochastic optimization. arXiv preprint arXiv:1412.6980 (2014)
15. Long, J., Shelhamer, E., Darrell, T.: Fully convolutional networks for semantic segmentation. In: Proceedings of the IEEE Conference on Computer Vision and Pattern Recognition, pp. 3431–3440 (2015)

16. Neubeck, A., Van Gool, L.: Efficient non-maximum suppression. In: 18th International Conference on Pattern Recognition (ICPR 2006), vol. 3, pp. 850–855. IEEE (2006)
17. Ren, S., He, K., Girshick, R., Sun, J.: Faster R-CNN: towards real-time object detection with region proposal networks. In: Advances in Neural Information Processing Systems, pp. 91–99 (2015)
18. Ronneberger, O., Fischer, P., Brox, T.: U-net: convolutional networks for biomedical image segmentation. In: Navab, N., Hornegger, J., Wells, W.M., Frangi, A.F. (eds.) MICCAI 2015. LNCS, vol. 9351, pp. 234–241. Springer, Cham (2015). https://doi.org/10.1007/978-3-319-24574-4_28
19. Simonyan, K., Zisserman, A.: Very deep convolutional networks for large-scale image recognition. arXiv preprint arXiv:1409.1556 (2014)
20. Smith, R.: An overview of the tesseract OCR engine. In: Ninth International Conference on Document Analysis and Recognition (ICDAR 2007), vol. 2, pp. 629–633. IEEE (2007)
21. Sudre, C.H., Li, W., Vercauteren, T., Ourselin, S., Jorge Cardoso, M.: Generalised dice overlap as a deep learning loss function for highly unbalanced segmentations. In: Cardoso, M.J., et al. (eds.) DLMIA/ML-CDS -2017. LNCS, vol. 10553, pp. 240–248. Springer, Cham (2017). https://doi.org/10.1007/978-3-319-67558-9_28
22. Szegedy, C., Ioffe, S., Vanhoucke, V., Alemi, A.A.: Inception-v4, inception-resnet and the impact of residual connections on learning. In: Thirty-First AAAI Conference on Artificial Intelligence (2017)
23. Tian, S., Pan, Y., Huang, C., Lu, S., Yu, K., Lim Tan, C.: Text flow: a unified text detection system in natural scene images. In: Proceedings of the IEEE International Conference on Computer Vision, pp. 4651–4659 (2015)
24. Tian, Z., Huang, W., He, T., He, P., Qiao, Y.: Detecting text in natural image with connectionist text proposal network. In: Leibe, B., Matas, J., Sebe, N., Welling, M. (eds.) ECCV 2016. LNCS, vol. 9912, pp. 56–72. Springer, Cham (2016). https://doi.org/10.1007/978-3-319-46484-8_4
25. Yin, X.C., Yin, X., Huang, K., Hao, H.W.: Robust text detection in natural scene images. IEEE Trans. Pattern Anal. Mach. Intell. **36**(5), 970–983 (2013)
26. Zhou, X., et al.: EAST: an efficient and accurate scene text detector. In: Proceedings of the IEEE Conference on Computer Vision and Pattern Recognition, pp. 5551–5560 (2017)

Face Detection in Thermal Images with YOLOv3

Gustavo Silva[1]([⊠]), Rui Monteiro[1], André Ferreira[2], Pedro Carvalho[3],
and Luís Corte-Real[1,3]

[1] Faculty of Engineering, University of Porto, Porto, Portugal
silva95gustavo@gmail.com, ruipauloaraujomonteiro@gmail.com,
lreal@fe.up.pt
[2] Bosch Car Multimedia Portugal, S.A., Braga, Portugal
andre.ferreira2@pt.bosch.com
[3] INESC TEC, Porto, Portugal
pedro.carvalho@inesctec.pt

Abstract. The automotive industry is currently focusing on automation in their vehicles, and perceiving the surroundings of an automobile requires the ability to detect and identify objects, events and persons, not only from the outside of the vehicle but also from the inside of the cabin. This constitutes relevant information for defining intelligent responses to events happening on both environments. This work presents a new method for in-vehicle monitoring of passengers, specifically the task of real-time face detection in thermal images, by applying transfer learning with YOLOv3. Using this kind of imagery for this purpose brings some advantages, such as the possibility of detecting faces during the day and in the dark without being affected by illumination conditions, and also because it's a completely passive sensing solution. Due to the lack of suitable datasets for this type of application, a database of in-vehicle images was created, containing images from 38 subjects performing different head poses and at varying ambient temperatures. The tests in our database show an AP_{50} of 99.7% and an AP of 78.5%.

Keywords: Thermal imaging · Face detection · Computer vision · Deep learning · YOLOv3 · Transfer learning

1 Introduction

In an autonomous driving environment, solutions for interior vehicle monitoring become a necessity, namely to monitor occupants and car interior, tasks that are mainly associated to the driver in modern transportation systems.

A possible approach for in-vehicle interior sensing considers the visible domain, namely the use of RGB cameras. These images greatly depend on external conditions, namely light. This introduces a considerable limitation if we aim

Supported by Bosch Car Multimedia Portugal, S.A. and INESC TEC Porto, Portugal.

G. Bebis et al. (Eds.): ISVC 2019, LNCS 11845, pp. 89–99, 2019.
https://doi.org/10.1007/978-3-030-33723-0_8

to monitor the vehicle during the 24 hours of a day. With this in mind, other modalities are being explored, that can be used independently or in conjunction. An example is near-infrared (NIR), robust to lack of lighting but requires a dedicated source of IR light and filters and is also sensible to different lens exposures [6]. The modality we explore in this document, thermal images, is a passive solution robust to any external light conditions.

Face detection is an object detection task with the specific goal of detecting faces in images. It is the first and one essential step for other more complex tasks, such as face verification and person identification, and so it can be used in many areas such as bio-metrics, security and entertainment.

In the visible domain, traditional approaches include the Viola-Jones framework [10], developed in 2004 and capable of performing in real-time. In the thermal domain, researchers were able to enhance and apply the same method to thermal images [1]. They employed and tested different types of features and concluded that the performance of the system was better using LBP features [7]. Recently, deep convolutional neural networks (CNNs) are being used to improve those results. In [4], transfer learning using a pre-trained Inception model [9] on visible images was successfully applied to thermal face detection, achieving a Positive Predictive Value (PPV) of 99.5%.

2   Dataset

In order to have training and test data for the algorithms described in this document, and due to the lack of labeled and suitable datasets for this application in the thermal domain, a database was created by capturing images inside a vehicle. This dataset is not limited to data important for the purposes of this paper, but also includes subjects performing activities that are relevant for the development of other monitoring algorithms.

The setup consisted of a camera operating both in the infrared thermal and in the visible light spectrum. For this purpose, the FLIR ONE Pro camera was chosen, mainly due to the fact that it combines both modalities in a small device and ensures calibration between frames. This camera has a thermal resolution of 160×120 and an RGB resolution of 1440×1080, capturing frames at a rate of 8.7 per second with a FOV of $55° \times 43°$ $±1$. The thermal sensor operates in the 8–14 µm waveband, measuring temperatures between $-20\,°C$ and $400\,°C$ with a thermal sensitivity of $0.15\,°C$. The camera was placed in front of the passenger using a folding arm, connected via USB to a Linux-running machine (NVIDIA Jetson TX2). Since the camera was designed to be controlled with a smartphone, a driver had to be developed to connect it to an embedded device, and also to extract raw temperature values provided by the capturing device with the highest thermal resolution (14bit). The described setup can be seen in Fig. 1.

The participants were asked to perform some specific actions and activities, namely head movements in multiple axis, simulating facial expressions, simulating fatigue, wearing glasses, smoking, entering the vehicle and leaving the

Fig. 1. The recording setup.

vehicle. Additionally, in the middle of the session, the air conditioning system of the vehicle was adjusted to change the cabin temperature.

In total, the database contains recordings of 38 subjects. In terms of gender distribution, data was captured from 33 males and 5 female subjects of white ethnicity. The average age of the recorded population is 28.8 with standard deviation of 10.1 years, and the average height is 1.76 m with a standard deviation of 0.10m. Regarding hair size, there were 3 bald subjects, 27 with short hair, 3 with medium hair and 5 with long hair. Furthermore, 63% of the subjects had a beard and 66% had a mustache.

In total, the database contains 87286 frames, where 5361 images were auto-labeled with facial bounding boxes using an RGB face detetor [11] and manually filtered to remove incorrect labels generated by the automatic labeling process. Example images can be seen in Fig. 2.

3   Implementation

Our face detection algorithm is based on the YOLOv3 [8] real-time general object detector. The feature extractor of YOLOv3 is pre-trained on a large amount of visible images from ImageNet [2] and the full object detection framework is then trained on COCO [5] database. In order to perform face detection in thermal images, we take advantage of those pre-trained weights and adapt them to our scenario where the input is a single-channel temperature matrix and the output is the bounding boxes of all faces. We studied and compared different ways of adapting the network to our input, which are further discussed in this article. In all our experiments, the pre-trained were loaded and all the layers were trained.

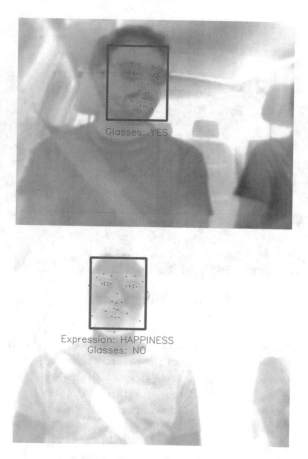

Fig. 2. Example images taken (a) in a "cold" environment and (b) in a "hot" environment. Additionally, ground truth labels of the dataset are shown (facial landmarks, facial expression and glasses usage).

In order to retrain the network, not only facial images are required, but also negatives. In the context of thermal imaging, these usually are high-temperature objects that could be confused with our target class. Most of the databases of infrared images have a clean background (cold) and are not suitable for good learning of negatives. Therefore, we collected and hand-labeled a total of 2075 additional images (some including faces and others not) in multiple scenarios, but ensuring that no appearing subject is included in the data reserved for testing. These images, together with the images from the database described in Sect. 2, were used as training data in our experiments. The validation of all models reported in this section was performed using the Monte Carlo method for subject-wise cross-validation (leave-group-out validation, with a group size of 8) and only the best model was chosen to be tested on the test set.

For the pre-trained output to match the objective of face detection, the network should be adjusted so that each bounding box only predicts one class. Additionally, since facial bounding boxes have a certain aspect ratio, we run the K-means algorithm to cluster the sizes of all faces in the dataset and generate anchor boxes that are better tuned for the use case, unlike the pre-trained version of YOLOv3 which is prepared to receive multiple classes of objects of varying size.

3.1   Model Selection

Since the input of YOLOv3 is the three RGB channels of visible images, our single-channel thermal input needs to be adapted. We have experimented and compared different ways of performing this. One possible method is to apply a color palette to the input, so that the number of channels matches the input of the network. We chose for this purpose a palette where the hottest pixels are orange, yellow or white, similar to the facial skin color. The expectation is that it better mimics the colors of the pre-trained version of YOLO in RGB images. This model achieved an AP_{50} of 99.64% and an AP of 78.41% in the test set.

Our next experiment was to feed the network directly with the thermal image, without preprocessing it with a color palette. A disadvantage of the previous model is that color mapping the temperatures does not introduce any new information when compared to an input composed solely of the pixel temperatures. Therefore, we experimented tripling the single-channel input in order to match the number of input channels of the pre-trained network, without applying any palette or making any other change to it. We take advantage of the fact that all the images in our dataset contain temperature information, and we do not perform any kind of equalization to avoid losing that important data, considering that the facial temperatures have a limited expected range [3]. This experiment improved the accuracy of the model when compared to the initial attempt with YOLOv3 using a color palette, resulting in an AP_{50} of 99.89% and an AP of 79.21%.

To avoid the need of tripling the input, we experimented passing only one channel and making the necessary adjustments to the network. This channel corresponds to the temperature matrix captured by the thermal camera. In order to prepare the network for the new input, it is important to understand how the first convolutional layer of YOLOv3 works and how it can be adapted to accept the new input. The output of a convolution layer is visualized in Fig. 3. In YOLOv3, the first layer contains 32 filters, also known as kernels, of size 3×3, which means that each value in the output convolved feature is a linear combination of the pixel values in a 3×3 square around it. A kernel is therefore defined by 9 trainable weights and, considering 3 color channels, there are 32 * 3 = 96 kernels.

Since the input shape suffered a reduction in the number of channels from 3 to 1, we discarded the weights corresponding to the kernels of the first convolutional layer and initialized them with random values. Comparing the results of this model to the triple thermal input version, we noticed a decrease in AP_{50} to

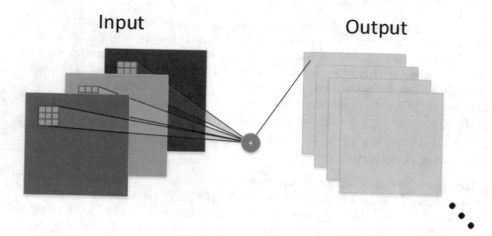

Fig. 3. Convolutional layer connected to RGB input.

99.59%, and in AP to 76.28%, but also a decrease of 6ms in inference time, due to the smaller number of input channels.

To improve those values, we tried to take advantage of the old weights of the convolutional kernels of the first layer. Since there are 3 kernels per filter (one for each color channel), it is necessary to properly combine the weights of those kernels into one. Convolutional layers calculate the output values of each filter according to the formula

$$h_j^n = max(0, \sum_{k=1}^{K} h_k^{n-1} * w_{kj}^n),$$ (1)

where h is a feature map, n is the index of the convolutional layer in the model, j is the index of a filter, K is the total size of the kernel and w is a weight matrix. Note that the output of a convolutional layer for a multi-channel input is related to the sum of the convolution operation on each channel, and not to its mean. For this reason, we sum the weights of each kernel for each filter to adapt from a multi-channel to a single-channel input, in an attempt to feed similar data to the rest of the network, and therefore taking as much advantage as possible from the previously learned weights. This resulted in an AP_{50} of 99.75%, and AP of 78.26%.

3.2 Optimizing for Speed

In the context of this paper, we are not very interested in detecting small objects, as we assume a minimum size of the faces of the vehicle occupants and distance to the camera (<60 cm). Therefore, it is possible that parts of the network are not contributing to the overall accuracy, because we do not have small objects in our dataset. To test this hypothesis, we grabbed the weights of our single-channel predictor with adapter weights and pruned part of the network. The high-level architecture of YOLOv3 is represented in Fig. 4.

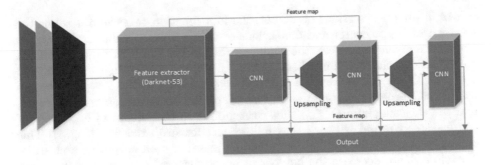

Fig. 4. High-level architecture of YOLOv3. Note that its output is generated from 3 different parts of the network.

The first output of YOLOv3 is given by the 82nd layer and the second output (medium-sized objects) is given by the 94th layer, so the rest of the network can be eliminated for our purposes. Inferences with this pruned model result in a similar accuracy, scoring minus 0.03% in AP_{50} and minus 0.02% in AP. Indeed, the last few layers of the network are not a high contribution to the prediction accuracy. The big advantage of making this conclusion is that we can predict in the pruned model, which means a considerable improvement in terms of speed with a low sacrifice in accuracy. In our implementation, the full model takes 35 ms to predict one frame of resolution 416×416, while the pruned one only takes 25 ms, which means we get a reduction of 29% in inference time. We also experimented ignoring the output of the second output layer, but the results deteriorated.

3.3 Training Without Last Output

Since we have concluded that the last layer of YOLOv3 is not helpful in our use case, we were able to increase its speed at inference time, but it is also possible to totally prune it during training so that it no longer contributes to the total loss (and decreasing training times). The loss function used for training of the model is defined in Eq. 2.

$$
\sum_{l=0}^{L} (\lambda_{coord} \sum_{i=0}^{S^2} \sum_{j=0}^{B} \mathbb{1}_{ij}^{obj} [(x_i - \hat{x}_i)^2 + (y_i - \hat{y}_i)^2
$$

$$
+ \lambda_{coord} \sum_{i=0}^{S^2} \sum_{j=0}^{B} \mathbb{1}_{ij}^{obj} [(\sqrt{w_i} - \sqrt{\hat{w}_i})^2 + (\sqrt{h_i} - \sqrt{\hat{h}_i})^2]
$$

$$
+ \sum_{i=0}^{S^2} \sum_{j=0}^{B} \mathbb{1}_{ij}^{obj} - \hat{C}_i log(p_i(C_i))
$$

$$
+ \lambda_{noobj} \sum_{j=0}^{B} \mathbb{1}_{ij}^{noobj} - \hat{C}_i log(p_i(C_i))
$$

$$
+ \sum_{i=0}^{S^2} \mathbb{1}_{ij}^{obj} \sum_{c \in classes} - c_i log(p_i(c)))
$$

(2)

As in previous versions of YOLO, the loss function takes into account the correctness of the center and dimensions of the predicted bounding boxes, the confidence given to objects, the confidence when there are no objects and the correctness of classification when there is an object. The changes with version 3 of YOLO are in the way the last three components of the loss function are calculated, using logistic regression instead of the previous squared difference, and the enclosing sum ($\sum_{l=0}^{L}$) that corresponds to the output of each layer of the feature pyramid network that follows the feature extractor (Fig. 4). This sum is responsible for adding the individual losses of each output at each scale. Therefore, if we decrease the number of output layers, L, from 3 to 2, we are effectively excluding the loss of the last output in the overall loss function. Our experiments show a reduction in training times of around 26%, but a decrease in AP_{50} of 2.3% and 4.1% in AP. For this reason, we decided not to exclude the last layer from the training process.

3.4   Comparison of Results

Table 2 presents a comparison of results between the different transfer learning techniques experimented, each being briefly described in Table 1. In terms of inference time, models C and D are 6 ms faster than the others, due to the smaller number of input channels. In accuracy, model C has the worst performance, which leads to the conclusion that adapting the weights to different images is better than random initialization. The results we obtained during cross-validation were similar, and we decided to choose model D due to the good compromise between speed and accuracy. Then, for testing, we used the model D that performed best during cross-validation, reaching an AP_{50} of 99.71% and an AP of 78.52%. A prediction example is provided in Fig. 5.

Table 1. Model description

Model	Description
A	YoloV3 with palette
B	YoloV3 grayscale with 3 channels
C	YoloV3 grayscale with 1 channel and random weights
D	YoloV3 grayscale with 1 channel and reused weights

After manual observation of the output of the face detector, it is noticeable that the score on the AP metric is limited by the fact that the labeling process was automatic and the face detector used for RGB images sometimes produces bounding boxes with slightly incorrect boundaries. For this reason, although the face detector reaches 97.14% in AP_{75}, it is harder for the algorithm to exactly match the ground truth and reach such values when the IoU (Intersection over Union) threshold is higher.

Table 2. Mean of test results obtained with different transfer learning techniques, predicting without the last output layer. The last row reports the test score of the model D that performed best during cross-validation.

Model	AP25	AP50	AP75	AP	Inference time
A	99.71%	99.60%	97.16%	78.38%	31 ms
B	99.89%	99.78%	97.34%	79.20%	31 ms
C	99.78%	99.52%	95.37%	76.25%	25 ms
D	99.85%	99.75%	97.33%	78.25%	25 ms
Best D	99.85%	99.71%	97.14%	78.52%	25 ms

Fig. 5. Example of a successful face detection in a very hot vehicle interior. The red bounding box represents the ground truth and the green box refers to the prediction of our model, together with its confidence value. (Color figure online)

4   Conclusions

Our results show that it is possible to develop an accurate face detector in thermal images using transfer learning with neural networks developed for RGB images. Furthermore, one possible reason to why the detector does not score higher in the AP metric is the fact that the ground truth information is generated automatically and the limits of the bounding boxes are not perfectly defined. Overall, we argue that our work compares ways of transferring existing algorithms from RGB to thermal and demonstrates good results in a vehicle scenario.

Further work can be considered. Model A uses a color palette to map the temperatures to different colors and there is the possibility of experimenting different palettes and see how they impact the prediction accuracy. Additionally, at the moment, the face detection algorithm here presented for thermal images relies on pre-trained weights fitted to RGB images from ImageNet and adapted to work with thermal images. Instead, we could retrain the whole YOLOv3 neural network with the grayscale version of those images, so that the network is prepared from scratch to accept input in a single-channel format, therefore removing the necessity of readjusting the weights from a three-color system to single-color. Furthermore, experiments can be conducted to understand how the input resolution affects the accuracy of the predictor, and what is the expected trade-off between inference speed and quality of predictions. Moreover, in the context of this work we focused on a maximum distance of $\sim 60\,\text{cm}$, which means the algorithm is not prepared to handle small objects. Larger distances could be considered by using scale augmentation or adding to the database images of faces further from the camera.

References

1. Basbrain, A.M., Gan, J.Q., Clark, A.: Accuracy enhancement of the viola-jones algorithm for thermal face detection. In: Huang, D.-S., Hussain, A., Han, K., Gromiha, M.M. (eds.) ICIC 2017. LNCS (LNAI), vol. 10363, pp. 71–82. Springer, Cham (2017). https://doi.org/10.1007/978-3-319-63315-2_7
2. Deng, J., Dong, W., Socher, R., Li, L.-J., Li, K., Fei-Fei, L.: ImageNet: a large-scale hierarchical image database. In: 2009 IEEE Conference on Computer Vision and Pattern Recognition (2009). https://doi.org/10.1109/CVPRW.2009.5206848
3. Korukçu, M.Z., Kilic, M.: The usage of IR thermography for the temperature measurements inside an automobile cabin. Int. Commun. Heat Mass Transf. **36**(8), 872–877 (2009). https://doi.org/10.1016/j.icheatmasstransfer.2009.04.010
4. Kwásniewska, A., Rumiński, J., Rad, P.: Deep features class activation map for thermal face detection and tracking. In: Proceedings - 2017 10th International Conference on Human System Interactions, HSI 2017, pp. 41–47 (2017). https://doi.org/10.1109/HSI.2017.8004993
5. Lin, T.-Y., et al.: Microsoft COCO: common objects in context. In: Fleet, D., Pajdla, T., Schiele, B., Tuytelaars, T. (eds.) ECCV 2014. LNCS, vol. 8693, pp. 740–755. Springer, Cham (2014). https://doi.org/10.1007/978-3-319-10602-1_48
6. Nonaka, Y., Yoshida, D., Kitamura, S., Yokota, T., Hasegawa, M., Ootsu, K.: Monocular color-IR imaging system applicable for various light environments. In: 2018 IEEE International Conference on Consumer Electronics (ICCE), pp. 1–5. IEEE, Las Vegas (2018). https://doi.org/10.1109/ICCE.2018.8326238
7. Ojala, T., Pietikäinen, M., Harwood, D.: A comparative study of texture measures with classification based on feature distributions. Pattern Recogn. **29**(1), 51–59 (1996). https://doi.org/10.1016/0031-3203(95)00067-4

8. Redmon, J., Farhadi, A.: YOLOv3: an incremental improvement (2018). https://doi.org/10.1109/CVPR.2017.690
9. Szegedy, C., Vanhoucke, V., Ioffe, S., Shlens, J., Wojna, Z.: Rethinking the inception architecture for computer vision. In: Proceedings of the IEEE Conference on Computer Vision and Pattern Recognition, pp. 2818–2826 (2015). https://doi.org/10.1109/CVPR.2016.308
10. Viola, P., Jones, M.J.: Robust real-time face detection. Int. J. Comput. Vision **57**(2), 137–154 (2004). https://doi.org/10.1023/B:VISI.0000013087.49260.fb
11. Zhang, K., Zhang, Z., Li, Z., Qiao, Y.: Joint face detection and alignment using multitask cascaded convolutional networks. IEEE Signal Process. Lett. **23**(10), 1499–1503 (2016). https://doi.org/10.1109/LSP.2016.2603342

3D Object Recognition with Ensemble Learning—A Study of Point Cloud-Based Deep Learning Models

Daniel Koguciuk[1]([✉]) [iD], Łukasz Chechliński[1] [iD], and Tarek El-Gaaly[2]

[1] Faculty of Mechatronics, Warsaw University of Technology,
Boboli 8, 05-525 Warsaw, Poland
daniel.koguciuk@gmail.com, lukasz.chechlinski@gmail.com
[2] Voyage, Palo Alto, CA, USA
tgaaly@gmail.com

Abstract. In this study, we present an analysis of model-based ensemble learning for 3D point-cloud object classification. An ensemble of multiple model instances is known to outperform a single model instance, but there is little study of the topic of ensemble learning for 3D point clouds. First, an ensemble of multiple model instances trained on the same part of the *ModelNet40* dataset was tested for seven deep learning, point cloud-based classification algorithms: *PointNet, PointNet++, SO-Net, KCNet, DeepSets, DGCNN,* and *PointCNN*. Second, the ensemble of different architectures was tested. Results of our experiments show that the tested ensemble learning methods improve over state-of-the-art on the *ModelNet40* dataset, from 92.65% to 93.64% for the ensemble of single architecture instances, 94.03% for two different architectures, and 94.15% for five different architectures. We show that the ensemble of two models with different architectures can be as effective as the ensemble of 10 models with the same architecture. Third, a study on classic bagging (*i.e. with different subsets used for training multiple model instances*) was tested and sources of ensemble accuracy growth were investigated for best-performing architecture, *i.e. SO-Net*. We measure the inference time of all 3D classification architectures on a *Nvidia Jetson TX2*, a common embedded computer for mobile robots, to allude to the use of these models in real-life applications.

Keywords: Point cloud · Point set · Classification · Ensemble learning · 3D Deep Learning

1 Introduction

Over the last few years with the rapid development of sensor technology, processing of three–dimensional data (3D) has become an important topic of research. High quality, long range laser scanners are widely used in autonomous cars, and the availability of cheap RGB-D sensors has resulted in significant progress in 3D

© Springer Nature Switzerland AG 2019
G. Bebis et al. (Eds.): ISVC 2019, LNCS 11845, pp. 100–114, 2019.
https://doi.org/10.1007/978-3-030-33723-0_9

mobile robots perception. Accurate object detection, segmentation, and classification from 3D point-clouds are challenging problems, especially so in real-world settings, and crucial for performing robotic tasks.

A lot of the handcrafted approaches to 3D point cloud analysis have been developed previously [6,13]; however, in recent years, deep learning – based approaches have increased in popularity [10,14]. The study of using these deep neural networks in ensemble learning for 3D point cloud recognition is lacking.

In point cloud classification task we assume that the object is already segmented, which means that all the points belong to that single-class object. There are 3 main approaches to point cloud classification:

- 3D ConvNets—point cloud is converted to voxel grid with a given resolution. This approach is not memory efficient in case of large volumes. The sparsity of 3D data leads to inefficient and redundant computation. However, some octree- or kd-tree–based approaches reduce these disadvantages and provide encouraging results [21].
- Rendering a set of 2D views of the 3D object—the problem is transformed into a set of 2D vision problems. View-pooling layer [17] may be used to aggregate features from different views. This technique leverages the performance of 3D ConvNets, but the loss of information during rendering makes this approach impractical in point-level segmentation task [14].
- Direct point cloud processing—architectures that directly process point-clouds in an order-invariant manner, first presented by the *PointNet* architecture. This approach does not require any data transformation, but processing of unordered data is not obvious.

A comparison between a representative technique for each modality is presented in [18]. In this paper, we focus on the direct point cloud processing, because such architectures can perform well not only in classification, but also in segmentation and detection tasks. Seven architectures are used in our experiments: *PointNet* [10], *PointNet++* [11], *SO-Net* [7], *KCNet* [15], *DeepSets* [22], *DGCNN* [20], and *PointCNN* [8]. We chose these because of their prominence and the availability of author's implementations that are open to the research community.

For object classification, two types of datasets can be considered. The first type is based on 3D CAD models: *PrincetonSB* [4], *ModelNet* [21], *ShapeNet* [2], and many others. The second type are datasets of 3D objects/scenes acquired from the real world with depth sensors [3,5,16]. In this work, we focus on *ModelNet40* [21], because it is one of the most popular benchmarks for object classification. It contains 40 classes of objects' CAD models

Above mentioned architectures are getting more and more complicated. For example, *PointNet* is a special case of later introduced *PointNet++* with 1.5% increase of instance classification accuracy on *ModelNet40*. However, one can achieve half of this accuracy increase with the ensembling of ten *PointNet* models. We do not want to prove there is no need for further architecture exploration; rather, thanks to ensemble learning we want to gain more insights into those architecture and the task itself.

Ensemble learning [9] increases performance of the prediction by leveraging multiple models. Several methods are reported in the literature: bagging, boosting, stacking, a bucket of models, Bayesian methods, and many others. In this paper, we focus on bagging, also known as bootstrap aggregating. We test three voting methods: direct output averaging, soft voting, and hard voting. We compare the ensemble of model instances trained on the same training set and its different subsets and evaluate their performance.

Our experiments show that an ensemble of neural networks trained on the whole training set is better than bagging using random parts of the training set. An ensemble of *different* model with different architectures can even further improve performance. In addition, we examine the number of trainable parameters and inference execution times on *NVIDIA Jetson TX2* platform for each approach. According to previous studies [19], using the *Jetson* platform as a high-level driver is a reasonable choice for energy-efficient mobile robotic applications.

2 Related Work

To the best of our knowledge, there are no studies reporting on the strict influence of different ensemble methods and the number of aggregated models to the prediction accuracy for direct point cloud classification architectures. Su et al. [18] studied a model combining different types of representations, but since there are fast advances in this field, there are more and more models in the point cloud classification zoo. A previous article [1] has reported significant performance gain while using an ensemble of 10 instances of one voxel-based, deep learning architecture, introduced in that article.

2.1 Comparison of Classification Architectures

All architectures can be split into the following groups: *DeepSets* [22] and *Point-Net* [10] as pionering approaches using global shape feature, *PointNet++* [11] and *SO-Net* [7] as hierarchical pointnets, *KCNet* [15] and *DGCNN* [20] as learnable local feature extractors and *PointCNN* [8] as hierarchical feature extractor.

The general idea behind *PointNet* and *DeepSets* approaches is similar, but they differ mostly in weight-sharing schemes in the *MLP* network and affine transformation matrix prediction by a *T-Net* network in *PointNet*. Authors call it a mini-network, but in fact there are two *T-Net* modules used in *PointNet* (for points and features transformation) and they consist of about 75% of the whole network parameters. Without *T-Net* modules *PointNet* has a similar number of network parameters to *DeepSets*. Both architectures are prominent works in the field but do not explicitly use local structure information.

PointNet++ and *SO-Net* both apply *PointNet* hierarchically but differ in the sampling and grouping strategy. *PointNet++* samples centroids of local regions using farthest point sampling algorithm (*FPS*) and *SO-Net* uses a Self-Organizing Map (SOM). Both algorithms reveal the spatial distribution of points, but SO-Net implementation provides deterministic sampling, whereas in *Point-Net++* sampled points depend on the choice of the starting point of *FPS*. Secondly, in *SO-Net* each point is assigned into k nearest SOM nodes, which ensure regions to be overlapped. On the other hand grouping in *PointNet++* is done by a ball query within a specified radius – the radius should be picked carefully so the regions will overlap slightly. The third difference is multi-resolution or multi-scale grouping strategy used in *PointNet++*. *SO-Net* does not have any similar strategy, but experiments with the former show that the strategy does not increase classification accuracy much, rather it helps in robustness against missing points in a point cloud.

KCNet and DGCNN both add local structure information, which is learnable—not designed by hand like in *PointNet++* or *SO-Net*. *KCNet* uses interesting kernel correlation technique, where *DGCNN* uses feature extraction form graph edges by traditional *MLP*. The former is define only in $\Re^3$, whereas the latter can operate on high dimensional input, thus can be applied hierarchically. Authors of *KCNet* introduce feature pooling via graphs, which tend to be more effective than max-pool in *PointNet*. *KCNet* and *DGCNN* architectures can be viewed as a *PointNet* working on points with learnable local features and having more effective feature aggregation scheme than original max-pool.

PointCNN is the only architecture truly working in hierarchical manner with 4 repeated χ-*conv* operations applied and 3 *FC* layers on top. However, there is a fixed number of neighbors, and they are found using *K-Nearest Neighbor*, which assume an equal distribution of points in the whole point cloud. Besides, there is no clever way of sampling points—rather they are sampled randomly. Despite all the assumptions *PointCNN* is different from the rest of the architectures because of the permutation invariance approach: it tries to sort points in canonical order rather than using a symmetric function like max-pool.

2.2 Ensemble Learning with Bagging and Boosting

An ensemble consists of a set of individually trained models, whose predictions are combined. It is well known that ensemble methods can be used to improve prediction performance [9,12].

Individual models may be trained using different training sets. In bagging, the training sets are selected independently for each classifier from the full training set. The selected set can be a subset of the entire training set (later referred to as bagging without replacement) or can have the same size, but samples can repeat (bagging with replacement). However, the result of neural network training depends on several random factors so that the ensemble can consist of classifiers trained on the same training set, which we refer to as a *simple* ensemble.

In Boosting approaches a series of classifiers are trained, with the training set (or samples loss weights) of the next classifier focusing on the samples with a higher error for the previous classifier. This can reduce errors, but noise in the training data often results in boosting overfitting [9].

Given the output of the individual classifier, the output of the ensemble can be calculated in different ways. Boosting uses individual weight for each of the classifier in series. Stacking trains a learning algorithm to combine predictions. In bagging and *simple* ensembles, all classifiers are equivalent, so three aggregation methods are commonly used in classification task: direct output averaging, soft voting (sum of activation of all hypothesis for each sample equals to one) and hard voting (each classifier output is in one-hot form, *i.e.* each classifier votes for one hypothesis).

3   Ensemble Learning for 3D Object Recognition

We performed several experiments during the conduct of this study. The whole setup with exact versions of all libraries and code version used has been shared online[1]. Seven deep network architectures were selected: *PointNet, PointNet++, SO-Net, KCNet, DeepSets, DGCNN*, and *PointCNN*. All networks were tested on one task, *i.e. ModelNet40* object classification. All these networks take a raw 3D point cloud as an input and output a vector of class scores for a given object, which can be denoted as follows:

$$F : \{p_i \in \Re^3, i = 1, \ldots, N\} \to \Re^C \tag{1}$$
$$F = \{f_j, j = 1, \ldots, C\} \tag{2}$$

where N is the number of points in the point cloud, and C is the number of classes in the classification task.

One set of hyper–parameters is selected for each network based on the authors' settings. 10 model instances are trained for each architecture. The influence of the number of models in the *simple* ensemble is tested for each architecture, which is described in Subsect. 3.1. An *SO-Net* architecture achieved the highest accuracy, so it was selected for further bagging tests. We tested the classification accuracy for bagging with and without replacement in Subsect. 3.3.

The ensemble of several model instances is computationally expensive. However, a deep network architecture can be viewed as an encoder (transforming sample to a feature vector) followed by a classifier (e.g. *MLP*, calculating class probabilities based on a feature vector). The question arises, whether classification accuracy can be improved by an ensemble of classifiers, based on the same feature vector. This was tested for *SO-Net* architecture according to Subsect. 3.4.

Our work shows that a *simple* ensemble of several model instances of the same architecture increases classification performance. Random factors cause differences between model instances. Influence of each factor is evaluated in Subsect. 3.5.

3.1   *Simple* Ensemble of Model Instances

We experiment with the *simple* ensemble, which is a special case of bagging, with the full training dataset being used to train every model instance. The

---

[1] https://github.com/dkoguciuk/ensemble_learning_for_point_clouds.

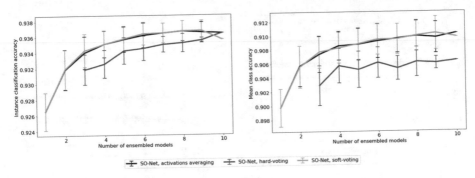

Fig. 1. Dependency between instance classification accuracy (left) or mean class accuracy (right) and k-number of ensemble models. For visibility, only results for best-performing architecture (*SO-Net*) are plotted. Results for soft-voting and activation ensemble are approximately equal, usually outperforming hard-voting.

ensembling is performed by averaging the raw output activation, soft voting, or hard voting (denoted as F, S, and H respectively):

$$F_e = \{f_j = \tfrac{1}{K} \sum_{k=1}^{K} f_{kj}, j = 1, \ldots, C\} \tag{3}$$

$$S_e = \{f_j = \tfrac{1}{K} \sum_{k=1}^{K} \frac{\exp(f_{kj})}{\sum_{n=1}^{C} \exp(f_{kn})}, j = 1, \ldots, C\} \tag{4}$$

$$H_e = \{f_j = \tfrac{1}{K} \sum_{k=1}^{K} \begin{cases} 1, & \text{if } j = l, \{l \mid f_{kl} = \min_{l'} f_{kl'}\}. \\ 0, & \text{otherwise.} \end{cases}, j = 1, \ldots, C\} \tag{5}$$

Where each model instance is denoted as: $F_k = \{f_{kj}, j = 1, \ldots, C\}$, where k is a model index.

For each architecture, 10 model instances were trained. Tests were performed for $K = 1, \ldots, 10$. For each value of K, all $\binom{10}{K}$ model instances' combinations were selected. Mean and standard deviation for each value of K are reported in the experimental results.

Figure 1 shows the comparison of voting methods. One needs at least three votes for hard-voting to contribute any useful information. With the infinite number of ensembled models, all voting methods are expected to produce asymptotically same results, but for a finite number of ensembled models, raw activation averaging equals approximately to soft-voting and usually outperforms hard-voting. The difference could be caused by the inflexibility of hard-voting: if a particular model outputs high scores for two classes, a small score change means the instability of the output class. For simplicity, only activation averaging is used in the rest of this paper.

Figure 2 presents the instance and mean class accuracy as a function of the number of models in the ensembles for each architecture, along with their standard deviation. As one can observe, with the increasing number of models in the

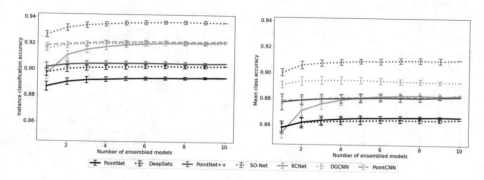

Fig. 2. Dependency between instance classification accuracy (left) or mean class accuracy (right) and k-number of ensemble models. We have learned each approach independently 10 times (70 different models), then for each k possible number included in the ensemble classifier we have randomly chosen ten different k-subsets and have reported mean accuracy with its standard deviation across those k-subsets. As one can observe, using the ensemble learning makes the output more stable and classification accuracy rise slightly.

ensemble, the classification accuracy is slightly rising, and the standard deviation of classification accuracy is getting smaller, which means that the output is more stable and not so much dependent on a single learning session.

Table 1 shows the numerical comparison of classification accuracy increase between all approaches. The *simple* ensemble of *KCNet* instances has a noticeably higher increase in the classification accuracy (2.52%), then second *SO-Net* (0.99%) and other architectures (with mean instance accuracy increase equal to 0.50%).

Some classes are easy to classify and all approaches achieve 100% accuracy (for example, airplane and laptop). However, interestingly, there are classes where the *PointNet* approach does better than others, despite the smallest accuracy

Table 1. Average instance and mean class accuracy for each architecture. Results for the single model, *simple* ensemble of 10 models and the accuracy increase are detailed. The *simple* ensemble of *KCNet* instances has a high increase in the classification accuracy (2.52%).

	Instance accuracy (reported)	Instance accuracy mean	Instance accuracy ensemble	Class accuracy mean	Class accuracy ensemble	Instance accuracy increase	Class accuracy increase
PointNet	89.20	88.65	89.38	85.77	86.62	0.74	0.86
PointNet++	90.70	90.14	90.48	87.71	88.19	0.34	0.48
DeepSets	90.30	89.71	90.27	85.79	86.46	0.56	0.67
KCNet	**91.00**	**89.62**	**92.14**	**85.38**	**88.28**	**2.52**	**2.89**
SO-Net	93.40	92.65	93.64	89.98	91.02	0.99	1.05
DGCNN	92.20	91.55	92.02	89.0	89.30	0.47	0.27
PointCNN	92.20	91.82	92.22	87.85	88.36	0.41	0.50

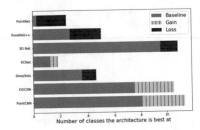

Fig. 3. Number of classes where certain architecture is the best for a version without ensemble, its gain (light gray), or loss (dark gray). High gain of *DGCNN* and *PointCNN* architectures suggests they can be much better in classifying some classes and much worse in other ones.

of overall classification (for example, glass box and stool). This suggests that different methods can be focused on various aspects of point clouds, in particular, focusing on local structure leads to overfitting for some classes with more discriminative global shape.

One can ask one more interesting question about those approaches and their ensembles: in how many classes a particular model has the highest accuracy? Figure 3 answers that question and shows how this number is changed after *simple* ensemble (if N classes reach same best accuracy, each of them scores $1/N$ in this rank). Note that the order of architectures is different than that given in Table 1.

3.2   Ensemble of Different Models

We evaluate ensembles of pairs of different models. First, an ensemble of output scores were calculated for pairs of architectures using weighted sum formula $F_{pair} = k_1 \cdot F_1 + k_2 \cdot F_2$, where $k_1 + k_2 = 1$ and $k_1 = 0.1, 0.2, \ldots, 0.9$. Note that each output of the architecture is scaled to have identity standard deviation for the training set. The ensemble of different models improved both instance and mean class accuracy. Top pairs consist of *SO-Net* model with higher weight and the second architecture. Ensemble results are calculated for 10 model instances: 5 of one architecture and 5 of the other. Table 2 shows the results. As two model instances are used in the ensemble to calculate its accuracy, results for two SO-Net instances ensemble are plotted for reference.

Ensemble of all considered architectures with the best-performing *SO-Net* was tested using the same principle as for pairs of architectures, but *SO-Net* weight was the highest $k_{so-net} > 0.4$ and weights of all other architectures were equal to $k = 0.0, 0.05, \ldots, 0.35$.

Note that this is the ensemble of different architectures including only one training instance of each architecture. The obtained models are further tested in the aspect of multiple training instances learning as described in Subsect. 3.1. The ensemble of all architectures with the major role of *SO-Net*, achieves the highest overall accuracy. The results of the ensemble are calculated for five

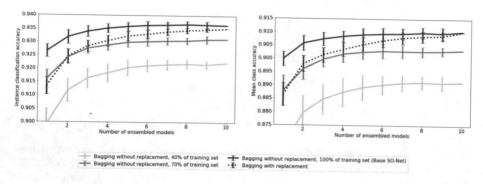

Fig. 4. Results of the *simple* ensemble, bagging without replacement for different training subset sizes and bagging with replacement. Results for *SO-Net* architecture, instance (left) and class (right) classification accuracy. The biggest gain is achieved for the smallest training subset size, but the overall classification accuracy is the best for *simple* ensemble (aka bagging without replacement with 100% of the training set).

instances for each architecture with the nonzero factor. Table 3 shows the most interesting results.

3.3 Ensemble Learning with Model Bagging

For the *SO-Net* architecture, which achieves the highest overall accuracy, model bagging was tested. For bagging with replacement, 10 training sets were generated by randomly sampling with replacement of a number of samples equal to the size of the training set. For bagging without replacement, $S = 9$ training subset sizes were used in experiments, denoted as follows: $s_i = k \cdot size(T_{train}), k = 0.1, 0.2, \ldots, 0.9$. For each s_i, 10 training set splits were generated (sampled without replacement), and one model instance was trained. Output of each model for a given s_i was aggregated as detailed in subsection 3.1.

Figure 4 shows the results. The biggest gain is achieved for the smallest training subset size. Accuracy increase for bagging with replacement is higher than

Table 2. Example results for ensemble of models with two different architectures.

F_1	F_2	k_1	k_2	Instance accuracy mean	Instance accuracy ensemble	Class accuracy mean	Class accuracy ensemble
SO-Net	*PointNet*	0.7	0.3	93.23%	93.65%	90.95%	91.44%
SO-Net	*PointNet++*	0.7	0.3	93.41%	93.75%	91.33%	91.61%
SO-Net	*KCNet*	0.8	0.2	93.21%	93.73%	90.62%	90.99%
SO-Net	**DGCNN**	**0.9**	**0.1**	**93.64%**	**93.95%**	**91.59%**	**92.00%**
SO-Net	*PointCNN*	0.8	0.2	93.55%	94.03%	90.97%	91.50%
SO-Net	*SO-Net*	0.5	0.5	93.18%	93.64%	90.57%	91.02%

that of without replacement. However, none of the bagging methods outperforms *simple* ensemble in the given task.

3.4 *Simple* Ensemble of Last Layers

The *SO-Net* architecture consists of the explicitly defined encoder (computationally expensive) and (fast) classifier. Now, we can check whether the accuracy growth of ensemble learning or SO-Net architecture is determined mostly by encoder or classifier part. In the case of the latter, one could learn the ensemble of classifiers only and thus save learning time by a significant factor. To check this, for each of the 10 *SO-Net* encoder instances, 5 additional classifiers were trained, with the same hyper–parameters, constant encoder weights, and 31 training epochs. The average result of 5–classifier ensemble is compared to the average result of model with a single classifier (both averages are calculated for 10 encoder instances).

Table 4 shows the results. According to the results, the encoder causes the major advantage of the ensemble. This means that computationally cheaper classifier ensemble does not result in rewarding accuracy gain.

3.5 Influence of Random Factors in *Simple* Ensembles

We identified four random factors in *SO-Net* model training:

- The order of training samples and random data augmentation (note that eliminating this factor means that samples are shuffled between training epochs but in the same way for every model instance);
- Initial values of weights and biases of the neural network;
- Random dropout regularization (eliminating this factor means fixing the dropout seed so certain neuron would be dropped, for example, always in epoch number 3, 7, 17, etc.);
- Random order of massively parallel computations, resulting in different summation order, which is not alternating for floating point numbers.

Table 3. Example results for ensemble of models with different architecture.

$k_{pointnet}$	$k_{pointnet++}$	k_{kcnet}	k_{dgcnn}	$k_{pointnet}$	k_{so-net}	Instance accuracy mean	Instance accuracy ensemble	Class accuracy mean	Class accuracy ensemble
–	0.1	–	–	0.2	0.7	93.73%	94.13%	91.24%	91.77%
0.05	0.05	–	–	0.25	0.65	93.74%	94.14%	91.17%	91.57%
–	0.05	–	0.05	0.3	0.6	93.88%	94.14%	91.52%	91.92%
–	0.05	–	–	0.2	0.75	93.65%	94.15%	91.14%	91.76%
0.05	0.05	–	–	0.2	0.7	93.67%	94.15%	91.12%	91.71%
–	0.3	–	0.05	–	0.65	93.73%	94.04%	91.66%	92.20%
0.05	0.3	–	0.05	–	0.6	93.78%	94.04%	91.79%	92.20%
–	0.15	–	0.1	0.05	0.7	93.76%	94.03%	91.69%	92.21%
–	0.15	–	0.1	–	0.75	93.70%	94.05%	91.64%	92.22%
–	0.2	–	0.1	–	0.7	93.68%	94.06%	91.60%	92.24%

Table 4. The influence of classifiers ensemble with one encoder for *SO-Net* architecture. Five classifiers were trained for each of the 10 encoders. As one can see, the computationally cheaper classifier ensemble does not result in rewarding accuracy gain.

Parameter	Mean	Standard deviation
Instance accuracy mean	92.43%	0.19%
Instance accuracy ensemble	92.69%	0.28%
Class accuracy mean	89.80%	0.21%
Class accuracy ensemble	89.98%	0.28%
Instance accuracy increase	0.25%	0.12%
Class accuracy increase	0.18%	0.12%

The first three factors can be eliminated, whereas the last one cannot be eliminated. To verify the influence of each factor, five *SO-Net* model instances were trained for each configuration with one, two, or three random factors eliminated.

The experiments were time-consuming (35 additional training sessions), but the results, presented in Table 5, are coarse because only one constant order of values for each factor was considered. However, one can observe that the increase in the accuracy can be observed even if all model instances in the ensemble were trained with the same training data order and augmentation, initial weights, and dropout order. This leads to the conclusion that for *SO-Net* architecture, diversity in models is caused mainly just by the numerical issues of massively parallel computations.

3.6   Comparison of Computational Runtime

We benchmark the speed of all the architectures on the *Jetson TX2* platform. We chose a mini-batch of four point clouds because it seemed to be a reasonable amount of segmented objects visible in a typical mobile robot environment. One has to keep in mind that we have not performed any target-specific optimization. All approaches used (*NVIDIA CUDA*) acceleration and three different deep learning frameworks, based on the original authors' implementations of these methods.

Inference time of deep neural networks depends on many aspects including the number of parameters, depth, number of operations, target-specific optimizations and more. In-depth implementation analysis of considered architectures is beyond the scope of this article, as we want to give a general view on their performance. As depicted in Fig. 5, *DeepSets* has the smallest number of parameters and is significantly faster than that of the other approaches, on the other hand *PointNet* has a considerable amount of parameters but is also pretty fast. The results could be explained by the design and types of operations, where *DeepSets* and *PointNet* has simple *MLP-like* structures thus are the fastest, *KCNet* is also pretty fast probably because of small number of parameters, *PointNet++* and *SO-Net* are slower probably because of hierarchical design, and *DGCNN* and *PointCNN* are the slowest since they have graph-based structures, which are expensive to build and convolve over. In the end, it is worth pointing out that an increase in a few percentages of classification accuracy (i.e., *SO-Net* or *PointCNN*) is occupied by significantly longer execution times.

Table 5. The influence of random factors in model instances training to ensemble accuracy gain. One can observe that accuracy increases even if results of massively parallel computations are the only one (irremovable) random factor. One can observe all removable random factors in the training procedure have little influence on classification accuracy in ensemble learning.

Training data	Weights initialization	Dropout	Instance accuracy mean	Instance accuracy ensemble	Class accuracy mean	Class accuracy ensemble	Instance accuracy increase	Class accuracy increase
Const	Const	Const	92.34%	93.19%	89.58%	90.96%	0.85%	1.38%
Const	Const	Random	92.48%	93.11%	89.89%	90.36%	0.63%	0.48%
Const	Random	Const	92.50%	93.15%	90.10%	90.58%	0.65%	0.48%
Random	Const	Const	92.51%	93.07%	89.88%	90.40%	0.56%	0.52%
Random	Random	Const	92.20%	92.99%	89.62%	90.25%	0.79%	0.63%
Random	Const	Random	92.47%	93.35%	89.78%	90.51%	0.88%	0.73%
Const	Random	Random	92.49%	93.15%	89.84%	90.65%	0.66%	0.81%
Random	Random	Random	92.65%	93.57%	89.98%	90.87%	0.92%	0.90%

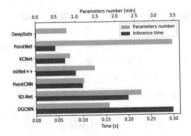

Fig. 5. Comparison of the time of inference on the *Jetson TX2* platform (on the bottom) and the number of parameters (on the top) for each tested model. *DeepSets* has the smallest number of parameters and is significantly faster than that of the other approaches.

4   Conclusion

In this article, we focus on the examination of ensemble learning on 3D point cloud classification with seven most popular architectures using raw point sets. We examine the possibility to leverage the classification accuracy of each of the seven cited models by ensemble learning. First, we observe which voting policy is the best for the task. Second, we found slightly better classification accuracy with the increasing number of models in ensemble along with smaller standard deviation. It proves that the ensemble's output is more stable and reliable. The biggest mean instance classification accuracy gain was observed for *KCNet*—(2.52%), *SO-Net*—(0.99%), and other for architectures—(0.50%) on average. Significant increase in classification accuracy achieved by *KCNet* in comparison with all other architectures could be caused by different underlying working principle of kernel correlation as a measure of neuron activation. Or could suggest there is some more space for hyperparameters tweaks in *KCNet*, e.g. the number of filters (sets of kernels).

We also show that the ensemble models with different architectures can further leverage the overall accuracy. We found that the *SO-Net* got the highest instance and mean class classification accuracy, but *PointCNN* wins in the number of classes in which given network obtained the highest accuracy after ensemble (this score is also high for *DGCNN*). This suggests that the latter can be much better in classifying some classes and much worse in other ones. This could also explain why the ensemble of only two model instances with different architectures lead to approximately 1.% of instance classification accuracy increase compared to the state of the art results. This increase is equal to one obtained while using 10 instances of *SO-Net* model. Further gain can be achieved while using multiple model instances for each of mixed architectures. Instance accuracy of 94.03% can be obtained for two architectures and 94.15% while combining three or four architectures.

We tested the source of randomness in ensemble learning analysis for *SO-Net*. We observed that numerical issues of massively parallel computations in deep neural networks are essential and beneficial in ensemble learning. The ensemble of several classifiers with the same encoder does not result in a significant performance gain. *Simple* ensemble outperforms classic bagging for tested approaches.

In addition we provide some tips for implementing point cloud classification into a mobile robot equipped with the *Jetson TX2* platform by comparing inference time for all the tested models.

There are more questions one can ask around the topic of ensemble learning for point cloud processing. In our opinion, results of this study could leverage the benefit of knowledge distillation in real-world 3D object detection for autonomous cars and mobile robots.

Acknowledgements. This research was partially supported by the Dean of Faculty of Mechatronics (Grant No. 504/03731 and Grant No. 504/03272). We want to thank authors of all architectures for providing a public repository. We would also like to gratefully acknowledge the helpful comments and suggestions of Tomasz Trzciński and Robert Sitnik.

References

1. Arvind, V., Costa, A., Badgeley, M., Cho, S., Oermann, E.: Wide and deep volumetric residual networks for volumetric image classification. arXiv preprint arXiv:1710.01217 (2017)
2. Chang, A.X., et al.: ShapeNet: an information-rich 3D model repository. Technical report. arXiv:1512.03012 [cs.GR], Stanford University – Princeton University – Toyota Technological Institute at Chicago (2015)
3. Dai, A., Chang, A.X., Savva, M., Halber, M., Funkhouser, T., Nießner, M.: ScanNet: richly-annotated 3D reconstructions of indoor scenes (2017). arxiv:1702.04405
4. Gan, Y., Tang, Y., Zhang, Q.: 3D model retrieval method based on mesh segmentation. In: Proceedings of SPIE - The International Society for Optical Engineering, vol. 8334, p. 120 (2012). https://doi.org/10.1117/12.961239
5. Geiger, A., Lenz, P., Stiller, C., Urtasun, R.: Vision meets robotics: the KITTI dataset. Int. J. Rob. Res. (IJRR) (2013)
6. Himmelsbach, M., Luettel, T., Wuensche, H.J.: Real-time object classification in 3D point clouds using point feature histograms. In: IEEE/RSJ International Conference on Intelligent Robots and Systems, IROS 2009, pp. 994–1000. IEEE (2009)
7. Li, J., Chen, B.M., Lee, G.H.: SO-Net: self-organizing network for point cloud analysis. In: Proceedings of the IEEE Conference on Computer Vision and Pattern Recognition, pp. 9397–9406 (2018)
8. Li, Y., Bu, R., Sun, M., Wu, W., Di, X., Chen, B.: PointCNN: convolution on X-transformed points. In: Bengio, S., Wallach, H., Larochelle, H., Grauman, K., Cesa-Bianchi, N., Garnett, R. (eds.) Advances in Neural Information Processing Systems 31, pp. 828–838. Curran Associates, Inc. (2018)
9. Opitz, D., Maclin, R.: Popular ensemble methods: an empirical study. J. Artif. Intell. Res. **11**, 169–198 (1999)
10. Qi, C.R., Su, H., Mo, K., Guibas, L.J.: PointNet: deep learning on point sets for 3D classification and segmentation. In: Proceedings Computer Vision and Pattern Recognition (CVPR), vol. 1, no. 2, p. 4. IEEE (2017)
11. Qi, C.R., Yi, L., Su, H., Guibas, L.J.: PointNet++: deep hierarchical feature learning on point sets in a metric space. In: Advances in Neural Information Processing Systems, pp. 5099–5108 (2017)
12. Rokach, L.: Ensemble-based classifiers. Artif. Intell. Rev. **33**(1–2), 1–39 (2010)
13. Rutzinger, M., Höfle, B., Hollaus, M., Pfeifer, N.: Object-based point cloud analysis of full-waveform airborne laser scanning data for urban vegetation classification. Sensors **8**(8), 4505–4528 (2008)
14. Sfikas, K., Pratikakis, I., Theoharis, T.: Ensemble of PANORAMA-based convolutional neural networks for 3D model classification and retrieval. Comput. Graph. **71**, 208–218 (2018)
15. Shen, Y., Feng, C., Yang, Y., Tian, D.: Mining point cloud local structures by kernel correlation and graph pooling. In: Proceedings of the IEEE Conference on Computer Vision and Pattern Recognition, vol. 4 (2018)
16. Song, S., Lichtenberg, S.P., Xiao, J.: SUN RGB-D: A RGB-D scene understanding benchmark suite. In: 2015 IEEE Conference on Computer Vision and Pattern Recognition (CVPR), pp. 567–576. IEEE (2015)
17. Su, H., Maji, S., Kalogerakis, E., Learned-Miller, E.: Multi-view convolutional neural networks for 3D shape recognition. In: Proceedings of the IEEE International Conference on Computer Vision, pp. 945–953 (2015)

18. Su, J., Gadelha, M., Wang, R., Maji, S.: A deeper look at 3D shape classifiers. CoRR abs/1809.02560 (2018)
19. Tang, J., Ren, Y., Liu, S.: Real-time robot localization, vision, and speech recognition on Nvidia Jetson TX1. CoRR abs/1705.10945 (2017)
20. Wang, Y., Sun, Y., Liu, Z., Sarma, S.E., Bronstein, M.M., Solomon, J.M.: Dynamic graph CNN for learning on point clouds. arXiv preprint arXiv:1801.07829 (2018)
21. Wu, Z., et al.: 3D ShapeNets: a deep representation for volumetric shapes. In: 2015 IEEE Conference on Computer Vision and Pattern Recognition (CVPR), pp. 1912–1920, June 2015. https://doi.org/10.1109/CVPR.2015.7298801
22. Zaheer, M., Kottur, S., Ravanbakhsh, S., Poczos, B., Salakhutdinov, R.R., Smola, A.J.: Deep sets. In: Advances in Neural Information Processing Systems, pp. 3391–3401 (2017)

Virtual Reality II

Designing VR and AR Systems with Large Scale Adoption in Mind

Amela Sadagic[1]($\boxtimes$), Jesse Attig[2], John Gibson[2], Faisal Rashid[3],
Nicholas Arthur[2], Floy Yates[2], and Cody Tackett[2]

[1] Naval Postgraduate School, Monterey, CA, USA
asadagic@nps.edu
[2] United States Marine Corps, Washington, DC, USA
[3] Pakistan Air Force, Islamabad, Pakistan

Abstract. Large scale adoption of novel solutions is the ultimate goal in many domains, and numerous factors need to be addressed to reach that success. This process is even more challenging when those systems are intended for human operators. Not only the technical performance of the system needs to be of the desired quality, but a range of other characteristics also gets scrutinized as well. The design and development of learning and training solutions will be encumbered by additional factors characteristic of learning and training processes. Current adoption of learning and training solutions is far from the desired state: the extent to which learning and training solutions became an every-day practice of their intended users is still much lower than the investment made in this domain. Our research suggests that a good part of that blame can be laid on elements of system design that did not match users' needs, skills, and expectations. In this paper, we report the results and lessons learned in multiple efforts focused on design and prototyping of a diverse set of training systems that used both immersive and non-immersive virtual reality technologies and a variety of 3D user interface solutions. Approaches discussed and suggested in this paper are equally applicable to the design of systems intended for other human activities in both civilian and military domains.

Keywords: Virtual environments · VR · AR · Training systems · Diffusion of innovation

1 Introduction

Large scale adoption of any solution is the ultimate goal in many domains—having tools that are widely and effectively adopted by a majority of intended users creates the necessary conditions for a paradigm shift in terms of dramatic change in the way those people operate. Having the majority of firefighters exposed to training solutions that effectively teach life-saving skills, providing the surgeons with alternative ways of practicing their surgical skills in as near-realistic conditions as possible, are essential goals that Virtual Reality (VR) and Augmented Reality (AR) communities aspire.

Numerous factors need to be addressed to reach that success. Some factors will depend on characteristics specific to the innovation itself, and some will be entirely

G. Bebis et al. (Eds.): ISVC 2019, LNCS 11845, pp. 117–128, 2019.
https://doi.org/10.1007/978-3-030-33723-0_10

outside of that innovation [1]. The elements that influence the adoption of novel solutions are even more varied when those systems are intended for human operators. Not only systems' technical performance will need to be of the desired quality, but a range of other issues will also be scrutinized including users' attitudes and expectations, satisfaction with the functionality of the system, ease of use, learnability, flexibility in supporting large audiences and high throughput, to name just a few.

Research activities done in VR and AR domains can be qualified as a cornucopia of interdisciplinary efforts done in numerous domains. The ultimate test of their collective success is the extent to which VR and AR manage to benefit masses of intended end-users. The true value of VR and AR will be reflected in new ways in which they operate, making them more efficient while saving precious resources, enabling practices that were not previously possible, and in extreme cases even contribute to saving lives. This point in time is also unique by the fact that we have easy access to a range of VR consumer solutions—both hardware and software—that are of high quality, reliable, and available at affordable prices; all those are necessary conditions for their large scale adoption.

The domains that are particularly well-positioned to benefit from such advances are domains of learning and training. While VR and AR solutions will not represent the entire spectrum of learning and training environments, they will inevitably be a large part of it. That is especially the case in situations where there is no other alternative available to address the needs of human operators. For example, flight simulators are currently the only solutions that offer the safe practice of emergency procedures. It is, therefore, no surprise that those systems are given the status of mandatory training solutions.

So far, only a few domains of human activity were capable of providing a range of well-crafted professional learning and training solutions equipped and proven to build a diverse set of skills needed by human operators. Training of astronauts is one such profession—the criticality of astronauts' missions and stringent standards of human performance demanded such an approach. Before reaching the point when astronauts train on near-identical mock-up of the spaceship that provides an opportunity for full skill integration, they are requested to go through a series of high-quality part-task trainers, where each training system focuses on one or several skills critical for the success of the final operation [2, 3]. Once they master those skills, they proceed to the next computer-supported part-task trainer and eventually graduate on the most sophisticated training environment available to them—a near-identical mock-up of the spaceship. The proliferation and affordability of VR and AR solutions finally bring about the possibility of other domains of human endeavor getting the same high-quality learning and training capabilities. The quality and a range of solutions that so far were reserved for the training of astronauts could become available to masses of users in other domains.

Our research agenda focuses on the needs of diverse groups of domain users, with the majority of those solutions directed towards the design of novel VR and AR training solutions. The operators of those systems range from submarine and ship navigators, pilots, firefighters, ground troops, and maintenance crews to name just a few. In this paper, we present a unified understanding of our multiple studies conducted in this domain. We summarize lessons learned, and introduce a framework for the design of VR and AR systems that are mindful of large scale adoption issues. We also hope that elements of our discussion will serve as a motivation to research community to engage with domain users more often, and help advance our collective knowledge about the needs of real people and real situations.

2 Diffusion of Innovation and Large Scale Adoption

2.1 Diffusion of Innovation Model

Adoption of novel ideas, physical artifacts, processes, has been a subject of study for quite a long time. The first direct demonstration of that work was published in the 19th century by Gabriel Tarde (Jean-Gabriel De Tarde), French sociologist, lawyer, and judge who viewed diffusion as "the law of imitation." [4] One of the most known modern theories is Diffusion of Innovations [1] that was established by E. M. Rogers and his team; the first edition of this seminal work was published in 1962.

The specifics of different domains, like technology, were brought in by other authors to enrich the initial Diffusion of Innovations model. Modified models included user acceptance processes (Technology Acceptance Model (TAM) introduced by Davis [5–7]), more specific details of 'perceived usefulness' (TAM2 model by Venkatesh and Davis [8]), and intention and usage (Unified Theory of Acceptance and Use of Technology or UTAUT by Venkatesh et al. [9]), to name just a few frequently used models. A common denominator for many of those models is the fact that they identify users' attitudes towards innovations as a key ingredient. It is, therefore, the attitudes and opinions of adopters (so both correct and incorrect opinions, from an objective standpoint) that are confirmed to have a considerable impact on the final adoption process. In our work, we operate with the original model by Rogers [1] and augment it with the specifics of technology domains and communities of interest.

2.2 Training-Centered Diffusion of Innovation Model (TC-DIM)

The technology adoption model that we designed and use in our studies incorporates all elements of Rogers' Diffusion of Innovation model. We extended it with elements that have been identified as significant for training with simulations. We named it the Training-Centered Diffusion of Innovation Model (TC-DIM) [10]. We intend to continue collecting the data related to the adoption of those systems and validate the elements of the model. As it is the case with the diffusion of innovation, this type of studies are always longitudinal (no adoption happens overnight, especially not in a large group of potential adopters), and so multiple years of consistent data collections among diverse groups of potential adopters are needed to achieve that goal.

2.3 Diffusion of Innovation: Our Data Sets

Our user studies regularly include the elements that concern the adoption of technology; in our case, those are most often training simulations. We collected initial data set in Marine Air Ground Task Force Training Command (MAGTFTC), Twentynine

Palms, CA, in Summer 2013. Since then, we kept collecting data in smaller studies, and the next large scale data collection has been planned for 2020.

The data set from 2013 tells us an interesting story about the users of training solutions (details of the study are reported in [10, 11]). The individuals we surveyed declared to use training systems to a very low level (number of surveyed individuals did not even know that there was a Battle Simulation Center in their base). However, they still appeared to be avid users of digital technology. In the case of young marines, they individually own three relatively expensive devices—a smartphone (90.91% of surveyed marines), a laptop or desktop (78.64%), and a game console (73.18%). They also pay for an internet connection to their rooms (81.36%), play first-person shooter games (77.27%), and engage in online multiplayer game tournaments. We were also explained that it is not uncommon that young marines would set-up an ad-hoc wireless network and play with each other. That means that they have considerable technical skills that are untapped, as well as undeniable interest and motivation to use those same tools in their work environments. We assume that with a passage of time, it is highly likely that their ownership and the use of applications will only increase.

2.4 Application of Diffusion of Innovation Model on Elements of Large Scale Adoption

The elements that constitute adopter-perceived attributes of innovation defined in Rogers' model [1] are worth explaining in more detail as we apply them very directly when we design novel training solutions that are intended to be effectively adopted and used by masses of users. Those elements are listed with examples we identified while working with domain users:

- **Relative advantage**: Perceived benefits over the current solution—bigger the benefits, faster the adoption. The new solutions should, therefore, convey a clear message of a substantial difference (advantage) that they bring over the existing solution. Examples for training systems include indication about new system effectiveness (faster, more precise, safer, more robust, and less error-prone), but also capable of doing things that were not possible before.
- **Compatibility**: The degree of being consistent with the current system of values— if a new solution is more compatible with the current solution, it is easier to get it adopted. Elements of current solutions that are highly regarded and appreciated by masses of their current users should therefore not be disregarded. Examples from the training domain include codified domain techniques and procedures, format and order in which some information needs to be provided to the user to support their operation optimally, and connectivity to data sources that adopters are used to having available.
- **Complexity**: Simpler to understand and simpler to use—faster the adoption. This can be directly connected with the complexity of an interface. A part of the system that is always visible to the users is its interfaces—the issues with the system are most often associated with the interface, as that is the only thing that users' see. The transition from an old interface to an entirely new interface will be tough for masses of potential adopters. This issue could potentially be less important if they know

they are transitioning to the new system with more significant relative advantage—that relative advantage would justify the effort that users need to invest in learning the new interface.

- **Trialability**: Ability to adopt innovation in incremental fashion results with easier adoption. Transitions to a new system that involves significant investments and perhaps even create a situation when adopters are unable to 'go back,' are always troublesome. Adopting some solutions in stages, testing it, and seeing if it fits their needs, is a far more productive approach for masses of adopters. That, again, may not play so much importance if adopters recognize significant relative advantage in that transition.
- **Observability**: Results being visible to other adopters, best 'advertising' and faster adoption. Advertising the use and successes of peer-adopters is a major tool for increasing the observability of the novel solution.

3 Designing Training Systems: Our Approaches and Experience

3.1 Study of User Needs

The design of any new system should not be done without conducting a detailed analysis of user needs beforehand. In our experience, no amount of effort invested in this work is too much. Information derived from multiple sources will provide a rationale on why a new solution is needed, it will help identify major capabilities and features that the new solution should provide, define expected performance levels of both technical systems and human operators, and even offer ideas for scenarios and new capabilities that should be supported in future system. A thorough scan of user needs expressed in both objective measures and enriched with user perception of their needs, will be crucial if a new solution aims to bring significant benefits to the users' current practices. Relative advantage (as perceived by the users) that new solutions offer when compared with the current solution will need to be significant if the goal is to persuade a large number of users to invest time, energy and resources and switch to the new system.

Our efforts explored multiple avenues of acquiring information to support our design process, and make sure that the relative advantage of the new system over the current solution is indeed very high. We list several examples of resources that can serve for that purpose:

1. **Official databases and reference documents freely available to the public**. Both governmental and non-governmental agencies and groups provide a wealth of information that is freely available for public review. One of our recent studies searched and analyzed data sets that could help us design novel training approaches and scenarios for the training of firefighters. According to NIOSH, "The United States depends on about 1.1 million firefighters to protect its citizens and property from fire. Approximately 336,000 are career firefighters, 812,000 are volunteers, and 80 to 100 die in the line of duty each year." [12] While significant technological

advances were made to make the job of firefighters safer, the firefighters are still losing their lives inside burning structures [13]. Public records that were searched for that purpose were stored in Fire Fighter Fatality Investigation Reports published by The National Institute for Occupational Safety and Health (NIOSH) [12]; this resource offered sufficient basis for suggesting a range of novel training solutions that could address training gaps illuminated in NIOSH Reports.

2. **Reports and information available to the public on demand**. Information about the number and nature of mishaps and catastrophic events that are recorded by different government agencies can be requested under the Freedom of Information Act (FOIA) [14]. While some mishaps may result in minimal or no damage made, other mishaps may cause substantial material damage, injury or death of human operators. Class A Mishap, for example, is defined as a mishap where "the total cost of damages to Government and other property is $2 million or more..." or an injury to human operator resulted in a "...fatality or total permanent disability" [15]. The time it takes to receive this type of report will vary, and depending on the complexity of the search, it can take even many months. The charge for searching those government records also applies, but it can be waived if a requestor can explain how likely it is that disclosure of requested information will create significant value towards public understanding of the government operations and activities [16]. Once the report is generated, special attention should be given to instances of mishaps that happened due to the human error or human error contributed to it, and situations that the research team is interested in addressing by creating new solutions for human operation. All those cases will help identify opportunities for new tools, systems, and training solutions that may address situations that, according to official reports, too frequently resulted in costly mishaps. Some of those solutions may have the power of dramatically affecting practices and outcomes in those domains, making them less costly, less prone to human error, safer and even have the potential to save human lives.

3. **Interviews with subject matter experts (SMEs).** The majority of our studies are done by individuals who pursue a master's degree at the Naval Postgraduate School (NPS), Monterey, California, and who are subject matter experts in domains central to their thesis research. While they have extensive professional expertise in their respective domains, those understandings are only used as starting points, and a search for more comprehensive information not specific to individual researchers is always requested. Interviews with SMEs in the domain—both instructors and practitioners who reached high levels of mastery and experience in given domains —are therefore frequently used. Results obtained from informal discussions with SMEs help us define the most pertinent questions that, later on, are presented to a larger population of domain users through the formal surveys.

4. **A formal survey of the user base**. Whenever possible, our research teams approach large groups of domain users and look for information that can assist in the design of novel solutions. Past studies included pooling information that concerns attitudes and opinions of Landing Signal Officers (LSOs) [17], pilots who provide instruction and pilots who receive instruction for Close Air Support (CAS) [18, 19], and pilots who receive training for instrument approach procedures [20]. When conducting those studies, it is prudent to approach a diverse set of users.

If the goal is to design a novel training system then the views of both trainers (providers of instruction who are typically expert users) as well as trainees (recipients of instruction, typically novices) should be collected and analyzed. It is not uncommon that their views on the same topics differ; if that happens, then additional investigation, most likely in-depth interviews, should be conducted as a follow-on activity.

5. **Literature and resources provided by representatives of domain users**. Many institutions provide periodic reviews and a list of technology and training gaps. In the case of DoD, all services list their interest areas and domains in which more superior solutions would be highly welcome.
6. **Research literature**. Publications devoted to past research efforts offer ample information about user needs. Studies that used the domain (end) users should be favored, especially in cases where the specifics of the application domain, users' background, skillset and even subjects' motivation to learn and train, for example, were crucial in obtaining more relevant results.

3.2   Task Analysis

A set of answers that we look for when we conduct task analysis extends beyond knowing the steps (actions) of the task that the system needs to address, their order and relative importance within the task. Additional elements that need to be identified and decided upon include but they are not limited to: operator's goals and what they do to achieve those goals, characteristics of the human operator (physical characteristics, age, gender, skills, abilities, levels of expertise, familiarity with technology), environmental conditions in which task could be performed (terrains, type of the scenes, weather, visibility), standards of performance for humans (typically expressed as accuracy, completeness, sequence or speed), system performance, interaction and communication with other human operators (in case of team task), use of other tools to perform essential task, exceptional cases of operation (what happens when things go wrong?), issues and difficulties typically experienced by the operators, health and safety issues, what data (if any) is used and what data (if any) gets generated and potentially shared, desired capabilities (beyond what current operation provides), current learning and training practices (including thorough understand of processes that generate very good learning and training outcomes as well as practices that are in need of improvement).

An important result of task analysis is a review of sensory cues and interactive modalities associated with each step of the task in a context of the overall objective that a system is expected to supports. The questions we need to answer (and we often test in our user studies) are related to a necessity of, for example, having haptic sensory stimuli by means of the passive or active haptic device as a part of the solution. One of our studies was focused on a design of a prototype that had to support the training of individuals who operate Man Portable Air Defense Systems (MANPADS), a system that allows firing of shoulder-launched surface-to-air missiles [21]. Close analysis of MANPADS operation suggested that a heavy launcher had to be held by the operator (thus affecting his posture and balance), and that important cues like vibration had to be received by the gunner when his cheekbone is in contact with the launcher (vibration of bone transducer suggested target acquisition). Additionally, a trigger had to be reached and activated by the gunner at a certain point during the operation. That type of requirements was hard to satisfy with all-virtual setup, and we opted for passive haptics that incorporated everything that an individual who is wearing head-mounted display would be able to touch and feel: body of the launcher, gripstock assembly with trigger switch and its physical button for simulating the uncage switch, trigger assembly (with HTC Vive controller attached), a prop that simulated optical sight, battery and coolant unit. This prototype also included an audio tone where its clarity and intensity represented the seeker level of infrared acquisition of the target.

3.3 User Interface: Family of Training Solutions

One approach that could help address compatibility and complexity as elements of adopter-perceived attributes of innovation is to pursue the design of a family of training solutions. The goal is to have solutions that are similar in look and feel both in terms of the interfaces and interactive modalities they enable. When appropriate, for example, the navigation in one environment should be the same as navigation in another simulated environment, thus minimizing learning time.

We identified a set of characteristics that a set of simulations should incorporate to be called a family of training solutions (details reported in [23]):

1. Training solutions should represent **effective bridges between training phases**. Individual systems should ideally cover all phases of training regimen, with overlap only where that is deemed necessary.
2. Whenever possible, training solutions should maintain **constancy in look and feel**. That would make a transition from one system to another, much easier.
3. Whenever possible, training solutions should maintain **constancy in interactive modalities**, thus minimizing time to learn them.
4. Training solutions should be **compatible with systems in the same family**. Getting input from those systems, and producing output for other systems and even connect with systems at run time should be possible.

Figure 1 illustrates several configurations of the same training simulation - Virtual Part-task Trainer for Close Air Support (CAS) [18]: (a) map and smartphone serving as a knee-pad (typical training setup for the pilots), (b) smartphone-only, (c) tablet with a keyboard and touchscreen capability, (d) large screen powered by the tablet, with a keyboard.

Figure 2 illustrates another aspect that can strengthen and support the concept of a family of training solutions, and consequently influence the adoption of this type of training solutions. In this case, the interface of CAS training system incorporates the look and feel of the tools that are available to the pilots inside the cockpit: moving map display, communications/data unit (CDU), and compass heading indicator with a timer. We were cautious not to add any tool that would not be available to the pilots in their operational environment (this helps avoid negative training transfer). Preliminary user studies also showed that a communications/data unit (CDU) and compass heading indicator had to be repositioned (Fig. 3) [19].

Fig. 1. A diverse set of configurations that support user's needs for training of CAS operations: (a) a map and smartphone serving as a knee-pad, (b) smartphone-only, (c) tablet with a keyboard and touchscreen capability, (d) large screen powered by the tablet, with a keyboard.

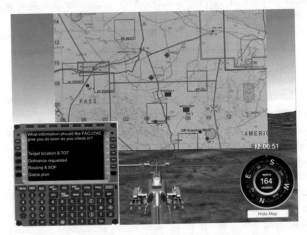

Fig. 2. CAS Execution Scenario Cockpit with three tools available at the same time: moving map display, communications/data unit (CDU) in the lower left corner, and compass heading indicator with a timer above it in the lower right corner [19].

3.4 Choice of the Platform

A choice of the platform that will be used to support the trainees' experience is one of the major decisions that need to be made.

A need for the fully-fledged training systems that mimic all aspects of the operational environment in as realistic manner as possible is well understood; they are often considered to be the ultimate training environments in many domains. Those training solutions frequently take the shape of the large setups that include a set of physical elements like instrument panels and elaborate dome projections used to visualize a three-dimensional environment. That type of setups inevitably makes them very complicated in terms of their maintenance and support (in constant need of dedicated instructors and maintenance crews). They are often situated in specially-designated

Fig. 3. The user study suggested a need for the increased size of communications/data unit (CDU) and repositioning of compass heading indicator [19].

places capable of providing a necessary support infrastructure, and in the end extremely expensive. While this type of training solutions are undeniably valuable as they provide the best opportunity to train in conditions that are as close to operational environment as it is possible, they are also known to be the bottlenecks in the training regimen, providing each trainee with very little time to acquire an extremely complex set of skills.

Insufficient availability of such large simulators is typically the main reason why less complicated but more portable solutions are sought after. A number of our studies explored the use of commercial off-the-shelf (COTS) solutions while designing the prototypes of training systems [17–22]. The choice of COTS was reflected not only in hardware setups that prototype used but also a range of software tools that were used to develop those applications.

Another reason why we frequently opt for part-task trainers and COTS is in fact that part-task trainers are ideal transition and step between a classroom training that does not use computer-supported systems and a fully-fledged simulator in which a trainee has to demonstrate all skills in an integrated fashion. Compared to full-fledged training systems, part-task trainers typically focus on a subset of skills. Training can often be conducted in a self-paced manner by an individual trainee in a fashion that is known as 'training any time, anywhere.' A unique characteristic of contemporary times is the availability of inexpensive commercial-off-the-shelf (COTS) technologies that make the promise of large-scale production and adoption of training solutions very realistic. Modern part-task trainers, therefore, fill several roles: they are teaching tools, much-needed bridge between the training in the classroom and in large training solutions, and they can also serve as a tool that available to refresh trainees' skill levels before they go to the operational environment.

An additional choice to consider when deciding on the type of platform to be used will concern the use of either fully immersive or non-immersive form of VR display [24]. While this will be heavily dictated by the training objectives and training needs analysis, it is certainly worth reminding ourselves that actual training sessions do not last 15–30 min as user studies tend to keep exposure to VR/AR system. It is therefore quite unrealistic that during such short exposure, the experimenters will be able to record a manifestation of the phenomena they are looking for, including the symptoms of discomfort (cybersickness). The typical training session lasts much longer, sometimes stretching to several hours, which increases the possibility of experiencing some discomfort that may significantly impact user performance and health. That being said, one needs to be critical with the setup that gets selected, and minimize potential risks that the users of that system will be exposed.

4   Conclusion

This paper reviews the results of our recent studies centered around the design of training solutions, and it discusses several vital activities done in the context of large scale adoption. We commented on the main postulates of diffusion of innovation models and provided the recommendations on how to approach the study of user needs, task analysis, how to design user interfaces, and how to select the display platform with a large scale adoption of training systems in mind. Approaches discussed and suggested in this paper are equally applicable to the design of systems intended for other human activities and operations in both civilian and military domains.

The results collected in our study represent only a small fraction of what VR and AR community needs to know and practice to fully deliver the promise of that technology to its users. We hope to inspire other researchers to engage in working with domain users and study the needs of real-world operations. We believe that going back to the actual, domain users, will inevitably serve as the best grounding mechanism and a powerful test for how far we have gotten in making VR and AR technologies a powerful and indispensable tool for human use.

References

1. Rogers, E.M.: Diffusion of Innovations, 4th edn. Free Press, New York (1995)
2. National Aeronautics and Space Administration: Astronaut Selection and Training. https://www.nasa.gov/centers/johnson/pdf/606877main_FS-2011-11-057-JSC-astro_trng.pdf. Accessed 10 July 2019
3. National Aeronautics and Space Administration: Astronauts in Training. http://www.nasa.gov/audience/forstudents/5-8/features/F_Astronauts_in_Training.html. Accessed 10 July 2019
4. Tarde, E.: The Laws of Imitation, Translated from the Second French Edition by Parsons, E. C. Henry Holt and Company, New York (1903)
5. Davis, F.D.: Technology acceptance model for empirically testing new end-user information systems: theory and results. MIT Ph.D. thesis (1986)
6. Davis, F.D.: Perceived usefulness, perceived ease of use, and user acceptance of information technology. MIS Q. **13**(3), 319–339 (1989)
7. Davis, F.D.: User acceptance of information technology: system characteristics, user perceptions and behavioral impacts. Int. J. Man Mach. Stud. **38**(3), 475–487 (1993)
8. Venkatesh, V., Davis, F.D.: A theoretical extension of the technology acceptance model: four longitudinal field studies. Manage. Sci. **46**(2), 186–204 (2000)
9. Venkatesh, V., Morris, M.G., Davis, G.B., Davis, F.D.: User acceptance of information technology: toward a unified view. MIS Q. **27**(3), 425–478 (2003)

10. Sadagic, A., Yates, F.: Large scale adoption of training simulations: are we there yet? In: Interservice/Industry Training, Simulation, and Education Conference (I/ITSEC), Orlando, FL (2015)
11. Yates, F.: Diffusion and large-scale adoption of computer-supported training simulations in the military domain. In: Naval Postgraduate School, Master thesis, September 2013, http://calhoun.nps.edu/handle/10945/37746
12. Fire Fighter Fatality Investigation Reports, The National Institute for Occupational Safety and Health. https://wwwn.cdc.gov/NIOSH-fire-fighter-face/. Accessed 10 July 2019
13. McDevitt, D.: Searching for effective training solutions in firefighting domain: the analysis of emergency responses and line of duty death reports for low frequency, high-risk events, In: Naval Postgraduate School, Master thesis, September 2017. https://calhoun.nps.edu/handle/10945/56157
14. The Freedom of Information Act, 5 U.S.C. § 552, The United States Department of Justice. https://www.justice.gov/oip/freedom-information-act-5-usc-552. Accessed 10 July 2019
15. DoD Accident/Mishap/Incident Classification - DODI 6055.07 6 June 2011, Attachment 17 – DoD Accident/Mishap/Incident Classification, Reporting Guide, and CSSO List. http://www.dcma.mil/Portals/31/Documents/Policy/8210-1c/A17_DoD_Accident_Mishap_Classification_Tool_and_CSSO_List_Jan_2017_2.pdf. Accessed 10 July 2019
16. Freedom of Information Act, Frequently Asked Questions, Office of Information Policy (OIP), U.S. Department of Justice. https://www.foia.gov/faq.html. Accessed 10 July 2019
17. Greunke, L., Sadagic, A.: Taking immersive leap in training of landing signal officers. IEEE Trans. Visual Comput. Graphics 22(4), 1482–1491 (2016)
18. Attig, J.: Proof-of-concept part-task trainer for close air support procedures. In: Naval Postgraduate School, Master thesis, June 2016. http://calhoun.nps.edu/handle/10945/49487
19. Gibson, J.: Marine light attack helicopter close air support trainer for situation awareness. In: Naval Postgraduate School, Master thesis, June 2017. https://calhoun.nps.edu/handle/10945/55601
20. Arthur, N.: Proof-of-concept part-task trainer to enhance situation awareness for instrument approach procedures in aviation domain. In: Naval Postgraduate School, Master thesis, June 2017. https://calhoun.nps.edu/handle/10945/55508
21. Rashid, F.: Use of VR technology and passive haptics for MANPADS training system. In: Naval Postgraduate School, Master thesis, September 2017. https://calhoun.nps.edu/handle/10945/56170
22. Tackett, C.: Development of a prototype virtual reality trainer for tactical vehicle ground-guiding procedures. In: Naval Postgraduate School, Master thesis, March 2019. https://calhoun.nps.edu/handle/10945/62303
23. Attig, J., Sadagic, A.: Virtual part-task trainer for close air support leveraging COTS. In: Interservice/Industry Training, Simulation, and Education Conference (I/ITSEC), Orlando, FL (2016)
24. Sadagic, A.: Design and choice of visual display solutions in the training domain. IEEE Comput. Graph. Appl. Mag. 36(6) (2016)

VRParaSet: A Virtual Reality Model for Visualizing Multidimensional Data

Ngan V. T. Nguyen[✉], Lino Virgen, and Tommy Dang

Texas Tech University, Lubbock, TX 79409, USA
{Ngan.V.T.Nguyen,Lino.Virgen,tommy.dang}@ttu.edu

Abstract. Visual analytics relies heavily on two-dimensional graphical representations. Going beyond 2D is useful as we can utilize additional dimensions to present complex data sets but requires more user efforts to navigate/rotate to the appropriate views. Moreover, multidimensional visual analytics in immersed environments has not been fully explored. In this paper, we present a virtual reality model for visualizing multidimensional data in parallel coordinates, called *VRParaSet*. Our approach stacks polylines traveling in the similar paths between two consecutive dimensions. We anchor the lines at the vertices to reduce occlusions, offer esthetic appearance, and reveal data-based structures not evident in 2D panels or contours. The proposed model is compared to its 2D and 3D equivalences through a user study of 19 participants. The results show that the virtual reality model, while potentially useful, requires a lot of cares, especially on navigation and interaction within the virtual space.

Keywords: Multidimensional visual analytics · Parallel coordinates · WebVR · Google Cardboard · Virtual Reality · Oculus Rift

1 Introduction

Big Data is nowadays the source of wealth for thousands of companies. According to a 2017 report made by NewVantage Partners, where they surveyed senior business and technology executives from international and modern companies, 48.4% of executives found the use of data "highly successful" for their businesses [21]. Data is also the backbone of many recent scientific studies, particularly multidimensional data. One such case is in microbiology, where large sets of organisms and environmental data are studied to explain certain behaviors of microbial ecology [22]. Thus, the understanding of large data has become increasingly imperative for both business and knowledge.

Two methods of data analysis that have been used for centuries are visual analytics and data visualization. It was during the 18th and 19th centuries when visual thinking started to take shape. Most of the first large data sets referred to the social aspect of the communities, such as people, economics, and medicine, where diagrams such as nomograms were used to represent them [12]. As information got more complex, different approaches and techniques surged. Some of

© Springer Nature Switzerland AG 2019
G. Bebis et al. (Eds.): ISVC 2019, LNCS 11845, pp. 129–140, 2019.
https://doi.org/10.1007/978-3-030-33723-0_11

these focus on illustrating multiple data fields by increasing the dimensions of the visualization. Hence, varying degrees of 3D visualizations started to be implemented for distinct purposes. The use of Virtual Reality (VR), consequently, started to be extensively discussed for data analysis.

Experiments have been carried out to test the usability of 3D over 2D data visualization. Throughout these experiments, advantages and disadvantages have been explained for each type of visualization. Specifically, they have exposed the best instances for which each visualization is better suited for. Such findings will be mentioned in the Related Work section of this paper. Nevertheless, data keeps growing into higher levels of dimensionality for which 2D and 3D visualizations are not always suited to represent. It has been confirmed that VR excels in multidimensional data, particularly on spatial dimensions, as well as providing a sense of awareness, interactivity [10], and collaborative properties [19]. Additionally, its challenges have been recognized and tested [4].

This paper aims to examine and compare 2D, 3D, and VR data visualizations on specific use cases of the multidimensional data analysis. Thereby, this paper introduces *VRParaSet*, a model to visualize categorical data in a virtual space. The features of the model will also be outlined. Moreover, the paper will present a use case study of the *VRParaSet*, reporting how effective and efficient each data visualization was. Criteria for this evaluation will also be explained. Finally, a comparison will be drawn between each visualization, and a conclusion will be reached upon.

2   Related Work

Beginning with 2D and 3D data visualizations, Dubel et al. [11] noted that distinct forms of visualizations have their weaknesses and strengths. Pure and mixed forms of visualization were classified and evaluated. A3 + R2 is one of these classifications, and it refers to graphs consisting of 3D objects (data) in 2D planes (grid). They established the following criteria for their study: occlusion, cluttering, distortion, and scalability. It was found that 2D visualizations outperform in precise measurement and interpretations, while 3D displays outperform in navigation and relative positioning. In like manner, VR technology has been the topic of several studies intended to describe its potential in the data visualization field and its numerous applications.

Ribarsky et al. [23] introduced possible applications for VR in information visualization back in 1994. They developed a system of virtual graphical objects bound to data or glyphs that enabled users to interact with them. They also explored the concept of human-scale virtual environments, such as a construction site; and non-human-scale visualizations, such as a virtual book.

Van Dam et al. [4] reviewed Immersive Virtual Reality (IVR) properties by conducting experiments on the matter. They concluded that VR environments highly depend on immersive senses. They also noted the challenges for non-human-scale scientific visualization. These challenges included abstract data representations, large amounts of data, and interactivity, among others.

Most recently, software systems have been developed to demonstrate the true scientific relevance of immersive data visualization.

Donalek et al. [10] directed a study on immersive data visualization (IDV). They presented an IDV application, iViz, that placed the user in a virtual space where a 3D scatter plot was shown. The virtual space allowed the user to interact with the 3D plot by selecting and shuffling data axis. The application provided "the first insight into the potential of immersive VR as a scientific data visualization platform." Moran et al. [19] developed a tool to visualize spatial Big Data. The authors incorporated data analytics to this tool to exalt the power of VR data visualizations.

A couple of recent academic papers have dealt with the comparison of different dimensions of DV and the evaluation of Non-Human-Scale VR visualization. These studies have left several questions when evaluating their usability.

Firstly, Sullivan's master thesis [25] consisted of a use case study comparing solely 2D and VR data visualizations. He developed a 3D scatter plot in a VR environment. Next, he surveyed users regarding a series of tasks they were asked to do. These tasks consisted of localizing and estimating data in the VR and the 2D visualizations. It was concluded that users with previous VR experience felt more comfortable in the VR environment. Nevertheless, most users were more successful localizing and estimating the data in the 2D plot. It is to be mentioned that the VR application was developed for the Oculus Rift VR Headset and a desktop keyboard. Thus, it was noted on the user studies that users had problems using the multiple buttons of the keyboard while wearing the headset. Moreover, the scatter plot design had some downfalls, such as the labeling and the scale of the graph.

Lastly, Gustafsson's master thesis [14] comprised of a use case study to evaluate the viability of Non-Human-Scale visualization. This use case study involved the creation of a scatterplot in a VR environment. A high interaction was achieved by adding extensive controls for the user. He resolved that useful VR visualization depended on a high degree of freedom (DoF).

Multiple website and blogs are in existence, where they display original data visualization applications. One of these is "Night at the Museum" by Arwa Mboya [17]. This application allows the user to view a scatter graph, a timeline, and a visual music model through VR. While the music visualization feature is not scientifically faithful, the scatter graph and the timeline are. The timeline, for instance, offers the user a different perspective of time awareness by scaling the chart to human-sized. While users can navigate through the music history and request for details on demand, the VR timeline does not provide users an overview or compare the kinds of music at different periods of time.

Another application by the company Datavized [18] implemented a globe model and column chart to represent geographically-linked data. The spatial data representation property of VR DV was again tested and successfully implemented.

3   The *VRParaSet* design

VRParaSet is a tool developed to aid in a data visualization use case study. It allows the user to view and contrast a categorical dataset in 2D, 3D, and 3D in a virtual space (using Google Cardboard and Oculus Rift). The tool was implemented using the Three.js [20] library with multiple perspective [2] and control [28] exported modules. The application is hosted in GitHub [15], and the VR feature is compatible with Google Cardboard [13]. *VRParaSet*'s VR mode compatible with Oculus Rift [27] was implemented using the previous resources on top of an A-Frame [1] framework. The use of A-Frame has been shown to be an effective means of creating and sharing VR/AR experiences in [26]. This mode is hosted in GitHub [16]. The 3D graph generated by the application is a categorical stacked parallel coordinate plot as described by Dang et al. [7].

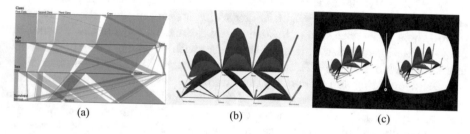

(a)   (b)   (c)

Fig. 1. Parallel sets visualization of the Titanic data set [24] on different models: (a) 2D, (b) 3D, and (c) VR on Google Cardboard.

3.1   *VRParaSet* features

The *VRParaSet* can be accessed from anywhere with an internet connection. The first screen prompts the user for a tag name to identify his/her answers and the starting category of the dataset. The start category is used to color-code the categorical data graph. The use case study begins when the play button is clicked. There are three modes to this tool: the 2D mode, the 3D mode, and the VR mode. When the user starts the application, one of the modes will begin at random. The 2D and 3D modes are meant to be experienced using a desktop or laptop. Thus, a use case study question is prompted at the top of the page where the user has an input text to enter his/her answer and continue to the next. There are ten questions in total. After all of them are answered, the next random mode begins automatically.

VRParaSet is a natural extension of Parallel Sets [9], hence, the 2D model is implemented using such library. As seen in Fig. 1(a), the categorical data is modeled vertically. Each category is categorized by the top category and represented by a color scheme. Such data categorization features are shared by the 3D model as well. Moreover, this library allows the user to highlight a particular category by clicking on the color code for a particular field. This feature also highlights the data based on the category level. For instance, if a user clicks on the third class adult male section, the female and child sections for the third class will not be highlighted. It is also possible to reset the highlight by clicking on empty space.

VRParaSet's 3D mode extends the classification methodology of Davis' Parallel Sets [9] by integrating additional dimensions into the visual space. Based on the description by Dang et al. [7], *VRParaSet* includes a categorical stacked parallel coordinate plot. This visualization contains stacked parabolas and stacked columns that represent the number of people. The parabolas connect two adjacent categories, and their heights represent the number of people pertaining to those categories, whereas the columns represent the number of people pertaining to a single category. The color scheme is also based on the first category data. Furthermore, the graph has data filtering capabilities as well. By clicking on a parabola, the user can filter out all records that do not contain the fields represented by the parabola. Similarly, clicking on a column also filters the data based on that column's field. To represent the filtered data in the graph, the tally of a "new" data set is computed. Henceforth, the heights of the parabolas and columns are recomputed given the categories i, j, and k and the category values c, u, and v, each one pertaining to the given features respectively. The updated height measurements are then denoted by

$$|\{w|w \in D, w_i = c, w_j = u, w_k = v\}|$$

where w is a sequence of values $(w_1, w_2, ..., w_n)$, n is the number of categories, and D is the original multiset of sequences. To reset the graph, the user has to click on an empty space in the scene. An instance of a data filtering can be seen in Fig. 2. The whole plot is centered on the screen and can be rotated by clicking on the scene and moving it to the desired angle view.

Finally, *VRParaSet* includes a VR mode as depicted in Fig. 1(c). The VR mode is supported by mobile devices and the Google Cardboard set [13]. This mode presents the 3D categorical plot in a virtual space where the user can navigate through it. The plot properties are exactly the same as in the 3D model, but the controls are different. Firstly, the scene provides a fixed center pointer, so the user knows where he/she is looking at. Secondly, the Cardboard sole button is used for both clicking and navigating. When the pointer is on top of the graph, the user can click the button to filter its content. The user can also click over an empty space to reset the graph. The only movement possible is forward, and that is achieved by keeping the button pressed. The user will move in the direction that the user is pointing to.

4   Use Case Study

By conducting case studies, understandings of the benefits and shortcomings of distinct categorical data visualizations were to be established. Accordingly, a user case study was performed with 14 individuals. They all trained with the *VRParaSet* controllers, as Sullivan's study, had demonstrated that useful VR

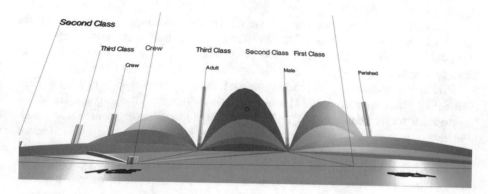

Fig. 2. *VRParaSet* VR visualization (A-Frame) of the Titanic dataset: filtered by male passengers.

applications are greatly bound by the user's experience in VR technologies [25]. The study was expected to illustrate how multidimensional categorical data is perceived differently under varying visual dimensions, particularly, utilizing an affordable and low-complex headset such as the Google cardboard for the VR stage. This was important to highlight due to previous studies using expensive and cumbersome VR headsets with numerous and confusing controllers [14,25]. The medium through which the 2D, 3D, and VR data visualizations were tested was the *VRParaSet* tool. Moreover, the dataset employed in the use case study was a Titanic dataset. This was chosen as this same dataset was employed for the initial 3D categorical stacked parallel coordinate plot [7], and questions regarding the data were easy to formulate.

4.1 Participants and Dataset

We recruited 14 researchers within the computer science and computer engineering department at a university. The age of our participants ranged between 20 and 36 years, with a mean age of about 26 years. The study computer was an iMac (Retina 5K, Late 2015) 3 GHz Dual-Core equipped with a standard 27-in. screen of resolution of $2,560 \times 1,444$ pixels used for the 2D and 3D visualizations and a Google Pixel 2 phone with Google Cardboard for the VR visualizations.

Regarding the test data, we opted for the Titanic data set [7,9] containing information of 2,202 passengers: *Class* (Crew, First Class, Second Class, and Third Class), *Age* (Adult vs. Child), *Sex* (Male vs. Female), and *Survived* (Survived vs. Perished). Studied parallel coordinates are color-coded by the *Class* attributes.

4.2 Procedure

In this user study, participants observed the graphed data on three different models and answered a series of 10 questions regarding the data displayed.

Each session, one per participant, began by explaining the purpose of the study and what was expected from him/her. They were then explained how the data was represented in each parallel coordinate plot. They were also taught how to use the controls for each model by having them practice with them. This introductory section lasted 10 min. Afterward, they were asked to begin the actual examination.

For the examination, each participant was shown each visualization model in random order. For each one of the models, each participant was asked a set of 10 questions. They then typed the answer to each question in an input box to be recorded along with the time they took to answer. Each visualization took approximately 10 min to be completed. Once the question examination ended, they were asked about each model's strengths and weaknesses. The entire session lasted approximately 45 min.

4.3 Questionnaire

The following is the list of questions each participant was asked to answer for each visualization model.

1. Which class was the least populated?
2. Which class had the most survivors?
3. Which sex suffered the most deaths?
4. Which class suffered the most deaths?
5. Which class had the most children?
6. Which class had the most adult male survivors?
7. Did the second class children perished or survived?
8. Did most adult female perished or survived?
9. Which class had the most male survivors?
10. Which class had more female perished than female survivors?

4.4 Hypotheses

Based on our analysis of meaningful features for pattern recognition, we hypothesized that 3D and VR would perform better than the equivalent 2D model on the same set of data as we can utilize an additional dimension to present complex data sets.

- H1—3D data visualization will have a higher percentage of questions answered correctly.
- H2—3D data visualization will have the least amount of completion time.

4.5 Results

After calculating the completion time and accuracy percentage of each participant, the following results were obtained. The accuracy of the responses was highest on the 3D model, while the lowest was on the VR model, as shown

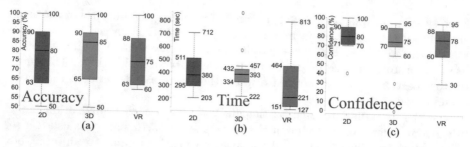

Fig. 3. Study results: (a) accuracy, (b) completion time, and (c) user confidence on 2D, 3D, and VR on Google Cardboard.

by Fig. 3(a). Although the accuracy results support the initial hypothesis H1, all visualizations had close accuracy percentages with very similar percentage variance. In fact, all ranges of variation are between 25% and 27%. It is worth noticing that the overall accuracy percentage among all visualizations concur with our expectations that categorical data visualizations are difficult to understand. This was made evident as most participants asked for clarifications on what each component of both 2D and 3D plots represented. For instance, the number of people was represented by the width of the colored region in the 2D plot while in the 3D plot it was represented by the height of the parabolas and columns.

Furthermore, and perhaps more interestingly, the completion time of some model sessions varied a lot from user to user, as illustrated in Fig. 3(b). The visualization phase that took the least amount of time on average was the VR while the longest one was the 3D visualization. This completely contradicts hypothesis H2. Despite the similarity in accuracy variance, variance in time spent varied tremendously. The most consisted one was the 3D, and the least consisted was the VR. This is supported by the fact that most users believed the information in the 3D model was "easy to find" while the VR model, even though it had the same plot, had a frustrating and at times confusing navigation. This means that people tended to spend more time on the more difficult model (2D) and spent less time on the easier one (3D). However, people performed worse on the VR model even though most of them, as shown by the average, spent little time on it. Hence, it can be inferred that participants deliberately answer the questions quickly regardless of the accuracy of the answer.

4.6   Qualitative Evaluation

Every participant was asked which model was overall preferable after the examination was over. Their preference was based on the ability to find data and the ability to compare data. Out of 14, 9 participants preferred the 3D data visualization model. They claimed the 3D model allowed the data to be organized and easy to find. They also mentioned that the rotating and filtering features were very helpful in localizing other data regions in the plot. The last 5 participants preferred the 2D model. They noted that the 2D visualization allowed all data to be visible at the same time. This comment supports the 2D graph description of Dubel et al. [11]. These participants also mentioned that the 2D model was simpler due to the lack of controls needed to navigate the visualization.

4.7   Discussions and Limitations

Participants also noted many of the weaknesses and limitations of each model. The VR model had the most critics. Participants thought the navigation was highly impractical. They thought adding a button to move back was needed. It was also suggested to implement movement sensors instead of movement buttons. Moreover, several of the participants felt motion sickness at various degrees after trying it. They mentioned that not having a reference point, like a floor, made "navigating through a floating graph very unreal and confusing." Nevertheless, they found the VR model interesting and believe it has great potential. The 3D faced some of the same issues as the VR one. Some participants mentioned that 3D objects were usually obstructed by other 3D objects. The perception of the data was also an issue for one of the participants.

Finally, for the 2D visualization, most users thought the graph was too crowded. They had a hard time finding certain data among the chart. Consequently, users felt it was challenging to compare data values. This becomes worse for higher-dimensional data as the *Class* (or colored) attributed will be split into many smaller portions as we travel to further dimensions.

4.8   *VRParaSet* A-Frame Extension

An extension to *VRParaSet* was developed to incorporate the feedback from the previous Google Cardboard session and to take advantage of the positional tracking and high-accuracy of more robust VR tools. This extension renders all of Three.JS (3D) objects in an A-Frame scene making the application compatible with most VR headset, including Google Cardboard and the Oculus Rift.

In order to use the Oculus Rift, first, the Supermedium [3] browser was added to the Oculus library. Supermedium is a free Oculus application that allows the user to access web pages with virtual reality content. Once the website is loaded in the Supermedium browser, the user will spawn in front of the chart which is on top of a gray table. An important improvement to the original *VRParaSet* is the navigation which is achieved by simply walking. One can also get a closer look at the chart by walking towards it, giving the user an immersive sensation. Filtering is achieved by using the pointer in the middle of the screen, which is controlled by the head movement and clicking the trigger button of the right-hand controller. Chart additions include a table underneath the chart and a floor for spatial reference, a color legend, lighting and shadows to improve realism, and high chart labels to avoid label obstruction.

A second part use case study was conducted with 4 participants who had tested the original *VRParaSet* and five new participants. They were all university graduate students. The use case study procedure was repeated for this second part as they were all explained the categorical data chart and given time to test the application using the Oculus Rift. The series of questions was also the same as in the first part. Each season, one per participant, lasted approximately 15 min.

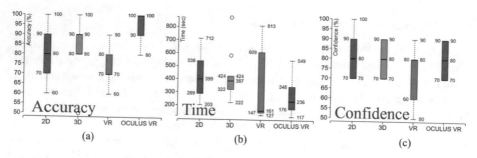

Fig. 4. Study results: (a) accuracy, (b) completion time, and (c) user confidence on 2D, 3D, and VR models compared with A-Frame extension

Significant improvements through the utilization of a robust VR headset such as the Oculus Rift is evident. Both accuracy in Fig. 4(a) and average time in Fig. 4(b) are better than not only the Google cardboard VR, but as good or even higher than the 2D and 3D model measures. This is intriguing since more than half of the second part user case participants had not seen the parallel coordinate chart before and performed as good as those who had seen it previously as demonstrated by the boxplot boundaries. Average confidence level in Fig. 4(c) using the Oculus is also sufficiently higher than the Google cardboard to assume users have a more accurate understanding of the data representation.

Moreover, the participants had previously participated in the first part of the user case study did comment that the visualization in A-Frame using the Oculus was tremendously better. They said that the navigation and interactions with the chart were "intuitive" and felt as if they were "seeing the graph on their actual desk." They also said that they felt little to no dizziness compared to the Google cardboard VR model. All of them mentioned that this VR visualization was better than their preference in the first case study. The new participants found the chart difficult to understand at the beginning but thought the concept of data visualization through VR was highly interesting and promising. Overall, most of them believe that this type of data visualization has enormous potential, especially for complex information such as multidimensional data. A couple of participants did add that they would like more motion interactions with the chart, such as moving it with the Oculus controllers from side to side or up and down.

5   Conclusion and Future Work

This paper presents a user study of multidimensional categorical data on 4 data visualization models utilizing the *VRParaSet* tool. The *VRParaSet* supports four modes: 2D mode, 3D mode, a VR mode for Google Cardboard, and a VR mode for Oculus Rift through an A-Frame extension. The *VRParaSet* was evaluated on a qualitative study of 19 users which lead to conclusions on the viability of three distinct data visualizations. It was found that 2D, 3D, and VR settings do not greatly affect the ability of a user to find and examine data. It was observed that a 3D parallel coordinate plot outperforms a 2D plot due to the organization of the data and its neat representation. Nevertheless, it was concluded that a VR visualization requires enough controls to move around the scene comfortably and that space where the plot spans should have reference points. If that were not the case, users tend to get frustrated and confused when analyzing the visual data.

The current user studies on multidimensional visual analytics models are limited to categorical data. In the future, more extensive studies on complex data set (higher dimensional and different data types) should be conducted to have broader views/conclusions as there are various visualization techniques for high-dimensional data [8], such as scatter plot matrices [29] and their variances [5,6]. Additionally, testing other VR headsets capabilities such as hand trackers would allow for the exploitation of the benefits of VR technologies for non-human-scale data visualizations. Overall, it would be ideal to also implement practical extensions of this technology in areas such as education or project management.

References

1. Ngo, K.: A-Frame (2018). https://aframe.io/
2. AlteredQualia: Stereoeffect (2018). http://alteredqualia.com
3. Marcos, D., Ngo, D.G.K.: Supermedium (2018). https://www.supermedium.com/
4. van Dam, A., Laidlaw, D.H., Simpson, R.M.: Experiments in immersive virtual reality for scientific visualization. Comput. Graphics **26**, 535–555 (2002)
5. Dang, T.N., Murray, P., Forbes, A.G.: PathwayMatrix: visualizing binary relationships between proteins in biological pathways. BMC Proc. **9**(6), S3 (2015)
6. Dang, T.N., Wilkinson, L.: ScagExplorer: exploring scatterplots by their scagnostics. In: Proceedings IEEE Pacific Visualization Symposium, PACIFICVIS 2014, pp. 73–80. IEEE Computer Society, Washington, DC, USA (2014). https://doi.org/10.1109/PacificVis.2014.42
7. Dang, T.N., Wilkinson, L., Anand, A.: Stacking graphic elements to avoid overplotting. IEEE Trans. Visual Comput. Graphics **16**(6), 1044–1052 (2010). https://doi.org/10.1109/TVCG.2010.197
8. Dasgupta, A., Kosara, R.: Pargnostics: screen-space metrics for parallel coordinates. IEEE Trans. Visual Comput. Graphics **16**, 1017–2626 (2010)
9. Davies, J.: Parallel sets: a visualisation technique for multidimensional categorical data (2018). https://www.jasondavies.com/parallel-sets/
10. Donalek, C., et al.: Immersive and collaborative data visualization using virtual reality platforms. CoRR **abs/1410.7670** (2014). http://arxiv.org/abs/1410.7670
11. Dübel, S., Röhlig, M., Schumann, H., Trapp, M.: 2D and 3D presentation of spatial data: a systematic review. In: 2014 IEEE VIS International Workshop on 3DVis (3DVis), pp. 11–18, November 2014. https://doi.org/10.1109/3DVis.2014.7160094

12. Friendly, M., Denis, D.: Milestones in the History of Thematic Cartography, Statistical Graphics, and Data Visualization: An Illustrated Chronology of Innovations. Statistical Consulting Service, York University (2008). https://books.google.com/books?id=cTjCjwEACAAJ
13. Google: Google cardboard (2018). https://vr.google.com/cardboard/
14. Gustafsson, M., Odd, O.: Virtual reality data visualization: concepts, technologies and more. Master's thesis, Halmstad University (2018)
15. idVL, T.: Vrparallelset (2018). https://git.io/fjjDw
16. idVL, T.: Vrparallelset aframe (2018). https://git.io/fjjDV
17. Mboya, A.M.: Data visualization in virtual reality - a VR demo project, December 2017. https://medium.com/inborn-experience/data-visualization-in-virtual-reality-a-vr-demo-project-a31c577aaefc
18. Metzler, K.: Experimenting with data visualization in VR, June 2018. http://ocean.sagepub.com/blog/2018/6/20/experimenting-with-data-visualization-in-vr
19. Moran, A., Gadepally, V., Hubbell, M., Kepner, J.: Improving big data visual analytics with interactive virtual reality. In: 2015 IEEE High Performance Extreme Computing Conference (HPEC), pp. 1–6 (2015)
20. Mrdoob: Three.js (2018). https://threejs.org
21. NewVantage-Partners: Big data executive survey 2017 (2017). http://newvantage.com/wp-content/uploads/2017/01/Big-Data-Executive-Survey-2017-Executive-Summary.pdf
22. Ramette, A.: Multivariate analyses in microbial ecology. FEMS Microbiol. Ecol. **62**(2), 142–160 (2007)
23. Ribarsky, W., Bolter, J., den Bosch, A.O., van Teylingen, R.: Visualization and analysis using virtual reality. IEEE Comput. Graphics Appl. **94**(1), 10–12 (2002)
24. Singh, A., Saraswat, S., Faujdar, N.: Analyzing titanic disaster using machine learning algorithms. In: 2017 International Conference on Computing, Communication and Automation (ICCCA), pp. 406–411, May 2017. https://doi.org/10.1109/CCAA.2017.8229835
25. Sullivan, P.: Graph-based data visualization in virtual reality: a comparison of user experiences. Master's thesis, California Polytechnic State University (2016)
26. Nguyen, V.T., Hite, R., Dang, T.: Web-based virtual reality development in classroom: from learner's perspectives. In: 2018 IEEE International Conference on Artificial Intelligence and Virtual Reality (AIVR), pp. 11–18, December 2018. https://doi.org/10.1109/AIVR.2018.00010
27. Facebook Technologies: Oculus rift (2018). https://www.oculus.com/rift/
28. W3C: Deviceorientation (2018). https://w3c.github.io/deviceorientation/
29. Wilkinson, L., Anand, A., Grossman, R.: Graph-theoretic scagnostics. In: Proceedings of the IEEE Information Visualization 2005, pp. 157–164. IEEE Computer Society Press (2005)

Occlusion and Collision Aware Smartphone AR Using Time-of-Flight Camera

Yuan Tian$^{(\boxtimes)}$, Yuxin Ma, Shuxue Quan, and Yi Xu

OPPO US Research Center, 2479 E Bayshore Rd, Palo Alto, CA 94303, USA
{yuan.tian,yuxin.ma,shuxue.quan,yi.xu}@oppo.com

Abstract. The development of Visual Inertial Odometry (VIO) systems such as ARKit and ARCore has brought smartphone Augmented Reality (AR) to mainstream. However, interactions between virtual objects and real objects are still limited due to the lack of 3D sensing capability. Recently, smartphone makers have been touting Time-of-Flight (ToF) cameras on their phones. ToF cameras can determine depth information in a photo using infrared light. By understanding the 3D structure of the scene, more AR capabilities can be enabled. In this paper, we propose practical methods to process ToF depth maps in real time and enable occlusion handling and collision detection for AR applications simultaneously. Our experimental results show real time performance and good visual quality for both occlusion rendering and collision detection.

Keywords: Augmented Reality · Time-of-flight · Visual occlusion · Collision detection · Depth up-sampling

1 Introduction

Augmented Reality (AR) superimposes virtual contents on top of a user's view of the real world. With the development of ARKit and ARCore, mobile industry has brought smartphone AR to mainstream. Both ARKit and ARCore provide 6 Degree-of-Freedom (DoF) camera tracking capability. A user can scan the environment using a mobile phone's camera, while the phone performs VIO in real time. Once camera pose is tracked continuously, virtual objects can be placed into the scene to create an illusion that real objects and virtual objects are merged together. VIO systems only create a sparse representation of the real world. This makes it difficult to solve the challenging problems of visual occlusion and collision detection as shown in Fig. 1. There have been some previous works to address real-time occlusion computation [9,31] and collision detection [36] for AR applications, however they all rely on the presence of visual features of the real objects. Moreover, none of them solve both problems within the same framework. To address both problems effectively, ideally one needs dense depth information in real time. It is very challenging to generate such information solely from a single RGB camera.

© Springer Nature Switzerland AG 2019
G. Bebis et al. (Eds.): ISVC 2019, LNCS 11845, pp. 141–153, 2019.
https://doi.org/10.1007/978-3-030-33723-0_12

Fig. 1. Occlusion and collision aware AR: (left) the virtual object is occluded when an occluder is present; (right) collision detection is fundamental for enabling interactions between virtual objects and real objects.

Recently some smartphone manufacturers start to equip their phones with depth sensors (ToF or structured light) to support novel photography and AR applications. A ToF camera measures the round trip time of emitted light, and then resolves the depth value (distance) for a point in the real-world scene [18]. Such cameras can provide dense depth data at 30–60 frames per second (fps). Although it is a straightforward step to apply depth data for visual occlusion and collision detection, there are still many critical challenges. First, most smartphone AR applications require real-time performance using limited computing resources. Second, ToF cameras have a unique sensing architecture, and contain systematic and non-systematic bias [18]. Specifically, depth maps captured by ToF cameras have low depth precision and low spatial resolution, and there are errors caused by radiometric, geometric and illumination variations. Furthermore, the depth maps also need to be up-sampled and registered to the resolution of RGB camera to enable smartphone AR applications.

In this work, we propose a processing pipeline that uses the RGB and ToF cameras on a smartphone to compute visual occlusion and collision detection. We first process the ToF depth maps to remove outliers and overcome sensor bias and errors. Then a densification algorithm is applied to up-sample the low-resolution depth map. An alpha map is also generated for blending between virtual objects and real objects along the occluding boundaries. A light-weighted voxelization representation of the real-world scene is also built from the depth maps to enable fast collision detection. The main contributions of the proposed methods are as follows:

- a system that exploits the ToF camera on smartphones for two essential AR applications with computational efficiency and plausible visual performance;
- a ToF depth map processing method that removes outlier, densifies the depth map, and enables blending at the occlusion boundaries between real objects and virtual objects; and
- a light-weighted 3D representation of the scene and corresponding collision detection algorithm.

2   Related Work

In this section, related works in depth map up-sampling, visual occlusion in AR, online 3D reconstruction, and collision detection are discussed.

Depth Up-Sampling: The main goal of depth up-sampling is to convert a depth map from low resolution to high resolution, often to that of a pairing RGB camera. Normally, the procedure includes projecting depth samples from depth camera to RGB camera's space using extrinsic parameters, and then filling in the missing depth samples at the high resolution. This is also called *depth densification* or *depth completion*. Many previous works have relied on joint bilateral filtering to fill the holes in sparse depth map [6,23,24]. Median filtering can also be used to perform depth completion to achieve temporal stability [17]. Some previous works transform the depth up-sampling/completion task into an optimization problem that estimates the proper depth values for the unknown pixels [15,19,33]. Recently, deep neural networks have also been applied for depth completion problem with guidance from color image [11,26,37]. Guided methods depend on the quality of the associated color image and are usually computationally expensive. Non-guided methods process depth data directly. In general they are more friendly towards real-time applications [10,30,34,35]. The work of [13] uses well-designed traditional image processing operations and achieves competitive results for depth completion. In our paper, we apply similar image processing steps to perform depth up-sampling so that the entire system can run in real time.

Visual Occlusion in AR: Enabling visual occlusion in AR has significant impact on user experience. A foreground object should occlude a virtual object placed behind it with temporal coherence. Walton and Steed [32] use a RGBD camera to enable occlusion for AR. However, they assume simple color model of the foreground occluder to compute a cost map and then filter the cost map into a matte for image compositing. [25] combines semantic segmentation and optical flow based depth estimation to handle occlusion using a visibility-based rendering method. [16] proposes a RGBD-based occlusion handling method that extracts region of interest and uses guided filtering for depth densification on HoloLens. Recently, progress has been made on dense depth estimation using monocular camera for visual occlusion on smartphones. [31] applies stereo matching to calculate sparse depth, then densifies the depth map using bilateral solver. [9] obtains sparse depth map produced by DSO SLAM [8]. It then extracts soft depth edges using optical flow and solves depth densification as an optimization problem with edge constraints. Apple Inc.'s ARKit3 SDK [2] supports human occlusion, which enables realistic rendering of AR contents that are placed behind people.

Online 3D Reconstruction: With the development of depth sensors, many research works have focused on online 3D reconstruction using RGBD cameras. The seminal work of KinectFusion [20] reconstructs 3D scenes in real time using Kinect camera. In this method, a Truncated Signed Distance Function (TSDF) data structure is used to store the implicit 3D surface of a static scene. [21] applies a spatial hashing function [7,28] together with TSDF to enlarge reconstructed space and improve storage efficiency. [12] applies voxel hashing data structure to realize 3D reconstruction on board of a mobile device. [36] proposes an adaptive multi-scale voxel hashing scheme for mobile AR applications. In our method, voxel hashing is also used to approximate the scene efficiently.

Collision Detection: Collision detection is a traditional topic of computer graphics. Numerous works have been proposed for different applications such as continuous collision detection [5], deformation interaction [27], and self-collision [4]. There have been a few attempts to enable collision detection for AR, but they either require a digital model of the real environment [1,3] or only address the problem in 2D [14]. For collision detection on smartphones, [36] proposes a mutli-scale voxel structure that forms a bounding volume hierarchy around the sparse 3D point cloud data reconstructed by ARKit. This method does not work with featureless areas of the scene. As an implicit data structure, TSDF supports fast collision detection. For example, [29] applies ray casting for 3 DoF collision detection between a haptic avatar and TSDF. [3] was the first research that addresses both occlusion and collision detection for AR. Their method relies on digital models of the real world scene. Our method also focuses on these two AR applications, and enables them on a smartphone for unknown real-world scenes.

3   Overview

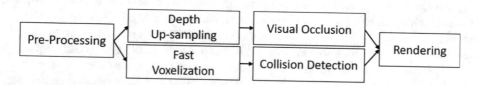

Fig. 2. Overview of the proposed occlusion and collision aware processing pipeline.

Figure 2 shows our ToF-based processing pipeline. In the pre-processing stage, depth map is processed to remove outliers. After that, it is further processed in two streams. In one stream, depth up-sampling is performed to generate high-resolution depth map for occlusion rendering. In the other stream, fast voxelization module converts the real-world scene into a 3D representation for collision detection. In the following chapters, Sect. 4 introduces the pre-processing method for ToF depth data. Section 5 describes how to up-sample the depth image and perform visual occlusion between virtual objects and real-world scene. Section 6 discusses a fast voxelization and collision detection approach. Experimental results and conclusion are discussed in Sects. 7 and 8 respectively.

4   Data Pre-processing

Both visual occlusion and collision detection require that each pixel of the RGB image has a reasonable depth value. However depth data from ToF camera is often quite noisy due to systematic and non-systematic errors. Specifically, systematic errors include infra-red (IR) demodulation error, amplitude ambiguity and temperature error. Usually, longer exposure time increases signal-to-noise ratio (SNR); however this will lower the frame rate. Researchers tend to apply filters to reduce noise. For example [22] removes outliers around the boundaries by comparing a depth sample with neighboring ones in a fixed-size local window.

In a typical AR application, a user often moves the camera slowly. Therefore, outliers due to IR saturation and 3D structure distortion are dominant. Such outliers exist along the depth discontinuity between foreground and background. Specifically, pixels on background object along the occlusion boundary tend to have abnormally smaller depth value. The larger the depth gap between background and foreground is, the larger the affected region. Based on this observation, we use morphology-based image processing to remove such outliers. To treat foreground and background differently, image segmentation is often used. However, accurate segmentation is an expensive process. For computational efficiency, we directly divide a depth image into multiple layers with thresholding. We found this simple approach works well.

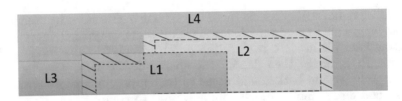

Fig. 3. Illustration of a sample depth image with 4 layers.

As shown in Fig. 3, each layer contains only pixels within a specific range. Each layer has thickness of $\lambda = d_{max}/l$, where d_{max} is the maximal working distance of the ToF camera and l is the number of layers. L_1 is the nearest layer and L_l is the farthest. Diagonally shaded regions represent the distortion region along depth edges. If the two sides of a depth edge are on consecutive layers, such as L_1 and L_2, the depth edge has less depth distortion and noisy region is small. If two sides are on non-consecutive layers, the depth distortion can be severe depending on the gap. As shown in Fig. 3, the distortion region between L_1 and L_4 is bigger than that between L_2 and L_4. When dividing the depth map into layers, if the number of pixels on one layer is smaller than a threshold t_{pixel}, this layer will ignored. Based on the gaps between different layers, morphological dilation is performed on the depth layers from far to near. The purpose of dilation is to propagate the depth values from far layer to the distortion region on the nearer layer which should belong to the far layer if not for the depth distortion problem. The detailed algorithm is shown as Algorithm 1. We assume that depth distortion between consecutive layers can be ignored (i.e., L_{i-1} will not be affected by L_i).

Algorithm 1: Multi-Layer Pre-Processing

Data: Depth image D is divided into l multiple layers $L_1, L_2...L_l$, and corresponding non-zero masks $M_1, M_2, ...M_l$.

1   $D_{out} \leftarrow L_l$, $i \leftarrow 3$;
2   **while** $i \leq l$ **do**
3     $j \leftarrow i - 2$, $L_{cur} = L_i$;
4   **while** $j \geq 1$ **do**
5   Dilation operation on L_{cur};
6   **if** L_j *exists* **then**
7         $L_{temp} \leftarrow L_{cur}$ masked by M_j;
8   **if** *number of non-zero pixel of* $L_{temp} > t_{pixel}$ **then**
9          $D_{out} \leftarrow D_{out} + L_{temp}^{nonzero}$, $j \leftarrow j - 1$;

10   $D_{out} \leftarrow D_{out} + L_{cur}^{nonzero}$, $i \leftarrow i + 1$

---

5   Depth Up-Sampling and Visual Occlusion

After outlier removal, depth maps need to be further processed for visual occlusion handling. Due to hardware limitation, ToF cameras typically have low spatial resolution. We need to register the depth samples to the frame of high-resolution RGB image then densify the sparse depth map. The depth edge between occluder and background needs to be temporally smooth while maintaining good discontinuity. Finally, we also need to complete the processing in real time on a smartphone with limited computing resources. To overcome these challenges, we propose a pipeline as shown in Fig. 4.

A. Depth Registration: Standard depth-RGB registration is performed using camera calibration data. We use OPPO R17 Pro smartphone since it has a back facing ToF camera. The ToF camera has a low resolution of 240×180. For AR application, we set RGB image at a higher resolution (1920×1280). In

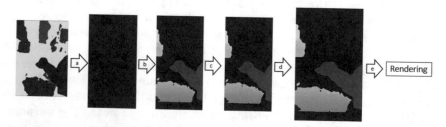

Fig. 4. The visual occlusion pipeline including 5 steps: a. registration, b. morphology-based depth densification, c. smooth filtering, d. up-sampling, e. alpha blending.

order to complete the entire pipeline in real time, We only register depth maps with a down-sampled RGB image at 480×320.

B. **Depth Densification:** We use a non-guided depth up-sampling method similar to [13], which is computationally fast. Three morphology operations are applied for depth densification. First, a dilation is performed with a diamond kernel to fill in most of the empty pixels. Then, a full kernel morphological close operation is applied to fill in the majority of holes. Finally, to fill in larger holes (usually very rare), a large full kernel dilation is performed. Note the kernel sizes need to be carefully tuned based on different ToF cameras.

C. **Filtering:** During densification, morphological operations might generate incorrect depth values. Therefore, smoothing is necessary to remove noises while keeping local edge information. We apply a median filter for this purpose. We then create a foreground mask for occluders using simple depth thresholding. Then Gaussian blur is applied to the mask to create an alpha map and also smooth the edges in depth image.

D. **Up-Sampling:** The filtered depth map (480×320) is up-sampled to full RGB resolution (1920×1080) to enable visual occlusion rendering. This is done in GPU with nearest interpolation. At the same time, the alpha map is also scaled to full resolution.

E. **Occlusion Rendering:** In the rendering step, with a full-resolution depth image and alpha map, alpha blending is utilized for compositing final image. Algorithm 2 shows per-pixel rendering algorithm implemented on GPU.

Algorithm 2: Per-Pixel Occlusion Rendering with Alpha Blending

---

Data: For pixel i: d_i - depth value from ToF; m_i - alpha map value; c_i - color from RGB camera; d_i^o: - depth of virtual object from depth buffer; c_i^o: - shaded color of virtual object.

Result: Final color of current pixel: c_i^r

1   **if** $d_i <= d_i^o$ **then**
2 | $\alpha = 1 - m_i/255$
3   **else**
4 | $\alpha = 1.0$
5   $c_i^r = (1 - \alpha)c_i + \alpha c_i^o$

---

6   Fast Voxelization and Collision Detection

There are a few representations for 3D data, such as point cloud, polygonal mesh, volumetric mesh, signed distance functions (SDF), etc. Truncated Signed Distance Function (TSDF) was first proposed by [20] and became popular in 3D tracking and mapping. Later spatial hashing is applied for scalability [28]. Our goal is to use the depth information captured by smartphone ToF camera for fast 3D representation, while the data structure shall support fast collision detection. Our method uses voxels to represent the coarse shape of the 3D scene. Compared with explicit mesh structures, our approach requires lower storage. Compared with implicit SDFs, our approach has faster construction speed and supports fast collision detection. Although our data structure lacks geometric details, in general detailed geometry is not necessary for collision detection unless accurate response is needed.

Cubes are used as unit voxels of the proposed data structure. The resolution of the data structure can be adjusted by changing the size of the unit voxel. A two-level voxel data structure is built as illustrated in Fig. 5 (left). First level of the structure stores large voxels which are indexed by a spatial hashing function, as defined in Eq. 1 [28].

$$H(x, y, z) = (x \cdot p_1 \oplus y \cdot p_2 \oplus z \cdot p_3) \bmod n \tag{1}$$

where $\oplus$ is XOR operation, p_1, p_2, p_3 are large prime numbers (e.g., $p_1 = 73856093$, $p_2 = 19349663$, $p_3 = 83492791$) and n is the hash table size. In the second level, each big voxel is subdivided into smaller voxels, with the resolution of $m * n * l$. Then each small voxel is also indexed by a regular hash function.

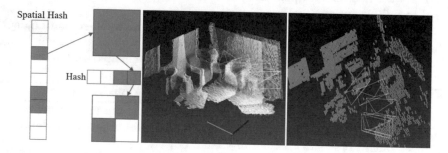

Fig. 5. (Left) 2D illustration of the two-level data structure; (Middle) Point cloud representation; (Right) Visualization of second level voxels.

When an AR session starts, a user scans the environment by moving the smartphone around. Once the SLAM module successfully initializes, 6DoF pose of the camera is continuously tracked. The proposed method performs 3D data structure reconstruction on each ToF frame at 30 fps. Using the camera pose, ToF depth frame is first transformed into a point cloud in the coordinate frame of the AR session. A plane detection step is simultaneously performed to detect the horizontal supporting plane using RANSAC-based plane detection algorithm. The supporting plane is where the 3D model will be placed on. The 3D point samples belonging to this plane are removed in this process. This speeds up the voxelization and reduces data storage. By using motion sensing hardware on the smartphone, we can obtain the direction of gravity. This enables us to find the horizontal plane efficiently.

For each remaining point, its coordinates (x, y, z) are then divided by the first-level grid cell size c, and rounded down to integer index (i, j, k). Then the integer index is hashed using Eq. 1 to check whether the first-level voxel exists. If not, a new voxel is created and hash map is updated. If a voxel exists, then (x, y, z) is transformed and rounded into integer index of the second level: (i', j', k'). This index will be hashed again to check whether the second level voxel exists. If not, a second-level voxel is created.

To improve robustness and temporal consistency, a queue with s-bit is stored in each second-level voxel. Each bit stores an binary value to represent whether this voxel is "seen" or not by the current ToF frame. When processing a ToF frame, the oldest bit is popped from the queue and a new bit is inserted. If the number of 1 bits is bigger than a threshold t_s, then this voxel will be used for collision detection for the current frame. Figure 5 visualizes the voxelization, where each depth frame is transformed into a point cloud (middle) and voxelization is generated (right).

Our two-level data structure can be used for fast collision detection, because each voxel is essentially an Axis-Aligned Bounding Box (AABB). In AR application, a virtual object can also be represented by an AABB. During collision detection, we first find all the first-level voxels that potentially intersect with the virtual object's AABB. Then we look for these voxels in the hash map using the spatial hashing function. Each lookup can be done in constant time. If one voxel exists in the map, second-level valid voxels are checked for collision detection. We iterate all the $m * n * l$ voxels and check whether such voxel exists in the map. If any voxel exists, intersection test is performed between the second-level voxel and the AABB of the virtual object. To improve robustness, a collision is detected only when the number of collided voxels is larger than a threshold t_c. Once the collision is detected between the static scene and the moving virtual object, the motion of the object will be stopped to simulate the visual effect of collision avoidance.

7 Results

To validate the proposed methods, we use an OPPO R17 Pro smartphone with a ToF camera. This smartphone uses SDM 710 processor, with an Adreno 616 GPU and 8 GB RAM. The operating system is Android 8.1. OPPO ARunit SDK, which is similar to ARcore and ARkit, is utilized for 6 DoF tracking. In this section, visual results are shown for visual occlusion and collision detection. More results can be found in the demo video: video link 1.

The ToF camera on OPPO R17 Pro has a resolution of 240×180, and the working range is 0.5 m to 3.5 m. The pre-processing step divides depth image into l layers. In our experiements, 5 layers produce good results for indoor scenes and for ToF camera with 3.5 m working range. For morphology operation, a cross kernel with kernel size 3×3 is applied. The pre-processing step aims to remove depth outliers. Figure 6 shows a result that compares the segmented foreground before and after depth pre-processing. As can be seen, before processing, the pixels that belong to the background object have abnormally small depth values. They are mitigated by the proposed method.

Fig. 6. Foreground layer using simple depth thresholding. (Left) without pre-processing. (Right) with proposed pre-processing.

Fig. 7. Screenshots of visual occlusion between a human hand and a 3D digital model.

The proposed up-sampling method registers and up-samples the depth image to the resolution of RGB image. In our experiment setting, depth image at 240 × 180 is first registered to RGB image at 480 × 320. Then this sparse depth map is densified and up-sampled to 1920 × 1080. A 3 × 3 diamond kernel is used for dilation operation. A 5 × 5 full kernel is used for morphological close operation. Finally, a large 21 × 21 full kernel dilation is performed to fill in large holes. In smoothing stage, 5 × 5 kernel is used for both the median filter and the Gaussian filter. These kernel sizes are carefully tuned specially for OPPO R17 Pro camera. Figure 7 shows visual results of occlusion handling. The average running time of occlusion thread is about **10 ms per frame**.

Figure 8 shows the visual result of voxelization of the scene. In this setting, the second-level voxel size is set to 1 cm. First level voxel contains 8 × 8 × 8 second-level voxels. The fast voxelization is performed for each original ToF frame at low resolution. Since hash map query time is constant, time complexity of voxelization depends on the resolution of the depth map. Threshold t_s is set to 30 to make sure the voxelization is focusing on the current view angle by only looking at past 30 frames. The running time is about **5 ms per frame** in our case. Overall, the running time of both occlusion and collision with separate threads is about **12 ms per frame**.

To validate collision detection and avoidance, a digital object is moved by hand on the supporting plane. The movement is stopped when there is collision detected. Note that if voxel size is large, the movement stops far from the actual object. There is a trade-off between the voxelization resolution (level of geometric details) and

Fig. 8. Screenshots of voxelization and collision detection. To better visualize voxels, a shrinked transparent 3D cube is rendered at the voxel center. RANSAC plane removal function is also disabled for visualization purpose. The rightmost image shows that the virtual 3D model intersects with some voxels, and its motion is stopped.

running time. As shown in Fig. 8, the digital object collides with the voxelized data structure and stops. The detection threshold t_c is set to be 10.

8 Conclusion and Future Work

In this work, we propose a pipeline for occlusion and collision aware AR applications. This pipeline is capable of handling occlusion and collision detection in real time using smartphone ToF camera. In this pipeline, a multi-layer preprocessing method is first performed to remove outliers of ToF image. Then, the processed ToF data is utilized in two streams simultaneously. On one hand, depth image is up-sampled, filtered and then utilized for AR visual occlusion rendering. On the other hand, ToF data is integrated into a voxelization data structure and used for fast and efficient collision detection.

With regard to limitations, in the proposed work, an image processing method is used to remove outliers in ToF data. However it cannot overcome all ToF systematic errors. The other limitation comes from the proposed data structure for scene reconstruction and collision detection. The lackness of geometric details prevents certain physics simulation that requires high-resolution geometry.

For future work, ToF outlier handling can be improved. For example, multipath error, IR saturation, and boundary ambiguity can be handled separately. In this work, the non-guided image processing is utilized to densify ToF depth map. To further improve performance, guided image filtering and instance segmentation can be integrated while meeting real-time requirements. Currently, our voxelization data structure is only applied for static scene. It can be further adapted for dynamic scenes.

References

1. Aliaga, D.G.: Virtual and real object collisions in a merged environment. In: Proceedings of Virtual Reality Software and Technology 1994, pp. 287–298 (1994)

2. Apple: ARKit3 (2019). https://developer.apple.com/augmented-reality/arkit/
3. Breen, D.E., Whitaker, R.T., Rose, E., Tuceryan, M.: Interactive occlusion and automatic object placement for augmented reality. Comput. Graph. Forum **15**(3), 11–22 (1996)
4. Bridson, R., Fedkiw, R., Anderson, J.: Robust treatment of collisions, contact and friction for cloth animation. ACM Trans. Graph. (ToG) **21**(3), 594–603 (2002)
5. Brochu, T., Edwards, E., Bridson, R.: Efficient geometrically exact continuous collision detection. ACM Trans. Graph. (ToG) **31**(4), 96 (2012)
6. Chen, L., Lin, H., Li, S.: Depth image enhancement for Kinect using region growing and bilateral filter. In: Proceedings of the 21st International Conference on Pattern Recognition, pp. 3070–3073 (Nov 2012)
7. Curless, B., Levoy, M.: A volumetric method for building complex models from range images. In: Proceedings of SIGGRAPH 1996, pp. 303–312 (1996)
8. Engel, J., Koltun, V., Cremers, D.: Direct sparse odometry. IEEE Trans. Pattern Anal. Mach. Intell. **40**(3), 611–625 (2018)
9. Holynski, A., Kopf, J.: Fast depth densification for occlusion-aware augmented reality. ACM Trans. Graph. **37**(6), 194 (2019)
10. Hornácek, M., Rhemann, C., Gelautz, M., Rother, C.: Depth super resolution by rigid body self-similarity in 3D. In: 2013 IEEE Conference on Computer Vision and Pattern Recognition, pp. 1123–1130, June 2013
11. Hui, T.-W., Loy, C.C., Tang, X.: Depth map super-resolution by deep multi-scale guidance. In: Leibe, B., Matas, J., Sebe, N., Welling, M. (eds.) ECCV 2016. LNCS, vol. 9907, pp. 353–369. Springer, Cham (2016). https://doi.org/10.1007/978-3-319-46487-9_22
12. Klingensmith, M., Dryanovski, I., Srinivasa, S., Xiao, J.: Chisel: Real time large scale 3D reconstruction onboard a mobile device using spatially hashed signed distance fields. In: Robotics: Science and Systems, vol. 4, p. 1 (2015)
13. Ku, J., Harakeh, A., Waslander, S.L.: In defense of classical image processing: fast depth completion on the CPU. In: 2018 15th Conference on Computer and Robot Vision (CRV), pp. 16–22, May 2018
14. Lee, D., Lee, S.G., Kim, W.M., Lee, Y.J.: Sphere-to-sphere collision estimation of virtual objects to arbitrarily-shaped real objects for augmented reality. Electron. Lett. **46**(13), 915–916 (2010)
15. Li, Y., Min, D., Do, M.N., Lu, J.: Fast guided global interpolation for depth and motion. ECCV **2016**, 717–733 (2016)
16. Luo, T., Liu, Z., Pan, Z., Zhang, M.: A virtual-real occlusion method based on GPU acceleration for MR. In: 2019 IEEE Conference on Virtual Reality and 3D User Interfaces (VR), pp. 1068–1069, March 2019
17. Matyunin, S., Vatolin, D., Berdnikov, Y., Smirnov, M.: Temporal filtering for depth maps generated by Kinect depth camera. In: 2011 3DTV Conference: The True Vision - Capture, Transmission and Display of 3D Video, pp. 1–4, May 2011
18. Miles, H., Seungkyu, L., Ouk, C., Radu, H.: Time-of-Flight Cameras: Principles, Methods and Applications. Springer, London (2012). https://doi.org/10.1007/978-1-4471-4658-2
19. Min, D., Choi, S., Lu, J., Ham, B., Sohn, K., Do, M.N.: Fast global image smoothing based on weighted least squares. IEEE Trans. Image Process. **23**(12), 5638–5653 (2014)
20. Newcombe, R.A., et al.: KinectFusion: real-time dense surface mapping and tracking. In: 2011 10th IEEE International Symposium on Mixed and Augmented Reality, pp. 127–136, October 2011

21. Nießner, M., Zollhöfer, M., Izadi, S., Stamminger, M.: Real-time 3D reconstruction at scale using voxel hashing. ACM Trans. Graph. (ToG) **32**(6), 169 (2013)
22. Park, J., Kim, H., Tai, Y.-W., Brown, M.S., Kweon, I.: High quality depth map upsampling for 3D-TOF cameras. In: 2011 International Conference on Computer Vision, pp. 1623–1630, November 2011
23. Qi, F., Han, J., Wang, P., Shi, G., Li, F.: Structure guided fusion for depth map inpainting. Pattern Recogn. Lett. **34**(1), 70–76 (2013)
24. Richardt, C., Stoll, C., Dodgson, N.A., Seidel, H., Theobalt, C.: Coherent spatiotemporal filtering, upsampling and rendering of RGBZ videos. Comput. Graph. Forum **31**(2), 247–256 (2012)
25. Roxas, M., Hori, T., Fukiage, T., Okamoto, Y., Oishi, T.: Occlusion handling using semantic segmentation and visibility-based rendering for mixed reality. In: Proceedings of the 24th ACM Symposium on Virtual Reality Software and Technology, VRST 2018, pp. 20:1–20:8. ACM, New York (2018)
26. Song, X., Dai, Y., Qin, X.: Deep depth super-resolution: learning depth super-resolution using deep convolutional neural network. In: Lai, S.-H., Lepetit, V., Nishino, K., Sato, Y. (eds.) ACCV 2016. LNCS, vol. 10114, pp. 360–376. Springer, Cham (2017). https://doi.org/10.1007/978-3-319-54190-7_22
27. Tang, M., Curtis, S., Yoon, S.E., Manocha, D.: ICCD: interactive continuous collision detection between deformable models using connectivity-based culling. IEEE Trans. Visual Comput. Graphics **15**(4), 544–557 (2009)
28. Teschner, M., Heidelberger, B., Mueller, M., Pomeranets, D., Gross, M.: Optimized spatial hashing for collision detection of deformable objects. In: Proceedings of the Vision, Modeling, Visualization (VMV), pp. 47–54 (2003)
29. Tian, Y., Li, C., Guo, X., Prabhakaran, B.: Real time stable haptic rendering of 3D deformable streaming surface. In: Proceedings of the 8th ACM on Multimedia Systems Conference, MMSys 2017, pp. 136–146. ACM, New York (2017)
30. Uhrig, J., Schneider, N., Schneider, L., Franke, U., Brox, T., Geiger, A.: Sparsity invariant CNNs. In: 2017 International Conference on 3D Vision (3DV), pp. 11–20, October 2017
31. Valentin, J.P.C., et al.: Depth from motion for smartphone AR. ACM Trans. Graph. **37**(6), 193 (2019)
32. Walton, D.R., Steed, A.: Accurate real-time occlusion for mixed reality. In: Proceedings of the 23rd ACM Symposium on Virtual Reality Software and Technology, VRST 2017, pp. 11:1–11:10. ACM, New York (2017)
33. Weerasekera, C.S., Dharmasiri, T., Garg, R., Drummond, T., Reid, I.D.: Just-in-time reconstruction: inpainting sparse maps using single view depth predictors as priors. In: International Conference on Robotics and Automation, pp. 1–9 (2018)
34. Xie, J., Feris, R., Sun, M.T.: Edge-guided single depth image super resolution. IEEE Trans. Image Process. **25**(1), 428–438 (2016)
35. Xie, J., Feris, R., Yu, S.S., Sun, M.T.: Joint super resolution and denoising from a single depth image. IEEE Trans. Multimedia **17**(9), 1525–1537 (2015)
36. Xu, Y., Wu, Y., Zhou, H.: Multi-scale voxel hashing and efficient 3D representation for mobile augmented reality. In: Proceedings of the IEEE Conference on Computer Vision and Pattern Recognition Workshops, pp. 1505–1512 (2018)
37. Zhang, Y., Funkhouser, T.: Deep depth completion of a single RGB-D image. In: 2018 IEEE/CVF Conference on Computer Vision and Pattern Recognition, pp. 175–185, June 2018

Augmenting Flight Imagery
from Aerial Refueling

James D. Anderson[1], Scott Nykl[2]([⊠]), and Thomas Wischgoll[1]

[1] Wright State University, Dayton, OH 45435, USA
{anderson.10,thomas.wischgoll}@wright.edu
[2] Air Force Institute of Technology, Dayton, OH 45435, USA
scott.nykl@afit.edu
http://www.avida.cs.wright.edu

Abstract. When collecting real-world imagery, objects in the scene may be occluded by other objects from the perspective of the camera. However, in some circumstances an occluding object is absent from the scene either for practical reasons or the situation renders it infeasible. Utilizing augmented reality techniques, those images can be altered to examine the affect of the object's occlusion. This project details a novel method for augmenting real images with virtual objects in a virtual environment. Specifically, images from automated aerial refueling (AAR) test flights are augmented with a virtual refueling boom arm, which occludes the receiving aircraft. The occlusion effects of the boom are quantified in order to determine which pixels are not viable for stereo image processing to reduce noise and increase efficiency of estimating aircraft pose from stereo images.

Keywords: Augmented reality · Virtual reality simulation · Vision occlusion

1 Introduction

Virtual 3D graphic environments offer the opportunity to simulate the real-world in a deterministic, controlled manner. These environments are also capable of playing back data collected from real-world experiments and introduce conditions and constraints not possible during data collection. For instance, images captured from real cameras can be augmented with virtual objects overlaid. This augmentation visualizes how the scene would appear had the virtual object been present during initial data collection. When analyzing the augmented images, the effects of the virtual object can be taken into account when comparing the augmented image to the original image.

Work on Automated Aerial Refueling (AAR) has focused on utilizing a stereo vision camera system to accurately inform the flight crew with relative position

Supported by Air Force Research Labs - Aerospace Systems (AFRL/RQ).

G. Bebis et al. (Eds.): ISVC 2019, LNCS 11845, pp. 154–165, 2019.
https://doi.org/10.1007/978-3-030-33723-0_13

data of the aircraft involved. The receiver is the airplane requesting fuel, and the tanker provides the fuel to the receiver via a boom arm. The tanker aircraft is equipped with such a boom and a stereo camera system located on the bottom of the fuselage, behind the boom and facing toward the rear and around 25° down from horizontal. Figure 1 depicts a virtual rendering of a refueling approach as well as the frusta of the stereo cameras.

Fig. 1. Virtual rendering of tanker based on a 767 airframe and a Beechcraft as receiver. The stereo camera frusta are visualized pointed toward the boom and receiver.

This paper details work on augmenting images taken from test flights of refueling approaches with a virtual rendering of the boom arm. During the test flights, two Beechcraft airplanes acted as both receiver and tanker. Since it is infeasible to attach a boom to a Beechcraft, the real world test flight images do not contain the boom. However, as depicted in Fig. 1, the boom arm occludes the receiver from the perspective of the cameras. This occlusion introduces difficulties when attempting to determine the position and orientation of the receiver relative to the tanker's stereo vision system. Augmenting the images with a virtual boom lets researchers deterministically test various occlusion solutions using real imagery.

When augmenting the images with a virtual boom, the number of pixels in the left and right stereo images which occlude the vision of the receiver can be quantified. Additionally, because of the nature of stereo vision, certain features visible by one camera are obscured in the other camera. These features are not viable for utilization with stereo vision but can be exploited by monocular vision. Rendering the virtual boom allows the capability to quantify not only pixels obscured in both cameras but also to measure the pixels seen in one camera but not the other.

The work presented in this paper makes the following contributions: (1) development of a real-time approach to augmenting real-world images with 3D virtual objects, (2) utilizing augmented images to test occlusion effects of objects not present in the original images, and (3) quantifying the intersection and disjunction of pixels being occluded with a stereo vision system.

2 Related Work

Typically, when discussed in augmented reality literature, occlusion refers to virtual objects occluding the user's vision of objects in the real world [12,20]. For example, a user may be wearing augmented reality glasses, and a virtual menu might appear, blocking the user's view of the real world located behind the menu. Work done in this field has focused on reducing the occlusion by either making the virtual objects transparent, or by utilizing smart computing methods to place the objects such that they do not occlude important features of the real world. Additionally, real objects may appear to occlude virtual objects, confusing the users' perception. In contrast, the approach toward occlusion with respect to AAR relates to a physical object blocking the view of the desired target object. Specifically, the tanker's boom arm occludes the cameras' view of the approaching receiver.

Virtual 3D environments are ubiquitous for simulating real-world scenarios. AAR is a natural candidate for such work as the flight approaches can be deterministically replicated. In the real world, deterministically repeating identical approaches is infeasible; furthermore, real test flights with two aircraft flying refueling approaches is prohibitively expensive. Simulation environments detailed in [3,6,19] for refueling unmanned aerial vehicles (UAV) provide the capability to generate virtual images that vision techniques can utilize.

With respect to utilizing computer vision algorithms to aid in AAR, [2] produces pose estimations from Gaussian least squares differential correlation (GLSDC) [11], while [10] utilizes an extended Kalman filter. Instead of using vision algorithms to determine the receiver pose with respect to the tanker, [13] compares the performance of point matching algorithms to determine the tanker's pose from the point of view of the receiver. In [7,8], virtual 3D environments simulate AAR with the capability of capturing virtual images via a Digital Frame Grabber which in turn are sent to various feature and pose estimation algorithms.

Previous approaches at the Air Force Institute of Technology (AFIT) have focused on utilizing computer vision techniques such as stereo block matching to generate disparity maps that produce a sensed point cloud [15,16]. A truth point cloud generated from the known geometry of the receiver (shown in Fig. 2) can then be registered with the sensed point cloud via iterative closest point (ICP). The six degrees of freedom (DoF) vector returned is the relative $x, y, z, roll, pitch, yaw$ between the tanker and receiver – this is the most important product from the vision system. Work has been done with electro-optical (EO) and infrared (IR) sensors [5]; however, this project focuses solely on augmenting the EO imagery.

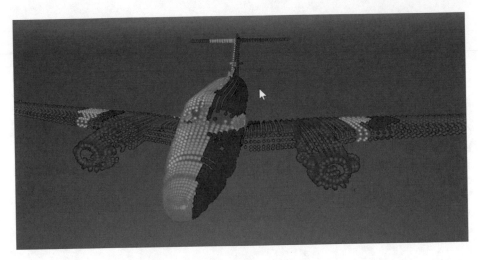

Fig. 2. Visualization of shadow volume method for determining occluded areas. (Color figure online)

Other work undertaken at AFIT, specifically in the AAR domain to reduce the boom's effect on stereo image processing, has involved calculating the volume of space occluded by the boom. In [18], shadow volumes were generated by casting rays from the point of view of the camera. Since these volumes represent the space occluded in either camera [4], any features detected within the volume can be discarded. An example of this technique is shown in Fig. 2 where red points can be seen by both cameras, green points by neither, and cyan and blue points can only be seen from one camera's point of view. In contrast to this method, augmenting the real images transforms a 3-dimensional problem into just 2-dimensions, whereas the shadow volume approach is done entirely in 3-dimensions. Additionally, the features detected within the shadow volume must go through stereo block matching first before they are discarded as viable points. With the augmented images, occluded pixels can be detected before the vision algorithm. Reducing the number of pixels input to the stereo vision algorithm decreases the computational time for stereo feature matching. Finally, pixels corresponding to the boom will not be matched to features on the plane since those pixels are not utilized in the image processing, increasing the accuracy of feature matching.

With respect to object occlusion, literature typically discusses methods to reconstruct the occluded object as seen in [9] where structure-from motion techniques are utilized for aiding robotic systems. This example demonstrates the capability to extend work done augmenting real imagery with virtual objects into other fields such as robotics. Another approach detailed in [21] utilizes single view approaches to generate 3D point clouds and model occlusion. A technique is presented in [1] to reduce the weight of occluded pixels during feature mapping with stereo matching. The work on augmented boom images can similarly improve matching algorithms by rejecting certain pixels that are known to be subject to occlusion.

3   Methodology

Previous work on AAR at AFIT has resulted in a simulation environment capable of playback of truth data collected from Global Positioning System (GPS) and inertial measurement unit (IMU) devices as well as visualization of point-clouds generated from stereo vision image processing. The application development has been realized with AfterBurner [14], a graphics engine built in C++ utilizing OpenGL for rendering. In addition, the stereo vision pipeline utilizes OpenCV. Figures 1, 2, 4 and 6 were generated with the AfterBurner engine.

Simulating the AAR approaches in the virtual world, the aircraft position and orientation can be replayed from data logs to accurately visualize the approach. Virtual cameras are placed on the refueling tanker, and with their orientation and view frusta conforming to their real-world counterparts, the images captured by these virtual cameras will be identical to the real images.

3.1   Test Flights

In March of 2019, researchers conducted aerial refueling test flights at Edwards Air Force Base. The aircraft involved in these flights were two Beechcraft, one as the receiver and one as the tanker with stereo EO and IR cameras attached. Figure 3 depicts the stereo camera setup for the test flights with the cameras mounted to the underbelly of the aircraft below the co-pilot's seat. Imagery was captured from these cameras and linked to truth data collected from GPS and IMU devices, resulting in accurate pose truth data for each aircraft.

Since a Beechcraft substituted an actual tanker in the test flights, it was impractical to attach a boom. Thus, the test images do not contain a boom occluding the receiver. In order to examine the effects of occlusion from the real test flights, an augmented reality solution detailed below was conceived with the goal of quantifying the occlusion of the receiver caused by the boom.

3.2   Virtual Cameras

In synthesizing real images with virtual objects, one objective is to render the virtual 3D models geometrically perspective-correct onto the real images. To achieve this result, a virtual construct is generated consisting of a quad or virtual "green screen" (see Fig. 4). The quad is simply a 2D textured planar rectangle serving as a surface to render the real images. This quad is placed near the far plane of a virtual frustum which shares the same aspect ratio and field of view as a virtual camera. The quad is oriented and locked with respect to the frustum such that it remains static when viewed from the frustum origin. The scene is then rendered with an OpenGL frame-buffer object (FBO) with the camera position and direction set to the frustum pose. Thus, as long as the field of view of the frustum is identical to the real world cameras capturing imagery, any virtual objects within the view frustum can be rendered perspective-correct into the real images. A summary of the image pipeline is shown in Fig. 5.

Fig. 3. Reference image of stereo EO and IR cameras mounted underneath the co-pilot.

Figures 4 and 6 depict the virtual camera arrangement for creating augmented images of aerial refueling test flight images. The images appearing in the upper corners are the raw image data captured during the test flight. Below the aircraft are visualizations of the stereo camera frusta, and positioned just in front of the far plane, quads utilize the raw stereo images as textures. The rationale for placing the quads just in front of the far plane (the distance from the frustum origin to the quad is 99% the distance to the far plane) is to minimize any errors caused by floating point precision loss which may cause the quad to not correctly render from the perspective of the virtual camera.

Near the bottom of Fig. 6 and appearing with black borders are the resulting render from the point of view of the virtual cameras located on the bottom of the plane. For this figure, the boom has been selectively rendered into the FBOs, whereas the Beechcraft model was excluded from the render. If the Beechcraft model were rendered, it would perfectly align with its real-world counterpart when visualized inside the augmented images. Note that since Fig. 6 is rendered with the world camera's pose different than the virtual cameras', the virtual Beechcraft is not aligned with the real aircraft. If the virtual model did not line up with the real aircraft image, it could be indicative of an error in the camera's parameters such as the position and rotation. Thus, the augmented image system also allows researchers to visually validate the correctness of the truth data collected during the test flights.

Some camera parameters were chosen based on the real camera measurements, while some were arbitrary. The near-plane for the virtual camera was set to 1 m as no objects, real nor virtual, came within 1 m of the camera. The far-plane distance and virtual quad position were set to 100 m from the camera.

Fig. 4. Depiction of virtual quad with real imagery rendered into it. The top two quads contain the raw image, and the quads behind the image use the raw image as their texture.

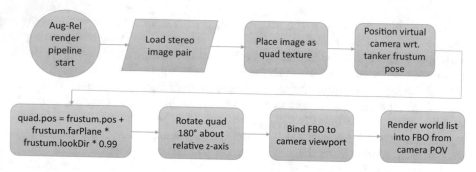

Fig. 5. Augmented reality render pipeline

This value was influenced by two factors. First and most importantly, the refueling envelope begins at 100 m from the tanker, thus the test flights focused on approaches with the receiver closer than 100 m. Second, a larger far-plane value would significantly increase the size of the quad and texture and likely decrease performance of the visualization. The horizontal field of view of the cameras utilized during the test flights was 56°. The aspect ratio of the real cameras was 4:3, and the resolution was 1280 by 960. The virtual camera was given this same aspect ratio, and the FBO texture the augmented images were rendered into were set to the same resolution.

Because the real image augmented with the virtual boom goes through the OpenGL rendering pipeline, the resulting composite image can go through multisample anti-aliasing (MSAA). As shown in [17], when stereo vision processes are

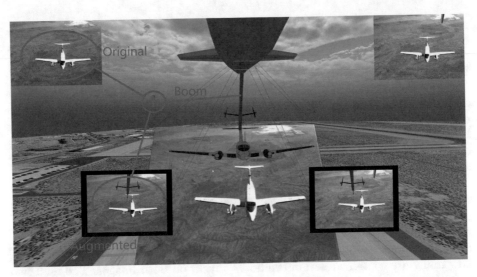

Fig. 6. A virtual model of a Beechcraft is placed in the truth location with respect to the tanker. Although this object falls within the frusta, it can be omitted from rendering into the augmented textures, which are rendered at the bottom with black borders.

performed on virtual objects, performing MSAA on the images before imparting them to the vision pipeline significantly reduces the error in the resulting point cloud.

4   Results

To evaluate the augmented images, simple image processing was performed to create masks for the boom and receiver. The boom mask was obtained by subtracting the original image from the augmented image. Since the pixels in the augmented image correspond to those in the original image that have the same value, they will become zero. Elsewhere, the pixels will likely be non-zero and thus can be utilized to create a mask. The original images were captured with a resolution of 1280 by 960, and Figs. 7a, b, c and 8a and b depict cropped segments of the original, so the resolutions will be less than 1280 by 960.

Figure 7a, b and c depict the masks created by subtracting the augmented images from the original images in RGB color-space. The figures have been cropped, focusing on the boom to enhance visibility. The left and right masks are colored cyan and blue, respectively, and when these two images are again subtracted, the overlapping areas appear green as shown in Fig. 7b. From this method, it is easy to visualize which pixels in each image are unavailable for stereo image processing. Black pixels are not occluded in either camera. Green pixels represent features occluded by the boom in both images, thus they are unsuitable for stereo image processing. Cyan and blue pixels correspond to features the boom occludes in either just the left or right image. These features are also unsuited for stereo processing since the boom blocks the feature in exactly one of the cameras; however, this feature could be utilized with monocular vision processing such as object or motion tracking if it were matched to the previous frame.

In addition to measuring the number of pixels occluded by the boom, the augmented imagery may be utilized to visualize and quantify areas of a specific object occluded by the boom. In Fig. 8a and b the masks from Fig. 7a and c have been added to the mask of the plane in RGB color-space. In Fig. 8a, the overlapping pixels of the plane and boom appear white, while in Fig. 8b, they appear magenta.

Table 1 presents data from one image pair regarding the number and percentage of pixels quantified by the masks. The first four entries show the number and percent of pixels which the plane and boom cover in the left and right images, respectively. The fifth entry shows the number of pixels overlapping from the left and right boom images. The percentage is how many pixels overlap compared to how many are contained within the boom masks on both images. The final two entries are how many pixels the boom occludes the plane in the left and right images, and the percentage shown is the percentage of how many pixels of the plane are occluded.

(a) Boom rendered cyan from POV of left camera.

(b) Combined render of boom from left and right cameras; green pixels are where boom overlaps in each camera.

(c) Boom rendered blue from POV of right camera.

Fig. 7. Masks generated of boom from POV of left and right cameras (Color figure online)

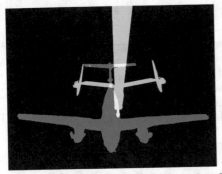

(a) From left camera POV, mask of boom (cyan) and plane (red), added creating overlapping pixels (white).

(b) From right camera POV, mask of boom (blue) and plane (red), added creating overlapping pixels (magenta).

Fig. 8. Visualization of pixels occluded in each camera frame (Color figure online)

Table 1. Pixel counts and percentages of image masks

Image	Pixels	Percent	Percent reference
Plane left (red pixels in Fig. 8a)	1164420	31.59%	Whole image
Plane right (red pixels in Fig. 8b)	1164983	31.60%	
Boom left (cyan pixels in Fig. 7a)	40970	1.11%	
Boom right (blue pixels in Fig. 7c)	42710	1.16%	
Boom overlap (green pixels in Fig. 7b)	5609	7.18%	Boom pixels
Boom occlusion left (white pixels in Fig. 8a)	2866	0.25%	Plane pixels
Boom occlusion right (magenta pixels in Fig. 8b)	3270	0.28%	

5   Conclusion

Combining real world imagery with virtual 3D models provides simulations with the capability to examine the obscuring effect caused by those objects if they had been present in the original scene. In order to accurately place the virtual objects into the real scene, the models must be rendered perspective-correct with respect to how the original images were captured. By placing the real imagery as a texture behind the virtual objects and locking the texture with respect to the camera's view point, the scene can be rendered with the blend of real and virtual objects. In the case of AAR, images captured from actual test flights can be enhanced to visualize and test the effect a boom arm occludes. This process can also be utilized to mitigate the effect the boom has on stereo vision processing by eliminating specific pixels from further feature matching, since it is known those pixels are being occluded by the boom. While this process was developed specifically for augmenting refueling images, it could be extended to other topics such as robotics and augmented reality.

References

1. Bobick, A.F., Intille, S.S.: Large occlusion stereo. Int. J. Comput. Vision **33**, 181–200 (1999). https://doi.org/10.1023/A:1008150329890
2. Campa, G., Mammarella, M., Napolitano, M.R., Fravolini, M.L., Pollini, L., Stolarik, B.: A comparison of pose estimation algorithms for machine vision based aerial refueling for UAVs. In: 14th Mediterranean Conference on Control and Automation, MED 2006 (2006). https://doi.org/10.1109/MED.2006.328769
3. Campa, G., Napolitano, M.R., Fravolini, M.L.: Simulation environment for machine vision based aerial refueling for UAVs. IEEE Trans. Aerosp. Electron. Syst. **45**, 138–151 (2009). https://doi.org/10.1109/TAES.2009.4805269
4. Crow, F.C.: Shadow algorithms for computer graphics. ACM SIGGRAPH Comput. Graphics **11**, 242–248 (2005). https://doi.org/10.1145/965141.563901
5. Dallmann, W.E.: Infrared and electro-optical stereo vision for automated aerial refueling. Master's thesis, Air Force Institute of Technology (2019)
6. Duan, H., Zhang, Q.: Visual measurement in simulation environment for vision-based UAV autonomous aerial refueling. IEEE Trans. Instrum. Meas. **64**, 2468–2480 (2015). https://doi.org/10.1109/TIM.2014.2343392
7. Fravolini, M.L., Brunori, V., Ficola, A., La Cava, M., Campa, G.: Feature matching algorithms for machine vision based autonomous aerial refueling. In: 14th Mediterranean Conference on Control and Automation, MED 2006 (2006). https://doi.org/10.1109/MED.2006.328792
8. Fravolini, M.L., Campa, G., Napolitano, M.R.: Evaluation of machine vision algorithms for autonomous aerial refueling for unmanned aerial vehicles. J. Aerosp. Comput. Inf. Commun. **4**, 968–985 (2008). https://doi.org/10.2514/1.17269
9. Huang, X., Walker, I., Birchfield, S.: Occlusion-aware reconstruction and manipulation of 3D articulated objects. In: Proceedings - IEEE International Conference on Robotics and Automation (2012). https://doi.org/10.1109/ICRA.2012.6224911
10. Johnson, D.T., Nykl, S.L., Raquet, J.F.: Combining stereo vision and inertial navigation for automated aerial refueling. J. Guidance Control Dyn. **40**, 2250–2259 (2017). https://doi.org/10.2514/1.g002648
11. Kimmett, J., Valasek, J., Junkins, J.: Autonomous aerial refueling utilizing a vision based navigation system. In: AIAA Guidance, Navigation, and Control Conference and Exhibit. American Institute of Aeronautics and Astronautics (2002). https://doi.org/10.2514/6.2002-4469
12. Lepetit, V.: On computer vision for augmented reality. In: Proceedings - International Symposium on Ubiquitous Virtual Reality, ISUVR 2008 (2008). https://doi.org/10.1109/ISUVR.2008.10
13. Mammarella, M., Campa, G., Napolitano, M.R., Fravolini, M.L.: Comparison of point matching algorithms for the UAV aerial refueling problem. Mach. Vis. Appl. **21**, 241–251 (2010). https://doi.org/10.1007/s00138-008-0149-8
14. Nykl, S., Mourning, C., Leitch, M., Chelberg, D., Franklin, T., Liu, C.: An overview of the STEAMiE educational game engine. In: Proceedings - Frontiers in Education Conference, FIE (2008). https://doi.org/10.1109/FIE.2008.4720454
15. Parsons, C.A.: Improving automated aerial refueling stereo vision pose estimation using a shelled reference model. Master's thesis, Air Force Institute of Technology (2017)
16. Parsons, C., Nykl, S.: Real-time automated aerial refueling using stereo vision. In: Bebis, G., et al. (eds.) ISVC 2016. LNCS, vol. 10073, pp. 605–615. Springer, Cham (2016). https://doi.org/10.1007/978-3-319-50832-0_59

17. Parsons, C., Paulson, Z., Nykl, S., Dallman, W., Woolley, B.G., Pecarina, J.: Analysis of simulated imagery for real-time vision-based automated aerial refueling. J. Aerosp. Inf. Syst. **16**(3), 77–93 (2019). https://doi.org/10.2514/1.I010658
18. Paulson, Z., Nykl, S., Pecarina, J., Woolley, B.: Mitigating the effects of boom occlusion on automated aerial refueling through shadow volumes. J. Defense Model. Simul. **16**, 175–189 (2019). https://doi.org/10.1177/1548512918808408
19. Pollini, L., Campa, G., Giulietti, F., Innocenti, M.: Virtual simulation set-up for UAVs aerial refuelling. In: AIAA Modeling and Simulation Technologies Conference and Exhibit. American Institute of Aeronautics and Astronautics (2012). https://doi.org/10.2514/6.2003-5682
20. Shah, M.M., Arshad, H., Sulaiman, R.: Occlusion in augmented reality. In: 8th International Conference on Information Science and Digital Content Technology (ICIDT 2012) (2012)
21. Zanfir, A., Sminchisescu, C.: Large displacement 3D scene flow with occlusion reasoning. In: Proceedings of the IEEE International Conference on Computer Vision (2015). https://doi.org/10.1109/ICCV.2015.502

Object
Recognition/Detection/Categorization

Hierarchical Semantic Labeling with Adaptive Confidence

Jim Davis[1]([⊠]), Tong Liang[1], James Enouen[1], and Roman Ilin[2]

[1] Ohio State University, Columbus, OH 43210, USA
{davis.1719,liang.693,enouen.8}@osu.edu
[2] AFRL/RYAP, Wright-Patterson AFB, Dayton, OH 45433, USA
rilin325@gmail.com

Abstract. In real-world applications with semantic classification labels ('dog', 'car', 'chair', etc.), it would be advantageous to identify any unconfident classification and then determine if a less specific label could instead be reliably established. In this work, we present a hierarchical estimation and inference approach using a semantic concept tree to provide an appropriate generalized label when needed. The proposed method has several advantages, including the ability to work with any logit/softmax-based semantic label classifier, the ability to correct many misclassified labels while not introducing any new errors, and a statistical guarantee of confidence for the final labels. We additionally provide a new set of hierarchical metrics to properly evaluate the approach. Multiple synthetic and real datasets are examined to demonstrate how the framework can quickly and efficiently resolve unconfident predictions.

Keywords: Semantic Concept Tree · Classification confidence

1 Introduction

Current deep learning approaches to semantic segmentation and image classification show compelling results across multiple challenging datasets (e.g., [2,5,11,14]). However, standard comparative performance metrics (accuracy, intersection-over-union, etc.) typically restrict the task and comparison to a "best-guess" for each pixel/image, though the predicted label may not be uniquely plausible. This forced-choice classification approach is obviously useful for current benchmarking purposes, but as no classifier is perfect (or ever will be) this approach can be problematic in real deployment scenarios. We believe it is important to identify an unreliable prediction and seek to find a reliable label from a set of more general options. Employing instead a top-N criteria, where credit is given if the correct answer is within the classifier's N best guesses, is still problematic as the label to choose and act upon is still unknown.

This work was supported by the U.S. Air Force Research Laboratory contract #GRT00044839/60056946. We acknowledge Sam Lerner for development insights.

G. Bebis et al. (Eds.): ISVC 2019, LNCS 11845, pp. 169–183, 2019.
https://doi.org/10.1007/978-3-030-33723-0_14

We base our approach on the natural categorical relationships of semantic labels and employ a concept tree representation that hierarchically organizes labels using IS-A relationships. For example, the initial terminal-level label 'chair' may be deemed unconfident due to a confusion with another label ('sofa'), occlusion, poor view-angle, etc. In this case, the parent concept 'Seat' would next be considered (which is composed of the related terminal descendants 'chair' and 'sofa'). If 'Seat' is also unconfident, the tree will be traversed upward through increasingly generalized labels, such as 'Furniture' and 'Object', until a confident assessment can be found. Reaching the root node ('Unknown') represents a withdrawn classification, which still has practical importance since it allows one to not act on any likely false label. This approach is based on underlying label confusions, but can still address misclassifications related to occlusion, view, etc.

Consider the task of image indexing, which searches for similar images using either concept-based methods based on textual descriptions (e.g., keywords, captions, etc.) or content-based approaches using image features. One can bridge these two approaches by employing semantic segmentation to automatically derive a list of objects present in the image to use for indexing. If the forced best-guess results are used, the list of uniquely predicted labels may be corrupt due to classification errors. Hence, the image retrieval process will be sub-optimal. Alternatively, one could use a score on each pixel classification and simply discard any predictions with a low score. However, with the removal of unconfident predictions, important object labels may be missed. Instead, a method that can produce a fuller list of highly-confident, specific and generalized labels will be more descriptive and powerful.

We present a principled approach to construct a concept tree for a set of semantic labels using the natural relationships provided in a lexical database. We also provide a Bayesian method to estimate confidence throughout the concept tree using the learned posterior probability of labels given softmax values provided by a base classifier. The posterior for a given label is compared to a specified confidence threshold to determine if the label should be generalized or not. The proposed framework has multiple contributions and advantages:

- Applicable to any base classifier that outputs semantic labels and corresponding logit/softmax scores.
- Provides a statistical guarantee to meet a given level of confidence.
- Withdraws from any forced classification if a sufficiently confident label cannot be found.
- Does not produce additional incorrect classifications, and has potential to correct errors made by the base classifier.
- Enables fast and efficient label inference.
- Presents new hierarchical metrics for evaluation.

We will outline the framework and computational efficiencies, and demonstrate the effectiveness of the approach with multiple classification tasks, models, and datasets.

2   Related Work

The foundation of our work is based on a hierarchical organization of semantic labels, which we refer to as a concept tree. Other related work with such label hierarchies have been proposed. In [12], the hierarchy is used to encode prior knowledge about class similarities for knowledge transfer during training, especially for classes that have insufficient training examples. However, only terminal labels are produced in the final classification, unlike our approach which provides both terminal and non-terminal labels when needed. The top-down strategy in [8] progresses through multiple classifications (from general to specific) to reach a final terminal label. Similarly, [10] uses a tree of labels for classification by multiplying conditional probabilities along the path from the root to a particular label. For detection within a selected bounding box, the tree is traversed downward, taking the highest confidence path at every split until a threshold is reached. In these approaches, any classification error or poorly modeled conditional probability occurring early (high) in the tree will drive the decision process down a wrong branch. Our approach instead begins with the original terminal classification and softens upward through the tree only as needed until a confident label is found. In [15], pixel features are mapped to a word embedding space for label retrieval within a concept hierarchy. When used to predict terminal-only labels, the performance was lower than state-of-the-art. Their main advantage was demonstrated in zero-shot learning (not addressed in this work), where novel objects were able to be labeled to generalized concepts when their features shared enough similarity to known objects at higher levels.

Another important aspect of this work is the use of a confidence measure on classification. The softmax value associated with the best classification label is often taken as a measure of confidence. But as presented in [4], modern deep neural networks are not well calibrated, i.e., $P(l|s) \neq s$ for the softmax value s of the argmax-selected label l. Several approaches to calibrate softmax values into true probabilities have been proposed (see overview in [4]), which include histogram-based precision methods and temperature scaling of the logits (before the softmax operation). However, issues can arise in the histogram approaches when very few true and false positive predictions are available in a particular softmax bin for a class (their ratio is unstable). Also, temperature scaling is designed to calibrate either over-confident or under-confident classifications, but a class may actually be both (at different softmax ranges). Rather than attempting to calibrate with these issues, we instead take a direct Bayesian approach to measure the posterior probability of a class label given the softmax value.

3   Framework

Our proposed approach employs a semantic concept tree, which defines the hierarchical relationship between the terminal labels for a given dataset and higher, more generalized, label concepts. A measure of confidence is used to evaluate an initial label hypothesis and guide generalization upward through the tree until a sufficiently confident concept is found. The overall framework is composed of a separate estimation and inference procedure.

3.1 Concept Tree Generation

Any semantic concept tree can be employed, with more levels offering a larger range of label generalization possibilities, and the tree will necessarily be dictated by the particular application at hand. Rather than manually creating a list of ad hoc concepts and tree, we employed a non-biased, repeatable technique on each examined dataset. Our approach is based on WordNet [9], which has an internal hierarchical structure of words based on grammar usage. Other lexical relational databases or other techniques could also be used, but we chose WordNet as it is a well-established resource with existing connections to datasets and has an available Python binding (nltk).

To begin, one must select a particular WordNet definition for each terminal label, referred to as a *synset*, as certain labels are semantically ambiguous. For example, the noun 'mouse' in a dataset could refer to a rodent (n.01) or perhaps a hand-operated electronic device (n.04). Once the appropriate synset definition (n.xx) is assigned to each label, the bottom-up tree building process begins.

For each possible pairing of labels, we find their Lowest Common Subsumer (LCS), which is the deepest generalized label in WordNet where the two labels merge. For example, LCS('chair', 'sofa') = 'Seat'. We then select the label pair (l_i, l_j) having the deepest LCS in the WordNet hierarchy. For that label pair, we assign their LCS as their direct parent in the concept tree. The label pair is then removed from the list of labels to examine and their LCS is added to the list (if not already present). We again generate the LCS for all pairs in the new label list, and the deepest LCS is to added to the concept tree. Note that if one terminal label is a parent of another terminal label in WordNet, then we retain a separate terminal and non-terminal version of that parent label in the hierarchy. This process is repeated until only one label remains (root node), which we assign to 'Unknown'. This automatic approach is particularly advantageous for constructing a meaningful tree with a large label set that would otherwise be manually prohibitive.

3.2 Label Confidence

A classification confidence is required at each label/node in the concept tree. As previously mentioned, modern deep learning classifiers produce softmax values s (for the argmax selected labels l) that are uncalibrated, hence $P(l|s) \neq s$. A calibration transform can be attempted with the hope of attaining $P(l|\text{Calib}(s)) = \text{Calib}(s)$, but as previously described, issues related to sample sizes and both over- and under-confidence within a class can produce undesirable results.

Instead we directly compute and evaluate $P(l|s)$, the posterior probability of a class label l given the example's softmax value s associated with that class (initially selected via argmax of the softmax vector). Using Bayes' Rule on the posterior with a two-class $\{l, \neg l\}$ context, we have

$$P(l|s) = \frac{P(s|l)P(l)}{P(s)} = \frac{P(s|l)P(l)}{P(s|l)P(l) + P(s|\neg l)P(\neg l)} \tag{1}$$

To compute the posterior distribution for a terminal node in the concept tree, we need to estimate its associated positive and negative class likelihoods and priors (to be described in the next section). With the posteriors being computed from known ground-truth class data, we do not have the previously mentioned under-sampling issue that can be present in histogram-based calibration.

3.3 Estimation Procedure

To compute the priors $P(l)$ and $P(\neg l)$ for each label l in the concept tree, class proportions found in the training set or uniform (non-informative) priors could be used. To estimate the posterior distribution, we additionally need to compute its associated positive and negative likelihood distributions. We employ a histogram-based approach, but other kernel density estimation methods could be used. For this task it is import to use validation data, which was not used to train the base classifier, as to reduce any overfitting.

For validation example x with ground-truth label l, we extract its corresponding classifier softmax value s for class l. The value of s is quantized to index into a histogram bin for this label and softmax value. As the range of softmax values is $0 \leq s \leq 1$, we can quantize s into n_b bins using $s_q = \min(\text{FLOOR}(s \cdot n_b), n_b - 1)$. With this index, the *positive* histogram bin $H_l^+[s_q]$ is incremented.

Next, we need to increment the *positive* histograms for all label ancestors of l in the concept tree. Each ancestor label a will be a generalization of l and also of certain other terminal labels. For example x, we create a's softmax value using the sum of all the classifier softmax values in x for the terminal label descendants of a. This aggregated softmax value is quantized to s_q and used to increment the positive histogram bin $H_a^+[s_q]$. This process is repeated for each ancestor of l in the concept tree.

We must also increment the *negative* histograms for each label d in the set corresponding to the other terminals and non-ancestor labels/nodes of l. The associated terminals for d are identified and their corresponding classifier softmax values in x are summed, quantized, and used to index and increment the negative histogram bin $H_d^-[s_q]$.

After all validation examples have been processed, the likelihood distributions are formed by L1-normalizing the respective histograms ($P(s_q|l) = H_l^+ / |H_l^+|_1$, $P(s|\neg l) = H_l^- / |H_l^-|_1$). Finally, to compute the posterior for label l, Eq. 1 is used with $P(l|s_q) = P(s_q|l)P(l)/(P(s_q|l)P(l) + P(s_q|\neg l)P(\neg l))$. The overall estimation algorithm is shown in Algorithm 1.

3.4 Inference Procedure

To make the final (confident) prediction, the inference algorithm starts with estimating the posterior probability of the base classifier's initial argmax-selected

---

Algorithm 1: Estimation

```
 1  Organize concept tree for label set 𝓛
 2  Compute label priors from training data (or set equal)
 3  foreach validation example x do
 4  │   l = ground-truth(x)                                    // ground-truth label of x
 5  │   sm = classifier_softmax(x)                             // classifier softmax vector of x
 6  │   s = sm[l]                                              // corresponding softmax value
 7  │   s_q = quantize(s, n_b)                                 // quantize into set of n_b bins
 8  │   H_l^+[s_q]++                                           // increment positive histogram for l
 9  │   foreach label a in ancestors(l) do
10  │   │   𝒥 = get_terminals(a)                              // get set of all terminals of a
11  │   │   s = Σ_{j∈𝒥} sm[j]                                 // sum their softmax values
12  │   │   s_q = quantize(s, n_b)                             // quantize into set of n_b bins
13  │   │   H_a^+[s_q]++                                       // increment positive histogram for a
14  │   end
15  │   foreach label d in 𝓛 \ ({l} ∪ ancestors(l)) do
16  │   │   𝒥 = get_terminals(d)                              // get set of all terminals of d
17  │   │   s = Σ_{j∈𝒥} sm[j]                                 // sum their softmax values
18  │   │   s_q = quantize(s, n_b)                             // quantize into set of n_b bins
19  │   │   H_d^-[s_q]++                                       // increment negative histogram for d
20  │   end
21  end
22  foreach label l in 𝓛 do
23  │   L1-Normalize H_l^+ and H_l^- into likelihoods
24  │   Compute posterior P(l|s_q), ∀q using Bayes with likelihoods and priors
25  end
```

---

label l (at a terminal node in the concept tree) using its corresponding softmax value s. Since modern deep learning classifiers typically perform well (more often correct than incorrect), we expect the label selected via argmax to be a reasonable initial label hypothesis, to be generalized as needed. Even if the initial hypothesis is incorrect, the approach may still have an opportunity to generalize to a correct label.

The softmax value s for the initial label l is quantized to s_q and used to index into the posterior $P(l|s_q)$. If the posterior is deemed unreliable (below the given confidence threshold T), there must exist other competing terminal label proposals. Therefore, we next examine the immediate parent of l with the hope of merging those competing terminal proposals. As this parent label is a generalization of the initial label and other related terminal labels, we sum all of the classifier softmax values associated with this parent. This new softmax sum is quantized and indexed into the parent label's posterior distribution. If the parent label posterior is also unconfident, we continue the process upward until a sufficiently confident label is found or the root node is reached, which by default has the label 'Unknown' with 100% confidence.

Importantly, with this method any originally *incorrect* prediction from the base classifier may be re-assigned to a valid (non-root) label that is actually an ancestor to the ground-truth label, thus *correcting* the initial error. Also, no originally *correct* prediction can be corrupted to an incorrect label as it cannot move off the upward path of the ground truth. Any initial label (either correct or incorrect) can however be removed/discarded from classification and set to

'Unknown' if no reliable label can be found. The overall inference approach is provided in Algorithm 2 and is quite efficient and fast.

Algorithm 2: Inference

Input : Test example x, confidence threshold T
Output: Confident label l for x

1	$sm = $ classifier_softmax(x)	// classifier softmax vector of x
2	$l = $ argmax sm	// choose best class
3	$s = sm[l]$	// corresponding softmax value
4	$s_q = $ quantize(s, n_b)	// quantize into set of n_b bins
5	Conf $= P(l\|s_q)$	// compute posterior confidence
6	**while** Conf $<$ T **do**	// not sufficiently confident
7	$\quad l = $ get_parent(l)	// use parent label
8	$\quad \mathcal{J} = $ get_terminals(l)	// get set of all terminals of parent
9	$\quad s = \sum_{j \in \mathcal{J}} sm[j]$	// sum their softmax values
10	$\quad s_q = $ quantize(s, n_b)	// quantize into set of n_b bins
11	$\quad Conf = P(l\|s_q)$	// compute posterior confidence
12	**end**	
13	Assign $x \to l$	// final classification

3.5   Hierarchical Metrics

An appropriate means is needed to evaluate the method's ability to hierarchically soften/generalize, correct, and withdraw labels. There exist related metrics such as hierarchical Precision, Recall, and F-score [15]. Also, the ImageNet ILSVRC2010 competition [6,11] used the depth of WordNet's LCS between the predicted and ground-truth label. However, these metrics give partial credit for predictions that are not on the correct IS-A ancestral path of the ground truth. We instead propose a new collection of hierarchical metrics to more precisely and strictly measure various important aspects of the tree-based labeling process. In all cases, we assign no credit for a prediction off the tree path of the ground-truth. The metrics are divided into two categories related to the change in originally correct (C) and originally incorrect (IC) base predictions:

- **C-Persist** is the fraction of predictions in the set S_c (initially *correct* predictions of the base classifier) that do not change: C-PERSIST $= \frac{1}{|S_c|} \sum_{i \in S_c}$ IS-TERMINAL(l_i), where the logical IS-TERMINAL(l_i) is 1 (TRUE) if l_i is a member of the original terminal label set, else it is 0 (FALSE). Higher proportions are desired.
- **C-Withdrawn** is the fraction of initially *correct* predictions assigned to the root 'Unknown': C-WITHDRAWN $= \frac{1}{|S_c|} \sum_{i \in S_c}$ IS-ROOT(l_i), where IS-ROOT(l_i) is 1 (TRUE) if the label is assigned to the root 'Unknown' node. Lower proportions are desired.
- **C-Soften** is the fraction of originally *correct* terminal predictions that were generalized to a valid (non-root) non-terminal label: C-SOFTEN $= 1 - ($C-PERSIST $+$ C-WITHDRAWN$)$. More softened than withdrawn predictions is desired.

- **C-SoftDepth** (of C-SOFTEN) is the ratio of the tree depth between a softened label and its ground-truth, averaged over all softened labels. Larger proportions close to 1 are desired (closer to the terminal) and smaller values signify more generalization toward the root.
- **IC-Remain** is the fraction of set S_{ic} (initially *incorrect* predictions) that remain at an incorrect, non-root label: IC-REMAIN = $\frac{1}{|S_{ic}|}\sum_{i \in S_{ic}}$ ¬IS-SUBSUMER$(l_i, gt_i) \wedge$¬IS-ROOT(l_i), where IS-SUBSUMER(l_i, gt_i) is 1 (TRUE) if label l_i is an ancestor of its ground-truth label gt_i. Lower proportions are desired.
- **IC-Withdrawn** is the fraction of initially *incorrect* predictions assigned to the root 'Unknown': IC-**withdrawn** = $\frac{1}{|S_{ic}|}\sum_{i \in S_{ic}}$ IS-**root**(l_i). Lower proportions are desired, but as these predictions were originally incorrect, a large withdrawal is possible.
- **IC-Reform** is the fraction of initially *incorrect* predictions that are generalized to a correct, non-root label: IC-REFORM = $1 - ($IC-REMAIN + IC-WITHDRAWN$)$. Larger proportions are desired.
- **IC-RefDepth** (of IC-REFORM) is the ratio of the tree depth between a reformed label and its deepest possible corrected label, averaged over the set of all reformed labels $S_{ic \to c}$: IC-REFORMDEPTH = $\frac{1}{|S_{ic \to c}|}\sum_{i \in S_{ic \to c}}$ DEPTH$(l_i)/$DEPTH(l_i^*), where l_i^* is the LCS of the original prediction and its ground-truth. Larger proportions close to 1 are desired.

4   Experiments

To evaluate the framework, we employed a synthetic classification dataset and multiple standard datasets with existing prediction models for semantic segmentation and image classification. For semantic segmentation, we examined the PASCAL VOC 2012 dataset [3] with DeepLabv3+ [2] and the ADE20K Scene Parsing dataset [1,16] with UperNet-101 [14]. The ImageNet ILSVRC 2012 dataset [7,11] with ResNet-152 [5] was used for image classification. All pre-trained prediction models are publicly available. In all experiments, we pass a single image through the model (with no additional scales or crops) to produce the base classification.

Many existing pre-trained models have been constructed using the *entire* training set, without properly using (or reporting) a validation hold-out set during the training procedure. The official validation set is commonly treated as a test set, due to unavailability of ground-truth for the actual test set. As our approach is based on the use of a validation set to properly estimate the concept tree posteriors, we therefore need to separate out a pseudo-validation and psuedo-test set from the official validation set. Rather than using a single random split, we instead employed a standard N-fold cross-validation approach. In all experiments with the real datasets, we randomly divide the validation set into N = 3 partitions, then repeatedly model the posteriors on 2 partitions and test on the remaining partition. Hence, it is not straightforward to compare with other reported results (other than results of the base classifiers employed), and we therefore present average scores for the newly defined metrics.

4.1 Synthetic Experiment

We created a simple synthetic dataset to illustrate the basics of the approach. Three terminal classes (A, B, C) were each assigned 100 examples (equal priors). A tree was defined by merging terminals B and C into non-terminal D, and merging A and D into the root ('Unknown'). We set the softmax vectors for the ground-truth examples for class A all to $[.8, .1, .1]$, for class B evenly split to $\{[.1, .5, .4], [.1, .4, .5]\}$, and for class C evenly split to $\{[.1, .4, .5], [.1, .5, .4]\}$. With the argmax as the base classification, the accuracies of A, B, and C are 100%, 50%, and 50%, respectively, simulating a strong confusion between B and C.

Initially, the data are used to estimate the posterior distribution for each node (A, B, C, D), as outlined in Sect. 3.3. For class A, this results in a simple posterior with $P(A|s_A = .8) = 1$ and $P(A|s_A \neq .8) = 0$. For class B, we have $P(B|s_B = \{.4, .5\}) = .5$ and $P(B|s_B \neq \{.4, .5\}) = 0$. Similarly, for class C, $P(C|s_C = \{.4, .5\}) = .5$ and $P(C|s_C \neq \{.4, .5\}) = 0$. For non-terminal D, $P(D|s_D = .4 + .5 = .9) = 1$ and $P(D|s_D \neq .9) = 0$. The inference stage begins with the argmax classification results (no cross-validation is used in this experiment) which are then generalized as needed given a confidence threshold. For this example, we employed the same synthetic data for testing as to confirm the expected behavior. We report the results in Table 1.

Table 1. Hierarchical metric scores for synthetic data within two confidence ranges.

	Confidence	
	≤50%	>50%
C-Persist	1	.5
C-Withdrawn	0	0
C-Soften	0	.5
C-SoftDepth	–	.5
IC-Remain	1	0
IC-Withdrawn	0	0
IC-Reform	0	1
IC-RefDepth	–	1
% Valid (¬root)	100	100
% Correct	66.7	100

With any confidence threshold ≤50%, the approach is equivalent to the base classification result (i.e., no classifications change). As given in the left confidence column (≤50%) in Table 1, C-Persist = 1 shows all correct argmax predictions remained at their respective terminal nodes (thus C-Soften = C-Withdrawn = 0) and IC-Remain = 1 denotes all incorrect predictions remained unchanged (thus IC-Reform = IC-Withdrawn = 0). Overall, every classification is a valid (non-root) label and two-thirds of them (66.7%) are correct.

With any confidence threshold >50% (right column of Table 1), *all* correct/incorrect classifications of B and C are generalized to D, while all of A remain at the correct terminal node. Hence, C-PERSIST $= .5$ (i.e., $100/(100+50+50)$). Since half of B and C were originally correctly classified, but generalized to D, the value of C-SOFTEN $= .5$ (i.e., $(50+50)/(100+50+50)$). The average softening depth C-SOFTDEPTH $= .5$ reflects that those softened are halfway down the tree branch to the correct terminal. In this threshold range, all originally incorrect predictions for B and C are now at D (a correct label), hence IC-REFORM $= 1$ (i.e., $(50+50)/(50+50)$). As all reformed labels are at their deepest correct label possible, IC-REFDEPTH $= 1$. There are no remaining incorrect predictions (IC-REMAIN $= 0$). No labels were withdrawn to the root. In this example, the original accuracy of 66.7% (from the base classifier) was increased to 100% when the confidence is selected to be >50%.

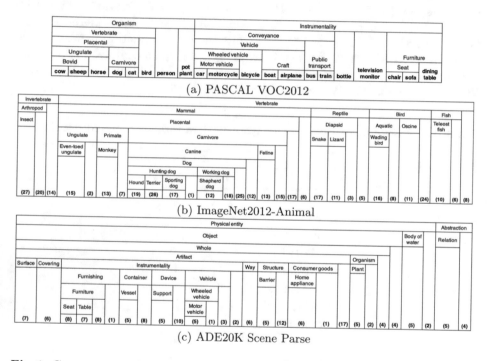

(a) PASCAL VOC2012

(b) ImageNet2012-Animal

(c) ADE20K Scene Parse

Fig. 1. Concept trees. Default root node ('Unknown') is not shown. Values in parentheses denote number of terminals.

4.2 PASCAL VOC2012/DeepLabv3+

In this experiment the PASCAL VOC2012 dataset [3] and Google's DeepLabv3+ [2] pretrained model were employed. The limited VOC2012 dataset was extended with the standard trainaug labelings [13]. We ignored all 'background' and 'void' pixels as these unused pixels do not adhere to a semantic hierarchy. All estimation/inference and evaluation procedures are based on the valid 20 object labels by removing DeepLab's output logits for the unused labels and performing softmax on the remaining logits. We made the following label changes for use with WordNet: 'aeroplane' → 'airplane', 'motorbike' → 'motorcycle', 'tv/monitor' → 'television monitor', and 'potted plant' → 'pot plant'. All labels were bound to the default WordNet noun definition (n.01).

The automatically generated concept tree using the technique in Sect. 3.1 is shown in Fig. 1(a), which depicts a natural and meaningful hierarchy of labels. We computed the average hierarchical metrics using cross-validation on the resulting labelings given by our approach using priors learned from training data. A 0% confidence threshold returns the original base classification results of 97.0% accuracy (C-PERSIST = IC-REMAIN = 1). Table 2 (left) presents the average results for multiple increasing confidences. Both C-PERSIST and IC-REMAIN monotonically decrease, while C-WITHDRAWN and IC-WITHDRAWN monotonically increase (softening is based on their relative rates of change). At higher confidences, approximately 50% of the incorrect examples were corrected. The bottom two rows in Table 2 show that nearly all of the classifications were retained (small overall withdrawal) and that a very high percentage of them are now correct. Depending on the dataset, at 100% confidence all labels may be set to 'Unknown' (as happens here) or some non-root labels may still be selected.

Table 2. Hierarchical metric scores for multiple confidence thresholds across datasets.

	VOC2012 Confidence:					ImageNet-Animal Confidence:					ADE20K Confidence:				
	50%	75%	90%	95%	99%	50%	75%	90%	95%	99%	50%	75%	90%	95%	99%
C-PERSIST	.996	.979	.923	.911	.808	.853	.762	.669	.640	.620	.935	.838	.493	.126	.004
C-WITHDRAWN	.000	.004	.014	.017	.017	.001	.003	.007	.010	.039	.004	.013	.021	.021	.021
C-SOFTEN	.003	.017	.063	.072	.174	.146	.235	.324	.349	.341	.061	.149	.487	.853	.975
C-SOFTDEPTH	.703	.610	.692	.703	.480	.766	.765	.749	.728	.670	.766	.663	.767	.645	.439
IC-REMAIN	.924	.616	.365	.284	.205	.598	.408	.290	.267	.235	.764	.457	.325	.121	.063
IC-WITHDRAWN	.009	.096	.202	.227	.228	.010	.024	.041	.052	.142	.033	.062	.101	.102	.102
IC-REFORM	.067	.287	.433	.489	.567	.393	.568	.669	.680	.624	.204	.482	.573	.777	.835
IC-REFDEPTH	.992	.968	.978	.981	.650	.976	.964	.936	.910	.842	.987	.941	.943	.890	.619
% Valid (¬root)	99.9	99.3	98.1	97.7	97.6	99.8	99.4	98.8	98.3	94.6	99.0	97.8	96.4	96.3	96.3
% Correct	97.2	98.1	98.8	99.1	99.3	91.0	93.8	95.6	95.9	96.3	84.8	90.8	93.3	97.5	98.7

An image containing the highly confusable ground-truth labels 'chair' and 'sofa' is shown in Fig. 2(a) and its ground-truth in Fig. 2(b). The DeepLab base prediction mistakenly labels most of one chair region as 'sofa' (see Fig. 2(c)). At a 95% confidence threshold our approach reasonably generalizes (softens and reforms) both chair regions to 'Seat' (see Fig. 2(d)). We note that pixels on object borders (removed in VOC2012) in most images are typically weakly predicted by a base classifier and are thus highly generalized by our approach. Furthermore, some regions may be composed of both specific and generalized labels. Additional post-processing of the final labeled image is the subject of future work.

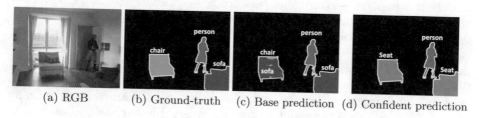

(a) RGB   (b) Ground-truth   (c) Base prediction (d) Confident prediction

Fig. 2. VOC2012 example result. (a) RGB image. (b) Ground-truth labeling. (c) Base prediction with 'chair'/'sofa' errors, and (d) Softening and reforming of 'chair' and 'sofa' to 'Seat' at 95% confidence.

To examine the effect of the tree itself, we employed the same tree structure but randomly shuffled the bottom 20 terminal labels. The hierarchical metrics were collected at 95% confidence and shown in the leftmost results of Table 3. As expected, C-PERSIST was unchanged, C/IC-WITHDRAWN increased, and IC-REFORM significantly decreased. The use of the meaningless tree structure (for the shuffled terminals) clearly shows degraded performance.

Table 3. Additional results at 95% confidence with normal vs. randomized/shuffled tree, posterior (w/ equal priors) vs. softmax confidence, and learned vs. equal priors.

	PASCAL VOC2012		ImageNet-Animal		ADE20K	
	Normal	Shuffled	Posterior	SoftMax	Learned	Equal
C-PERSIST	.911	.911	.640	.178	.126	.041
C-WITHDRAWN	.017	.026	.010	.256	.021	.020
C-SOFTEN	.072	.063	.349	.566	.853	.939
C-SOFTDEPTH	.703	.557	.728	.370	.645	.653
IC-REMAIN	.284	.379	.267	.051	.121	.152
IC-WITHDRAWN	.227	.415	.052	.450	.102	.100
IC-REFORM	.489	.206	.680	.499	.777	.748
IC-REFDEPTH	.981	.984	.910	.494	.890	.918
% Valid (¬root)	97.7	96.3	98.3	71.5	96.3	96.4
% Correct	99.1	98.8	95.9	98.9	97.5	96.9

(a) Softened to 'Snake' (b) Withdrawn (c) Reformed to 'Canine'

Fig. 3. ImageNet-Animal inference results at 95% confidence. (a) C-Soften: 'vine snake' → 'Snake'. (b) IC-Withdrawn: 'conch' → 'Unknown' (truth: 'chiton'). (c) IC-Reform: 'timber wolf' → 'Canine' (truth: 'white wolf', direct child of 'Canine').

4.3 ImageNet-Animal/ResNet-152

For this experiment, we focused on the subset of 398 animal types within the larger ImageNet ILSVRC 2012 dataset [7,11]. Microsoft's ResNet-152 [5] pre-trained model was used to give the base predictions, where all non-animal classes were removed from the output logits before computing the softmax. All animal labels were bound to their default WordNet noun definition (n.01), except for 25 labels that needed to be specified as the animal meaning (e.g., the dog 'boxer' is n.04). During the generation of the concept tree, we removed any non-terminal labels/nodes having less than 10 terminal descendants to give the more compact tree shown in Fig. 1(b).

Table 2 (middle) presents the average results using cross-validation with equal priors. The base classifier (0% confidence) has an accuracy of 85.0%, and we see that even at 50% confidence nearly all (99.8%) of the labels remain valid (non-root) and that 91% of them are correct. At higher confidences, more than 60% of the incorrect examples were reformed/corrected. A few example images are shown in Fig. 3. Notably, the withdrawn example is not clearly, or singularly, distinguished (it is a chiton on top of a mollusk) and the reformed image is relabeled more generally, yet correctly, as 'Canine' for the wolf confusion.

We also compared our posterior confidence to a baseline method directly using the softmax value as the confidence. Results at a 95% confidence threshold are presented in Table 3 (middle) and show that using softmax values alone produce much worse results, with a dramatically reduced C-Persist and IC-Reform. Testing with different thresholds on the softmax values could potentially improve these results, but would no longer be representative of a meaningful confidence measure. These results further reinforce the uncalibrated nature of softmax values, as described in [4].

4.4 ADE20K/UperNet-101

The ADE20K Scene Parsing Benchmark [1,16] contains natural images with 150 semantic labels. The particular WordNet synset definition (n.xx) was determined from the provided label information. Twenty labels were not uniquely matched and were manually assigned. The following label changes were made: 'water' →

'body of water', 'kitchen island' → 'kitchen table', and 'arcade machine' → 'slot machine' to better map to the WordNet concepts and hierarchy. The resulting concept tree with a constraint of at least 5 terminals associated with each non-terminal is shown in Fig. 1(c).

The UperNet-101 [14] pre-trained model was used as the base classifier, which produced an initial (0% confidence) accuracy of 80.3%. The hierarchical metrics with cross-validation and priors learned from training data are shown in Table 2 (right). We see a similar trend as in the previous experiments, but with much weaker scores at higher confidence ($\geq$90%). The small C-PERSIST values at high confidences can be explained by the fact that most terminal nodes have weak posteriors. For example, at 95% confidence the majority (81%) of terminal nodes cannot reach the confidence threshold (at any softmax value). In comparison, the learned posteriors for VOC2012 and ImageNet-Animal have only 10% and 2%, respectively, of terminals not able to meet the 95% threshold. Thus the UperNet-101 base classifier is not strongly confident in many cases.

We also compared the use of learned (from training data) vs. equal priors in the posterior calculation. Results at a 95% confidence threshold are presented in Table 3 (right) and show the preference for learned priors, as particularly reflected in C-PERSIST and IC-REFORM. The difference is even more pronounced at lower confidence due to the constrained posterior values in this dataset.

5   Summary

We presented an approach that provides a useful alternative to forced-choice classification when the labels have semantically meaningful relationships that can be hierarchically organized. Instead of removing unconfident labels, the approach attempts to produce more generalized and informative labels when possible. When a label is encountered that cannot meet the required confidence at any generalization, the label is withdrawn from classification.

We outlined a bottom-up label generalization method based on WordNet to create a semantic concept tree. A Bayesian posterior confidence employing classifier softmax predictions is used to determine the level of label generalization. A separate estimation and inference process was outlined that is applicable to any base classifier producing semantic labels with logit/softmax scores. Results with multiple synthetic and real datasets demonstrated the ability to correct many errors while only mildly generalizing correctly predicted labels. The approach can be widely used with a variety of existing models and tasks to provide high confidence predictions with informative, semantic labels.

References

1. ADE20K Scene Parse dataset. http://sceneparsing.csail.mit.edu/
2. Chen, L.-C., Zhu, Y., Papandreou, G., Schroff, F., Adam, H.: Encoder-decoder with atrous separable convolution for semantic image segmentation. In: Ferrari, V., Hebert, M., Sminchisescu, C., Weiss, Y. (eds.) ECCV 2018. LNCS, vol. 11211, pp. 833–851. Springer, Cham (2018). https://doi.org/10.1007/978-3-030-01234-2_49

3. Everingham, M., van Gool, L., Williams, C., Winn, J., Zisserman, A.: The PASCAL Visual Object Classes Challenge 2012 (VOC2012). http://host.robots.ox.ac.uk/pascal/VOC/voc2012/
4. Guo, C., Pleiss, G., Sun, Y., Weinberger, K.: On calibration of neural networks. In: ICML (2017)
5. He, K., Zhang, X., Ren, S., Sun, J.: Deep residual learning for image recognition. In: CVPR (2015)
6. ImageNet Large Scale Visual Recognition Challenge 2010. http://image-net.org/challenges/LSVRC/2010/
7. ImageNet Large Scale Visual Recognition Challenge 2012. http://image-net.org/challenges/LSVRC/2012/
8. Liang, X., Zhou, H., Xing, E.: Dynamic-structured semantic propagation network. In: CVPR (2018)
9. Princeton University: WordNet. https://wordnet.princeton.edu/
10. Redmon, J., Farhadi, A.: YOLO9000: better, faster, stronger. In: CVPR (2017)
11. Russakovsky, O., et al.: ImageNet large scale visual recognition challenge. Int. J. Comput. Vision 115(3), 211–252 (2015)
12. Srivastava, N., Salakhutdinov, R.: Discriminative transfer learning with tree-based priors. In: NIPS (2013)
13. VOC2012 trainaug annotations. https://www.sun11.me/blog/2018/how-to-use-10582-trainaug-images-on-DeeplabV3-code/
14. Xiao, T., Liu, Y., Zhou, B., Jiang, Y., Sun, J.: Unified perceptual parsing for scene understanding. In: Ferrari, V., Hebert, M., Sminchisescu, C., Weiss, Y. (eds.) ECCV 2018. LNCS, vol. 11209, pp. 432–448. Springer, Cham (2018). https://doi.org/10.1007/978-3-030-01228-1_26
15. Zhao, H., Puig, X., Zhou, B., Fidler, S., Torralba, A.: Open vocabulary scene parsing. In: ICCV (2017)
16. Zhou, B., Zhao, H., Puig, X., Fidler, S., Barriuso, A., Torralba, A.: Scene parsing through ADE20K dataset. In: CVPR (2017)

An Active Robotic Vision System with a Pair of Moving and Stationary Cameras

S. Pourya Hoseini A.$^{(\boxtimes)}$ (iD), Janelle Blankenburg, Mircea Nicolescu, Monica Nicolescu, and David Feil-Seifer

University of Nevada, Reno, NV 89557, USA
hoseini@nevada.unr.edu

Abstract. Vision is one of the main potential sources of information for robots to understand their surroundings. For a vision system, a clear and close enough view of objects or events, as well as the viewpoint angle can be decisive in obtaining useful features for the vision task. In order to prevent performance drops caused by inefficient camera orientations and positions, manipulating cameras, which falls under the domain of active perception, can be a viable option in a robotic environment.

In this paper, a robotic object detection system is proposed that is capable of determining the confidence of recognition after detecting objects in a camera view. In the event of a low confidence, a secondary camera is moved toward the object and performs an independent detection round. After matching the objects in the two camera views and fusing their classification decisions through a novel transferable belief model, the final detection results are obtained. Real world experiments show the efficacy of the proposed approach in improving the object detection performance, especially in the presence of occlusion.

Keywords: Active perception · Active vision · Robotics · PR2 · Dual-camera · Transferable belief model · Dempster-Shafer · Occlusion

1 Introduction

An important component of robotic platforms is their sensing capability. Through the sensory data, robots can interpret their surroundings. Analyzing the inputs from visual sensors, i.e. cameras, can specifically be used in determining the type of objects or events around the robot. Gaining knowledge about the existing objects or events happening around a robot can be cornerstone of many robotic applications, such as robotic manipulation, vision-based simultaneous localization and mapping (SLAM), rescue robots, social robots, etc.

In a vision system, a correct detection, among other factors, depends on obtaining distinctive features for the specific task at hand. Inadequate distinguishable features or occlusions may deteriorate a vision system's detection performance. To alleviate such problems in real world robotic platforms, trying to get a new viewpoint or moving the camera closer or farther from the event or object of interest can be advantageous. However, in real world conditions it is not practical to capture data in all possible orientations and positions around the robot. It would be energy and time inefficient to

G. Bebis et al. (Eds.): ISVC 2019, LNCS 11845, pp. 184–195, 2019.
https://doi.org/10.1007/978-3-030-33723-0_15

move the cameras to all possible poses around the robot. Moreover, adding a lot of cameras on robots to process their inputs at the same time to accomplish only one task would be infeasible, due to physical, computational, and energy limits of robots. Active perception, or active vision as it is known in the computer vision community, can be the answer to these issues. Active vision is a technique to manipulate cameras to help in better performing the vision-related tasks.

Relocating cameras based on a bioinspired approach is discussed in [1], where authors analyzed the head movement of barn owls and adopted it to actuate a depth camera installed on a robot. An active object detection and pose estimation method with dynamic camera location planning is presented in [2]. The sensor used was an Asus Xtion RGB-D camera mounted on the PR2 robot's wrist. This method tries to balance the amount of energy needed to move the camera and the added chance of getting a better object detection. In [3] a relative navigation system for space robotics by means of a monocular camera is presented, which benefits from an active leader robot tracking by means of a Dual Quaternion-based controller. An active head (and camera) rotation is also implemented in [4] for humanoid soccer robots to obtain useful data for each player robot. Also, a leader-follower robotic arrangement is realized in [5] with active tracking capability of the leader through dynamically rotating a pan-controlled camera. In another work [6], an active vision system is employed on a quadrotor to detect gaps. As the quadrotor moves, optical flow is computed by considering different captures of the same scene. Subsequently, contours of the gaps are detected from the resulting optical flow.

In our work, we designed an object detection system that works with two cameras. It is implemented on a PR2 humanoid robot, with a camera mounted on the robot's head (main camera) and the other one (secondary camera) installed in the robot's arm. The main camera is a Kinect v1 3D camera, while the secondary camera is an ordinary RGB camera. In the beginning, the proposed vision system detects objects in the view seen by the main camera only. In addition to detecting objects, it also computes the confidence on recognition of the detected objects. In the case of any uncertainty in the detections, it dynamically asks for another round of detection by the secondary camera. Before getting the assistive detections from the secondary camera, it moves the arm of the robot, and with it the secondary camera, to a pose suitable for capturing another viewpoint of the object with an uncertain detection. The detections made in the two scenes viewed by the dual-camera system are matched together and then combined via a novel transferable belief model, a decision fusion method based on the Dempster-Shafer evidence theory.

The contributions of this work can be summarized in three parts, which are: (1) dynamic allocation of cameras to improve detection performance while trying to keep number of detection efforts minimum, (2) a distance-based matching scheme to associate the detection between the two camera views, and (3) a decision fusion technique to combine the classification results of the two cameras. In the rest of this paper, the proposed active perception-based robotic vision system is described in Sect. 2. In Sect. 3, the experimental results are presented and analyzed, while Sect. 4 concludes the discussion.

2   The Proposed Vision System

Figure 1 shows the main components of the proposed vision system. They are clustered in the a few main phases that are demonstrated in the left vertical bar of Fig. 1. The flowchart of Fig. 1 shows that after an initial preprocessing and denoising stage to eliminate impulsive noise through a median filter, objects in the scene viewed by the main camera are detected by means of a sliding window technique. Since the main goal of this project is to enhance the detection performance by incorporating active perception, we chose to use a simple, yet effective, detection method in our case. For every candidate object, a feature vector containing a color histogram and a histogram of oriented gradients (HOG) [7] is constructed. HOG captures edge-based appearance, whereas the color histogram is generated by merging two flattened 2D histograms in the CIELUV [8] and HSV (i.e. Hue, Saturation, Value) color spaces. The 2D histogram of the CIELUV color space is computed from the u and v channels, while the 2D histogram of the HSV color space only considers the hue and saturation channels. In contrast to the two discarded channels, value (V) and L, which contain brightness information, these channels encode the color information of pixel.

After feature extraction, a stage of feature reduction based on the Principal Component Analysis (PCA) method is used to prevent curse of dimensionality. In other words, it ensures the subsequent classifier sees a moderate number of features given the number of available training samples. To classify the input features a non-linear multi-class Support Vector Machine (SVM) classifier with one-versus-rest strategy and a Radial Basis Function kernel is used in our method. For every trained object category, the classifier outputs mass values. It will be explained later that mass values are counterparts of probabilities in terms of the Dempster-Shafer theory, and represent the belief of the classifier concerning the similarity to the trained object categories.

In the proposed method, first the detection procedure is applied to the main camera frames. Subsequently, a confidence measure is computed by dividing the maximum mass value in the output mass vector to the second largest mass value. A low confidence value occurs when there are at least two strong candidate categories, which typically is the result of lack of discriminating features in the appearance of the candidate object. By comparing the confidence measure with a threshold value, the classification of detected objects in the main view is deemed "reliable" or "unreliable". In the case of an unreliable classification, the secondary camera is directed to perform object detection on its input frames, otherwise the reliable detection result is regarded final.

Prior to starting the second round of object detection, the secondary camera should be moved to a pose with respect to the object with unreliable detection to have it in its perspective. After the secondary camera's detections are done, the detections in the two camera views are matched and their classification results are fused and converted to probability values to form the final probability vectors. The classification output of each object is then the winner category with the highest probability.

In order to keep the computational load of the proposed vision method suitable for real-time applications, median flow tracker [9] is embedded in the system. It handles the tracking of the objects between every two successive object detections.

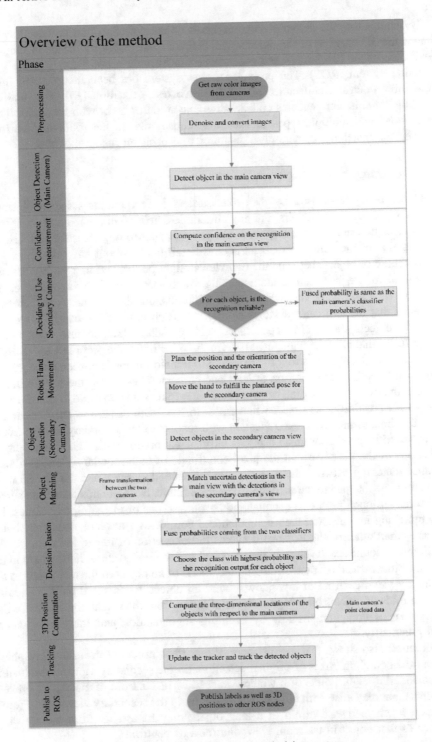

Fig. 1. Main steps of the proposed vision system.

By completing the active perception-based object detection, the proposed system obtains the 3D location of the objects with respect to the robot by means of the point cloud data of the 3D camera and publishes them to other robotic nodes in the robot operating system (ROS). The proposed vision system has been incorporated into a multi-robot control architecture for collaborative task execution [15]. This real-time distributed architecture enables collaborative execution of tasks with hierarchical representations and multiple types of execution constraints. In the following we focus more on the matching, camera pose planning, and decision fusion modules.

2.1   Matching

To enable fusing the decisions of the two classifiers, it is required to associate objects in both views to form object pairs. For any unreliable detection in the main view, if there is an association in the secondary view, the pair of matched objects is formed, else the classification of the main view object is considered final without any fusion.

Matching of objects between the two views might be fulfilled in a variety of ways. Among them we can enumerate matching of shape, keypoints, appearance, etc. Although they may work very well in some situations, but since in our work there is no guarantee that the two camera views are close to each other, there can be large variations in objects shape, size, appearance or keypoints, which in turn may hamper proper functionality of the matching [10]. On the other hand, the proposed active vision system is implemented on a robot with access to transformations between its coordinate frames and depth information on at least one camera. Thus, given the transformation between the two corresponding camera coordinate frames it is possible to transform the relative 3D position of an object with respect to the depth camera to another camera. After this transformation, the 3D location with respect to the secondary camera can be converted to its pixel coordinate using its intrinsic calibration data. The accessibility to detections of the main view in the pixel coordinate of the secondary view, facilitates distance matching between the detections of the secondary view and the detections of the main view mapped to the secondary camera's frame. Not only this technique avoids the aforementioned problems encountered by other types of matching techniques, but also by taking into account their computational complexity, distance matching should be faster than other methods, since it avoids the extraction of image features.

Figure 2 delineates the steps in the proposed matching algorithm. It is evident in the flowchart that instead of transforming all the pixels of an object in the main view to the secondary view, centroid of a window around an object is converted only. Assuming that centroids of objects have high chances of being from the actual object surface this strategy keeps computations low by avoiding segmentation and transformations in pixel granularity.

Figure 2 also shows that the distances of any transformed centroid to eight points around the bounding boxes of original detections in the secondary view are evaluated. By considering eight points of a window instead of its centroid to match, we prevent problems that may arise with objects that look long in the secondary viewpoint. From a secondary perspective, centroid of a long object may be too far from the viewable surface of that object in the main viewpoint (and its centroid).

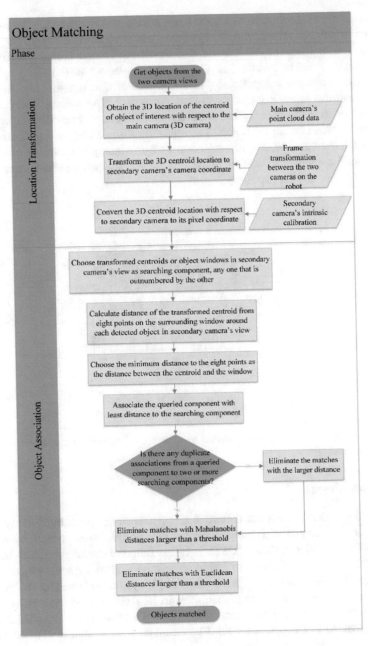

Fig. 2. Flowchart of the proposed object matching

2.2   Camera Pose Planning

Whenever there is an unreliable detection, the secondary camera should be planned to be moved to a proper pose to have a clear view of the object. Figure 3 shows a schematic of the PR2 robot, in which the main parameters for planning the robot's arm are shown in red. Distance of the object to the shoulder joint is computed by using the point cloud data from the 3D camera and the robot's inner frame transformations. Camera angle, forearm length, and upper arm length are also known in advance. Through the geometric computations, it is possible to find the shoulder lift and flex joints to have the secondary camera toward the object. The forearm roll (rotation) is determined relative to the computed shoulder joint values to keep the forearm camera (secondary camera) facing the object. The elbow flex angle and the upper arm rotation are set to a fixed value to simplify calculations by reducing the number of degrees of freedom in the planner. Detailed discussion about the geometric computations is beyond the scope of this paper.

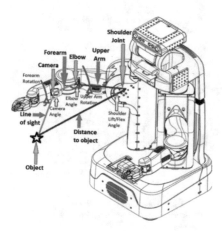

Fig. 3. Schematic of the parameters needed to plan the movement of the secondary camera. (Color figure online)

2.3 Decision Fusion

Typically, a multiclass classifier outputs a one-dimensional probability array. It constitutes a set of singleton (mutually exclusive) probabilities, which in terms of Dempster-Shafer evidence theory (DST), is called frame of discernment (Ω). Instead of merely relying on Ω, DST decision fusion alternatively allows for the power set of Ω and attributes a value called mass in the range of $[0, 1]$ to any element of the power set. Here, masses can be compared to probabilities in Bayesian fusion. Any element of the power set with mass value greater than zero is called a focal element. Additionally, the sum of all masses in the power set must be equal to 1, as shown in (1):

$$\sum_{\Psi \in 2^\Omega} m(\Psi) = 1 \tag{1}$$

where Ψ is an element of the power set of Ω and $m(.)$ is a mass value for it. Because in our work there are two sets of classification results from the two classifiers, we have two frames of discernments to combine. In the proposed fusion method, the power set is designed to have $n + 1$ focal elements, in which n elements are the singleton object categories and the last one is the universe of object categories. By defining the power set this way, we have masses for each object class that work like probabilities of that object class, while there is a mass value for the set of all the training samples [11]. We call this extra category, *unknown* class, because it actually represents how a classifier believes an object of interest is similar to all of the objects in its training set. Due to the larger size of the training samples for the *unknown* class, a balancing scheme by using weights relative to the training set size of each object category is used in the optimization formulae of the SVM classifier.

To fuse the two mass vectors from the main and secondary view classifiers, the unnormalized rule of combination [12] is used, as shown in the following:

$$m(\Psi) = \sum_{\alpha \cap \beta = \Psi} m_A(\alpha) * m_B(\beta), \quad \forall \Psi \subseteq \Omega, \ \alpha \in A, \ \beta \in B \tag{2}$$

where $m(\Psi)$ is mass of category Ψ, and sets A and B are mass vectors of the main view and the secondary view, respectively. Focal elements α and β are each a category from the mass vector of the main view and the secondary view classifiers in order. As an example, by considering (2) in our application, a category α in the mass vector A, except the class *unknown*, has intersection with two βs, namely the *unknown* category of the mass vector B and the corresponding element in B (the same label in B).

The proposed Dempster-Shafer fusion is a transferable belief model as a result of using an unnormalized rule of combination [12]. To convert the combined mass vector to a probability vector, we employ the pignistic transformation described in [13]:

$$P(\omega) = \sum_{\Psi \in \Phi} \frac{m(\Psi)}{|\Psi|}, \quad \forall \omega \in \Omega, \ \Phi = \{\Psi \mid \Psi \subseteq \Omega, \ \omega \in \Psi\} \tag{3}$$

where $P(\omega)$ is the probability of an object class ω, excluding the *unknown* category. In addition, Ψ is a focal element of the power set of object classes and $|\Psi|$ designates the number of object classes in Ψ. The above equation shows that any mass of belief is distributed among its comprising class probabilities [14].

Generally speaking, the two classifiers feeding the DST fusion provide a mass value for an *unknown* category besides actual the classes of objects present in the training. This specific mass value can be considered as indicating to the fusion module the uncertainty of the classifier about its recognition results. Considering the combination rule in (2) and the fact that sum of all masses resulted from a classifier is 1 (as stated in (1)), we observe not only that an increase in the mass of the *unknown* category of a classifier decreases other masses of that classifier, but also it weighs more toward the masses of the other classifier, with which it has a non-empty intersection. In contrary, a more resolute classifier that contributes more to the final fusion result is obtained when the *unknown* mass of the classifier is low.

3 Experimental Results

The proposed active vision system was implemented on a PR2 robot. Figure 4 shows a sample situation where there are three objects in the scene viewed by the main camera. One of the objects, though, (Tea Pot) is partially occluded. Each of the three parts of the figure, show the output of the proposed system in a different time. The bottom left image in the system output is the processed main view, while the bottom right is the secondary view, and the top left is the output of the active vision system superimposed on the scene viewed in the main view. In the beginning (Fig. 4a), there is an incorrect detection in the main view for the occluded object (Tea Pot is recognized as Sugar.) The active perception system has found it as an unreliable detection and marked it with a red bounding box. After that (Fig. 4b), the active vision system moves an arm with the secondary camera on it toward the object and detects objects in the secondary view. The detections in the secondary view are matched with those in the main view, and only the one which has been matched with an unreliable detection in the main view is shown (Tea Pot). We observe that it is correctly detected there as it has a clearer view of the object compared to the main view. The fusion result (top left of Fig. 4b) demonstrates the system was successful in correcting the initial erroneous detection. Consequently in Fig. 4c, the manipulation section receives the object detection and position information from the proposed system and based on that starts to manipulate the objects with the other arm.

Our method was tested in fifteen different real-world benchmarks. In the tests, objects were placed in front of the robot in various table-top settings in different lighting conditions. The benchmarks were also divided into two types: those with objects being partially occluded and those without any obstacles in viewpoint of the main camera. Table 1 shows the test results in terms of precision, recall, accuracy, and F_1 score (harmonic mean of precision and recall) for three scenarios: a single camera only (main camera), the proposed system without any secondary camera movement, and the system with its complete functionality. Macro-averaging in Table 1 means the measure is calculated separately for each object category and is averaged over the results. In contrary, micro-averaging is the process of computing the measures for all the object categories collectively. Micro-averaging results were not included in Table 1, because micro-averaging precision and recall are equal to accuracy in the case of multi-class classifiers.

Table 1 indicates large improvements in the performance of the proposed system in comparison to the conventional single camera configuration. In accurately detecting the non-occluded objects, the proposed method outperforms the traditional single camera setup by 12.9%, 12.2%, 13.1%, and 12.5% in precision, recall, accuracy, and F_1 score, respectively. These enhancements bring the percentage of the four measures to over 97.7%. In the tests consisting of only partially occluded objects, the active vision system was even more successful in ameliorating over the traditional single camera robotic vision with 18.3%, 15.5%, 17.1%, and 16.9% increases in precision, recall, accuracy, and F_1 score, respectively. The reason is that, the active vision had access to more informative viewpoints via its use of the secondary camera. Furthermore, it is obvious in Table 1 that the proposed method with the dynamic secondary camera

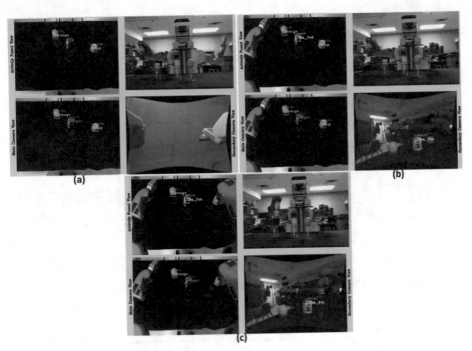

Fig. 4. A sample situation involving active perception through the proposed vision system and manipulation of objects. (a) Before using the secondary camera, (b) After completing the active detection, (c) Subsequent manipulation of objects based on the provided information from the vision system. (Color figure online)

movement works better than the same system with fixed secondary camera. The accuracy of the vision system increased by 4.4% and 2.2% in the benchmarks with non-occluded and occluded objects, respectively, when the secondary camera pose planning and movement was added to the proposed system. This proves, not only using cameras in different viewpoints contributes to a better detection performance, but also planning and moving the extra views help in further improvements.

In order to evaluate the efficacy of the transferable belief model (TBM) decision fusion proposed in this paper, we implemented our method with the fusion module replaced with Bayesian fusion [11] instead. Table 2 shows the results obtained for the same tests we conducted for Table 1. By comparing them to those illustrated in Table 1, we observe that without any fusion taken place (single camera only) the vision system with the classifier trained for the Bayesian fusion works better. The reason is probability the added *unknown* category in the classifier for TBM, which reduces the probability of other object categories before any fusion is taken place. In spite of a weaker single camera performance, the proposed TBM fusion, however, is superior in the final results obtained after the decision fusion are applied.

Table 1. Performance results of the proposed active vision system.

Performance measure	Single camera		Active perception (no camera motion)		Active perception (with camera motion)	
	Non-occluded	Partially occluded	Non-occluded	Partially occluded	Non-occluded	Partially occluded
Macro-averaging precision	0.860	0.745	0.944	0.903	0.989	0.928
Macro-averaging recall	0.855	0.700	0.933	0.833	0.977	0.855
Accuracy	0.846	0.684	0.933	0.833	0.977	0.855
F_1 score	0.857	0.721	0.938	0.866	0.982	0.890

Table 2. Performance results of the proposed active vision system with Bayesian fusion.

Performance measure	Single camera		Active perception (no camera motion)		Active perception (with camera motion)	
	Non-occluded	Partially occluded	Non-occluded	Partially occluded	Non-occluded	Partially occluded
Macro-averaging precision	0.884	0.765	0.922	0.878	0.967	0.907
Macro-averaging recall	0.877	0.722	0.911	0.811	0.955	0.833
Accuracy	0.868	0.706	0.911	0.811	0.955	0.833
F_1 score	0.880	0.742	0.916	0.843	0.960	0.868

4   Conclusion

In this paper, a dual-camera robotic object detection system based on the idea of active perception was presented. It is implemented on a PR2 humanoid robot. The contributions of the work are the dynamic switching capability between cameras, which is accomplished automatically, a fast matching algorithm between the cameras, and a decision fusion method established on the basis of Dempster-Shafer evidence theory. The experimental results in real-world tests prove the efficiency of the proposed method in enhancing the vision performance of robots. The accuracy of the presented vision approach is 13.1% more than a traditional single camera robotic vision system. The practicality of the proposed decision fusion is also verified in the tests. The presented method is useful in making robotic vision more robust when there is more than one camera present. It is especially applicable in dealing with partial occlusions as shown in the tests.

A future work can be adding the ability of handling complete occlusion of objects. Another future direction can be extending the functionalities of the current system to the field of activity and intent recognition.

Acknowledgment. This work has been supported by Office of Naval Research Award #N00014-16-1-2312.

References

1. Barzilay, Q., Zelnik-Manor, L., Gutfreund, Y., Wagner, H., Wolf, A.: From biokinematics to a robotic active vision system. Bioinspiration Biomimetics **12**(5), 056004 (2017)
2. Atanasov, N., Sankaran, B., Le Ny, J., Pappas, G.J., Daniilidis, K.: Nonmyopic view planning for active object classification and pose estimation. IEEE Trans. Rob. **30**(5), 1078–1090 (2014)
3. Zhang, G., Kontitsis, M., Filipe, N., Tsiotras, P., Vela, P.A.: Cooperative relative navigation for space rendezvous and proximity operations using controlled active vision. J. Field Robot. **33**(2), 205–228 (2016)
4. Mattamala, M., Villegas, C., Yáñez, J.M., Cano, P., Ruiz-del-Solar, J.: A dynamic and efficient active vision system for humanoid soccer robots. In: Almeida, L., Ji, J., Steinbauer, G., Luke, S. (eds.) RoboCup 2015. LNCS (LNAI), vol. 9513, pp. 316–327. Springer, Cham (2015). https://doi.org/10.1007/978-3-319-29339-4_26
5. Chen, X., Jia, Y.: Adaptive leader-follower formation control of non-holonomic mobile robots using active vision. IET Control Theory Appl. **9**(8), 1302–1311 (2015)
6. Sanket, N.J., Singh, C.D., Ganguly, K., Fermuller, C., Aloimonos, Y.: GapFlyt: active vision based minimalist structure-less gap detection for quadrotor flight. IEEE Robot. Autom. Lett. **3**(4), 2799–2806 (2018)
7. Dalal, N., Triggs, B.: Histograms of oriented gradients for human detection. In: IEEE Conference on Computer Vision and Pattern Recognition (CVPR). IEEE, San Diego (2005)
8. CIE 015:2018: Colorimetry. 4th edn., International Commission on Illumination
9. Kalal, Z., Mikolajczyk, K., Matas, J.: Forward-backward error: Automatic detection and tracking failures. In: International Conference on Pattern Recognition, Istanbul (2010)
10. Hoseini A., S.P., Nicolescu, M., Nicolescu, M.: Active object detection through dynamic incorporation of Dempster-Shafer fusion for robotic applications. In: International Conference on Vision, Image and Signal Processing (ICVISP), Las Vegas (2018)
11. Hoseini A., S.P., Nicolescu, M., Nicolescu, M.: Handling ambiguous object recognition situations in a robotic environment via dynamic information fusion. In: IEEE Conference on Cognitive and Computational Aspects of Situation Management, Boston (2018)
12. Smets, P.: The combination of evidence in the transferable belief model. IEEE Trans. Pattern Anal. Mach. Intell. **12**(5), 447–458 (1990)
13. Smets, P., Kennes, R.: The transferable belief model. Artif. Intell. **66**(2), 191–243 (1994)
14. Denoeux, T.: A neural network classifier based on Dempster-Shafer theory. IEEE Trans. Syst. Man Cybern. Part A Syst. Hum. **30**(2), 131–150 (2000)
15. Blankenburg, J., et al.: A distributed control architecture for collaborative multi-robot task allocation. In: International Conference on Humanoid Robotics, Birmingham (2017)

Background Modeling Through Spatiotemporal Edge Feature and Color

Byeongwoo Kim[1], Adín Ramírez Rivera[2], Oksam Chae[1],
and Jaemyun Kim[1(✉)]

[1] Department of Computer Science and Engineering, Kyung Hee University, 1732,
Deogyeong-daero, Giheung-gu, Yongin-si, Gyeonggi-do 17104, South Korea
{byeongwoo,oschaeg,jaemyunkim}@khu.ac.kr
[2] Institute of Computing, University of Campinas (UNICAMP), Campinas, Brazil
adin@ic.unicamp.br

Abstract. In this paper, we propose a new spatiotemporal edge feature for background modeling that can extract spatial and temporal (motion) features by considering the background model and current information. Previous work on background modeling considers mainly the spatial domain, which misses key temporal information. In our proposal, we create spatiotemporal edge features by using current and past background information by identifying the amount of change from past to present. By finding these differences, we can accurately detect the movement of objects that is more robust to noise and illumination variations. Moreover, our proposed background-modeling technique adapts to background changes that occur over time through a dynamic model update strategy. Additionally, we are enhancing the spatiotemporal edge features with color to maintain the characteristics of each other. Finally, we evaluated our proposed method on the publicly available CDNET 2012 dataset and compared with state-of-the-art methods. Our extensive evaluation and analysis show that our method outperforms previous methods on this dataset.

Keywords: Background modeling · Spatiotemporal · Fusion

1 Introduction

Detection of foreground objects from videos is an initial step for many computer vision applications, like surveillance, activity recognition, human pose estimation, traffic flow estimation, etc. One of the widely used methods for this task is Background Subtraction (BS). Typically, this method requires to create a background model and then new frames from the videos are compared with that model to detect the foreground. Thus, it is important to generate a background

Funded in part by the Brazilian National Council for Scientific and Technological Development (CNPq) under grant No. 307425/2017-7.

G. Bebis et al. (Eds.): ISVC 2019, LNCS 11845, pp. 196–208, 2019.
https://doi.org/10.1007/978-3-030-33723-0_16

model that contains the background information of the scene by including its different variations. If the background model includes consistent background information, then the foreground can be detected by comparing the current frame with the model. However, since the real video images contain various obstacles, such as illumination variations, shadows, waving trees, or flowing water, it is impossible to accurately detect the foreground by using a difference between RGB pixel values.

Since there are several sources of movement within a video, we have to decide which of these situations will be detected as foreground. Therefore, the goal of background modeling is to detect the motion of the moving objects by accepting non-interesting motions (e.g., the waving trees, flowing water, and illumination variations) as a moving background. To detect the foreground, it is common to extract spatial features from the image and compare them. Therefore, there are extensive studies on spatial descriptors for background modeling.

One of the typical background modeling techniques is texture-based background modeling. Local Binary Pattern (LBP) [3] compares the intensity between the center pixel and neighboring pixels and encode them in binary code. It is robust to illumination variations but is very sensitive to noise. Local Binary Similarity Pattern (LBSP) [1] encodes similarity rather than direct intensity comparison with adjacent pixels to solve the LBP problem. However, it is sensitive to shadows and background variations and degrades performance in flat regions. Local Binary Similarity Segmenter (LOBSTER) [9] tried to solve the problem by using both LBSP and color information together alongside a random background update strategy based on Sample Consensus (SACON) [12]. Furthermore, the Self-Balanced Sensitivity Segmenter (SubSENSE) [10] attempted to adapt quickly to changes by dynamically adjusting its internal parameters. However, it is still sensitive to noise and when the color of the background and foreground are similar, and then its performance degrades in flat regions.

Edge-based background modeling is robust to illumination variations but sensitive to noise. Also, edges in the same position in continuous frames are not always with the same magnitude and direction. To solve this problem, an edge-segment-based method was proposed [7,8]. It uses edge magnitude and shape information by connecting adjacent edges. However, it is difficult to accurately detect the inside of the foreground due to a lack of edge information in flat regions. Local Hybrid Pattern (LHP) [5] tried to solve this problem by using edge and color information together, but using only one direction did not show characteristics in various directions. Local Top Directional Pattern (LTDP) [6] uses the compass masks instead of pixel information to accurately extract changes of an edge in different directions and encodes only the direction with the largest edge response. Therefore, it can extract straight lines, edge, and other shapes.

Pixel-based background modeling uses the intensity and color information of each pixel. It is sensitive to changes caused by the appearance of new objects, but also sensitive to illumination variations. This method cannot capture the background variations. Mixture of Gaussians (MoG) [11] used k Gaussian-models to solve this problem. However, the disadvantage of MoG is that it is difficult to determine the value of k between the fast and slow variations. Pixel Based Adaptive Segmenter (PBAS) [4] creates the background model based on the pixel intensity recorded recently. PBAS determines the background and foreground with different thresholds and uses a random update strategy. Moreover, the thresholds are dynamically adjusted to show high performance.

In this paper, we use the spatiotemporal edge feature and color information based on SuBSENSE to detect the foreground. This can accurately detect pixel changes due to the existence of moving objects. The spatiotemporal edge feature is the average of the differences between the pixels of the current frame and the pixels of the past frames in the background model. Besides, we use five spatiotemporal edge features in different directions by comparing the pixels in the 7×7 block in the current frame and the pixels of the background model. Therefore, it is robust to noise and can detect the object's change in any direction. LOBSTER and SuBSENSE use LBSP and color information to detect different foreground and use the **and** operator to detect the foreground again. However, we try to use both the spatiotemporal edge feature and color simultaneously using a fusion method that uses a sigmoid graph with the edge magnitude in the x-axis.

2 Spatiotemporal Edge Feature

Previous background modeling methods create features with information from a single frame and within consecutive frames. Then, the created features are compared with those in the background model to detect the foreground. However, features created with information extracted in this manner are not robust enough to accurately detect pixel variations due to the foreground and moving background. Moreover, it is difficult to create features with accurate information in flat or complex regions. We present a solution to this problem by proposing a spatiotemporal edge feature that is generated based on the change between the current frame and the stable background information held in the background model.

We propose the spatiotemporal edge feature that by jointly modeling the appearance and motion of the objects in the frame obtains higher accuracy when detecting moving objects. Given the neighborhoods of two pixels p and q, their difference is

$$D(\mathcal{N}_p, \mathcal{N}_q) = \frac{1}{9} \sum_{\substack{i \in \mathcal{N}_p, \\ j \in \mathcal{N}_q}} |i - j|, \tag{1}$$

where i and j are parallel indexed pixels over the neighborhoods $\mathcal{N}_p$ and $\mathcal{N}_q$ (of size 3×3) centered at pixels p and q, respectively, i.e., i and j are the values of their respective neighborhoods that are traversed at parallel locations. The differences are performed channel-wise. Hence, the final element will contain the same amount of channels as the original pixel (these were omitted for brevity). We are computing the difference between a neighborhood centered at pixel p, $\mathcal{N}_p$, and subtracting it to another neighborhood centered at pixel q, $\mathcal{N}_q$. We

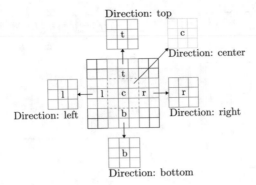

Fig. 1. Directions of a 3×3 neighborhood used to create the spatiotemporal edge features.

define the feature in terms of neighborhoods since we take advantage of our background model, instead of densely computing the features for every frame. To obtain robust motion-features, we use five directions to get variations of the current neighborhood at the pixel of interest. Hence, for every pixel p and given a neighborhood $\mathcal{N}_q$ for comparison, we define a set of features

$$\mathcal{F}(p, \mathcal{N}_q) = \{D(\mathcal{N}_r, \mathcal{N}_q) : r \in \mathcal{D}(p)\} \tag{2}$$

based on five directions defined by

$$\mathcal{D}(p) = \{(p_x, p_y), (p_x \pm \Delta_x, p_y), (p_x, p_y \pm \Delta_y)\}, \tag{3}$$

where p is the pixel's position with horizontal and vertical components p_x and p_y, respectively, and where Δ_x and Δ_y are the displacements on each axis. In our definition of 3×3 blocks, we used a displacement $\Delta_x = \Delta_y = 2$ to minimize the overlap between the blocks, and still maintain consistency over the regions. We show an illustration of the five directions in Fig. 1.

3   Background Modeling

Model Definition. We model the scene pixel-wise through a set of codebooks that represent the local context of the pixel by including its spatiotemporal and color information. Let $\mathcal{B}_i(p)$ be the ith background model at pixel p's position as the tuple of the spatiotemporal edge features at p, $\mathcal{F}(p, \mathcal{N}^*)$, and the current pixel's neighborhood information, $\mathcal{N}_p$, such as

$$\mathcal{B}_i(p) = (\mathcal{F}(p, \mathcal{N}^*), \mathcal{N}_p). \tag{4}$$

Note that we need a reference neighborhood $\mathcal{N}^*$ to compute the features for the given pixel. Given a match with the jth background model at pixel p (cf. Sect. 4), the corresponding neighborhood $\mathcal{N}^* \in \mathcal{B}_j(p)$ will be our reference neighborhood

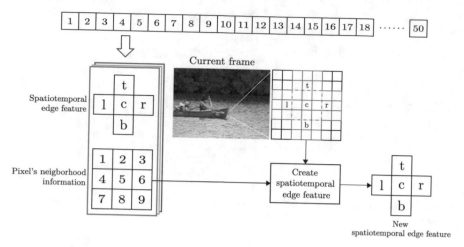

Fig. 2. The background model consists of the five-direction spatiotemporal edge features and the pixels within the 3×3 block. Given a new frame, the new five-direction spatiotemporal edge features are created using nine pixels of the 3×3 block in the background model.

for the model. Moreover, the use of past background models as reference points for the features, instead of frame-to-frame features, creates a more robust representation of the changes between the current frame and the model. For initialization, we use a background frame that serves as reference neighborhoods for the first frame of the sequence. The whole background model for every pixel p is the set $\mathbb{B}(p) = \{\mathcal{B}_i(p)\}_{i=1}^{N}$ for a set number of codebooks N. In our proposal, we maintain a similar number of models per pixel as previous works [10], i.e., $N = 50$, that is supported by our experimental results on parameter selection. We illustrate the model in Fig. 2.

Model Matching. If a pixel is matched against $M_{\min}$ or more models within its set of codebooks for that particular pixel, then we consider it as background. Otherwise, it is considered as foreground. If the pixel is considered background, its information is used to randomly replace one of the N models. We performed an analysis of the parameters settings of our method in Sect. 5.1.

To match a pixel from the incoming frames with its set of models, we measure the distance of its features against each model. If the distance is close enough (according to a threshold, see below for details on their computation), we consider it a match. First, we compute the feature of the current frame at each pixel using the background models at its location as a reference. That is, at pixel p, for one of its background models, we use its neighborhood $\mathcal{N}^* \in \mathcal{B}(p)$ to compute the features of the current pixel $C = \mathcal{F}(p, \mathcal{N}^*)$. Then, we compare the distance against the background model's features $B = \mathcal{F}(\cdot, \cdot) \in \mathcal{B}(p)$ by

$$d_f(p, \mathcal{B}) = d_f(C, B) = \frac{1}{5} \sum_{\substack{c \in C \\ b \in B}} \sum_{n=1}^{3} |c[n] - b[n]|, \tag{5}$$

where the difference between the codes is performed channel-wise (n), and the codes are selected from the same direction in both sets C and B (the indexing was omitted for brevity). Similarly, we compute the difference between the color of the current pixel, $c_c = \mathcal{N}_p(\mathtt{c})$, where $\mathtt{c}$ represents the center position of the neighborhood $\mathcal{N}_p$, and the background color $c_b = \mathcal{N}_b(\mathtt{c})$, where $\mathcal{N}_b \in \mathcal{B}(p)$ is the neighborhood information stored on the background model, by

$$d_c(p, \mathcal{B}) = d_c(c_c, c_b) = \sum_{n=1}^{3} |c_c[n] - c_b[n]|, \tag{6}$$

where a color comprises three channels: R, G, and B. The range for both distances is within 0–765.

In contrast to existing methods [10] that use intersection between different detection maps, we propose to rely on a distance fusion method defined by

$$d^*(p, \mathcal{B}) = \alpha(p)d_f(p, \mathcal{B}) + (1 - \alpha(p)) d_c(p, \mathcal{B}), \tag{7}$$

where α is determined by a saturated edge magnitude of the current pixel to combine d_f and d_c, $\mathcal{B}$ is one of the N models for the pixel p. Given the edge magnitude $e(p)$ at pixel p's position, we compute the scaling parameter by

$$\alpha(p) = \frac{0.8}{1 + \exp\left(-6e(p) + 2.8\right)} + 0.2, \tag{8}$$

where the parameters of the function define a minimum of 0.2 and a maximum of 0.8 for the sigmoid function. (These values give soft step function.) This is to prevent drastic changes in regions where feature or color is unilaterally strong. Hence, we allow a mixture of both distances within those limiting proportions.

Model Update. If the current pixel is determined to be background, the information of the current pixel is updated into the background model by randomly replacing one of its N models at the pixel's position. Similarly, a random adjacent pixel is selected too, and one of its models is also randomly updated. This random update is similar to the SuBSENSE method [10].

4   Foreground Detection

We do the foreground detection at two steps based on our match confidence. At the first step, we compare the spatiotemporal edge feature (5) and color information (6) independently, and select pixels that we consider foreground with high confidence for both features. Otherwise, we use the fused information (7) to make an informed decision.

We define our foreground function (1 is foreground, 0 is background) as

$$F\left(p, \mathbb{B}\left(p\right)\right) = \begin{cases} 1 & \exists_{M_{\min}} \mathcal{B} \in \mathbb{B} : d_f(p, \mathcal{B}) > T_f^H(p) \text{ and } d_c(p, \mathcal{B}) > T_c^H(p), \\ 0 & \forall \mathcal{B} \in \mathbb{B} : d_f(p, \mathcal{B}) < T_f^L(p) \text{ and } d_c(p, \mathcal{B}) < T_c^L(p), \\ 1 & \exists_{M_{\min}} \mathcal{B} \in \mathbb{B} : d^*(p, \mathcal{B}) > T_*(p), \end{cases} \tag{9}$$

where $\mathbb{B}(p)$ corresponds to the set of models for the pixel p, and $\exists_{M_{\min}}$ represents the existence of at least $M_{\min}$ elements. For the spatiotemporal edge features, we use two thresholds (high and low) $T_f^H(p)$ and $T_f^L(p)$, respectively, per pixel p. Similarly, for the color features we use $T_c^H(p)$ and $T_c^L(p)$. For the fused distance, we have a singular threshold $T_*(p)$. The first two cases correspond to the certain cases in which both features agree on foreground or background by been higher or lower than its respective thresholds for one or all of the models, respectively. The third case is when there is a disagreement between the features (we omit the negation of the two previous conditions for brevity). Consequently, we use the fused distance to reach a consensus.

The thresholds reflect the tails on the distribution of distances that represent, either, foreground or background at the seen contexts per pixel. However, defining the threshold that best divides them is not trivial. Instead of setting the thresholds, we set the proportion of learned distributions of these distances. That is, given a prior distribution (σ^0) we maintain and update a running standard deviation each frame. Let $\sigma^t(p)$ be the standard deviation at time t and pixel p. We define its update as

$$\sigma^t(p) = \beta d(p) + (1 - \beta)\sigma^{t-1}(p), \tag{10}$$

were β represents the learning rate for the distributions, and $d(p)$ the distance that corresponds to the distribution of σ. We set $\beta = 0.05$ for a quick adaptation in the first 100 frames. After that, we set $\beta = 0.01$ to adapt slower to sequence the changes. We will maintain three parameters, one per distance (5, 6, and 7), namely, σ_f^t, σ_c^t, and σ_*^t at each time frame (we omit the frame t henceforth for brevity). Each distribution is updated (10) throughout the sequence to represent the changes in the scene.

We define the thresholds based on a factor of how far is the distance from the mean (based on standard deviations) by

$$T_{\{f,c\}}^{\{H,L\}}(p) = \sigma_{\{f,c\}}(p)F_{\{f,c\}}^{\{H,L\}}, \tag{11}$$

$$T_*(p) = \sigma_* F_*, \tag{12}$$

where $F_{\{f,c\}}^{\{H,L\}}$ and F_* are five the factors, one per threshold. We found the best factors experimentally, cf. Sect. 5.1.

5 Experimental Results

To evaluate the performance of the proposed approach, we use F_1 measure [5,6] as a standard evaluation metric. We conduct background subtraction experiments on the Change Detection dataset 2012 (CDNET) [2]. This dataset is considered as challenging since the videos have diverse real-world scenes captured by CCTV surveillance cameras, and are categorized into six groups: baseline, camera jitter, dynamic background, intermittent object motion, shadow, and thermal. The dataset provides pixel-wise ground-truth information for all frames of videos.

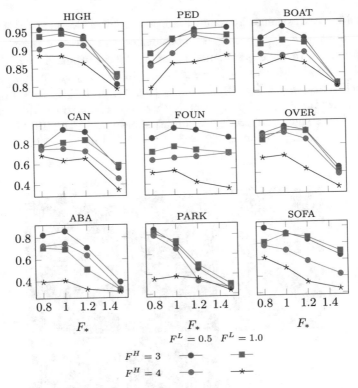

Fig. 3. The effect of varying the factors F^H, F^L, and F_* on the performance of the proposed method measured by F_1 on the CDNET database.

In our evaluations, we make use of nine videos taken from three categories: Highway (HIGH), Pedestrians (PED), Boats (BOAT), Canoe (CAN), Fountain (FOUN), Overpass (OVER), Abandoned Box (ABA), Parking (PARK), and Sofa (SOFA). It should be noted that videos along with moving objects contain several other complications affecting the performance of the detection: illumination variations in the frames of HIGH and PED; dynamic backgrounds like waving in trees and water in BOAT, CAN, FOUN, and OVER; as well as sudden changes in background, and stopping of moving objects in ADA, PARK, and SOFA.

5.1 Parameter Setting

There are several important parameters of the proposed approach that should be set appropriately to expect reliable performance. We consider parameters related to the thresholds mentioned in Sect. 4. We perform experiments in various cases with different values to determine these best parameters.

Threshold Parameters. Through empirical studies, we attempt to find the optimal values of $F_{\{f,c\}}^{\{H,L\}}$ and F_* by considering the effect of the threshold on the performance. In the experiments, the factors were grouped by high and low, such as $F_f^H = F_c^H = F^H$ and $F_f^L = F_c^L = F^L$, to simplify the parameter search. Our search space was $F^H \in \{3, 4\}$, $F^L \in \{0.5, 1\}$, and $F_* \in \{0.8, 1.0, 1.2, 1.5\}$. Figure 3 shows the F_1 measure of each dataset according to the different factors in 16 cases. We show the average of all F_1 measures in the Table 1. Thus, we found the best configuration at $F^H = 3$, $F^L = 0.5$, and $F_* = 1.0$.

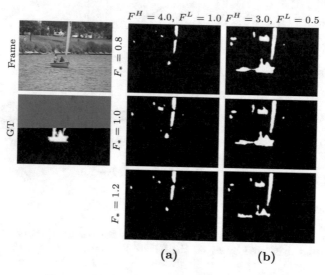

Fig. 4. Example of F^H and F^L effects in the BOAT dataset. (a) Detections when the foreground is not correctly detected (too many false negatives). And (b) detections when the foreground is over detected (too many false positives).

Table 1. Mean of F_1 measure by changing the different factor parameters.

F_*	(F^H, F^L)			
	$(3, 0.5)$	$(4, 0.5)$	$(3, 1.0)$	$(4, 1.0)$
0.8	0.807 ± 0.113	0.744 ± 0.139	0.712 ± 0.172	0.554 ± 0.269
1.0	$\mathbf{0.846 \pm 0.151}$	0.767 ± 0.151	0.702 ± 0.197	0.564 ± 0.252
1.2	0.772 ± 0.229	0.709 ± 0.224	0.645 ± 0.256	0.508 ± 0.278
1.5	0.549 ± 0.318	0.528 ± 0.303	0.487 ± 0.305	0.391 ± 0.315

From these experiments we can see that if F^H or F^L is too high the foreground regions are reduced (false negatives increase). Conversely, if F^H and F^L are too low, dynamic backgrounds and shadows appear as foreground (false positives increase). For example, when $F^H = 4$ and $F^L = 1$ the foreground is not detected properly, and when $F^H = 3$ and $F^L = 0.5$ the foreground is over detected, as shown in Fig. 4.

Background Model Parameters. We also conducted experiments to understand the effect of background model parameters. Table 2 shows the F_1 measures of the average of the CDNET sequences while varying N and $M_{\min}$ in 12 cases. We set our search space as $N \in \{30, 40, 50, 60\}$ and $M_{\min} \in \{2, 3, 4\}$. When N is too large there is a drop in performance due to the large model size. Conversely, if it is too small, the background cannot be modeled exactly. In the case when $M_{\min}$ is too large, it is easy to detect the exact background, but if it is too small, the foreground can be detected as background. We selected $N = 50$ and $M_{\min} = 3$ as the optimal configuration.

Table 2. Mean of F_1 measure by changing the different background model parameters.

N	$M_{\min}$		
	2	3	4
30	0.791 ± 0.161	0.819 ± 0.166	0.809 ± 0.163
40	0.800 ± 0.165	0.824 ± 0.161	0.819 ± 0.165
50	0.812 ± 0.163	$\mathbf{0.850 \pm 0.141}$	0.838 ± 0.140
60	0.804 ± 0.175	0.838 ± 0.160	0.830 ± 0.153

Table 3. Quantitative evaluation based on F_1 measure of different features on our background modeling setup.

Methods	LBP	LDP	LBSP	Proposed
HIGH	0.914	0.949	0.944	**0.955**
PED	0.907	0.953	0.954	**0.955**
BOAT	0.656	0.636	0.693	**0.758**
CAN	0.756	0.884	0.792	**0.939**
FOUN	0.905	0.906	0.944	**0.954**
OVER	0.806	0.793	0.857	**0.929**
ABA	0.656	**0.879**	0.849	0.859
PARK	0.405	**0.528**	0.444	0.504
SOFA	0.695	0.732	0.742	**0.761**
Avg.	0.744	0.807	0.802	**0.846**

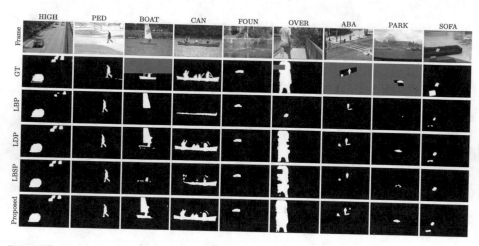

Fig. 5. Detection examples on the sequences of CDNET when using different features on the proposed setup. GT stands for ground truth.

5.2 Performance Analysis

To demonstrate the efficiency of proposed features, we compare our proposed spatiotemporal edge feature against well-know descriptors, such as LBP, LDP, and LBSP, by using such features instead of our proposal in our setup. Table 3 shows the F_1 measures on the different categories. The results demonstrate that our spatiotemporal edge features outperform others in most of the experiments. Although LDP shows a better result in ABA and PARK categories, the proposed approach provides comparable results with more stable performance, as shown by the higher average F_1 measure.

Table 4. Quantitative evaluation by comparing F_1 measures of several methods on CDNET.

Methods	ViBe	PBAS	GMM	SuBSENSE	Proposed
HIGH	0.855	0.945	0.924	0.944	**0.955**
PED	0.808	0.936	0.954	0.954	**0.955**
BOAT	0.433	0.361	0.729	0.693	**0.758**
CAN	0.779	0.720	0.882	0.792	**0.939**
FOUN	0.714	0.936	0.803	0.944	**0.954**
OVER	0.746	0.793	0.872	0.857	**0.929**
ABA	0.614	0.690	0.539	0.849	**0.859**
PARK	0.388	0.174	**0.749**	0.444	0.504
SOFA	0.546	0.738	0.645	0.742	**0.761**
Avg.	0.654	0.699	0.789	0.802	**0.846**

Along with quantitative results, we also provide qualitative results in Figs. 5 and 6. In Fig. 5, we can see over-detection due to the sensitivity to pixel illumination changes (i.e., shadows) in ABA and PARK videos.

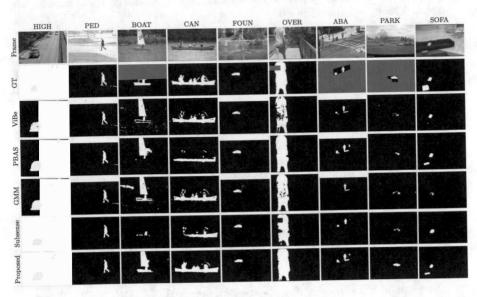

Fig. 6. Detection examples on the sequences of CDNET when comparing other methods. GT stands for ground truth.

Figure 6 is a comparison of the proposed method with the other methods. Additionally, we show a quantitative comparison in Table 4. In PARK, F_1 measures of GMM is higher, but the proposed method is better overall.

6   Conclusion

In this paper, we propose a spatiotemporal edge features that take advantage of both spatial and temporal domains. This feature is robust to noise while being responsive to detect pixel variations occurring due to foreground appearance changes. We combine the spatiotemporal edge and color features to improve the prediction of foreground based on a set of adaptive thresholds. Thus, the foreground is detected by complementing the weak points of each other feature. Besides, internal parameters can be adjusted dynamically to quickly adapt to illumination or background variations. This shows that the overall proposed method provides better performance in different situations.

References

1. Bilodeau, G.A., Jodoin, J.P., Saunier, N.: Change detection in feature space using local binary similarity patterns. In: International Conference on Computer and Robot Vision, pp. 106–112 (2013)
2. Goyette, N., Jodoin, P.M., Porikli, F., Konrad, J., Ishwar, P.: Changedetection.net: a new change detection benchmark dataset. In: IEEE Computer Society Conference on Computer Vision and Pattern Recognition Workshops, pp. 1–8. IEEE (2012)
3. Heikkila, M., Pietikäinen, M.: A texture-based method for modeling the background and detecting moving objects. IEEE Trans. Pattern Anal. Mach. Intell. **28**(4), 657–662 (2006)
4. Hofmann, M., Tiefenbacher, P., Rigoll, G.: Background segmentation with feedback: the pixel-based adaptive segmenter. In: 2012 IEEE Computer Society Conference on Computer Vision and Pattern Recognition Workshops (CVPRW), pp. 38–43. IEEE (2012)
5. Kim, J., Ramírez Rivera, A., Ryu, B., Chae, O.: Simultaneous foreground detection and classification with hybrid features. In: Proceedings of the IEEE International Conference on Computer Vision, pp. 3307–3315 (2015)
6. Arefin, M.R., Makhmudkhujaev, F., Chae, O., Kim, J.: Background subtraction based on fusion of color and local patterns. In: Jawahar, C.V., Li, H., Mori, G., Schindler, K. (eds.) ACCV 2018. LNCS, vol. 11366, pp. 214–230. Springer, Cham (2019). https://doi.org/10.1007/978-3-030-20876-9_14
7. Murshed, M., Ramírez Rivera, A., Chae, O.: Statistical background modeling: an edge segment based moving object detection approach. In: 2010 7th IEEE International Conference on Advanced Video and Signal Based Surveillance, pp. 300–306. IEEE (2010)
8. Ramírez Rivera, A., Murshed, M., Kim, J., Chae, O.: Background modeling through statistical edge-segment distributions. IEEE Trans. Circ. Syst. Video Technol. **23**(8), 1375–1387 (2013)
9. St-Charles, P.L., Bilodeau, G.A.: Improving background subtraction using local binary similarity patterns. In: IEEE Winter Conference on Applications of Computer Vision, pp. 509–515. IEEE (2014)
10. St-Charles, P.L., Bilodeau, G.A., Bergevin, R.: SuBSENSE: a universal change detection method with local adaptive sensitivity. IEEE Trans. Image Process. **24**(1), 359–373 (2015)
11. Stauffer, C., Grimson, W.E.L.: Adaptive background mixture models for real-time tracking. In: IEEE Computer Society Conference on Computer Vision and Pattern Recognition, vol. 2, pp. 246–252. IEEE (1999)
12. Wang, H., Suter, D.: A consensus-based method for tracking: modelling background scenario and foreground appearance. Pattern Recogn. **40**(3), 1091–1105 (2006)

Fast Object Localization via Sensitivity Analysis

Mohammad K. Ebrahimpour$^{(\boxtimes)}$ and David C. Noelle

EECS, University of California, Merced, USA
{mebrahimpour,dnoelle}@ucmerced.edu

Abstract. Deep Convolutional Neural Networks (CNNs) have been repeatedly shown to perform well on image classification tasks, successfully recognizing a broad array of objects when given sufficient training data. Methods for object localization, however, are still in need of substantial improvement. In this paper, we offer a fundamentally different approach to the localization of recognized objects in images. Our method is predicated on the idea that a deep CNN capable of recognizing an object must implicitly contain knowledge about object location in its connection weights. We provide a simple method to interpret classifier weights in the context of individual classified images. This method involves the calculation of the derivative of network generated activation patterns, such as the activation of output class label units, with regard to each input pixel, performing a sensitivity analysis that identifies the pixels that, in a local sense, have the greatest influence on internal representations and object recognition. These derivatives can be efficiently computed using a single backward pass through the deep CNN classifier, producing a *sensitivity map* of the image. We demonstrate that a simple linear mapping can be learned from sensitivity maps to bounding box coordinates, localizing the recognized object. Our experimental results, using real-world data sets for which ground truth localization information is known, reveal competitive accuracy from our fast technique.

Keywords: Object localization · Sensitivity analysis · Neural networks

1 Introduction

Deep Convolutional Neural Networks (CNNs) have been shown to be effective at image classification, accurately performing object recognition even with thousands of object classes when trained on a sufficiently rich data set of labeled images [11]. One advantage of CNNs is their ability to learn complete functional mappings from image pixels to object categories, without any need for the extraction of hand-engineered image features [17]. To facilitate learning through stochastic gradient descent, CNNs are (at least approximately) differentiable with regard to connection weight parameters.

Image classification, however, is only one of the problems of computer vision. In the task of image classification, each image has a single label, associated with

© Springer Nature Switzerland AG 2019
G. Bebis et al. (Eds.): ISVC 2019, LNCS 11845, pp. 209–220, 2019.
https://doi.org/10.1007/978-3-030-33723-0_17

Fig. 1. Examples of sensitivity maps, displaying the sensitivity of network internal representations to individual pixels, providing information about the locations of the main objects in the source images.

the class identity of the main object in the image, and the goal is to assign correct labels in a manner that generalizes to novel images. This can be accomplished by training a machine learning classifier, such as a CNN, on a large data set of labeled images [4]. In the object localization task, in comparison, the output for a given image is not a class label but the locations of a specified number of objects in the image, usually encoded as bounding boxes. Evaluation of an object localization system generally requires ground truth bounding boxes to compare to the system's output. The object detection task is more difficult than the localization task, as the number of objects is not predetermined [17].

In this paper, we focus on object localization, identifying the position in the image of a recognized object. As is common in the localization literature, position information is output in the form of a bounding box. Previously developed techniques for accomplishing this task generally involve searching the image for the object, considering many candidate bounding boxes with different sizes and locations, sometimes guided by an auxiliary algorithm for heuristically identifying regions of interest [8,10,17]. For each candidate location, the sub-image captured by the bounding box is classified for object category, with the final output bounding box either being the specific candidate region classified as the target object with the highest level of certainty or some heuristic combination of neighboring or overlapping candidate regions with high classification certainty. These approaches tend to be time consuming, often requiring deep CNN classification calculations of many candidate regions at multiple scales. Efforts to speed these methods mostly focus on reducing the number of regions considered, typically by using some heuristic region proposal algorithm [8,10,14].

A noteworthy alternative approach is to directly train a deep CNN to produce outputs that match ground truth localization bounding boxes, using a large image data set that provides both category and localization information for each image. It appears as if some form of this method was used with AlexNet [11], though details concerning localization, rather than image classification, are difficult to discern from the published literature. A natural approach would be to cast the learning of bounding boxes as a simple regression problem, with targets being the four coordinates that specify a bounding box (e.g., coordinates of upper-left and lower-right corners, or region center coordinates along with region width and height). It is reasonable to consider sharing early layers of a deep CNN, such as those performing convolution and max pooling, between both an image classification network and an object localization network. Indeed, taking such a multitask learning approach [2] can allow for both object category and object location training data to shape connection weights throughout the network. Thus, the deep CNN would have "two heads", one for image classification, using a classification cross-entropy loss function, and one for object localization, reducing the ℓ_2 norm between ground truth and predicted bounding box coordinates [11]. While this approach can produce a network that quickly outputs location information, extensive training on large data sets containing ground truth bounding box information is necessary to produce good generalization.

In this paper, we introduce an approach to object localization that is both very fast and robust in the face of limited ground truth bounding box training data. This approach is rooted in the assertion that any deep CNN for image classification must contain, implicit in its connection weights, knowledge about the location of recognized objects [16]. The goal, then, is to interpret the flow of activation in an object recognition network when it is performing image classification so as to extract information about object location. Furthermore, the goal is to do this quickly. Thus, this approach aims to leverage location knowledge that is already latent in extensively trained and tuned image classification networks, without requiring an additional complex learning process for localization.

Our method makes use of the notion of a *sensitivity analysis* [21]. We propose estimating the sensitivity of the category outputs, or activation patterns at internal network layers, of an image classification CNN to variance in each input pixel, given a specific input image. The result is a numeric value for each pixel in the input image that captures the degree to which small changes in that pixel (locally, around its current value) give rise to large changes in the output category. Together, these numeric values form a *sensitivity map* of the image, encoding image regions that are important for the current classification. Our proposed measure of sensitivity is the partial derivative of activity with regard to each pixel value, evaluated for the current image. For a deep CNN that formally embodies a differentiable mapping (at least approximately) from image pixels to output categories, this partial derivative can be quickly calculated. While many tools currently exist for efficiently calculating such derivatives, we provide a simple algorithm that computes these values through a single backward pass through the image classification network, similar to that used to calculate unit error (delta) values in the *backpropagation of error* learning algorithm [15]. Thus, we can generate a sensitivity map for an image in about the same amount of time as it takes the employed image classification network to produce an output. Some example sensitivity maps are shown in Fig. 1.

The idea of using sensitivity information, like that in our sensitivity maps, for a variety of tasks, including localization, has previously appeared in the literature [16,19,23]. Indeed, some of these past efforts have used more sophisticated measures of sensitivity. In this paper, we show that even our very simple sensitivity measure can produce strong localization performance, and it can do so quickly, without any modifications to the classification network, and even for object categories on which the classification network was not trained. The relationship of the results reported here to previously reported work is discussed further in Sect. 4.

As previously mentioned, object localization methods typically encode object location as a bounding box. Since our sensitivity maps encode location differently, in terms of pixels, we propose learning a simple linear mapping from sensitivity maps to bounding box coordinates, allowing our method to output a bounding box for each classified image. We suggest that this linear mapping can be robustly learned from a relatively small training set of images with ground truth bounding boxes, since the sensitivity maps form a much more simple input than the original images.

The primary contributions of this paper may be summarized as follows:

- We propose a new general approach to performing object localization, interpreting a previously trained image classification network by performing a sensitivity analysis, identifying pixels to which the category output, or a more general internal representation, is particularly sensitive.
- We demonstrate how a linear function from the resulting sensitivity maps to object location bounding box coordinates may be learned from relatively small set of training images containing ground truth location information.
- We provide a preliminary assessment of our approach, measuring object localization performance on the ImageNet and PASCAL VOC data sets using the VGG16 image classification CNN, showing strong accuracy while maintaining short computation times.

2   Method

Calculating Pixel Sensitivities in a Trained CNN. Calculating derivatives of a function of network output with regard to network parameters, such as connection weights, is a standard part of CNN training. It is common for learning in a deep CNN to involve stochastic gradient decent, which involves such derivatives. In that case, the derivatives are of an objective function with regard to connection weight values. In image classification networks, the objective function is designed to have optima where training images are correctly classified. In the case of object localization, a similar objective function could be designed to minimize differences between output bounding box coordinates and provided ground truth bounding box coordinates, for all images in an appropriately labeled training set. For example, given N training images, stored in the matrix $\mathbf{X}$, with the ground truth 4-dimensional bounding box vector for image x_i being y_i, and $G(x_i; \mathbf{w})$ being the CNN output vector for image x_i given connection weights $\mathbf{w}$, an appropriate loss function would be:

$$\ell(\mathbf{X}, \mathbf{w}) = \frac{1}{N} \sum_{i=1}^{N} \|y_i - G(x_i; \mathbf{w})\|_2^2 \qquad (1)$$

The CNN will produce good estimates of the training image bounding boxes when this loss function is minimized with regard to $\mathbf{w}$. Network weight parameters that minimize this loss, $\mathbf{w}^*$, may be sought through stochastic gradient decent, incrementally updating $\mathbf{w}$ according to the gradient of $\ell(\mathbf{X}, \mathbf{w})$ with regard to $\mathbf{w}$. A primary drawback of this approach is that it requires a large and representative sample of images with ground truth bounding box information.

Consider that, once weights are found, the gradient of $\ell(\mathbf{X}, \mathbf{w}^*)$ with regard to $\mathbf{X}$ would provide information about the sensitivity of the bounding box loss function with regard to the pixels in the images. This gradient can be calculated as efficiently as the gradient of the loss with regard to the weights, with both depending on the gradient of $G(x_i; \mathbf{w})$ with regard to a subset of its arguments. This means that the gradient of $G(x_i; \mathbf{w}^*)$ with regard to x_i can be efficiently computed, and that gradient would capture the sensitivity of bounding box coordinates with regard to the specific pixels in image x_i. Note that this gradient can be calculated for images beyond those in the training set. Knowing which pixels in a novel image play an important role in determining the bounding box provides useful information for object localization. Using this calculation to address the object localization task makes little sense, however, as $G(x_i; \mathbf{w}^*)$ provides an estimate of object location without a need to consider pixel sensitivity.

Rather than training a deep CNN to output bounding boxes, requiring extensive labeled data, we propose calculating the same gradient for a different network – one successfully trained to perform image classification. If we now see $G(x_i; \mathbf{w}^*)$ as the output of such an image classification network, its gradient with regard to x_i would provide information about the sensitivity of the assigned category to individual pixels. Pixels with the largest absolute values of this derivative will, around the input x_i, produce the largest changes in the classification decision of the CNN. This can be seen as one measure of how important pixels are for classifying the object in the image. Consider that the object class output is not immediately affected by changes to pixels with a derivative of zero.

The calculation of this gradient can be performed as efficiently as a single "backward pass" through the classification network. This is well illustrated by considering the case of a simple layered backpropagation network [15] in which the "net input" of unit i, η_i, is a weighted sum of the activations of units in the previous layer, and the activation of unit i is $g(\eta_i)$, where $g(\cdot)$ is the unit activation function. In this case, we can define a sensitivity value for each unit, s_i, as the derivative of the network output with regard to η_i. Using the chain rule of calculus, it is easy to show that the sensitivity of an output unit is $g'(\eta i)$, and, for units in earlier layers the gradients are computed as follows:

$$s_i = g'(\eta_i) \sum_k w_{ki} \, s_k \tag{2}$$

where k iterates over all units in the immediately downstream layer from unit i and $\mathbf{w}_{ki}$ is the connection weight from unit i to unit k. This calculation may be performed, layer by layer, from outputs to inputs, until s_i values for each pixel input unit are available.

This demonstrates how efficiently pixel sensitivity values can be calculated for a given classified image. Of course, there are currently a variety of software packages that include tools for calculating gradients. In the evaluation of our approach in Sect. 3, we report results using the tools provided by TensorFlow [1].

Sensitivity of the Attention Map. We have proposed using a previously trained image classification network as a source of information about object location, focusing on the gradient of the network output with regard to image pixels. It is interesting to note that it might not be necessary to perform the sensitivity calculation using the full classification network. There is a growing body of research that suggests that, in a well trained image classification CNN, the features that are extracted at the "attention map" layer (i.e., the output of the last convolutional layer) tend to be generally useful for learning a variety of image analysis tasks [5,13]. Inspired by these results, we have investigated the possibility of substituting the gradient of the classifier output with regard to pixels with the gradient of the attention map with regard to pixels. This avoids calculations involving final fully connected layers and any classification softmax layer. Generating image sensitivity maps from the attention map layer is slightly faster than our original proposal, but, more importantly, it is possible that general knowledge about object location might be found in the attention map, and using the attention map as the basis of the sensitivity map might actually generalize beyond the categories on which the image classification CNN was trained. We have not yet done a formal comparison of these two approaches to constructing the sensitivity map, but example results using both approaches are reported in Sect. 3. When computing these gradients, we refer to the aggregated values of the last convolutional layer as the Gestalt Total, which is computed as follows [6].

$$GT = \frac{1}{H \times W \times C} \sum_{i,j,k} A_n(i,j,k) \tag{3}$$

where A_n is the activation map of the last convolution layer.

Aggregating Across Color Channels. The sensitivity map calculations that have been described, so far, provide a scalar sensitivity value for each *input* to the image classification deep CNN. Color images, however, are regularly provided to such networks using multiple inputs per image pixel, often encoding each pixel over three color channels. Thus, the gradient calculation will actually produce three sensitivity values for each pixel. Since we hope to produce a sensitivity map that focuses in a general way on location information, it seems reasonable to aggregate the three sensitivity values into one. Since the direction of the sensitivity relationship with the class output is irrelevant, a good first step is to take the absolute value of each derivative. Given that dependence on even a single color channel suggests that a pixel is important for identifying the object, an argument can be made that a pixel should be labeled with the maximum of the three absolute derivatives. Alternatively, it could be argued that all color channels should be taken into account when producing the sensitivity map, in which case it might be better to average the three absolute derivatives. We have explored both of these aggregation methods, with results appearing in Sect. 3.

Learning to Produce Bounding Boxes. Object localization algorithms typically output the four coordinates of a bounding box to communicate the location of the target object. Such a bounding box is not intrinsic to a sensitivity map, however. Heuristic techniques could be used to identify a rectangular region that captures the majority of the high sensitivity pixels, while avoiding low sensitivity pixels, but we have taken a different approach. We have opted to learn a linear mapping from sensitivity maps to bounding box coordinates, using training images with ground truth location information.

It is important to note that learning this mapping is not the same as learning to map from the original images to bounding box coordinates, as has been done in some other object localization systems. Sensitivity maps contain much less information than the original images, so using the sensitivity maps as inputs both reduces the dimensionality of the input to this mapping and makes for a more simple functional relationship between pixels and bounding box coordinates. We expect that this simplification will allow the mapping to bounding box coordinates to be successfully learned using a far smaller set of training images labeled with ground truth object locations. Indeed, we expect that a simple linear mapping could perform well.

Formally, we define the parameters of the linear mapping to the four bounding box coordinates as a $4 \times M$ matrix, $\hat{W}$, (where M is the number of pixels in an image) and a 4-dimensional vector of "bias weights", $\hat{w}$. Given a sensitivity map, s, the output is $(\hat{W}s + \hat{w})$. Given a training set of N images, the mapping is found by minimizing the following objective function with regard to $\hat{W}$ and $\hat{w}$:

$$\frac{1}{N} \sum_{i=1}^{N} \frac{1}{4} \sum_{j=1}^{4} \|B_{i,j} - (\hat{W}s_i + \hat{w})\|_2^2 \qquad (4)$$

where s_i is the sensitivity map for the ith image, and $B_{i,j}$ is the jth coordinate of the bounding box for the ith image. This learning process amounts to four independent linear regression problems, which can be solved efficiently.

Once learned, mapping from sensitivity maps to bounding box coordinates can be done very quickly. With sensitivity map formation requiring only a single backward pass through the image classification network, the whole process – from image, to classification, to sensitivity map, to bounding box – can be performed in little more than twice the time it takes for the network to do object recognition.

3   Results

The code and the sensitivity maps for the ImageNet and PASCAL VOC datasets will be publicly available.

Data Sets and Performance Measures. We evaluated our proposed method for object localization on two challenging data sets: the PASCAL VOC 2007 [7] data set and the ImageNet 2012 [4] data set. The PASCAL VOC 2007 data set was selected due to its use in the existing object localization literature. The ImageNet data set is one of the largest publicly available data sets. It also contains many images annotated with ground truth bounding boxes.

We followed the literature with regard to the evaluation criterion applied to our method, using *CorLoc*, which has been used for weakly supervised localization. The CorLoc metric is defined as the percentage of images in a data set that are correctly localized based on the PASCAL criterion, in which a given localization is considered correct if and only if the *intersection over union (IOU)* area of the predicted and ground truth bounding boxes is greater than one half:

$$IOU = \frac{area(\beta_p \cap \beta_{gt})}{area(\beta_p \cup \beta_{gt})} > 0.5 \tag{5}$$

... where β_p is the predicted bounding box and β_{gt} is the ground truth bounding box [22].

Pre-trained Image Classification Deep CNN. To demonstrate that our approach works with an image classification deep CNN that was in no way specialized for our localization method, we opted to use a publicly available VGG16 network. This network provides ImageNet object classes as output, allowing us to calculate sensitivity maps based on the network classification when examining ImageNet data. For the PASCAL VOC 2007 data set, we used the previously described method of calculating derivatives based on the attention map of VGG16, since there is not consistent class correspondence between the PASCAL VOC 2007 classes and the classes on which VGG16 was trained. To produce sensitivity maps for the PASCAL VOC 2007 data set, we aggregated across color channels by using the maximum absolute derivative across the three inputs for each pixel. For the ImageNet data set, we averaged the absolute derivatives across the three inputs in order to produce pixel sensitivity values.

For generating sensitivity maps, we have used a pretrained VGG 16 network, and we have used the whole network architecture while we were experimenting on the ImageNet dataset, otherwise we have removed the last 3 fully connected layers and computed the Gestalt Total at the last convolution layer. The derivatives in either case were computed using just one backward pass to the original pixels. For learning bounding boxes we have used the aggregated sensitivity maps as an input. To learn the mapping from sensitivity maps to bounding box coordinates, we performed linear regression using stochastic gradient decent. Updates were performed in batches of 2,048. The learning rate was initialized to 0.1 and decayed by a factor of 10 every 10,000 iterations. The experiment was run on 1 GPU for 4 days.

Performance on PASCAL VOC 2007. The full PASCAL VOC 2007 data set includes 12,608 training set images and an equal number of testing set images [7]. Each image contains an object of 1 of 20 different categories. We applied our object localization method to this full data set. Table 1 compares the localization performance of our method with that of other approaches. Note that our method, while being very fast, outperforms the comparison algorithms.

Fig. 2. Results of the proposed method on the first 10 classes of PASCAL VOC 2007. The green boxes are the ground truth, and the red ones are the predicted bounding boxes. (Color figure online)

Examples of the bounding boxes selected by our method, compared to ground truth, for all 20 classes in the PASCAL VOC 2007 data set are shown in Fig. 2. Qualitatively, it appears as if our approach is most accurate when there is a single target object with little crowding. However, if the target object is small and in a crowded region of the image, performance is less reliable.

Several of the comparison methods display better localization performance than our approach for some classes, but it is important to keep in mind that the comparison cases had some important advantages, including taking the time to use a sliding window and access to the class labels on which the network was trained. Recall that our sensitivity maps were produced, in this case, by calculating the sensitivity of the network attention map activity to pixel values. Thus, this comparison illustrates trade-offs between speed, performance, and generalization. To illustrate that sensitivity maps can be used without learning a linear mapping from the maps to bounding box coordinates, we also examined a heuristic method for producing bounding boxes from maps. We used a Gaussian smoothing filter to smooth out the sensitivity maps, and then we picked up the top 20% of the pixels, heuristically drawing the bounding box so as to surround those pixels, as other researchers have done before [16,23]. We noticed that this heuristic approach could damage the mean CorLoc by 3% in our best observations. However, this process highly depends on the smoothing parameter σ. The obtained results from different σ values are reported in Table 2.

Performance on ImageNet. ImageNet is a large image data set that has been systematically organized by object category [4]. We executed a large scale evaluation of our approach by using all images in ImageNet that are annotated with ground truth localization information. This subset contains 300,916 images

Table 1. PASCAL VOC 2007 test detection results. The proposed method performed favorably against state of the art methods.

Method	MeanCL	areo	bike	bird	boat	bottle	bus	car	cat	chair	cow	table	dog	horse	mbike	person	plant	sheep	sofa	train	tv
[20]	30.2	45.8	21.8	30.9	20.4	5.3	37.6	40.8	51.6	7.0	29.8	27.5	41.3	41.8	47.3	24.1	12.2	28.1	32.8	48.7	9.4
[18]	36.2	67.3	54.4	34.3	17.8	1.3	46.6	60.7	68.9	2.5	32.4	16.2	58.9	51.5	64.6	18.2	3.1	20.9	34.7	63.4	5.9
[9]	38.8	56.6	58.3	28.4	20.7	6.8	54.9	69.1	20.8	9.2	50.5	10.2	29.0	58.0	64.9	36.7	18.7	56.5	13.2	54.9	59.4
OM [12]	31.8	50.4	30	34.6	18.2	6.2	39.3	42.2	57.3	10.8	29.8	20.5	41.8	43.2	51.8	24.7	20.8	29.2	26.6	45.6	12.5
PBRM [3]	36.6	50.3	42.8	30.0	18.5	4.0	62.3	64.5	42.5	8.6	49.0	12.2	44.0	64.1	57.2	15.3	9.4	30.9	34.0	61.6	31.5
Sensitivity Maps	40.1	63.8	55.1	41.2	23.3	34.2	58.6	72.7	36.9	23.3	49.7	11.5	29.6	50.1	65.9	11.8	42.2	39.7	18.1	51.0	41.2

Table 2. Average CorLoc Performance on Pascal VOC 2007 using the heuristic bounding box (σ is the smoothing parameter.)

σ	CorLoc
10	27.2%
20	38.4%
30	32.5%

involving 478 object classes. We divided this data set into a training set, a test set, and a validation set by sampling without replacement (i.e., the intersection between each pair of the three sets was empty). There were 225,687 images (75%) in the training set, and there were 45,137 images in each of the other two sets.

We compared the performance of our approach with two methods discussed in Tang et al. [22] for which ImageNet results are explicitly reported: Top Objectiveness Box & Co-Localization. Also, we noted that many images in this data set presented the target object in the middle of the image, providing a bias that could be leveraged by learned localization systems. Thus, as a baseline of performance, we calculated the CorLoc performance for a system that blindly offered the same bounding box in the middle of the image, with average size, for every input. The results are shown in Table 3. Once again, note the relatively high accuracy performance of our efficient method. Also note that the baseline was comfortingly low. As might be expected, performance varies with class. Our algorithm appears to do well on some objects, such as balls and dogs. One might suspect that failures arise in the linear mapping from sensitivity maps to bounding box coordinates, but a perusal of the sensitivity maps, themselves, suggests that the pixel sensitivity values vary in utility across different object categories. Still, our method performs fairly well across the classes. Note that the IOU did not fall below 0.62 for any class. This suggests that, while some individual images may be problematic, the overall performance for each class is quite good. This universally strong class-specific performance is also displayed in Table 3.

The sensitivity analysis approach gives us the sensitivity of single pixels in all channels in the RGB images. Since we are in need of locations, we need to aggregate among channels. We proposed two methods, an average function, and a maximum function. The first approach calculates the sensitivity as the average

Table 3. CorLoc Performance on ImageNet (478 Classes)

Method	Average CorLoc
Constant Center Box Baseline	12.34%
Top Objectiveness Box	37.42%
Co-Localization	53.20%
Sensitivity Maps	**68.76%**

among channels, and the second method uses the maximum absolute derivatives among channels. We didn't notice a significant difference between these two methods in localization performance. The only insight is that generating sensitivity maps based on the average function is a bit smoother in a visual sense than the maximum function. The CorLoc between average and maximum aggregation functions on the ImageNet dataset are 68.7 and 67.9 respectively, and the results for these two aggregation operators on the PASCAL VOC dataset is 39.2 and 40.1, respectively.

4   Conclusion

We have presented an approach to object localization based on performing a sensitivity analysis of a previously trained image classification deep CNN. Our method is fast enough to be used in online applications, and it demonstrates accuracy that is superior to some methods that are much slower. It is likely that even better accuracy could be had by incorporating sensitivity analysis information into a more sophisticated bounding box estimator.

As previously noted, the idea of using sensitivity information has appeared in previously published work. There are ways in which the results reported in this paper are distinct, however. We have moved beyond visualization of the network function using sensitivity (or *saliency*) [19] to performing direct comparisons between different methods on the localization task. We have shown that using a fast and simple measure of sensitivity can produce comparable performance to that of much slower methods. Our approach produces good generalization without modifying the classification network, as is done in *Class Activation Mapping (CAM)* [23]. With our PASCAL VOC 2007 results, we have shown that our approach can successfully be applied to attention maps, even when the image contains objects belonging to a class on which the classification network was not trained, distinguishing it from *Grad-CAM* [16]. In short, we have demonstrated the power of a simple sensitivity measure for performing localization.

Note that our approach may be used with image classifiers other than CNNs. The proposed sensitivity analysis can be conducted on any differentiable classifier, though performance will likely depend on classifier specifics. Indeed, at a substantial time cost, even a black box classifier could be approximately analyzed by making small changes to pixels and observing the effects on activation patterns.

References

1. Abadi, M., et al.: TensorFlow: large-scale machine learning on heterogeneous systems (2015). Software available from tensorflow.org
2. Caruana, R.: Multitask learning. Mach. Learn. **28**, 41–75 (1997)
3. Cho, M., Kwak, S., Schmid, C., Ponce, J.: Unsupervised object discovery and localization in the wild: part-based matching with bottom-up region proposals. In: CVPR (2015)

4. Deng, J., Dong, W., Socher, R., Li, L.J., Li, K., Fei-Fei, L.: ImageNet: a large-scale hierarchical image database. In: CVPR. IEEE (2009)
5. Donahue, J., et al.: DeCAF: a deep convolutional activation feature for generic visual recognition. In: ICML (2014)
6. Ebrahimpour, M.K., et al.: Ventral-dorsal neural networks: object detection via selective attention. In: WACV, pp. 986–994 (2019)
7. Everingham, M., Van Gool, L., Williams, C.K.I., Winn, J., Zisserman, A.: The PASCAL visual object classes challenge 2007 (VOC 2007) results (2008)
8. Girshick, R.: Fast R-CNN. In: CVPR (2015)
9. Gokberk Cinbis, R., Verbeek, J., Schmid, C.: Multi-fold mil training for weakly supervised object localization. In: CVPR (2014)
10. He, K., Gkioxari, G., Dollár, P., Girshick, R.: Mask R-CNN. In: CVPR (2017)
11. Krizhevsky, A., Sutskever, I., Hinton, G.E.: ImageNet classification with deep convolutional neural networks. In: NIPS (2012)
12. Li, D., Huang, J.B., Li, Y., Wang, S., Yang, M.H.: Weakly supervised object localization with progressive domain adaptation. In: CVPR (2016)
13. Razavian, A.S., Azizpour, H., Sullivan, J., Carlsson, S.: CNN features off-the-shelf: an astounding baseline for recognition. In: CVPR (2014)
14. Ren, S., He, K., Girshick, R., Sun, J.: Faster R-CNN: towards real-time object detection with region proposal networks. In: NIPS (2015)
15. Rumelhart, D.E., Hinton, G.E., Williams, R.J.: Learning representations by back-propagating errors. Nature **323**, 533–536 (1986)
16. Selvaraju, R.R., Cogswell, M., Das, A., Vedantam, R., Parikh, D., Batra, D.: Grad-CAM: visual explanations from deep networks via gradient-based localization. See https://arxiv.org/abs/1610.02391 v3 7(8) (2016)
17. Sermanet, P., Eigen, D., Zhang, X., Mathieu, M., Fergus, R., LeCun, Y.: OverFeat: integrated recognition, localization and detection using convolutional networks. arXiv:1312.6229 (2013)
18. Shi, Z., Hospedales, T.M., Xiang, T.: Bayesian joint topic modelling for weakly supervised object localisation. In: CVPR (2013)
19. Simonyan, K., Vedaldi, A., Zisserman, A.: Deep inside convolutional networks: visualising image classification models and saliency maps. arXiv preprint: arXiv:1312.6034 (2013)
20. Siva, P., Russell, C., Xiang, T.: In defence of negative mining for annotating weakly labelled data. In: Fitzgibbon, A., Lazebnik, S., Perona, P., Sato, Y., Schmid, C. (eds.) ECCV 2012, Part III. LNCS, vol. 7574, pp. 594–608. Springer, Heidelberg (2012). https://doi.org/10.1007/978-3-642-33712-3_43
21. Sobol, I.: Sensitivity estimates for nonlinear mathematical models. Math. Model. Comput. Exp. **1**(4), 407–414 (1993)
22. Tang, K., Joulin, A., Li, L.J., Fei-Fei, L.: Co-localization in real-world images. In: CVPR (2014)
23. Zhou, B., Khosla, A., Lapedriza, A., Oliva, A., Torralba, A.: Learning deep features for discriminative localization. In: CVPR (2016)

On the Salience of Adversarial Examples

Amanda Fernandez[(⊠)]

Department of Computer Science,
University of Texas at San Antonio (UTSA), San Antonio, USA
amanda.fernandez@utsa.edu

Abstract. Adversarial examples are beginning to evolve as rapidly as the deep learning models they are designed to attack. These intentionally-manipulated inputs attempt to mislead the targeted model while maintaining the appearance of innocuous input data. Countermeasures against these attacks that take a global approach tend to be lossy to the original data, or ineffective in removing the perturbations. Localized approaches have proven effective, however it is difficult to identify affected areas in the data in order to apply a targeted cleaning algorithm. For image data, visual saliency estimation models identify important features in an image, and provide a targeting mechanism for countering adversarial examples. In this work, we examine the effectiveness of state-of-the-art saliency models on complex scenes, in their original and perturbed forms. In a thorough range of standard metrics, we compare performance on clean image data with adversarial examples to demonstrate the vulnerability of deep learning-based saliency models to adversarial examples.

Keywords: Adversarial examples · Visual saliency · Image processing · Deep learning

1 Introduction

As machine learning models increase in popularity, malicious inputs in the form of adversarial examples are also on the rise. Attacks have caused models to misclassify images [16], misinterpret audio [33], and misidentify network intrusions as benign normal activity [41]. Similar attacks are demonstrable even in the real-world, by printing adversarial images as a physical prop in order to, for example, reduce the effectiveness of security cameras for face recognition [36], or alter the way an autonomous vehicle interprets traffic signs [11].

The goals of these attacks vary, generally categorized as white-, gray-, or black- box attacks depending on their level of access and prior knowledge of the targeted learning system. With direct access to a learning model, and/or critical information regarding its training data or a popular backbone model, attacks can be efficient and effective. However most of the most recent examples identified above are black-box attacks, those without direct access to this information.

© Springer Nature Switzerland AG 2019
G. Bebis et al. (Eds.): ISVC 2019, LNCS 11845, pp. 221–232, 2019.
https://doi.org/10.1007/978-3-030-33723-0_18

In order to evade further detection, adversarial examples additionally aim to visually resemble the original data as closely as possible. Perturbation algorithms such as fast gradient sign method (FGSM) [15], iterative FGSM (I-FGSM) [21], DeepFool [27], and CWL2 [5] generate noise which can be slight enough to be imperceptible. Countermeasures to these attacks must reduce the affected areas of an image without further altering the underlying content. Approaches that are focused globally across an image, such as jpeg compression and bit-depth reduction, alter the data globally and increase the potential for loss [17]. Localized approaches such as image quilting and SHIELD [8] focus on uniform patches within an image to apply a compression or similar technique to reduce the perturbations. For a more targeted approach to localization, visual saliency models have been leveraged as mechanisms against adversarial examples. When salient regions of an image are identified, the countermeasures against attacks can be applied in specific and relevant regions [23,26].

However, solutions are predicated on the assumption that the saliency estimation models are unaffected by the perturbations. The main contributions of this work include: (i) examination of the effects of perturbations on state-of-the-art saliency algorithms, both traditional and deep learning models; (ii) identification of conditions for decreased performance of saliency algorithms on adversarial examples.

The following section identifies in detail a range of existing approaches for estimating visual salience, and applies several to adversarial examples. The subsequent sections set up and evaluate a series of experiments to better understand the impact of these examples on the performance of saliency models, across two challenging real-world datasets.

2   Modeling Visual Salience

Visual saliency estimation models emulate the attention mechanisms in the human visual system, identifying low-level features as in the early visual system, as well as higher-level features further on [7]. These models similarly take after fundamental stages in our visual system: pre-attentive (stimulus-driven) and attentive (task-driven).

Image processing and machine learning approaches to modeling salience may require some feature selection by hand. The top-down models are task-driven, performing well when there will be particular known salient objects in both training and testing [18]. The bottom-up models are stimulus-driven, with a challenging goal of identifying salient or important data without a given task. A global approach to bottom-up models developed by Cheng et al. [6] is based upon contrast, for example. Improvements to bottom-up methods have combined local and global approaches, to identify salient regions at multiple scales [1,34].

In this work, the bottom-up model proposed by Erdem et al. [10] is leveraged in comparison with other categories of salience models. In this model, a localized patch-based approach identifies salient regions of an image. The saliency S of a patch p within an image is determined by the distance d' from that patch p to all others, defined as:

$$S(p_i) = \frac{1}{m} \sum_{j=1}^{M} d'(p_i, p_j) \tag{1}$$

Where p_i and p_j are patches centered at pixels i and j respectively, and the distance metric d' is defined in terms of the feature vectors $\Psi(c)$:

$$d'(p_i, p_j) = \frac{||\Psi(c_i) - \Psi(c_j)||}{1 + ||x_i - x_j||}$$

In another category of salience estimation, context-awareness in models leverages prior knowledge of some (potentially unrelated) domain of data in order to provide some previously understood context to new stimuli [14,19]. Fusion models take advantage of context awareness for stimulus-driven tasks, noting that prior context does not guarantee performance (i.e. models trained on character recognition data are not improved for complex scene analysis). This work leverages a model proposed by Danko et al. [7] which combines both a pre-attentive approach and some prior context in order to improve patch-based modelling:

$$S(p_i) = \frac{1}{m} \sum_{j=1}^{M} d'(p_i, p_j) + [1 - exp\{d''(p_i, p_j)\}] \tag{2}$$

The distance function d'' between these patches is defined as follows [14]:

$$d''(p_i, p_j) = \frac{d_{color}(p_i, p_j)}{1 + c \cdot d_{position}(p_i, p_j)}$$

More recently, deep learning models provide the advantage of feature engineering, and are increasingly robust to real-world data. Visual salience estimation models built on generative adversarial networks employ two or more neural networks to generate salience maps and continuously improve results [13,28]. Context-aware deep learning models aim to identify salient data in the conditions which it appears [44]. These deep models consist of two parts, a predictive module and a refinement module [24,25]. Its prediction module is an Encoder-Decoder [35] for both low-level and high-level feature extraction. The second module is largely similar to the first, a simpler residual refinement module (RRM) often employed for boundary refinement [31]. In contrast, a recent cascaded partial decoder (CPD) [39] reduces the lower-level features and instead favors high-level features in an image, and a boundary-aware salient object detection network (BASNet) [32] emphasizes edges. Other recent approaches aim to refine the capabilities of convolutional and recurrent neural networks, such as the progressive attention guided recurrent network (PAGRN) [43] and aggregate multi-level convolutional features (Amulet) [42].

These approaches highlight the need for quality datasets, as ground truth saliency maps are required to quantitatively measure performance between models. Datasets with a focus on complex images such as ECSSD [37], SALICON [19], salient objects in clutter (SOC) [12], DUT-OMRON [40], HKU-IS [22], and others have established a challenge for new deep learning methods.

In this work, we compare deep learning approaches CPD [39] and BASNet [32] with earlier approaches by Erdem et al. [10] and Danko et al. [7], in an effort to demonstrate the effects of adversarial examples on both categories of models. In particular, we chose BASNet [32] and CPD [39] models as they have demonstrated improved results over other models identified here, on the same datasets. We implement these models with the ECSSD [37] and SALICON [19] images as a subset of the more popular and standard saliency estimation datasets for comparison.

2.1 Salience of Adversarial Examples

As an example of these diverse approaches, Fig. 1 illustrates visual results of related works in these categories of visual salience estimation. The top row is an original image, a given fixation map, and an adversarial example, which is almost visually indistinguishable from the original. Dataset details and adversarial example generation methods are discussed in the following section. The second row conveys the saliency maps generated on the original image using two deep learning models, BASNet [32] and CPD [39], as well as a bottom-up approach by Erdem et al. [10] and a fusion model by Danko et al. [7]. In contrast, the last row demonstrates the saliency maps from the adversarial example. In this example, only minor differences are visible in the salience maps generated before/after perturbation. The following sections examine further the extent to which this is true, and under which circumstances adversarial perturbation affects the accuracy of recent saliency estimation models.

3 Experiments and Results

In this section, the experimental setup is described first, including the data, algorithms, and metrics of evaluation used in this work. The subsequent section evaluates quantitative and qualitative results of these experiments.

3.1 Setup

Two popular image datasets were chosen for their difficulty for salience algorithms: ECSSD [37] and SALICON [19]. The Extended Complex Scene Saliency Dataset (ECSSD) [37] contains 1,000 complex real-world images and their corresponding ground truth masks. ECSSD was developed for more rigorous evaluation of saliency models on structurally complex images from the Internet. The binary ground truth masks were created in average by five participants.

The Saliency In Context (SALICON) Dataset [19], contains 15,000 images, and corresponding ground truth masks and fixations. In this work, 500 images were selected from the 15,000 in the SALICON dataset to evaluate models and

Fig. 1. Saliency maps on the SALICON dataset. Top row: original image, ground truth map, adversarial example (original perturbed by FGSM). Middle row: Saliency maps on the original image, from BASNet [32], CPD [39], fusion model [7], and bottom-up model [10]. Bottom row: Saliency maps from the same models on the perturbed image.

attacks. The corresponding ground truth maps and fixation data for these images is available, labeled by human participants.

The popular fast gradient sign method (FGSM) [15] was chosen as a means of adversarial example generation. This approach has been the basis for popular attacks and demonstrates improved performance over the Jacobian saliency map attack method (JSMA) [29,30]. In this approach, the adversarial example x_{adv} is calculated as the addition of perturbations to the original image x.

$$x_{adv} = x + \epsilon sign(\nabla_x L(\theta, x, y)) \tag{3}$$

Where y is the known label for the image, L is the loss function of the model under attack, and θ represents the parameters of the model. Keeping with the common and most popular components for learning models, the VGG16 [38] model was chosen as a backbone, pre-trained on ImageNet [9] data to create the adversarial examples in this work. Implementations for all models and evaluation in MATLAB and Python, using Keras, TensorFlow, and PyTorch libraries.

Metrics for evaluation in this work include the MIT Saliency Benchmark [3,4], encompassing area under the curve (AUC) [2,20], Pearsons Correlation Coefficient (CC), KL-divergence (KLD), normalized scanpath saliency (NSS), similarity score (SIM), and receiver operator characteristics (ROC). Statistical metrics for precision, recall, and confusion matrices are additionally included.

We implemented each of the four models previously identified and applied them to the ECSSD and SALICON datasets to generate saliency maps.

Adversarial examples were also generated from the images in both datasets, using the FGSM [15] method. Finally, saliency maps for all adversarial examples were generated, and all maps were evaluated against ground truth data.

3.2   Results and Discussion

In contrast to Fig. 1 in the previous section, Fig. 2 demonstrates an example of adversarial perturbation of an image interfering with the performance of saliency estimation. The first column of the figure includes the original image and the ground truth. The second column contains the saliency maps generated by BAS-Net [32] on the original (top) and adversarial (bottom) image. While the original map is almost identical to the ground truth, the map of the perturbed image includes other structures within the original image. The third column contains the saliency maps generated by CPD [39]. After perturbation of the image, the model is less confident in the salience of the boat, as noted in the bottom image. The final two columns contain saliency maps generated by a fusion model [7] and a bottom-up model [10] respectively. Both models take a local patch-based approach to saliency estimation, and the maps generated show more global interest. A blurring of features can be identified in both sets of maps between the original and perturbed images.

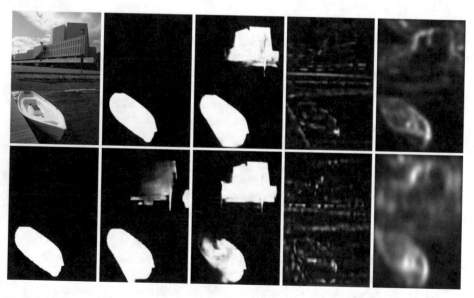

Fig. 2. Saliency maps on the ECSSD dataset. Top row: original image, saliency maps on this image generated by BASNet [32], CPD [39], fusion model [7], and bottom-up model [10]. Bottom row: ground truth fixation map, saliency maps generated on the perturbed image via the same estimation models.

Confusion matrices describe the performance of classification-type tasks, useful for identifying correctly and incorrectly labeled values. In the context of fixation maps, the confusion matrix identifies (in)correctly labeled pixels, compared with a ground truth. The following Figs. 3 and 4 show the performance of the visual saliency models on two datasets via confusion matrices. Ideally, the saliency models would score high values for the true positives and true negatives, and corresponding low values for false positives and false negatives.

In Fig. 3, each model shows relatively low false-positive scores and high true-negative scores. These values indicate the saliency methods tend to agree with the ground truth map on the background, or less salient regions in the image. The second row of this figure shows the confusion matrices for the perturbed image across all models. In this result, the largest change across all models is in the false negative values - there is an appreciable increase in the deep learning models. This increase in false negatives indicates a decrease in the confidence of the saliency model in the salient object within the image.

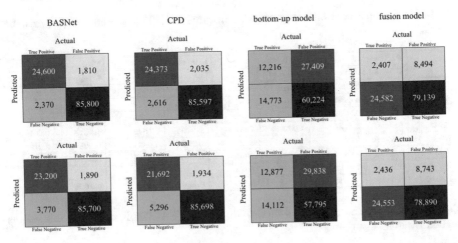

Fig. 3. Confusion matrices for models on ECSSD and perturbed image data.

Figure 4 contains similar confusion matrices for the SALICON dataset. With more intricate scenes in this dataset, the bottom-up saliency model had difficulty separating the background and resulted in a high number of false positives.

A comparison of each model on the original ECSSD data versus its performance on the perturbed images is shown in Table 1. On the original images, the deep learning models outperform across most metrics. However, these models were significantly impacted by the perturbations in the adversarial images. The distance metrics KL-divergence and normalized scanpath saliency indicated the largest difference in performance from these models.

Table 2 displays a similar comparison for all models on the SALICON dataset leveraged in this work. In this set of results, none of the four models were as significantly impacted by the adversarial perturbations as in the previous dataset.

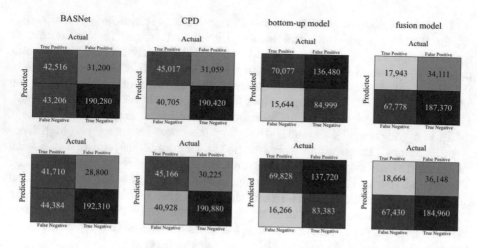

Fig. 4. Confusion matrices for models on SALICON and perturbed image data.

Table 1. Comparison of salience models on original ECSSD data and images perturbed by FGSM.

	BASNet [32]		CPD [39]		Bottom-up model [10]		Fusion model [7]	
	Original	Adversarial	Original	Adversarial	Original	Adversarial	Original	Adversarial
AUCB	**0.8454**	0.8250	0.8428	0.8067	0.5761	0.5777	0.5055	0.5054
AUCJ	**0.7388**	0.6964	0.7348	0.6532	0.0693	0.0718	0.1614	0.1614
CC	**0.9114**	0.8721	0.9053	0.8369	0.4033	0.4169	0.1449	0.1410
KLD	1.5295	2.5773	**1.1595**	2.7435	1.2129	1.1946	1.9578	1.9414
NSS	**1.9778**	1.8987	1.9674	1.8322	0.9622	0.9821	0.3282	0.3192
SIM	**0.8843**	0.8369	0.8747	0.7961	0.3805	0.3742	0.2670	0.2657
Precision	**0.9219**	0.9117	0.9103	0.9034	0.4276	0.4223	0.4162	0.4088
Recall	**0.9263**	0.8764	0.9245	0.8353	0.6301	0.6521	0.1600	0.1611

Table 2. Comparison of salience models on original SALICON data and images perturbed by FGSM.

	BASNet [32]		CPD [39]		Bottom-up model [10]		Fusion model [7]	
	Original	Adversarial	Original	Adversarial	Original	Adversarial	Original	Adversarial
AUCB	0.5650	0.5678	0.5756	**0.5756**	0.5196	0.5162	0.5019	0.5018
AUCJ	0.1570	0.1096	0.0865	0.0865	0.4464	0.4794	0.6335	**0.6342**
CC	0.4279	0.4241	0.4611	**0.4611**	0.3075	0.3006	0.1454	0.1438
KLD	10.920	10.918	8.9516	8.9688	**1.0242**	1.0296	1.4847	1.4825
NSS	0.3429	0.3640	0.3971	**0.3971**	0.3712	0.3591	0.1463	0.1431
SIM	0.4015	0.4046	0.4347	0.4347	**0.4434**	0.4381	0.3457	0.3449
Precision	0.6455	0.6657	0.6648	**0.6706**	0.3705	0.3709	0.4347	0.4285
Recall	0.4938	0.4785	0.5257	0.5256	**0.8516**	0.8476	0.2397	0.2483

The deep learning models had similar performance across the distance metrics and images. One cause for this is the relative structural complexity of the SALICON dataset in comparison with the ECSSD dataset. Figure 5 contains saliency maps for an image in the ECSSD dataset which is visually complex.

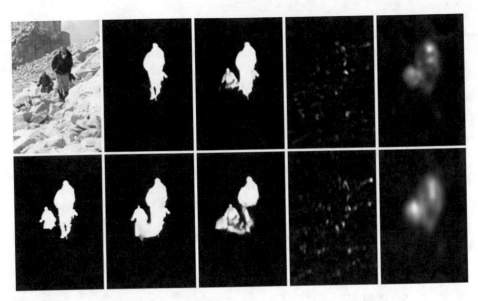

Fig. 5. Qualitative comparison of saliency maps generated on the ECSSD dataset. Top row: original image, saliency maps on this image generated by BASNet [32], CPD [39], fusion model [7], and bottom-up model [10]. Bottom row: ground truth fixation map, saliency maps generated on the perturbed image via the same estimation models.

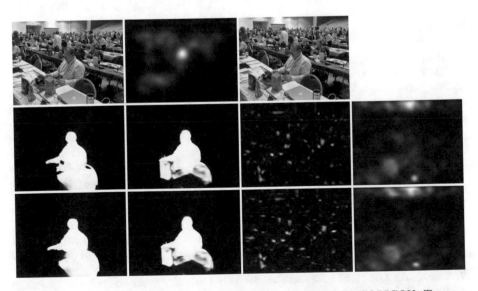

Fig. 6. Qualitative comparison of saliency maps generated from SALICON. Top row: original image, ground truth map, adversarial example. Middle row: Saliency maps on the original image, from BASNet [32], CPD [39], fusion model [7], and bottom-up model [10]. Bottom row: Saliency maps from the same models on the perturbed image.

In comparison, Fig. 6 demonstrates a structurally complex image from the SAL-ICON dataset. While both images are of real-world scenes, the latter motivates the need for improved salience modeling in cluttered environments. The ground truth map, second image in the top row, indicates the salient data to be some of the crowd, with a focus on the man in the foreground.

4   Conclusions and Future Work

Adversarial examples are malicious input to the learning models, and are becoming increasingly prevalent. Countermeasures that are applied globally across an image can be either quickly ineffective or broadly damaging. Visual saliency models attempt to localize application of countermeasures to improve their potency and reduce loss of critical image data. However, in this work saliency models are shown to also suffer some consequences of the perturbations in the adversarial images.

Saliency algorithms built upon deep learning models are particularly vulnerable to attack on less-complex image scenes, as visually demonstrated in Fig. 2 on the complex scenes from ECSSD. These models suffer a measured reduction in performance across all metrics used in this work, with the most severe impacts in KL-divergence and normalized scanpath saliency. In future work, we will investigate a more broad range of saliency estimation models, and applications to video object tracking, audio analysis, and real-world adversarial attacks.

References

1. Borji, A., Itti, L.: Exploiting local and global patch rarities for saliency detection. In: 2012 IEEE Conference on Computer Vision and Pattern Recognition (2012)
2. Borji, A., Sihite, D.N., Itti, L.: Quantitative analysis of human-model agreement in visual saliency modeling: a comparative study. IEEE Trans. Image Process. 22(1), 55–69 (2013)
3. Bylinskii, Z., Judd, T., Durand, F., Oliva, A., Torralba, A.: MIT saliency benchmark. http://saliency.mit.edu/
4. Bylinskii, Z., Judd, T., Oliva, A., Torralba, A., Durand, F.: What do different evaluation metrics tell us about saliency models? arXiv preprint: arXiv:1604.03605 (2016)
5. Carlini, N., Wagner, D.: Towards evaluating the robustness of neural networks. In: 2017 IEEE Symposium on Security and Privacy (SP), pp. 39–57. IEEE (2017)
6. Cheng, M., Mitra, N.J., Huang, X., Torr, P.H.S., Hu, S.: Global contrast based salient region detection. IEEE Trans. Pattern Anal. Mach. Intell. 37(3), 569–582 (2015)
7. Danko, A., Lyu, S.: Fused methods for visual saliency estimation. In: SPIE Image Processing: Machine Vision Applications VIII, vol. 9405 (2015)
8. Das, N., et al.: Shield: fast, practical defense and vaccination for deep learning using JPEG compression. In: Proceedings of the 24th ACM SIGKDD International Conference on Knowledge Discovery and Data Mining, pp. 196–204. ACM (2018)
9. Deng, J., Dong, W., Socher, R., Li, L.J., Li, K., Fei-Fei, L.: ImageNet: a large-scale hierarchical image database. In: CVPR 2009 (2009)

10. Erdem, E., Erdem, A.: Visual saliency estimation by nonlinearly integrating features using region covariances. J. Vis. **13**(4), 11 (2013)
11. Eykholt, K., et al.: Robust physical-world attacks on deep learning visual classification. In: Proceedings of the IEEE Conference on Computer Vision and Pattern Recognition, pp. 1625–1634 (2018)
12. Fan, D.-P., Cheng, M.-M., Liu, J.-J., Gao, S.-H., Hou, Q., Borji, A.: Salient objects in clutter: bringing salient object detection to the foreground. In: Ferrari, V., Hebert, M., Sminchisescu, C., Weiss, Y. (eds.) ECCV 2018, Part XV. LNCS, vol. 11219, pp. 196–212. Springer, Cham (2018). https://doi.org/10.1007/978-3-030-01267-0_12
13. Fernando, T., Denman, S., Sridharan, S., Fookes, C.: Task specific visual saliency prediction with memory augmented conditional generative adversarial networks. In: IEEE Winter Conference on Applications of Computer Vision (WACV) (2018)
14. Goferman, S., Zelnik-Manor, L., Tal, A.: Context-aware saliency detection. IEEE Trans. Pattern Anal. Mach. Intell. **34**(10), 1915–1926 (2011)
15. Goodfellow, I., Shlens, J., Szegedy, C.: Explaining and harnessing adversarial examples. In: International Conference on Learning Representations (2015)
16. Goodfellow, I.J., Shlens, J., Szegedy, C.: Explaining and harnessing adversarial examples. arXiv preprint: arXiv:1412.6572 (2014)
17. Guo, C., Rana, M., Cisse, M., Van Der Maaten, L.: Countering adversarial images using input transformations. arXiv preprint: arXiv:1711.00117 (2017)
18. Itti, L., Koch, C., Niebur, E.: A model of saliency-based visual attention for rapid scene analysis. IEEE Trans. Pattern Anal. Mach. Intell. **20**(11), 1254–1259 (1998). https://doi.org/10.1109/34.730558
19. Jiang, M., Huang, S., Duan, J., Zhao, Q.: SALICON: saliency in context. In: The IEEE Conference on Computer Vision and Pattern Recognition (CVPR) (2015)
20. Judd, T., Durand, F., Torralba, A.: A benchmark of computational models of saliency to predict human fixations. MIT Technical report (2012)
21. Kurakin, A., Goodfellow, I., Bengio, S.: Adversarial examples in the physical world. arXiv preprint: arXiv:1607.02533 (2016)
22. Li, G., Yu, Y.: Deep contrast learning for salient object detection. In: IEEE Conference on Computer Vision and Pattern Recognition (CVPR), pp. 478–487 (2016)
23. Li, H., Li, G., Yu, Y.: ROSA: robust salient object detection against adversarial attacks. IEEE Trans. Cybern., 1–13 (2019)
24. Liu, N., Han, J.: DHSNet: deep hierarchical saliency network for salient object detection. In: Proceedings of the IEEE Conference on Computer Vision and Pattern Recognition, pp. 678–686 (2016)
25. Liu, N., Han, J., Yang, M.H.: PiCANet: learning pixel-wise contextual attention for saliency detection. In: Proceedings of the IEEE Conference on Computer Vision and Pattern Recognition, pp. 3089–3098 (2018)
26. Luo, Y., Boix, X., Roig, G., Poggio, T., Zhao, Q.: Foveation-based mechanisms alleviate adversarial examples. arXiv preprint: arXiv:1511.06292 (2015)
27. Moosavi-Dezfooli, S.M., Fawzi, A., Frossard, P.: DeepFool: a simple and accurate method to fool deep neural networks. In: Proceedings of the IEEE Conference on Computer Vision and Pattern Recognition, pp. 2574–2582 (2016)
28. Pan, J., et al.: SalGAN: visual saliency prediction with adversarial networks. In: CVPR Scene Understanding Workshop (SUNw) (2017)
29. Papernot, N., McDaniel, P., Goodfellow, I., Jha, S., Celik, Z.B., Swami, A.: Practical black-box attacks against machine learning. In: Proceedings of the 2017 ACM on Asia Conference on Computer and Communications Security, pp. 506–519 (2017)

30. Papernot, N., McDaniel, P., Jha, S., Fredrikson, M., Celik, Z.B., Swami, A.: The limitations of deep learning in adversarial settings. In: 2016 IEEE European Symposium on Security and Privacy (EuroS&P), pp. 372–387. IEEE (2016)

31. Peng, C., Zhang, X., Yu, G., Luo, G., Sun, J.: Large kernel matters improve semantic segmentation by global convolutional network. In: 2017 IEEE Conference on Computer Vision and Pattern Recognition (CVPR), pp. 1743–1751, July 2017

32. Qin, X., Zhang, Z., Huang, C., Gao, C., Dehghan, M., Jagersand, M.: BASNet: boundary-aware salient object detection. In: The IEEE Conference on Computer Vision and Pattern Recognition (CVPR), June 2019

33. Qin, Y., Carlini, N., Cottrell, G., Goodfellow, I., Raffel, C.: Imperceptible, robust, and targeted adversarial examples for automatic speech recognition. In: International Conference on Machine Learning, pp. 5231–5240 (2019)

34. Rantalankila, P., Kannala, J., Rahtu, E.: Generating object segmentation proposals using global and local search. In: Proceedings of the IEEE Conference on Computer Vision and Pattern Recognition, pp. 2417–2424 (2014)

35. Ronneberger, O., Fischer, P., Brox, T.: U-Net: convolutional networks for biomedical image segmentation. In: Navab, N., Hornegger, J., Wells, W.M., Frangi, A.F. (eds.) MICCAI 2015, Part III. LNCS, vol. 9351, pp. 234–241. Springer, Cham (2015). https://doi.org/10.1007/978-3-319-24574-4_28

36. Sharif, M., Bhagavatula, S., Bauer, L., Reiter, M.K.: Accessorize to a crime: real and stealthy attacks on state-of-the-art face recognition. In: Proceedings of the 23rd ACM SIGSAC Conference on Computer and Communications Security (2016)

37. Shi, J., Yan, Q., Xu, L., Jia, J.: Hierarchical image saliency detection on extended CSSD. IEEE Trans. Pattern Anal. Mach. Intell. $\mathbf{38}$(4), 717–729 (2016). https://doi.org/10.1109/TPAMI.2015.2465960

38. Simonyan, K., Zisserman, A.: Very deep convolutional networks for large-scale image recognition. arXiv preprint: arXiv:1409.1556 (2014)

39. Wu, Z., Su, L., Huang, Q.: Cascaded partial decoder for fast and accurate salient object detection. In: Proceedings of the IEEE Conference on Computer Vision and Pattern Recognition, pp. 3907–3916 (2019)

40. Yang, C., Zhang, L., Lu, Huchuan, R.X., Yang, M.H.: Saliency detection via graph-based manifold ranking. In: 2013 IEEE Conference on Computer Vision and Pattern Recognition (CVPR), pp. 3166–3173. IEEE (2013)

41. Yang, K., Liu, J., Zhang, C., Fang, Y.: Adversarial examples against the deep learning based network intrusion detection systems. In: MILCOM 2018 - 2018 IEEE Military Communications Conference (MILCOM), pp. 559–564, October 2018

42. Zhang, P., Wang, D., Lu, H., Wang, H., Ruan, X.: Amulet: aggregating multi-level convolutional features for salient object detection. In: Proceedings of the IEEE International Conference on Computer Vision, pp. 202–211 (2017)

43. Zhang, X., Wang, T., Qi, J., Lu, H., Wang, G.: Progressive attention guided recurrent network for salient object detection. In: Proceedings of the IEEE Conference on Computer Vision and Pattern Recognition, pp. 714–722 (2018)

44. Zhao, R., Ouyang, W., Li, H., Wang, X.: Saliency detection by multi-context deep learning. In: Proceedings of the IEEE Conference on Computer Vision and Pattern Recognition, pp. 1265–1274 (2015)

Posters

Entropy Projection Curved Gabor with Random Forest and SVM for Face Recognition

Eucássio G. Lima Júnior[1], Luis H. S. Vogado[1]([✉]), Ricardo A. L. Rabelo[1],
Cornélia J. P. Passarinho[2], and Daniela M. Ushizima[3,4]

[1] Federal University of Piauí, Teresina, Brazil
eucassiojr@gmail.com, lhvogado@gmail.com, ricardoalr@ufpi.edu.br
[2] State University of Piauí, Piripiri, Brazil
janaynapassarinho@gmail.com
[3] University of California, Berkeley, CA, USA
[4] Lawrence Berkeley National Laboratory, Berkeley, CA, USA
dushizima@lbl.gov

Abstract. In this work, we propose a workflow for face recognition under occlusion using the entropy projection from the curved Gabor filter, and create a representative and compact features vector that describes a face. Despite the reduced vector obtained by the entropy projection, it still presents opportunity for further dimensionality reduction. Therefore, we use a Random Forest classifier as an attribute selector, providing a 97% reduction of the original vector while keeping suitable accuracy. A set of experiments using three public image databases: AR Face, Extended Yale B with occlusion and FERET illustrates the proposed methodology, evaluated using the SVM classifier. The results obtained in the experiments show promising results when compared to the available approaches in the literature, obtaining 98.05% accuracy for the complete AR Face, 97.26% for FERET and 81.66% with Yale with 50% occlusion.

Keywords: Face recognition · Face occlusion · Curved Gabor · Features selection

1 Introduction

One of the many goals of face recognition is the identification of individuals in crowds with security cameras. However, to create an ideal recognition system, the methodology should satisfy the following requirements: (1) effective differentiation of individuals (a large inter-class variation) while accepting variations between representations of the same individual (intra-class variation); (2) extraction of face images precisely through quick processing; and (3) low dimensional space to reduce computational costs as part of the classification process [17]. A task of major importance in these systems is detection under face occlusion [29].

© Springer Nature Switzerland AG 2019
G. Bebis et al. (Eds.): ISVC 2019, LNCS 11845, pp. 235–246, 2019.
https://doi.org/10.1007/978-3-030-33723-0_19

This face variation is seldom easy or even impossible to recognize an individual through accessories and lighting conditions [26]. The problem presented by the occlusion linked to the difficulty of obtaining a feature vector with an ideal dimensionality are two of significant obstacles to the development of a robust system.

In this work, we propose a reduced feature vector face recognition workflow for images with face occlusions. The Entropy Curved Gabor Random Forest methodology consists in extracting the features using the Curved Gabor Entropy Projection. This allows a representation of the face in different degrees of orientation, scale, and translation. Recent proposals as in [14] used Curved Gabor Entropy Projection with vectors of high dimensionality, which made this face recognition algorithm unfeasible to recognize an individual in real time when using complex image databases. This paper describes how we use Random Forest (RF) [1] to select the most relevant features and make a representative and robust feature vector for real-time recognition. In the classification stage, we use the Support Vector Machine (SVM) [22] and evaluate the performance on three images database: AR-Face [18], FERET [20,25] and Yale B database [7]. The obtained results are compared with other approaches existing in the state-of-the-art.

In Sect. 2 several works that include potential solutions for face recognition in complex environments are presented. In Sect. 3 describes the proposed approach and tests performed as part of model evaluation, including all the parameters used to set up the curved Gabor filter, entropy, random forest, and SVM to obtain the results. We describe the image database used in the tests and present results and the experiments in Sect. 4. In Sect. 5 we discuss the results obtained by the proposed methodology. Lastly, Sect. 6 we show the potential limitations of this methodology and describe the perspectives of further research projects.

2   Related Work

Convolutional Neural Networks (CNNs) has integrated new workflows to solve tasks in image recognition, including faces, and objects recognition, and the diagnosis of medical images. In 2014, Parkhi et al. [19] proposed VGG-Faces, a CNN for the sole purpose of recognizing faces. However, after its creation, CNN's most powerful were presented, and at a specific instant, the creation of these powerful architectures stagnated. CNN's main problem is the large number of data to carry out the training process [9]. From this, techniques were proposed with the use of CNN's without performing all the training of the network. The approach proposed by Ghazi and Ekenel [8] presents a face recognition solution using transfer learning with pre-trained CNNs. The authors used the VGG-Faces and Lightened CNN by extracting the fully-connected layer of each model. In addition to face recognition, the authors proposed an evaluation of the deep learning techniques in different representations of the face in variations of illumination and occlusion.

The authors in [15], highlight the main challenges related to face recognition in images. Among them are: distortions caused by lighting and variations of face expression, head position and occlusion which all bring uncertainties. As this work is an approach proposed to solve such issues, a new regression model (Discriminative and Compact Coding - DCC) is developed that provides multi scale error measurement, compactness and interclass collaboration. This approach has demonstrated significant improvements in results from experiments using several image databases. However, the accuracies obtained for faces with occlusion were lower than those from other state of the art approaches.

A feature-sign search (FSS) in [16] presents an issue when using sparse coding in large image databases due to the high computational cost. The authors in this work developed a new algorithm, which iteratively solves two problems of convex optimization by searching for the best base vector for image representation. The approach performed robustly to occlusion problems in continuous blocks located on the inferior portion of the face. Accuracy values were 95.38% for recognition of individuals using the AR Face image database for scarf occlusion. However, the approach presented difficulties mostly when handling occlusions on the region around the eyes.

The Sparse Representation-based Classification (SRC) [24] and Correntropy-based Sparse Representation (CESR) [11] approaches do not acquire all the image features available but randomly select small amounts of information sufficient to rebuild the image. CESR was presented in [11] to deal with noise and occlusion problems in face recognition. In CESR, non-negative sparse representation is combined to the maximum correntropy criterion. Other works, which were used to compare with this approach, are founded upon linear regression. Linear Regression Classification (LRC) [24], FSS, Structured graphical lasso (SGLasso) [27] and DCC consider the test image as a linear combination of some of the training images.

Among the approaches mentioned above, all of them presented difficulties when performing face recognition dealing with continuous occlusions on regions around the eyes and mouth. That can be attributed to the holistic aspect of those approaches. In practice, holistic feature vectors do not perform very robustly to variations of lighting, face expression, head position and local deformation [23].

3   Proposed Methodology

In this paper, we propose a face recognition methodology based on feature selection using the Random Forest from a vector consisting of the Gabor Filter Bank response, entropy calculation, and classification with SVM. We present the flowchart of the proposed methodology in Fig. 1.

3.1   Features Extraction

In the feature extraction step, we subdivided the creation of the vector into three stages. In the first one, we used the result of the Gabor filter bank convolution with the input image to create an initial representation of the vector. In the second one, we apply block segmentation to subdivide the result from the previous

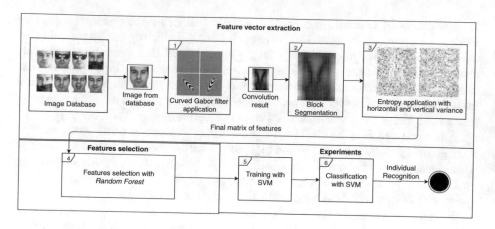

Fig. 1. General flowchart of the proposed methodology.

stage in order to reduce the feature vector dimensionality using entropy in the third stage.

Curved Gabor Filter Application: Initially proposed in [6] for 1D and later 2D signal processing [5]. Gabor has several configurations used in state of the art and among them, curved Gabor. This provides the extraction of contour features associated with regions that present curves on the face, such as the eyes, nose, mouth, and cheeks. Given this, we believe that curved Gabor is more appropriate than traditional Gabor [12].

The curved Gabor filter banks were created with frequencies (u) and orientations (v), where the number of orientations varies according to the degree of curvature of c, as seen in the state-of-the-art works. For the degree of curvature a set $c = \{0; 0.05; 0.1; 0.2\}$ was defined, which produces a curved Gabor filter bank [10,12]. To determine the values of c, a series of experiments were performed, varying $c = 0$ to 0.5. For $c > 0.2$, the curved Gabor filter bank presented acute deformations that reduced the quality of the generated feature vectors. For c different from 0, the number of orientations should be 16, twice the number of no curved filters due to the asymmetric features of the curved filter.

The curved Gabor bank uses 16 orientations while the traditional filter uses only 8. This is due to the asymmetry of the curved filter bank, which requires twice the amount of filters.

After the curved Gabor filter bank is built, the convolution of each filter belonging to the bank, through the input image. Thereby the magnitude of the curved Gabor filter bank responses is generated, and contains the initial set of features of the face. This set of responses from the curved Gabor is the final product in the first stage (Fig. 1.1).

Block Segmentation: Since images of different individuals can have the same histogram sequence and share the same log energy entropy, both images can be incorrectly identified as belonging to the same person [28]. Another possible approach to solve this problem is the segmentation of curved Gabor filter magnitude responses, obtained in stage 1, into small non-overlapping blocks (Fig. 1.2). Then each block, although from the same original image, will have different intensities. Computationally, this segmentation technique is fast, simple, and is not based on detection of essential areas of the face like the eyes, nose and mouth [2].

Entropy: The third stage uses the combination of Local Variance Projection Log Energy Entropy (LVP-LEE) features. The concept of entropy introduced by Shannon in [21] was initially used in studies on communication systems. After considering the components of those systems as probabilistic components, it was then used in other fields such as image processing [3]. The LVP-LEE as presented in [28], its function is to work as a feature extractor and a dimensionality reducer for feature vectors obtained in stage 2.

After the segmentation of the curved Gabor filter magnitude responses into non-overlapping blocks, a dimensionality reduction technique can be applied. Here, LVP-LEE was chosen, because at the same time as it extracts features it creates more representative features vectors. For each block in curved Gabor magnitude response, the method based on the entropy is applied. By applying the LVP-LEE on each curved Gabor filter bank response, two new data matrices are produced, representing the entropy of variance projection in the horizontal and vertical directions. After they are concatenated into only one feature vector, they are able to be used by a classifier to recognize a face (Fig. 1.3).

3.2   Features Selection with Random Forest

The features extraction step provides many features. In this way, it is necessary to reduce the features vector size using face image representation. For this it is necessary to identify the most relevant elements of the vector, making use of a features selection technique.

Among several algorithms that provide the relevance of each element to the classification, we use Random Forest [1] in this work. Its choice is due to its extensive use in the selection of variables in problems involving large amounts of data [13]. The feature vector, provided by step 1, is divided into s sub-vectors of size t. The k elements of each sub-vector most relevant to the classification are selected using the Random Forest. In this process, the number of trees for 250 was defined, according to tests performed with the parameter varying in 1, 25, 50, 250, and 1000.

According to our experiments, there was no significant increase with values above 250 for the number of trees. Then, we concatenate the elements then selected in each sub-vector, forming a new candidate vector that is subjected to the same procedure described. Thus, in the second iteration a new vector is got, thus being considered the final representation of the individual.

The choices of the values of the parameters s and k are of fundamental importance to get a relevant feature vector. For the best choice of these values, we performed a set of experiments on face databases. The experiments have to change the values of s and k and then execute step 2 of the methodology, getting the value of the accuracy. In the execution of the procedure, we observed the maximization of precision and minimization of the vector size. We identify that for the proposal, the best values in the first iteration are $k = 100$ and $s = 32$, totalizing a features vector of size 3200. In the second iteration, the best values are $k = 100$ and $s = 28$. The vector produced in this iteration is considered the face representation.

3.3   Classification

A Support Vector Machine is a powerful technique for pattern classification [22]. A SVM creates a hyperplane or a set of hyperplanes in a high-dimensional space, which can be used for classification by supervised learning. In step 2, the features representing diverse individuals from the image database are submitted to the classifier. After the training, the SVM generates the result as a data prediction model for the image classification.

Lastly, a vector generated is classified by the SVM and, consequently, the identification of the individual is made. The LIBSVM library [4], with a kernel Radial function, was used as a tool to support the SVM performance as a classifier. At this step, the k-fold cross-validation technique was used to estimate any error generated by the classifier. At the end of this process, the accuracy for face recognition of this approach, as well as the parameters used in SVM, is obtained. At the end of cross-validation, the best values given by the proposed approach for the following parameters of SVM were: penalty $C = 8$ and parameter $\gamma = 3.0517578125 \cdot 10^{-5}$ of the RBF kernel.

4   Datasets and Experimental Results

In order to compare our results, we used three public databases: AR-Face Database, FERET, and Extended Yale B. We evaluated the proposed methodology using k-fold cross-validation with $k = 10$ in three public databases that present occlusion. Among the various techniques of face recognition are the follow approaches: SRC [24], LRC [16], CESR [11], FSS [16], SGLasso [27], DC, CC and DCC [15] that were used to compare the approach proposed in this work. For the AR-Face database, we include results obtained by Ghazi and Ekenel [8], and the methodology with only the Curved Gabor + Entropy (CGEP), without the features selection. For the execution of the experiments, we used MATLAB and the Scikit-learn library in an Intel®Core™i5-8350U CPU @ 1.70 GHz × 8 computer with 16 GB RAM.

4.1   AR Face

The AR Face Database, which consists of over 4,000 colored images of 126 people (70 men and 56 women) in total. The images in this database are frontal pictures of faces with different facial expressions, lighting conditions and occlusions. The main feature of this face database is the occlusion caused by glasses and scarves worn by the individuals. The pictures were resized to 48×56 pixels for our experiments in order to turn the dimensions similar to other algorithms used as comparison. This database was partitioned into 6 different subsets in order to group different features in the tests. Face images with different facial expressions, lighting and occlusion are grouped to enable a more robust experiment of the proposed approach in different scenarios.

In Table 1, we present the results obtained by the proposed methodology in the AR Face database. For the lighting variations subset, the best result was obtained by the CGEP methodology. However, due to the features vector of high dimensionality, the proposed methodology in this work becomes more interesting because it presents an accuracy above 99% and a vector with only 2800 features. In occlusion by sunglasses subset, we observed that the best result was obtained by the proposed methodology, with 96%. This result demonstrates the robustness of our methodology for several types of occlusion and presents the gain obtained through the selection of attributes.

Table 1. Comparisons between the results and state-of-the-art methodologies in AR Face database

Database	LRC	SRC	CESR	FSS	SGLasso	DC	CC	DCC	Ghazi and Ekenel [8]	CGEP [14]	Proposed methodology
Lighting variations	31.37	45.80	48.74	44.96	38.24	45.24	79.83	71.01	x	100.00	99.50
Occlusions by sunglasses	25.21	28.99	68.49	28.99	21.85	74.79	3.78	72.69	35.45	76.00	96.00
Occlusion by scarf	94.96	95.38	96.64	95.38	93.28	97.06	68.49	97.06	89.09	84.50	96.50
Illumination + sunglasses	8.19	15.13	20.80	14.50	11.55	23.95	3.15	22.48	x	94.75	96.50
Illumination + occlusion by scarf	18.28	29.41	36.76	27.31	21.22	29.20	63.87	45.80	x	98.25	99.25
Facial expressions variations	x	x	x	x	x	x	x	x	x	98.25	99.00
Complete basis	x	x	x	x	x	x	x	x	x	99.14	98.05

The occlusion created in the occlusion by scarf subset occurs throughout the lower part of the image, being cut at 50% of its height, getting a new image that in the classification. In this experiment, all the methodologies presented got high settling rates, of which six presented values above 94%. DC and DCC got the best accuracy with 97.06%, and the proposed methodology reached 96.50%. Such metrics are justified by the significant reduction in the size of the final image used in the tests. Therefore, suggesting that the level of dimensionality reduction applied to the images should be adjusted regarding the image size. The occlusion created in the occlusion subset per scarf occurs throughout the lower part of the image, being cut at 50% of its height, obtaining a new image that is used in the classification.

From the lighting variations and occlusions generated in the first subsets of the database. Two new subsets have been created that combine the features presented and increase the difficulty in recognizing the individual. The proposed methodology obtained the best results in both subsets, demonstrating Gabor's ability to extract features in images that have light variation. In illumination + occlusion by sunglasses we obtained 96.50%, and in illumination + occlusion by scarf, it reached 99.25%.

The last subset presented has variations of facial expressions. In this subset segregate the faces that represent neutral expressions, smile, anger, and fright, enabling the verification in an environment closer to the real world. State-of-the-art approaches do not mention the results obtained for this subset. However, we conducted experiments in order to determine the applicability of our methodology in this type of problem. The proposed methodology reached 99.00%.

4.2 FERET

The FERET database consists of 1400 face images. This database has as main feature the occlusion of the face through changes in lighting. The imaging database was the result of the US Department of Defense's same-name program aimed at developing a standard image database for testing and evaluating face recognition algorithms. In the experiment presented, the face region of the original image was manually cut, and the images were resized to 48×56 pixels, similar to those used in the other comparison approaches.

Table 2 presents the results of the accuracy of the various approaches in the FERET database. The proposed approach obtains the best results with the accuracy of 97.26%, followed by DCC with 92.84%. As a result, precision and recall of 97.26% are obtained indicating that the proposed approach has the same ranking of individuals as false positives and false negatives, a characteristic appropriate for a balanced database.

Table 2. Comparisons between the results and state-of-the-art methodologies in FERET database

Methodology	LRC	SRC	CESR	FSS	SGLasso	DC	CC	DCC	Proposed
Accuracy	79.22	86.37	92.35	86.27	82.35	92.55	64.02	92.84	**97.26**

4.3   Extended Yale B

Extended Yale B database corresponds to 2496 frontal facial images of 38 people, photographed in gray-scale on 64 controlled variations of illumination. From the base, 30 faces per subject were randomly selected and overlaid with a fixed image of a baboon. The size of the occlusion generated ranges from 10%, 20%, 30%, 40%, 50%, 60%, 70% and 80% while the position of the occlusion occurs randomly. The new base generated is exemplified in Fig. 2. Due to the random characteristic of occlusion positioning, the Yale B database used in each experiment are different regarding the positioning of the occlusion.

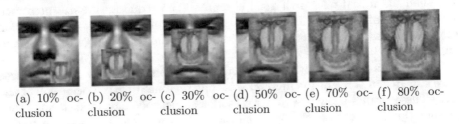

(a) 10% oc- (b) 20% oc- (c) 30% oc- (d) 50% oc- (e) 70% oc- (f) 80% occlusion   clusion   clusion   clusion   clusion   clusion

Fig. 2. Faces from Extended Yale B database.

In Fig. 3, we present the results obtained by the methodology in the Extended Yale B database with occlusion generated by the baboon. These data point out that in all compared approaches, as occlusion increases, the accuracy decreases. However, in our work, we obtained results ranging from 96.22% with 10% occlusion to 50.87% with 80% occlusion. These values surpass all the approaches used in the comparison for all occlusion variations. This demonstrates the robustness of the proposed methodology in high percentages of occlusion.

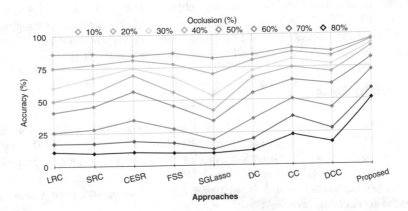

Fig. 3. Comparison of the results of the proposed methodology with approaches on the Yale base with occlusion.

During the execution of the experiments, we calculated the time required to extract the features for a single image. Given this, we obtained 3.98 s with sequential processing of the images. We believe that with the use of parallelism, this time will decrease considerably.

5   Discussion

The feature vector created after the extraction stage results in 94080 elements for images of size 48×56 pixels. From this representation, we use Random Forest for feature selection in stage 4. As a result, the new generated vector has a smaller size than the initial one, with 2800 elements. The reduction in size presented a percentage of 97.024%. The low dimensionality of the image representation provides the use of less storage space and fewer times for image retrieval and identification.

The results obtained by the methodology proposed for the AR Face base were superior in three of the four subsets that presented partial occlusion of the face. These results show the robustness of the methodology in situations that present this type of uncontrolled condition. For the other subsets, the results obtained proved superior or equivalent to those of state of the art. In situations involving light variation and change of facial expressions, the results obtained were higher than 98%. The result presented for the complete base allows us to infer that the created vector is representative enough to classify the faces in different conditions although they are in the same set.

The experiments with occlusion performed at the Yale base have the objective of creating conditions of uncontrolled environments in a controlled database. From the results obtained, we can evaluate positively the results achieved. These experiments were performed with the random overlap of the baboon in each image. Since in the work of [15], the authors do not specify whether the image of the baboon is in the same position, varying only the percentage of occlusion. Thus, the methodology had to adapt to occlusions in different positions and from this, to identify the individual. Among the state-of-the-art methodologies, CC achieved the best results, followed by DCC. However, the proposed methodology exceeded the accuracy values of all state-of-the-art approaches.

6   Conclusions

In this work, we propose a pipeline methodology for face recognition under occlusion conditions. The Gabor curved filter bank forms the methodology as a descriptor, local variance projection function entropy as dimensionality reducer, Random Forest as attribute selector and SVM as the classifier. From three consolidated public bases, several experiments were created, and their results were compared to those of state-of-the-art methodologies.

Among the main contributions of the methodology we have, the robustness in images of faces that present occlusion and the creation of a more representative vector and with lower dimensionality. With the use of the entropy and the bank of curved Gabor filters, we were able to create a robust vector with the presence of occlusion. This is demonstrated by their results that when compared to state of the art, were superior. As for the dimensionality of the characteristics vector, the selection through Random Forest allowed the most relevant and most representative characteristics to be kept in the vector and the rest discarded. Such disposal provided the increase or stability of the accuracy depending on the base used. The selection also allowed for vector reduction by a little over 97% when compared to that provided by Curved Gabor + Entropy.

However, limitations are still found, and some ideas are proposed to complement this study. Among them, we perform experiments on non-controlled image databases and the implementation of other classifiers, as well as the use of GPUs in the feature extraction stage.

Acknowledgments. This research is funded in part by the Gordon and Betty Moore Foundation through Grant GBMF3834 and by the Alfred P. Sloan Foundation through Grant 2013-10-27 to the University of California, Berkeley. Algorithmic work is partially supported by the Office of Science of the US Department of Energy (DOE) under Contract No. DE-AC02-05CH11231, Advanced Scientific Computing Research (ASCR) Early Career Award. Any opinions, findings, and conclusions or recommendations expressed in this material are those of the authors and they do not necessarily reflect the views of DOE or the University of California.

References

1. Breiman, L.: Random forests. Mach. Learn. **45**(1), 5–32 (2001)
2. Chan, T.H., Jia, K., Gao, S., Lu, J., Zeng, Z., Ma, Y.: Pcanet: a simple deep learning baseline for image classification? IEEE Trans. Image Process. **24**(12), 5017–5032 (2015)
3. Chang, C.I., Du, Y., Wang, J., Guo, S.M., Thouin, P.: Survey and comparative analysis of entropy and relative entropy thresholding techniques. IEE Proc. Vision Image Signal Process. **153**(6), 837–850 (2006)
4. Chang, C.C., Lin, C.J.: LIBSVM: a library for support vector machines. ACM Trans. Intell. Syst. Technol. **2**(3), 1–27 (2011)
5. Daugman, J.G.: Uncertainty relation for resolution in space, spatial frequency, and orientation optimized by two-dimensional visual cortical filters. JOSA A **2**(7), 1160–1169 (1985)
6. Gabor, D.: Theory of communication part 1: the analysis of information. J. Inst. Electr. Eng.-Part III Radio Commun. Eng. **93**(26), 429–441 (1946)
7. Georghiades, A.S., Belhumeur, P.N., Kriegman, D.J.: From few to many: illumination cone models for face recognition under variable lighting and pose. IEEE Trans. Pattern Anal. Mach. Intell. **23**(6), 643–660 (2001)
8. Ghazi, M.M., Ekenel, H.K.: A comprehensive analysis of deep learning based representation for face recognition. In: The IEEE Conference on Computer Vision and Pattern Recognition (CVPR) Workshops, pp. 34–41. IEEE (2016)
9. Grm, K., Štruc, V., Artiges, A., Caron, M., Ekenel, H.K.: Strengths and weaknesses of deep learning models for face recognition against image degradations. IET Biometrics **7**(1), 81–89 (2018)

10. Haghighat, M.B.A., Namjoo, E.: Evaluating the informativity of features in dimensionality reduction methods. In: 2011 5th International Conference on Application of Information and Communication Technologies (AICT), pp. 1–5. IEEE (2011)
11. He, R., Zheng, W.S., Hu, B.G.: Maximum correntropy criterion for robust face recognition. IEEE Trans. Pattern Anal. Mach. Intell. **33**(8), 1561–1576 (2011)
12. Hwang, W., Huang, X., Li, S.Z., Kim, J.: Face recognition using Extended Curvature Gabor classifier bunch. Pattern Recogn. **48**(4), 1247–1260 (2015)
13. Janitza, S., Tutz, G., Boulesteix, A.L.: Random forest for ordinal responses. Comput. Stat. Data Anal. **96**(C), 57–73 (2016)
14. Júnior, E.G.L., Vogado, L.H.S., Rabelo, R.A.L., Passarinho, C.J.P.: Curved gabor projection entropy for face recognition. In: 2018 International Joint Conference on Neural Networks (IJCNN 2018), pp. 2611–2618. IEEE (2018)
15. Lai, Z.R., Dai, D.Q., Ren, C.X., Huang, K.K.: Discriminative and compact coding for robust face recognition. IEEE Trans. Cybern. **45**(9), 1900–1912 (2015)
16. Lee, H., Battle, A., Raina, R., Ng, A.Y.: Efficient sparse coding algorithms. In: Advances in neural information processing systems, pp. 801–808 (2006)
17. Li, S.Z., Jain, A.K. (eds.): Handbook of Face Recognition. Springer, London (2011). https://doi.org/10.1007/978-0-85729-932-1
18. Martínez, A., Benavente, R.: The ar face database. Technical report 24, Computer Vision Center, Bellatera, June 1998. http://www.cat.uab.cat/Public/Publications/1998/MaB1998, cites in Scholar Google: http://scholar.google.com/scholar?hl=en&lr=&client=firefox-a&cites=15042646876214698 12
19. Parkhi, O.M., Vedaldi, A., Zisserman, A.: Deep face recognition. In: Xianghua Xie, M.W.J., Tam, G.K.L. (eds.) Proceedings of the British Machine Vision Conference (BMVC), pp. 1–12. BMVA Press, September 2015
20. Phillips, P.J., Moon, H., Rizvi, S.A., Rauss, P.J.: The FERET evaluation methodology for face-recognition algorithms. IEEE Trans. Pattern Anal. Mach. Intell. **22**(10), 1090–1104 (2000)
21. Shannon, C.: A mathematical theory of communication. Bell Syst. Tech. J. **27**(3), 379–423 (1948). https://doi.org/10.1002/j.1538-7305.1948.tb01338.x
22. Vapnik, V.N., et al.: The Nature of Statistical Learning Theory. Information Science and Statistics. Springer, New York (1995)
23. Weng, R., Lu, J., Tan, Y.P.: Robust point set matching for partial face recognition. IEEE Trans. Image Process. **25**(3), 1163–1176 (2016). https://doi.org/10.1109/TIP.2016.2515987
24. Wright, J., Yang, A.Y., Ganesh, A., Sastry, S.S., Ma, Y.: Robust face recognition via sparse representation. IEEE Trans. Pattern Anal. Mach. Intell. **31**(2), 210–227 (2009)
25. Yang, W.H., Dai, D.Q.: Two-dimensional maximum margin feature extraction for face recognition. IEEE Trans. Syst. Man Cybern. Part B (Cybern.) **39**(4), 1002–1012 (2009)
26. Yu, Y.F., Dai, D.Q., Ren, C.X., Huang, K.K.: Discriminative multi-scale sparse coding for single-sample face recognition with occlusion. Pattern Recogn. **66**, 302–312 (2017)
27. Yuan, M., Lin, Y.: Model selection and estimation in regression with grouped variables. J. Roy. Stat. Soc.: Ser. B (Stat. Methodol.) **68**(1), 49–67 (2006)
28. Zhang, J.S., Chen, C.J.: Local variance projection log energy entropy features for illumination robust face recognition. In: 2008 International Symposium on Biometrics and Security Technologies, ISBAST 2008, pp. 1–5. IEEE (2008)
29. Zhang, L., Verma, B., Tjondronegoro, D., Chandran, V.: Facial expression analysis under partial occlusion: a survey. ACM Comput. Surv. **51**(2), 1–49 (2018)

Guitar Tablature Generation Using Computer Vision

Brian Duke and Andrea Salgian[✉]

The College of New Jersey, Ewing, NJ 08628, USA
{dukeb2,salgian}@tcnj.edu

Abstract. Traditionally, automatic music transcription uses audio recordings to generate the score of a musical piece. However, extracting pitch from an audio recording can be difficult. Vision-based approaches can address this by tracking the musician's gestures, and generating the score based on the way the musician plays the instrument.

In this paper we present a system that uses a vision-based approach to generate musical notation for guitar. Most guitar transcription systems to date rely on machine learning, specialized gear, or drawn-on markers. Our approach is vision based, yet markerless. We track the guitar's strings and frets, and in each frame we use skin detection to localize the guitarist's fingers on the fretboard. We use this information to generate tablature notation, a guitar specific notation that shows which strings and frets should be played for every beat.

The approach achieves a significantly higher accuracy than similar systems described in the literature. The system runs and displays tablature in real time, making it especially useful for educational purposes.

Keywords: Guitar fingering recognition · Guitar tablature · Automatic music transcription

1 Introduction

Writing musical notation can be a tedious process. A number of software applications are available to automatically transcribe audio files into staff notation that can then be read by musicians playing various instruments. Since audio processing is not an easy task, newer approaches have looked at vision-based methods, where musical notation is generated based on the gestures performed by the musician playing the instrument. This is especially important for the guitar, which is different from most instruments in that the same sound can be produced in multiple ways.

The tablature notation, described in more detail in Sect. 2, is a musical notation specific to the guitar, which shows which strings and frets should be played for every beat. This notation is difficult to extract from audio files. Verner [14] uses a midi guitar, with different midi channels associated to each string. Such guitars are expensive and not readily available to all musicians. Traube [13] uses

© Springer Nature Switzerland AG 2019
G. Bebis et al. (Eds.): ISVC 2019, LNCS 11845, pp. 247–257, 2019.
https://doi.org/10.1007/978-3-030-33723-0_20

the timbre of the guitar, since two notes with the same pitch can have different timbre. The drawback of this method is the need for a-priori knowledge about the timbre of the guitar.

Existing vision-based transcription systems rely on markings or specialized gear that make guitar playing cumbersome. In [4], Burns and Wanderley describe a system where a webcam is mounted on the headstock of the guitar to get a stabilized, close-up view of the hand. The downside is that the mounted webcam can only capture the first five frets, and its weight disturbs the player. Kerd-vibulvech's system [7] used two webcams, colored fingertips, and an ARTag. Scarr and Green [11] used a markerless approach and showed promise during preliminary testing. However, the system had difficulties because of the lack of fretboard tracking and reliance on individual finger detection.

Multi-modal systems combine the analysis of audio and image data. An early multi-modal system described by Paleari et al. [10] relies mainly on computer vision and uses audio analysis to resolve ambiguous situations. However, the system was only tested on single notes.

In this paper we describe a vision-based automated music transcription system that generates tablature (or tab, for short) notation using a video recording of a guitar player. Using a simple webcam and computer vision techniques, our system detects the strings and frets of the guitar and the location of the guitarist's fingertips, generating the tab notation with a higher accuracy than previously published systems. We show results on three different video recordings, for a total of 2298 frames.

2   Background

2.1   Guitar Tablature

Musical score for most instruments is recorded in staff notation as sheet music. Staff notation is an arrangement of notes of various durations played at various times, which amounts to pitches and their durations and attack times. This type of notation is suitable for instruments where there is a unique way to play each pitch, such as the piano.

Fretted instruments, such as the guitar, can produce the same pitch from different fingerings. For example, on a guitar in standard tuning, the fifth fret held down on the low E string produces the same pitch as the A string played openly. If the A note were represented in staff notation, a guitar player would have to decide which fingering to use. While a classically trained player may be able to sight-read staff notation and determine appropriate fretting positions on the fly, this is a time-consuming task for others. For this reason, amateur guitar players often prefer tablature.

A tablature shows the combination of frets and strings that should be played on a given beat. The six lines represent the six strings from the perspective of a player looking down at their guitar, with the low E string on the bottom and the high E string on the top. The numbers represent the fret position that should be held down [6].

Along with being easier to read, guitar "tabs" can be created without special software. Players type tabs using the ASCII character set and share them on websites such as [2]. Figure 1 shows the staff notation and tablature for a chord progression in C major.

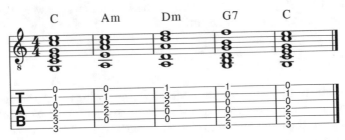

Fig. 1. Staff notation and corresponding tablature for a chord progression in C major.

2.2   Recording Preparation

An ideal video recording for our system is one where the guitar is the main subject of the frame. To achieve this, a player can sit at a close distance in front of the camera, or the camera's lens can be zoomed in. To make sure that the fingertips of the player are not obscured by the rest of their hand, the camera should be positioned at a slightly higher elevation than the guitar. Figure 2a shows an image obtained using a poor camera angle. Since the fingertips are not visible, the system would have to rely on the positioning of the knuckles, leading to many errors.

(a) An example of a poor camera angle.   (b) Correct setup.

Fig. 2. Setting up for a recording session

A setup that can provide contrast between the fretboard and background is recommended. The background should not be cluttered. Our videos were recorded in front of a solid white wall. To maintain the contrast of the scene, the guitarist should avoid wearing a patterned or striped shirt. The color of the fretboard of the guitar should not be the same as the player's skin tone.

The color balance/white balance of the video should be set to ensure proper skin detection. This can be done within the camera's settings, or using the Gray World algorithm. The latter would add overhead to the system's runtime.

Videos were recorded by a camera mounted on a tripod and scaled down to have a width of 1280 pixels. No sensors or drawn-on markers were used.

Figure 2b shows the correct setup.

3   Methodology

Our system starts by detecting and tracking the strings and the frets on the fretboard of the guitar. We then use skin color segmentation to detect the fingers, and we use their positioning relative to the strings and frets to obtain the tablature notation for the given frame.

We explain our algorithms in more detail below.

3.1   Fretboard Detection

The first step of the algorithm is to find lines that represent the fret bars, strings, and outline of the guitar fretboard. The accuracy of these lines is crucial for the system's performance. A classical guitar, such as the Yamaha guitar used in the test videos, allows for easy detections due to the thickness and contrast of the nylon strings. Strings on a steel-string acoustic guitar are harder to detect because they are thinner. Strings could also be rusted or missing.

We started by extracting the edges in each frame, using OpenCV's Canny edge detector [5], and carefully selecting hysteresis threshold values to minimize the amount of extraneous edges. Figure 3 shows a frame and the results of the Canny edge detection.

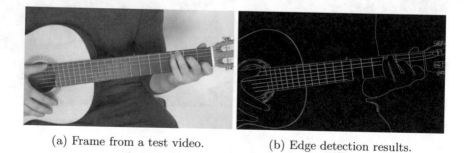

(a) Frame from a test video.   (b) Edge detection results.

Fig. 3. Original frame and Canny edge detector results.

We then use the Progressive Probabilistic Hough Transform (PPHT) algorithm to extract straight lines. Just like for the Canny edge detection, thresholds were determined experimentally, to maximize accuracy. Lines are extrapolated to fill in gaps and to extend them to edges of the fretboard. Lines that are very close and have similar slopes are averaged, as they usually represent multiple detections of the same string or fret bar.

The positions of strings can be predicted using knowledge of the top and bottom of the fretboard wood, using the formulas below:

$$\frac{\text{Outer gap}}{\text{Fretboard height}} = 0.086 \tag{1}$$

$$\frac{\text{Inner gap}}{\text{Fretboard height}} = 0.17 \tag{2}$$

The outer gap is the distance between the top or bottom string and the top or bottom of the board. The inner gap is the distance between two adjacent strings. Equation (1) can be used to predict the positions of the first and sixth string, while Eq. (2) can predict the position of an inner string.

While these predictions are not accurate enough to replace line detection, they can be used to remove duplicate detections, or to signal undetected strings.

Fret bar lines can also be predicted using a luthier's formula [1], but they will be even less accurate due to camera lens distortion or the guitar not being flat against the lens.

To address the problem of occasionally undetected strings or fret bars, we use tracking. We start by picking a calibration frame at the beginning of the video sequence, before the player places their hand over the fretboard. Lines from this frame are used to initialize the tracking values. Future detections are compared to the previously tracked values. If the string lines' y coordinates or the fret lines' x coordinates fall within a close pixel distance of the tracked values, the tracked values can be updated with the current frame's detections. Otherwise, lines were probably not properly detected, and the tracked values from the previous frame should be used in the current frame.

This process allows the system to perform well on frames where the hand obscures the fret bars and prevents them from being detected.

Figure 4a shows the lines detected using PPHT, while Fig. 4b shows the strings and frets detected after line correction.

(a) PPHT detected line segments.   (b) Detected strings and frets.

Fig. 4. Fretboard detection.

Finally, the angle of the fourth (middle) string is used to rotate the frame of the video so that strings are horizontal, and fret bar lines are vertical. Once the fingertips are detected, this positioning will allow us to determine their correct location on the fretboard with less calculation.

3.2   Finger Detection and Localization

The second objective of the algorithm is to detect the guitar player's fingers, and determine where the fingertips are in relation to the guitar's strings and the frets.

Skin pixels are detected using their RGB values, according to the Kovac model [8]. A pixel is considered skin if its RGB values follow these rules:

$$R \geq 95$$
$$B \geq 20 \tag{3}$$
$$G \geq 40$$

The procedure is followed by a Gaussian blur to remove noise. Finally, pixels with R and G values that fall within a distance of 15 from each other are eliminated.

Results are shown in Fig. 5. The body and the headstock of the guitar were classified as skin. Since we are only interested in the fingers placed on the fretboard, and the fretboard has already been detected, we remove other parts of the image from consideration. We then use Suzuki's border following algorithm [12], as implemented in OpenCV, to find the contour of the fingers. Figure 6 shows the results of this step.

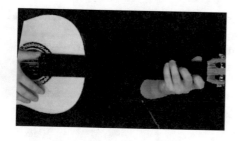

Fig. 5. Skin detection and segmentation.

Fig. 6. Finger isolation and contour detection.

Next, we keep only the top half of the contour, and detect the fingertips at the local maxima of the y coordinate. Figure 7 shows the process. This approach is more robust than other approaches which require detection of each finger, and can fail when fingers are touching [11]. Then, we produce a tablature by analyzing where the points are in relation to the strings and frets. The system output is shown in Fig. 8.

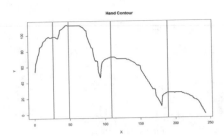

Fig. 7. Fingers contour with fingertips located at local maxima.

Fig. 8. System output. Tablature notation was flipped to correspond with strings in the video.

4 Results

We tested our approach on three video recordings: a chord progression in C major whose notes are shown in Fig. 1 (659 frames), an open C major scale followed by an E major scale that begins on the seventh fret (533 frames), and a chord progression from "Autumn Leaves", a jazz standard popular with beginner guitar players (1106 frames). The videos were manually transcribed by a volunteer who, for each frame, recorded what appeared to be the current fretting position in tablature notation. The volunteer also noted which frets had a finger hovering over them.

We then compared the manually transcribed tab to the system's output. Correct detections were those where the fret for a string matched the one listed in the manually transcribed tab. Hovering notes were also checked for correctness. Open notes, where there are no fingers on a given string, marked as 0 in tab notation, were not considered in the performance calculation, as they would have unfairly inflated performance numbers.

Tables 1, 2 and 3 show the performance of the system on each of these videos, separated by strings. Since the tab output lists the fret for each string, we reported separate performances for each string, as well as an overall average performance. Since open notes are not considered, the number of frames compared varies from string to string.

While testing on "Autumn Leaves" is unique to our paper, other systems were tested on the chord progression in C major and the C major scale. Table 4 shows a comparison between our results and results published in [11] and [3].

Our system's best performance was on the C major chord progression, where the overall accuracy was 86%. This is significantly higher than the performance of Scarr's proposed system [11], which achieved a 52% accuracy on the same chord progression, or Burns' system [3], with an accuracy of 14%.

"Autumn Leaves" had the worst performance at 71% (Table 3). This is mainly due to the fact that in several chords the little finger was under the ring finger, and our approach failed to detect its tip (see Fig. 9). In addition, hovering fingers are ambiguous, as it is hard to tell whether the finger is pressing down on a string

Table 1. Chord progression in C major. 659 frames.

	String					
	1	2	3	4	5	6
Errors	2	126	28	40	131	12
Frames compared	383	384	382	275	622	302
Accuracy	99%	67%	93%	85%	79%	96%
Overall accuracy	86%					

Table 2. Open C major scale followed by an E major scale that begins on the seventh fret. 533 frames.

	String					
	1	2	3	4	5	6
Errors	–	7	30	56	103	–
Frames compared	–	102	188	183	330	–
Accuracy	–	93%	84%	69%	69%	–
Overall accuracy	76%					

Table 3. "Autumn Leaves". 1106 frames.

	String					
	1	2	3	4	5	6
Errors	81	188	283	318	–	–
Frames compared	571	574	962	857	–	–
Accuracy	85%	67%	71%	63%	–	–
Overall accuracy	71%					

Table 4. Comparison between our results and previous methods

Video	Burns' method	Scarr's method	Our method
C major scale	34%	78%	76%
C major chords	14%	52%	86%
Autumn Leaves	N/A	N/A	71%

or not. This problem is usually solved by assuming that the highest detected fret on a string is the one being played. However, that assumption can backfire when a scale is played.

Fig. 9. Missed fifth finger detection on the first chord of "Autumn Leaves."

As our initial goal was to assess transcription accuracy, we did not put too much effort into optimization. Nevertheless, our system runs in real-time. Processing time can be further reduced by cutting down the number of frames that are analyzed, as described below.

When playing a chord, a guitarist's fretting hand remains mostly still, while their strumming hand moves. In the current version of the system, tab output is calculated at every frame, even as it stays constant for the duration of a note. This results in unnecessary overhead, as well as an occasional jitter in the output due to a detection glitch. To address this problem, we are currently working on using key frames, i.e. frames where the guitarist's fretting hand moves significantly relative to the previous frame. These can be detected by calculating pixel differences in consecutive frames, as described by Wang and Ohya [15].

5   Conclusion and Future Work

In this paper we presented a real-time, computer vision-based, markerless system for transcribing guitar music. Our approach starts by detecting and tracking the strings and frets of the guitar. It then uses skin detection and contour following to extract and localize the fingertips on the guitar's fretboard.

We tested the system on three recordings of well-known guitar pieces, and achieved accuracies of 86%, 76%, and 71% on the C major chord progression, C major and E major scales, and the "Autumn Leaves" piece respectively. In particular, the 86% performance on the C major chord progression is significantly higher than that achieved by other systems. This can be attributed mostly to the fact that our system does not rely on detecting individual fingers. Instead, it localizes fingertips based on local maxima of the hand contour.

Tracking the guitar strings and frets from one frame to the next, rather than relying solely on detection in individual frames, also improves performance.

Another advantage of our system is that it can display the tablature output in real time, making it especially useful for educational purposes.

Future work includes implementing key frames as described in the previous section, as well as improvements to tracking and skin detection. Using optical flow based tracking such as the Lucas-Kanade [9] algorithm can make the system more robust to unexpected, fast moves by the guitarist. Skin detection could be improved to handle more varied skin tones.

Finally, better results could be obtained by analyzing the other hand of the guitarist to determine if strings are picked or strummed, and by using a multi-model approach that combines audio and video data.

Acknowledgment. The authors would like to thank Matthew Van Soelen for manually annotating the video files and helping with the error analysis.

References

1. Calculating fret positions. https://www.liutaiomottola.com/formulae/fret.htm. Accessed 10 Jun 2019
2. Ultimate guitar tabs - 1,100,000 songs catalog. https://www.ultimate-guitar.com. Accessed 10 Jun 2019
3. Burns, A.M.: Computer vision methods for guitarist left-hand fingering recognition (2007)
4. Burns, A.M., Wanderley, M.M.: Visual methods for the retrieval of guitarist fingering. In: Proceedings of the 2006 Conference on New Interfaces for Musical Expression, pp. 196–199. IRCAM-Centre Pompidou (2006)
5. Canny, J.: A computational approach to edge detection. In: Readings in Computer Vision, pp. 184–203. Elsevier (1987)
6. Harrison, E.: Challenges facing guitar education. Music Educators J. **97**(1), 50–55 (2010)
7. Kerdvibulvech, C., Saito, H.: Real-time guitar chord estimation by stereo cameras for supporting guitarists. In: Proceeding of 10th International Workshop on Advanced Image Technology (IWAIT 2007), pp. 256–261 (2007)
8. Kovac, J., Peer, P., Solina, F.: Human skin color clustering for face detection, vol. 2. IEEE (2003)
9. Lucas, B., Kanade, T.: An iterative image registration technique with an application to stereo vision. In: Proceedings of Image Understanding Workshop, pp. 121–130. IEEE (1981)
10. Paleari, M., Huet, B., Schutz, A., Slock, D.: A multimodal approach to music transcription. In: 2008 15th IEEE International Conference on Image Processing, pp. 93–96. IEEE (2008)
11. Scarr, J., Green, R.: Retrieval of guitarist fingering information using computer vision. In: 2010 25th International Conference of Image and Vision Computing New Zealand, pp. 1–7. IEEE (2010)

12. Suzuki, S., et al.: Topological structural analysis of digitized binary images by border following. Comput. Vis. Graph. Image Process. **30**(1), 32–46 (1985)
13. Traube, C.: An Interdisciplinary Study of the Timbre of the Classical Guitar. Ph.D. thesis, McGill University (2004)
14. Verner, J.A.: Midi guitar synthesis: yesterday, today and tomorrow. Recording Mag. **8**(9), 52–57 (1995)
15. Wang, Z., Ohya, J.: Tracking the guitarist's fingers as well as recognizing pressed chords from a video sequence. Electron. Imaging **2016**(15), 1–6 (2016)

A Parametric Perceptual Deficit Modeling and Diagnostics Framework for Retina Damage Using Mixed Reality

Prithul Aniruddha[1], Nasif Zaman[1], Alireza Tavakkoli[1(✉)], and Stewart Zuckerbrod[2]

[1] University of Nevada, Reno, NV 89557, USA
tavakkoli@unr.edu
[2] Houston Eye Associates, Houston, TX 77801, USA

Abstract. Age-related Macular Degeneration (AMD) is a progressive visual impairment affecting millions of individuals. Since there is no current treatment for the disease, the only means of improving the lives of individuals suffering from the disease is via assistive technologies. In this paper we propose a novel and effective methodology to accurately generate a parametric model for the perceptual deficit caused by the physiological deterioration of a patient's retina due to AMD. Based on the parameters of the model, a mechanism is developed to simulate the patient's perception as a result of the disease. This simulation can effectively deliver the perceptual impact and its progression to the patient's eye doctor. In addition, we propose a mixed-reality apparatus and interface to allow the patient recover functional vision and to compensate for the perceptual loss caused by the physiological damage. The results obtained by the proposed approach show the superiority of our framework over the state-of-the-art low-vision systems.

Keywords: Macular damage · Parametric modeling · Perceptual deficit · Mixed reality

1 Introduction

There are several age-related eye diseases and conditions that drastically affect one's quality of life by causing permanent vision loss [6, 19]. These include: Age-related Macular Degeneration (AMD), Diabetic Eye Diseases, and Glaucoma, to name a few. According to the National Eye Institute an estimated 37 million adults in the U.S. over the age of 40 suffer from an age-related eye condition, such as, age-related Macular Degeneration (AMD), Glaucoma, Diabetic Retinopathy, and Cataracts [20]. The leading condition affecting people over 40 is cataracts (24.4 million cases), followed by AMD (20 million cases), Diabetic Retinopathy (7.7 million cases), and Glaucoma (2.7 million cases). The total number of AMD, Diabetic Retinopathy, Cataract, and Glaucoma cases in the U.S. is expected to

G. Bebis et al. (Eds.): ISVC 2019, LNCS 11845, pp. 258–269, 2019.
https://doi.org/10.1007/978-3-030-33723-0_21

double between 2010 and 2050, according to the data from the National Eye Institute [21].

There is an effective surgical procedure to remove cataracts and treat patients. However, for other age-related conditions, such as AMD and other retinal diseases, there are no effective treatments to completely recover lost vision. Diabetic Retinopathy is the most common cause of vision loss in people with diabetes [15], while advanced AMD is the leading cause of irreversible blindness and visual impairment in otherwise healthy individuals in the U.S. [3]. The blindness caused by AMD or Diabetic Retinopathy is due to the damage to the patient's retina that result in central vision loss [10]. However, the damage caused to the optic nerve as a result of Glaucoma produces gradual loss of peripheral vision in one or both eyes [10]. In this paper, our main focus is on central vision loss but the methodologies developed within this project can easily be expanded to cover peripheral vision loss.

1.1 Motivations

As mentioned above, central vision loss is caused by the gradual deterioration of the center of the retina [14]. Currently several tests, including, Humphrey Visual Field (HVF) Testing, Fluorescein Angiography, Visual Acuity Testing, and Optical Coherence Tomography (OCT), are administered by eye care professionals to determine the affected area on the patient's retina. While these tests could provide physicians with physiological impacts of the affected area within the eye, they fall short of providing a measurement of the perceptual impact on the patient's vision. Although the location and the physiological extent of the damage can be determined, the current assistive technologies such as NuEyes [22], eSight [8,9], and Vivid Vision [29], do not utilize this information to provide site specific visual aid.

Current research indicates that there are a number of barriers that prevent the current technologies to provide each individual patient with specialized assistance in enhancing the remaining vision [16]. For example, there is a need to systematically examine how acuity level and visual field loss is associated with specific eye conditions, and how to utilize this connection to deliver specialized visual aid. There is also a need to utilize computer vision to enhance the provided visual aid to specific areas where the deficit in vision occurs. In this paper we address this gaps in the literature and develop a framework to significantly improve the current state of visual aid technologies for patients suffering from central vision loss.

2   Literature Review

Fundus photography is typically a great diagnostic tool for determining the physiological damage caused to the retina as a result of Age-related Macular Degeneration (AMD) – Fig. 1(a). In conjunction with visual field perimetry results (shown in Fig. 1(b)), physicians determine the physiological damage caused by the disease and track the progression of the condition.

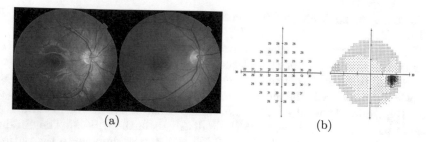

Fig. 1. (a) Retina damage caused by AMD (left), and Healthy retina (right). (b) Visual field perimetry shows a map of the visual field and the areas within the visual field that may be affected.

The main problem is the difficulty in interpreting the perceptual impact of the physical damage. For example, AMD can cause a number of different perceptual effects in patient's vision, as shown in Fig. 2. Therefore, the main question to address in developing a model of perceptual deficit is, what does the patient see as a result of the physical damage to the retina, and can we correct it?

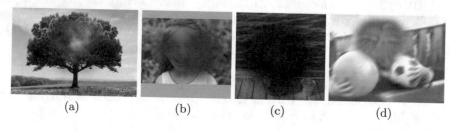

Fig. 2. Different perceptual impacts of AMD on vision.

Many commercially available kits try to simulate various vision loss phenomenons [11,12]. Usually they make use of goggles with easily changeable lenses to simulate different anomalies. Almutleb et al. used contact lenses to simulate central scotoma [1]. Although these techniques, specially the ones that use goggles, are inexpensive, their setup is rather cumbersome with each disease requiring a different hardware setup. Moreover they cannot be modified anymore once built and therefore will lose their effectiveness as the disease progresses.

Thus, software-based simulation techniques could be employed to obtain more flexibility. In recent years, many software simulators have been developed. Lewis et al. developed a simulation inside Unreal Engine 3 to visualize six impairments including AMD [17]. Currently a multitude of websites also provide interactive ways to simulate various impairments online [25,28,30]. However, these simulations work on a regular monitor. Moreover, they fall short of providing a complete binocular and stereoscopic simulation, thus are not an accurate and immersive representation of the visual loss.

Augmented Reality (AR) environments could be employed to deliver a more accurate simulation of the visual impairment. Velázquez et al. developed a simulator of several visual impairments for the normally sighted individuals [27]. However, the system used camera feed from a single camera and therefore is not stereoscopic in nature. SimViz solved this problem by mounting two PlayStation eye cameras [26] on an Oculus VR HMD to create a see-through AR display [2].

Most of the above mentioned simulators are capable of visualizing central vision loss. However, none can accurately model the perceptual loss caused by actual physiological damage impacting an individual's retina. Therefore, although the state-of-the-art simulators may be used as tools, for example assisting in development of other applications with accessibility in mind [5], they cannot be employed to model a patient's perceptual vision loss nor are they capable of recovering functional vision caused by the disease.

Wearable AR HMD technology is still in it's infancy and most traditional approaches to low-vision, such as SimVis, deliver ad-hoc solutions. The Microsoft Hololens [13] and the Magic Leap One [18] are among promising AR technologies on the horizon. However, while the potential is there, these devices are quite expensive and potentially out of reach for many patients [24].

In order to alleviate the current roadblocks in the software and hardware technology for developing a unified infrastructure to allow for both simulation and vision recovery, we propose the computation of a parameterised model for the perceptual deficit generated by the patients themselves. In order to accomplish this, there needs to be an easy way to integrate various parameters of the model into an intuitive interface for patients, most of whom are advanced in age.

Current literature on interaction techniques in VR deals with 3D movement. Chatterjee et al. describe a hand gesture based interaction technique for desktop environments [4] and Pfeuffer et al. take a similar approach but introduce a VR environments [23]. Both of these techniques, however, rely on eye gaze to focus on objects of interest. This can potentially cause problem for patients suffering from central vision loss, since fixation could be difficult for this population. Thus, in this paper, we focus on the development of a hand gesture based mechanism as a more appropriate design for our application.

3   The Proposed Approach

In this paper we utilize advances in the fields of Virtual Reality (VR) and Computer Vision (CV) in conjunction with the knowledge from current practices in the field of Ophthalmology to deliver transformative contributions to answer these questions. Specifically, this paper solves the problem of parameterizing the perceptual impairment and vision deficit in different AMD types based on the localized physiological damage. We will utilize the locus of the physiological damage to create parametric models for the visual deficit. This will lead to a VR central vision loss simulator for a variety of impairments associated with AMD.

3.1 Modeling Perceptual Deficit

We propose a parametric model for the perceptual loss as a 4-tuple of the following form:

$$\mathcal{P} = (\mathbf{\Gamma}, \mathbf{\Omega}_\lambda, \mathbf{R}_\theta, \mathbf{\Psi}) \tag{1}$$

where $\mathbf{\Gamma}$ represents luminance degradation, $\mathbf{\Omega}_\lambda$ represents a parametrization of the visual field loss region with λ as the cut-off value for the degradation determining the boundaries of $\mathbf{\Omega}_\lambda$, $\mathbf{R}_\theta$ is the rotational distortion matrix within $\mathbf{\Omega}_\lambda$, and $\mathbf{\Psi}$ is the a Sinusoidal mapping function representing the spatial distortion.

Modeling Luminance Degradation Effects. We propose a Gaussian Mixture Model (GMM) [7] as a representative model for the degradation in luminance caused as a result of damage to the cone photoreceptors. Therefore, the proposed model for luminance degradation, $\mathbf{\Gamma}$, will be of the following form:

$$\mathbf{\Gamma} = \sum_{i=1}^{N} \omega_i \cdot \mathcal{N}_{\vec{\mu}_i, \sigma_i}(u, v) \tag{2}$$

where u and v are the coordinate locations on the 2-D visual field, N is the number of Gaussian kernels (Normal distributions) modeling the deficit in the luminance perception in the visual field, and ω_i is the amount of luminance deficit caused by each Gaussian kernel. Each Gaussian is represented by $\mathcal{N}_{\vec{\mu}_i, \sigma_i}(\cdot)$, where $\vec{\mu}_i = [\mu_i^u, \mu_i^v]^T$ represents the center and σ represents the standard deviation of the distribution.

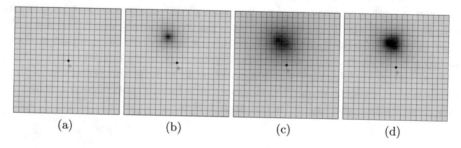

(a)   (b)   (c)   (d)

Fig. 3. Illumination degradation $\mathbf{\Gamma}$, represented by the proposed parametric model.

Figure 3 shows the results of the proposed illumination degradation model in affecting the vision on the Amsler grid (Fig. 3(a)). Figure 3(b) shows the illumination degradation modeled by a single Gaussian. A significant advantage of the proposed parametric model is in its ability to represent complex illumination degradations caused by the progressive retina damage. As shown in Fig. 3(c) and (d), with the progression of the disease a complex mathematical formulation than a single Gaussian will be needed to model the degradation. Note that for each Gaussian kernel, the luminance deficit is the highest at the central location of that kernel ($\vec{\mu}$).

Modeling Perceptual Deficit Region. Once the luminance degradation model is established in Eq. (2), it will be easy to determine the region in the visual field in which the perceptual impact is significant (see Fig. 4). Let's call this region Ω. Setting a cutoff value $0 < \lambda < 1$, the region Ω can be determined as the following:

$$\Omega = \left\{ (u, v) \in \mathbb{R}^2_{[0,1]} | \boldsymbol{\Gamma}(u, v) \leq \lambda \right\} \tag{3}$$

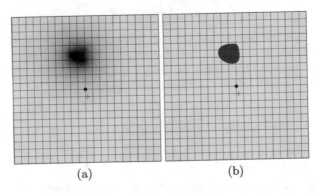

(a)   (b)

Fig. 4. Perceptual deficit region Ω, represented by the proposed parametric model. The area within the solid blue region represents illumination degradation of more than λ percent. (Color figure online)

The solid blue area in Fig. 4(b) shows the perceptual deficit region Ω for the modelled illumination degradation of Fig. 4(a). Note that since λ is a free parameter, it can control the boundary of the perceptual deficit region Ω. The larger the value of λ, the broader the regions Ω will be. We can also visualize multiple regions with different prominent levels of illumination degradation (Fig. 5).

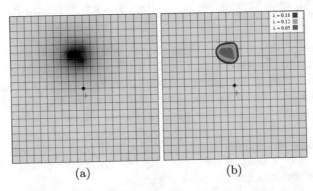

(a)   (b)

Fig. 5. Different perceptual deficit region Ω at various levels of degradation prominence λ. The area within the solid blue, green, and red regions represents illumination degradation of more than $\lambda = 18\%$, $\lambda = 12\%$, and $\lambda = 5\%$, respectively. (Color figure online)

Modeling Rotational Distortion. With the Loci of the perceptual damage determined by the cental positions ($\vec{\mu}_i$) of each Gaussian distribution in Eq. (2), we can model the rotational distortion as a result of physiological damage. Recall from Eq. (1) that rotational distortion, $\mathbf{R}_\theta$, is one of the components of the perceptual loss model, $\mathcal{P}$. Let θ be the angle of rotation, each point in the visual field will be rotated by the following rotation matrix:

$$\hat{\mathbf{R}}_\theta = \begin{bmatrix} \cos\theta & -\sin\theta \\ \sin\theta & \cos\theta \end{bmatrix} \tag{4}$$

However, since the perceptual impact decreases as we get farther away from the central location of each Gaussian kernel, the rotational distortion becomes less and less prominent. Therefore, we model the rotational distortion within the damaged region Ω for each of the Gaussian kernels as:

$$\mathbf{R}_\theta = \sum_{i=1}^{N} \omega_i \mathcal{N}_{\vec{\mu}_i, \sigma_i}(u, v) \hat{\mathbf{R}}_{\theta_i} \tag{5}$$

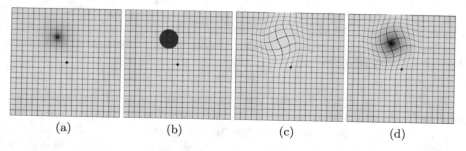

(a)   (b)   (c)   (d)

Fig. 6. Modeling rotational distortion: (a) A single Gaussian kernel illumination degradation. (b) The perceptual impact regions with $\lambda = 0.5$. (c) the Rotational distortion with $\frac{\pi}{2}$ angle. (d) Both illumination degradation and rotational distortion.

The effects of this rotational distortion within the affected region of the visual field may be observed from Fig. 6. In Fig. 6(a) the model utilizes a single Gaussian kernel with its impact region shown in Fig. 6(b) at $\lambda = 0.5$. A rotation of $\theta = \frac{\pi}{2}$ will cause the rotational distortion shown in Fig. 6(c). The effects of both the illumination degradation and rotational distortion can be observed in Fig. 6(d).

Figure 7 shows the advantage of the proposed parameterized framework in modelling the progression of both the illumination degradation and rotational distortion as a result of the disease progression.

Modeling Spatial Distortion. The final component of the perceptual deficit is the spatial distortion model $\mathbf{\Psi}$. This model represents the spatial shift perceived by the patient as a result of the damage to the retina that is not captured by the

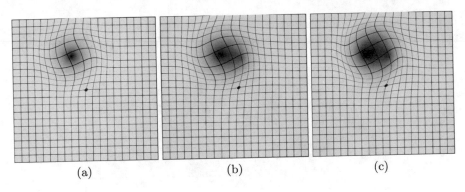

(a)   (b)   (c)

Fig. 7. Rotational distortion and illumination degradation as the disease progresses.

rotational distortion model described in Sect. 3.1. This model is represented by a vector field dictating the spatial translation of points within the visual field. The complete spatial distortion vector field $\mathbf{\Psi}$ is defined as:

$$\mathbf{\Psi} = \sum_{i=1}^{N} \mathcal{N}_{\vec{\mu}_i, \sigma_i}^{i}(u, v) * \mathbf{I_2} * \left[\begin{pmatrix} u - \mu_u^i \\ v - \mu_v^i \end{pmatrix} \right] \tag{6}$$

where $\mathcal{N}^i$ represents each of the Gaussian deficit models with the mean of $\vec{\mu}_i$ and standard deviation of σ_i. $\mathbf{I_2}$ represents the 2×2 identity matrix, and u and v are coordinates within the visual field. To illustrate this spatial distortion effect, suppose we have a single scotoma at the central location of the visual field (i.e., $[u \quad v]^T = \mathbf{0}$). The vector field representing the spatial distortion model will be of the following form (and shown in Fig. 8(a)):

$$\mathbf{\Psi} \approx \left[\begin{matrix} e^{-\frac{(u-\mu_u)^2+(v-\mu_v)^2}{2\sigma^2}} * (u - \mu_u) \\ e^{-\frac{(u-\mu_u)^2+(v-\mu_v)^2}{2\sigma^2}} * (v - \mu_v) \end{matrix} \right] \tag{7}$$

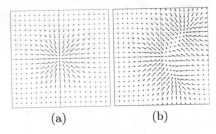

(a)   (b)

Fig. 8. Vector fields representing the spatial distortion maps, as modeled by: (a) a single Gaussian kernel, and (b) multiple Gaussian kernels.

Figure 8 shows the vector fields representing spatial transformations that the visual field undergoes as a result of the physiological damage. A single Gaussian kernel will generate a simple vector field shown in Fig. 8(a), while a more complex spatial distortion will require a Gaussian Mixture Model as seen in Fig. 8(b).

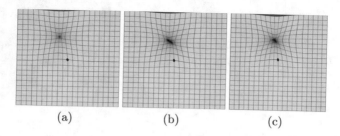

(a)   (b)   (c)

Fig. 9. Spatial distortion of the Amsler grid as represented by the Ψ component of the proposed model. Note the model adaptation and its ability to capture disease progression: modeling spatial distortion with (a) a single Gaussian kernel, (b) two Gaussian kernels, and (c) three Gaussian kernels.

The strength of the proposed model for representing the spatial distortions caused by the disease can be seen from Fig. 9. At the early stages of the disease a single Gaussian kernel may be sufficient to model the distortions (Fig. 9(a)), but as the disease progresses more complex models will be required. The proposed mixture model shows the flexibility to represent the distortion changes as the disease progresses without the need to fundamentally change the model, but rather increase the number of Gaussian kernels (Fig. 9(b) and (c)).

(a)   (b)

Fig. 10. (a) The diagnostic interface allowing the patient to establish the perceptual deficit model and populate its parameters in the Diagnostic VR environment. (b) The functional vision recovery allowing the video feed from a webcam corrected by the patient's perceptual deficit model and mapped to patient's eye.

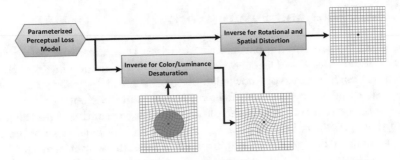

Fig. 11. The dichoptic solution for vision compensation by enhancing the remaining vision in the affected eye determines the vision loss region (W) and the parameters of the perceptual loss from Model $\mathcal{P}$.

4   Experimental Results

The proposed framework is a comprehensive diagnostic and vision recover system. Therefore, the patients will utilize the system in two phases: The VR Diagnostic Mode, and the AR Vision Compensation Mode.

In the first mode (shown in Fig. 10(a)) the Amsler grid is shown to the patient in a neutral VR environment with the proposed user interfaces to allow the patient to interact with parameters of their perceptual deficit model. Changing the parameters updates the material being rendered for the patient's eyes in real-time. Our goal here is to have the user closely mimic what they see with their affected eye in order to populate the parameters of their perceptual deficit model in the affected eye.

Once the the patient accurately model their perceptual deficit, the remainder of the operation for recovering functional vision will take place in the AR mode. In this mode the VR HMD works as an AR glass, by presenting the patient with the live video of the environment captured through the stereoscopic video cameras. The images in the video feed shown to the unaffected eye is, however, distorted by with the perceptual loss model that the user came up in the Amsler grid mode. This gives the user an opportunity to test how the distortion looks in real life. Figure 10(b) shows the uncorrected vision of a patient as observed by a physician. The inverse of the parametric model is applied and the patient sees the environment as if their eye were not affected.

Based on the model generated by the proposed framework in the VR Diagnostics mode, an inverse function for the perceptual vision loss is calculated. This inverse model is then applied in the AR mode to the live-stream videos recorded and rendered to each individual eye. The process is shown in Fig. 11. As seen in the figure, the inverse function for the parametric vision loss will compensate for the perceptual impact of the vision loss to recover as much functional vision as possible.

5   Conclusions and Future Work

In this paper we presented a parametric model for the perceptual deficit caused by Age-related Macular Degeneration (AMD). This model bridges the gap between our current state of knowledge about the physiological damage caused to the retina and its perceptual effect on the patient's vision. We developed a mixed-reality system that allows the patient to configure and update the parameters of their perceptual deficit in a VR mode. Once the patient's unique vision loss is modeled, the system is employed in AR mode to perform the inverse model on the affected eye to compensate for the perceptual deficit and recover functional vision. The experiments show that the proposed system captures the patient's vision loss and allows for significant recovery of the functional vision.

One future direction to this work includes modeling other vision loss and visual anomalies such as Glaucoma, Diabetic Retinopathy, etc. Our team is also conducting human trails in order to validate the usability, efficacy, and acceptability of the proposed system.

References

1. Almutleb, E., Bradley, A., Jedlicka, J., Hassan, S.: Simulation of a central scotoma using contact lenses with an opaque centre. Ophthalmic Physiol. Opt. **2018**(38), 76–87 (2017)
2. Ates, H.C., Fiannaca, A., Folmer, E.: Immersive simulation of visual impairments using a wearable see-through display. In: Proceedings of the Ninth International Conference on Tangible, Embedded, and Embodied Interaction, pp. 225–228. ACM (2015)
3. Bressler, N.M.: Age-related macular degeneration is the leading cause of blindness. JAMA **291**(15), 1900–1901 (2004)
4. Chatterjee, I., Xiao, R., Harrison, C.: Gaze+ gesture: expressive, precise and targeted free-space interactions. In: Proceedings of the 2015 ACM on International Conference on Multimodal Interaction, pp. 131–138. ACM (2015)
5. Choo, K.T.W., Balan, R.K., Wee, T.K., Chauhan, J., Misra, A., Lee, Y.: Empath-d: empathetic design for accessibility. In: Proceedings of the 18th International Workshop on Mobile Computing Systems and Applications, pp. 55–60. ACM (2017)
6. Congdon, N., et al.: Causes and prevalence of visual impairment among adults in the united states. Arch. Ophthalmol. **122**(4), 477–485 (2004). (Chicago, Ill.: 1960)
7. Cootes, T.F., Taylor, C.J.: A mixture model for representing shape variation. Image Vis. Comput. **17**(8), 567–573 (1999)
8. Devenyi, R.: Wearable technology expands mobility for visually impaired. Ophthalmology Times (2016)
9. eSight: eSight. https://www.esighteyewear.com/homex. Accessed 2018
10. Evans, K., Law, S.K., Walt, J., Buchholz, P., Hansen, J.: The quality of life impact of peripheral versus central vision loss with a focus on glaucoma versus age-related macular degeneration. Clin. Ophthalmol. **3**, 433 (2009). (Auckland, NZ)
11. Fork in the Road Website: Fork in the road: low vision simulators. https://www.lowvisionsimulators.com/collections/find-the-right-low-vision-simulator/, Accessed 24 Mar 2019

12. Good-lite: Visualeyes vision simulator glasses. https://www.good-lite.com/Details. cfm?ProdID=766. Accessed 24 Mar 2019
13. Microsoft hololens mixed reality technology for business. https://www.microsoft. com/en-us/hololens. Accessed 13 May 2019
14. Jager, R.D., Mieler, W.F., Miller, J.W.: Age-related macular degeneration. N. Engl. J. Med. **358**(24), 2606–2617 (2008). https://doi.org/10.1056/NEJMra0801537. pMID: 18550876
15. Kahn, H.A., Hiller, R.: Blindness caused by diabetic retinopathy. Am. J. Ophthalmol. **78**(1), 58–67 (1974)
16. Kinateder, M., Gualtieri, J., Dunn, M.J., Jarosz, W., Yang, X.D., Cooper, E.A.: Using an augmented reality device as a distance-based vision aid-promise and limitations. Optometry Vis. Sci. **95**(9), 727 (2018)
17. Lewis, J., Brown, D., Cranton, W., Mason, R.: Simulating visual impairments using the unreal engine 3 game engine. In: 2011 IEEE 1st International Conference on Serious Games and Applications for Health (SeGAH), pp. 1–8. IEEE (2011)
18. Magic Leap Inc.: Magic leap one (2019). https://www.magicleap.com/magic-leap-one
19. Massof, R.W.: A systems model for low vision rehabilitation. II. Measurement of vision disabilities. Optometry Vis. Sci. **75**(5), 349–373 (1998). Official Publication of the American Academy of Optometry
20. National Eye Institute: Prevalence of adult vision impairment and age-related eye diseases in America. https://nei.nih.gov/eyedata/adultvision_usa. Accessed 15 Sept 2018
21. National Eye Institute: Statistics and data: the most common eye diseases: NEI looks ahead. https://nei.nih.gov/eyedata. Accessed 15 Sept 2018
22. NuEyes Inc.: NuEyes. https://nueyes.com/nueyes-pro/. Accessed 2018
23. Pfeuffer, K., Mayer, B., Mardanbegi, D., Gellersen, H.: Gaze+ pinch interaction in virtual reality. In: Proceedings of the 5th Symposium on Spatial User Interaction, pp. 99–108. ACM (2017)
24. Robertson, A.: I tried magic leap and saw a flawed glimpse of mixed reality's amazing potential, August 2018. https://www.theverge.com/2018/8/8/17662040/magic-leap-one-creator-edition-preview-mixed-reality-glasses-launch
25. Vision Loss Simulator: Vision loss simulator (2019)
26. Stocker, S.: Playstation eye, a little more info (2007). https://blog.us.playstation. com/2007/10/10/playstation-eye-a-little-more-info/
27. Velázquez, R., Sánchez, C.N., Pissaloux, E.E.: Visual impairment simulator based on the Hadamard product. Electron. Notes Theor. Comput. Sci. **329**, 169–179 (2016)
28. Vision disorders. https://www.genworth.com/aging-and-you/health/vision-disorders.html#/. Accessed 22 Mar 2019
29. Vivid Vision: Vivid Vision. https://www.seevividly.com/. Accessed 30 Sept 2018
30. World Health Organization: Blindness and vision impairment. https://www.who. int/news-room/fact-sheets/detail/blindness-and-visual-impairment. Accessed 22 Mar 2019

Topologically-Guided Color Image Enhancement

Junyi Tu[ID] and Paul Rosen[✉][ID]

University of South Florida, Tampa, FL 33620, USA
{junyi,prosen}@mail.usf.edu

Abstract. Enhancement is an important step in post-processing digital images for personal use, in medical imaging, and for object recognition. Most existing manual techniques rely on region selection, similarity, and/or thresholding for editing, never really considering the topological structure of the image. In this paper, we leverage the contour tree to extract a hierarchical representation of the topology of an image. We propose 4 topology-aware transfer functions for editing features of the image using local topological properties, instead of global image properties. Finally, we evaluate our approach with grayscale and color images.

Keywords: Image editing · Topological Data Analysis · Contour tree

1 Introduction

Image enhancement techniques aim to provide users maximal control in directing the improvements of the appearance of an image. They are widely used in photography post-processing (i.e., retouching), medical image processing, and object recognition. Many image editing platforms, such as Adobe Photoshop, utilize region selection, similarity, and/or thresholding to determine groups of pixels to edit. Then, editing options (e.g., contrast or brightness) that only consider global image properties are provided, never considering the topological structure of an image. Topological information provides a new perspective on the "shape" of the image and new capabilities for manipulating it [14].

In this paper, we leverage a tool from Topological Data Analysis (TDA) [6], specifically the contour tree [3], to extract a hierarchical representation of key features of an image (i.e., critical points) and the monotonic regions connecting those features (i.e., Morse cells). The contour tree of a scalar function defined on a simply connected domain (i.e., an image) is obtained by encoding the evolution of the connectivity of the level sets induced by the scalar function. The key property of contour tree that makes it a viable tool for image enhancement is its graph-based representation that captures the changes of topology in image data. The contour tree can therefore be searched, modified, and pruned locally, in a quantifiable way, while retaining the global structures in the image. Using the contour tree, topology-aware transfer functions provide new image enhancement

© Springer Nature Switzerland AG 2019
G. Bebis et al. (Eds.): ISVC 2019, LNCS 11845, pp. 270–282, 2019.
https://doi.org/10.1007/978-3-030-33723-0_22

functionalities for editing images using local topological properties, instead of using global image properties.

The contributions of this paper are: (1) we provide a mapping of color images to the *contour tree* for extracting the topological structure of the image; (2) we describe an interface for selecting topological features for image editing; and (3) we provide 4 topology-aware transfer function modalities for image editing: brightness enhancement, contrast enhancement, denoising, and gamma correction.

2   Capturing the Topology of an Image

Let $f : \Omega \subset \mathbb{R}^2 \to \mathbb{R}$ be a continuous function on a simply connected domain Ω. The level set of a single isovalue z is $f^{-1}(z) = \{(x, y) : f(x, y) = z\}$, and a contour is a connected component of a level set. The most familiar context of contours are topographic maps (see Fig. 1), where f is the elevation, and contours are shown at selected values. The contour tree tracks the creation, merging, splitting, and destruction of contours as a plane is swept across f.

Consider the example height map in Fig. 1(c) and contour tree in Fig. 1(d). First, a plane z is swept from $-\infty \to +\infty$. As the plane sweeps up, when it reaches local minima, nodes are created in the contour tree, denoted by labels m, l, and d, since these represent the "birth" of a contour. As the plane continues its sweep up, one can observe that at $z = f_{red-plane}$ there are 3 independent contours, each represented by an edge in the contour tree.

At $z = f_h$, a special event occurs, where the contour of l and d merge together. The merge, called a *join event*, represents the "death" of the contour that was born more recently, in this case l. The event creates the *feature pair* l/h. Similarly, at $z = f_o$, the contours of m and d join and m "dies", creating the m/o pair.

The birth/death relationships are important, because they segment the space into a hierarchy of regions of uniform (i.e., monotonic) behavior. Furthermore,

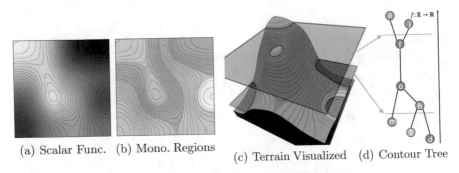

(a) Scalar Func.   (b) Mono. Regions   (c) Terrain Visualized   (d) Contour Tree

Fig. 1. (a) A scalar function defined on a simple domain (with contours shown for demonstration purposes only) (b) has monotonic regions differentiated by color. The function, (c) visualized as terrain with 2 isovalues highlighted (i.e., the red and blue planes), (d) produces a contour tree, where the nodes represent critical points and edges represent regions of monotonic behavior. (Color figure online)

the difference between the birth and death, $|f_{birth} - f_{death}|$, of a contour is known as the *persistence* of the feature. Persistence is an important measure in our context, as it captures the amplitude/magnitude of a feature.

Likewise, we also consider a sweep plane z that goes from $+\infty \rightarrow -\infty$. As the plane sweeps downwards, new contours are born at local maxima, such as a and j. For downward sweeps, when the contours merge together at $z = f_f$, this is called a *split event*. Similarly to join events, the split represents the "death" of the feature born more recently, in this case j/f. With splits, $f_{birth} > f_{death}$.

Finally, the global minimum and maximum are paired into a special feature, captured twice as d/a and a/d, representing the range of values.

2.1   Computing the Contour Tree

We briefly describe the computation of the contour tree. For a detailed description and efficient algorithm, see [4,15].

As the previous section implies, the construction is split into 2 phases: an upward and downward sweep, implemented as join tree (see Fig. 2(c)) and split tree (see Fig. 2(e)) construction, respectively. To find the join and split trees, the construction first finds the *augmented join tree* and *augmented split tree*.

Using the scalar field in Fig. 2(a), which is a downsampled version of Fig. 1(a), the augmented join tree construction is shown in Fig. 2(b). First, the pixels are sorted by values, $f_d < f_c < f_m < f_l < \ldots < f_f < f_j < f_a$. Pixels are inserted 1 at a time into the augmented join tree. As they are inserted, connected components are tracked by connecting with neighboring pixels already in the augmented join tree. In our implementation we consider the ring of 8 neighbors surrounding a given pixel. In this example, we only consider 4 (i.e., left/right/up/down) neighbors. If a pixel joins 1 or more existing components, it is connected to the top of those components in the augmented join tree. If it joins no component, it starts a new connected component. For example, when d is added to the tree, no connected components exist, so it creates one. When

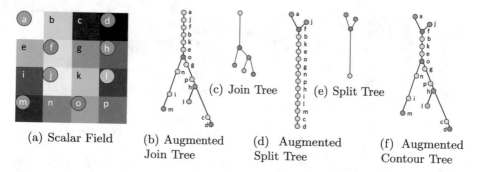

(a) Scalar Field   (b) Augmented Join Tree   (c) Join Tree   (d) Augmented Split Tree   (e) Split Tree   (f) Augmented Contour Tree

Fig. 2. (a) A low resolution version of Fig. 1(a) has its (b) augmented join and (d) split trees generated. (f) The trees combine into an augmented contour tree. The critical points of the augmented trees generate the (c) join, (e) split, and (Fig. 1(d)) contour trees of the scalar field.

c is inserted, it joins the $\{d\}$ component, since they are neighbors in the image. Continuing forward, when h is inserted, it links the $\{l\}$ component to the $\{c, d\}$ component.

Augmented split tree construction is performed nearly identically, except it starts at the largest valued pixel first. The augmented contour tree is constructed by pealing leaf nodes off of the join/split trees and adding them to the augmented contour tree, as described in [4]. The join/split/contour trees consist of only critical nodes (i.e., nodes that cause birth and death events). They are calculated by removing "regular" nodes, those having only 1 upward and 1 downward edge, from the augmented tree. Finally, using the contour tree, the critical points are paired into birth/death units using the approach in [16].

This construction assumes that all pixels have unique values, which is not the case in real images. There are 2 cases of equal valued pixels we consider. When equal valued pixels are non-adjacent, no special handling is required—the pixels can be processed in arbitrary order, but the output is still deterministic. However, adjacent pixels of equal value are problematic, since changing their insertion order can change the contour tree structure. This is resolved by grouping adjacent equal-valued pixels into "super-pixel" units that are processed together.

2.2 Feature Subtree Extraction

Extracting the regions of monotonic behavior requires selecting a subtree from the augmented contour tree for a given feature pair. Given a join/split node and local minimum/maximum pair, starting at the join/split, find the 3 subtrees extending from it. The selected subtree for the feature pair is the one containing the local minimum/maximum node. For example, in Fig. 2(f), the m/o feature pair contains join node o and local minimum m. Join node o has 3 subtrees: up, down-left, and down-right. The down-left subtree contains the local minimum node m, making it the feature subtree, containing nodes $\{m, i, n, o\}$. The selection can be seen in Fig. 4(a).

2.3 Using the Contour Tree of Color Images

The contour tree requires $f : \mathbb{X} \to \mathbb{R}$ (i.e., a single color channel). However, considering color images in RGB (Red, Green, Blue) colorspace, 3 channels map to each pixel. We consider each channel, red, green, and blue independently, generating 3 contour trees. We also consider HSB (Hue, Saturation, Brightness) colorspace. Saturation and brightness each map to their own contour trees. However, hue maps to $\mathbb{S}^1$ (i.e., circular coordinates), and the contour tree does not work in $\mathbb{S}^1$. Resolving this limitation requires additional theoretical studies. Other colorspaces are possible, when channels map to $\mathbb{R}$.

3 Image Processing via Contour Trees

The basic procedure for topology-based enhancement of an image is: (1) first, the user selects a set of feature pairs of interest; (2) next, the feature pairs are used to automatically select pixels for editing; (3) finally, the image is edited by the user, and the contour trees are recalculated so the process can restart.

3.1 Visualizing the Contour Tree

Direct visualization of the contour tree is generally not advisable, as the size and complexity of the tree is unmanageable for even moderately sized data. To select features to edit, each contour tree is displayed using 2 interactive interfaces—the persistence diagram and persistence-volume diagram.

Persistence Diagram. A standard practice in TDA represents the contour tree with birth/death feature pairs in a scatterplot display, called a *persistence diagram* [5]. In a persistence diagram, the x-axis is tied to the feature birth value, while the death value is tied to the y-axis. Figure 3(a) (left) shows an example for the contour tree in Fig. 1(d). Join features (i.e., l/h and m/o) are on the upper left, while split features (i.e., j/f) are on the lower right. Features are also colored by their type—join features blue and split features red. The persistence diagram provides 2 powerful selection hints. First, features on the lower left are darker pixels, while those on the upper right are brighter pixels, since the birth and death are parameterized by pixel value. Second, the distance of the point from the diagonal is an analog of the *persistence* of the feature pair. In other words, features with larger magnitude are farther from the diagonal.

Persistence-Volume Diagram. The persistence diagram primarily captures the amplitude of a selected feature. The volume (i.e., the pixel count of a feature) is sometimes important as well. The *persistence-volume diagram* (see Fig. 3(a) (right)) is an alternative representation that encodes persistence (i.e., $|f_{birth} - f_{death}|$) on the x-axis using a linear scale and volume on the y-axis using a log scale. Volume is calculated by counting the number of nodes/pixels in the feature subtree. For example, the m/o contains 4 nodes/pixels, m, i, n, and o.

3.2 Subtree Selection

Once the contour trees are generated and visualized, user interaction can proceed. Many topological features come from an image, so while individual selection is possible, selection of multiple features is desirable. We provide a brushing mechanism on both the persistence diagram and persistence-volume diagram for selecting a *set* of features of interest. As the mouse is clicked-and-dragged, the features and feature subtrees are gathered for further processing. For example, brushing across the middle of the persistence-volume diagram in Fig. 3(a) would select feature m/o and its subtree, as shown in Fig. 3(b). Features of the contour tree are hierarchical, thus, if more than one feature is selected, those features may be inclusions (i.e., one feature may be a subsets of another). In that case, only the larger/outermost feature is processed.

The selected feature pairs and their associated subtrees are relatively easy to use for segmentation. Starting with a full resolution binary mask, the nodes/pixels of each selected feature is marked in the mask. Figure 4(f) shows how this would work given the selection of the m/o feature from Fig. 1.

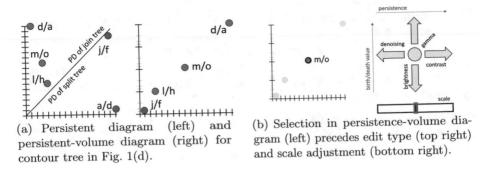

(a) Persistent diagram (left) and persistent-volume diagram (right) for contour tree in Fig. 1(d).

(b) Selection in persistence-volume diagram (left) precedes edit type (top right) and scale adjustment (bottom right).

Fig. 3. (a) The main interfaces used for selecting topological features use the persistence diagram (left) and persistence-volume diagram (right). (b) Once features a selected (left) the editing interface enables selecting the type and scale of edits (right).

3.3 Subtree Modification as Image Editing

From a segmentation mask, global image editing options (i.e., contrast enhancement, brightness enhancements, etc.) could be easily executed. However, this misses an opportunity for modifications based upon local topology, by using subtree information. For subtree-based modification, we provide 4 transfer function options that utilize the properties of the subtree.

Contrast Enhancement. Contrast enhancement fixes value of the feature pair join/split node and linearly stretches rest of the subtree. For a given node $\sim$ in the subtree and a contrast scale factor $s \geq 1$, the value $f'_\sim = f_{death} + (f_\sim - f_{death}) \cdot s$. Figure 4(b) shows an example of the operation, where the local contrast enhancement fixes the death value of a feature, while lowering the birth value.

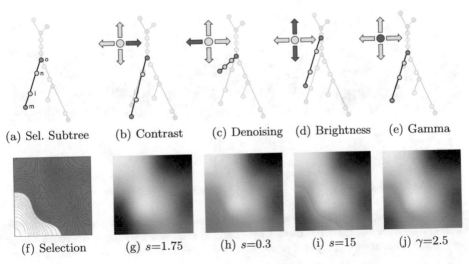

(a) Sel. Subtree   (b) Contrast   (c) Denoising   (d) Brightness   (e) Gamma

(f) Selection   (g) $s=1.75$ (h) $s=0.3$ (i) $s=15$ (j) $\gamma=2.5$

Fig. 4. Using the (a/f) selected subtree, (b/g) contrast enhancement, (c/h) denoising, (d/i) brightness enhancement, and (e/j) gamma correction operations are shown.

Denoising. Denoising linearly collapses the subtree, such that all pixels eventually have the same value, f_{death}. The calculation of denoising is identical to contrast enhancement—for a given node $\sim$ in the subtree and a denoising scale factor $0 \leq s \leq 1$, the value $f'_\sim = f_{death} + (f_\sim - f_{death}) \cdot s$. Figure 4(c) shows an example, where the death value is fixed and the values of other nodes/pixels are increased.

Brightness Enhancement. The brightness of the entire subtree can be modified up or down uniformly. For a given node $\sim$ in the subtree and a brightness scale factor $-255 \leq s \leq +255$, the value $f'_\sim = f_\sim + s$. Figure 4(d) shows an example.

Gamma Correction. Gamma correction provides a nonlinear modification, which is usually applied to the luminance of an image. For a given node $\sim$ in the subtree and a gamma correction value γ, where $\gamma > 0$, the value of a pixel $f_\sim$ is first normalized and gamma corrected $\overline{f}_\sim = \left(\frac{f_\sim - f_{death}}{f_{birth} - f_{death}} \right)^\gamma$. The final value of the pixel is then linearly interpolated, $f'_\sim = f_{death} \cdot (1 - \overline{f}_\sim) + f_{birth} \cdot (\overline{f}_\sim)$. Figure 4(e) shows an example, where $\gamma = 2.5$.

Interface. The interface for selecting the editing mode and scale is shown in Fig. 3(b). The interface designed represents how a chosen function modifies the persistence of the feature (horizontally) and the birth and death of a feature (vertically). For example, contrast enhancement increases persistence, while denoising decreases it. Brightness enhancement modified both the birth and death of a feature, leaving persistence unchanged. Finally, gamma correction changes nothing about the birth, death, or persistence. To use this interface, the user simply selects the button (i.e., the arrow or the circle) for the edit type they prefer. Finally, the level of the transfer function is selected using a slider.

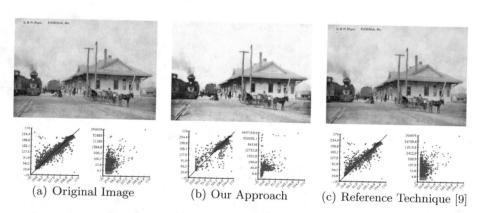

(a) Original Image   (b) Our Approach   (c) Reference Technique [9]

Fig. 5. *Florala dataset.* The (a) original, (b) cleaned by a combination of denoised, contrast enhancement, and gamma correction, is compared to (c) a reference image from [9]. A persistence (left) and persistence-volume (right) diagram is shown for each.

Topology Preservation. It is important to note that many of these edits will ultimately modify the local topology (i.e., within a subtree) and/or global topology (i.e., entire contour tree) of the image. Contrast enhancement and denoising change the persistence of local topology, and they can change feature pairs in the global context. Brightness enhancement makes no modification of the local topology, but significant changes can occur in the global topology (e.g., creation of new features, changes in persistence, etc.). Finally, gamma correction can modify the persistence of local topology, but it will have no effect on the global topology. To handle these cases, as part of the normal process of image editing, the contour trees are recalculated after an edit is applied to the image.

4   Examples

We have implemented a prototypes of our approach using Java. Images were generated using a 2017 MacBook Pro. All aspects of our approach are interactive, except the construction of the contour trees and extraction of feature pair subtrees, which took between 5 and 30 s, depending upon the size and complexity of the image. Before considering the quality of an enhancement, context, such as how the image will be utilized, needs to be taken into account. We do not consider this context in our analysis, and instead only provide examples enhancements.

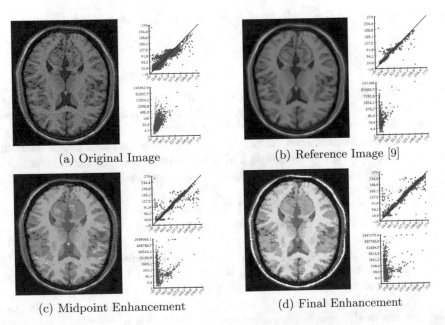

(a) Original Image   (b) Reference Image [9]

(c) Midpoint Enhancement   (d) Final Enhancement

Fig. 6. *Brain dataset* cleaned using a combination of all 4 functions. Each image include its persistence diagram (top) and persistence-volume diagram (bottom).

Synthetic Example. Our synthetic example, based upon the selection of the m/o feature from Fig. 3(b), has the operations outlined in Fig. 4 applied: contrast enhancement (Fig. 4(g)), denoising (Fig. 4(h)), brightness enhancement (Fig. 4(i)), and gamma correction (Fig. 4(j)).

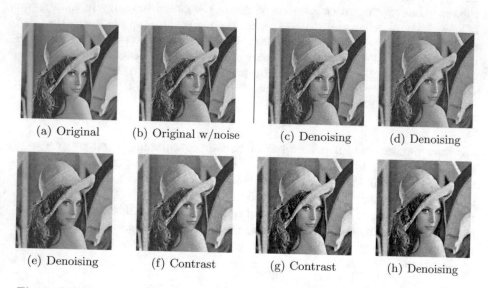

| (a) Original | (b) Original w/noise | (c) Denoising | (d) Denoising |

| (e) Denoising | (f) Contrast | (g) Contrast | (h) Denoising |

Fig. 7. (a/b) *Lenna Grayscale.* (c–h) Series of denoising and contrast enhancement.

4.1   Grayscale Images

Since contour trees operate on a single channel, grayscale images are a natural way to demonstrate this functionality. For the following datasets, the brightness channel of the HSB colorspace was used for editing.

The *Florala dataset*, seen in Fig. 5(a), is a photograph of Florala Alabama, retrieved from [9]. The photograph had a series of denoising, contrast enhancement, and gamma correction steps applied to recover the final image in Fig. 5(b). The persistence and persistence-volume diagrams are shown for comparison.

The *Brain dataset*, seen in Fig. 6(a), is a noisy and low contrast MRI scan of a brain, retrieved from [9]. The figure shows a midpoint (Fig. 6(c)) and the final version (Fig. 6(d)) after a combination of 12 contrast, brightness, gamma correction, and denoising steps. The final image removes noise and highlights important features, such as the skull, white matter, and grey matter. The persistence and persistence-volume diagrams are shown for comparison.

The *Lenna Grayscale Dataset*, seen in Fig. 7 shows a series of 7 edits to a noisy version of the classic Lenna dataset.

(a) Original Data

(b) Reference Method [7]

(e) Brightness Channel

(c) Green Channel

(d) Saturation Channel

Fig. 8. (a) *Notre Dame dataset.* (b) Reference method [7] is compared to a version modified using (c) the green channel, then (d) saturation, and finally (e) the brightness. (Color figure online)

4.2 Color Images

The *Notre Dame dataset*, retrieved from [7] and shown in Fig. 8(a), is a photo with an underexposed foreground. For this dataset, we first performed a (virtually invisible) brightness enhancement to the green color channel, to make the foliage a green hue (see Fig. 8(c)). Next, we performed a denoising and contrast enhancement to the saturation channel of the HSB colorspace (see Fig. 8(d)). Finally, denoising, gamma correction, and contrast enhancement were applied to the brightness channel of HSB. Persistence and persistence-volume diagram are not shown due to the number of diagrams involved (10 total—2 × red, green, blue, saturation, and brightness). This is compared to a reference image (Fig. 8(b)) generated using a high-dynamic range technique (i.e., using significantly more data than our approach).

The *Swan dataset*, shown in Fig. 9(a) is a photograph of a swan with a mix of light and shadow, retrieved from [7]. We perform a series of enhancements that include denoising of the brightness channel (see Fig. 9(c)); followed by brightness enhancement in the saturation channel (see Fig. 9(d)); and contrast enhancement and gamma correction of the brightness channel (see Fig. 9(e)). This is compared to a reference image (Fig. 9(b)) generated using a high-dynamic range technique.

The *Lenna Color Dataset*, seen in Fig. 10 shows a series of 11 edits to a noisy version of the classic color Lenna dataset.

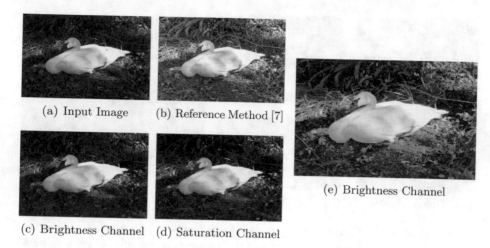

Fig. 9. (a) *Swan dataset*. (b) Reference method [7] is compared to image enhanced using (c) denoising of brightness, then (d) brightness enhancement of saturation, and finally (e) contrast enhancement and gamma correction of the brightness. (Color figure online)

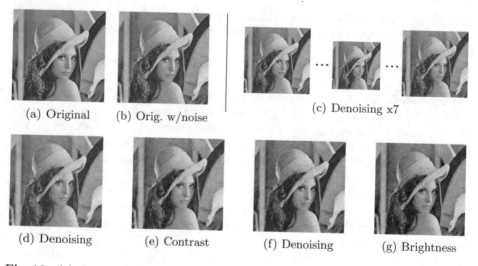

Fig. 10. (a) *Lenna Color* with noise added. (b–f) A series of denoising, contrast enhancement, and brightness enhancement steps. (Color figure online)

5   Prior Work and Conclusions

We have presented a new approach to image enhancement based upon the topology of an image. Our approach provides a high-level of control to users, while not requiring an extensive number of interactions to achieve desirable results.

Like with most other image enhancement algorithms, artifacts are important concern. Our approach does not introduce new artifacts, per se, but instead it may emphasize existing image artifacts. For example in Fig. 5, blocking artifacts appear due to lack of detail for generating a smooth result. In Fig. 6, artifacts occur due once again to missing contrast and detail that lead to small differences in intensity ending up emphasized.

Much of the prior work on image enhancement has focused on automated techniques. A number approaches have addressed segmentation. For example, algorithms for edge detection and image segmentation detected "contours" (i.e., edges) in a hierarchical manner for segmentation [1]. Supervised learning, such as the hierarchical merge trees model in [12], is popular in image segmentation. Contrast enhancement has been proposed as an optimization problem that maximizes the average local contrast of an image [13]. Recently, deep learning has been leveraged to automatically retouch images [8]. These approaches provide high quality results, but they offer limited opportunity for tuning the output.

TDA has also been used previously in image processing. The first use of the contour tree on a binary image was [2]. Edge detection and Delaunay triangulation were performed to decompose images into regions indexed by radius of a disk and persistence [11]. Finally, persistence-based segmentation of noisy 2D point clouds has been studied in [10]. Our approach in this paper is different from these prior works in that it not only captures the structure of images, but it also enables a variety of methods for manipulating the segmented regions of grayscale and color images.

Acknowledgments. This project was supported in part by the National Science Foundation (IIS-1513616 and IIS-1845204).

References

1. Arbelaez, P., Maire, M., Fowlkes, C., Malik, J.: Contour detection and hierarchical image segmentation. IEEE Trans. Pattern Anal. Mach. Intell. **33**(5), 898–916 (2011)
2. Aydogan, D.B., Hyttinen, J.: Binary image representation by contour trees. In: Medical Imaging 2012: Image Processing, vol. 8314, p. 83142X (2012)
3. Boyell, R.L., Ruston, H.: Hybrid techniques for real-time radar simulation. In: Proceedings of 1963 Fall Joint Computer Conference, pp. 445–458 (1963)
4. Carr, H., Snoeyink, J., Axen, U.: Computing contour trees in all dimensions. Comput. Geom. **24**(2), 75–94 (2003)
5. Cohen-Steiner, D., Edelsbrunner, H., Harer, J.: Stability of persistence diagrams. Discrete Comput. Geom. **37**(1), 103–120 (2007)
6. Edelsbrunner, H., Letscher, D., Zomorodian, A.J.: Topological persistence and simplification. Discrete Comput. Geom. **28**, 511–533 (2002)
7. Fattal, R., Lischinski, D., Werman, M.: Gradient domain high dynamic range compression. ACM Trans. Graph. (TOG) **21**(3), 249–256 (2002)
8. Hu, Y., He, H., Xu, C., Wang, B., Lin, S.: Exposure: a white-box photo postprocessing framework. ACM Trans. Graph. (TOG) **37**(2), 26 (2018)
9. Kervrann, C., Boulanger, J.: Patch-based image denoising (2019). https://www.irisa.fr/vista/Themes/Demos/Debruitage/ImageDenoising.html
10. Kurlin, V.: A fast persistence-based segmentation of noisy 2D clouds with provable guarantees. Pattern Recogn. Lett. **83**, 3–12 (2016)

11. Letscher, D., Fritts, J.: Image segmentation using topological persistence. In: Kropatsch, W.G., Kampel, M., Hanbury, A. (eds.) Computer Analysis of Images and Patterns, pp. 587–595 (2007)

12. Liu, T., Seyedhosseini, M., Tasdizen, T.: Image segmentation using hierarchical merge tree. IEEE Trans. Image Process. **25**(10), 4596–4607 (2016)

13. Majumder, A., Irani, S.: Contrast enhancement of images using human contrast sensitivity. In: Applied Perception in Graphics and Visualization, pp. 69–76 (2006)

14. Robles, A., Hajij, M., Rosen, P.: The shape of an image - a study of mapper on images. In: International Conference on Computer Vision, Imaging and Computer Graphics Theory and Applications (VISIGRAPP), pp. 339–347 (2018)

15. Rosen, P., Tu, J., Piegl, L.A.: A hybrid solution to parallel calculation of augmented join trees of scalar fields in any dimension. Comput. Aided Design Appl. **15**(4), 610–618 (2018)

16. Tu, J., Hajij, M., Rosen, P.: Propagate and pair: a single-pass approach to critical point pairing in Reeb graphs. In: International Symposium on Visual Computing (2019)

A Visual Analytics Approach for Analyzing Technological Trends in Technology and Innovation Management

Kawa Nazemi$^{(\boxtimes)}$ and Dirk Burkhardt

Research Group on Human-Computer Interaction and Visual Analytics,
Darmstadt University of Applied Sciences, Darmstadt, Germany
{kawa.nazemi,dirk.burkhardt}@h-da.de

Abstract. Visual Analytics provides with a combination of automated techniques and interactive visualizations huge analysis possibilities in technology and innovation management. Thereby not only the use of machine learning data mining methods plays an important role. Due to the high interaction capabilities, it provides a more user-centered approach, where users are able to manipulate the entire analysis process and get the most valuable information. Existing Visual Analytics systems for Trend Analytics and technology and innovation management do not really make use of this unique feature and almost neglect the human in the analysis process. Outcomes from research in information search, information visualization and technology management can lead to more sophisticated Visual Analytics systems that involved the human in the entire analysis process. We propose in this paper a new interaction approach for Visual Analytics in technology and innovation management with a special focus on technological trend analytics.

Keywords: Visual Analytics · Information visualization · Trend analytics · Analysis approach · User-centered design

1 Introduction

Visual Analytics and information visualization are widely used to identify, detect and predict early technological trends for strengthening the competitiveness of enterprises. There exist a variety of methods for analyzing emerging or decreasing trends and predict possible future scenarios. From the visualization point of view, the human with his cognitive abilities plays an essential role in the analysis process. This aspect of so called human-in-the-loop approach, is crucial for the interaction design of every interactive visual application and in particular for complex analytical visualizations. Interactive visualizations for trend analytics and technology and innovation management commonly focus on processing data and integrating algorithms for detecting trends. The interaction capabilities are

© Springer Nature Switzerland AG 2019
G. Bebis et al. (Eds.): ISVC 2019, LNCS 11845, pp. 283–294, 2019.
https://doi.org/10.1007/978-3-030-33723-0_23

limited and a real exploration and discovery is not supported by involving the human in the analysis process. On one the hand there exist a number of search and exploration approaches of interactive visualizations or in technology and innovation management system that include humans in the analytics loop. These systems commonly are either designed to solve general visualization tasks or enable humans to solve trend analytics tasks without visualizations. So there exist a gap between the given approaches coming form economics and the human- and task-centered approaches in information visualizations and Visual Analytics.

We propose in this paper a new approach for Visual Trend Analytics that in particular includes the economic tasks in a human-centered way by investigating the different perspectives on trend analytics. We therefore first introduce the state-of-art in trend visualization and interactive Visual Trend Analytics. Thereafter, we propose a general approach for Visual Trend Analytics that aims at bringing together the different viewpoints of economy, analytics, search, exploration, technology and innovation management with interactive visualization and will illustrate the way how this approach was applied to Visual Analytics system for technology and innovation management.

2   Literature Review

Current trend mining methods provide useful indications for discovering trends. Nevertheless, the interpretation and conclusion for serious decision making still requires the human and his knowledge acquisition abilities. Therefore, the representation of trends is one of the most important aspects for analyzing trends. Common approaches often include basic visualization techniques. Depending on the concrete results, line graphs, bar charts, word clouds, frequency tables, sparklines or histograms are utilized to impart different aspects of trends. *ThemeRiver* and *Tiara* represents thematic variations over time in a stacked graph visualization with a temporal horizontal axis [1]. The variation of the stream width indicates the strength of a specific topic over time [2]. *ParallelTopics* [3] includes a stacked graph for visualizing topic distribution over time. Although the system was not designed for discovering trends but rather for analyzing large text corpora, it allows users to interactively inspect topics and their strengths over time and thus allows the exploration of important trend indicators in the underlying text collection. *Parallel Tag Clouds* (PTC) is based on multiple word clouds that represent the contents of different facets in the document collection [4]. Temporal facets can be used to identify the difference of certain keywords over time and to infer the dynamics of themes in a text collection. Another extension of word clouds is *SparkClouds* that includes a sparkline for each word [5]. These sparklines indicate the temporal distribution of each term and allow conclusions about the topic trends. A user study reveals that participants are more effective with SparkClouds compared to three other visualization techniques in tasks related with trend discovery [5]. A similar approach [6] also includes co-occurrence highlighting. In contrast to SparkClouds, this technique includes a histogram for representing the temporal relevance of each tag. Additional overlays in the histograms show the co-occurrences over time for a selected word to enable a more comprehensive analysis of trend indicators. Han et al. introduce with *PatStream* a visual trend analysis system for technology management [7]. Their system measures similarity between pairs of patents using the cosine metrics and extents the work of Heimerl et al [8] in particular in regards of visualization. The evolution and structure of topics that indicates the trends is visualized through a *Streamgraph* [1] using a river metaphor, it shows the evolution of topic-specific corpus structure.

Wei et al. [9] placed word clouds onto the streams to convey the topic content and Heimerl et al. [8] extended stream graphs to visually link topics in a scientific literature corpus with the cited communities to enable a joint analysis. In contrast to this previous works, *Patstream* breaks down the streams into vertical time slices, which represents periods of years. These time slices are based on their introduced concept that uses the term score, the ratio between the radiative frequency of a term in the given patent collection and its relative frequency in a general discourse reference corpus [7]. Although, their concept makes use of term frequencies, *title score* and *claims score* [7], the most useful approach seems to be the term score, thus it relies on a relative score and investigates the entire document or patent corpus. Beside the main visual representation, the stream visualization, they provide four further visual representation, such as a scatterplot with brushing and linking [7]. The most advanced interactive visual representation is *PatStream* [7]. It provides more than one view, makes use of relative scores and co-occurrences and visualize the temporal spread of the topics with the related categories. Furthermore, it provides a kind of process of functionalists to support trend analysis and technology management in particular for patents. They propose a five-step approach derived from the works of Ernst [10] and Joho et al. [11] that starts with (1) obtaining an overview of different technology topics in a given field, (2) identifying relevant trends according to individual information needs, (3) evaluating the importance of technological trends, (4) observing the behavior and productivity of different players relevant to specific trend, and (5) spotting new technologies related to a trend.

As the literature review revealed, there are already a number Visual Analytics systems for analyzing and visualizing trends. We could outline that existing systems do not really make use of the huge interaction capabilities of Visual Analytics and the human in the loop.

3   General Analysis Approach

Different approaches from information visualization, Visual Analytics, search behavior and from the area of technology and innovation management arose to support the analysis process in particular through visual interactive systems. One of the main works in this area is the "Visual Information Seeking Mantra" proposed by Shneiderman [12] with the basic principle of an interactive visualization to give first an overview, then zoom and filter functionalities and then details on demand [12]. In context of large graph-visual exploration to support users with their degree of interest, van Ham and Perer [13] proposed a more bottom-up approach, starting with search, then showing the context of a certain graph and expanding this on demand. Although, this work is proposed for large graph exploration, the main idea can be adapted to a more user-centered approach and complement the basic principle of Shneiderman in particular by the "search" task. From the area of search and exploration, Marchionini [14] proposed an exploratory search approach based on Bloom's taxonomy [15]. With three kinds of search activities, *Lookup*, *Learn*, and *Investigate*, he proposed that the activities are overlapping and searchers may be involved in more than one activity in parallel. *Lookup* is the lowest level while Learn is the next step of his search process model, which is assigned together with *Investigate* as exploratory activities. This search activity involves multiple iterations of searching and result evaluation to enhance the knowledge about a certain domain or topic. The most complex cognitive activity in the search process is *Investigate* that includes tasks as analysis, synthesis and evaluation. This search activity includes not only finding and acquiring new knowledge and information. It involves analytical tasks such as discovering gaps in the knowledge domain. In this process of knowledge discovery they [14, 16] construct knowledge by investigating various sources and ideas [17].

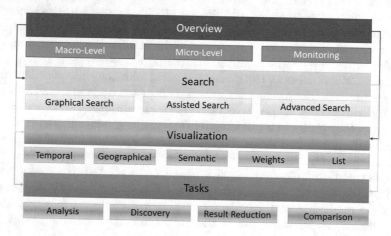

Fig. 1. General visual-interactive analysis approach for trend analytics.

From the viewpoint of technology and innovation management and trend analytics a number of processes arose that should enable strengthening the market position of enterprises through a well-defined analytics process. In this context, commonly patents are used as data corpus and as technology trigger. Bonino et al. [18] proposed that the tasks pursued by patent information users can be subdivided into the three main classes of *search*, *analysis* and *monitoring*. They correlated five *search* tasks to three main questions of *when*, *why* and *what*, and a "focus" that can be either specific or broad. Considering the introduced works the broad-focus can be seen as exploratory search [14]. Such a correlation matrix could be *portfolio survey* as search task, "when" is set to *business planning*, "why" to *identifying the technical portfolio of different players*, "what" to *patents, scientific and technical publications in a given technology area*, and the focus is *broad. Analysis* is subdivided according to Bonino et al. into *micro-* and *macro-analysis*. Thereby micro-analysis involves a single (patent) document, while macro-analysis investigates a portfolio of documents (patents in their case) [18]. The analysis is usually performed to evaluate and assess the Intellectual Property (IP), to map and chart the IP, to identify trends and competitors and also to identify new areas of potential to exploit. The analysis task is therewith pretty similar to the definition of Marchionini's exploratory investigation step [14]. The *monitoring* task is about keeping the users up to date about new upcoming (patent) information in the specified domain of interest [18]. Joho et al. [11] used the classification of Bonino et al. and investigated in an empirical study beside demographic aspects, question on how search tasks are performed, which search functionalities are perceived as important, and what the ideal (patent) search system is. They first derived from these questions "important system features" that were then roughly grouped into (1) *query formulation*, (2) *result assessment and result navigation*, and (3) *search management, organization and history. Query formulation* included aspects like Boolean search, query expansion, field operators etc., while *result assessment and result navigation* focused on highlighting, navigation and relevance score, and *search management, organization and history* included aspects of combining queries, search or navigation history and timeliness. In their evaluation they could find out that users of such analytics systems are willing to adopt and leverage functionality in contrast to web searchers [11]. Nazemi et al. [19], proposed the following main question in Visual Analytics systems for technology and innovation management: (1) *when* have technologies or topics emerged and when established? (2) *"where* are the key-players and key-locations, (3) *who* are the key-players, (4) *what* are the core-topics (4) *how* will the technologies or topics evolve, and (5) *which* technologies or topics are relevant for an enterprise?" [19, p. 4].

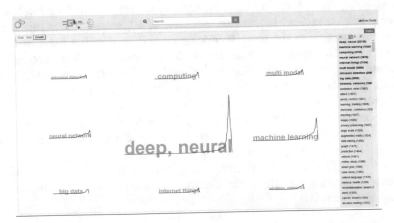

Fig. 2. Overview on macro-level: emerging trends of a certain data-set (in this example the entire DBLP database) at a glance.

Based on the above approaches and models, we derived a more general approach for investigating the entire analysis process for visual trend analytics. Figure 1 illustrates the four main steps of "Overview", "Search", "Visualization" and "Tasks". The first two steps of *overview* and *search* can be assigned as the initial steps, a user is performing during the analysis process. So the first steps are either searching for a certain term or getting an overview of the data or the sub-set of data. The results are then visualized that enables solving different tasks. Our approach combines more abstract tasks like *analysis* or *discovery* with specific tasks that are commonly performed during the analysis process, e.g. *result reduction* or *comparison*. Although, these tasks are not at the same level of *analysis* or *discovery*, dedicated functionalities for the analysis process are required as the introduced models showed.

4   Overview

The *overview* step is based on the initial work of Shneiderman [12] and aims at giving an overview to entire data-set or a sub-set of data to gain an overall overview of the underlying data. We integrated three overview levels according to the work of Bonino et al. [18], namely overview on macro-level, on micro-level and for monitoring. In trend analytics the overview on macro-level should give an initial overview of emerging trends [20] out of the entire data base. Figure 2 illustrates such an overview on macro-level. Thereby the emerging trends gathered through topic modeling is illustrated as *SparkCloud* [5] and the users are able to see the most emerging trends at a glance. On the right side, other topics of interest can be selected. The user can further choose an overview of the most appeared topics in the entire data-set or the topics with the highest climax. The overview on macro-level is interactive, so that the user is able to get details-on-demand with one click on a certain SparkCloud.

Overview on micro-level in trend analytics contains the temporal spread of topics (trends) for a certain key-term that is either searched or selected from the macro-level overview. It gives an overview of all related topics in a temporal manner and insights of the main technologies and approaches for a certain key-term. Figure 3 illustrates one example of an overview on micro-level. The user has chosen the term "Information Visualization" from the overview on macro-level and gets the temporal spread of the related technologies and approaches ranked based on the frequency of the topics in related documents.

For monitoring as overview, we integrated a personalized word cloud that illustrates the most search or selected terms for a single person. Thereby a simple user model with a *bag-of-words* approach is implemented and enables the user to select the terms that wants to monitor. Figure 4 illustrates the word-cloud for two different persons and illustrates clearly that the amount of monitored terms can vary significantly.

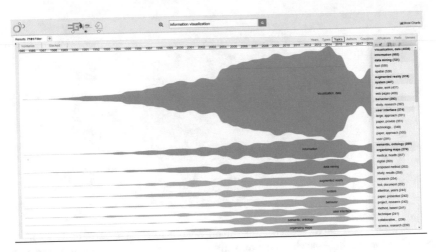

Fig. 3. Overview on micro-level: temporal spread of related topics for a single key-term (in this example for information visualization).

Fig. 4. Overview - monitoring: personalized word-clouds of two different persons.

5   Search

Search functionalities are essential in particular if the amount of the underlying data are large. We have integrated different search approaches to assist users in the search process. A novel approach is the "graphical search" functionality (see Fig. 5). Thereby the initial search term (or selected term) is visualized as a circle in the center of the screen. Users are able to define further search terms as "points-of-interest" (POI), whereas each POI is visualized as a small circle with a certain color. These POIs can be dragged into the initial search circle that illustrates the amount of results including both search terms. The graphical search functionality further enables a nested search, so that more than two circles can be dragged. With this action, the amount of the results is always the amount of all nested POIs.

The assisted search was applied according to Nazemi et al. [19] and extends the search functionalities beside traditional linguistic methods with a topic-based approach. The approach incorporates the information of the generated topics to

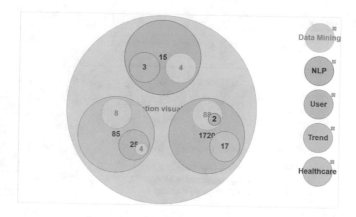

Fig. 5. Search - graphical search: the initial search-term is represented as a circle, users can define further search terms and drag them into the initial search-term to get a nested number of combined search.

enhance search-terms from the query. The topics provide N-Grams, which are the most used phrases within each topic. These phrases often represent different ways to articulate the idea of the topic and consequently can be used as a key phrase to represent the topic. We use data from the phrases and choose the top five most used phrases as additional search-terms to extend the result set. Based on the initial users' search the most dominant topic in the result set is identified. In the next step, semantically similar phrases are extracted based on the identified dominant topic. Additional searches are performed by the system using the semantically similar phrases as search-terms. The functionality can be activated with one click on top next to the search field. The advanced search is detecting automatically all data rows in the database and provides dedicated search in those tables.

6   Visualization

We integrated a set of different visualizations in particular to respond to the questions according to Nazemi et al. [19]: (1) *when* have technologies or topics emerged and when established? (2) *"where* are the key-players and key-locations, (3) *who* are the key-players, (4) *what* are the core-topics (4) *how* will the technologies or topics evolve, and (5) *which* technologies or topics are relevant for an enterprise?" [19, p. 4]. To address these questions, we integrated different data models that are the foundation of the underlying visual structures. The visualizations are automatically detecting the data model and visualize the data in appropriate manner. A semantic data model serves as the primary model for all other data models. The visualization step includes a set of temporal, geographical, semantic and topic (weights) visual layouts that are all interactive and enable solving different tasks. A simple list-view is added to select single entities. Figure 6 illustrates examples of the integrated visualizations that lead to solve different analytical tasks. The visualizations can be used as single interactive visual interface or be combined in dashboards.

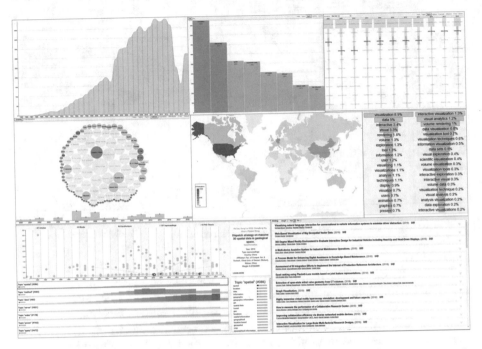

Fig. 6. Visualization: examples of integrated temporal, geographical, semantic, weight and list visualizations.

7   Tasks

The visualizations and the overall user interface enables user to solve different tasks. The tasks vary in every domain and is strongly dependent to the users of a visual system. The analysis tasks in our approach responds mainly to the questions according to Nazemi et al. [19] (see Sect. 6). Whereas aspects of predicting technologies, detecting emerging trends [20] and strengthening the market position of enterprises plays an essential role. The analysis tasks incorporates solving a complex analytical task with a specific goal in order to strengthen the potentials of an enterprise or other institution. The discovery tasks aims at detecting unexpected patterns, topics, technologies or correlations in data. This tasks can be best supported by aspect-oriented visualizations, where the user gets insights from different perspectives and detects a new correlation. Result reduction as first main task is essential for every research task, e.g. researching for related technologies or competitors. To support this tasks, we integrated a dynamic faceting that is further supported by each of the visual layouts. So the user can explore starting a huge amount of data related to a certain field and reduce the amounts based on his requirements.

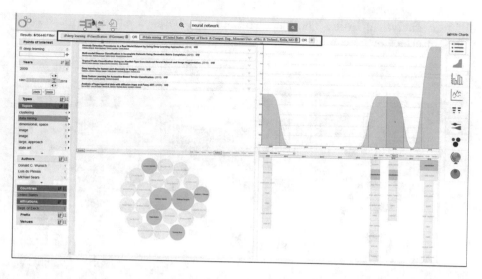

Fig. 7. Tasks: result reduction.

Figure 7 illustrates the user interface of our application including the faceting and visual reduction. The user started with a search-term with about 60,000 results (top left of the screen). He used the graphical search, faceting and visual interactions to reduce the amount to only six relevant papers and chose four visualization to see the results. The faceting is visualized on left and the result reduction is on top (highlighted with a blue rectangle).

The comparison as second main task can be performed on two different levels: Comparison on data-subset with two same visual layouts or comparison of different databases. This differentiation is similar to the proposed micro-level and macro-level overview. Based on the requirements, a user is able to set up a campaign and compare the entire data stored in different database. This way of comparison enable to compare for example enterprise data with scientific publications and see the results at a glance. Figure 8 illustrates a comparison on macro-level through different databases and the visual layout is a macro-level overview too, so that he is able to see the emerging trends in two different databases.

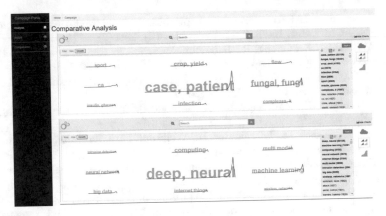

Fig. 8. Tasks: comparison on macro-level by using macro-level overview visual layouts.

8   Conclusion

We proposed in this paper an approach for Visual Trend Analytics that included the economic tasks in a human-centered way. We therefore first introduced the state-of-art in trend visualization and interactive visual trend analytics. Thereafter, we proposed a general approach for visual trend analytics that aimed at bringing together the different viewpoints of economy, analytics, search, exploration, technology and innovation management with interactive visualization. In this context the different approaches was be described let us derive a general approach for Visual Analytics in technology and innovation management. We applied and illustrated each step of our approach with a Visual Analytics system for technology and innovation management with two main contributions: a general approach that brings the different viewpoints together to enhance the state-of-the-art in visual trend analytics and the application of the approach to a complex Visual Analytics system for detecting early trends in technology an innovation management.

Acknowledgments. This work was partially funded by the Hessen State Ministry for Higher Education, Research and the Arts within the program "Forschung für die Praxis" and was conducted within the research group on Human-Computer Interaction and Visual Analytics (https://vis.h-da.de). The presentation of this work was supported by the Research Center for Digital Communication & Media Innovation of the Darmstadt University of Applied Sciences.

References

1. Havre, S., Hetzler, E., Whitney, P., Nowell, L.: ThemeRiver: visualizing thematic changes in large document collections. IEEE TVCG **8**(1), 9–20 (2002). http://dx.doi.org/10.1109/2945.981848

2. Liu, S., et al.: TIARA: interactive, topic-based visual text summarization and analysis. ACM Trans. Intell. Syst. Technol. **3**(2), 25:1–25:28 (2012)
3. Dou, W., Wang, X., Chang, R., Ribarsky, W.: ParallelTopics: a probabilistic approach to exploring document collections. In: VAST 2011 (2011)
4. Collins, C., Viegas, F., Wattenberg, M.: Parallel tag clouds to explore and analyze faceted text corpora. In: VAST 2009 (2009)
5. Lee, B., Riche, N.H., Karlson, A.K., Carpendale, S.: SparkClouds: visualizingtrends in tag clouds. IEEE TVCG **16**, 1182–1189 (2010)
6. Lohmann, S., Burch, M., Schmauder, H., Weiskopf, D.: Visual analysis of microblog content using time-varying co-occurrence highlighting in tag clouds. In: Proceedings of the International Working Conference on Advanced Visual Interfaces, AVI 2012, pp. 753–756. ACM, New York (2012)
7. Han, Q., Heimerl, F., Codina-Filba, J., Lohmann, S., Wanner, L., Ertl, T.: Visual patent trend analysis for informed decision making in technology management. World Patent Inf. **49**, 34–42 (2017)
8. Heimerl, F., Han, Q., Koch, S., Ertl, T.: CiteRivers: visual analytics of citation patterns. IEEE Trans. Vis. Comput. Graph. **22**(1), 190–199 (2016)
9. Wei, F., et al.: TIARA: a visual exploratory text analytic system. In: Proceedings of the 16th ACM SIGKDD International Conference on Knowledge Discovery and Data Mining, KDD 2010, pp. 153–162. ACM, New York (2010)
10. Ernst, H.: Patent information for strategic technology management. World Patent Inf. **25**(3), 233–242 (2003)
11. Joho, H., Azzopardi, L.A., Vanderbauwhede, W.: A survey of patent users: an analysis of tasks, behavior, search functionality and system requirements. In: Proceedings of the Third Symposium on Information Interaction in Context, IIiX 2010, pp. 13–24. ACM, New York (2010)
12. Shneiderman, B.: The eyes have it: a task by data type taxonomy for information visualizations. In: VL, pp. 336–343 (1996)
13. van Ham, F., Perer, A.: Search, show context, expand on demand: supporting large graph exploration with degree-of-interest. IEEE Trans. Vis. Comput. Graph. **15**, 953–960 (2009)
14. Marchionini, G.: Exploratory search: from finding to understanding. Commun. ACM **49**(4), 41–46 (2006)
15. Bloom, B.S.: Taxonomy of Educational Objectives. David McKay Co., Inc., New York (1956)
16. White, R.W., Roth, R.A.: Exploratory Search: Beyond the Query-Response Paradigm. Synthesis Lectures on Information Concepts, Retrieval, and Services. Marchionini, G. (ed.), vol. 1. Morgan & Claypool Publishers (2009)
17. Bruner, J.S.: The act of discovery. Harvard Educ. Rev. **31**, 21–32 (1961)
18. Bonino, D., Ciaramella, A., Corno, F.: Review of the state-of-the-art in patent information and forthcoming evolutions in intelligent patent informatics. World Patent Inf. **32**(1), 30–38 (2010)
19. Nazemi, K., Retz, R., Burkhardt, D., Kuijper, A., Kohlhammer, J., Fellner, D.W.: Visual trend analysis with digital libraries. In: Proceedings of the 15th International Conference on Knowledge Technologies and Data-driven Business - i-KNOW 2015. ACM Press (2015). https://doi.org/10.1145/2809563.2809569
20. Nazemi, K., Burkhard, D.: Visual analytics for analyzing technological trends from text. In: 2019 23rd International Conference Information Visualisation (IV), pp. 191–200. IEEE (2019)

A Framework for Collecting and Classifying Objects in Satellite Imagery

Aswathnarayan Radhakrishnan[1], Jamie Cunningham[1], Jim Davis[1(✉)], and Roman Ilin[2]

[1] Ohio State University, Columbus, OH 43210, USA
{radhakrishnan.39,cunningham.844,davis.1719}@osu.edu
[2] AFRL/RYAP, Wright-Patterson AFB, Dayton, OH 45433, USA
rilin325@gmail.com

Abstract. A major issue with data-hungry deep learning algorithms is the lack of annotated ground truth for specific applications. The high volume of satellite imagery available today, coupled with crowd-sourced map data can enable a new means for training and classifying objects in wide-area imagery. In this work, we present an automated pipeline for collecting and labeling satellite imagery to facilitate building custom deep learning models. We demonstrate this approach by automatically collecting labeled imagery of solar power plants and building a classifier to detect the structures. This framework can be used to collect labeled satellite imagery of any object mapped by spatial databases.

Keywords: Satellite imagery · Data generation · Automated ground truthing · OpenStreetMap · Deep learning · Solar power plants

1 Introduction

Advancements in deep learning for image classification, segmentation, and object detection are creating profound changes in methods for analysis and inference of imagery. Supervised machine learning tasks are highly dependent on the availability of large, labeled training datasets. Hence, there is always a need to find a dataset which is sufficiently large enough to train a model and broad enough to contain diverse data samples to ensure better generalization performance. Satellite imagery is one such source of expansive and rich data.

Remote sensing is an Earth observation technique by which information about a feature on the Earth's surface is gathered without making physical contact. Earth Observation (EO) satellites are launched into space with their primary mission being remote sensing and providing satellite imagery of the Earth's surface from low Earth orbits. The number of EO satellites has increased

This work was supported by the U.S. Air Force Research Laboratory under contract #GRT00044839/60056946.

exponentially over recent years. The data from these satellites have various applications in fields such as environmental monitoring, disaster management, agricultural engineering, cartography, and military intelligence. EO satellites have instruments capable of sensing a wide range of bands in the electromagnetic spectrum. Another important property of satellite imagery is the frequency in which new data is captured. A primary advantage of satellite imagery is that archived imagery of multiple spectral bands at high resolution can be collected and processed.

Although there has been a considerable increase in the volume of publicly available satellite imagery, it remains difficult to find a dataset that contains examples of a specific object for a particular task. Similarly, generating new datasets leads to the additional overhead of annotation. Manual annotation is a time-consuming task that becomes difficult with large amounts of imagery. However, public geographical databases and crowd-sourced map information can be used to automatically locate objects and label the ground truth. In this work, we present a generic framework for extracting satellite imagery of specified object categories using public databases. We demonstrate the approach by automatically extracting satellite imagery of solar power plants (though other object classes can be used) from around the world and building a classifier to detect them in novel satellite imagery.

2   Related Work

The availability of satellite imagery has already promoted the use of deep learning algorithms for analyzing remote sensing data. In [1], they focused on predicting land use (cropland, residential, forest, etc.) in satellite imagery of urban areas. However, they were restricted to train with a small, manually-created dataset for 6 European cities. Similarly, in [9] a classifier was trained to predict crop types using satellite imagery having manual ground truth. In [6], solar power plants were detected in geographically restricted satellite imagery and the ground truth classes were manually annotated. Also, there was a large bias between the number of positive and negative examples. Crowd-sourced map information has become widely available today and OpenStreetMap (OSM) [18] is one such popular crowd-sourced spatial database primarily used for the purpose of land use mapping. In [7], they used existing OSM datasets for labeling water, farm, grass, etc. on Landsat imagery. In [15], OSM data were used for filling gaps in existing land cover maps. In [2], OSM raster images were used to superimpose land use labels on satellite imagery. Similarly, in [8], OSM raster data were used to superimpose labels of roads and buildings on existing satellite imagery to perform semantic image segmentation. In [20], OSM data were integrated with high spatial resolution imagery to classify types of buildings.

Overall, most of these approaches suffered from the lack of large problem-specific labeled training examples, which has been a bottleneck for applying deep learning techniques. Also, those employing OSM data used existing filtered OSM datasets. Our proposed framework can dynamically query the OSM database for

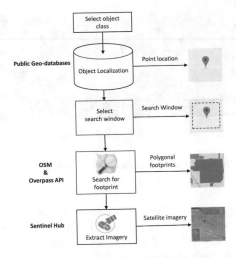

Fig. 1. Data generation pipeline architecture.

the required data thus bypassing having to download and filter the entire OSM database. Additionally, our proposed model extracts OSM data in vector format allowing us to work with the object boundaries (points, lines, or polygons). We can also exploit the broader categories of features mapped by OSM. Furthermore, we exploit the use of additional geo-location data sources to help localize the objects.

3   Data Generation Pipeline

We developed a modular framework for collecting satellite imagery of a specified object class using public geographical databases and crowd-sourced labels. The different modules of our framework are shown in Fig. 1 and explained below.

3.1   Satellite Imagery

In this work, we employ the European Space Agency's Sentinel-2 (A and B) [5] constellation of twin satellites. It is a wide-swath, high-resolution, multi-spectral imaging mission supporting Copernicus Land Monitoring studies (monitoring vegetation, soil, and water cover, as well as observation of inland waterways and coastal areas). The Sentinel-2 Multispectral Instrument samples thirteen spectral bands in the visible, near-infrared, and short-wave infrared part of the spectrum with a spatial resolution of 10 m per pixel for the four optical and near-infrared (NIR) bands, 20 m for the six red edge and shortwave infrared (SWIR) bands, and 60 m for the three atmospheric correction bands.

Sentinel Hub's [17] Open Geospatial Consortium (OGC) API can be used to provide services for data access, display, and processing within hours of image acquisition. The `sentinelhub` Python package facilitates OGC web requests to

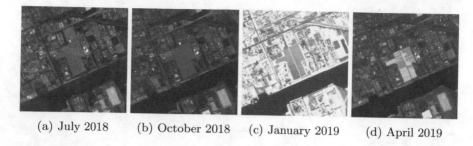

(a) July 2018   (b) October 2018   (c) January 2019   (d) April 2019

Fig. 2. Sentinel-2 imagery of the same area acquired at four different times.

download and process satellite imagery in batch scripts thus circumventing the need to manually download Sentinel-2 data from the web. Sentinel Hub's Web Map Service (WMS) is used to request downloads of certain Sentinel bands using different settings such as maximum cloud coverage, time range of imagery acquisition, image format, size, etc. The region of interest to be downloaded is represented as a bounding box in geo-coordinates. This enables the extraction of satellite imagery for any particular region of interest at any required time period, thus avoiding time mismatches between imagery and any ground truth data. Figure 2 shows some examples of Sentinel-2 RGB imagery acquired at four different times highlighting the variations in the image across different climatic conditions (notice the snow cover in Fig. 2(c)).

3.2   Object Localization

An object in satellite imagery can be a building, forest, industrial area, etc. selected to train a classifier. The geo-coordinates of many types of objects can be found using publicly available resources, such as a catalog of street addresses or a database containing geo-coordinates. Given a list of addresses, open-source Geocoders such as Nominatim [13] can be used to determine their geo-coordinates. Python's geopy package supports several popular geocoding web services. Also, some public geo-databases exist that already provide a geo-coordinate for a category of interest (e.g., power plant database [3]). However, such data sources may have only an approximate (inaccurate) location for the object. We therefore will need to search for the object near the given geo-coordinate. For this, we use a global spatial database which contains object footprints to identify bounding regions.

3.3   OpenStreetMap

OpenStreetMap (OSM) [11] is a collaborative project used to create a crowd-sourced spatial database of the world. It was started in 2004 with the simple idea of multiple contributors with local knowledge collaborating to create a detailed labeled map. We employ OSM as our auxiliary data source to extract polygonal footprints for the given geo-location of objects obtained from public databases.

Forest
Wood
Golf course
Park
Residential area
Common and
meadow
Retail area
Industrial area
Commercial area
Heathland
Lake and reservoir
Farm
Brownfield site
Cemetery
Allotments
Sports pitch
Sports centre
Nature reserve
Military area
School and
university

Fig. 3. OSM region with land use labels.

The OSM data model consists of three basic data structures: *Nodes*, *Ways*, and *Relations*. A *Node* represents a geographic point expressed in latitude and longitude. A *Way* constitutes at least two *Nodes* (polyline or polygon). A *Relation* is a logical collection of *Ways* and *Nodes* (multipolygon). The physical features on the Earth's surface are described by OSM using tags with key-value pairs attached to its basic data structures (*Nodes*, *Ways*, and *Relations*). The key is used to describe a topic, category, or feature type (e.g., building), and the value details the specific form of the key (e.g., residential). The OSM Map Features pages on the OSM wiki [12] lists the tags agreed upon by the OSM community. Figure 3 shows an example OSM urban area with land use labels.

There are multiple methods for downloading data from OSM. It is possible to get the data in the form of XML formatted .osm files. OSM also provides its entire database as a Planet.osm file which is updated weekly to reflect new changes to its database. But often we do not need to work with the entire database when there is a specific region of interest. In such cases, the Overpass API [14] can be used, which is a read-only, web-based service that accepts queries to download custom filtered datasets. Python's `overpy` package provides Python bindings to the Overpass API.

We use the object's initial geo-coordinate to restrict our search space in OSM to avoid the overhead of having to search throughout the entire planet to localize our object footprints. We next define a search space around the object's geo-coordinate. We build a query in the Overpass Query Language which contains the search criteria and a bounding box defining the search window. We use a pre-determined size for the search window based on the average size of our objects. We then search within the window using the Overpass API for the polygonal footprint of the object class.

We search for both *Relations* and *Ways*, as some objects might be represented as *Relations* (multipolygon) which are made up of multiple *Ways* (polygons). In such cases, we extract all *Ways* which are a member of a *Relation*. The *Ways* are made up of an ordered list of *Nodes* which form the vertices of the object's polygonal footprint. A bounding box is fit to the entire footprint using the min and max latitude and longitude extents. Sentinel Hub is then used to download the satellite imagery corresponding to the footprint bounding box generated for the object.

Using the various packages related to Sentinel and OSM, a batch script can be used to extract imagery of a selected object type from the associated list of geo-coordinate locations. We can use this same approach to generate negative (non-object) examples by querying OSM using the Overpass API to ensure the absence of an object.

4   Example and Experiments

We demonstrate the proposed framework by procedurally generating a training and testing dataset with positive and negative examples of solar power plants. To show the applicability of the extracted dataset, we train an image classifier using a Convolutional Neural Network (CNN) to detect the selected object class. The main focus of this work is the automatic generation of annotated imagery (other object classes and classification models could be used).

4.1   Solar Power Plants

We leverage the World Resources Institute's Global Power Plant Database (GPPD) [3], which is a comprehensive, open-source database of power plants around the world. Each power plant listed has information on its geo-location, capacity, generation, ownership, and fuel type. It is continuously updated as new information becomes available. The database version used in this work includes over 28K power plants. However as previously mentioned, some of the geo-locations are only approximate and may not even exist on the footprint of the power plant.

We center our search region in OSM on the provided geo-coordinate of a solar power plant from the database. We define our search window by ±0.2 decimal degrees in latitude and longitude around the geo-coordinate (approximately a 16 × 16 km area centered around that geo-coordinate). We then search through OSM using the Overpass API in the search window for *Relations* and *Ways* with the tags **'generator:source = solar'** or **'plant:source = solar'** (standard tags for solar power plants in OSM, note that other key-value tags for different objects can be used). We extract all *Ways* which are a member of *Relations*. The *Ways* give us the desired polygonal footprints of the solar power plants. Figure 4(a) shows multiple polygons that make up an OSM relation representing a solar power plant.

4.2   Image Collection

The next step is to extract the satellite imagery for the located object footprints. We selected to evaluate the RGB and NIR bands as they have the highest spatial resolution (10 m) among the bands in the Sentinel-2 imagery. Also, the solar power plants were visually more distinct in the RGB and NIR bands to the human eye (NIR is closer to the visible range than thermal). Other bands may be more applicable to different object classes. Figure 4(b) and (c) show the corresponding Sentinel-2 RGB and near-infrared band imagery for the OSM polygonal footprint of a solar power plant (see Fig. 4(a)). Table 1 lists the central wavelength, bandwidth, and spatial resolution for each of the Sentinel-2 bands used.

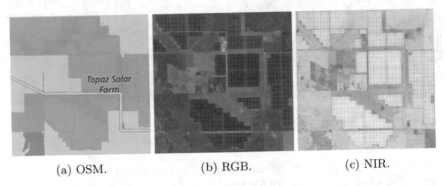

(a) OSM.   (b) RGB.   (c) NIR.

Fig. 4. OSM polygonal footprint and its corresponding Sentinel-2 RGB and NIR band imagery.

Table 1. Spectral band properties for Sentinel-2 (A and B).

Sentinel-2 bands	Sentinel-2A		Sentinel-2B		Spatial resolution (m)
	Central wavelength (nm)	Bandwidth (nm)	Central wavelength (nm)	Bandwidth (nm)	
B02: Blue	492.4	66	492.1	66	10
B03: Green	559.8	36	559.0	36	10
B04: Red	664.6	31	664.9	31	10
B08: NIR	832.8	106	832.9	106	10

Positive Examples. To extract multiple positive examples of each solar power plant, we randomly sampled 5 points within each polygonal footprint and extracted a 256 × 256 sized image chip centered around each of these points

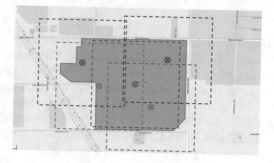

Fig. 5. Randomly sampled points and their cropping windows.

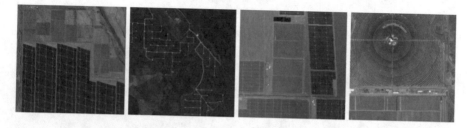

Fig. 6. Positive examples of solar power plants.

(see Fig. 5). To download the Sentinel-2 imagery, we used Sentinel Hub's WMS request. We downloaded imagery for July 2018, October 2018, January 2019, and April 2019 to account for variations in the appearance across different climatic conditions (as seen in Fig. 2). We additionally set the maximum cloud cover percentage to 30% to filter out imagery where the solar power plant may be occluded by clouds. Since the cloud coverage is estimated on larger Sentinel-2 tiles (100 km × 100 km areas), and not just for the region defined by a footprint bounding box, heavily clouded imagery might still be present in the smaller image chips. Also, a part of the image might contain white (empty) regions if that particular data acquisition only partially intersected the specified footprint's bounding box. We manually removed such corrupt images from our collection.

We generated approximately 20K positive samples from 400 solar power plants as our training data and another 500 positive samples from 100 different solar power plants for testing purposes. We created a validation set by randomly sampling 2K images from the training set. Figure 6 shows a few positive samples of solar power plants generated by this method.

Negative Examples. The negative samples consist of land regions with no solar power plants, but contain a diverse collection of urban as well as randomly sampled land areas. We sampled from two separate world cities databases of urban areas across the world. We used the freely available World Cities Database [16] (provides an accurate and up-to-date database of the world's cities and towns) for training data and Nordpil's World Database of Large Urban Areas [10] which contains a different set of geo-coordinates of urban areas for generating test data. Both databases provide a single geo-coordinate for geo-referencing cities and towns. The remaining negative samples are located by randomly generating a geo-coordinate on the Earth's surface and verifying with OSM that the randomly generated point is over land (not over water).

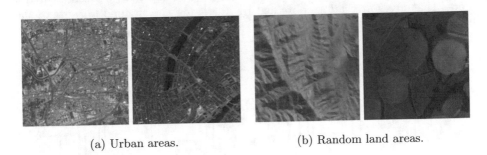

(a) Urban areas.   (b) Random land areas.

Fig. 7. Negative examples.

We extracted 256 × 256 sized image chips centered on the geo-coordinates of the selected urban and random land areas. We again use the Overpass API to query the OSM database to ensure that the bounding boxes contain no solar power plants. Several heavily clouded image chips remained in our negative samples. We collected approximately 20K negative samples for training and another 500 negative samples (250 urban areas, 250 randomly sampled land areas) for testing. As before, we randomly sampled 2K images from the negative training set with an equal proportion of images from urban areas and randomly sampled land areas for the validation set. Some negative examples from urban and random land areas are shown in Fig. 7.

4.3   Image Classification Model Architecture

We employed a standard CNN architecture to train our image classification model. The network employs three downsampling blocks, each composed of a convolutional layer (Conv) with 32 filters of size 3 × 3 and ReLU activation, followed by a 2 × 2 max pooling layer (MaxPool). The output from the final downsampling block is flattened and fed to 2 fully-connected layers (FC) having 512 nodes each with ReLU activation. The output layer consists of a single node with a sigmoid activation function. Separate models were trained for NIR (1 channel), RGB (3 channels), and RGBNIR (4 channels). The input to the network is the image chip of size 256 × 256 and the number of input channels is equal to the number of bands being used to train the model. The model architecture is shown in Fig. 8 and takes an input of size 256 × 256 with either 1, 3, or 4 channels.

Each image was preprocessed by normalizing the pixel values to the range [−1, 1]. The model was trained using stochastic gradient descent with a batch size of 32 images and momentum of 0.9. We initialized the weights in each layer using Xavier initialization and the biases were initialized with values drawn from a normal distribution with zero mean and unit standard deviation. The learning rate was initialized to 0.001 and adjusted using "Poly" learning rate adaptation [4,19]. We trained each model for 30 epochs and selected the model from the epoch which had the highest validation accuracy. In addition, we also created a model that gives predictions obtained by averaging the sigmoid outputs of the individual RGB and NIR models (RGB+NIR).

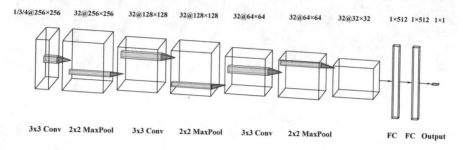

Fig. 8. CNN Model architecture.

Table 2. Comparison of results from models trained on different bands.

Bands	Accuracy	Precision	Recall	F1 score	Parameters
NIR	0.92	0.98	0.86	0.91	17,059,905
RGB	0.96	0.98	0.93	0.95	17,060,481
RGB+NIR	0.96	0.98	0.94	0.96	34,120,386
RGBNIR	**0.97**	**0.99**	**0.94**	**0.97**	17,060,769

4.4 Results

The results of the various models on the solar power plants are summarized in Table 2. The best performance was given by the model trained on all the four bands together (RGBNIR), with an accuracy of 0.97 and an F1 score of 0.97. As expected, the joint RGBNIR model with early fusion (at the input) incorporating inter-dependency was better than the individual models. It was also slightly better than the independent late fusion approach (RGB+NIR). The RGBNIR model had an increase of 288 parameters over the RGB model and 864 parameters over the NIR model, but it had nearly half of the parameters of the dual late-fusion approach (RGB+NIR). This shows that the model's performance improves as we increase the number of bands used for training, advocating the use of potentially even more bands provided by Sentinel.

4.5   Alternate Object Classes

The above framework can be used to collect satellite imagery of other object classes by swapping the public data source used to extract the point location of the required object class and then using their corresponding OSM tags to search for their polygonal footprints. Figure 9 shows imagery generated using the framework for airports, reservoirs, and ports.

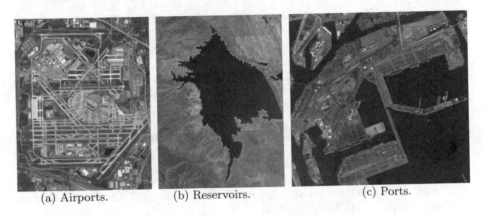

(a) Airports.   (b) Reservoirs.   (c) Ports.

Fig. 9. Example imagery collected for alternate object classes.

5   Summary

Manually generating and annotating imagery is a time-consuming task and a commonly faced problem. This task becomes more complicated with the use of supervised deep learning models which require large volumes of labeled training data. In this work, we presented a general framework employing existing geographical databases and satellite imagery to automatically generate labeled imagery of a selected object class for a classification task. We demonstrated this method by selecting solar power plants as our object class, though other classes could also be used with the framework. We achieved compelling results with multiple image bands which validate the proposed pipeline. We next plan on leveraging the framework to examine the use of the polygonal footprints to label each pixel in the image to facilitate semantic image segmentation. We expect the use of deep learning on satellite imagery to increase as more avenues are opening for automated annotation.

References

1. Albert, A., Kaur, J., Gonzalez, M.C.: Using convolutional networks and satellite imagery to identify patterns in urban environments at a large scale. In: Proceedings ACM SIGKDD (2017)

2. Audebert, N., Le Saux, B., Lefèvre, S.: Joint learning from earth observation and openstreetmap data to get faster better semantic maps. In: Proceedings CVPR Workshop: Large Scale Computer Vision for Remote Sensing Imagery (2017)
3. Byers, L., et al.: A global database of power plants. World Resources Institute, p. 18 (2018)
4. Chen, L.C., Papandreou, G., Kokkinos, I., Murphy, K., Yuille, A.L.: DeepLab: semantic image segmentation with deep convolutional nets, atrous convolution, and fully connected CRFs. IEEE Trans. Pattern Anal. Mach. Intell. **40**(4), 834–848 (2017)
5. European Space Agency: Copernicus Sentinel-2 data (2019). https://sentinel.esa.int/web/sentinel/missions/sentinel-2
6. Ishii, T., et al.: Detection by classification of buildings in multispectral satellite imagery. In: ICPR (2016)
7. Johnson, B.A., Iizuka, K.: Integrating OpenStreetMap crowdsourced data and Landsat time-series imagery for rapid land use/land cover (LULC) mapping: case study of the Laguna de Bay area of the Philippines. Appl. Geogr. **67**, 140–149 (2016)
8. Kaiser, P., Wegner, J.D., Lucchi, A., Jaggi, M., Hofmann, T., Schindler, K.: Learning aerial image segmentation from online maps. IEEE Trans. Geosci. Remote Sensing **55**(11), 6054–6068 (2017)
9. Kussul, N., Lavreniuk, M., Skakun, S., Shelestov, A.: Deep learning classification of land cover and crop types using remote sensing data. IEEE Geosci. Remote Sensing Lett. **14**(5), 778–782 (2017)
10. Nordpil: World database of large urban areas, pp. 1950–2050 (2019). https://nordpil.com/resources/world-database-of-large-cities/
11. OpenStreetMap contributors: Planet dump (2017). https://planet.osm.org, https://www.openstreetmap.org
12. OpenStreetMap Wiki: Map Features (2019). https://wiki.openstreetmap.org/w/index.php?title=Map_Features&oldid=1819914
13. OpenStreetMap Wiki: Nominatim (2019). https://wiki.openstreetmap.org/w/index.php?title=Nominatim&oldid=1848597
14. OpenStreetMap Wiki: Overpass API (2019). https://wiki.openstreetmap.org/w/index.php?title=Overpass_API&oldid=1872170
15. Schultz, M., Voss, J., Auer, M., Carter, S., Zipf, A.: Open land cover from OpenStreetMap and remote sensing. Int. J. Appl. Earth Observ. Geoinf. **63**, 206–213 (2017)
16. SimpleMaps- Pareto Software, LLC: World Cities Database (2019). https://simplemaps.com/data/world-cities
17. Sinergise Ltd.: Modified Copernicus Sentinel data. Sentinel Hub (2019). https://sentinel-hub.com/
18. Sui, D., Goodchild, M., Elwood, S.: Volunteered geographic information, the exaflood, and the growing digital divide. In: Sui, D., Elwood, S., Goodchild, M. (eds.) Crowdsourcing Geographic Knowledge, pp. 1–12. Springer, Dordrecht (2013). https://doi.org/10.1007/978-94-007-4587-2_1
19. Zhao, H., Shi, J., Qi, X., Wang, X., Jia, J.: Pyramid scene parsing network. In: Proceedings of CVPR (2017)
20. Zhao, W., Bo, Y., Chen, J., Tiede, D., Thomas, B., Emery, W.J.: Exploring semantic elements for urban scene recognition: deep integration of high-resolution imagery and OpenStreetMap (OSM). ISPRS J. Photogram. Remote Sensing **151**, 237–250 (2019)

Moving Objects Segmentation Based on DeepSphere in Video Surveillance

Sirine Ammar[1,2]([✉]), Thierry Bouwmans[2], Nizar Zaghden[1], and Mahmoud Neji[1]

[1] Lab. MIRACL, Univ de Sfax, Sfax, Tunisia
[2] Lab. MIA, Univ de La Rochelle, La Rochelle, France
ammarsirine3@gmail.com

Abstract. Segmentation of moving objects from video sequences plays an important role in many computer vision applications. In this paper, we present a background subtraction approach based on deep neural networks. More specifically, we propose to employ and validate an unsupervised anomaly discovery framework called "DeepSphere" to perform foreground objects detection and segmentation in video sequences. Deep-Sphere is based on both deep autoencoders and hypersphere learning methods to isolate anomaly pollution and reconstruct normal behaviors in spatial and temporal context. We exploit the power of this framework and adjust it to perform foreground objects segmentation. We evaluate the performance of our proposed method on 9 surveillance videos from the Background Model Challenge (BMC 2012) dataset, and compare that with a standard subspace learning technique, Robust Principle Component Analysis (RPCA) as well as a Deep Probabilistic Background Model (DeepPBM). Experimental results show that our approach achieved successful results than other existing ones.

Keywords: Background subtraction · Unsupervised anomaly discovery · DeepSphere · DeepPBM · RPCA

1 Introduction

Motion detection is a fundamental process for video surveillance systems. It consists of extracting moving objects in a video recorded using a surveillance camera. Motion detection is applied for many applications such as video surveillance, human motion analysis, robotics applications, etc. The main approaches used for motion detection can be categorized into three groups: the temporal difference approaches, optical flow analysis, and the background subtraction (BS) methods. In this paper, we focused on the last one.

The basic approaches of motion detection calculate the time difference between two consecutive images to extract moving region [1]. This method is computationally fast, but produces noisy segmentation results and the objects are partially detected. Optical flow based approaches provide all information

© Springer Nature Switzerland AG 2019
G. Bebis et al. (Eds.): ISVC 2019, LNCS 11845, pp. 307–319, 2019.
https://doi.org/10.1007/978-3-030-33723-0_25

about the motion [2]. However, these approaches suffer from the complexity of real-time scenarios and the slowness of flow estimation. A BS method has generally four components: a background initialization step that generates a model of the background of the scene which represents the static parts. The detection image is obtained by calculating the difference between the current frame and the reference frame. The model is updated to adapt to changes in the scene and finally a threshold operation is applied to categorize the pixels as 'background' or 'foreground'. Foreground detection often suffers from some limitations such as the environmental changes, the noise of acquisition and digitization, the homogeneous areas. To overcome this, many approaches have been proposed for objects segmentation based on powerful models, like RPCA models introduced by Candès et al. [3], neural networks models and filter based models. The most easy way to initialize a background is to calculate the temporal average, temporal median or the histogram over time. But, these algorithms are sensitive to camera jitter, illumination changes and dynamic backgrounds. To address this issue, statistical models based on Gaussian distribution are proposed such as single Gaussian [4], Gaussian Mixture Model [5] and Kernel based Density Estimation [6]. Fuzzy concept approaches like Type-2 fuzzy sets [7], Sugeno integral [8] and Choquet integral [9] are robust to dynamic backgrounds. Principal Component Analysis(PCA) [10] were suggested to learn the background in an unsupervised way. Subspace learning [11], support vector machines [12] and deep neural networks are also used to perform segmentation tasks. To avoid the sensibility of subspace methods to noise and missing data, an RPCA [13] has been proposed. But, it can't run in real-time because it need batch algorithms. To overcome this, dynamic RPCA as well as robust subspace tracking [14] have been suggested to achieve real-time accuracy.

Since the work of Xu et al. [15], Neural Networks have received considerable interest in the field of background subtraction. Due to the large availability of labeled data, Convolutional neural networks (CNNs) [16], have been considered for moving object segmentation. Many approaches were also proposed as cascaded CNNs [17], deep CNNs [18] and structured CNNs [19]. Xu et al. [15] employed deep autoencoder networks to perform a similar task and Zhang et al. [20] used a Stacked Denoising Auto-Encoder (SDAE) to learn robust spatial characteristics and the static scene is modeled with density analysis. Deep autoencoders have proved their success in detecting non-linear features. Many applications have been proposed based on RPCA [21,22].

In this paper, to avoid the limitations of RPCA, we propose to perform foreground objects segmentation based on an anomaly discovery framework called "DeepSphere" proposed by Teng et al. [23]. Since the work of Braham and Van Droogenbroeck in 2016 [16], numerous studies have demonstrated the important interest of deep neural networks in the field of BS. The main contribution of this paper is to provide a new approach for moving objects segmentation by adapting "DeepSphere" to the task of background subtraction. Then, we compare our proposed method with both DeepPBM and RPCA.

The rest of this paper is organized as follows. Section 2 presents the different methods based on deep neural networks for background subtraction. In Sect. 3, we detail our proposed approach based on DeepSphere to segment moving objects. We also provide a comparison with some state-of-the-art methods. Section 4 concludes the paper.

2   Related Research

Motion Detection is a fundamental research topic in Computer Vision. In this section, we provide a summary of the previous deep learning approaches used for moving object segmentation. Current BS approaches are mainly of four types: Methods based on Convolutional Neural Network, Multi-scale and Cascaded CNN, Generative Adversarial Network and Encoder-decoder Network.

In recent years, deep learning methods based on CNNs have achieved great performance in BS tasks. CNNs have been first proposed by Braham and Droogenbroeck [16] for BS. This model called ConvNet has the same structure as LeNet-5 [24]. The reference frame is extracted for a specific scene using a temporal median. Bautista et al. [25] detect and classify vehicles based on CNN using poor quality traffic video sequences. Yan et al. [26] apply a deep neural network (DNN)to detect pedestrians on the urban scene. A post-processing operation is performed to smooth the detection frame. This method can handle partial occlusions and illumination changes. Babaee et al. [18] proposed an approach based on deep CNN for BS task. Background model initialization and feature learning using CNN are applied. The image patches from the current frame are associated with the corresponding reference frame patches and transmitted into CNN. Then, a median filter is applied. Although CNNs present significant improvements in BS performance, they still have some limitations. They present a high computational cost and they often require image processing step. CNNs can not consider the long-term dependencies of the input videos as it uses a small number of input frames. They usually produce blurry foreground region. Subsequent methods have attempted to address these limitations, which are the main challenges of using DNN.

The second category of BS methods includes Multi-scale and Cascaded CNN approaches. The authors in [17] learn the appearance of the background and the foreground objects in order to produce the ground truths by manually outlining a small amount of moving objects. In Lim and Keles [27], a method is suggested termed FgSegNet-M which uses a triplet CNN and a transposed convolutional neural network (TCNN) attached to the end of the network in an encoder–decoder structure. First, VGG-16 Net [28] is adapted under a triplet network as a feature encoder in multiple scales. A decoder network produces a collection of pixel-wise segmentation probability maps which are transmitted to TCNN to learn the weights used for decoding the feature maps. Only a few training samples are used to train this network. An extension of FgSegNet-M is then proposed by Lim and Keles [29] called FgSegNet-S. A Feature Pooling Module (FPM) is added to model a triplet convolutional network and a feature in multiple scales. Lim et al. [30] suggested an extended variant to the previous method called FgSegNet-V2. An adjusted FPM module is proposed with feature fusion. But, these methods usually need a large number of annotated samples. To solve this, Liao et al. [31] proposed a multi-scale cascaded scene-specific (MCSS) BS method, which combines both ConvNets and the multiscale cascaded architecture.

Generative Adversarial Networks have been successfully used to segment foreground objects. Bakkay et al. [32] proposed a BS method based on conditional Generative Adversarial Network (cGAN). The generator maps from the reference frame and the current frame to get the foreground mask. These produced maps are trained with the discriminator by comparing the ground truth with the estimated result by considering the entered frame and the background. The encoder part includes own-sampling layers followed by convolutional filters. In the decoder part, up-sampling layers as well as deconvolutional filters are used. In Zheng et al. [33], a Bayesian GAN (BGAN) approach is proposed. To generate the reference frame, a median filtering operation is applied. Each pixel is categorized as foreground or background by training a network using BGAN. Both the generator and the discriminator networks are built based on Deep CNNs. Bahri et al. [34] proposed a Neural Unsupervised Moving Object Detection (NUMOD) method which uses two fully connected networks. The first network approximates the reference image from the input frame, while the second network produces a reference frame from an illumination invariant image.

Despite the performance of CNNs in images segmentation, they are unable to use temporal information which have long-term dependencies. The dense pixel-wise estimation is a big challenge for a CNN due to the big memory and the huge amount of parameters required to learn the time correlations. To overcome this, Choo et al. [35] proposed a Multi-Scale Recurrent encoder–decoder Neural Network (MSRNN), which compresses the spatial and temporal characteristics at the encoder and reconstructs them to the original size at the decoder. The recurrent layers are convolutional long short-term memory LSTM used to learn the temporal features from the subsequent frames and generate the dense predictions. Farnoosh et al. [36] exploited the power of Variational Autoencoders (VAEs) [37] and proposed a Deep Probabilistic Background Model (DeepPBM) approach. DeepPBM generates background model by computing backgrounds of a specific-scene in lighting changes and background motion. The background model is constructed as lying in a lower dimensional space with a series of latent variables which is processed based on a non-linear mapping of the data fit to a Gaussian distribution. The encoder learns and maps a powerful representation of the entered data into a lower dimensional subspace. To recuperate the original data, the decoder uses the probabilistic latent variables from the encoder. Finally, the authors compare the input data with the reconstructed output to get the final result.

Zhou and Paffenroth [21] suggested a model called Robust Deep Autoencoder (RDA) based on the concept of an RPCA proposed by [3]. The entered data is divided into two parts A = L + S. The hidden layer represents very well L which can then be reconstructed and S groups the anomalies and noise in the data. This split makes regular deep autoencoder more robust. Similarly, in Chalapathy et al. [22], a Robust Convolutional Autoencoder (RCAE) is proposed to learn non-linear subspace containing the large number of samples, but it often generates noisy segmentation masks. These two methods acquire the ability of autoencoder to learn non-linear representation as well as the capacity to discriminate RPCA anomalies. Dai et al. [38] proposed an extension to RPCA models called Variational AutoEncoders (VAE), which are able to learn corrupted non-linear manifolds. A linear deep autoencoder network has the same function as a dimension-reduction technique (PCA). Many approaches have been proposed based on RPCA method for foreground segmentation [39]. However, even RPCA based techniques can be trained successfully, they suffer from some limitations, especially when the background is static and when the foreground motion is fast. RPCA based methods are computationally complex and with global optimization. To address this problem, in this paper, we take advantages from an unsupervised anomaly discovery framework called DeepSphere proposed by Teng et al. [23], which has no requirement for anomaly sparsity and adapt it to the task of foreground objects segmentation. DeepSphere is an unified algorithm which does not require any optimization steps. This work demonstrates how DeepSphere can capture well foreground objects.

RPCA has the ability to distinguish anomalies by splitting the input data into a low rank matrix and a sparse matrix which contains the outliers of the dataset. The input splitting gives a loss function which is not exploitable by calculation. Whereas DeepSphere has no requirements for anomaly sparsity, it is, more specifically an end-to-end unified learning model that does not need any optimization technique. Despite the supervised methods require clean data in training phase, DeepSphere trains an unsupervised model to deal with the lack of labels and polluted data as presented in Ammar et al. [40]. DeepSphere add an hypersphere learning component to prevent anomalies and then keep high quality reconstruction of normal behaviors. Unlike the general foreground-background separation task in computer vision research, here we consider the problem of detecting foreground objects without using additional image processing or background learning.

DeepSphere aims to discover the anomalous cases in networks and explore the case's anomalous structure in spatial and temporal aspect. DeepSphere does not need any labeled samples or clean data. To create an unsupervised and computationally performant solution to BS challenges, we present a new method, which exploits the power and flexibility of deep neural networks, especially DeepSphere [23], to detect anomalies in videos and then well capture and segment foreground objects. The proposed method shows high performance in the majority of the scenes in the BMC 2012 dataset [41]. To do this, we propose a foreground activity detection algorithm based on both hypersphere learning and deep autoencoders to solve the problem of interfering learning process caused by anomaly pollution which can significantly reduce the quality of neural network. It excludes anomaly pollution by defining a compact limit separating normal and abnormal examples.

The basic idea consists of detecting foreground activities in the video sequences and then thresholding the outcome of the subtraction. We compare our approach with both RPCA and DeepPBM which both estimate a deterministic low dimensional representation of the background in videos.

3   Proposed Approach

In this section, we describe the proposed method in detail. It can be summarized as follows: based on a subset of frames in which foreground moving objects were presented, our method trains a foreground background model based on an anomaly discovery framework "DeepSphere" to do foreground objects segmentation. The objects are segmented by thresholding the difference between the reconstructed image and the input frame. The goal of our method is: (1) get segmentation results sufficiently accurate by employing an anomaly discovery algorithm and (2) compare those results with RPCA and DeepPBM.

DeepSphere can identify the anomalous cases and explore the cases' anomalous structure localized in spatial and temporal aspect. DeepSphere combines both deep autoencoders and hypersphere learning to clean the data by removing the anomalies and then rebuild normal situations. Unlabelled data may be corrupted by some anomalies that can affect learning process and reduce the quality of data. To overcome this, hypersphere learning is proposed to exclude anomaly pollution by learning a limit between normal and abnormal samples. The flowchart of our algorithm is presented in Fig. 1.

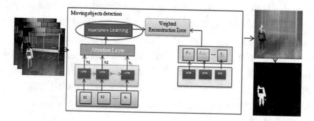

Fig. 1. The pipeline of our proposed background subtraction approach.

3.1   DeepSphere Architecture

DeepSphere proposed by Teng et al. [23] combines both autoencoders and hypersphere learning. On one hand, DeepSphere exploits the ability of hypersphere learning to remove anomalies and then enhance the quality of autoencoders; on the other hand, DeepSphere takes advantage from the ability of autoencoders to capture the temporal and spatial dependencies between elements to rebuild the normal situations from anomalous entered samples. Figure 1 shows the entire DeepSphere architecture. For a dynamic graph, let $\{\chi_k, k = 1, ..., m\}$ present a set of historical observations, (i.e. training data), a model is trained based on the training data, and then applied to unseen data (i.e. test data) $\{\chi_k, k > m\}$. A sample case χ is sliced into a series of matrices $\{X_t, t = 1, ..., T\}$ corresponding to a sequence of graphs. They are transmitted into an LSTM encoder [42] and a series of internal states $\{h_t, t = 1, .., T\}$ can be generated. The $\{h_t\}$ contains the information about the source sequence $\{X_t\}$. To learn the dependency structure more efficiently, the attention mechanism is used i.e., z = $P_t \, w_t \, h_t$, where z is the embedded representation, and w_t is the attention weight at time t. Hypersphere learning is assigned to learn a spherically shaped limit around the encoded representations $\{z_k\}$ to separate anomaly pollution Fig. 1. To reduce the risk of accepting abnormal cases, the objective function is defined as follows:

$$\phi = r^2 + \gamma \sum_{k=1}^{k=m} \xi_k + \frac{1}{m} \sum_{k=1}^{k=m} \| z_k - a \|^2 \tag{1}$$

All normal tensors should be mapped onto the centroid a of the hypersphere. The hypersphere learning layer output ϕ, d and r. The latent representations z lying outside of the hypersphere with large distances are considered as anomalous, while the ones inside of the hypersphere of small distances lies to be normal. The reconstruction error function is modified for LSTM as follows:

$$\Psi = \sum_{k=1}^{k=m} \eta_k \| \chi_k - \hat{\chi}_k \|^2 \tag{2}$$

where χ_k is reconstructed through LSTM decoder, and the η_k indicates weights computed through a heuristic function $\eta(d_k, r)$.
   The overall objective function is defined as:

$$\min_{\Theta} = \{\phi + \lambda \Psi\} \tag{3}$$

where λ is the trade-off parameter between these two items, and $\Theta = \{a, r, w, \theta, \phi\}$ contains the hypersphere centroid a, the radius r, the attention parameter w and the neural network parameters θ, Φ for LSTM encoder and decoder. DeepSphere is able to reconstruct its normal behavior even via $\{h_t\}$ is an anomalous input. By computing the reconstruction difference, the anomalies are discovered in spatial and temporal dimensions.

3.2   Performance Assessment

We evaluated the performance of our proposed method based on DeepSphere for BS on the BMC 2012 dataset [41] which contains 9 real videos, 20 synthetic videos and ground truths masks for a subset of frames in each video. They are recorded on outdoor situations with weather and illumination variations. We used this dataset to compare the quality of our method against DeepPBM and RPCA. Figure 2 shows the segmentation output using our proposed method in BMC 2012 dataset [41]. The three metrics that we used are:

$$Recall(Re) : TP/(TP + FN) \tag{4}$$

314   S. Ammar et al.

(a)   (b)   (c)   (d)

Fig. 2. (a) Background frame (b) Video input frame (c) DeepSphere output (d) Segmentation output

Table 1. The performance values of the proposed method compared to the other methods in the BMC 2012 Dataset [41]

Video	Method	Recall	Precision	F-measure
Video_001	RPCA	0.1786	0.6512	0.2803
	DeepPBM	0.3690	0.3690	0.5386
	Proposed method	0.5576	0.9590	**0.7051**
Video_002	RPCA	0.4333	0.8740	0.5794
	DeepPBM	0.4367	0.9856	0.6052
	Proposed method	0.5667	0.5667	**0.7190**
Video_003	RPCA	0.2803	0.8566	0.4223
	DeepPBM	0.5987	0.9863	0.7451
	Proposed method	0.6242	0.9680	**0.7590**
Video_004	RPCA	0.3179	0.8339	0.4603
	DeepPBM	0.3579	0.9820	0.5246
	Proposed method	0.5267	0.9827	**0.6858**
Video_005	RPCA	0.1538	0.6850	0.2513
	DeepPBM	0.5385	0.9255	0.6808
	Proposed method	0.5769	0.9304	**0.7122**
Video_006	RPCA	0.3251	0.9120	0.4794
	DeepPBM	0.4053	0.9891	0.5750
	Proposed method	0.4485	0.9677	**0.6129**
Video_007	RPCA	0.2321	0.2321	0.3038
	DeepPBM	0.3074	0.9761	0.4676
	Proposed method	0.3684	0.3684	**0.5345**
Video_008	RPCA	0.2914	0.9702	0.4482
	DeepPBM	0.2914	0.9271	**0.4738**
	Proposed method	0.2980	0.9409	0.4526
Video_009	RPCA	0.4119	0.9627	0.5769
	DeepPBM	0.4206	0.9891	0.5902
	Proposed method	0.5218	0.9572	**0.6754**

$$Precision(Pr) : TP/(TP + FP) \tag{5}$$

$$F - measure(Fm) : 2(Pr * Re)/(Pr + Re) \tag{6}$$

where TP = number of true positives, TN = number of true negatives, FN = number of false negatives, and FP = number of false positives.

The quantitative results of our method in BS compared to the RPCA and DeepPBM for each video of BMC 2012 dataset [41] are reported in Table 1.

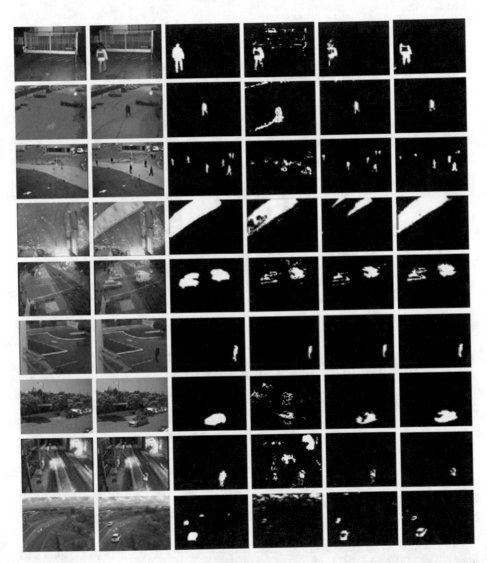

Fig. 3. Typical segmentation results for all sequences of BMC 2012 dataset [41]. Columns from left to right show the background image, the input image, the ground truth and the segmentation masks of RPCA, DeepPBM, Our proposed approach.

We computed the average metric for each video. Figure 3 illustrates segmentation mask outputs of applying DeepPBM, RPCA and our method. Our method is more successful in detecting foreground objects in these videos, and provides acceptable results, while RPCA and DeepPBM both fail to detect efficient foreground masks. Graphical values of our proposed method are enough successful than other methods Fig. 4. The proposed method attains the highest quantitative values such as the F-measure exceeds 68 % in the majority of the videos.

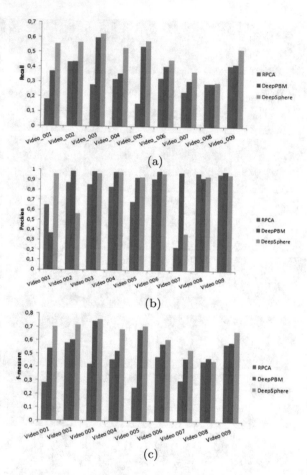

Fig. 4. Results obtained with the proposed scheme and other methods for the BMC 2012 dataset [41]. (a) Recall (b) Precision (c) F-measure.

As reported by the results, our proposed method outperformed both DeepPBM [36] and RPCA [3] on BMC 2012 dataset.

4   Conclusion

In this paper, we have presented our background subtraction approach using an unsupervised anomaly discovery framework DeepSphere for detecting and then segmenting moving objects in videos. We evaluated the efficiency of our method in the task of BS. From the visualized results and the quantitative and qualitative measurements, our proposed method outperformed both RPCA and DeepPBM known as well-performed subspace learning methods in foreground objects segmentation in terms of quality of the detected moving objects.

References

1. Shuigen W., Zhen C., and Hua D. Motion detection based on temporal difference method and optical flow field. In: Second International Symposium on Electronic Commerce and Security, pp. 85–88 (2009)
2. Mahraz, M.A., Riffi, J., Tairi, H.: Motion estimation using the fast and adaptive bidimensional empirical mode decomposition. J. Real-Time Image Process. 9(3), 491–501 (2014)
3. Candès, E., Li, X., Ma, Y., Wright, J.: Robust principal component analysis? Int. J. ACM 58(3), 11 (2011)
4. Wren, C., Azarbayejani, A.: Pfinder: real-time tracking of the human body. IEEE Trans. Pattern Anal. Mach. Intell. 19, 780–785 (1997)
5. Pulgarin-Giraldo, J., Alvarez-Meza, A., Insuasti-Ceballos, D., Bouwmans, T., Castellanos-Dominguez, G.: GMM background modeling using divergence-based weight updating. In: Conference Ibero-American Congress on Pattern Recognition (2016)
6. Zivkovic, Z.: Efficient adaptive density estimation per image pixel for the task of background subtraction. Pattern Recogn. Lett. 27(7), 773–780 (2006)
7. Bouwmans, T., El Baf, F.: Modeling of dynamic backgrounds by type-2 fuzzy gaussians mixture models. J. Basic Appl. Sci. 1(2), 265–276 (2009)
8. Zhang, H., Xu D.: Fusing color and gradient features for background model. In: International Conference on Signal Processing, vol. 2, no. 7 (2006)
9. Baf, F.E., Bouwmans, T., Vachon, B.: Fuzzy integral for moving object detection. In: IEEE International Conference on Fuzzy Systems, pp. 1729–1736 (2008)
10. Oliver, N., Rosario, B., Pentland, A.: A Bayesian computer vision system for modeling human interactions. In: ICVS (1999)
11. Dong, Y., DeSouza, G.: Adaptive learning of multi-subspace for foreground detection under illumination changes. Comput. Vis. Image 115, 31–49 (2011)
12. Bouwmans, T., Sobral, A., Javed, S., Jung, S.: Decomposition into low-rank plus additive matrices for background/foreground separation:a review for a comparative evaluation with a large-scale dataset. Comput. Sci. Rev. 23, 1–71 (2017)
13. Guyon, C., Bouwmans, T., Zahzah, E.: Foreground detection by robust PCA solved via a linearized alternating direction method. In: International Conference on Image Analysis and Recognition, ICIAR (2012)
14. Vaswani, N., Bouwmans, T., Javed, S., Narayanamurth, P.: Robust subspace learning: robust PCA, robust subspace tracking and robust subspace recovery. IEEE Signal Process. Mag. 35(4), 32–55 (2018b)

15. Xu, P., Ye, M., Liu, Q., Li, X., Ding, J.: Motion detection via a couple of auto-encoder networks. In: International Conference on Multimedia and Expo, ICME (2014)
16. Braham, M., Droogenbroeck, M.V.: Deep background subtraction with scene-specific convolutional neural networks. In: International Conference on Systems, Signals and Image Processing, IWSSIP, pp. 1–4 (2016)
17. Wang, Y., Luo, Z., Jodoin, P.: Interactive deep learning method for segmenting moving objects. Pattern Recogn. Lett. **96**, 66–75 (2016)
18. Babaee, M., Dinh, D., Rigoll, G.: A deep convolutional neural network for background subtraction. Pattern Recogn. (2017)
19. Lim, K., Jang, W., Kim, C.: Background subtraction using encoder-decoder structured convolutional neural network. In: IEEE International Conference on Advanced Video and Signal Based Surveillance, AVSS (2017)
20. Zhang, Y., Li, X., Zhang, Z., Wu, F., Zhao, L.: Deep learning driven blockwise moving object detection with binaryscene modeling. Neurocomputing **168**, 454–463 (2015)
21. Zhou, C., Paffenroth, R.: Anomaly detection with robust deep autoencoders. In: KDD (2017)
22. Chalapathy, R., Menon, A., Chawla, S.: Robust, deep and inductive anomaly detection. Preprint (2017)
23. Teng, X., Yan, M., Ertugrul, A., Lin, Y.: Deep into hypersphere: robust and unsupervised anomaly discovery in dynamic networks. In: International Joint Conference on Artificial Intelligence, IJCAI, pp. 2724–2730 (2018)
24. Cun, Y.L., Bottou, L., Haffner, P.: Gradient-based learning applied to document recognition. Proc. IEEE **86**, 2278–2324 (1998)
25. Bautista, C.M., Dy, C.A., Manalac, M.I., Orbe, R.A., Cordel, M.: Convolutional neural network for vehicle detection in low resolution traffic videos. TENSYMP **9**(11), 277–281 (2016)
26. Yan, Y., Zhao, H., Kao, F., Vargas, V., Zhao, S., Ren, J.: Deep background subtraction of thermal and visible imagery for pedestrian detection in videos. In: International Conference on Brain Inspired Cognitive Systems, BICS (2018)
27. Lim, L., Keles, H.: Foreground segmentation using a triplet convolutional neural network for multiscale feature encoding. Preprint (2018)
28. Simonyan, K., Zisserman, A.: Very deep convolutional networks for large-scale image recognition. In: International Conference on Learning Representation (2015)
29. Lim, L., Keles, H.: Foreground segmentation using convolutional neural networks for multiscale feature encoding. Pattern Recogn. Lett. **112**, 256–262 (2018)
30. Lim, L., Ang, l., Keles, H.: Learning multi-scale features for foreground segmentation. Preprint (2018)
31. Liao, J., Guo, G., Yan, Y., Wang, H.: Multiscale cascaded scene-specific convolutional neural networks for background subtraction. In: Pacific Rim Conference on Multimedia, PCM, pp. 524–533 (2018)
32. Bakkay, M., Rashwan, H., Salmane, H., Khoudour, L., Puig, D., Ruichek, Y.: BSCGAN: deep background subtraction with conditional generative adversarial networks. In: International Conference on Image Processing, ICIP (2018)
33. Zheng, W., Wang, K., Wang, F.: Background subtraction algorithm based on Bayesian generative adversarial networks. Acta Automatica Sinica **44**, 878–890 (2018)
34. Bahri, F., Shakeri, M., Ray, N.: Online illumination invariant moving object detection by generative neural network. Preprint (2018)

35. Choo, S., Seo, W., Jeong, D., Cho, N.: Multi-scale recurrent encoder-decoder network for dense temporal classification. In: ICPR, pp. 103–108 (2018)
36. Farnoosh, A., Rezaei, B., Ostadabbas, S.: DeepPBM: deep probabilistic background model estimation from video sequences. Preprint (2019)
37. Doersch, C.: Tutorial on variational autoencoders. Preprint (2016)
38. Dai, J., Wang, Y., Aston, J., Wipf, D.: Connections with robust PCA and the role of emergent sparsity in variational autoencoder models. J. Mach. Learn. Res. (JMLR) **19**, 1–42 (2018)
39. Liu, X., Zhao, G., Yao, J., Qi, C.: Background subtraction based on low-rank and structured sparse decomposition. Trans. Image Process **24**, 2502–2514 (2015)
40. Ammar, S., Zaghden, N., Neji, M.: A framework for people re-identification in multi-camera surveillance systems. In: International Conference on Cognition and Exploratory Learning in Digital Age CELDA (2017)
41. Vacavant, A., Chateau, T., Wilhelm, A., Lequièvre, L.: A benchmark dataset for outdoor foreground/background extraction. In: Park, J.-I., Kim, J. (eds.) ACCV 2012. LNCS, vol. 7728, pp. 291–300. Springer, Heidelberg (2013). https://doi.org/10.1007/978-3-642-37410-4_25
42. Baytas, M., Xiao, C., et al.: Patient subtyping via time-aware LSTM networks. In: SIGKDD, vol. 19, pp. 65–74 (2017)

Benchmarking Video with the Surgical Image Registration Generator (SIRGn) Baseline

Michael Barrow[1]($\boxtimes$), Nelson Ho[2], Alric Althoff[3], Peter Tueller[1], and Ryan Kastner[1]

[1] University of California, San Diego, La Jolla, CA 92093, USA
{mbarrow,ptueller,rkastner}@eng.ucsd.edu
[2] VMware, Palo Alto, CA 94304, USA
hon@vmware.com
[3] Leidos, San Diego, CA 92127, USA
aalthoff@eng.ucsd.edu

Abstract. Augmented Reality (AR) surgical image guidance overlays preoperative data into the surgeon's view in real time during the procedure. Non-rigid 3D registration is a critical and often challenging step for AR surgical image guidance. Since surgical environments vary greatly and registration must by done quickly and accurately, it is unlikely that one registration technique will work well over different surgical scenarios. Unfortunately, it is currently challenging to evaluate the accuracy and effectiveness of 3D registration techniques on surgical scenes. In this work, we provide a novel method to benchmark quality of non-rigid 3D surface registration. Our method provides a triangular mesh overlay representing the quality of registration and can highlight areas of unacceptably poor registration performance given some specified tolerance. We use the method to evaluate the quality of two existing non-rigid registration approaches on surgical video.

Keywords: Benchmarking · Registration · Augmented Reality · Image guidance

1 Introduction

Augmented Reality (AR) has significant potential for enhancing surgical procedures. For example, the ability to superimpose landmarks like major internal vessels onto the surface of an organ provides immense value for surgical image guidance. There are many therapeutic uses for AR guidance in laparoscopic surgery [1–5] and other closely related intervention types such as telerobotic surgery where AR enhances the pre-existing feedback from robotic tools [6,7].

A key challenge for AR surgery is registration, which provides the relationship between a preoperative model (e.g., CT or MRI scan) and the surgical video feed. Figure 1 illustrates the registration process. The three images/frames on the left

© Springer Nature Switzerland AG 2019
G. Bebis et al. (Eds.): ISVC 2019, LNCS 11845, pp. 320–331, 2019.
https://doi.org/10.1007/978-3-030-33723-0_26

are collected in real-time during the procedure from a camera. Each frame must be registered onto the preoperative 3D model on the right. After that, features from the preoperative 3D model are overlaid onto the surgeons view.

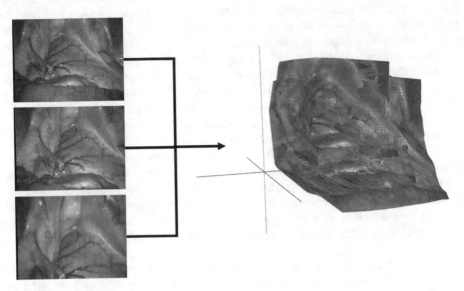

Fig. 1. Registration maps video frames (left) onto a 3D model (right). The video frames should be mapped in real-time onto the 3D model allowing any features from the model to be projected into the surgeons view.

Surgical augmented reality is particularly challenging since it must be done in real time with high accuracy. A surgical scene can be extremely complex: tissues deform, lighting varies dramatically, and features quickly come in and out of the field of view. Every laparoscope, every lighting solution, and every type of surgery have unique idiosyncrasies. Consequently, custom registration algorithms are needed for the unique challenges arising from a given combination of factors in a particular surgery. It can be difficult to tune the performance of a registration algorithm to the surgeon's needs since benchmarks that account for specific idiosyncrasies of that surgery do not exist. Because of these challenges, surgery-specific heuristics are needed to perform high quality dense surface registration in real-time. However, it is impossible to measure the effectiveness of these heuristics without a baseline quality measure. A useful quality measure must be *dense, granular,* and *convenient.*

Many quality metrics have been applied to clinical registration. The canonical approach is Target Registration Error (TRE) which involves computing $L2$ or some other distance between corresponding feature points after registration [8–12]. Feature separation distances can be highly representative of registration error if the features are appropriately chosen, but such metrics have no concept of a global coordinate system to track drift in a stream of registrations. Besides distance measures, global similarity metrics based on intensity have broad clinical applications [13–16]. These qualitative measures combine intensities of the registered images into one image. A clinician can then judge the quality of registration through experienced observation of the resulting overlay of images. Because of this reliance on clinical experience, intensity metrics are not used in applications where registration accuracy is critical as they cannot represent the warp function in a physically meaningful way.

Landmark registration metrics judge registration quality by an objective function weighted by pre-defined feature points. These consider rigid registration [17] and/or fiducial markers [18] rather than tissue only landmarks and can be used to focus the metric on registration regions of clinical interest. Hoffmann et al. [19] develop such a quality metric. Unfortunately, they do not attempt large surface area coverage, they rely on a small number of landmarks, and their technique is applied to CT scans rather than video. Recently Thompson et al. [20] proposed an AR specific registration evaluation focused on accurately positioning sub-surface landmarks. Unfortunately shifting focus from surface registration to sub-surface features requires that assumptions are made on the biomechanics of the organ when estimating landmark positions. Because such assumptions often break down [21], quantitative surface registration quality metrics are more robust.

Surgical Image Registration Generator (SIRGn) is a novel dense, granular baseline quality metric for video registration algorithms. Figure 2 shows how SIRGn works. It evaluates the registration of a set of images/frame (Fig. 2a) by creating a heat map that shows regions of poor registration quality (Fig. 2b) that can be subsequently overlaid onto the scene (Fig. 2c) for visual inspection of the quality of result of the registration algorithm.

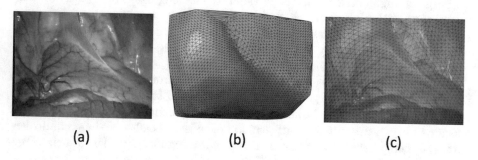

(a)   **(b)**   **(c)**

Fig. 2. Illustration of the SIRGn concept. Assume a 3D registration algorithm is run on the video frame shown in Fig. 2a. SIRGn evaluates the quality of the registration by creating a covariance mesh (Fig. 2b) and overlaying that as a "heat map" (Fig. 2c) where high heat indicates poor registration quality, e.g., as seen in the upper left corner.

The novelty of SIRGn lies in the fact that it combines the physically meaningful metric of TRE with the clinically useful dense image coverage of an intensity type measure. Additionally, unlike the aforementioned approaches, SIRGn is well suited for image guidance benchmarking since real time registration algorithms are evaluated using a global coordinate system, which allows it to compare across multiple frames. Our method can be applied in situations where no suitable database of videos exists or where synthetic simulation is intractable. Also, it can be applied to many types of surgery and it does not rely on physical simulation or biomechanical tissue information.

In this manuscript we describe the SIRGn method and an experiment that uses SIRGn to compare performance of two non-rigid 3D registration algorithms on laparoscopic video from a database [22]. Our experiment models the exploratory phase of AR image guidance where several approaches are tried to accurately track the clinically significant portion of a surgical scene over time. Specifically we show that SIRGn is advantageous in evaluating the accuracy of different registration methods by comparing a SIRGn work flow with the conventional TRE and RMSE error metrics. Registration performance is evaluated using landmark correspondences [23]. Although it is desirable in clinical image registration to use expert landmark correspondences, our goal is convenience[1] and so we provide tools for automated global reference feature extraction from 2D and 3D laparoscopic video.

The remainder of this paper is organized as follows. Section 2 gives an overview of the baseline generation method and evaluation of 3D registration quality using SIRGn as a baseline. Section 3 gives an appraisal of SIRGn as a simple and flexible baseline generation method. We conclude in Sect. 4.

2   Method

SIRGn provides a way to evaluate a given registration algorithm on a surgical 3D video data set. For this, we must create a metric that describes the quality of the registration. An ideal metric would work for any registration algorithm and data set. It would allow us to compare the quality of different registration algorithms on that data set. And it would provide a location specific quality measure. We describe our metric in the context of stereo laparoscopic cameras since we anticipate SIRGn's greatest applicability to be in image guided surgery. However our methodology can be applied to conventional 2D surgical video data.

The insight motivating SIRGn is that surfaces in surgical scenes are smooth with very few exceptions. Therefore given a smooth surface, a point that is heavily warped by registration with respect to surrounding "known-good" points is less likely to be accurate. In order to formalize this intuition, we rely on two sets of points. The first, G, is a set of expert landmarks that we assume as correct a priori; these could be human labeled by a surgeon or provided by a reliable feature detection algorithm. The second, C, contains points that require heavy warping to align well on a global model M. Points in C are chosen by searching points enclosed within the triangulation of G. Specifically, a set of candidate points to be registered is masked using a triangle from G to project onto M space. After registration the point that required the largest registration warping

---

[1] Example code and data available at: https://github.com/KastnerRG/SIRGn.git.

transform to M space is added to C. Any point that requires substantial warping is likely due to an incorrect registration, and similarly any points that require a small amount of warping are likely correctly registered. Thus, the key is to determine how to evaluate these warp functions for any registration algorithm and to derive a method to efficiently locate points C that must be heavily warped. We describe this in more detail in the following.

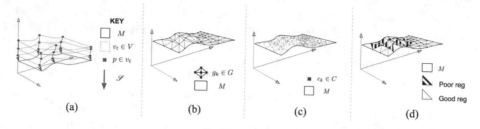

Fig. 3. Steps to compute the SIRGn quality metric are, in order: (a) Construct a 3D model M and warp $\mathscr{S}$ using points $g_k \in G$ and all 3D scans $v_t \in V$. (b) Project expert-labeled landmarks $g_i \in G$ onto M. (c) Find heavily-warped registered points $c_i \in C$. (d) Label a mesh with vertices G showing registration quality. The labels/coloring are a function of G, C and ε tolerance and can be visualized, e.g., as done in Figs. 5d to f.

The four major components to SIRGn are shown graphically in Fig. 3. Figure 3a computes a non-rigid warping function $\mathscr{S}$ that projects G from the video frames V to the 3D model M. That is, the warp function $\mathscr{S}$ describes the relationship between the landmarks G in the stereo video frames V and those same landmarks on the 3D model M. One can view M as containing the average location of all the landmarks within G over time. Figure 3b computes a Delaunay triangulation between each landmark g_i on the 3D model M. Figure 3c finds the most heavily warped points for each surface triangle. Figure 3d assigns a value to each triangle computed from these sets to faces of a Delaunay triangulation to form a "correlation mesh". This is the output that indicates how well the worst case points correlate with the landmarks. If there is high correlation, then the worst case points correspond well to the assumed high quality landmarks, and thus are more likely to indicate that the registration was accurate. This correlation mesh is very useful for comparing the performance of different registrations with one another since it highlights regions of relatively poor performance.

Once a candidate algorithm has been selected using the correlation mesh, SIRGn can be re-run and set to report mean registration error of the G triangulation for a candidate registration in another mesh. We set an acceptable error threshold based on the registration accuracy desired. This is typically defined by the needs of a clinical AR application, i.e., 5 mm is typical abdominal surgeries [24]. Unacceptable regions of the candidate registration are highlighted in a second mesh. This work flow is demonstrated in Sect. 3.

2.1   SIRGn Registration Quality Measure

In order to use SIRGn, an evaluator must first run a global registration algorithm, which we call ALG. ALG is chosen to be highly accurate, i.e., real time constraints do not apply in order to maximize the registration quality. Because AR registration is performed in $\mathscr{R}3$, SIRGn should be run after a stereo reconstruction algorithm on stereoscopic laparoscopes although it can be run directly on 3D scopes. ALG returns a dense global registration model M by performing a global registration optimization that minimizes the transform distance of the set of G points for all 3D video frames $v_t \in V$, such that

$$M = \text{ALG}(V, G) \tag{1}$$

Global Warping Function: Once we have computed M, we obtain a dense benchmark registration over M. To do this, we compute a function $\mathscr{S}$ mapping from scans V to the space of M to allow every point in 3D depth scans $v_t \in V$ to be mapped to the dense surface. We choose the method used by Global Non-Rigid Alignment (GNRA) [25] using thin plate spline (TPS) interpolation that is regularized to produce a smooth function. We prefer this method as a warp baseline both for its stability and the guarantee that $\mathscr{S}$ is a smooth bijective transform. The resulting $\mathscr{S}$ is the global warping function, such that $\mathscr{S}(p; t) = \bar{p} \in M$ for any point p in a 3D scan v_t. $\mathscr{S}$ is therefore useful when building the C set as detailed later.

Landmark Distance Vectors: SIRGn builds a set $\mathcal{D}_G$ of landmark distance vectors consisting of one vector ℓ_k for each expert landmark in the set of all landmarks G. Note that landmark points g_k in some 3D scan v_t correspond to each other throughout scans $v_t \in V$, and to one $\bar{g}_k$ in the space of the global model M. We compute index t of these vectors ℓ_k as the distance between $g_k \in v_t$ and $\bar{g}_k \in M$. That is,

$$\ell_k[t] = \|g_k - \bar{g}_k\|_2, \text{ s.t. } g_k \in v_t \tag{2}$$

for each global landmark $\bar{g}_k \in M$. Then $\mathcal{D}_G = \{\ell_k : 1 \leq k \leq |G|\}$ is the set of landmark distance vectors.

Warping Distance Vectors: SIRGn computes a mesh of M via Delaunay triangulation using G as mesh vertices. Then, for each triangular face Δ_{c_k} of the mesh we define points $c_{k,t}$ in frames v_t as the *most heavily warped in* Δ_{c_k} at time t. Formally,

$$c_{k,t} = \text{argmax}_{p \in \Delta_{c_k}} \mathscr{S}^{-1}(p; t) \tag{3}$$

Note that since $\mathscr{S}$ is bijective and everywhere differentiable, $\mathscr{S}^{-1}$ is well-defined for each t, and Eq. (3) can be solved using standard optimization techniques. We choose these points $c_{k,t}$ because a point on the model surrounded by expert landmarks on the surface of an organ that undergoes a different warp than these landmarks is unlikely to track the tissue surface well. We form a set C_t of these "worst points" $c_{k,t}$, one for each triangle in the mesh, by projecting c_k's enclosing triangle to form a planar region of interest (ROI) and then performing gradient ascent on $\mathscr{S}^{-1}$ within these ROIs. Once C_t is determined, the set $\mathcal{D}_{C_t}$ of warping distances is computed identically to $\mathcal{D}_G$ with $c_{k,t}$ and $\bar{c}_{k,t}$ replacing g_k and $\bar{g}_k$ in Eq. (2).

Correlation Mesh: In order to make our metric dense over the registration surface, we define Delaunay mesh face-values as the linear correlation between vectors $\omega_{k,t} \in \mathcal{D}_{C_t}$, and averages of those vectors corresponding to the vertices of Δ_{c_k} from $\mathcal{D}_G$. That is,

$$\text{SIRGn}(\Delta_{c_k}) = \frac{1}{n} \sum_t \text{corr}(\omega_{k,t}, \hat{\ell}_k) \tag{4}$$

where $\text{corr}(u, v)$ is the linear correlation (normalized covariance) between vectors u and v, and $\hat{\ell}_k = (\ell_a + \ell_b + \ell_c)/3$ where $\ell_a, \ell_b, \ell_c \in \mathcal{D}_G$ are the three vectors corresponding to those g_k that are the vertices of Δ_{c_k}, and n is the number of frames containing c_k. Good registration in the local region Δ_{c_k} is indicated by a large correlation between the vectors for that particular Δ_{c_k}. In this way we obtain a quality score that is both *dense*, because the whole model surface is covered, and *granular*, so that each region can be specifically highlighted for easy localization of unacceptable registration errors.

Labeling: This correlation mesh can be transformed into a binary accept/reject by taking a tolerance parameter ε to define what level of error is acceptable. We can also display the linear correlation on the mesh faces directly via coloring for final visualization. Labeling the Delaunay triangle set of G is the final step in generating the SIRGn quality metric.

3   Experiments and Results

We track respiration motion in a laparoscopic surgery scene accurately in order to best place image guidance landmarks on a live patient. We use SIRGn and the conventional metrics of RMSE and TRE to compare two 3D surface registration algorithms on laparoscopic video from the Hamlyn data set [22]. Our goal is to use each of the comparison metrics to understand which registration algorithm was best suited to tracking the non-rigid respiration motion in the scene. Our findings detailed in this section showed that SIRGn meshes offered a simple way to compare registration in specific regions of interest in a case where traditional metrics were more difficult to interpret.

We ran all metrics on two algorithms under test. The first, "$ICP(V)$", is a non-rigid ICP variant based on Amberg's work [26]. The second, "$GEO(V)$", uses Chen's geodesic approach [27]. Geodesic registration is suited to non-rigid problems but is typically computed offline due to its complexity. However, a real time implementation was recently described, making it interesting to compare with ICP [28].

SIRGn was run on the algorithms under test using the following steps. First the $ALG(V, G)$ inputs were generated from a laparoscopic video data base [22] using a stereo reconstruction specialized to laparoscopic video (V) [29] and a robust global SIFT tracker (G). Although mixed manual methods for extracting ground truth are more desirable, these must be applied during video acquisition which was not possible in our case [30,31]. Next, C and M were generated by running $ALG(V, G)$.

Correlation: We applied Eq. 4 to the output from $ICP(V)$ and $GEO(V)$ to generate relative quality meshes as shown in Figs. 5b and c. Yellow is weak correlation with the benchmark and deep blue is strong correlation with the benchmark. The color map of the figures was normalized to the algorithms under test for ease of visual comparison.

Labeling: After using SIRGn to compare $ICP(V)$ and $GEO(V)$ quality meshes, we ran SIRGn with a labeling threshold ε. The ε was set to reject error $\geq 10,5$ and 3 mm as shown in Figs. 5d, e and f respectively. Mesh triangle registration errors of ε and above were greyed out.

SIRGn runtime varied from 5 to 12 min depending on $ALG(V, G)$ input size. An example implementation is available under the BSD license at *Omitted for blind review*. Figure 4 summarizes the results of all metrics where $|G| = 1155$ and $|V| = 180$ which were the largest input we used for 6 s of video.

Traditional Metrics: Traditional metrics were computed frame to frame as they are not designed for global registration. Completely global RMSE and TRE metrics (Fig. 5i) cannot represent time and it was not possible to use them in assessing how stable either $ICP(V)$ or $GEO(V)$ might have been. In addition registration drift could not be accounted for which led to misleadingly low error reports. Even when a time dimension is added to RMSE as in Fig. 5g it was not possible to isolate the respiratory ROI.

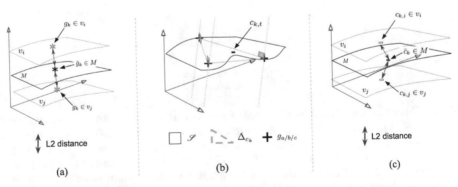

Fig. 4. (a) Indices i and j of the landmark distance vector ℓ_k corresponding to $\bar{g}_k$ are computed as the Euclidean (L2) distance from the corresponding points $g_k \in v_i$ and $g_k \in v_j$. (b) The most heavily warped point $c_{k,t}$ are computed for a single time point t as the maximum warp $\mathscr{S}$ required to send the point $p \in \Delta_{c_k}$ to the model M. (c) Warping distance vectors ω_k are computed similarly to landmark distance vectors, except $c_{k,t}$ is used instead.

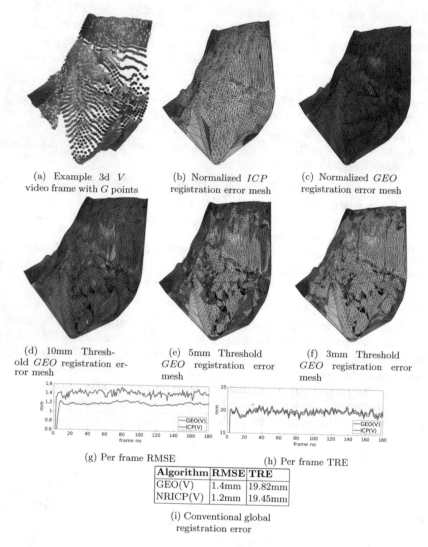

(a) Example 3d V video frame with G points

(b) Normalized ICP registration error mesh

(c) Normalized GEO registration error mesh

(d) 10mm Threshold GEO registration error mesh

(e) 5mm Threshold GEO registration error mesh

(f) 3mm Threshold GEO registration error mesh

(g) Per frame RMSE

(h) Per frame TRE

Algorithm	RMSE	TRE
GEO(V)	1.4mm	19.82mm
NRICP(V)	1.2mm	19.45mm

(i) Conventional global registration error

Fig. 5. Example use of SIRGn to compare two non-rigid 3D registration approaches (Figs. 5a to c), alongside traditional error metrics (Figs. 5g to i). Figure 5a shows a priori known good points (G) rendered on one video frame in green. Figure 5b and c are the quality meshes for the $ICP(V)$ and $GEO(V)$ video registrations respectively. According to SIRGn, $ICP(V)$ showed a far greater variation than $GEO(V)$ from the baseline in the region of video with most movement. Figure 5d, e and Fig. 5d show the results of SIRGn set to color the $GEO(V)$ error mesh white. based on different triangle registration error thresholds. Important parts of the scene can be inspected at the desired threshold setting to see if registration is acceptable. Comparatively, traditional metrics shown in Fig. 5i, g and h do not show the variation of registration performance with area which was less informative than SIRGn for evaluating quality of registration around the region of interest in the video clip.

Although we could use our G and C points to define mean TRE per frame as shown in Fig. 5h, it was still not trivial to isolate the ROI. In contrast, the SIRGn overlays in Figs. 5b and c clearly show regional variations of registration quality between $ICP(V)$ and $GEO(V)$ on the respiratory region, which was colored yellow for $ICP(V)$. SIRGn was most reflective of the more rigid registration $ICP(V)$ implemented with respect to $GEO(V)$ of all the evaluated metrics. In addition the ε threshold of SIRGn allowed us to see that the GEO algorithm was likely unsuitable for an abdominal AR guidance application requiring sub 5 mm accuracy. This is in contrast to our evaluations with traditional metrics of RMSE and TRE where it is difficult to know if sub 5 mm accuracy is possible in regions of interest.

4 Conclusion

We describe SIRGn – a novel metric for evaluating the quality of nonrigid registration algorithms on surgical 3D video. SIRGn indicates the quality of the registration for different parts of the 3D model by generating an overlay mesh that highlights areas where the registration approach succeeds and fails. This can serve as a way to evaluate different registration algorithms (both new and old) in various surgical scenarios. The ultimate goal is to provide a metric by which different registration algorithms crucial to enabling surgical augmented reality can be compared and evaluated. Our experiments demonstrate how SIRGn can be used to compare different registration methods. SIRGn evaluates a given registration algorithm by creating a mesh of registration quality over a 3D surgical video sequence using known good landmarks and our novel warp variance interpolation. We demonstrate how a SIRGn mesh can show relative registration quality between algorithms under evaluation, and also how an error tolerance can be specified when generating a registration quality mesh to highlight regions of unacceptable registration accuracy for a given application.

References

1. Pessaux, P., Diana, M., Soler, L., Piardi, T., Mutter, D., Marescaux, J.: Towards cybernetic surgery: robotic and augmented reality-assisted liver segmentectomy. Langenbeck's archives of surgery **400**(3), 381–385 (2015)
2. Ieiri, S., et al.: Augmented reality navigation system for laparoscopic splenectomy in children based on preoperative CT image using optical tracking device. Pediatr. Surg. Int. **28**(4), 341–346 (2012)
3. Onda, S., et al.: Short rigid scope and stereo-scope designed specifically for open abdominal navigation surgery: clinical application for hepatobiliary and pancreatic surgery. J. Hepato-Biliary-Pancreat. Sci. **20**(4), 448–453 (2013)
4. Kowalczuk, J., et al.: Real-time three-dimensional soft tissue reconstruction for laparoscopic surgery. Surg. Endosc. **26**(12), 3413–3417 (2012)
5. Schoob, A., Kundrat, D., Kleingrothe, L., Kahrs, L.A., Andreff, N., Ortmaier, T.: Tissue surface information for intraoperative incision planning and focus adjustment in laser surgery. Int. J. Comput. Assist. Radiol. Surg. **10**(2), 171–181 (2015)

6. Hughes-Hallett, A., Mayer, E.K., Pratt, P., Mottrie, A., Darzi, A., Vale, J.: The current and future use of imaging in urological robotic surgery: a survey of the european association of robotic urological surgeons. Int. J. Med. Robot. Comput. Assist. Surg. **11**(1), 8–14 (2015)

7. Volonté, F., et al.: Console-integrated stereoscopic osirix 3D volume-rendered images for da vinci colorectal robotic surgery. Surg. Innov. **20**(2), 158–163 (2013)

8. Fitzpatrick, J.M.: Detecting Failure, Assessing Success. CRC Press, New York (2001)

9. Hong, J., Matsumoto, N., Ouchida, R., Komune, S., Hashizume, M.: Medical navigation system for otologic surgery based on hybrid registration and virtual intraoperative computed tomography. IEEE Trans. Biomed. Eng. **56**(2), 426–432 (2009)

10. Shekhar, R., et al.: Live augmented reality: a new visualization method for laparoscopic surgery using continuous volumetric computed tomography. Surg. Endosc. **24**(8), 1976–1985 (2010)

11. Krucker, J.F., LeCarpentier, G.L., Fowlkes, J.B., Carson, P.L.: Rapid elastic image registration for 3-D ultrasound. IEEE Trans. Med. Imaging **21**(11), 1384–1394 (2002)

12. Grachev, I.D., et al.: A method for assessing the accuracy of intersubject registration of the human brain using anatomic landmarks. NeuroImage **9**(2), 250–268 (1999)

13. Nanayakkara, N.D., Chiu, B., Samani, A., Spence, J.D., Samarabandu, J., Fenster, A.: Twisting and bending model-based nonrigid image registration technique for 3-D ultrasound carotid images. IEEE Trans. Med. Imaging **27**(10), 1378–1388 (2008)

14. Tamura, Y., et al.: Surface-based registration accuracy of CT-based image-guided spine surgery. Eur. Spine J. **14**(3), 291–297 (2005)

15. Parsai, E.I., Ayyangar, K.M., Dobelbower, R.R., Siegel, J.A.: Clinical fusion of three-dimensional images using bremsstrahlung spect and CT. J. Nucl. Med. **38**(2), 319 (1997)

16. Nelson, S.J., et al.: Alignment of volume MR images and high resolution [18f] fluorodeoxyglucose pet images for the evaluation of patients with brain tumors. J. Comput. Assist. Tomogr. **21**(2), 183–191 (1997)

17. Fitzpatrick, J.M., West, J.B., Maurer, C.R.: Predicting error in rigid-body point-based registration. IEEE Trans. Med. Imaging **17**(5), 694–702 (1998)

18. West, J.B., Fitzpatrick, J.M., Toms, S.A., Maurer Jr., C.R., Maciunas, R.J.: Fiducial point placement and the accuracy of point-based, rigid body registration. Neurosurgery **48**(4), 810–817 (2001)

19. Hoffmann, C., et al.: Accuracy quantification of a deformable image registration tool applied in a clinical setting. J. Appl. Clin. Med. Phys. **15**(1), 237–245 (2014)

20. Thompson, S., et al.: In vivo estimation of target registration errors during augmented reality laparoscopic surgery. Int. J. Comput. Assist. Radiol. Surg. **13**(6), 865–874 (2018)

21. Wong, V.W.S., et al.: Diagnosis of fibrosis and cirrhosis using liver stiffness measurement in nonalcoholic fatty liver disease. Hepatology **51**(2), 454–462 (2010)

22. Imperial College, London: Hamlyn centre laparoscopic/endoscopic video datasets (2019). http://hamlyn.doc.ic.ac.uk/vision/. Accessed 15 Jan 2019

23. Castillo, R., et al.: A framework for evaluation of deformable image registration spatial accuracy using large landmark point sets. Phys. Med. Biol. **54**(7), 1849 (2009)

24. Bernhardt, S., Nicolau, S.A., Soler, L., Doignon, C.: The status of augmented reality in laparoscopic surgery as of 2016. Med. Image Anal. **37**, 66–90 (2017)

25. Brown, B.J., Rusinkiewicz, S.: Global non-rigid alignment of 3-d scans. In: ACM Transactions on Graphics (TOG), vol. 26, no. 21. ACM (2007)
26. Amberg, B., Romdhani, S., Vetter, T.: Optimal step nonrigid ICP algorithms for surface registration. In: IEEE Conference on Computer Vision and Pattern Recognition, 2007, CVPR 2007, p. 1–8. IEEE (2007)
27. Chen, Q., Koltun, V.: Robust nonrigid registration by convex optimization. In: Proceedings of the IEEE International Conference on Computer Vision, pp. 2039–2047 (2015)
28. Barrow, M., Burns, S.M., Kastner, R.: A FPGA accelerator for real-time 3D nonrigid registration using tree reweighted message passing and dynamic Markov random field generation. In: 2018 28th International Conference on Field Programmable Logic and Applications (FPL), pp. 335–3357. IEEE (2018)
29. Chang, P.-L., Stoyanov, D., Davison, A.J., Edwards, P.E.: Real-time dense stereo reconstruction using convex optimisation with a cost-volume for image-guided robotic surgery. In: Mori, K., Sakuma, I., Sato, Y., Barillot, C., Navab, N. (eds.) MICCAI 2013. LNCS, vol. 8149, pp. 42–49. Springer, Heidelberg (2013). https://doi.org/10.1007/978-3-642-40811-3_6
30. Padoy, N., Blum, T., Ahmadi, S.A., Feussner, H., Berger, M.O., Navab, N.: Statistical modeling and recognition of surgical workflow. Med. Image Anal. **16**(3), 632–641 (2012)
31. Bouarfa, L., Jonker, P.P., Dankelman, J.: Discovery of high-level tasks in the operating room. J. Biomed. Inform. **44**(3), 455–462 (2011)

Towards Fine-Grained Recognition: Joint Learning for Object Detection and Fine-Grained Classification

Qiaosong Wang[✉] and Christopher Rasmussen

Department of Computer and Information Sciences,
University of Delaware, Newark, DE, USA
{qiaosong,ras}@udel.edu

Abstract. Fine-grained classification is a challenging problem due to subtle differences between intra-class categories. In practice, fine-grained classification is often used in conjunction with object detection algorithms to locate and identify object categories. Despite recent achievements in both fine-grained classification and object detection, few works have demonstrated datasets or solutions to simultaneously handle both tasks. We make two contributions to this problem. Firstly, we construct a fine-grained classification and detection benchmark. Secondly, we show an end-to-end convolutional neural networks (CNNs) architecture to detect and classify fine-grained objects. Experimental results verify that our networks perform favorably against alternatives.

Keywords: Object detection · Fine-grained classification

1 Introduction

Locating and identifying objects is important for many computer vision applications. For example, one could develop automated computer vision software to process live surveillance videos and recognize brand and model of a vehicle for identifying traffic violations. For environmental monitoring, locating and recognizing wildlife could generate statistics to help protecting endangered species. However, even for car enthusiasts or bird-watching experts, it is still difficult to identify a specific car model or bird species accurately.

Recent advances in deep learning have shown promising results for image classification and detection. PASCAL VOC [3] and ImageNet [11] are widely used to evaluate classification/detection performance. Both datasets provide annotations for generic object classification and detection. In contrast to generic object classification, fine-grained classification aims at identifying objects within the same fine-grained category (or subcategory). Stanford Cars [10] and Caltech-UCSD Birds 200 (CUB-200) [24] are the two most popular benchmarks for evaluating such tasks. Comparing to the generic classification task, images in fine-grained datasets usually exhibit small inter-class and large intra-class variations in visual

© Springer Nature Switzerland AG 2019
G. Bebis et al. (Eds.): ISVC 2019, LNCS 11845, pp. 332–344, 2019.
https://doi.org/10.1007/978-3-030-33723-0_27

appearances. The small inter-class variation is due to the natural of fine-grained classification task, where all objects belonging to the same category share similar appearances. The large intra-class variation is introduced by the dataset, where objects are often presented in close-up photos with a combination of pose, viewpoint, illumination and background changes. A simple change in the camera perspective may lead to dramatic visual differences which could easily fool a neural network model trained on generic classification datasets.

While fine-grained datasets composed of close-ups are often geometrically warped comparing to photos from generic classification datasets, it enables learning of features more robust to variations in camera perspective and pose. Humans are able to rapidly identify the model of a car from key visual features such as the shape of the taillight or logo [27]. However, CNNs struggle on learning the fine details because it only learns the object appearance and lacks understanding of keypoint location, pose and geometry [7]. Recent work has shown that CNNs have remarkable capabilities to learn geometry-related information in convolutional layers [31], but final fully-connected layers weaken this ability and tend to keep only category-level information. Based on this finding, researchers propose several two-stage object detectors [4, 20] to use shared convolutional layers to find object proposals and output final predictions.

This leads to an open question: can we utilize a single network to learn both object-level localization information as well as stable fine-grained features invariant to imaging conditions and pose deformations? We address this question by creating a unified framework to perform *fine-grained object recognition*, subsuming the problems of object detection and fine-grained classification. Although many deep learning methods have been proposed for each task, we are not aware of any framework that directly train on both fine-grained classification and generic object detection datasets. By learning both spatial locations and intra-class diversities of an object, we enable the network to produce quality feature vectors with high distinctiveness. Additionally, as most convolutional layers in our network are shared for both tasks, we introduce very little computational overhead to achieve combined goals of efficiency and accuracy.

The rest of this paper is organized as follows. Section 2 discusses related work. Section 3 details our overall framework based on the proposed method. We show experimental results in Sect. 4 and conclude in Sect. 5.

2   Related Work

Visual Object Classification: Visual object classification aims at predicting class labels from a given image. Deep convolutional neural networks (DNNs) have led to tremendous success in visual recognition [5, 11]. Deep networks naturally enforce features from different levels and can be trained easily in an end-to-end fashion to reach high accuracy. Highway Networks [22] were the first to introduce bypassing paths to tackle the gradient vanishing problem. ResNet further utilizes identity mapping as bypassing paths and achieved remarkable performance in benchmark datasets such as ImageNet and Microsoft COCO [5]. Experiments

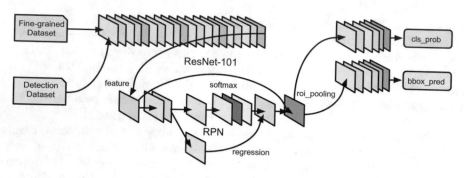

Fig. 1. Architecture of our network. Our network is based on Faster-RCNN and branches after ROI Pooling layer for fine-grained classification.

have shown that ResNet is able to converge on as many as 1000 layers. In the mean time, researchers also attempt to make the network wider. [23] proposes wider residual blocks to achieve better accuracy.

Fine-Grained Classification: Fine-grained recognition is the process of identifying objects within the same category. Various fine-grained classification datasets have been proposed, including bird species classification [9] and recognition of car brand, year and model [10,27]. [28] was among the first to employ deep object detection networks for fine-grained classification. [6] leverages a convolutional networks to locate multiple object parts and a two-stream classification network to encode object and part level information. Spatial transformer networks [7] explicitly allow spatial manipulation of training data, giving neural networks the ability to actively transform the region of interest. Other research directions include attention models and feature pooling. Attention models aim at focusing the network on only a few distinctive image parts/keypoints [30] while feature pooling collects second-order or higher-order statistics to form a more distinctive feature vector for better classification results [13].

Object Detection: Object detection aims at finding locations of object instances in a scene. Recent work shows CNN has sufficient power to learning geometric representations to predict both the class label and geometric information of an object [4,17,20,31]. Modern detectors can be categorized as one-stage or two-stage frameworks. The one-stage detection framework [14,18] is free of object proposals and can be trained in an end-to-end fashion. At test time, the entire network is only evaluated once, achieving real-time performance. The two-stage detection framework [4,20], on the other hand, includes a class-agnostic region proposal generator and a classifier. Generally speaking, one-stage frameworks exhibit better efficiency and run at a higher frame rate, while two-stage frameworks are more accurate and are capable of locating smaller objects. Also, there is a growing interest in converting these frameworks into more compact versions for real-time/embedded systems [12].

Fig. 2. Randomly selected sample images from our FGR-4K benchmark. Compared to the Stanford Cars [10] dataset, our benchmark contains more real-life images with complex background.

Weakly-Supervised Object Localization: The recent progress of deep learning is largely due to advances in high-power computing hardware and the availability of large-scale, high-quality annotated datasets. However, the annotation of ground truth labels is expensive and labor-intensive, and sometimes even impossible considering the scale of today's massive visual data. Therefore, it is important to develop unsupervised or weakly-supervised approaches to enable continuous learning. Researchers have investigated weakly-supervised object localization by studying maximal activations in the network layers [17,31]. Our work attempts to learn from both detection and classification benchmarks without full annotation.

3   Approach

3.1   Network Architecture

In [20], Ren *et al.* designed the Faster-RCNN network which is composed of a Region Proposal Network (RPN) and a backbone CNNs. To improve efficiency, they also combined the RPN and the CNNs into a single network with a large number of shared layers. Faster-RCNN exhibits excellent tradeoff of speed and accuracy. It runs at near real-time speed (5 fps) on a single GPU, while achieving state-of-the-art detection accuracy. Although Faster-RCNN gives perfect results on detection benchmarks, it can not be directly applied to the task of learning both detection and fine-grained classification. Therefore, we build upon the Faster-RCNN network architecture and made a few modifications. Firstly, we use ResNet-101 [5] as the backbone CNNs as it is deeper and gives better accuracy compared to the ZF or VGG16 network used in the original paper. Next, we made a new branch after the ROI Pooling layer for predicting fine-grained categories. Therefore, apart from the original RPN stream which predicts bounding box coordinates, the additional steam simultaneously predicts fine-grained class labels. Our network structure is illustrated in Fig. 1.

3.2   Fine-Grained Recognition Benchmark

Existing fine-grained classification benchmarks such as Stanford Cars [10] only contain one object per image. Also, a large portion of the dataset is composed of stock images with clean/white background. To provide a fair technical benchmark for evaluating fine-grained classification and object detection performance, We introduce a new dataset called FGR-4K (Fine-grained Recognition 4K). We plan to open-source this dataset for research purposes. Our dataset is annotated using the same labels from the Stanford Cars dataset (see Fig. 2). This dataset is constructed for testing only, as training and validation data could be obtained from Stanford Cars or PASCAL VOC car class. Our dataset provides 3818 images crawled from Google image search API. These images are filtered to include only those permitted for commercial reuse. We also run automated deduplication, white background detection and text detection algorithms to remove images not suitable for annotation. The deduplication is done by removing images with the same SHA256 checksum on RGB values. White background is identified by

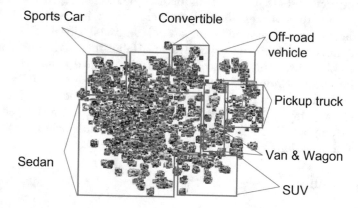

Fig. 3. t-SNE visualization [16] of features extracted from the joint model on Stanford Cars test set (Best viewed zoomed in and in color). The similarities are calculated purely based on visual feature embeddings. This illustrates that our joint model is able to preserve fine-grained semantics information after dimensionality reduction. (Color figure online)

Algorithm 1. Training Strategy

Parameters: $\mathcal{M} \leftarrow$ CNNs Model
$\mathcal{D} \leftarrow$ Dataset

procedure TrainingStrategy($\mathcal{D}_{fg+det}$)
   $\mathcal{M}_{fg} \leftarrow$ LearningPolicy($\mathcal{M}_{ImageNet}, \mathcal{D}_{fg}$)
   $\mathcal{M}_{det} \leftarrow$ LearningPolicy($\mathcal{M}_{ImageNet}, \mathcal{D}_{det}$)
   $\mathcal{M}_{joint} \leftarrow$ netsurgery($\mathcal{M}_{fg}, \mathcal{M}_{det}$)
   $\mathcal{M}_{joint} \leftarrow$ LearningPolicy($\mathcal{M}_{joint}, \mathcal{D}_{fg+det}$)
   return $\mathcal{M}_{joint}$
end procedure

---

converting the image to a binary map using 33% above its median pixel value as the threshold. If white pixels occupy more than 50% of the image then we will remove it from the candidate set. We use the open source text detection library [2] to remove images detected with any words or letters. After the automatic filtering, we manually clean up the dataset to choose only real-life images with complex background. Next, we send the candidate set to human annotators to draw rectangles around all car objects that fall into the given 196 fine-grained categories. Compared to the Stanford Cars dataset, our benchmark contains more real-life images with complex backgrounds which are challenging for both fine-grained classification and object detection tasks.

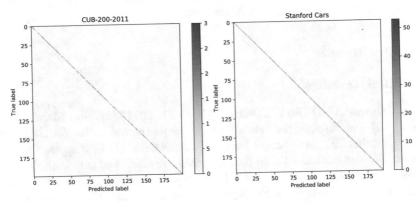

Fig. 4. Confusion matrix on the CUB-200 and Stanford Cars datasets. The vertical axis shows the groundtruth labels while the horizontal axis shows the predicted labels. Note that our model makes more false positive predictions on the CUB-200 dataset compared to the Stanford Cars dataset. This is because CUB-200 contains non-rigid transformations with larger intra-category variance on object pose and appearance.

3.3   Training Strategy

Because of the high diversity in fine-grained classes, we use on-the-fly data augmentation during training. The augmentation includes random cropping, resizing and rotation up to 30°. We also included random smooth filtering and JPEG compression varying from 50% to 90% quality. The online augmentation is only applied to training while the validation/testing accuracy is still reported on the original dataset. Due to the difficulty in training initial weights for the whole network, we first train a ResNet model on the fine-grained dataset and a Faster-RCNN model on the detection dataset separately. Note that these two networks are using the same ResNet-101 backbone and the only difference between them is the RPN network inserted between Res4b and Res5a layers. Once both models converge, we freeze all layers in the detection model by setting learning rate to 0 for all bottom layers below the ROI Pooling layer. Next, we append all top layers above res4b from the fine-grained model to the detection model as a separate branch for finetuning. During training, we define the maximum number of iterations as max_iter and iterations per step as $step\_size$. The learning rate will drop by a factor of 10 (*i.e.* multiplied by lr_decay where $lr\_decay = 0.1$). Once the step size is reached, the learning rate decreases by 10. The accuracy jumps when learning rate changes. This is because the solver has been optimizing at a certain learning rate for a certain number of iterations to find the local optimum. The weight of the whole model stabilizes for the duration of a consistent learning rate. After the learning rate reduces, it is easier for the neural networks to capture fine details and increase accuracy. Assuming the initial warm-up learning rate to be lr_init, when we reach the max_iter the learning rate will be $lr\_init \times lr\_decay^{max\_iter/step\_size}$. When the accuracy saturates, we will only fine-tune softmax layers to obtain the joint model. We illustrate the details of our training strategy in Algorithm 1.

4 Experiments

4.1 Initial Training

We use Caltech-UCSD Birds-200-2011 (CUB-200-2011) [24] and Stanford Cars dataset [10] for fine-grained classification experiments. The CUB-200-2011 dataset contains 200 fine-grained bird categories with 11788 images. The Stanford Cars dataset contains 16185 images with 196 classes of cars including year, make and model. Details of the datasets are shown in Table 1. For both datasets, We fine-tune on the ImageNet ResNet-101 model. The model is trained with the base learning rate of 0.01, gamma of 0.5, momentum of 0.9 and weight decay of 0.0001. Next, we start fine-tuning this model. Once the training accuracy is saturated, we fix all bottom layer weights and only fine-tune the softmax layer. The final accuracy is 81.0%. A comparison to related work is shown in Table 1.

For object detection, We build our approach based on the state-of-the-art Faster-RCNN [20] detection framework. We start training the modified Faster-RCNN network explained in Sect. 3 with ResNet-101 backend. The weights of ResNet-101 is initialized with pre-trained ImageNet weights. We train our model with base learning rate of 0.001, gamma of 0.1, momentum of 0.9 and weight decay of 0.0005. The training is performed on the combined PASCAL VOC 07+12 dataset on a single class (car or bird). After 1000K iterations the tested mAP is 71.99% on VOC 07 and 77.85% on VOC 12 for the bird class. We repeat the same procedure for the car class on VOC 07 and 12 and the final mAP for the car class is 75.15% and 78.06%, respectively. Quantitative evaluations can be found at Table 1. Note that our accuracy is reported on images only containing the bird or car class with all other annotations removed, while the accuracy reported by all other algorithms still consider classes other than bird or car. Qualitative results are shown in Fig. 7.

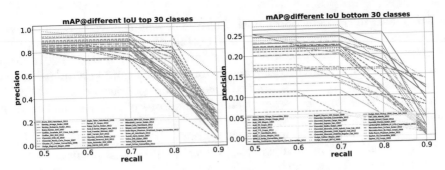

Fig. 5. Precision-recall curve of our joint model on the FGR-4K dataset (Best viewed electronically and zoomed in). Left: PR curve on the top-performing 30 classes. Right: PR curve on the lowest-performing 30 classes. Note that our model is robust to stricter IoU criterias and the performance starts to degrade when IoU is increased to more than 0.7.

Table 1. Results on fine-grained classification and object detection benchmarks. Our methods handles both tasks at the same time, while performs favorably against alternative methods designed specifically for each task.

Classification accuracy (%)				Detection MAP (%)				
Bird (CUB-200)		Car (Stanford)		Bird (VOC)		Car (VOC)	Train	Test
Xiao et al. [25]	69.7	Krause et al. [9]	**92.8**	Faster-RCNN (VGG16) [20]	70.9	**84.7**	0712	07
Simon et al. [21]	81.0	Lin et al. [13]	91.3	Faster-RCNN (ResNet50) [20]	74.3	75.9	0712	12
Kong et al. [8]	84.2	Zhang et al. [29]	88.4	SSD300 [14]	70.5	76.1	0712	07
Liu et al. [15]	**85.4**	Xie et al. [26]	86.3	YOLO [18]	57.7	55.9	0712	12
				YOLOv2 544 [19]	74.8	76.5	0712	12
Ours initial	81.0	90.1		72.0		75.2	0712	07
Ours Joint	72.6	86.2		**77.9**		78.0	0712	12

4.2   Joint Training

Now that we obtained models for both detection and fine-grained classification, we start merging the models for joint training. During inference time, the network will produce bounding box locations in an image, as well as fine-grained class labels for each bounding box. We freeze all layers in the detection model by setting learning rate to 0 for all bottom layers below the roi_pool5 layer. Next, we append all top layers above res4b from the fine-grained classification model to roi_pool5 layer in the detection model. Because of weight discrepancies between the original bottom layers and the new bottom layers trained on the object detection dataset, the test accuracy of the joint model on CUB-200-2011 drops from 81.0% to 67.5%. After joint training for another round (1000K iterations, freezing bottom layers) the fine-grained classification accuracy goes up to 72.6%. We performed the same net-surgery and training procedures for the car class. The final classification accuracy for cars is 86.2%. The detection accuracy stays the same since we are only training the fine-grained branch with all other weights fixed. We found that this training schedule leads to the best results comparing to alternative approaches such as adjusting weights for all layers. The whole training process is illustrated in Algorithm 1. Next, we apply our joint model to the FGR-4K benchmark dataset. We show the precision-recall curve for the best and worst performing 30 categories in Fig. 5. This is done by varying the IoU threshold from 0.5 to 0.9 and recalculate mAP scores for all classes. We also compare our model with the commercial vehicle recognition service provided by Sighthound [1] on the FGR-4K dataset. Since Sighthound API only returns vehicle brand and model, we remove the year info from both the groundtruth and predicted results on the FGR-4K dataset for comparison. The final average mAP of our method is 62.59% while the average mAP of Sighthound is 56.88%. We show True /False predictions for each fine-grained class in Fig. 6. Note that the production Sighthound model is possibly trained on a enlarged dataset which includes more vehicle models than the FGR-4K dataset.

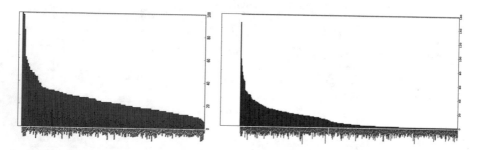

Fig. 6. mAP and TP/FP scores of our joint model on the FGR-4K dataset (Best viewed electronically). Left: True (green)/False (red) predictions using our approach. Right: True (green)/False (red) predictions obtained by Sighthound Cloud API for vehicle recognition [1]. The average mAP of our approach is 62.59% while the average mAP of the Sighthound Cloud API is 56.88 %. Note that our model predicts less false alarms comparing to the Sighthound production model. (Color figure online)

4.3   Analysis

For the fine-grained classification experiments, we show the confusion matrix on the CUB-200 and Stanford Cars datasets in Fig. 4. The CUB-200 contains objects with non-rigid transformations and is more challenging compared to the Stanford Cars dataset. Also, according to Table 1, there is a larger gap between the classification accuracy of our model and attention-based models [9,15] on CUB-200 compared to Stanford Cars. Furthermore, our joint model suffers more accuracy degradation on the CUB-200 dataset compared to the Stanford Cars dataset. Despite these limitations, our model is able to learn from two vastly distinctive datasets and demonstrate competitive performance compared to methods developed for each task. We apply t-SNE visualization [16] to features extracted from the joint model on Stanford Cars test set and visualize the embeddings in Fig. 3. This illustrates that our joint model is able to preserve fine-grained semantics information in the high-dimensional space. The t-SNE visualization also indicates that our learnt features are able to capture visual similarities but is less sensitive to pose variations. For the FGR-4K dataset, we evaluate the detector performance against varying IoU thresholds in Fig. 5. As can be seen from the figure, the mAP per category only starts decreasing when IoU is more than 0.7. This shows that our detector is robust to stricter evaluation criterias, which is generally more desirable for real life vision applications. We also notice that the best-performing class labels are mostly composed of visually distinctive car models from different manufacturers, while the lowest-performing classes are more often from the same manufacturer with similar car-model names. This implies that the current joint network is good at detecting objects but is still having difficulties capturing small partial details within the object.

We show qualitative results in Fig. 7(a) by running forward-inference on this joint model. Note that our model is able to predict fine-grained class labels not present in the PASCAL VOC dataset. As shown in Fig. 7(a), our joint network predicts accurate bounding box locations for all bird objects in an image. In addition, our network is good at recognizing subtle color (e.g. "Red headed woodpecker" in row 2 column 3, "Gray Catbird" in row 2 column 4, "Red bellied woodpecker" in row 3 column 2 and "White crowned sparrow" in row 3 column 3) and shape variations (e.g. difference between "Mallard" and "Herring Gull" in row 3 column 1). In Fig. 7(b), the model is able to recognize subtle differences between two similar-looking cars with the same color (e.g. "Jaguar XK XKR 2012" in row 2 column 1 vs. "BMW M6 Convertible 2010" in row 3 column 4) and partial object with occlusion (e.g. "Mercedes Benz SL Class Sedan 2012" in row 1 column 5). For object classes not present in the Stanford Cars dataset, the network is able to assign a label with a closest visual match (e.g. "Dodge Challenger SRT8 2011" in row 1 column 3).

(a) Results on PASCAL VOC 0712 bird class

(b) Results on PASCAL VOC 0712 car class

Fig. 7. Qualitative results on PASCAL VOC 0712 Bird and Car classes [3]. The labels are learnt from CUB-200-2011 [24] and Stanford Cars dataset [10], respectively.

5   Conclusion

In this work we have presented a framework to detect and classify fine-grained objects. To evaluate performance, we have created a new benchmark for fine-grained recognition. Experiments show that our approach performs favorably against competitive methods. In summary, our network structure provides more desirable characteristics for practical computer vision applications and reaches good balance between the model size, computational complexity and accuracy. Our system can be used to add visual intelligence to mobile devices. This feature is particularly useful for ornithologists or car enthusiasts who wish to identify or search for a particular object of interest. In the future, we plan to leverage post-training quantization techniques to compress our joint model and enable fast forward-inference on mobile apps.

References

1. Sighthound cloud API for vehicle recognition. https://www.sighthound.com/products/cloud
2. Tesseract open source OCR engine. https://github.com/tesseract-ocr/tesseract
3. Everingham, M., Van Gool, L., Williams, C., Winn, J., Zisserman, A.: The pascal visual object classes (VOC) challenge. IJCV **88**(2), 303–338 (2010)
4. He, K., Gkioxari, G., Dollár, P., Girshick, R.: Mask R-CNN. In: ICCV (2017)
5. He, K., Zhang, X., Ren, S., Sun, J.: Deep residual learning for image recognition. In: CVPR, pp. 770–778 (2016)
6. Huang, S., Xu, Z., Tao, D., Zhang, Y.: Part-stacked CNN for fine-grained visual categorization. In: CVPR, pp. 1173–1182 (2016)
7. Jaderberg, M., Simonyan, K., Zisserman, A., et al.: Spatial transformer networks. In: NIPS, pp. 2017–2025 (2015)
8. Kong, S., Fowlkes, C.: Low-rank bilinear pooling for fine-grained classification. In: CVPR, pp. 7025–7034. IEEE (2017)
9. Krause, J., Jin, H., Yang, J., Fei-Fei, L.: Fine-grained recognition without part annotations. In: CVPR, pp. 5546–5555 (2015)
10. Krause, J., Stark, M., Deng, J., Fei-Fei, L.: 3D object representations for fine-grained categorization. In: 3dRR, Sydney, Australia (2013)
11. Krizhevsky, A., Sutskever, I., Hinton, G.: Imagenet classification with deep convolutional neural networks. In: NIPS, pp. 1097–1105 (2012)
12. Li, Z., Peng, C., Yu, G., Zhang, X., Deng, Y., Sun, J.: Light-head R-CNN: in defense of two-stage object detector. arXiv preprint arXiv:1711.07264 (2017)
13. Lin, T.Y., RoyChowdhury, A., Maji, S.: Bilinear CNN models for fine-grained visual recognition. In: ICCV, pp. 1449–1457 (2015)
14. Liu, W., et al.: SSD: single shot MultiBox detector. In: Leibe, B., Matas, J., Sebe, N., Welling, M. (eds.) ECCV 2016. LNCS, vol. 9905, pp. 21–37. Springer, Cham (2016). https://doi.org/10.1007/978-3-319-46448-0_2
15. Liu, X., Wang, J., Wen, S., Ding, E., Lin, Y.: Localizing by describing: attribute-guided attention localization for fine-grained recognition. In: AAAI, pp. 4190–4196 (2017)
16. Maaten, L.V.D., Hinton, G.: Visualizing data using t-SNE. J. Mach. Learn. Res. **9**(11), 2579–2605 (2008)

17. Oquab, M., Bottou, L., Laptev, I., Sivic, J.: Is object localization for free?-weakly-supervised learning with convolutional neural networks. In: CVPR, pp. 685–694 (2015)
18. Redmon, J., Divvala, S., Girshick, R., Farhadi, A.: You only look once: unified, real-time object detection. In: CVPR, pp. 779–788 (2016)
19. Redmon, J., Farhadi, A.: Yolo9000: better, faster, stronger. arXiv preprint (2017)
20. Ren, S., He, K., Girshick, R., Sun, J.: Faster R-CNN: towards real-time object detection with region proposal networks. In: NIPS, pp. 91–99 (2015)
21. Simon, M., Rodner, E.: Neural activation constellations: unsupervised part model discovery with convolutional networks. In: ICCV, pp. 1143–1151 (2015)
22. Srivastava, R.K., Greff, K., Schmidhuber, J.: Highway networks. arXiv preprint arXiv:1505.00387 (2015)
23. Targ, S., Almeida, D., Lyman, K.: Resnet in resnet: generalizing residual architectures. arXiv preprint arXiv:1603.08029 (2016)
24. Welinder, P., et al.: Caltech-UCSD Birds 200. Technical report, CNS-TR-2010-001, California Institute of Technology (2010)
25. Xiao, T., Xu, Y., Yang, K., Zhang, J., Peng, Y., Zhang, Z.: The application of two-level attention models in deep convolutional neural network for fine-grained image classification. In: CVPR, pp. 842–850 (2015)
26. Xie, S., Yang, T., Wang, X., Lin, Y.: Hyper-class augmented and regularized deep learning for fine-grained image classification. In: CVPR, pp. 2645–2654 (2015)
27. Yang, L., Luo, P., Change Loy, C., Tang, X.: A large-scale car dataset for fine-grained categorization and verification. In: CVPR, pp. 3973–3981 (2015)
28. Zhang, N., Donahue, J., Girshick, R., Darrell, T.: Part-based R-CNNs for fine-grained category detection. In: Fleet, D., Pajdla, T., Schiele, B., Tuytelaars, T. (eds.) ECCV 2014. LNCS, vol. 8689, pp. 834–849. Springer, Cham (2014). https://doi.org/10.1007/978-3-319-10590-1_54
29. Zhang, X., Zhou, F., Lin, Y., Zhang, S.: Embedding label structures for fine-grained feature representation. In: CVPR, pp. 1114–1123 (2016)
30. Zheng, H., Fu, J., Mei, T., Luo, J.: Learning multi-attention convolutional neural network for fine-grained image recognition. In: ICCV, vol. 6 (2017)
31. Zhou, B., Khosla, A., Lapedriza, A., Oliva, A., Torralba, A.: Object detectors emerge in deep scene CNNs. arXiv preprint arXiv:1412.6856 (2014)

Foreground Object Image Masking via EPI and Edge Detection for Photogrammetry with Static Background

Chawin Sathirasethawong[1(✉)], Changming Sun[2,3], Andrew Lambert[1], and Murat Tahtali[1]

[1] School of Engineering and Information Technology, The University of New South Wales Canberra, Campbell, ACT 2612, Australia
c.sathirasethawong@student.adfa.edu.au, {a.lambert, m.tahtali}@adfa.edu.au
[2] CSIRO Data61, Marsfield, NSW 1710, Australia
changming.sun@csiro.au
[3] School of Computer Science and Engineering, The University of New South Wales, Sydney, NSW 2052, Australia

Abstract. In automated photogrammetry of a small object, rotating the object provides an easier setting and more stable camera positions than moving the camera around the object. However, the static features in the background can confuse the structure from motion, which leads to the failure of reconstruction. We are addressing the problem by proposing a masking algorithm based on light field epipolar-plane images (EPIs). Using a simple EPI analysis and edge detection technique, a single light field image is enough to create an initial mask, which acts as a region of interest for an edge image. Lastly, binary morphological techniques are applied to obtain the final mask image. The result shows promising performances of 93.84% recall and outperforms comparable algorithms in accuracy, precision, JI, and F1 scores with 98.39%, 97.75%, 91.86%, and 95.75%, respectively.

Keywords: Image masking · Foreground segmentation · Epipolar-plane image · Light field · Plenoptics

1 Introduction

Image masking is one of the digital image processing methods generally used in editing. A mask image defines where the region of interest (ROI) in the image is. Accurate scoping of the working area can be helpful in various algorithms. Manual masking, while providing results as accurate as humanly perceived, can be time-consuming. It is suitable for a task that requires high accuracy, for instance, generating ground truth data or specifying an area for method evaluation. Automatic masking, on the other hand, is much faster and no user interaction is required. The accuracy of the mask image varies

© Springer Nature Switzerland AG 2019
G. Bebis et al. (Eds.): ISVC 2019, LNCS 11845, pp. 345–357, 2019.
https://doi.org/10.1007/978-3-030-33723-0_28

from an algorithm to another depending on the type of images they are developed to process. For instance, for large object photogrammetry, such as a monument, region glowing was introduced to detect the foreground from heterogeneous background and it was used as a mask in cleaning the dense point clouds from the reconstruction in [1].

In structure from motion (SfM), a mask image is useful in feature extraction of the specific area. Especially when rotating the object is preferred to moving a camera around the object, such as in a small photogrammetry lab setting [2–4]. While feature points of a static background can confuse the camera pose estimation and fail the reconstruction, object-masked images will help ruling out those features and make a successful reconstruction, using for example, background subtraction [4], background illumination [3], automated background suppression via colour [2], and mask by HSV colour thresholding and support vector machine [5].

In this paper, a foreground masking algorithm via epipolar-plane images (EPIs) of a light field for photogrammetry of an object in a lab setting with a static background is introduced. We intend to create a flexible lab acquisition system which is less strict on the hardware setting by focusing on the algorithm to perform most of the work instead. Thus, the proposed algorithm does not rely on other images in creating a mask. The lab setting is easy to follow and no complicated preparations are required. The performance of the algorithm will be assessed and compared with manual ground truth and related algorithms.

2   Related Works

Light field imaging is a technique that captures not only the light intensities but also their directions as well [6], which makes it possible to render several viewpoints, called sub-aperture images, from a single shot. Applications and studies on light field spread widely in many topics such as depth estimation, view synthesis, and intrinsic decomposition [7]. Our masking algorithm is derived from the concept of depth estimation, which we adapted for our purpose.

Most depth estimation algorithms were proposed, all competitive in the accuracy of depth maps. EPI analysis [8] is one of the techniques popular for depth estimation because of the depth information contained within. While there are several existing depth estimation algorithms via EPI published in [9–18], only a few have developed masking algorithms from light field. Yücer et al. [19] demonstrated one closely related foreground object segmentation method from light field. By densely sampling the light field of over a thousand input images from a video, a static foreground object can be extracted. In spite of the promising result in foreground segmentation and 3D reconstruction, a smooth camera motion around the object is required for the acquisition of the video. In contrast, we propose in this paper a simple yet effective masking algorithm based on EPIs and edge detection using a single light field image.

3 Methods

In this section, the equipment and lab environment are described, followed by the acquisition of the light field images, and then image decoding. After that, the proposed method is presented. The first step is to create the initial mask from EPIs. Next, the initial mask with an edge detection technique is applied to create the final mask.

3.1 Equipment and Lab Setting

The lab was set up for the photogrammetry of small objects. A lightbox, as shown in Fig. 1, with a white backdrop was used as a mini studio for shooting. The object used in this experiment is the Stanford bunny [20] and was 3D printed with bounding box dimensions of 50 mm × 35 mm × 50 mm (length × width × height). Colour patches were randomly painted on the model to give texture. The bunny model was adhered on a Zaber's motorised rotary stage. A light field camera, a Lytro Illum, was attached to the mini-tripod and acted as the acquisition unit. Illumination was through a ring light, attached to the objective of the camera.

Fig. 1. The small object photogrammetry lab.

3.2 Image Acquisition and Image Decoding

In this paper, we aim for the masking technique and its performance over the 3D reconstruction. Therefore, instead of lots of views and angles for complete 3D reconstruction, only 36 images were captured with 10° apart, adding up to 360° around the object. Each image taken from a light field camera is in a LFR format, which contains raw light field image and metadata. Each light field image was decoded into a 4D light field by the Lytro power tool beta version 1.0.1, the official processing tool of the Lytro camera.

3.3 Epipolar-Plane Image Masking

The masking algorithm was developed and run in MATLABversion 2016a. For each 4D light field, selected sub-aperture images were converted to grayscale and then processed into EPI. A light field image is represented as a 4D function $L(s, t, x, y)$ as in [16], where (s, t) and (x, y) denote a viewpoint of sub-aperture images and a pixel position in that sub-aperture image, respectively. When a direction of viewpoints (s, t) and a direction of pixels (x, y) are fixed, stacking these slices together forms an EPI.

Figure 2 shows an example of fixed t^* and y^*, where the EPI is $L_{t^*\,y^*}(s, x) = L(s, t^*, x, y^*)$. From the available 14×14 sub-aperture images in the light field map, only eleven of those were used, where $t^* = 7$ and $s^* = 2$ to 12 to avoid vignetting. Then the Canny edge detection algorithm [21] is applied to the EPI.

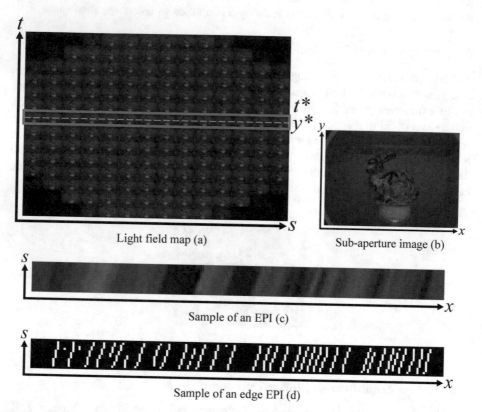

Light field map (a)   Sub-aperture image (b)

Sample of an EPI (c)

Sample of an edge EPI (d)

Fig. 2. A 14×14 sub-aperture images light field map (a). The red square shows all viewpoints with fixed t^*. The blue dash line indicates the fixed y^* pixel position. A single sub-aperture image (c). An EPI of $L_{t^*\,y^*}(s, x)$, (c). An edge image of EPI (d). (Color figure online)

Assuming that a straight line in the edge image of the EPI was formed by one connected component, the number of pixels in that connected component should be no less than the number of selected sub-aperture images; otherwise, the connected component is deleted. The remaining connected components were calculated for slopes of the lines and then passed through the thresholding to decide whether the line will be labeled as belonging to the object or to the background. Next, the area between each line is marked as belonging to an object or to the background. The area is marked as an object when it is between 2 object-marked lines. Otherwise, it is marked as background. After that, the masked EPI is converted back to the 4D light field. Then, binary image morphological operations [22] (image opening and closing) are applied to the center image to clear out the horizontal straight line which was thinner than the structural element and is used to fill the small holes.

3.4   Refine Image Masking

The resulting masking image obtained from the EPI is used as the initial mask in order to process the final mask. First of all, the Canny edge of the grayscale center image is obtained. The initial mask was then integrated to the edge image to scope down only the area of interest. The longest boundary of the connected components was calculated and converted to the mask image.

4   Results

Our dataset of 36 images was processed by the masking algorithm and gave the output of 36 mask images. These mask images were used as the prediction and assessed the performance with two binary ground truth images, which were manually created for each center image. One covered only the bunny as the object of the image, called ground truth without the base (GT-base). The other covered both the bunny and the base as the object, called ground truth with the base (GT+base). The base is simply the object to raise the bunny in the frame. The dataset are available at https://github.com/Chawin-S/Image-Masking-via-EPI/.

4.1   Performance Metrics

To assess the masking performance, predicted masking images were compared against the ground truth mask obtained manually. With the prediction and ground truth of each image, the confusion matrixes of the dataset and per-image were computed. The true positive (TP) in the confusion matrix is defined by the number of pixels that are correctly predicted as the object. False positive (FP) is the number of pixels which are falsely predicted as the object. Similarly, there are true negatives (TN) and false negatives (FN). While TN is the number of pixels which are correctly predicted as background, FN is the number of pixels that are falsely predicted as background. These values from the confusion matrix were used to compute the performance metrics as follow:

Accuracy is the proportion of correct predicted pixels to total pixels. Its value is calculated by

$$Accuracy = \frac{TP + TN}{TP + TN + FP + FN} \tag{1}$$

The *precision or positive predictive value* (PPV) indicates how many pixels are actually objects from the total object-predicted pixels. The percentage is the proportion of correct predicted pixels to all predicted pixels. For dataset precision, the value is calculated from the overall pixels in the dataset. Per-image precision is obtained from the calculation of pixels in each image and then averaged over all images.

$$Precision = \frac{TP}{TP + FP} \qquad (2)$$

Recall or sensitivity is the ratio of correctly predicted object to the real object. There are 2 values for this, one for the dataset and another one for per-image, similar to the precision. The recall is obtained by:

$$Recall = \frac{TP}{TP + FN} \qquad (3)$$

Jaccard similarity index (JI) *or the intersection over union* (IoU) shows the overlap between the predicted mask and the ground truth mask [23]. It is the ratio of the similarity between 2 masks. The dataset JI and per-image JI were calculated in our study.

$$JI = \frac{TP}{TP + FP + FN} \qquad (4)$$

F1-score (F1) *or Dice similarity coefficient* (DSC) is a harmonic mean of precision and recall. Both the precision and recall are taken into consideration. F1 balances the weight equally between precision and recall as shown in the equation. The F1 was computed only for per-image as in [23]

$$F1 = \left(\frac{Precision^{-1} + Recall^{-1}}{2} \right)^{-1} \qquad (5)$$

$$= \frac{2 \times TP}{2 \times TP + FP + FN} \qquad (6)$$

4.2   Algorithm Evaluation

As our method does not have the algorithm to differentiate the base from the bunny, both GT-base and GT+base were used for the computation of the performance metrics. Moreover, the output performance was compared with two different depth map estimation algorithms, even though they did not aim for the masking as ours. One is the depth map processed by the Lytro Power tool. The other is Jeon's algorithm [24], the sub-pixel-wise disparity estimation by the cost volume.

Optimum outcomes were obtained from all methods by the adjustment of their parameters. In our algorithm, the window size and the sigma of edge detection are the adjustable parameters which affect the outcome. Empirically, the window size = 5 and sigma = 3 were found to be working well in our case. For the other algorithms, depth estimation was run with their default parameters. After each depth map was obtained, the range of depth was set to create the mask. The range was specified manually to obtain the mask which covered the bunny at a similar percentage of recall as our algorithm compared with GT-base. To be fair with comparative algorithms which aimed for the depth estimation, only GT+base was used for their performance assessment because both the bunny and the base were located at the same depth.

The performance scores for our algorithm are shown in Table 1 together with Lytro's depth map and Jeon's disparity algorithm. We represented the performances of our algorithm when compared with GT-base and GT+base while other methods were compared with only GT+base as mentioned above. Scores in Table 1 are plotted as a bar chart in Fig. 3 for easy comparison. Focusing on our algorithm, the one which compared with GT-base has a higher score for the recall only. Comparison between methods with the same GT+base shows that our algorithm outperforms the others in all metrics except the recall which is highest by Lytro's. The scores between dataset and averaged per-image have only slight differences (less than 1%) in each metrics.

Table 1. Result of performance assessments.

Method	Accuracy (%)	Precision (%)		Recall (%)		JI (%)		F1 score (%)
		Dataset	Avg. per-image	Dataset	Avg. per-image	Dataset	Avg. per-image	
Our algorithm (GT-base)	94.70	72.01	71.80	99.31	99.29	71.65	71.43	83.30
Our algorithm (GT+base)	**98.39**	**97.75**	**97.78**	93.84	93.82	**91.86**	**91.86**	**95.75**
Lytro's depth map	87.65	61.14	61.15	**99.60**	**99.60**	60.99	60.99	75.73
Jeon's algorithm [24]	95.94	85.70	86.00	94.92	94.83	81.94	82.06	90.13

Furthermore, the precision-recall graph is plotted from the result which was compared with the GT+base (Fig. 4). In spite of having recall scores over 90% for all methods, only our algorithm that also has the precision score over 90%. Jeon's method comes with 85.70% of the precision score while the lowest shows 61.14% for Lytro's precision.

Additionally, a result of statistical analysis by ANOVA of each per-image metrics compared with GT+base for all algorithms are labeled in Fig. 3. The precision, JI, and F1 of our algorithm are higher than those of Lytro and Jeon's algorithm ($P < 0.001$). On the other hand, recall of our algorithm is lower than Jeon's algorithm ($P < 0.05$) and Lytro's depthmap ($P < 0.001$).

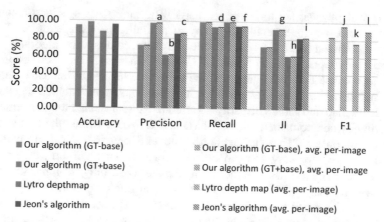

Fig. 3. The performance metrics of each algorithm. Significant differences between each algorithm are denoted by different letters (a, b = our algorithm (GT+base) compared to Lytro, $P < 0.001$; a, c = our algorithm (GT+base) compared to Jeon's algorithm, $P < 0.001$; d, e = our algorithm (GT+base) compared to Lytro, $P < 0.001$; d, f = our algorithm (GT+base) compared to Jeon's algorithm, $P < 0.05$; g, h = our algorithm (GT+base) compared to Lytro, $P < 0.001$; g, i = our algorithm (GT+base) compared to Jeon's algorithm, $P < 0.001$; j, k = our algorithm (GT +base) compared to Lytro, $P < 0.001$; j, l = our algorithm (GT+base) compared to Jeon's algorithm, $P < 0.001$).

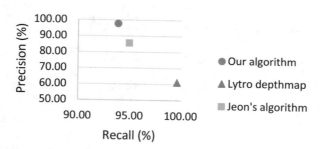

Fig. 4. Precision-recall plot of dataset scores between algorithms compared with GT+base.

5   Discussion

Our algorithm shows the masking result by using a mask image from EPIs as an initial ROI for edge detection, which was then linked together to create the final mask image (Fig. 5). The mask from EPIs by itself is, in fact, accurate to a certain degree. However, it has difficulty in detecting the background gap between parts of the object at the same horizontal row. Furthermore, separate processing each EPI results in lack of mask continuity in each horizontal row (Fig. 5b). Despite that, introducing this initial mask to the edge detection has the effect of overcoming some errors in masking (Fig. 5d). While this combination makes the mask more accurate and fits the real shape of the object, some errors may persist. Also, similar intensities of the edge of the object to the background decrease its likelihood to be detected as an edge, which leads to the erosion of the mask. We can exploit this by using similar colours as the background for an unwanted part like the base, as shown in Fig. 5e. However, this can be a drawback at the same time if it occurs at the edge of the object that has a similar colour to the background.

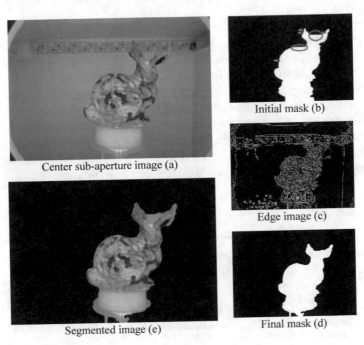

Fig. 5. A center sub-aperture image of the Stanford bunny (a). An initial mask from EPIs (b). The circles present background area that was masked as the object and the arrow points the part which lacks in object continuity. An edge image (c). A final mask (d). A segmented image (e).

The results in Table 1 show both dataset and averaged per-image metrics. While the dataset metrics represent the overall scores, averaged per-image metrics can differentiate algorithms that work well in specific conditions from the ones that work well in general settings. Besides, statistical analysis can also be carried out [23]. In our case, images in the dataset are similar in composition because the only difference between each image is the position of the object while the background stays the same. That is why there is not much difference between dataset and averaged per-image scores and also there is no difference in ranking among methods.

The results of our algorithm, when compared with different GTs (GT-base and GT +base), reveal the features of the algorithm. First of all, the recall of 99.31% when compared with GT-base shows that the final mask nearly perfectly covers the bunny, which is our main objective. On the other hand, the precision of 72.01%, JI of 71.65%, and F1 of 83.30% indicate that up to 30% of the mask covers the area other than the bunny, which is incorrect. Meanwhile, the algorithm has a lower recall score of 93.84%

354   C. Sathirasethawong et al.

when comparing with GT+base. Whereas, its other metrics (accuracy, precision, and F1) are higher than 95% and has the JI of more than 90%. That means no more than 5% of the mask covers the area other than the bunny and the base. Further, it has more than 90% similarity to the ground truth bunny with base. From the following results, it can also be said that the algorithm can detect almost all of the bunny areas and some parts of the base while very little (less than 3% of the mask) was incorrectly detected the background as the object.

For the comparison between methods, the GT+base was used as the ground truth for all methods. Even though other methods have their own goals which differ from ours, the depth estimation methods from light field images were selected for comparison. One of the reasons is that they use the same input as ours, which is the light field. Secondly, a depth map closely relates to a mask image for the condition and setting of our lab, which has the object located at the center of the image and has the distance between the object and the background. Thus, an accurate depth map can be converted to a mask image by setting the specific range of depth that covers only the object, which is the bunny with the base in this case. Therefore, the depth range of each depth map was specified manually to achieve the best object-covered mask as shown in Fig. 6.

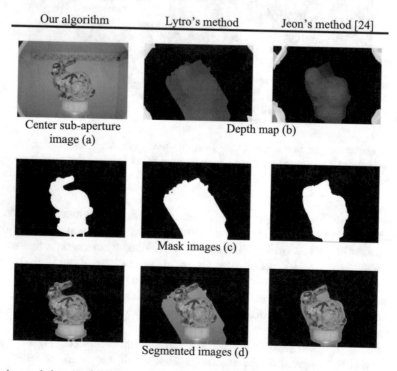

Fig. 6. A sample image of different methods. There are center sub-aperture image (a), depth maps of Lytro's and Jeon's methods (b), mask images (c), and segmented images of each method (d).

Considering the result between different methods with the same GT+base, our algorithm has scores of over 90% in all metrics. Moreover, almost all of them show better scores over other methods, as shown in Table 1. Whereas our recall ranks last among Lytro's and Jeon's, the 93.84% of recall is considered a high score. In comparison, Lytro's and Jeon's methods did well on the recall of 99.60% and 94.92%, respectively, while most of the other metrics show the scores below 90% except for the accuracy and F1 of Jeon's method, which score 95.94% and 90.13%, respectively. The following results show that Lytro's and Jeon's algorithms over masked the object as they have high recall while low on the precision. On the other hand, our algorithm sufficiently masked the object with slightly less recall, albeit with higher precision. The per-image analysis of precision, JI, and F1 show that our scores are higher than the other methods' scores significantly ($P < 0.0001$) as labeled in Fig. 4.

In terms of time efficiency, even though the exact processing time used in creating the mask was not taken into account, our algorithm took about 85 s for 36 images, which was about 2–3 s per image. Lytro spent about 20 s to export a depth map. Meanwhile, Jeon's method took about one hour to process one disparity map.

6   Conclusion

In summary, we presented an accurate masking algorithm based on EPIs of a light field image and edge detection. Our algorithm does not rely on other images to create a mask. Instead, only a single light field image is required to make its mask. It uses a simple slope estimation to mask the EPIs, which are later converted back to sub-aperture mask images. The center mask image then passes through morphological operators to clean up and fill the holes in the mask, called the initial mask. The initial mask scopes the ROI for edge detection which rules out the undesired area and brings out the potential of edge detection. Finally, binary morphological techniques link the edge together to create the final mask image. The performance of our algorithm reports high competitive recall of 93.84% to other comparable methods and also outperforms them in accuracy, precision, JI, and F1 scores with 98.39%, 97.75%, 91.86%, and 95.75%, respectively.

In a further study, more varieties of objects and differences in surfaces and structures will be introduced. Capturing more angles of the object and creating a complete 3D reconstruction will prove the usefulness of our algorithm, as it was our goal from the start. Finally, it would be interesting to integrate it to improve and compare between the conventional photogrammetry and light field 3D reconstruction methods, such as in [19, 25].

References

1. Sergeeva, A.D., Sablina, V.A.: Using structure from motion for monument 3D reconstruction from images with heterogeneous background. In: 7th Mediterranean Conference on Embedded Computing (MECO), pp. 1–4. IEEE (2018). https://doi.org/10.1109/meco.2018. 8406058

2. Sosa, G.D., et al.: 3D surface reconstruction of entomological specimens from uniform multi-view image datasets. In: 2016 XXI Symposium on Signal Processing, Images and Artificial Vision (STSIVA), pp. 1–8. IEEE (2016). https://doi.org/10.1109/stsiva.2016.7743319

3. Ströbel, B., Schmelzle, S., Blüthgen, N., Heethoff, M.: An automated device for the digitization and 3D modelling of insects, combining extended-depth-of-field and all-side multi-view imaging. ZooKeys 759, 1–27 (2018). https://doi.org/10.3897/zookeys.759.24584

4. Nguyen, C.V., et al.: 3D scanning system for automatic high-resolution plant phenotyping. In: 2016 International Conference on Digital Image Computing: Techniques and Applications (DICTA), pp. 1–8. IEEE (2016). https://doi.org/10.1109/dicta.2016.7796984

5. Scharr, H., et al.: Fast high resolution volume carving for 3D plant shoot reconstruction. Front. Plant Sci. 8, 1680 (2017). https://doi.org/10.3389/fpls.2017.01680

6. Levoy, M., Hanrahan, P.: Light field rendering. In: Proceedings of the 23rd Annual Conference on Computer Graphics and Interactive Techniques, pp. 31–42. ACM (1996). https://doi.org/10.1145/237170.237199

7. Zhu, H., Wang, Q., Yu, J.: Light field imaging: models, calibrations, reconstructions, and applications. Front. Inf. Technol. Electron. Eng. 18(9), 1236–1249 (2017). https://doi.org/10.1631/fitee.1601727

8. Bolles, R.C., Baker, H.H., Marimont, D.H.: Epipolar-plane image analysis: an approach to determining structure from motion. Int. J. Comput. Vis. 1(1), 7–55 (1987). https://doi.org/10.1007/bf00128525

9. Wanner, S., Goldluecke, B.: Globally consistent depth labeling of 4D light fields. In: 2012 IEEE Conference on Computer Vision and Pattern Recognition, pp. 41–48. IEEE (2012). https://doi.org/10.1109/cvpr.2012.6247656

10. Goldluecke, B., Wanner, S.: The variational structure of disparity and regularization of 4D light fields. In: Proceedings of the IEEE Conference on Computer Vision and Pattern Recognition, pp. 1003–1010 (2013). https://doi.org/10.1109/cvpr.2013.134

11. Zhang, Y., et al.: Light-field depth estimation via epipolar plane image analysis and locally linear embedding. IEEE Trans. Circuits Syst. Video Technol. 27(4), 739–747 (2016). https://doi.org/10.1109/tcsvt.2016.2555778

12. Lee, J.Y., Park, R.-H.: Depth estimation from light field by accumulating binary maps based on foreground–background separation. IEEE J. Sel. Top. Sig. Process. 11(7), 955–964 (2017). https://doi.org/10.1109/jstsp.2017.2747154

13. Monteiro, N.B., Barreto, J.P., Gaspar, J.: Dense lightfield disparity estimation using total variation regularization. In: Campilho, A., Karray, F. (eds.) ICIAR 2016. LNCS, vol. 9730, pp. 462–469. Springer, Cham (2016). https://doi.org/10.1007/978-3-319-41501-7_52

14. Lin, P.-H., Yeh, J.-S., Wu, F.-C., Chuang, Y.-Y.: Depth estimation for Lytro images by adaptive window matching on EPI. J. Imaging 3(2), 17 (2017). https://doi.org/10.3390/jimaging3020017

15. Diebold, M., Goldluecke, B.: Epipolar plane image refocusing for improved depth estimation and occlusion handling. In: Vision, Modeling & Visualization (VMV), pp. 145–152. The Eurographics Association (2013). http://dx.doi.org/10.2312/PE.VMV.VMV13

16. Suzuki, T., Takahashi, K., Fujii, T.: Disparity estimation from light fields using sheared EPI analysis. In: 2016 IEEE International Conference on Image Processing (ICIP), pp. 1444–1448. IEEE (2016). https://doi.org/10.1109/icip.2016.7532597

17. Wanner, S., Fehr, J., Jähne, B.: Generating EPI representations of 4D light fields with a single lens focused plenoptic camera. In: Bebis, G., et al. (eds.) ISVC 2011. LNCS, vol. 6938, pp. 90–101. Springer, Heidelberg (2011). https://doi.org/10.1007/978-3-642-24028-7_9

18. Tao, M.W., Hadap, S., Malik, J., Ramamoorthi, R.: Depth from combining defocus and correspondence using light-field cameras. In: Proceedings of the IEEE International Conference on Computer Vision, pp. 673–680 (2013). https://doi.org/10.1109/iccv.2013.89

19. Yücer, K., Sorkine-Hornung, A., Wang, O., Sorkine-Hornung, O.: Efficient 3D object segmentation from densely sampled light fields with applications to 3D reconstruction. ACM Trans. Graph. (TOG) **35**(3), 22 (2016). https://doi.org/10.1145/2876504

20. The Stanford 3D Scanning Repository. http://graphics.stanford.edu/data/3Dscanrep/

21. Canny, J.: A computational approach to edge detection. In: Readings in Computer Vision, pp. 184–203. Elsevier, Amsterdam (1987)

22. Gonzalez, R.C., Woods, R.E.: Digital Image Processing, 3rd Edn. Prentice-Hall Inc., Upper Saddle River (2006)

23. Csurka, G., Larlus, D., Perronnin, F., Meylan, F.: What is a good evaluation measure for semantic segmentation? In: British Machine Vision Conference (BMVC), pp. 32.31–32.11. Citeseer (2013). https://doi.org/10.5244/c.27.32

24. Jeon, H.-G., et al.: Accurate depth map estimation from a lenslet light field camera. In: Proceedings of the IEEE Conference on Computer Vision and Pattern Recognition, pp. 1547–1555 (2015). https://doi.org/10.1109/cvpr.2015.7298762

25. Zhang, Y., Yu, P., Yang, W., Ma, Y., Yu, J.: Ray space features for plenoptic structure-from-motion. In: Proceedings of the IEEE International Conference on Computer Vision, pp. 4631–4639 (2017). https://doi.org/10.1109/iccv.2017.496

Lidar-Monocular Visual Odometry with Genetic Algorithm for Parameter Optimization

Adarsh Sehgal⬤, Ashutosh Singandhupe, Hung Manh La$^{(\boxtimes)}$⬤,
Alireza Tavakkoli⬤, and Sushil J. Louis

University of Nevada, Reno, NV 89557, USA
hla@unr.edu
https://ara.cse.unr.edu

Abstract. Lidar-Monocular Visual Odometry (LIMO), an odometry estimation algorithm, combines camera and LIght Detection And Ranging sensor (LIDAR) for visual localization by tracking features from camera images and LIDAR measurements. LIMO then estimates the motion using Bundle Adjustment based on robust key frames. LIMO uses semantic labelling and weights of the vegetation landmarks for rejecting outliers. A drawback of LIMO as well as many other odometry estimation algorithms is that it has many parameters that need to be manually adjusted according to dynamic changes in the environment in order to decrease translational errors. In this paper, we present and argue the use of Genetic Algorithm (GA) to optimize parameters with reference to LIMO and maximize LIMO's localization and motion estimation performance. We evaluate our approach on the well-known KITTI odometry dataset and show that the GA helps LIMO to reduce translation error in different datasets.

Keywords: LIMO · Genetic Algorithm · Sensor odometry

1 Introduction

Motion estimation has long been a popular subject of research in which many techniques have been developed over the years. Much work has been done related to Visual Simultaneous Localization and Mapping (VSLAM), also referred to as Visual Odometry, which simultaneously estimates the motion of the camera and the 3D structure of the observed environment. A recent review of SLAM techniques for autonomous car driving can be found in [18]. Bundle Adjustment

This material is based upon work supported by the National Aeronautics and Space Administration (NASA) Grant No. NNX15AI02H issued through the NVSGC-RI program under sub-award No. 19–21, and the RID program under sub-award No. 19–29, and the NVSGC-CD program under sub-award No. 18–54. This work is also partially supported by the Office of Naval Research under Grant N00014-17-1-2558.

© Springer Nature Switzerland AG 2019
G. Bebis et al. (Eds.): ISVC 2019, LNCS 11845, pp. 358–370, 2019.
https://doi.org/10.1007/978-3-030-33723-0_29

is the most popular method for VSLAM. Bundle Adjustment is a procedure of minimizing the re-projection error between the observed point (landmarks in reference to LIMO) and the predicted points. Recent developments make use of offline VSLAM for mapping and localization [19].

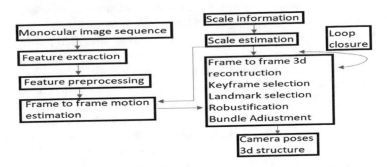

Fig. 1. VSLAM pipeline. The input is temporal sequence of images, and the system outputs a sparse reconstruction of the observed environment and the camera poses [13]. In this work, LIMO does not perform loop closure.

Figure 1 illustrates the structure of the VSLAM pipeline [13]. Algorithms such as ROCC [2] and SOFT [4] rely on pre-processing and feature extraction, which is in very contrast to most of the methods that obtain scale information from a camera placed at a different viewpoint. The former mentioned algorithms (SOFT and ROCC) extract robust and precise features and select them using special techniques, and have managed to attain high performance on the KITTI Benchmark [6], even without Bundle Adjustment.

LIght Detection And Ranging (LIDAR)-camera calibration is an expanding topic of research [8,14] with accuracy reaching a few pixels. Previous work has been done with VSLAM and LIDAR [24,25]. Lidar-Monocular Visual Odometry (LIMO) [13] uses feature tracking capability of the camera and combines it with depth measurements from a LIDAR but suffers from translation and rotation errors. Later on, we describe our approach for increasing LIMO's robustness to translation errors.

LIMO takes advantage of the depth information from LIDAR, which is to be used for feature detection in the image. Outliers are rejected if do not meet the local plane assumptions, and points on the ground plane are treated for robustness. As illustrated in Fig. 1, in the VSLAM pipieline, the depth information is fused with monocular feature detection techniques. Another approach is taken for prior estimation, landmark selection and key frame selection to fulfill real time constraints. Unlike the approach in [25], LIMO does not use any LIDAR-SLAM algorithms such as Iterative Closest Point (ICP). The major drawback of LIMO is that it has many parameters, which needs to be manually tuned. LIMO suffers from translation and rotation errors even more than existing algorithms such as Lidar Odometry and Mapping (LOAM) [24] and Vision-Lidar Odometry and Mapping (V-LOAM) [1]. Typically, researchers tune parameters (in LIMO as well) in order to minimize these errors but there always exists the possibility of finding better parameter sets that may be optimized for specific camera and LIDAR hardware or for specific scenarios. Hence, there is a need to use optimization algorithms to increase LIMO's performance. In this paper, we propose using a genetic algorithm (GA) to efficiently search the space of possible LIMO parameter values to find precise parameters that maximize performance. Our experiments with this new GA-LIMO algorithm show that GA-LIMO performs better than stock LIMO.

Much empirical evidence shows that evolutionary computing techniques such as GA work well as function optimizers in poorly-understood, non-linear, discontinuous spaces [10, 22]. GA and the GA operators of crossover and mutation have been tested on numerous problems. Closer to our research, GA has been applied to early SLAM optimization [5], multi-robot flocking [16], and deep reinforcement learning [17]. This provides good evidence for GA efficacy on localization problems, and our main contribution in this paper is a demonstration of smaller translation error when using a GA to tune LIMO parameter values compared to the stock LIMO Algorithm [13]. Our experiments show that translation error is non-linearly related to LIMO parameters, that is, translation error can vary non-linearly based on the values of the LIMO's parameters and thus suitable for GA search. The following sections describe the LIMO, the GA and GA-LIMO algorithms. We then show results from running LIMO with GA tuned parameters on the KITTI odometry data sequences [7].

2   Background

In this section, we present prior work related to our GA-LIMO algorithm. We first describe the VSLAM pipeline and then the LIMO algorithm.

2.1   Feature Extraction and Pre-processing

Figure 1 shows feature extraction's procedure in the pipeline. Feature extraction consists of tracking the features and associating the features using the Viso2 library [9]. It is further used to implement feature tracking, which comprises of non-maximum suppression, sub-pixel refinement and outlier rejection by flow. Deep learning is used to reject landmarks that are moving objects. The neighborhood of the feature point in a semantic image [3] is scanned, and if the majority of neighboring pixels categorize to a dynamic class, like vehicle or pedestrian, the landmark is excluded.

2.2   Scale Estimation

For scale estimation, the detected feature points from camera is mapped to the depth extracted from LIDAR. LIMO uses a one shot depth estimation approach. Initially LIDAR point cloud is transformed into the camera frame, and then it is projected onto the image plane. In detail, the following steps are executed for every feature point f:

1. A region of interest is selected around f, which is a set F consisting of projected LIDAR points.
2. A new set called foreground set F_{seg} is created by segmenting the elements of F.
3. The elements of F_{seg} are fitted with a plane p. A special fitting algorithm is used in case f belongs to the ground plane.
4. To estimate the depth, p is intersected with the line of sight corresponding to f.
5. For the previous estimated depth, a test is performed. Depth estimates that are more than 30 m are rejected since they could be uncertain. In addition, the angle between the line of sight of the feature point and the normal of the plane must be smaller than a threshold.

From the point clouds, neighborhoods for ordered point clouds can be selected directly. However, projections of the LIDAR points on the image are used, and the points within a rectangle in the image plane around f are selected in case the point clouds are unordered. Before the plane estimation is performed, the foreground F_{seg} is segmented. In the next step, a histogram of depth having a fixed bin width of $h = 0.3$ m is created and interpolated with elements in F. LIDAR points of the nearest bin is used to perform segmentation using all detected feature points. For estimating the local surface around f precisely, fitting the plane to F_{seg} can help. Three points are chosen from the points in F_{seg}, which traverse the triangle F_Δ with maximum area. Depth estimation is avoided if the area of F_Δ is too small, to evade incorrectly estimated depth.

However, the above technique cannot be used to estimate the depth of points on the ground plane because LIDAR has a lower resolution in the perpendicular direction than in a level direction. A different approach is followed to enable depth estimation for a relevant ground plane. For solving this, RANSAC with refinement is used on the LIDAR point cloud to extract the ground plane [21]. In order to estimate feature points on the road, points that corresponds to the ground plane are segmented. Outliers are extracted by allowing only local planes that lie close to the ground plane.

2.3   Frame to Frame Odometry

Perspective-n-Point-Problem [21] serves as the starting point of the frame to frame motion estimation.

$$\underset{x,y,z,\alpha,\beta,\gamma}{argmin} \sum_i \|\varphi_{i,3d\to2d}\|_2^2 \tag{1}$$

$$\varphi_{3d\to2d} = \bar{p}_i - \pi(p_i, P(x,y,z,\alpha,\beta,\gamma)), \tag{2}$$

where $\bar{p}_i$ is the observed feature point in the current frame, p_i is the 3D-point corresponding to $\bar{p}_i$, the transform from the previous to the current frame is denoted by freedom $P(x, y, z, \alpha, \beta, \gamma)$, which has three translation and three rotation degrees of freedom. While $\pi(.)$ is the projection function from the 3D to 2D domain. The extracted features with valid estimated depth from the environments that has low structure and large optical flow may be very small. LIMO introduces epipolar error as $\varphi_{2d \to 2d}$ [15].

$$\varphi_{2d \to 2d} = \bar{p}_i F(\frac{x}{z}, \frac{y}{z}, \alpha, \beta, \gamma) \bar{p}_i, \tag{3}$$

where fundamental matrix F can be calculated from the intrinsic calibration of the camera and from the frame to frame motion of the camera. LIMO suggests the loss function to be Cauchy function [15]: $\rho_s(x) = a(s)^2.log(1 + \frac{x}{a(s)^2})$, where $a(s)$ is the fix outlier threshold. For frame to frame motion estimation, the optimization problem can be denoted as:

$$\underset{x,y,z,\alpha,\beta,\gamma}{argmin} \sum_i \rho_{3d \to 2d}(\|\varphi_{i,3d \to 2d}\|_2^2) + \rho_{2d \to 2d}(\|\varphi_{i,2d \to 2d}\|_2^2). \tag{4}$$

2.4 Backend

LIMO proposes a Bundle Adjustment framework based on keyframes, with key components as selection of keyframes, landmark selection, cost functions and robustification measures. The advantage with this approach is that it retains the set that carries information, which is required for accurate pose estimation as well as excludes the unnecessary measurements. Keyframes are classified as required, rejected, and sparsified keyframes. Required frames are crucial measurements. Frame rejection is done when the vehicle does not move. The remaining frames are collected, and the technique selects frames every 0.3 s. Finally in keyframe selection, length of optimization window is chosen.

An optimal set of landmarks should be well observable, small, free of outliers and evenly distributed. Landmark selection divides all landmarks into three bins, near, middle and far, each of which have fixed number of landmarks selected for the Bundle Adjustment. Weights of the landmarks are then determined based on the semantic information. The estimated landmark depth is taken into consideration by an additional cost function,

$$\xi_{i,j}(i_i, P_j) = \begin{cases} 0, & if\ l_i\ has\ no\ depth\ estimate \\ \hat{d}_{i,j} - \begin{bmatrix} 0\ 0\ 1 \end{bmatrix} \tau(l_i, P_j), & else, \end{cases} \tag{5}$$

where l_i denotes the landmark, τ mapping from world frame to camera frame and $\hat{d}$ denotes the depth estimate. The indices i, j denote combination of landmark-pose. A cost function ν punishes deviations from the length of translation vector,

$$\nu(P_1, P_0) = \hat{s}(P_1, P_0) - s, \tag{6}$$

where P_0, P_1 are the last two poses in the optimization window and $\hat{s}(P_0, P_1) = \|translation(P^{-1}P_1)\|_2^2$, where s is a constant with value of $\hat{s}(P_1, P_0)$ before optimization.

While outliers need to be removed because they do not let Least-Square methods to converge [23], semantics and cheirality only does preliminary outlier rejection. The LIMO optimization problem can now be formulated as:

$$\underset{P_j \in P, l_i \in L, d_i \in D}{argmin} \quad w_0 \|\nu(P_1, P_0\|_2^2) +$$

$$\sum_i \sum_j w_1 \rho_\phi(\|\phi_{i,j}(l_i, P_i)\|_2^2) + w_2 \rho_\xi(\|\xi_{i,j}(l_i, P_j)\|_2^2), \tag{7}$$

where $\phi_{i,j}(l_i, P_j) = \bar{l}_{i,j} - \pi(l_i, P_j)$ is the re-projection error, and weights w_0, w_1 and w_2 are used to scale the cost functions to the same order of magnitude.

3   GA-LIMO Algorithm

In this section, we present the main contribution of our paper. The specific GA searches through the space of parameter values used in LIMO for parameter values that maximize performance and minimize translation error as a result of pose estimation. We are targeting the following parameters: outlier rejection quantile δ; maximum number of landmarks for near bin ϵ_{near}; maximum number of landmarks for middle bin ϵ_{middle}; maximum number of landmarks for far bin ϵ_{far} and weight for the vegetation landmarks μ. As described in the background section on rejecting outliers, δ, plays an important role in converging to minimum. Thus the weight of outlier rejection has notable impact on translation error. Landmarks are categorized into three bins, which also have great significance in translation error calculation. Trees that have a rich structure result in feature points that are good to track, but they can move. So, finding an optimal weight for vegetation can significantly reduce translation error. δ and μ range from 0 to 1, while ϵ_{near}, ϵ_{middle} and ϵ_{far} range from 0 to 999. We have set these ranges based on early experimental results. Our experiments show that adjusting the values of parameters did not decrease or increase the translation error in a linear or easily appreciable pattern. So, a simple hill climber will not do well in finding optimized parameters. We thus use a GA to optimize these parameters.

Algorithm 1 explains the combination of LIMO with the GA, which uses a population size of 50 runs for 50 generations. We used ranking selection [11] to select the parents for crossover and mutation. Rank selection probabilistically selects higher ranked (higher fitness) individuals. Unlike fitness proportional selection, ranking selection pays attention to the existence of a fitness difference rather than to the magnitude of fitness difference. Children are generated using uniform crossover, which are then mutated using flip mutation [12]. Chromosomes are binary encoded with concatenated parameters. δ and μ are considered up to three decimal places, which means a step size of 0.001, because changes in values of parameters cause considerable change in translation error. All the parameters require 11 bits to represent their range of values, so we have a chromosome length of 55 bits, with parameters arranged in the order: δ, ϵ_{near}, ϵ_{middle}, ϵ_{far}, μ.

Algorithm 1. GA-LIMO

1: Choose population of n chromosomes
2: Set the values of parameters into the chromosome
3: Run LIMO with the GA selected parameter values
4: **for** all chromosome values **do**
5:      Run LIMO on KITTI odometry data set sequence 01
6:      Compare LIMO estimated poses with ground truth
7:      Translation error σ_1 is found
8:      Run LIMO on KITTI odometry data set sequence 04
9:      Compare LIMO estimated poses with ground truth
10:     Translation error σ_4 is found
11:     Average error $\sigma_{avg} = \frac{\sigma_1 + \sigma_4}{2}$
12:     **return** $1/\sigma_{avg}$
13: **end for**
14: Perform Uniform Crossover
15: Perform Flip Mutation at rate 0.1
16: Repeat for required number of generations for optimal solution

---

The algorithm starts with randomly generating a population of n individuals. Each chromosome is sent to LIMO to evaluate. LIMO evaluates the parameter set represented by this individual by using those parameters to run on the KITTI dataset [6]. The KITTI benchmarks are well known and provide the most popular benchmark for Visual Odometry and VSLAM. This dataset has rural and urban scenes along with highway sequences and provides gray scale images, color images, LIDAR point clouds and their calibration. Most LIMO configurations are as in [13]. In our work, we focus on two sequences in particular: sequence 01 and 04. Sequence 01 is a highway scenario, which is challenging because only a road can be used for depth estimation. Sequence 04 is an urban scenario, which has a large number of landmarks for depth estimation. We consider both sequences for each GA evaluation because in this initial research we want a common set of parameters that works well with multiple scenes.

The fitness of each chromosome is defined as the inverse of translation error. This translates the minimization of translation error into a maximization of fitness as required for GA optimization. Since each fitness evaluation takes significant time, an exhaustive search of the 2^{55} size search space is not possible, hence we are using the GA. During a fitness evaluation, the GA first runs the LIMO with sequence 01. It then compares the LIMO estimated poses with ground truth (also found in [6]) and finds the translation error using the official KITTI metric [6]. The same steps are followed for sequence 04. The fitness value of each chromosome is the average of the inverse translation errors from the two sequences.

$$\sigma_{avg} = \frac{\sigma_1 + \sigma_4}{2}. \tag{8}$$

Selected chromosomes (ranked selection) are then crossed over and mutated to create new chromosomes to form the next population. This starts the next GA iteration of evaluation, selection, crossover, and mutation. The whole system takes significant time since we are running $50 \times 50 = 2500$ LIMO evaluations to determine the best parameters. The next section shows our experiments with individual and combined sequences, with and without the GA. Our results show that the GA-LIMO performs better than the results of LIMO [13].

4   Experimental Results

In this section we show our experiments with individual KITTI sequences, a combination of sequences, and overall results. First, we run the GA-LIMO with sequences 01 and 04 separately. We show the translation error and the error mapped onto the trajectory compared to the ground truth (reference) [7]. We then, show our results when GA-LIMO runs with evaluations on both sequences 01 and 04. Finally, we compare the values of parameters found by GA-LIMO versus LIMO. Figure 2 shows camera data while GA-LIMO is estimating the pose from that data in Fig. 3.

Fig. 2. Camera data while GA-LIMO is in action.

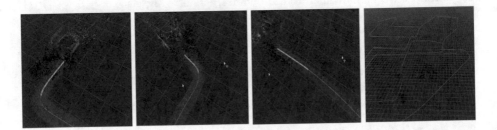

Fig. 3. GA-LIMO estimating the pose.

Figure 4 compares LIMO performance with GA-LIMO on sequence 04. Here the GA was run on this sequence individually to find the optimal parameters, as in Algorithm 2. Absolute Pose Error (APE) and Root Mean Squared Error (RMSE) are one of the important measures [20]. The translation error for each

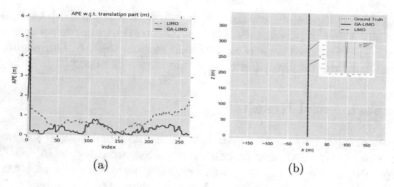

Fig. 4. Results comparison for sequence 04 (Algorithm 2). LIMO has 1.01% translation error, while GA-LIMO has about half this error with 0.56%. (a) Translation error comparison over the poses. (b) Trajectory comparison for sequence 04, when GA-LIMO was run on this sequence individually (Algorithm 2).

sequence is the RMSE calculated with respect to ground truth. Figure 4(a) compares the translation error over the poses, while Fig. 4(b) compares the error mapped onto the trajectory with the zoomed in trajectory. Our results show that the GA-LIMO trajectory is closer to ground truth compared to LIMO. We found that the translation error was 0.56% with GA-LIMO, in contrast to 1.01% with LIMO.

Algorithm 2. GA-LIMO individual

1: Choose population of n chromosomes
2: Set the values of parameters into the chromosome
3: Run LIMO with the GA selected parameter values
4: **for** all chromosome values **do**
5:     Run LIMO on individual KITTI odometry dataset sequence
6:     Compare LIMO estimated poses with ground truth
7:     Translation error σ is found
8:     **return** $1/\sigma$
9: **end for**
10: Perform Uniform Crossover
11: Perform Flip Mutation at rate 0.1
12: Repeat for required number of generations to find optimal solution

---

Figure 5 compares the performance of LIMO with GA-LIMO when the system is run on just sequence 01. Here first, the GA was run on sequence 01 (Algorithm 2) and the optimal parameters were used to test the same sequence. Table 1 compares the original and GA found parameter values. Figure 5(a) compares translation error, while Fig. 5(b) shows the error mapped onto the trajectory for LIMO and GA-LIMO. As shown in the zoomed in-Fig. 5(b), GA-LIMO is closer to the ground truth. The translation error for LIMO is found to be around

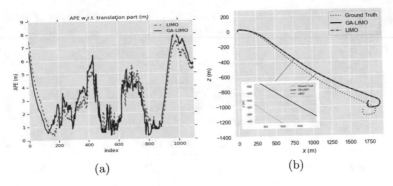

(a)   (b)

Fig. 5. Results comparison for sequence 01 (Algorithm 2). LIMO has 3.71% translation error, while GA-LIMO has 3.8%. (a) Translation error comparison over the poses. (b) Trajectory comparison.

3.71% and 3.8% in case of GA-LIMO, with sequence 01. GA found parameters that did not outperform the original parameters, when GA-LIMO was run on just sequence 01.

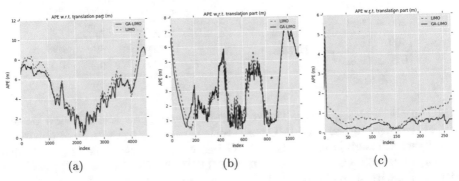

(a)   (b)   (c)

Fig. 6. (a) Translation error comparison over the poses for sequence 01. LIMO has 3.71% translation error while GA-LIMO has 3.59%. (b) Translation error comparison over the poses for sequence 00. LIMO has 5.77% translation error while GA-LIMO has 5.13%. (c) Translation error comparison over the poses for sequence 04. LIMO has 1.01% translation error while GA-LIMO has 0.65%. The parameters are found using GA-LIMO using combination of sequences 01 and 04 (Algorithm 1). These parameters are then tested on three sequences. In all three sequences GA-LIMO performs better than LIMO.

We finally ran the system with both sequences 01 and 04 as described in Algorithm 1. The fitness of each evaluation is the average of translation errors of the sequences when run using the input parameters. The parameters found in GA-LIMO as shown in Table 1, were then tested on sequences 00, 01 and 04, as shown in Figs. 6 and 7. It is evident that GA-LIMO performed better than

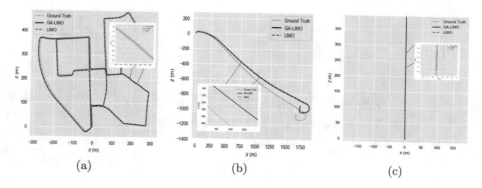

(a)   (b)   (c)

Fig. 7. Trajectory comparison when GA-LIMO was run as in Algorithm 1. In all three sequences GA-LIMO performs better than LIMO.

Table 1. LIMO vs. GA-LIMO parameters when GA ran on LIMO: (Left table)-with sequence 01 individually; (Middle table)-with combined sequence 01 and 04; (Right table)-with sequence 04 individually.

Param	LIMO	GA-LIMO	Param	LIMO	GA-LIMO	Param	LIMO	GA-LIMO
δ	0.95	0.958	δ	0.95	0.963	δ	0.95	0.986
ϵ_{near}	400	999	ϵ_{near}	400	999	ϵ_{near}	400	999
ϵ_{middle}	400	593	ϵ_{middle}	400	554	ϵ_{middle}	400	960
ϵ_{far}	400	877	ϵ_{far}	400	992	ϵ_{far}	400	859
μ	0.9	0.813	μ	0.9	0.971	μ	0.9	0.128

LIMO in all three sequences. The zoomed-in figures show a closer view on one part of the trajectories. GA-LIMO trajectories are closer to the ground truth and have lesser translation errors. GA-LIMO has a translation error of 5.13% with sequence 00, 3.59% with sequence 01 and 0.65% with sequence 04, in contrast with 5.77% with sequence 00, 3.71% with sequence 01 and 1.01% with sequence 04 using original parameters.

Our method helped to find common set of optimal parameters, which works better and hence lead to better performance in different kinds of environments.

5   Discussion and Future Work

This paper shows results that demonstrated that the GA can tune LIMO parameters to achieve better performance, reduced translation error, across a range of scenarios. We discussed existing work on VSLAM, presented an algorithm to integrate LIMO with GA to find LIMO parameters that robustly minimize translation error, and explained why a GA might be suitable for such optimization. Initial results had the assumption that GAs are a good fit for such parameter optimization, and our results show that the GA can find parameter values that lead to faster learning and better (or equal) performance. We thus provide further evidence that heuristic search as performed by genetic and other similar evolutionary computing algorithms are a viable computational tool for optimizing LIMO's performance. Open source code for this paper is available on our ARA Lab's github: https://github.com/aralab-unr/LIMOWithGA.

References

1. Balazadegan Sarvrood, Y., Hosseinyalamdary, S., Gao, Y.: Visual-lidar odometry aided by reduced IMU. ISPRS Int. J. Geo-Inf. **5**(1), 3 (2016)
2. Buczko, M., Willert, V.: Flow-decoupled normalized reprojection error for visual odometry. In: 19th IEEE International Conference on Intelligent Transportation Systems, pp. 1161–1167 (2016)
3. Cordts, M., et al.: The cityscapes dataset for semantic urban scene understanding. In: Proceedings of the IEEE Conference on Computer Vision and Pattern Recognition, pp. 3213–3223 (2016)
4. Cvišić, I., Petrović, I.: Stereo odometry based on careful feature selection and tracking. In: European Conference on Mobile Robots, pp. 1–6 (2015)
5. Duckett, T.: A genetic algorithm for simultaneous localization and mapping. In: IEEE International Conference on Robotics and Automation, pp. 434–439, September 2003
6. Geiger, A., Lenz, P., Stiller, C., Urtasun, R.: Vision meets robotics: the kitti dataset. Int. J. Robot. Res. **32**(11), 1231–1237 (2013)
7. Geiger, A., Lenz, P., Urtasun, R.: Are we ready for autonomous driving? the kitti vision benchmark suite. In: Conference on Computer Vision and Pattern Recognition (2012)
8. Geiger, A., Moosmann, F., Car, Ö., Schuster, B.: Automatic camera and range sensor calibration using a single shot. In: IEEE International Conference on Robotics and Automation, pp. 3936–3943 (2012)
9. Geiger, A., Ziegler, J., Stiller, C.: Stereoscan: dense 3D reconstruction in real-time. In: IEEE Intelligent Vehicles Symposium, pp. 963–968 (2011)
10. Gibb, S., La, H.M., Louis, S.: A genetic algorithm for convolutional network structure optimization for concrete crack detection. In: 2018 IEEE Congress on Evolutionary Computation (CEC), pp. 1–8 (2018)
11. Goldberg, D.E., Deb, K.: A comparative analysis of selection schemes used in genetic algorithms. In: Foundations of Genetic Algorithms, vol. 1, pp. 69–93 (1991)
12. Goldberg, D.E., Holland, J.H.: Genetic algorithms and machine learning. Mach. Learn. **3**(2), 95–99 (1988)
13. Graeter, J., Wilczynski, A., Lauer, M.: LIMO: lidar-monocular visual odometry. In: IEEE/RSJ International Conference on Intelligent Robots and Systems, pp. 7872–7879 (2018)
14. Gräter, J., Strauss, T., Lauer, M.: Photometric laser scanner to camera calibration for low resolution sensors. In: 19th IEEE International Conference on Intelligent Transportation Systems (ITSC), pp. 1552–1557 (2016)
15. Hartley, R., Zisserman, A.: Multiple View Geometry in Computer Vision. Cambridge university press, Cambridge (2003)
16. La, H.M., Nguyen, T.H., Nguyen, C.H., Nguyen, H.N.: Optimal flocking control for a mobile sensor network based a moving target tracking. In: IEEE International Conference on Systems, Man and Cybernetics, pp. 4801–4806, October 2009

370 A. Sehgal et al.

17. Sehgal, A., La, H., Louis, S., Nguyen, H.: Deep reinforcement learning using genetic algorithm for parameter optimization. In: IEEE International Conference on Robotic Computing, pp. 596–601 (2019)
18. Singandhupe, A., La, H.: A review of SLAM techniques and security in autonomous driving. In: IEEE International Conference on Robotic Computing, pp. 602–607 (2019)
19. Sons, M., Lategahn, H., Keller, C.G., Stiller, C.: Multi trajectory pose adjustment for life-long mapping. In: 2015 IEEE Intelligent Vehicles Symposium (IV), pp. 901–906 (2015)
20. Sturm, J., Engelhard, N., Endres, F., Burgard, W., Cremers, D.: A benchmark for the evaluation of RGB-D SLAM systems. In: 2012 IEEE/RSJ International Conference on Intelligent Robots and Systems, pp. 573–580 (2012)
21. Szeliski, R.: Computer Vision: Algorithms and Applications. Springer, London (2010). https://doi.org/10.1007/978-1-84882-935-0
22. Tavakkoli, A., Ambardekar, A., Nicolescu, M., Louis, S.: A genetic approach to training support vector data descriptors for background modeling in video data. In: International Symposium on Visual Computing, pp. 318–327 (2007)
23. Torr, P.H., Fitzgibbon, A.W.: Invariant fitting of two view geometry. IEEE Trans. Pattern Anal. Mach. Intell. **26**(5), 648–650 (2004)
24. Zhang, J., Singh, S.: LOAM: lidar odometry and mapping in real-time. In: Robotics: Science and Systems, vol. 2, p. 9 (2014)
25. Zhang, J., Singh, S.: Visual-lidar odometry and mapping: low-drift, robust, and fast. In: IEEE International Conference on Robotics and Automation, pp. 2174–2181 (2015)

Residual CNN Image Compression

Kunal Deshmukh$^{(\boxtimes)}$(iD) and Chris Pollett(iD)

San Jose State University, San Jose, CA 95192, USA
kunaldeshmukh27@gmail.com, chris@pollett.org

Abstract. We present a neural network architecture inspired by the end-to-end compression framework [1]. Our model consists of an image compression module, an arithmetic encoder, an arithmetic decoder, and an image reconstruction module. We evaluate the compression rate and the closeness of the reconstructed image to the original image for this model. Structural similarity metrics and peak signal to noise ratio are used to evaluate the image quality. We have also measured the net reduction in file size after compression and compared it with other lossy image compression techniques. Our architecture achieves better results in terms of these metrics compared to traditional and newly proposed image compression algorithms. In particular, an average PSNR of 28.48 and SSIM value of 0.86 are obtained as compared to 28.45 PSNR and 0.81 SSIM value in the previously mentioned network.

Keywords: Convolutional Neural Networks · Generative adversarial networks · Structural similarity metrics · Peak signal to noise ratio

1 Introduction

Several recently published articles [1,2] on image processing and compression frameworks have used deep learning networks. Parts and ideas from several of these frameworks seemed like they might augment each other to give better results. The present paper explore this by developing a new hybrid architecture which we show improves upon existing architectures for both efficiency and image quality metrics such as SSIM, PSNR while still being as time efficient as possible.

The first architecture we leveraged was Jiang et al. [1]. They consider an end to end image compression network in which a fully convolutional neural network (CNN) based encoder is used for image compression. Their inspiration was that in JPEG to achieve higher compression one uses bigger quantization steps. Unfortunately, these bigger steps result in blocking artifacts during decoding. Zhai et al. [3] and Foi et al. [4] had previously considered image based hand-crafted deblocking filters to reduce this problem. Jiang, et al propose instead that one should try to use a CNN to learn filters which would do the same job as efficiently as possible.

Jiang et al.'s architecture serves as our baseline model to compare with our approach. In Jiang et al.'s architecture, a smaller image is first constructed by

© Springer Nature Switzerland AG 2019
G. Bebis et al. (Eds.): ISVC 2019, LNCS 11845, pp. 371–382, 2019.
https://doi.org/10.1007/978-3-030-33723-0_30

the encoder. This image is nothing but a downsampled version of the original image. The decoder, called the re-constructor, is designed to generate an original image back from this smaller image.

Cavigelli et al. [2] propose a different architecture that is efficient at suppressing artifacts that are introduced during the image compression process. To do this their model makes use of skip connections. Our proposed architecture also makes use of skip connections. Besides suppressing artifacts, this helped our model converge 19.65% faster as compared to a network without skip connections. Space separable CNN layers such as pointwise and depthwise CNN layers are useful to speedup the training and inference. We used such CNN layers for some of the levels in our neural network. This further reduced the training as well as inference time by about 7% and 3% as compared to the network using vanilla CNN layers. We discuss what these layer types are and these result in detail in Sect. 2.3.

Finally, we have also designed a loss function in such a way that the images generated by the compression module have a very low variance in pixel values. This limits the pixel values the resultant compressed image can have. An arithmetic encoder is then used to process this compressed image. Since the compressed image now has a very small number of distinct values, the arithmetic encoder can use a lossless data compression algorithms such as entropy coding or RLE to further compress the results obtained from compression module.

In summary, our architecture at a high level starts with the base model of Jiang et al. Compression and decompression neural networks are trained simultaneously. The decompression network is larger and makes use of skip connections and space separable CNN layers which together with the choice of our loss function speed up training. To improve image quality of our decompression network we make use of an SRGAN sub-network.

We now discuss the organization of the rest of the paper. In the next section, we fix the definitions of some of the neural network layers we are considering as well as discuss prior models that have been considered in more detail. We also discuss image quality metrics in brief. We then have a section describing our proposed architecture in detail. This is followed by training methodology and experiments and, finally, there is a conclusion section.

2   Background

We assume the reader is familiar with Convolutional Neural Networks (CNNs), Recurrent Neural Networks (RNNs), etc. as well as the fundamental concepts in deep neural network training such as training and loss functions. Information on these topics can be found in Goodfellow et al. [5].

2.1   The Use of Convolutional Neural Networks in Image Compression

Our architecture relies heavily on CNNs to capture image artifacts. CNNs have been used recently in many image compression architectures.

Jiang et al. [1] use a fully convolutional auto-encoder to obtain a compressed representation of an image. Their auto-encoder consists of a series of two kinds of convolutional layers stacked one after the other to capture features of the image. The authors claim that, because of the use of multi-layer CNNs, this architecture maintains the structural composition of the image. The two distinct convolutional layers networks they use are called the ComCNN and the RecCNN. The ComCNN network is responsible for compressing images in such a way that the resultant images can be effectively reconstructed by a reconstruction network. The ComCNN network consists of three convolutional layers with the second layer followed by a batch normalization layer. Since the first convolutional layer uses a stride of two, the image size is reduced by half. The RecCNN layer uses twenty CNN layers. Apart from the first and the last layer, each layer in this architecture carries out convolutional and batch normalization operations. The authors train this network using 400 grayscale images for 50 epochs. The SSIM and PSNR metrics for these images are better than what is obtained by using JPEG. PSNR and SSIM values for 28.17 and 0.8206 respectively.

In lossy image compression techniques, artifacts of the compression are often visible in the images. One example class of artifacts is caused when tiling is used for quantization. In such images, the tile boundaries are often visible in the images. The CNN based architecture [2] proposed by Cavigelli et al. is a twelve layer image compression architecture designed to suppress such artifacts. Cavigelli et al. also give a new way to train deep neural network models which is adaptable to other low-level computer vision tasks. They propose the use of hierarchical skip connections together with a multiscale loss functions. Two advantages of skip connection are: In the forward pass, this method provides information that allows the network to obtain higher resolution images. In the backward pass, these skip connections allow gradient flow to skip middle layers and help train earlier layers more quickly. Using skip connections though does not eliminate the possibility of very long paths in the network. Hence, they calculate the loss function on many intermediate low-resolution images. The authors observes that batch normalization does not reduce the accuracy of their network.

2.2   The Use of GANs for Image Interpolation

Ledig et al. [6] use GANs to recover finer detail from an image that are lost because of compression. Their framework uses a perceptual loss function that consists of a content loss term and an adversarial loss term. We have used this idea as an efficient way to do image up-scaling.

Their architecture up-scales the images by a factor of four. The quality of images generated using this method are close to the quality of original images. This GAN's architecture uses a VGG network [7] as a Discriminator.

2.3   Space Separable Convolutional Neural Betworks

Our architecture makes use of two special types of CNN Layers: Point-wise and Depth-wise CNN layers. A point-wise convolutional operation is a special type of operation where the size of the kernel is always 1×1. This operation returns a layer of the same dimensions as that of its inputs. Depthwise CNNs work on depth. Each kernel can have any height and width, however, its depth is always one. Separate kernels act on each depth level. Stacking all these layers together results in an image.

Point-wise and Depth-wise convolutions involve fewer multiplications, hence, they are computationally efficient. However, shallow neural networks with space separable convolutions may fail to learn the underlying function.

2.4   Image Quality Metrics

Image quality metrics are used to measure how well an image compression architecture performs. Image quality metrics are of two types: Reference image quality metrics and non-reference image quality metrics. Reference image quality metrics require a reference image to compute; on the other hand, non-reference image quality metrics, such as Mean Subtracted Contrast Normalized (MSCN), do not require such a reference image.

Since we are going to compare the uncompressed image with the original image anyway for our loss function, we have used only reference image quality metrics. We next review some of these reference image quality metrics:

Mean Square Error (MSE): MSE calculates the sum of the squared differences between pixel values of two images of the same dimensions: $MSE = \frac{1}{MN} \sum_{y=1}^{M} \sum_{x=1}^{N} [I(x,y) - I'(x,y)]^2$. Here M and N are the width and height respectively of the images in pixels and $I(x,y)$ is the pixel intensity value at the image position (x,y). This is perhaps the simplest image quality metric to understand, however, it is not always a good metric to access image compression quality as it does not take into account the range of variations in pixel values in an image or the high and low-frequency components in an image, two factors which affect human perception of image quality.

Peak Signal to Noise Ratio (PSNR): PSNR is a measure of the peak error between the two images. It is computed using the equation: $PSNR = 10 \log_{10} \frac{R^2}{MSE}$ where R represents the maximum fluctuation in input image pixel values. Since PSNR uses Mean Square Error in its denominator, higher PSNR values represent a better quality compression.

Structural Similarity Index (SSIM): SSIM measures image quality degradation due to processing tasks such as compression. SSIM is considered to be a better metric for accessing degradation of images as it takes into account visible structures in an image. SSIM is calculated via the following formula:

$$SSIM(x,y) = \frac{(2\mu_x \mu_y + C_1) + (2\sigma_{xy} + C_2)}{(\mu_x^2 + \mu_y^2 + C_1)(\sigma_x^2 + \sigma_y^2 + C_2)} \tag{1}$$

Here x and y represent images, μ_x, μ_y are the average pixel value for each image, σ_{xy} is the co-variance between x and y, and σ_x^2, σ_y^2 are the variances of x and y.

3   Network Design

Our proposed architecture consists of four parts: an Image Compression Module (ICM), an Arithmetic Encoder, an Arithmetic Decoder, and an Image Reconstruction Module (IRM). The ICM and IRMs result in lossy image compression while the Arithmetic Encoder and Decoder are lossless. Both the ICM and the IRM are based on deep neural networks.

3.1   The Arithmetic Coder and Decoder

Our arithmetic coder and decoder make use of a Python implementation of Huffman coding [8]. Since the original data can be completely retrieved in the decoder part, it is a lossless compression algorithm and its introduction or removal does not affect the other neural network-based modules. Thus, for neural network training, we did not use the arithmetic coder or decoder so as to avoid unnecessary computational overhead.

3.2   The Image Compression Module

The CNN layers in the ICM are used to learn features and components of the image helpful for further image reconstruction tasks. These components include the overall structure of the image as well as some salient features such as edges and corners that cannot be regenerated by the reconstruction layer unless they are provided as inputs. Thus, this module acts as a filter through which only a few critical components are passed to an intermediate image. We have used a three layer CNN module as shown in Fig. 1. We specify this network in more detail below:

The first block consists of a CNN layer followed by a rectified linear unit (ReLU) non-linearity. It uses a 3×3 kernel of a depth 3 in the case of RGB compression and of depth 1 in the case of grayscale images. This layer has 3 feature maps. The second block has a CNN layer, a ReLU activation, and a layer for batch-normalization. This block's CNN uses a 2 padding, resulting in a tensor of half the size of the original image. This layer thus reduces the size and resolution of an image by half, when the stride is 2.

The resultant tensor is passed through a batch normalization layer which helps [9] avoid gradient overflow or underflow and makes the neural network less sensitive to the choice of random initializer and its variation. A single convolution layer is used for the third block of the network. The number of kernels used in this layer corresponds to the number of channels in the output image. The output of this layer is not subject to a non-linearity as the goal of this layer is to reproduce an image as close to the original image as possible.

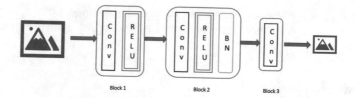

Fig. 1. Image compression module

The Image Compression Module was trained simultaneously with the Image Reconstruction Module. The goal of the compression network is to generate an intermediate representation of an original image that can be used by the reconstruction layers to generate an image as close to the original image as possible. The size of this intermediate result decides the compression factor of the compression algorithm. This compression factor can be changed by varying the stride and dilation values in the intermediate layer.

3.3 Image Reconstruction Module

The reconstruction module has two responsibilities: To resize the image to the original size and to improve the quality of the resized image.

Since this module is tasked with the reconstruction of a facsimile of the original image from the minimal information passed on by the compression module, this module requires more layers to try to detect residual information from the compressed image that might aid in reconstruction. These residuals are detected by the feature maps used in its convolutional layers. The first few of these layers are responsible for the reconstruction of basic shapes such as lines, points, corners etc. while further layers add more information about higher order combinations of these base features. The size of kernels used in this network is always 3×3 since all these features are local to a region and are less likely to have any impact on other parts of an image.

The framework in [1] uses a bicubic interpolation method to resize the compressed image to its original size. Our system uses an SRGAN (Super Resolution Generative Adverserial Network) [6] for this purpose. Our SRGAN network returns an image of size four times the size of the original image. This can be scaled down to the desired size using an interpolation technique before it is fed to the reconstruction module. The SRGAN paper shows these networks generate better quality images as compared to simple interpolation techniques, giving our network better input data for image enhancement.

Using an SRGAN allows us to use bad quality images to train the network for image enhancement. Slightly bad quality data is often generated as part of a data augmentation task for robust training. Using a bicubic interpolation instead of SRGAN during training alleviated the amount of data augmentation needed when training the reconstruction network. The SRGAN network that we used, was trained separately in its original proposed shape on the ImageNet dataset.

The IRM consists of five blocks each containing one convolutional layer and an optional batch normalization or ReLU layer.

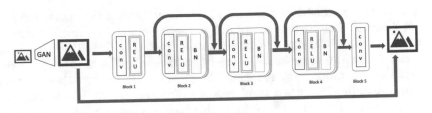

Fig. 2. Image reconstruction module.

The first block contains a CNN layer with ReLU activation function. For this layer, we used 64 features each of which had a 3×3 kernel with depth 3 for RGB images and 1 for grayscale. The second block consists of five concatenated sub-blocks each consisting of a CNN layer, a ReLU activation, and a batch normalization layer. Hence, overall, this block contains five CNN, ReLU, and batch normalization layers. The third and fourth blocks are identical to the second block. Pointwise and depthwise convolution functions are applied to the second block. The fifth and last block consists of a CNN layer which takes in 64 channels and outputs a tensor of size height $\times$ width$\times$ # of channels.

After the 2nd, 3rd, and 4th blocks, a skip connection is added as shown in Fig. 2. Then a ReLU is applied after this.

An interpolated image from the start of the network is added to the output of the fifth block. The resultant tensor is saved as an image. As we have discussed in previous section, skip connections are useful in backpropagation. The use of ReLU activations also ensures that the tensors passed in these layers are subjected to enough non-linearity so that the network weights in successive layers are not updated in a uniform manner during training. This activation function also ensures that the resultant values in tensors are restricted to the desired domain. Since we have used batch normalization layers in the network, the use of ReLU does not contribute to an exploding gradient problem. For skip connections, two tensors of same dimension are added and each new tensor is passed through at least one convolutional layer, this ensures that the convolutional layer weights are adjusted in the training phase so as to accommodate the values obtained from skip connections.

3.4 Loss Function

A loss function computes an error between the desired values and those output by a neural network. The training algorithm tries to adjust weights so as to minimize this function. For our training procedure, the loss function was calculated using the following formula:

$$L = \frac{1}{M} \sum_{y=1}^{M} [(\sum_{i,j} P_{ij}(y) - P_{ij}(\widehat{y}))^2 + |(P_{ij}(I_{in}) - P_{ij}(I_{out}))|] \qquad (2)$$

In Eq. 2, M is the number of images and the function $P_{i,j}(I)$ outputs the i, jth pixel of image I. The first term in Eq. 2 is the mean square error between the input image to the ICM and the output image from the IRM. The second term is the mean absolute error between the input image to the first CNN block of IRM and the output image after the fifth block of the IRM before they are added together. It can be viewed as a regularization term. I_{in} is after we have upscaled the compressed image. We do not want this image to be substantially different from the final output, so we add this as a penalty term.

4   Experiments

Experiments were conducted using the publicly available image datasets: STL10, CIFAR10, COCO and CLIC. We varied the dataset, the numbers of epochs and network sizes during our experiments, however, our best results were obtained for 50 epochs on the COCO dataset. Training required more than 110 h on a Google Cloud instance that had an Nvidia Tesla P 100 GPU. SRGAN and arithmetic encoder and decoders were not added to the network during training. We used an Adam optimizer [10] and Xavier initialization [11] for all experiments.

Our first experiment was a reimplementation of the baseline model of Jiang et al. [1]. We did not achieve exactly the same results as claimed by these authors as we could not obtain the original dataset for training used by authors. Instead, we trained our version on the STL10 and COCO datasets, the COCO dataset giving the better results. We implemented the image augmentation techniques as described in their paper. That is, we generated images from our starting images by random horizontal and vertical flips and by rotations of angles between 0 and 360°. Our results below are for the COCO dataset of 330 thousand images. All training images were 200 × 200 pixels. The COCO dataset contains a variety of image sizes 650 × 450, so we also performed image croppings by randomly choosing a base point from the image and then cropping out a 200 × 200 image at this base point. Each epoch during our training had 330 thousand images, where each image was generated from the COCO dataset image using the random processes just described. Twenty percent of the images were used in each epoch for validation. Finally, for testing we used the Kodak image dataset of 25 images where we re-scaled these images to 200 × 200.

For comparison, Jiang et al. used images of size 180 × 180. They created augmentations of 400 starting images and tested using 7 images from the Kodak dataset. We observe that our network performance increased when we increased the number of images in our augmented datasets.

Table 1. Baseline model results

Image name	PSNR	SSIM
Lenna	28.07	0.59
Peppers	27.9088	0.48
Parrots	28.036	0.61
Average	28.00	0.56

Table 2. Examples of baseline model results

Type	Lenna	Peppers	Parrots
Original Image			
Reconstructed Image			

Our baseline model results are shown in Tables 1 and 2. Overall, we obtained a PSNR 28.45 and an SSIM 0.81 for their model; whereas, their paper obtains a PSNR of 30.17 and an SSIM 0.88. However, to achieve comparable results we needed to use more data. This might be due to the particularities of their data set, which we did not have, as well as to tuning and initialization factors in their training. Table 2 shows some examples of compressed and uncompressed images we obtained on the test data for this experiment. Table 2 shows results only for grayscale images as only grayscale images were used by Jiang et al.

We next describe the experiments we conducted using our proposed neural network architecture. These experiments were also conducted using the COCO dataset with the same image augmentations. For these experiments we used color rather than grayscale images. Our results are given in Tables 3 and 4.

Table 3. Color image results for the proposed model

Image name	PSNR	SSIM
Baboon	27.7869	0.89
Lenna	29.26	0.86
Peppers	28.46	0.79
Parrots	28.33	0.69
Average	28.45	0.81

Table 4. Example color images using the proposed model

Type	Peppers	Parrots	Lenna
Original Image			
Reconstructed Image			

These results show some distortion in the color images as the IRM introduced errors during image regeneration. This distortion might be reduced if deeper neural networks were used in tandem with a larger dataset. It might also be reduced by using smoothing or removal of high-frequency areas. We conducted experiments for both color and gray scale images. Grayscale was used so we could compare our results to what was used in the baseline model. To handle grayscale we slightly modified the first and last layer of our networks so they dealt with only one channel. The grayscale results are shown in Tables 5 and 6.

Table 5. Grayscale results for the proposed model

Image name	PSNR	SSIM
Cameraman	27.34	0.78
Peppers	28.30	0.88
Lenna	29.88	0.87
Parrots	28.23	0.89
House	28.67	0.89
Average	28.48	0.86

Table 6. Example grayscale images using the proposed model

Type	Peppers	Parrots	Lenna
Original Image			
Reconstructed Image			

From our results, we see that the performance of our model on grayscale is better than on color images. For grayscale, each image pixel is represented by a single value, for RGB, three values are required to define a single pixel. This increases the possibility of error in color images. Grayscale images are generated using a two-dimensional tensor. Since the possibility of error is reduced by the factor of three, errors in grayscale are not easily perceived by a human eye. As the SSIM metric is modeled after human perception, understandably grayscale perform better for the SSIM metric as compared to PSNR. In addition to comparing the image quality of our proposed model with the baseline model, we also conducted experiments looking at the time to train our model, the time to carry out compression and decompression of images using our model, and the average compression sizes obtained via our model.

On the COCO dataset, the average time to train the baseline framework for one epoch was 173 min as compared to 139 min for our framework.

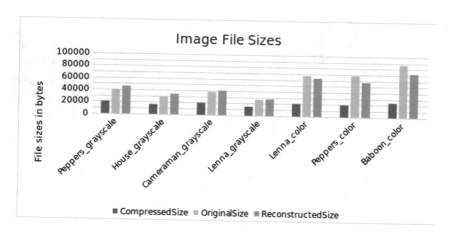

Fig. 3. Image file size before and after compression

Compression and decompression speeds were measured in images/second. We tested 200 images from COCO dataset. The average compression time for the baseline model was 3.2 and for the proposed architecture was 3.3. These were comparable as these networks were essentially the same. On the other hand, the average decompression time for the baseline model was 4.1 and for the proposed architecture was 3.4. The inference time is slower than the baseline model probably due to the evaluation of the SRGAN portion of the reconstruction as it add more than twenty layers to the model. Replacing this portion withta simpler bicubic upscaling, gave a value of 4.3 while worsening the image quality to an average PSNR of 28.44 and SSIM of 0.85. In terms of compressed files sizes, Fig. 3 shows that the file size of an image was substantially reduced after going through the image compression module and the arithmetic encoder. In this figure, the original size is that of the JPEG (already compressed) image from the data set.

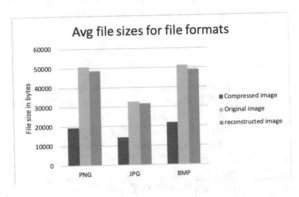

Fig. 4. Average file size for image file format

Figure 4 shows the compression achieved for images of various file types. The compressed image files were obtained by taking the original file, reading it into our compression neural network, computing its compressed image and then saving the result in the same file format as was input. So if the original image was PNG, we read it in, applied our neural network to obtain a compressed image, and then saved that compressed image as a PNG. Similarly, the decompressed file sizes were obtained by reading in the compressed image in some format X, applying our neural network, and writing out an image in format X. It can be concluded from this that our architecture is useful for a variety of file formats. The loss and overall quality for the image file formats do not vary substantially with a change in file formats. The same was true for implementation of a baseline model as well.

5   Conclusion

Autoencoders seem particularly useful for image compression and reconstruction. Using residual connections and space separable layers, reduced training by approximately 20% over the baseline model [1]'s training. Our model also achieves slightly better quality with a PSNR of 28.48 and SSIM of 0.86 are obtained as compared to 28.45 PSNR and 0.81 SSIM, with only a slight change in decompression time. A slightly lower quality version of our model where the SRGAN portion is replaced with bicubic interpolation actually gives a faster decompression time than the baseline with only a slightly reduction in quality of the output. Our method provides a way to achieve image compression after it is processed by traditional image compression algorithms such as JPEG. Hence, it can be used to supplement traditional image compression and encoding algorithms. We expect that in the future a variety of interesting experiments and improvements can be made in the field of neural network compression. For example, even without changing our model we might obtain faster training times for our network and potentially higher compression ratios by focusing on images coming from a single category such as just car images.

References

1. Jiang, F., Tao, W., Liu, S., Ren, J., Guo, X., Zhao, D.: An end-to-end compression framework based on convolutional neural networks. IEEE Trans. Circuits Syst. Video Technol. **28**(10), 3007–3018 (2018)
2. Cavigelli, L., Hager, P., Benini, L.: CAS-CNN: a deep convolutional neural network for image compression artifact suppression. In: International Joint Conference on Neural Networks (IJCNN), pp. 752–759 (2017)
3. Zhai, G., Zhang, W., Yang, X., Lin, W., Xu, Y.: Efficient image deblocking based on postfiltering in shifted windows. IEEE Trans. Circuits Syst. Video Technol. **18**, 122–126 (2008)
4. Foi, A., Katkovnik, V., Egiazarian, K.: Pointwise shape-adaptive DCT denoising with structure preservation in luminance-chrominance space. IEEE Trans. Image Process. **16**, 1395–1411 (2006)
5. Goodfellow, I., Bengio, Y., Courville, A.: Deep Learning. MIT Press, Cambridge (2016). http://www.deeplearningbook.org
6. Ledig, C., et al.: Photo-realistic single image super-resolution using a generative adversarial network. In: IEEE Conference on Computer Vision and Pattern Recognition, pp. 4681–4690 (2017)
7. Krizhevsky, A., Sutskever, I., Hinton, G.: Very deep convolutional networks for large-scale image recognition, arXiv preprint arXiv:1409.1556 (2014)
8. Knuth, D.: Dynamic huffman coding. J. Algorithms **6**(2), 163–80 (1985)
9. Ioffe, S., Szegedy, C.: Batch normalization: accelerating deep network training by reducing internal covariate shift, arXiv preprint arXiv:1502.03167 (2015)
10. Kingma, D., Ba, J.: Adam: A method for stochastic optimization, arXiv preprint arXiv:1412.6980, December 2014
11. Thimm, G., Fiesler, E.: Neural network initialization. In: International Workshop on Artificial Neural Networks, pp. 535–542 (1995)

CNNs and Transfer Learning for Lecture Venue Occupancy and Student Attention Monitoring

Antonie J. Smith[✉], Barend J. Van Wyk[✉], and Shengzhi Du[✉]

Tshwane University of Technology, Pretoria West, Gauteng, South Africa
{SmithAJ, VanWykB, DuS}@tut.ac.za

Abstract. Lower student success rates in higher education might, in some case, be due to the unprecedented increase of student numbers without a comparable increase in resources and funding. This paper proposes a face-based detection system to monitor occupancy and student attention in crowded classroom using state of the art deep Convolutional Neural Networks (CNN) architectures. The aim of the proposed system is to contribute to the increase of subject success rates by monitoring attendance and attention. The system utilizes a two-phased approach: The first phase determines the number of student faces in an image frame. The Haar Cascade, LBP, HOG, Resnet CNN, TinyFace CNN, and SSD were compared to determine the algorithm best suited to the detection of faces in crowded classroom scenes. In phase two, the orientations of the faces are determined using transfer learning. Faces are classified as "right", "left", or at the "center". This information is displayed on an augmented reality display to provide feedback to lecturers in semi real-time. It is hoped that this will assist lecturers to address problems related to student attention in crowded classrooms.

Keywords: Haar Cascade · LBP · HOG · CNN · Face detection

1 Introduction

In South Africa, as in many other developing countries, higher education numbers are increasing without a comparable increase in funding or other resources. At the Tshwane University of Technology, for example, student numbers increased by 27% since 2014, without a significant increase in lecturing positions or venues, resulting in an unprecedented growth in first-year class sizes and a drop in overall success rate of more than 10%. The effect of an increase in class size on student achievement has been studied by a number of authors, including Monks and Schmidt [1]. There seems to be consensus that unless additional interventions are implemented, a negative correlation between class size and student achievement is the norm.

By using computer vision and augmented reality technologies, the effect of increased classroom sizes can potentially be alleviated by providing lecturers with real-time student attention statistics. By providing lecturers with continuous feedback while they are in class, will increase the lecturer's ability to address attention problems when

© Springer Nature Switzerland AG 2019
G. Bebis et al. (Eds.): ISVC 2019, LNCS 11845, pp. 383–393, 2019.
https://doi.org/10.1007/978-3-030-33723-0_31

they occur. Basic classroom occupancy statistics can also be generated for class attendance monitoring and the optimal management of venue utilization.

The proposed system to enable lecture venue occupancy and student attention monitoring in a crowded classroom scenes, is shown in Fig. 1. Phase1 receives a video frame as an input. A video camera is placed in front of the classroom (where the lecturer is located) pointing towards the students. By implementing a face detection algorithm on the continues video feed, we are able to continuously monitor the number and position of all students in a classroom.

Once the position of each student is determined, the detected faces are sent to Phase2. Phase2 employs a Deep Convolutional Neural Network (CNN) that is trained to determine if a student is looking "left", "right" or straight at the camera ("center"). Potential distractions in the classroom are then be flagged by the system using an average class attention score.

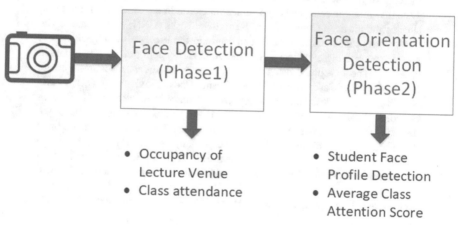

Fig. 1. Occupancy and student monitoring system overview

PHASE 1: Face Detection in Crowded Classroom Scenes

2 Face Detection in Crowded Classroom Scenes

Multiple face detection algorithms were developed over a period of 20 years. They range from classical methods such as Haar Cascade [7], Linear Binary Pattern (LBP) [8], and Histogram of Orientated Gradients (HOG) [9] to more complex and state of the art methods such as Convolutional Neural Networks and Single Shot Detectors. These algorithms were implemented on a Tshwane University of Technology classroom dataset. An example of a video frame is shown in Fig. 2.

The accuracy of each algorithm that was tested is shown in Table 1. These accuracies were determined by calculating the F1 score of each algorithm. To be able to calculate the F1 score successfully, the Precision (1) and Recall (2) of each algorithm is calculated as follows:

Fig. 2. Crowded classroom video frame

$$Precision(P) = \frac{True\,Positives}{True\,Positives + False\,Positives} \tag{1}$$

$$Recall(R) = \frac{True\,Positives}{True\,Positives + False\,Negatives} = \frac{True\,Positives}{Total\,Visible\,Students} \tag{2}$$

The F1 Score (3) is then calculated as follows:

$$F1\,Score = \frac{2 \times P \times R}{P + R} \tag{3}$$

From Table 1 it is seen that the TinyFace CNN implementation from Carnegie Melon University yielded the best results. The TinyFace CNN utilizes parallel CNNs that are optimized for different face sizes in the image frame. As a consequence the TinyFace CNN is able to detect subjects that are located close and far away from the camera. The TinyFace algorithm is therefore ideal to detect faces in a crowded classroom scene. In Fig. 3 example outputs of tested algorithms can be seen. Face detections are indicated with bounding boxes.

Table 1. Face detection test accuracies conducted on crowded classroom dataset.

Face detection algorithms	Accuracy (F1 score)
Haar Cascade (OpenCV [10])	0.48
LBP Cascade (OpenCV [10])	0.40
HOG (DLib [11])	0.26
ResNet CNN (DLib [11])	0.76
TinyFace CNN [12]	0.97
Single Shot Detector [13]	0.70

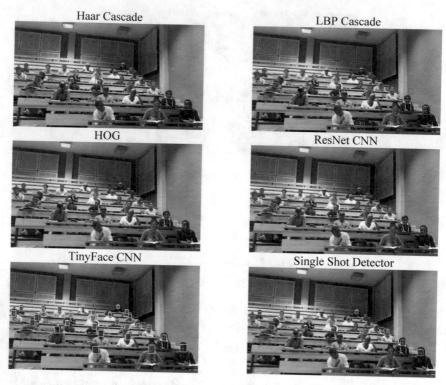

Fig. 3. Phase1: Video frame output for each face detection algorithm

PHASE 2: Face Side Profile Detection Using CNNs

3 Convolutional Neural Network Architectures

Convolutional Neural Networks (CNN) is a class of deep, feed-forward artificial neural networks that have been successfully implemented on images to detect and identify objects. CNNs are based on ordinary Neural Networks that are made up of neurons that have learnable weights and biases. The difference is that CNNs make the explicit assumption that the inputs are images, which allows us to encode specific properties into the architecture, making the forward function more efficient to implement and vastly reducing the number of parameters in the network.

CNNs arrange neurons in three dimensions (width, height, depth). Every layer of a CNN transforms the 3D input volume to a 3D output volume of neuron activations. Several layers are stacked to create an optimal solution.

CNNs have demonstrated recognition accuracies better than or comparable to humans in several visual recognition tasks including traffic signs [2], faces [3, 4], and hand-written digits [2, 5]. CNNs fall short against humans when noise and blurs are added to images [6]. CNNs are more computational intensive compared to traditional machine learning object recognition algorithms, but significantly more accurate.

For Phase2, a variety of CNN architectures have been investigated to find an architecture best suited to detect the side profiles of faces. Each architecture was trained and tested using the same data. The following CNN architectures were implemented: Alexnet; VGG19; Resnet101; Googlenet; Inception V3; InceptionResnet V2; and Densenet201.

3.1   Alexnet

Alexnet is a convolutional neural network designed by Krizhevsky [14]. Alexnet achieved a top-5 error of 15.3% at the ImageNet Large Scale Visual Recognition Challenge in September 2012. The depth of the model was credited for its high performance. Although computationally demanding, by training with GPUs the network becomes more feasible [15].

Alexnet consists of eight layers. The first 5 layers are convolutional layers with maxpooling and the last three layers are fully connected layers. Alexnet uses non-saturating ReLu activation functions.

3.2   VGG19

VGGNet was developed by the Visual Geomeetery Group at Oxford University and won the localization task at the ILSVRC 2014 competition. The VGGNet uses 2 layers of 3×3 filter that effectively covers a 7×7 area [16]. Larger filter sizes as used in AlexNet (11×11) and ZFNet (7×7) is therefore not needed. By reducing the filer size the number of parameters is also reduced. Fewer parameters have to be learned, it converges faster, and the over-fitting problem is reduced. The VGGNet consists of 16 convolutional layers and is very appealing because of its uniform architecture.

3.3   Resnet101

Deep residual learning for image recognition utilizes skip connection, or short-cuts to jump over layers. It is typical that a Resnet model employs double- or triple- layer skips that contain nonlinearities with batch normalization in between [17]. The Resnet model was the winner for 2015 at the ILSVRC competition with a top-5 error rate of 3.6%.

The main motivation for skipping over layers is to solve the vanishing gradients problem by reusing activations from previous layers until the adjacent layer learns its weights. Skipping layers effectively simplifies the network in the initial stages and speeds up learning. The network then gradually restores the skipped layers as it learns the feature space.

3.4   Googlenet/Inception V1

Googlenet (or also known as Inception V1) from Google was the winner of the ILSVRC 2014 competition. It achieved a top-5 error rate of 6.67%. The network uses a CNN model inspired by LeNet [18] but implements a novel element which is dubbed an inception module. It uses batch normalization, image distortions and RMSprop [19]. The Google net architecture consists of 22 layers but with only 4 million parameters compared to the 60 million parameters of Alexnet.

3.5   Inception V3

Google introduced the Inception V3 model with 42 layers. Inception V3 was the first runner up at the ILSVRC 2015 competition. The authors noted that the auxiliary classifiers didn't contribute much until near the end of the training process when accuracies were nearing saturation in the case of Inception V1 and V2. Thus Inception V3 focuses on factorization rather than batch normalization [20].

Inception V3 still utilizes all the optimizations introduced in V2 but incorporates the following optimizations as well: RMSprop optimizer; Factorized 7×7 convolutions; Batch normalization in the Auxiliary Classifiers; and Label Smoothing.

3.6   Inception Resnet V2

The Inception Resnet model is basically hybrid version of an Inception model and Resnet model. The premise of the Inception Resnet model is to introduce residual connections that add the output of the convolution operation of the inception module, to the input [21].

3.7   Densenet201

Problems arise with CNNs when they go deeper. This is because the path for the information from the input layer until the output layer becomes so big, that they can get vanished before reaching the other side. Densenets simplify the connectivity pattern between layers introduced in other architectures. Densenets utilizes several parallel skips to achieve this [22].

Instead of drawing representation power fro extremely deep or wide architectures, Densnets exploit the potential of the network through feature reuse. Densenets requires fewer parameters than an equivalent traditional CNN, as there is no need to learn redundant feature maps.

4   Training

The CVL face dataset [23] was used to train each Deep CNN model to classify a person looking "left", "right", and "center" (directly at the camera). The CVL dataset consists out of 114 subjects with 7 images of each subject. Samples of male and female subjects can be seen in Fig. 4. The dataset is reorganized into "left", "right" and "center". As an example, the first two images in Fig. 4 are categorized as "left", the last two as "right", and the middle three images as "center". This was done for all the individuals in the dataset.

The transfer learning method of retraining a CNN to determine new classifications was used. In most cases the fully connected layer (3rd last layer of the model) was replaced with a fully connected layer of size 3. The last layer of each model is the classification layer, which was replaced with a new classification layer of size 3 ("left", "right", and "center").

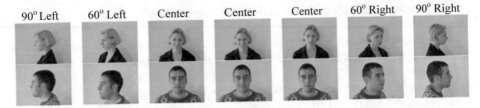

Fig. 4. CVL dataset

5 Testing

The Pointing face dataset [24] was used to test each algorithm to determine the accuracy of each Deep CNN. The Pointing dataset consists out of 15 subjects with 93 images per subject. 4 left, 4 right, and 4 center face profile images were selected from each subject and reorganized into the three categories. The adapted Pointing face dataset, therefore, comprise 60 test images for "left", "right", and "center". A sample of one subject from the Pointing database is shown in Fig. 5.

Fig. 5. Pointing face dataset

Table 2. Comparison of deep CNN models trained on the adapted CVL face dataset and tested on the adapted pointing face dataset.

Deep CNN models	Left profile	Center profile	Right profile	Total accuracy
Alexnet	0.73	0.86	0.98	0.86
VGG19	1.00	1.00	1.00	1.00
Resnet	0.76	0.88	1.00	0.88
GoogleNet	0.93	1.00	1.00	0.97
InceptionV3	0.85	0.98	1.00	0.94
InceptionResnetV2	0.90	0.68	1.00	0.88
Densenet201	1.00	0.93	1.00	0.97

The results of each deep CNN tested on the adapted Pointing dataset can be seen in Table 2.

The Pointing dataset was obtained in a strictly controlled environment with a neutral background. It was, therefore, necessary to also test the models in a real-world environment. A dataset at Tshwane University of Technology was used for this purpose. An example of two test subjects in a lecture hall is shown in Fig. 6. The subjects were recorded at 5 different positions from the camera when looking "left", "right" and "center" at each position. The faces were detected with the use of the TinyFace CNN (stage 1) and cropped out of the original images (Fig. 6) and tested on each Deep CNN model to get real-world accuracies. The results tested on the dataset is shown in Table 3.

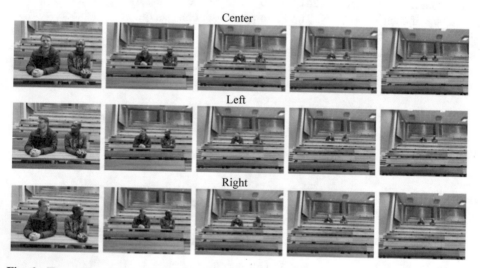

Fig. 6. Two subject looking left, right, and straight at the camera (center) at 5 different positions from the camera.

Table 3. Comparison of Deep CNN models trained on the adapted CVL dataset and tested on the dataset obtained at Tshwane University of Technology.

Deep CNN models	Left profile	Center profile	Right profile	Total accuracy
Alexnet	0.4	0.8	0.9	0.70
VGG19	0.4	1.0	1.0	0.80
Resnet	0.2	0.0	0.9	0.36
GoogleNet	0.3	0.8	1.0	0.70
InceptionV3	0.3	0.5	1.0	0.18
InceptionResnetV2	0.9	0.0	1.0	0.63
Densenet201	0.0	0.0	1.0	0.33

From Tables 2 and 3 we see that the VGG19 CNN model scored the best on each test. In both cases Googlenet obtained the second-best results. It is interesting to note that Googlenet consists of 4 million parameters compared to VGG that have 138 million parameters. It is also interesting to see the difference in accuracy for the Densenet between the two datasets.

Overall VGG19 is the preferred choice to determine if a subject is looking "left", "right", or at the camera in a classroom scenario.

6 Implementation

With the ability to determine how many students are in a classroom (Phase1) and the ability to determine if the students in a classroom are looking at the lecturer (Phase2) it was possible to create an Augmented Reality display for the lecturer in the classroom. This Augmented Reality display is shown in Fig. 7. Phase1 and Phase2 was implemented on a NVIDIA Jetson TX2 development board.

Fig. 7. Augmented reality video frame of a crowded classroom scene.

In Fig. 7 one can see that the students that are not paying attention (assuming that those not looking in the direction of the lecturer/camera are distracted) are indicated with a red box with red stripes. In the right bottom corner, the total number of students, and the average attention score (number of students looking at lecturer divided by the total number of detected students) is shown.

7 Conclusion

For Phase1, the TinyFace CNN face detection algorithm was the best suited to detect faces in crowded classroom scenes. By combining the TinyFace CNN in series with a trained Face Profile Detection VGG19 network, we were able to create an Augmented

Reality display with an attention metric. It is hoped that such an augmented reality display will enable lecturers to better handle larger classrooms and address student attention problems, ultimately improving the success rates of problematic subjects presented to large groups of students.

Acknowledgements. The face images used in this work have been provided by the Computer Vision Laboratory, University of Ljubljana, Slovenia [1, 2].

The training face images from CVL Face Database used in this work have been provided by the Computer Vision Laboratory, University of Ljubljana, Slovenia.

The test face images from Pointing Face Database used in this work has been provided by the ICPR, International Workshop on Visual Observation of Deictic Gestures, Cambridge, UK.

The merSETA chair in Intelligent Manufacturing at TUT is thanked for its financial support.

References

1. Monks, J., Schmidt, R.: The Impact of Class Size and Number of Students on Outcomes in Higher Education. Robins School of Business, University of Richmond. https://www.ilr.cornell.edu/sites/ilr.cornell.edu/files/WP136.pdf. Accessed July 2019
2. Ciresan, D., Meier, U., Schmidhuber, J.: Multi-column deep neural networks for image classification. In: CVPR (2012)
3. Taigman, Y., Yang, M., Ranzato, M., Wolf, L.: Deepface: closing the gap to human-level performance in face verification. In: CVPR (2014)
4. Sun, Y., Chen, Y., Wang, X., Tang, X.: Deep learning face representation by joint identification-verification. In: NIPS (2014)
5. Wan, L., Zeiler, M., Zhang, S., Cun, Y.L., Fergus, R.: Regularization of neural networks using dropconnect. In: ICML, pp. 1058–1066 (2013)
6. Dodge, S., Karam, L.: A study and comparison of human and deep learning recognition performance under visual distortions. arXiv:1705.02498v1 [cs.CV], May 2017
7. Viola, P., Jones, M.: Rapid object detection using a boosted cascade of simple features. In: Conference on Computer Vision and Pattern Recognition (2001)
8. Kushsairy, K., et al.: A comparative study between LBP and Haar-like features for face detection using OpenCV, pp. 335–339 (2014). https://doi.org/10.1109/ice2t.2014.7006273
9. Rekha, N., Kurian, M.Z.: Face detection in real time based on HOG. Int. J. Adv. Res. Comput. Eng. Technol. (IJARCET) 3(4), 1345–1352 (2014)
10. OpenCV. https://www.opencv.org/. Accessed July 2019
11. DLib. http://blog.dlib.net/. Accessed July 2019
12. Hu, P., Ramanan, D.: Finding Tiny Faces. Robotics Institute, Carnegie Mellon. arXiv:1612.04402v2 [cs.CV], April 2017
13. Liu, W., et al.: SSD: single shot multibox detector. In: Leibe, B., Matas, J., Sebe, N., Welling, M. (eds.) ECCV 2016. LNCS, vol. 9905, pp. 21–37. Springer, Cham (2016). https://doi.org/10.1007/978-3-319-46448-0_2. https://github.com/weiliu89/caffe/blob/ssd/README.md
14. Krizhevsky, A.: ImageNet Classification with Deep Convolutional Neural Networks. http://www.image-net.org/challenges/LSVRC/2012/supervision.pdf. Accessed July 2019
15. Krizhevsky, A., Sutskever, I., Hinton, G.E.: ImageNet classification with deep convolutional neural networks. Commun. ACM 60(6), 84–90 (2017). https://doi.org/10.1145/3065386. ISSN 0001-0782

16. Simonyan, K., Zisserman, A.: Very Deep Convolutional Networks For Large – Scale Image Recogntion. arXiv:1409.1556v6 [cs.CV], April 2015
17. He, K., Zhang, X., Ren, S., Sun, J.: Deep Residual Learning for Image Recognition. arXiv: 1512.03385 [cs.CV], December 2015
18. LeCun, Y., et al.: Gradient-based learning applied to document recognition. Proc. IEEE **86**(11), 2278–2324 (1998)
19. Szegedy, C., et al.: Going deeper with convolutions. arXiv:1409.4842v1 [cs.CV], September 2014
20. Szegedy, C., et al.: Rethinking Inception Architecture for Computer Vision. arXiv:1512. 00567v3 [cs.CV], December 2015
21. Szegedy, C., et al.: Inception-v4, Inception-ResNet and the impact of Risudual Connections on Learning. arXiv:1602.07261v2 [cs.CV], August 2016
22. Huang, G., Liu, Z., Weinberger, K.Q., van der Maaten, L.: Densely Connected Convolutional Networks. arXiv:1608.06993 [cs.CV], August 2016
23. Peer, P., et al.: Strategies for exploiting independent cloud implementations of biometric experts in multibiometric scenarios. Math. Probl. Eng. **2014**, 1–15 (2014)
24. Gourier, N., Hall, D., Crowley, J.L.: Estimating face orientation from robust detection of salient facial features. In: Proceedings of Pointing, ICPR, International Workshop on Visual Observation of Deictic Gestures, Cambridge, UK (2014)

Evaluation of the Interpolation Errors
of Tomographic Projection Models

Csaba Olasz[✉], László G. Varga, and Antal Nagy

University of Szeged, Árpád tér 2, Szeged, Hungary
{olaszcs,vargalg,nagya}@inf.u-szeged.hu

Abstract. Tomographic reconstruction algorithms perform reconstruction on a discrete grid, assuming a discrete projection model. However, such discrete assumptions bring artifacts into the reconstructed results, we call interpolation error. We compared eight projection models including the Joseph, Siddon or box-beam-integrated methods for analyzing their interpolation errors. We found that by selecting the proper projection model, one can gain significantly better reconstruction quality.

Keywords: Tomography · Projection · Reconstruction · Interpolation error

1 Introduction

The field of tomography is concerned with the imaging of the slices or intersections of objects [11] in a non-destructive way. This is usually performed by using mathematical tools for reconstructing the structure of the slices from some derived measurements (e.g., transmitted X-rays, reflected ultrasound waves, magnetic resonance, etc.).

In case of transmission tomography the measurements consist of the attenuation of penetrating radiation (X-rays or neutron rays) passing through the object. The attenuations of the beams are proportional to the density of the material along the rays. Therefore, one can calculate the summed density along paths of the beams. The measurements of lines having the same rotation angle are called projections. By taking projections from many different directions it is possible to calculate the densities of the material at each position of an image of a cross-sections.

Real world objects have structures of infinite detail which we cannot handle computationally. Therefore, the reconstruction is usually represented in a discrete digital image, and we also have a representation of the projections on the

We are grateful to the Nvidia Hardware Grant program for providing a GPU for the research. Ministry of Human Capacities, Hungary, grant 20391-3/2018/FEKUSTRAT is acknowledged. This research was supported by the project "Integrated program for training new generation of scientists in the fields of computer science", no EFOP-3.6.3-VEKOP-16-2017-0002. The project has been supported by the European Union and co-funded by the European Social Fund.

© Springer Nature Switzerland AG 2019
G. Bebis et al. (Eds.): ISVC 2019, LNCS 11845, pp. 394–406, 2019.
https://doi.org/10.1007/978-3-030-33723-0_32

discrete grid. This discrete representation results in structured artifacts – i.e., *interpolation error* – in the reconstructed results (see examples in Fig. 4).

Most common interpolation techniques are based on the intersection of projection beams and pixels or an approximation of the connections. For example the Siddon [17] and the Joseph [12] methods were compared on real data in [6], while in [8] the authors investigated the merits of three linear interpolation models. In [9] and [15] the authors used a different approach by representing the connection between voxels and projection lines by different basis-functions. In [9] several local basis-functions were inspected on a phantom. A thorough listing of techniques can be found in [16], where the authors introduced their distance-driven method. Some other approaches try to improve on the quality of reconstruction by improving on existing interpolation techniques. In [5] the authors performed an extensive study on combining Fourier-based and iterative methods against aliasing artifacts. In [20] hexagonal oversampling was applied to get a superior result compared to many interpolation and integration methods.

In this paper, we intend to give a comparison of eight commonly used interpolation techniques to find out their advantages and disadvantages. We evaluate the methods using analytic projections of our specifically designed geometrical phantoms, together with the well known Shepp-Logan, and Forbild head phantoms. We evaluate our findings with three error metrics in an experimental framework designed for assessing interpolation errors in reconstructions. Based on our results, one can find appropriate methods for tomographic reconstruction, and gain reconstructions of better quality.

2   Background

The general task of tomography is to determine the internal structure of an unknown object with the constraint that we know only the projections of the object at given directions [13]. The attenuation coefficients of the material in a two dimensional cross-section are represented by the $f : \mathbb{R}^2 \to \mathbb{R}$ function. The projections of f can be obtained by the Radon transform as

$$[\mathcal{R}f](\alpha, t) = \int_{-\infty}^{\infty} f(t\cos(\alpha) - q\sin(\alpha), t\sin(\alpha) + q\cos(\alpha))dq , \qquad (1)$$

where the (α, t) pair determines a line in the two dimensional space, by giving its direction and distance from the origin, respectively. In this paper we will use parallel beam geometry and assume that a projection consists of projection lines having the same α directions. With (1) the mathematical description of the reconstruction problem can be defined as finding an f', such that $[\mathcal{R}f'](\alpha, t) = [\mathcal{R}f](\alpha, t)$ for all measured (α, t) projection lines.

For the practical applicability we have to make two restrictions on the reconstruction. First, f' has a bounded support, i.e., $f'(u, v) = 0$, with $(u, v) \notin [n/2, n/2)^2$ for a large enough n constant integer. Second, f' takes a constant value on each unit square-shaped area determined by the two-dimensional integer lattice, i.e., $f'(u + a, v + b) = f(u + c, v + d)$, for all $u, v \in \mathbb{Z}$ and for all

$a, b, c, d \in [0, 1)$. With these restrictions the task is to reconstruct an n by n sized image. Note, that the problem of the interpolation error arises from this assumption of a discrete grid. We need this assumption to handle the task computationally, but it distorts the projection model and brings artifacts.

2.1   Reconstruction Techniques

One common approach to produce reconstructed images is the Filtered-Back-Projection (*FBP*) technique that is based on the inversion of the Radon-Transform. This technique gives highly accurate results in a short time provided that a large enough number of projections are available. This means that the projections should be equiangularly positioned on the half circle and we need at least

$$\mathbb{N}_n = \frac{n}{\sqrt{2}}\pi \ , \tag{2}$$

of them to get a theoretically perfect reconstruction [13]. Unfortunately, on a discrete representation the perfect reconstruction only exists in theory, and this technique is also affected by interpolation errors.

Another set of methods are based on reformulating the reconstruction task as a system of equations $\mathbf{Ax} = \mathbf{b}$, where the $\mathbf{A} \in \mathbb{R}^{m \times n^2}$ matrix represents the projection geometry, $\mathbf{b}$ denotes the measured projection vector with $\mathbf{b} \in \mathbb{R}^m$ and $\mathbf{x}$ contains the unknown image pixels to be reconstructed with size of n^2 where $\mathbf{x} \in \mathbb{R}^{n^2}$. The new model enables us to perform the reconstruction as solving a system of linear equations and opens up the way for using various equation system solvers for tomography [4]. From this set of methods, we specifically used the *SIRT* (Simultaneous Iterative Reconstruction Technique [18]) for the reconstructions.

3   Interpolation Methods

If we work with *FBP* we have to apply some interpolation method when we try to build the image from the projections. If we work with *SIRT* we meet with the same problem at the creation of the $\mathbf{A}$ matrix. Since the discretization is necessary, we are interested in finding the proper interpolation methods for a given reconstruction algorithm. In this paper we evaluate the following interpolation methods (the order of the methods in the listing is the same as the order of the methods in Figs. 3 and 8):

- Cubic interpolation with the MATLAB [2] iradon function (*MCubic*).
- Linear interpolation with the MATLAB iradon function (*MLinear*).
- Nearest-neighbor interpolation with the MATLAB iradon function (*MNearest*).
- Spline interpolation with the MATLAB iradon function (*MSpline*). Note, that MATLAB methods are using pixel supersampling.
- Line integral, also known as Siddon method or box-line-integrated using the ASTRA [3] Toolbox (*ALine*).

- Linear interpolation, also known as Joseph method or slice-interpolated using the ASTRA Toolbox (*ALinear*).
- Strip integral, also known as box-beam-integrated using the ASTRA Toolbox (*AStrip*).
- Gaussian-Distance-Interpolation method, which is equivalent to the Gaussian local basis-function based method in [9] (*GDI*), in our own implementation.

4   Performance Evaluation Metrics

The performance of the methods was tested with three error metrics. The Mean-Absolute-Error (MAE) compares an image to a ground truth original and therefore gives an accurate picture of how much pixels differ from the expected value on average. The perfect match is denoted by a value of 0, while there is no upper limit for the produced error, but we normalized the values, so it should be considered to be in the range of [0, 1]. The MAE measures the distortion of the reconstruction, but it does not show the structured error in the reconstructed results. Therefore, we use it to measure the basic goodness of the reconstructions.

The Structural Similarity (SSIM) index also compares an image to a ground truth, but it has been designed to model the people's visual perception as well [19]. The formula $\text{SSIM}(\mathbf{x}, \hat{\mathbf{x}}) = [l(\mathbf{x}, \hat{\mathbf{x}})]^\alpha [c(\mathbf{x}, \hat{\mathbf{x}})]^\beta [s(\mathbf{x}, \hat{\mathbf{x}})]^\gamma$, consist of three terms, namely the $l(\mathbf{x}, \hat{\mathbf{x}})$ luminance, the $c(\mathbf{x}, \hat{\mathbf{x}})$ contrast and the $s(\mathbf{x}, \hat{\mathbf{x}})$ structural term. Furthermore, $\mathbf{x}$ and $\hat{\mathbf{x}}$ are the pictures to be compared. By setting the α, β and γ parameters one can gain different types of information from the metric. By setting a high α exponent to the $l(\mathbf{x}, \hat{\mathbf{x}})$ luminance term, we get a measure that focuses on the difference in intensities. Doing this with a low β and γ value the luminance can suppress the other two terms, therefore, it works similar to the MAE. By omitting the luminance, on the other hand, we get a metric that only focuses on structural differences in the images. Therefore, we use the SSIM with $\alpha = 0$, $\beta = 1$ and $\gamma = 1$ values. Originally the range of the measure is $\text{SSIM}(\mathbf{x}, \hat{\mathbf{x}}) \in (-1, 1]$. If $\text{SSIM}(\mathbf{x}, \hat{\mathbf{x}}) = 1$, then the two compared images are identical. If $\text{SSIM}(\mathbf{x}, \hat{\mathbf{x}})$ is negative, then there is similarity, but in a complementer way. If $\text{SSIM}(\mathbf{x}, \hat{\mathbf{x}}) = 0$, then there is no similarity between the two images. As the applied reconstruction techniques are not designed to produce complementer reconstructions, negative values should be considered errors, and, we replaced negative values by 0. The SSIM is also capable of generating similarity maps, where one can observe the similarities of the images locally for each pixel. We will also be using such tools for depicting the interpolation errors. We will present the SSIM maps in an inverted form for better visibility.

The Haralick texture features evaluate one single image without a ground truth [10]. To define the Haralick features we have to calculate the co-occurrence matrix of one single image. The co-occurrence matrix contains the number of times when two pixel intensities appear together next to each other at a given offset. In our case the offset is always [0, 1], which means, that the two pixels to be examined are the pixel of interest and it's right neighbor. We will present the results of the Haralick Homogeneity feature (HHom), which is between the [0, 1] interval. For a constant image $\text{HHom}(\mathbf{x}) = 1$.

The application of the last two metrics is justified by the fact that the geometric distortions often appear in the form of typical textures or structures. For a better comparability we will be investigating artifacts on originally homogeneous areas. Therefore, we calculate the evaluation metrics in specified regions of interests (ROI), which will be defined later. The perfect reconstruction would have the error values $\mathtt{MAE} = 0$, $\mathtt{SSIM} = 1$ and $\mathtt{HHom} = 1$.

5   Experimental Setup

In our paper, we examined the *FBP* and *SIRT* reconstruction algorithms with the interpolation methods given in Sect. 3. We have involved various software phantoms specified in Sect. 5.1 and considered parameters of the reconstructions described in Sects. 5.2 and 5.3.

5.1   Test Dataset

Our test dataset can be divided in two parts: geometrical phantoms and head phantoms. We generated the sinograms of all test images analytically, calculating the line intersection of the geometrical shapes with the projection lines, with the help of [21]. These sinograms will be the inputs of all interpolation methods.

The geometrical phantoms have the size of 128×128 and they have one object on them. The object can be a circle, ellipsis, ring, rectangle, square or triangle, which are basic geometrical structures. Besides the structure, the objects are variable in size, location and (if possible) rotation angle for a more complete insight. Figure 1 shows some examples from our geometrical phantoms. In the case of geometrical phantoms we specified one ROI with the help of a mask, which excludes all object pixels and their few pixel vicinities. Therefore, the black pixels in Fig. 2(a) are ignored during the error metrics calculation.

Fig. 1. Examples of our geometrical images.

Apart from the geometrical phantoms, we used the Sheep-Logan [14] and the Forbild [21] head phantoms, which are classical test images in computed tomography. We examine the head phantoms with the size of 2048×2048 for better visibility. There are several objects on the head phantoms. For the evaluation we determined 15 ROI-s with the size of 36×36 for both head phantoms shown in Fig. 2.

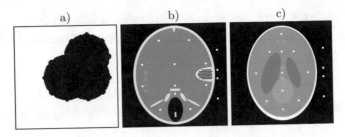

Fig. 2. The mask used for geometrical images shown in (a), while (b) and (c) are illustrations of Forbild and Shepp-Logan head phantoms and the used ROI-s (white squares).

5.2 Projection Number

We performed evaluations with 143, 285, and 428 projections in the case of the geometrical image database and 4550 projections with the head phantoms. Using only 143 projections might show aliasing according to (2), but the evaluation with 285, 428 and 4550 projections must have enough projections for an accurate reconstruction.

5.3 Random Noise of Projections

In practice, tomographic imaging is always exposed to some noise. Commonly accepted solution in simulation studies [7] is modeling the shot noise with Poisson distribution while the detectors electrical noise is usually modeled by Gaussian distribution. We examine both distribution types in our experiments, one at a time. Altogether, we have three noise levels with each distribution and the noiseless case. We set the noise levels based on the signal-to-noise (SNR) ratio of the sinogram. In the case of the geometrical phantoms, the noise levels are 36 dB, 42 dB and 48 dB, while in the case of the high resolution head phantoms the noise levels are 54 dB, 60 dB and 66 dB.

6 Results and Discussion

Here, we will discuss intersections of our results, showing our most important findings. Interested readers can find the full evaluation dataset at [1].

6.1 Geometrical Images

First, we evaluate the results of the geometrical phantoms. Figure 4 illustrates, that variable structures of the objects result in different interpolation error on the reconstructed images. One can notice, that interpolation error is stronger along the line of strong edges, which implies, that the object structure influences the quality of the reconstruction and the interpolation error itself. During this set of evaluations, we will use the average error value calculated for all geometrical phantoms. The results of geometrical phantoms are summarized in Fig. 3, and in Fig. 5.

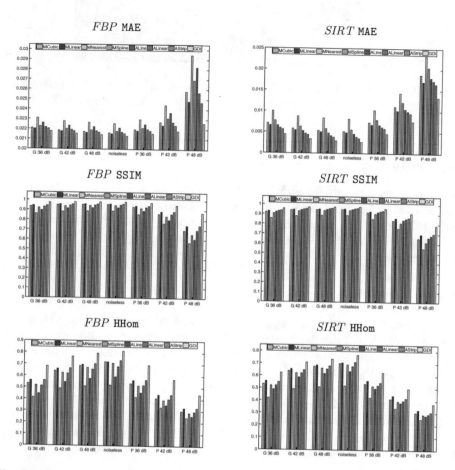

Fig. 3. There are six grouped bar charts in this figure. The columns show the results with *FBP* and *SIRT* algorithms respectively, while the rows correspond to the error metrics MAE, SSIM and HHom. The diagrams show the average error value of the error metrics for the geometrical phantoms with 285 projections. The bars denote the different interpolation methods, which are repeated in groups. In the middle group of the diagrams one can see the noise-free case. To the left form the noise-free case the Gaussian noise, while to the right the Poisson noise are increasing.

In case of 285 projections, looking at the noiseless part of the diagrams in Fig. 3 all the average MAE values are below 0.03, which shows us that the reconstructions quality is acceptable. According to the SSIM value the *MNearest* method preforms the worst in most of the cases. Besides that, the *MNearest* and *ALine* did not work well with *FBP*, while the *ALine* with the *SIRT* was

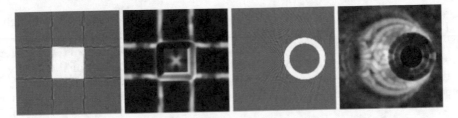

Fig. 4. Illustration of object structure influencing interpolation error. The first and third images show the result of the *ALine* method without noise with 285 projections and *FBP* algorithm. The second and fourth images show the corresponding SSIM maps.

performing much better. The results of the other methods are close to each other, but a notable difference was observed for the benefit of *GDI* method with both algorithms. Based on the HHom measurement the *GDI* method yields the best results with a significant difference.

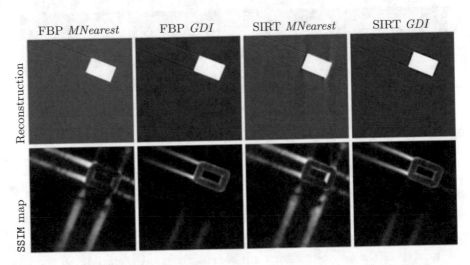

Fig. 5. Two examples of the geometrical phantoms with 285 projections. The first row shows the reconstructed images with the *MNearest* and *GDI* method which have in general the worst and best performance. In the second row one can see the SSIM maps belonging to images of the first row. The figure displays results of the *FBP* and *SIRT* algorithms.

If we look at the effects of noise in the diagrams in Fig. 3, we can say that most the reconstruction algorithm - interpolation method combinations are performing worse with increasing noise. This is however not to the same extent. Moreover it seems that the Poisson type of noise has a greater effect on the reconstruction quality then the Gaussian type. The *MLinear*, *AStrip* and *GDI* methods preform the best among all. Initially, the *GDI* method yields the highest SSIM and HHom values, which decreased to a lesser extent than the others, therefore in the end it has gained a lot of advantage. One can see an example for the effect of the noise on the reconstructions in Fig. 6. The effect of the interpolation error is clearly visible with the middle-level noise, and it is still noticeable with higher levels of noise.

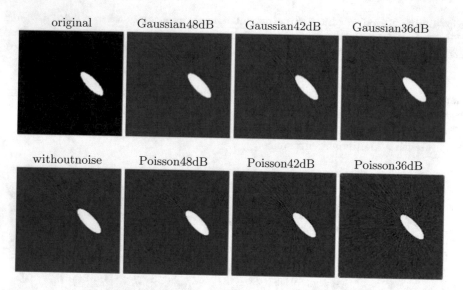

Fig. 6. The effect of noise in case of 285 projections using the *SIRT* reconstruction algorithm with the *ALine* method. In the first column we present the original image, and its reconstruction without noise. From the second column one can see the images with Gaussian noise in the first row, and with Poisson noise in the second row. The amount of noise grows from left to right.

With 428 projection the results are essentially the same as with 285 angles. The quality of the reconstructions are constantly good according to the MAE, while the relations between the performance of the interpolation techniques did not change. With 143 projections, some deterioration can be observed in every case. One can see an example on Fig. 7 to this statement, which was expected since 143 projection are bellow the sampling criteria. Apart from that, no significant changes occurred.

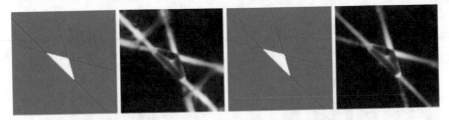

Fig. 7. This figure illustrates the deterioration of the quality with *ALine* method due to the reduced projection number using *FBP*. The first two images are the reconstructed images with 143 projections and its SSIM map, respectively. The second two images are the reconstruction with 285 projections and its SSIM map, respectively.

6.2   Head Phantoms

In case of the head phantoms, the error values were gained as the median value of the ROI-s, because the average value is not reliable if any algorithm performs better in a few ROI-s. Figure 8 summarizes the results of the head phantoms. In the case of the *FBP* and the Forbild head phantom the noiseless results looks similar like with the geometrical phantoms according to the SSIM and HHom. With an increasing noise the SSIM values are decreasing, but not equally. At the highest noise level, the *GDI* has the best performance followed by *AStrip* and *MLinear* with *FBP*. In the case of *SIRT* the differences among the methods are smaller than with *FBP*. This suggests that the iterative algorithm makes the reconstruction less sensitive to the interpolation method. With an increasing noise the HHom values are decreasing, while the differences are reducing between the methods.

In the case of the noiseless results of the Shepp-Logan head phantom the differences between the interpolation methods are barley noticeable with SSIM. But with the noisy case the observed relations were similar to the Forbild head phantom. With HHom the situation is just the opposite. One can see big differences without noise, which is decreasing with increasing noise. We argue this phenomena is natural, because the unstructured noise spoils homogeneity of the image resulting low HHom value with all methods. The noise, on the other hand, can amplify the structured interpolation noise in proportion to its initial size without noise.

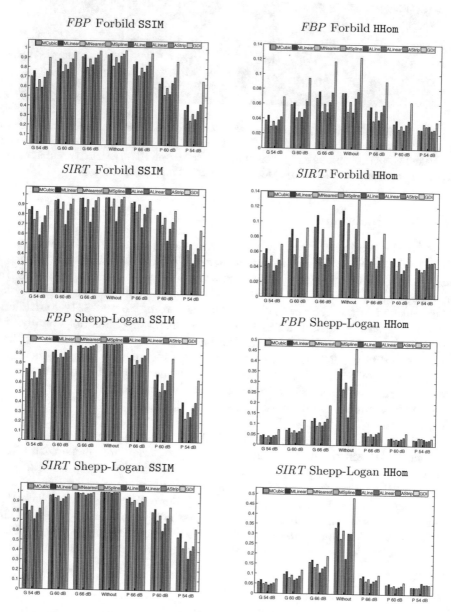

Fig. 8. There are eight grouped bar charts in this figure. The first four on the top shows the results with *FBP* algorithms, while the second four correspond to the results with *SIRT* algorithms. The diagrams show the median value of the previously presented ROI-s for the big images database. The bars denote the different interpolation methods, which are repeated in the groups. In the middle of the diagrams one can see the noise-free case. To the left form the noise-free case the Gaussian noise, while to the right the Poisson noise are increasing.

7   Conclusion

In this study, we examined the errors of discrete projection geometries with different interpolation methods. We did this using two well-known head phantoms in the field of computer tomography, and a set of new test phantoms, which were designed to compare the interpolation procedures. Our observations are, that an iterative algorithm was more robust to interpolation errors, and we can say that selecting the proper interpolation method for modeling the projection is important to gain good quality reconstructions. The more rudimentary interpolation methods like *Nearest* or *Line* produced significantly more artifact, which means that the crisp decisions in the projection models lead to interpolation errors. In our experiments we found, that the best projection geometries were the Linear interpolation-based one with pixel supersampling and the Gaussian-blob based distance driven approaches. In practice we recommend the usage of these two methods, or their combinations.

References

1. Dataset. https://urlzs.com/y1UG3
2. Matlab r2017b. The MathWorks Inc, Natick, Massachusetts, United States
3. van Aarle, W., et al.: Fast and flexible x-ray tomography using the astra toolbox. Opt. Express **24**(22), 25129–25147 (2016)
4. Andersen, A., Kak, A.: Simultaneous algebraic reconstruction technique (SART): a superior implementation of the art algorithm. Ultrason. Imaging **6**(1), 81–94 (1984)
5. Danielsson, P.E., Magnusson, M., Cvl, S.: Combining fourier and iterative methods in computer tomography: analysis of an iteration scheme. the 2D-case 49 (2004)
6. Flores, L., Vidal, V., Verdu, G.: System matrix analysis for computed tomography imaging. PLoS ONE **10**, 1252–1255 (2015)
7. Foi, A., Trimeche, M., Katkovnik, V., Egiazarian, K.: Practical poissonian-gaussian noise modeling and fitting for single-image raw-data. IEEE Trans. Image Process. **17**(10), 1737–1754 (2008)
8. Hahn, K., Schondube, H., Stierstorfer, K., Hornegger, J., Noo, F.: A comparison of linear interpolation models for iterative CT reconstruction. Med. Phys. **43**(12), 6455–6473 (2016)
9. Hanson, K.M., Wecksung, G.W.: Local basis-function approach to computed tomography. Appl. Opt. **24**, 4028 (1985)
10. Haralick, R., Shanmugam, K., Dinstein, I.: Textural features for image classification. IEEE Trans. Syst. Man Cybern. SMC **3**(6), 610–621 (1973)
11. Herman, G.: Fundamentals of Computerized Tomography: Image Reconstruction from Projections, 2nd edn. Springer, London (2009). https://doi.org/10.1007/978-1-84628-723-7
12. Joseph, P.: An improved algorithm for reprojecting rays through pixel images. IEEE Trans. Med. Imaging **1**(3), 192–196 (1982)
13. Kak, A., Slaney, M.: Principles of Computerized Tomographic Imaging. IEEE Press, New York (1999)
14. Shepp, L.A., Logan, B.F.: The fourier reconstruction of a head section. IEEE Trans. Nucl. Sci. **21**(3), 21–43 (1974)

15. Lewitt, R.: Alternatives to voxels for image representation in iterative reconstruction algorithms. Phys. Med. Biol. **37**(3), 705–716 (1992)
16. Man, B.D., Basu, S.: Distance-driven projection and backprojection in three dimensions. Phys. Med. Biol. **49**, 2463–2475 (2004)
17. Siddon, R.: Fast calculation of the exact radiological path for a three-dimensional ct array. Med. Phys. **12**, 252–255 (1985)
18. van der Sluis, A., van der Vorst, H.: SIRT- and CG-type methods for the iterative solution of sparse linear least-squares problems. Linear Algebra Appl. **130**, 257–303 (1990)
19. Wang, Z., Bovik, A., Sheikh, H., Simoncelli, E.: Image quality assessment: from error visibility to structural similarity. IEEE Trans. Image Process. **13**(4), 600–612 (2004)
20. Xu, F., Mueller, K.: A comparative study of popular interpolation and integration methods for use in computed tomography. In: 3rd IEEE International Symposium on Biomedical Imaging: Nano to Macro, vol. 4, pp. 1252–1255 (2006)
21. Yu, Z., Noo, F., Dennerlein, F., Wunderlich, A., Lauritsch, G., Hornegger, J.: Simulation tools for two-dimensional experiments in x-ray computed tomography using the for bild head phantom. Phys. Med. Biol. **57**(13), 237–252 (2012)

Skin Lesion Segmentation Based on Region-Edge Markov Random Field

Omran Salih, Serestina Viriri[✉], and Adekanmi Adegun

School of Mathematics, Statistics and Computer Science,
University of KwaZulu-Natal, Durban, South Africa
omran@aims.ac.za, {viriris,218082884}@ukzn.ac.za

Abstract. This paper presents a probabilistic model based on Markov Random Field (MRF) theory to achieve skin lesion segmentation. MRF theory plays a significant potential role in the image segmentation field. It has several models based on its theory such as region-based MRF model and edge-based MRF model to detect object, boundaries and other relevant information in an image. The proposed method aims to combine the advantages of these two models by computing the product of the regional likelihood function and edge likelihood function. Regional features and edge features are used to solve the maximum a posteriori (MAP) estimation problem to find the best estimation for better image segmentation. The algorithm starts from pre-processing obtained by convolution technique, and iteratively refines the segmentation by taking into account several metrics of region homogeneity under a probabilistic framework. The technical content is described in detail, and the algorithm was tested on the International Skin Imaging Collaboration (ISIC) database, showing its potential. The proposed method shows a significant improvement when compared with individual lesion segmentation methods in ISIC 2018 challenge with overall results achieved as Jaccard Index of 76.40%.

Keywords: Markov random field · Skin lesion · Segmentation

1 Introduction

Malignant melanoma is one of the very rapidly increasing incidences on earth and has a very high mortality rate. Early diagnosis is quite important because melanoma may be cured with prompt excision if detected early [19]. Dermoscopy images play a significant role in the noninvasive early detection of melanoma [4]. However, melanoma detection using human vision alone may be subjective, inaccurate and poorly reproducible even among experienced dermatologists. Obviously this is related to the challenges in interpreting images with diverse characteristics including lesions of varying sizes and shapes, lesions that will have fuzzy boundaries, different skin colors and the clear presence of hair [3]. Automatic analysis of dermoscopy images is therefore an invaluable aid for clinical decision making and for image based diagnosis to recognize diseases like melanoma.

© Springer Nature Switzerland AG 2019
G. Bebis et al. (Eds.): ISVC 2019, LNCS 11845, pp. 407–418, 2019.
https://doi.org/10.1007/978-3-030-33723-0_33

Doctors diagnose about 160,000 new cases yearly of melanoma worldwide. It is most commonly found in women compared to men with high rate of incidence found in Australia, New Zealand, North America, Latin America, etc. [7]. Melanoma is a cancer that starts in melanocytes and is curable if found at early stages. It is most likely to spread to other parts of the body where it is hard to treat and cure when not detected early. Science and technology has helped out to deal with these kinds of skin diseases [34]. One of the common methods which is widely used all over for the detection and the classification of this disease is automatic detection using Computer Aided Diagnosis System. This is the most promising technology now used for the early detection and identification of the disease.

MRF model is a probabilistic graphical model that it uses a statistical way to extract the image segmentation feature as the prior information. This model has been used for removing the noise and reducing the impact of intra-class variation [12–14,17]. MRF model was initially used to segment the image based on its pixels [1,2]. Since spatial neighbouring relationship among pixels is regular, the pixel-based MRF model could conveniently use the spatial contextual information on the lattice. However, the calculation of the pixel-based MRF model is time-consuming, and its small neighbourhood also limits the segmentation accuracy. Hence, many researches have been done to extend the MRF model from the pixel-based to another level such as the edge-based and the region-based [15–17].

Chen et al. [33] stated that region-based MRF models can not overcome all shortcoming of pixel-based MRF models because of various challenges that still effect the image segmentation result, such as the irregular spatial contextual neighbourhood of initial regions and the inaccuracy of the region. However, the region-based MRF can cover the macro texture pattern by employing the region-based information. But it suffers the irregular spatial context which could be solved using the edge-based MRF. Therefore, in this work, we propose a model that possesses the regular spatial context and the description of the macro texture pattern at the same time, by taking advantages of both region-based and edge-based MRF models to solve pitfalls of each model.

2   Related Work

In recent years image segmentation had different approaches based on MRF theory to improve the performance of the segmentation. Wong et al. used Iterative stochastic region merging method [32] that utilised merging strategy to solve an image segmentation problem. Automatic segmentation of skin lesion using MRF that presents a new method to segregate the skin lesions through level set concept with regard to the level of homogeneity and MRF was done by [10]. A hybrid method [11] was developed by combining particle swarm optimization and MRF methods, in order to delineate the border of the lesion area in the images. A Unified Markov Random Field (UMRF) model which is a probabilistic graphical method and provides statistical way to model the image information as the prior information was presented by [33]. Furthermore, the implementation of UMRF model has been used to detect skin lesion segmentation by the authors in [26]. This combines pixel-based and region-based MRF models. An Enhanced Unified Markov Random Field (EUMRF) model [27] which combines various skin lesion features achieved a good skin lesion segmentation accuracy.

Although several models for lesion segmentation have been proposed, but there is still a room of performance improvement. MRF theory has a significant potential role in image segmentation field. It uses (pixels, egions, edges)-based on MRF theory to detect objects, boundaries and other relevant information in an image. In this study we consider combining the benefits of (region, edge)-based on MRF theory instead of considering specific information such as pixel-based MRF theory [10] or the region-based MRF theory [8], or edge-based MRF theory [9]. The main purpose of this paper is to segment skin lesion image using the benefit of both (region, edge)-based MRF theory. Our work focuses on the fusion of complementary benefits in one method for better segmentation.

3 Materials and Method

The proposed method is a probabilistic model based on MRF theory. It take the combination of combines the benefits of two models based on MRF into its account. The proposed method put into account the advantages of two MRF models: the region-based MRF model, the edge-based MRF model. The general overview of the proposed method is as follows: first we apply pre-processing techniques to enhance an input image. Second, an enhanced image is used to extract the regional features, and the edge features. The regional feature is extracted using mean shift method or other methods such as segmented image algorithm (mean shift, Ncut, watershield, turbopixel), which is very important image since it could directly affect the desire segmentation accuracy. The edges of a color image is extracted by the max gradient method to obtain the edge features image. Finally, regional features, and edge features are used to solve the MAP estimation to obtain the best estimation which leads to the desire segmentation.

3.1 Problem Formulation

Let $S = \{s_i | i = 1, 2, \cdots, N \times M\}$ be an input image, where $N \times M$ denote the size of the image and s_i represents each pixel in the image. $X = \{X_s | s \in S\}$ represents the label random field defined on S. Each random variable X_s in X represents the class of pixel s, the class set is $\Lambda = \{1, 2, \cdots, n\}$, where n is the number of classes. $Y = \{y_s | s \in S\}$ represents the observed image defined on S. Let $x = \{x_s | s \in S\}$ an instantiation of the region label field. In the MRF method, the goal of segmentation is to find an optimal estimation of x given the observed image Y, formulated as the following MAP estimation problem:

$$\hat{x} = \arg \max_x P(x|Y), \tag{1}$$

where $P(x|Y)$ is the posteriori, using Bayes' theory, the posterior $P(x|Y)$ in Eq. (1) is equivalent to

$$\hat{x} = \arg\max_{x} P(Y|X)P(X). \tag{2}$$

The proposed method divides the observed image Y into the regional feature $Y^R = \{Y_s^R|s \in S\}$, and the edge feature $Y^R = \{Y_s^E|s \in S\}$ which means $Y = (Y^P, Y^E)$.

$$\hat{x} = \arg\max_{x} P(Y^R|X)P(Y^E|X)P(X). \tag{3}$$

For finding estimation of Eq. (3), the distribution of $P(Y^R|X)$, $P(Y^E, X)$ and $P(X)$ will be described below in details.

3.2   Probability of the Label Random Field

The probability of the label random field $P(X)$ is used to model the label random field X. According to the theory of Harmercley-Clifford [20], $P(X)$ is a Gibss distribution, which is given by

$$P(X = x) = \frac{1}{Z}\exp\left(-U(x)\right), \quad Z = \sum_{x} U(x) \tag{4}$$

where Z is the normalisation factor, $U(x)$ denotes the energy function, that is

$$U(x) = \sum_{s \in S} U(x_s, x_{N_s}), \text{ where } U(x_s, x_{N_s}) = \sum_{t \in N_s} V(x_s, x_t) \tag{5}$$

where N_s is the set of pixels neighbouring pixel s and each $V(x_s, x_t)$ is the potential function between pixel s and pixel $t, t \in N_s$. The potential function $V(x_s, x_t)$ is defined by the multilevel logistic (MLL) model [21], which is

$$V(x_s, x_t) = \begin{cases} \beta & \text{if } x_s = x_t \\ -\beta & \text{if } x_s \neq x_t \end{cases}, \text{ where } \beta > 0 \text{ and } t \in N_s \tag{6}$$

3.3   Conditional Probability Function

The likelihood function in our proposed method has been divided into two parts: The regional likelihood function, and the edge likelihood function. All these functions are described below in more details.

The Regional Likelihood Function. The proposed method used algorithm provided by [33], to extract the regional feature of an input image. It highlighted that one of over segmented should be used to obtain the initial segmentation because it is very important in the final segmentation accuracy. Several methods of over-segmented are proposed in the literature to provide a better over segmentation result, i.e., watershed [5], mean shift (MS) [6], normalisation cut (Ncut) [30], and tuberpixel [20]. In this paper, MS is used to extract the over-segmented.

Then the regional feature formula Y_s^R is applied to extract the spectral value information from over-segmented image for each pixel s. The regional feature Y_s^R is given as follows

$$Y_s^R = p_{R_s} \left[1 - \log(p_{R_s}) \right] + \frac{1}{|N_{R_s}|} \sum_{T \in N_{R_s}} p_T \left[1 - \log(p_T) \right], \tag{7}$$

where R_s represents the initial over-segmented region including s. p_{R_s} denotes the area ratio of the region R_s to the whole image, and N_{R_s} is the set of neighbour regions of R_s. On solving for the likelihood function of regional feature $P(Y_s^R|X)$, the Gaussian distribution have been used to determine the distribution of the likelihood function of $P(Y_s^P|X)$, which is given by

$$P(Y_s^R|X_s = h) = \frac{\sqrt{\alpha} \times \exp \left(\frac{-1}{2} (Y_s^P - \mu_h^P)^T \cdot (\Sigma_h^P/\alpha)^{-1} (Y_s^P - \mu_h^P) \right)}{(2\pi)^{D'/2} \sqrt{\det(\Sigma_h^P)}} \tag{8}$$

Here D' is the dimension of Y_s^R, μ_h^R, and Σ_h^R are the parameters of Gaussian distribution, $\det(\Sigma_h^R)$ is the determinant of Σ_h^R, $1 \le h \le n$, and α is proposed to show the interaction between the regional feature and the edge feature.

The Edge Likelihood Function. Edges of a color image by the max gradient method [9] is used, to extracts the edges of a color image without converting it to grayscale. This clearly shows that a significant amount of information is lost by the standard method, but it is recovered with the max gradient method [9]. The RGB color of each pixel is treated as a 3D vector, and the strength of the edge is the magnitude of the maximum gradient. This also works most especially when the image is in any other dimension (3-dimensional) color space. Direct formulas for the jacobian eigenvalues were used [25] to calculate the maximum eigenvalue (gradient magnitude), so this function is vectorized and yields good results without sacrificing performance.

Assume $f : R^2 \rightarrow rgb, (x, y) \in R^2$ is a continuous color image. The color components will be denote $r(x, y), g(x, y)$ and $b(x, y)$, so that the image as a whole can be denote $f = (r, g, b)$ or, more explicit, $f(x, y) = (r(x, y), g(x, y), b(x, y))$. Let J is the Jacobian, its elements are the partial derivatives of r, g, b with respect to x, y. The edge strength is the greatest eigenvalue of the product of Jacobian and its transpose.

$$J' * J = \begin{pmatrix} \frac{\partial r}{\partial x} & \frac{\partial g}{\partial x} & \frac{\partial b}{\partial x} \\ \frac{\partial r}{\partial y} & \frac{\partial g}{\partial y} & \frac{\partial b}{\partial y} \end{pmatrix} \begin{pmatrix} \frac{\partial r}{\partial x} & \frac{\partial r}{\partial y} \\ \frac{\partial g}{\partial x} & \frac{\partial g}{\partial y} \\ \frac{\partial b}{\partial x} & \frac{\partial b}{\partial y} \end{pmatrix} = \begin{pmatrix} J_x & J_{xy} \\ J_{xy} & J_y \end{pmatrix}. \tag{9}$$

The edge color image is obtained by finding the greatest eigenvalues of Eq. (9), which is given by the following formula:

$$Y^E = (J_x + J_y) + \sqrt{|(J_x^2 - 2J_xJ_y + J_y^2 + 4J_{xy}^2)|}. \tag{10}$$

where Y^E is the edge color image for a whole image. The partial derivatives is obtained using Sobel filter. For solving the likelihood function of edge feature $P(Y_s^E|X)$, the Gaussian distribution have been used to determine the distribution of the likelihood function of $P(Y_s^E|X)$, which is

$$P(Y_s^E|X_s = h) = \frac{\exp\left((Y_s^E - \mu_h^E)^T \cdot (\Sigma_h^E)^{-1} \cdot (Y_s^E - \mu_h^E)\right)}{(2\pi)^{D/2}\sqrt{\det(\Sigma_h^P)}} \tag{11}$$

where Y_s^E is the pixel feature for every pixel s, the Gaussian distribution parameters are μ_h^E, Σ_h^E, and D is the dimension of Y_s^E.

Parameters Setting. The proposed method has six parameters, $\mu_h^R, \Sigma_h^R, \mu_h^E$, and Σ_h^E are used in Eqs. (11) and (8) respectively. Furthermore, they are known as the mean value and the variance value for the Gaussian distribution, which can be calculated as follows.

$$\mu_h^R = \frac{1}{|X^h|} \sum_{s \in X^h} Y_s^R, \quad \Sigma_h^R = \frac{1}{|X^h|} \sum_{s \in X^h} \left(Y_s^R - \mu_h^R\right)' \left(Y_s^R - \mu_h^R\right). \tag{12}$$

$$\mu_h^E = \frac{1}{|X^h|} \sum_{s \in X^h} Y_s^E, \quad \Sigma_h^E = \frac{1}{|X^h|} \sum_{s \in X^h} \left(Y_s^E - \mu_h^E\right)' \left(Y_s^E - \mu_h^E\right). \tag{13}$$

β is the potential parameter in Eq. (6), which is used for finding $P(X)$, and α is used to reflect the interaction between $P(Y_s^R|X_s = h)$ and $P(Y_s^E|X_s = h)$.

   Algorithm 1 shows the steps of proposed practical implementation. Starting with pre-processing for an input images, then extracts the pixel, region, and edge features, finally obtains the segmentation result.

4   Performance Analysis

4.1   Data Sets

ISIC archive is the publicly available dermatology database in ISIC [18] which is used for experimental analysis in this paper. The ISIC has developed the ISIC Archive, an international repository of dermoscopic images, for both the purposes of clinical training, and for supporting technical research toward automated algorithmic analysis by hosting the ISIC Challenges.

4.2   Evaluation Metrics

Lesion segmentation researchers recommend several metrics for performance evaluation, for instance Jaccard Index (JI), Jaccard distance (JD) [23], Rand Index (RI) [24], global consistence error (GCE), and Variation of information (VI) [6]. The Jaccard similarity coefficient measures similarity between finite

---

Algorithm 1. Proposed Method

1: Use convolution technique to enhance an input image Y.
2: Use mean shift to get over-segmented image;
3: Extract the regional feature Y^R from over-segmented image;
4: Use the max gradient method to obtain the edge feature Y^E from pre-processing;
5: Get the initial label field X^0 by using k-mean algorithm the feature into n classes;
6: Start iteration. Set **itr** $= 0$;
7: **while** True **do**
8:     Estimate $\mu_h^R, \Sigma_h^R, \mu_h^E$ and Σ_h^E respectively, $\forall n$ classes given $X^{\mathbf{itr}}$;
9:     Compute: $P(Y_s^R|X_s = h), P(Y_s^E|X_s = h)$ and $P(X_s|X_{N_s})$;
10:    Obtain the best estimation $\hat{x} = \{\hat{x}_s | s \in S\}$ using Eq. (3);
11:    Set $X^{\mathbf{itr}+1} = \hat{x}$;
12:    **if** $X^{\mathbf{itr}+1} == X^{\mathbf{itr}}$ **then**
13:        Stop and $X^{\mathbf{itr}+1}$ is the best segmentation
14:    **if** $X^{\mathbf{itr}+1}! = X^{\mathbf{itr}}$ **then**
15:        **itr** $=$ **itr** $+ 1$
16:        repeat;

---

sample sets, and is defined as the size of the intersection divided by the size of the union of the sample sets:

$$JI(A, B) = \frac{|A \cap B|}{|A \cup B|} = \frac{|A \cap B|}{|A| + |B| - |A \cap B|}, \qquad (14)$$

where $JI(A, B)$ is Jaccard index $0 \leq JI(A, B) \leq 1$. Another Jaccard similarity coefficient is used to measure the similarity between finite sample sets, which is called the Jaccard distance:

$$JD(A, B) = 1 - JI(A, B) = \frac{|A \cup B| - |A \cap B|}{|A \cup B|}. \qquad (15)$$

Here $JD(A, B)$ is the Jaccard distance $0 \leq JD(A, B) \leq 1$.

The RI is a measure of the similarity between two images or (data clusterings). Let N_{TP}, N_{TN}, N_{FP} and N_{FN} represent the number of true positive, true negative, false positive and false negative, respectively. The metric can be defined as:

$$RI = \frac{N_{TP} + N_{TN}}{N_{TP} + N_{TN} + N_{FP} + N_{FN}}. \qquad (16)$$

The GCE measures the extent to which one segmentation can be viewed as a refinement of the other [29]. The related segmentations are considered to be consistent. Since they could represent the same image at different scales. Segmentation is basically a partition of an image into several homogeneous region and the segments are sets of pixels. If one segment is a proper subset of the other, then the pixel lies in an area of refinement, and the error should be zero. If there is no subset relationship, then the two regions overlap in an inconsistent manner. The formula for GCE is given as follows,

$$GCE = \frac{\min \left(\sum_i E(S_1, S_2, p_i), \sum_i E(S_2, S_1, p_i) \right)}{n}, \qquad (17)$$

where, GCE measure takes two segmentations S_1 and S_2 as input, and the output is a real value in the range $0 \leq GCE \leq 1$ where zero signifies no error. We consider the segments in S_1 and S_2 are contains a given pixel p_i.

The VI metric defines the distance between two segmentations as the average conditional entropy of one segmentation given the other, and thus measures the amount of randomness in one segmentation which cannot be explained by the other [29]. Assume we have two clustering (a division of a set into several subsets) X and Y where $X = \{x_1, x_2 \cdots x_k\}, p_i = |x_i|/n, n = \sum k|x_i|$. Then the variation of information between two clustering is:

$$VI = h(X) + h(Y) - 2I(X, Y), \tag{18}$$

where $h(X)$ is the entropy of X and $I(X, Y)$ is mutual information between X and Y. The mutual information of two clustering is the loss of uncertainty of one clustering if the other is given. Thus, mutual information is positive and bounded by $\{h(X), h(Y)\}_{\log 2(n)}$ [29]. The JI used in this paper as a main evaluation metric for segmentation performance same as in ISIC challenge. The other metrics are measured as reference.

4.3   Experimental Results

The proposed method has been implemented on a publicly available database on ISIC [18], showing its potential. Figure 1 shows a few samples of lesion images from our dataset. Furthermore, we assign our result based on extracting the region features and the edge features to address the challenges of skin lesion segmentation. In order to evaluate the segmentation effectiveness of our proposed method, we have presented several evaluation metrics for instance JI, RI, JD, GCE, and VI. In these metrics, large values of JI and RI, and small values for JD, GCE, and VI indicate good segmentation. Table 1 shows the evaluation metric result for the whole sample of the experiments which is depicted in Fig. 1.

4.4   Comparison with Benchmarks

In order to evaluate the segmentation performance of our proposed method, we compared it with several existing frameworks on ISIC. The proposed methods for lesion segmentation in ISIC are selected. The data-driven color augmentation techniques [36], supervised saliency map driven [35], algorithm based on preprocessing, thresholding and neural networks [37], semi-supervised learning technique [22], skin lesions based on fuzzy classification of pixels and histogram thresholding [31], and the k-means clustering and ensemble of regressions [28] are used for comparison. Table 2 shows the accuracy result for each method using two evaluation metric. JI and accuracy (AC) metrics which are used by ISIC for more confidence result. As we observe from Table 2, our proposed method achieved good result JI among the presented benchmark algorithms. The Jahanifar et al. [35] ranks second, i.e., 0.749 is achieved for JI. The proposed method produced the best JI (0.764) which is main evaluation metric in ISIC.

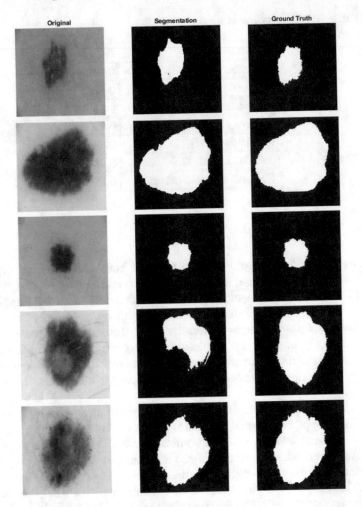

Fig. 1. Samples of lesion images from ISIC database and their segmentation. The first column shows the original images. The second row shows the segmentation result using the proposed method. The third column shows the ground truth of each images.

Table 1. Segmentation performance metric.

Metric	1st row image	2nd row image	3rd row image	4th row image	5th row image
JI	0.602468	0.885360	0.897308	0.579027	0.817017
RI	0.908325	0.896182	0.985626	0.751229	0.875963
JD	0.397532	0.114640	0.102692	0.420973	0.182983
GCE	0.078678	0.097544	0.012992	0.170074	0.118132
VI	0.474315	0.517928	0.094852	0.904797	0.671917

Table 2. Lesion segmentation performances of different frameworks.

Methods	JI	AC
Jahanifar et al. [35]	0.749	0.930
Galdran et al. [36]	0.735	0.922
Gutierrez et al. [37]	0.715	0.910
Alvarez et al. [28]	0.679	0.900
Garcia et al. [31]	0.665	0.884
Jaisakthi et al. [22]	0.665	0.910
Proposed method	**0.764**	**0.928**

5   Conclusion

In this paper, skin lesion segmentation method based on MRF theory is presented. The method combined the two MRF models in its account, which are the region-based MRF model and edge-based model. The proposed method starts from pre-processing of the input images by convolution technique, the algorithm then iteratively refines the segmentation by taking into account several metrics of region homogeneity under a probabilistic framework to address the challenges of skin lesion segmentation in image processing. The technical content is described in details, and the algorithm was tested on a publicly available database showing its potential.

There are two mainly contribution of the proposed method. First, we put into account various type of features, for instance the region size and the region context for the regional feature, and the boundary information for the edge feature. Secondly, this method has incorporated these various type of feature information into the product of the region likelihood function, and the edge likelihood function. The proposed method has been implemented on ISIC database. The results were compared with the frameworks that have been implemented on the ISIC dataset. The JI of the proposed method for skin lesion segmentation 0.764 outperforms the existing traditional algorithm frameworks, which demonstrates its excellent capacity for addressing the challenge. The model can be modified for better result in the future work.

References

1. Besag, J.: On the statistical analysis of dirty pictures. J. Roy. Stat. Soc.: Ser. B (Methodol.) **48**(3), 259–279 (1986)
2. Derin, H., Elliott, H.: Modeling and segmentation of noisy and textured images using Gibbs random fields. IEEE Trans. Pattern Anal. Mach. Intell. **9**(1), 39–55 (1987)
3. Celebi, M.E., et al.: Automatic detection of blue-white veil and related structures in dermoscopy images. Comput. Med. Imaging Graph. **32**(8), 670–677 (2008)

4. Celebi, M.E., et al.: A methodological approach to the classification of dermoscopy images. Comput. Med. Imaging Graph. **31**(6), 362–373 (2007)
5. Chien, S.Y., Huang, Y.W., Chen, L.G.: Predictive watershed: a fast watershed algorithm for video segmentation. IEEE Trans. Circ. Syst. Video Technol. **13**(5), 453–461 (2003)
6. Comaniciu, D., Meer, P.: Mean shift: a robust approach toward feature space analysis. IEEE Trans. Pattern Anal. Mach. Intell. **5**, 603–619 (2002)
7. Detmar, M.: Tumor angiogenesis. J. Invest. Dermatol. Symp. Proc. **5**(1), 20–23 (2000)
8. Jie, F., Shi, Y., Li, Y., Liu, Z.: Interactive region-based MRF image segmentation. In: 2011 4th International Congress on Image and Signal Processing (CISP), vol. 3, pp. 1263–1267. IEEE (2011)
9. Di Zenzo, S.: A note on the gradient of a multi-image. Comput. Vis. Graph. Image Process. **33**(1), 116–125 (1986)
10. Torkashvand, F., Fartash, M.: Automatic segmentation of skin lesion using Markov random field. Can. J. Basic Appl. Sci. **3**(3), 93–107 (2015)
11. Eltayef, K., Li, Y., Liu, X.: Lesion segmentation in dermoscopy images using particle swarm optimization and Markov random field. In: 2017 IEEE 30th International Symposium on Computer-Based Medical Systems (CBMS), pp. 739–744. IEEE (2017)
12. Krishnamachari, S., Chellappa, R.: Multiresolution Gauss-Markov random field models for texture segmentation. IEEE Trans. Image Process. **6**(2), 251–267 (1997)
13. Noda, H., Shirazi, M.N., Kawaguchi, E.: MRF-based texture segmentation using wavelet decomposed images. Pattern Recogn. **35**(4), 771–782 (2002)
14. Xia, Y., Feng, D., Zhao, R.: Semi-supervised segmentation of textured images by using coupled MRF model. In: TENCON 2005-2005 IEEE Region 10 Conference, pp. 1–5. IEEE (2005)
15. Xia, G.S., He, C., Sun, H.: An unsupervised segmentation method using Markov random field on region adjacency graph for SAR images. In: 2006 CIE International Conference on Radar, pp. 1–4. IEEE (2006)
16. Yu, Q., Clausi, D.A.: IRGS: image segmentation using edge penalties and region growing. IEEE Trans. Pattern Anal. Mach. Intell. **30**(12), 2126–2139 (2008)
17. Kuo, W.F., Sun, Y.N.: Watershed segmentation with automatic altitude selection and region merging based on the Markov random field model. Int. J. Pattern Recognit Artif Intell. **24**(1), 153–171 (2010)
18. ISIC: Skin Lesion Analysis Towards Melanoma Detection (2019). https://challenge2018.isic-archive.com/. Accessed 13 June
19. Jerant, A.F., Johnson, J.T., Demastes Sheridan, C., Caffrey, T.J.: Early detection and treatment of skin cancer. Am. Fam. Physician **62**(2), 381–382 (2000)
20. Levinshtein, A., Stere, A., Kutulakos, K.N., Fleet, D.J., Dickinson, S.J., Siddiqi, K.: Turbopixels: fast superpixels using geometric flows. IEEE Trans. Pattern Anal. Mach. Intell. **31**(12), 2290–2297 (2009)
21. Li, S.Z.: Markov Random Field Modeling in Image Analysis, 3rd edn. Springer, London (2009). https://doi.org/10.1007/978-1-84800-279-1
22. Jaisakthi, S.M., Chandrabose, A., Mirunalini, P.: Automatic skin lesion segmentation using semi-supervised learning technique. arXiv preprint arXiv:1703.04301 (2017)
23. Real, R., Vargas, J.M.: The probabilistic basis of Jaccard's index of similarity. Syst. Biol. **45**(3), 380–385 (1996)
24. Recasens, M., Hovy, E.: BLANC: implementing the Rand index for coreference evaluation. Nat. Lang. Eng. **17**(4), 485–510 (2011)

25. Rogers, H.W., Weinstock, M.A., Feldman, S.R., Coldiron, B.M.: Incidence estimate of nonmelanoma skin cancer (keratinocyte carcinomas) in the US population, 2012. JAMA Dermatol. **151**(10), 1081–1086 (2015)
26. Salih, O., Viriri, S.: Skin cancer segmentation using a unified Markov random field. In: Bebis, G., et al. (eds.) ISVC 2018. LNCS, vol. 11241, pp. 25–33. Springer, Cham (2018). https://doi.org/10.1007/978-3-030-03801-4_3
27. Salih, O., Viriri, S.: Skin lesion segmentation using enhanced unified Markov random field. In: Groza, A., Prasath, R. (eds.) MIKE 2018. LNCS (LNAI), vol. 11308, pp. 331–340. Springer, Cham (2018). https://doi.org/10.1007/978-3-030-05918-7_30
28. Alvarez, D., Iglesias, M.: k-Means clustering and ensemble of regressions: an algorithm for the ISIC 2017 skin lesion segmentation challenge. arXiv preprint arXiv:1702.07333 (2017)
29. Sathya, B., Manavalan, R.: Image segmentation by clustering methods: performance analysis. Int. J. Comput. Appl. **29**(11), 27–32 (2011)
30. Shi, J., Malik, J.: Normalized cuts and image segmentation. Departmental Papers (CIS), p. 107 (2000)
31. Garcia-Arroyo, J.L., Garcia-Zapirain, B.: Segmentation of skin lesions based on fuzzy classification of pixels and histogram thresholding. arXiv preprint arXiv:1703.03888 (2017)
32. Wong, A., Scharcanski, J., Fieguth, P.: Automatic skin lesion segmentation via iterative stochastic region merging. IEEE Trans. Inf Technol. Biomed. **15**(6), 929–936 (2011)
33. Chen, X., Zheng, C., Yao, H., Wang, B.: Image segmentation using a unified Markov random field model. IET Image Proc. **11**(10), 860–869 (2017)
34. Xu, L., et al.: Segmentation of skin cancer images. Image Vis. Comput. **17**(1), 65–74 (1999)
35. Jahanifar, M., Tajeddin, N.Z., Asl, B.M., Gooya, A.: Supervised saliency map driven segmentation of lesions in dermoscopic images. IEEE J. Biomed. Health Inf. **23**(2), 509–518 (2018)
36. Galdran, A., et al.: Data-driven color augmentation techniques for deep skin image analysis. arXiv preprint arXiv:1703.03702 (2017)
37. Gutierrez-Arriola, J.M., Gomez-Alvarez, M., Osma-Ruiz, V., Saenz-Lechon, N., Fraile, R.: Skin lesion segmentation based on preprocessing, thresholding and neural networks. arXiv preprint arXiv:1703.04845 (2017)

Centerline Extraction from 3D Airway Trees Using Anchored Shrinking

Kálmán Palágyi$^{(\boxtimes)}$ and Gábor Németh

Department of Image Processing and Computer Graphics,
University of Szeged, Szeged, Hungary
{palagyi,gnemeth}@inf.u-szeged.hu

Abstract. Centerline is a frequently applied 1D representation of 3D tubular and tree-like objects. This paper proposes a new curve skeletonization algorithm, which is computationally efficient, guarantees 1-point wide centerlines, and does not generate 'spurious' branches. The reported method is specifically targeting segmented intrathoracic airway trees but it is applicable to many other tasks. Our algorithm is based on iterative shrinking combined with branch-end detection and preservation.

Keywords: Skeletonization · 3D Centerline · Digital topology · Shrinking · Medical image analysis

1 Introduction

Skeletonization provides region-based shape descriptors, which represent the topology and the general shape of objects [16]. 3D skeleton-like shape features (i.e., medial surface, centerlines, and topological kernel) play important role in various applications in image processing, pattern recognition, and visualization [14].

Surface skeletonization methods produce medial surfaces (i.e., union of 1D and 2D structures), curve skeletonization algorithms are used to extract centerlines (i.e., descriptors containing only 1D structures), and kernel skeletonization provides topological kernels (i.e., minimal sets of points that are topologically equivalent [7] to the original objects). Medial surfaces are usually extracted from general shapes, while tubular and tree-like objects can be represented by their centerlines, and topological kernels are useful in topological description [10,14,17,18].

Thinning is a frequently used approach to produce medial surfaces and centerlines in a topology-preserving way: the outmost layer of an object is deleted, and the entire process is repeated until stability is reached [7,14,17]. Topological kernels are generally produced by (reductive) shrinking [5]. Shrinking is similar to thinning: it is also an iterative object reduction, but geometric constraints are not taken into consideration. Parallel thinning and shrinking algorithms can

© Springer Nature Switzerland AG 2019
G. Bebis et al. (Eds.): ISVC 2019, LNCS 11845, pp. 419–430, 2019.
https://doi.org/10.1007/978-3-030-33723-0_34

delete a set of object points simultaneously, while sequential algorithms scan the picture, and focus on the actually visited single point for possible deletion [5].

Tubular and tree-like structures (e.g., arterial and venous systems, intrathoracic airways, and gastrointestinal tract) are frequently found in living organisms, thus centerlines (as 1D structures) can serve as viewpoint trajectory for navigation purposes in virtual angioscopy, bronchoscopy, or colonoscopy, and help us to generate formal structures for the forthcoming analysis and measurements [9,14,19,20].

In this study, our attention is focussed on the centerline extraction from 3D tree-like objects. Some recent reviews on curve skeletonization are available in [6,13,17,18]. Note that most of the existing centerline extraction methods are rather sensitive to coarse object boundaries, and may produce several spurious side branches. In order to overcome this problem, the false segments included by the produced centerlines are removed by a pruning process (i.e., a post-processing step) [15]. We should note that some existing algorithms are time consuming, and cannot produce 1-point wide centerlines for all possible objects.

This paper proposes a new curve skeletonization algorithm. It guarantees 1-point wide centerlines, preserves the topology, and it is computationally efficient. In addition, its centerlines are free from 'spurious' branches, hence no post-pruning is required. Our algorithm is based on shrinking combined with branch-end detection and preservation. The new method is compared with two existing curve skeletonization algorithms. The two older algorithms also have computationally efficient implementations and they can produce 1-point wide centerlines, too. It is illustrated that the new algorithm is as fast as the two existing algorithms under comparison, but it produces 'more reliable' results.

2 Basic Notions and Results

In this work, we apply the fundamental concepts of digital topology as reviewed by Kong and Rosenfeld [7].

Let p be a point in the 3D digital space $\mathbb{Z}^3$. Let us denote $N_j(p)$ (for $j = 6, 18, 26$) the set of points that are j-adjacent to point p and let $N_j^*(p) = N_j(p)\backslash\{p\}$, see Fig. 1.

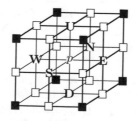

Fig. 1. Frequently used adjacencies in $\mathbb{Z}^3$. The set $N_6(p)$ contains point p and the six points marked **U**, **D**, **N**, **E**, **S**, and **W**. The set $N_{18}(p)$ contains $N_6(p)$ and the twelve points marked '□'. The set $N_{26}(p)$ contains $N_{18}(p)$ and the eight points marked '■'

The sequence of distinct points $\langle x_0, x_1, \ldots, x_n \rangle$ is called a *j-path* (for $j = 6, 18, 26$) of length n from point x_0 to point x_n in a non-empty set of points X if each point of the sequence is in X and x_i is j-adjacent to x_{i-1} for each $i = 1, \ldots, n$. (Note that a single point is a j-path of length 0.) Two points are said to be *j-connected* in the set X if there is a j-path in X between them. A set of points X is *j-connected* in the set of points $Y \supseteq X$ if any two points in X are j-connected in Y. A *j-component* of a set of points X is a maximal (with respect to inclusion) j-connected subset of X.

A $(26,6)$ 3D binary digital picture on is a quadruple $(\mathbb{Z}^3, 26, 6, B)$, where $B \subseteq \mathbb{Z}^3$ is the set of black points (consequently, $\mathbb{Z}^3 \setminus B$ is the set of white points), 26-adjacency and 6-adjacency are used for B and $\mathbb{Z}^3 \setminus B$, respectively. For practical purposes, we assume that all pictures are *finite* (i.e. they contain finitely many black points).

A *black component* or *object* is a 26-component of B, while a *white component* is a 6-component of $\mathbb{Z}^3 \setminus B$. In a finite picture there is a unique infinite white component, which is called the *background*. A finite white component is said to be a *cavity*.

A black point is called a *border point* in a $(26,6)$ picture if it is 6-adjacent to at least one white point. A border point is said to be a **U**-*border point* if the point marked **U** in Fig. 1 is white. We can define **D**-, **N**-, **E**-, **S**-, and **W**-border points in the same way. A black point is called an *interior point* if it is not a border point.

A *reduction* transforms a binary picture only by changing some black points to white ones (which is referred to as the deletion of black points). A reduction is *not* topology-preserving [7] if any object in the input picture is split (into several ones) or is completely deleted, any cavity in the input picture is merged with the background or another cavity, or a cavity is created where there was none in the input picture. There is an additional concept called *tunnel* (which donuts have) in 3D pictures [7]. Topology preservation implies that eliminating or creating any tunnel is not allowed.

A black point is *simple* if and only if its deletion is a topology-preserving reduction [7]. The following theorem states a characterization of simple points in $(26,6)$ pictures:

Theorem 1. [8,12] *A black point p is simple in picture $(\mathbb{Z}^3, 26, 6, B)$ if and only if all of the following conditions hold:*

1. *The set $N_{26}^*(p) \cap B$ contains exactly one 26–component.*
2. *The set $N_6(p) \setminus B$ is not empty (i.e., p is a border point).*
3. *Any two points in $N_6(p) \setminus B$ are 6–connected in the set $N_{18}(p) \setminus B$.*

Based on Theorem 1, the simplicity of a point p can be decided by examining the set $N_{26}^*(p)$ (i.e., it is a local property).

3D curve-thinning algorithms generally preserve curve-end points:

Definition 1. *A (simple) black point p in picture $(\mathbb{Z}^3, 26, 6, B)$ is a curve-end point of type if the set $N_{26}^*(p) \cap B$ contains exactly one point (i.e., p is 26-adjacent to exactly one further black point).*

Bertrand and Couprie proposed an alternative approach for curve-thinning by accumulating some curve interior points that are called isthmuses [2].

Definition 2. *A border point p in a picture $(\mathbb{Z}^3, 26, 6, B)$ is a curve-isthmus if the set $N_{26}^*(p) \cap B$ contains more than one 26–component.*

All curve-isthmuses are not simple points since Condition 1 of Theorem 1 is violated. Note that the characterization of curve-isthmuses examines the set $N_{26}^*(p)$ for a point p in question.

Figure 2 presents examples of simple, curve-end, and curve-isthmus points.

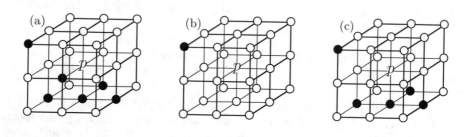

Fig. 2. Configuration in which the central black point p is a simple point (a), a curve-end point (b), and a curve-isthmus point (c). Black and white points are marked '●' and 'O', respectively

3 Curve Skeletonization Based on Shrinking

In this section the curve skeletonization algorithm **3D-CS-APS** is presented. The reported method is specifically targeting segmented intrathoracic airway trees but it is applicable to many other tasks. The input of our algorithm is a 3D $(26, 6)$ picture representing a segmented volumetric tree object. The method consists of the following four steps:

1. identification of the tree root as an anchor point (see Fig. 3a),
2. the first k iterations of anchor-preserving shrinking (see Fig. 3b),
3. detection of curve-end points as further anchor points (see Fig. 3c), and
4. anchor-preserving shrinking until stability is reached (see Fig. 3d).

These steps are now described in more detail.

Step 1: Root Detection
The root detection is not a critical phase of the process. Since we deal with intrathoracic airway trees segmented from volumetric CT (or MR) image data, a priori knowledge of the data set can be used to identify the tree root. In [9], the center of the topmost nonzero 2D slice in direction z (detected by 2D shrinking)

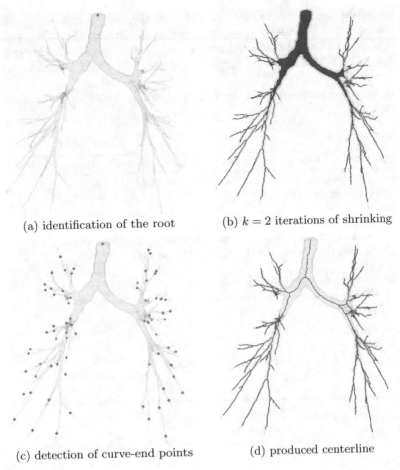

(a) identification of the root   (b) $k = 2$ iterations of shrinking

(c) detection of curve-end points   (d) produced centerline

Fig. 3. The four steps of algorithm **3D-CS-APS** for a human airway tree. The detected anchor points (a,c) and the resulted structures (b,d) are superimposed on the input tree

defines the root of the tree. (Note that the identified root point belongs to the trachea.) In other applications, different root identification approaches may be needed.

The detected root point (see Fig. 3a) acts as an *anchor point* in the remaining steps of the process (i.e., it cannot be deleted further on).

Step 2: Anchor Preserving Interrupted Shrinking

We make use of the fact that the trachea of a human airway tree is the thickest branch, and the terminating branches are the thinnest ones. Hence a given number of shrinking iterations produce 1-point wide terminating branches that end with curve-end points, and no further curve-end points are generated in the 'thicker' branches (see Fig. 3b).

Many researchers proposed 3D parallel shrinking algorithms [1,10]. Here we present a new 6-subiteration sequential anchor-preserving shrinking algorithm capable of producing 1-point wide structures. Hence, centerlines produced by algorithm **3D-CS-APS** contain only non-simple points and (simple) curve-end points.

One iteration step of our anchor-preserving shrinking is outlined by Algorithm 1.

Algorithm 1:   One Iteration Step of the Anchor-Preserving Shrinking

---

Input: picture $(\mathbb{Z}^3, 26, 6, X)$ and set of anchor points $Anchors \subseteq X$
Output: picture $(\mathbb{Z}^3, 26, 6, Y)$
$Y \leftarrow X$
foreach direction $d \in \{\mathbf{U,N,E,S,W,D}\}$ **do**
    // Subiteration according to the deletion direction d
    // Collecting potentially deletable points
    $Z \leftarrow \emptyset$
    foreach point $p \in (Y \setminus Anchors)$ **do**
        if p is a d-border and simple point in $(\mathbb{Z}^3, 26, 6, Y)$ **then**
            $\lfloor Z \leftarrow Z \cup \{p\}$
    // Deletion
    foreach point $p \in Z$ **do**
        if p is a simple point in $(\mathbb{Z}^3, 26, 6, Y)$ **then**
            $\lfloor Y \leftarrow Y \setminus \{p\}$

Algorithm 1 (i.e., one iteration step of our anchor-preserving shrinking algorithm) is decomposed into six successive subiterations according to the six main directions in 3D, and each subiteration consists of two phases. First, black points that are not anchor points are traversed. If the given point is a border point of the actual type and simple point (in the input picture), it is marked as a potentially deletable point. In the second phase, a marked point is deleted if it remains simple after the deletion of the previously visited marked points.

Depending on the 'thickness' of the terminating branches of the segmented tree, we apply k iterations of shrinking (and the iterative peeling is interrupted). In this step, the set of anchor points is singleton in each iteration, it contains only the root point (detected in the first step of the process).

Step 3: Detection of Curve-End Points

This step is fairly straightforward: all curve-end points (see Definition 1) in the structure produced by the second step of the process are to be identified (see Fig. 3c). These points and the root point form the set of anchor points for the last step.

Step 4: Anchor Preserving Final Shrinking
The proposed process is completed by anchor preserving shrinking until stability is reached. This step forms 1-point wide centerlines of airway trees by connecting the root point and the ends of terminating branches (see Fig. 3d).

Since the proposed sequential shrinking algorithm may delete just one simple point at a time, the entire process preserves the topology.

4 Computationally Efficient Implementation

One may think that the proposed curve skeletonization algorithm (see Sect. 3) is time-consuming, and it is rather difficult to implement it. That is why Algorithm 2 presents a computationally efficient implementation of the proposed algorithm **3D-CS-APS**. Note that similar implementation schemes were proposed by Palágyi et al. [9,10] for arbitrary sequential and parallel thinning algorithms.

The input of Algorithm 2 is array A which stores the $(26, 6)$ picture with the tree-like object to be represented. In input array A, the value '1' corresponds to black points and the value '0' is assigned to white ones. According to the proposed scheme, the input and the output pictures can be stored in the same array, hence array A will contain the produced centerline.

We use two lists to speed up the process: *border_list* stores the border points in the current picture (hence the repeated scans of the entire array A are avoided), and *potentially_deletable_list* is to collect all potentially deletable points in the current subiteration of the anchor preserving shrinking. (Note that *potentially_deletable_list* is a sublist of *border_list*.) In order to avoid storing more than one copy of a border point in *border_list*, and examining anchor points for possible deletion, array A represents a four-color picture:

- the value of '0' corresponds to white points,
- the value of '1' is assigned to (black) interior points,
- the value of '2' corresponds to (black) border points in the actual picture (i.e., elements of *border_list*), and
- the value of '3' is assigned to the detected (black) anchor points.

First, the root point (i.e., the initial anchor point) is identified by the function 'ROOT_DETECTION'. Then the input picture is scanned, and all the border points in it are inserted into the list *border_list*. We should note that it is the only time-consuming scan in the entire process.

The next step is the first k iterations of anchor-preserving shrinking. We use a pre–calculated look-up-table to encode simple points. Simple points in $(26, 6)$ pictures can be locally characterized; this property for a point p can be decided by examining the set $N_{26}^*(p)$ that contains 26 points (see Theorem 1). Hence the pre-calculated look-up-table has 2^{26} entries of 1 bit in size. It is clear that our look-up-table requires just 8 megabytes of storage space in memory.

Algorithm 2:   Efficient Implementation of Algorithm **3D-CS-APS**

Input: array A storing the segmented tree and number of iterations k
Output: array A containing the picture with the produced centerline
// Step 1 - identification of the tree root
$(x, y, z) \leftarrow$ ROOT_DETECTION (A); $A[x, y, z] \leftarrow 3$;
// Collect border points
$border\_list \leftarrow$ <empty list>;
foreach $p = (x, y, z)$ in array A **do**
    if $A[x, y, z] = 1$ and p is a border point **then**
        $border\_list \leftarrow border\_list + <p>$; $A[x, y, z] \leftarrow 2$;

// Step 2 - the first k iterations of anchor-preserving shrinking
for $i \leftarrow 1$ **to** k **do**
    foreach direction $d \in \{$**U,N,E,S,W,D**$\}$ **do**
        $potentially\_deletable\_list \leftarrow$ <empty list>;
        foreach point p in $border\_list$ **do**
            if p is a d-border and simple point **then**
                $potentially\_deletable\_list \leftarrow potentially\_deletable\_list + <p>$;

        foreach point $p = (x, y, z)$ in $potentially\_deletable\_list$ **do**
            if p is a simple point **then**
                $A[x, y, z] \leftarrow 0$; $border\_list \leftarrow border\_list - <p>$;
                foreach point $q = (x', y', z')$ that is 6-adjacent to p **do**
                    if $A[x', y', z'] = 1$ **then**
                        $A[x', y', z'] \leftarrow 2$; $border\_list \leftarrow border\_list + <q>$;

// Step 3 - detection of curve-end points
foreach point $p = (x, y, z)$ in $border\_list$ **do**
    if p is a curve-end point **then**
        $A[x, y, z] \leftarrow 3$; $border\_list = border\_list - <p>$;

// Step 4 - anchor-preserving shrinking
repeat
    $number\_of\_deleted\_points = 0$;
    foreach direction $d \in \{$**U,N,E,S,W,D**$\}$ **do**
        $potentially\_deletable\_list \leftarrow$ <empty list>;
        foreach point p in $border\_list$ **do**
            if p is a d-border and simple point **then**
                $potentially\_deletable\_list \leftarrow potentially\_deletable\_list + <p>$;

        foreach point $p = (x, y, z)$ in $potentially\_deletable\_list$ **do**
            if p is a simple point **then**
                $A[x, y, z] \leftarrow 0$; $border\_list = border\_list - <p>$;
                $number\_of\_deleted\_points = number\_of\_deleted\_points +1$;
                foreach point $q = (x', y', z')$ that is 6-adjacent to p **do**
                    if $A[x', y', z'] = 1$ **then**
                        $A[x', y', z'] \leftarrow 2$; $border\_list \leftarrow border\_list + <q>$;

until $number\_of\_deleted\_points = 0$;

Each subiteration of the anchor preserving shrinking is a 2-phase process: First, simple border points of the actual type that are added to the *potentially_deletable_list*. In the second phase, a point in the *potentially_deletable_list* is deleted if it remains simple after the deletion of the previously visited and deleted points. If a border point is deleted, all interior points that are 6-adjacent to it become border points. These brand new border points of the resulted picture are added to the *border_list*.

The third step of algorithm **3D-CS-APS** is fairly simple. Since all curve-end points are border points, only points in the *border_list* are to be examined. The detected curve-end points are removed from the *border_list* and the value of '3' is assigned to these new anchor points.

The last step of algorithm **3D-CS-APS** is the ultimate anchor preserving shrinking. The number of deleted points within an iteration step is stored in the variable *number_of_deleted_points*. The algorithm terminates when stability is reached (i.e., $number\_of\_deleted\_points = 0$). Then all points having a nonzero value belong to the produced centerline.

5 Experiments

In experiments, the proposed algorithm **3D-CS-APS** is compared with two existing curve skeletonization algorithms:

- Palágyi et al. [9] suggested a 6-subiteration sequential curve thinning algorithm named **PTHS_2006**. It uses endpoint-rechecking: a curve-end point (see Definition 1) can be deleted if at least t points of its 6-neighbors have been deleted during the actual subiteration. According to the experiences, setting $t = 1$ is suggested for human airway trees.
- In [11], Palágyi proposed an isthmus-based 6-subiteration sequential curve thinning algorithm named **P_2014**. This algorithm accumulates and preserves curve-isthmus points (see Definition 2), while non-accumulated curve-end points are deleted.

We selected these two existing algorithms, since they also have computationally efficient implementations. In addition, the selected algorithms can also produce 1-point wide centerlines for all possible 3D objects.

The three curve skeletonization algorithms (i.e., **PTHS_2006**, **P_2014**, and **3D-CS-APS**) were tested on various segmented intrathoracic airway trees. Due to the lack of space, here we can present just two illustrative examples, see Figs. 4 and 5. We can state that the existing algorithms **PTHS_2006** and **P_2014** generate some unwanted side branches due to the coarse object boundary. Thanks to the anchor-preserving shrinking, centerlines produced by the proposed algorithm **3D-CS-APS** are free from 'spurious' branches. Hence, our method do not require post-pruning. We should note that algorithm **3D-CS-APS** slightly trims the terminating branches.

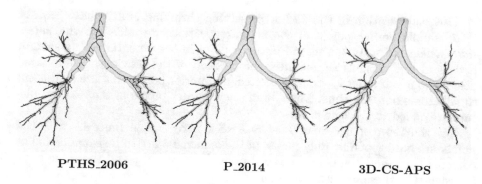

PTHS_2006   **P_2014**   **3D-CS-APS**

Fig. 4. Centerlines produced by the three curve skeletonization algorithms superimposed on a $512 \times 512 \times 509$ image of a segmented human airway tree (with 'noisy' boundary)

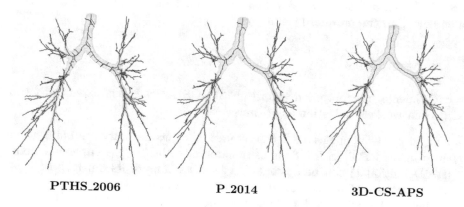

PTHS_2006   **P_2014**   **3D-CS-APS**

Fig. 5. Centerlines produced by the three curve skeletonization algorithms superimposed on a $512 \times 512 \times 490$ image of a segmented human airway tree (with 'noisy' boundary)

Table 1 illustrates the efficiency of the proposed algorithm **3D-CS-APS** on 12 human airway trees, and validates quantitatively its superiority over the two examined two methods. The examined algorithms were run on a usual PC under Linux (Fedora 27 - 64 bit), using a 3.30 GHz 4x Intel Core i5-2500 CPU. (Note, that just the centerline extraction process itself is considered here; reading the input volume and writing the output image are not taken into account.) We can state that the computational complexity of the selected three curve skeletonization algorithms are extremely low, they are much faster than the concurrent methods [3,4,6,19,20].

Table 1. Computation time (in sec.) by the three algorithms on 12 human airway trees (with 'noisy' boundaries). The image size ($512 \times 512 \times dim\_z$) and the number of branches (#branch) in the produced centerlines and are also given. Parameter settings: $t = 1$ for **PTHS_2006**, and $k = 1$ for **3D-CS-APS**. Note that the proposed algorithm **3D-CS-APS** does not produce visible unwanted side branches, and do not miss visually obvious branches.

Test object	Size (dim_z)	PTHS_2006		P_2014		3D-CS-APS	
		Time	#branch	Time	#branch	Time	#branch
Tree 1	436	0.31	120	0.30	93	0.29	75
Tree 2	537	0.36	111	0.35	90	0.35	74
Tree 3	557	0.34	37	0.34	32	0.33	27
Tree 4	490	0.30	44	0.30	38	0.29	31
Tree 5	490	0.33	135	0.32	116	0.32	93
Tree 6	459	0.29	57	0.29	49	0.28	42
Tree 7	387	0.24	26	0.23	22	0.23	19
Tree 8	349	0.22	45	0.22	31	0.21	23
Tree 9	389	0.25	53	0.24	37	0.24	32
Tree 10	509	0.34	83	0.33	72	0.32	61
Tree 11	509	0.40	124	0.38	100	0.39	82
Tree 12	556	0.34	63	0.33	47	0.32	41

6 Conclusions

In this paper, a new algorithm is proposed for producing centerlines from binary 3D tree-like objects. It is based on interrupted anchor-preserving shrinking, hence the produced centerlines do not contain 'spurious' branches. Our method is usable for tree-like objects in which each 'important' terminating branch ends with a curve-end points after a given number of shrinking iterations. The proposed algorithm is computationally efficient and preserves the topology. Quantitative experiments on intrathoracic airway trees have demonstrated that the new method outperforms two existing curve skeletonization algorithms.

Acknowledgments. This research was supported by the project "Integrated program for training new generation of scientists in the fields of computer science", no EFOP-3.6.3-VEKOP-16-2017-0002. The project has been supported by the European Union and co-funded by the European Social Fund.

References

1. Bertrand, G., Couprie, M.: Powerful parallel and symmetric 3D thinning schemes based on critical kernels. J. Math. Imaging Vis. **48**, 134–148 (2014)

2. Bertrand, G., Couprie, M.: Transformations topologiques discrètes. In: Coeurjolly, D., Montanvert, A., Chassery, J. (eds.) Géométrie discrète et images numériques, pp. 187–209. Hermès Science Publications (2007)
3. Bitter, I., Kaufman, A.E., Sato, M.: Penalized-distance volumetric skeleton algorithm. IEEE Trans. Vis. Comput. Graph. **7**, 195–206 (2001)
4. Bouix, S., Siddiqi, K., Tannenbaum, A.: Flux driven automatic centerline extraction. Med. Image Anal. **9**, 209–221 (2005)
5. Hall, R.W., Kong, T.Y., Rosenfeld, A.: Shrinking binary images. In: Kong, T.Y., Rosenfeld, A. (eds.) Topological Algorithms for Digital Image Processing, pp. 31–98. Elsevier Science B. V. (1996)
6. Jin, D., Chen, C., Hoffman, E.A., Saha, P.K.: Curve skeletonization using minimum-cost path. In: Saha, P.K., Borgefors, G., Sanniti di Baja, G. (eds.) Skeletonization: Theory, Methods and Applications, pp. 151–180. Academic Press (2017)
7. Kong, T.Y., Rosenfeld, A.: Digital topology: introduction and survey. Comput. Vis. Graph. Image Process. **48**, 357–393 (1989)
8. Malandain, G., Bertrand, G.: Fast characterization of 3D simple points. In: Proceedings of the 11th IEEE International Conference on Pattern Recognition, ICPR 1992, pp. 232–235 (1992)
9. Palágyi, K., Tschirren, J., Hoffman, E.A., Sonka, M.: Quantitative analysis of pulmonary airway tree structures. Comput. Biol. Med. **36**, 974–996 (2006)
10. Palágyi, K., Németh, G., Kardos, P.: Topology preserving parallel 3D thinning algorithms. In: Brimkov, V.E., Barneva, R.P. (eds.) Digital Geometry Algorithms. Theoretical Foundations and Applications to Computational Imaging, pp. 165–188. Springer, Dordrecht (2012). https://doi.org/10.1007/978-94-007-4174-4_6
11. Palágyi, K.: A sequential 3D curve-thinning algorithm based on isthmuses. In: Bebis, G., et al. (eds.) ISVC 2014. LNCS, vol. 8888, pp. 406–415. Springer, Cham (2014). https://doi.org/10.1007/978-3-319-14364-4_39
12. Saha, P.K., Chaudhury, B.B.: Detection of 3-D simple points for topology preserving transformations with application to thinning. IEEE Trans. Pattern Anal. Mach. Intell. **16**, 1028–1032 (1994)
13. Saha, P.K., Borgefors, G., Sanniti di Baja, G.: A survey on skeletonization algorithms and their applications. Pattern Recogn. Lett. **76**, 3–12 (2016)
14. Saha, P.K., Borgefors, G., Sanniti di Baja, G. (eds.): Skeletonization: Theory, Methods and Applications. Academic Press, Cambridge (2017)
15. Shaked, D., Bruckstein, A.: Pruning medial axes. Comput. Vis. Image Underst. **69**, 156–169 (1998)
16. Siddiqi, K., Pizer, S. (eds.): Medial Representations – Mathematics, Algorithms and Applications. Computational Imaging and Vision, vol. 37. Springer, Dordrecht (2008). https://doi.org/10.1007/978-1-4020-8658-8
17. Sobiecki, A., Jalba, A., Telea, A.: Comparison of curve and surface skeletonization methods for voxel shapes. Pattern Recogn. Lett. **47**, 147–156 (2014)
18. Tagliasacchi, A., Delame, T., Spagnuolo, M., Amenta, N., Telea, A.: 3D skeletons: a state-of-the-art report. In: Proceedings of the Conference on European Association for Computer Graphics, EG 2016, pp. 573–597 (2016)
19. Wan, M., Liang, Z., Ke, Q., Hong, L., Bitter, I., Kaufman, A.: Automatic centerline extraction for virtual colonoscopy. IEEE Trans. Med. Imaging **21**, 1450–1460 (2002)
20. Wong, W.C.K., So, R.W.K., Chung, A.C.S.: Principal curves for lumen center extraction and flow channel width estimation in 3-D arterial networks: theory, algorithm, and validation. IEEE Trans. Image Process. **21**, 1847–1862 (2012)

A 360° Video Virtual Reality Room Demonstration

Robin Horst[✉], Savina Diez, and Ralf Dörner

RheinMain University of Applied Sciences, Wiesbaden, Germany
{robin.horst,savina.diez,ralf.dorner}@hs-rm.de
http://www.hs-rm.de/

Abstract. The "third mission" of higher education institution demands them to closely engage with the general society and stakeholders in the economy. An established method to do so is giving demos of different laboratories at events like open house days. 360° Virtual Reality (VR) can be a valuable medium in such settings, especially when laboratories or exhibits in these rooms cannot easily be visited. A fundamental task in such VR applications is to highlight important elements in this room to guide the user's attention. The creation of these cues for highlighting in 360° video VR is already a non-trivial task itself. It is even more challenging for laymen in the field of VR who want to introduce their laboratory.

In this paper we propose a 360° demo concept that allows presenters to virtually introduce rooms, like laboratories, to laymen in the field of VR, such as visitors of open house events at universities. We describe an implementation of our demo concept and give insights in the authoring work flow. A challenge that arises during the authoring of video-based VR demos is the mandatory interdisciplinary knowledge. Programming skills and specific knowledge in the field of 3D modeling is necessary as for common 3D model-based VR. But furthermore, the recording of videos and the integration of domain-specific knowledge and involvement actors in these videos is crucial for VR demos. In an in-the-wild user study we evaluate our demo concept and show that it is well-accepted by the targeted audience.

Keywords: Virtual reality · Content creation · Authoring · Knowledge demonstration

1 Introduction

The integration of Virtual Reality (VR) and Augmented Reality (AR) as a novel medium in different educational [9] or marketing [20] related settings gains important in the recent decades. This trend also influences events at universities and similar institutions. The so called "third mission" [4,8] demands of these institutions to engage closely with the general society and stakeholders in the

© Springer Nature Switzerland AG 2019
G. Bebis et al. (Eds.): ISVC 2019, LNCS 11845, pp. 431–442, 2019.
https://doi.org/10.1007/978-3-030-33723-0_35

economy. VR and AR can be utilized within the field of Knowledge Demonstration (KD) for this purpose [14].

One way to engage people with the universities is to host events like open house days or to participate in public events. Giving research demos and introducing the associated laboratories are common procedures at these events. But this can not always be carried out easily. Depending on the type of research or laboratory, restrictions may apply. Demos may be dangerous for non-trained people and laboratory equipment may not be transportable at all. To illustrate this challenge we will take a look at an example: A professor for technical optics and photonics runs a laboratory within the university that contains a high performance femtosecond laser. The room itself contains stationary equipment. It furthermore is subject to strict safety regulations. The professor therefore (1) is dependent on visitors to come to this laboratory instead of bringing the laboratory equipment to a certain event and (2) is only able to guide very small groups through the laboratory at once.

In this paper, we propose a concept that makes use of current 360° video and mobile VR hardware to present virtual copies of existing rooms as such laboratories.

We make the following contributions:

1. We propose a demo concept that allows presenters to virtually present an existing room using only consumer-oriented and mobile VR hardware.
2. We give a proof-of-concept and describe the implementation for a specific use-case. Furthermore, we give insights in the authoring processes that were needed to implement our concept.
3. Within an in-the-wild user study we evaluate the acceptance of the target laymen users. We indicate that the demo was well-accepted by our participants.

This paper is organized as follows: After this introductory section we present related work that relates to presenting existing rooms with virtual technology. Section 3 describes the main concept of presenting a natural science laboratory in 360° video VR. In Sect. 4, we describe our prototype implementation and show the feasibility of the proposed concepts. In Sect. 5, we present the user study that evaluate the VR demo concept. A conclusion and future work section completes this paper.

2   Related Work

In this section, we relate our work to state of the art in the field of presenting an existing real-world room with the medium of VR.

Authoring for VR itself is an identified challenge in this field, from early work until today [7,10,11,17,19,21]. Specific challenges often depend on the actual application domain. Examples are archeology [2], history museums [22], assembly and maintenance prototyping [6] or prototyping for telecommunication products [16].

Recent work in demonstrating knowledge of spatial nature covers the presentation of existing real-world places in a VR. Application areas of this emerging sub-domain [14] are for example tourism, heritage sites [1,12,18], and virtual education places, such as libraries [3], lecture rooms [5] and museums [3,22].

Davies et al. [5] use 360° images of clinical rooms for student education. Students that participated in the evaluation mention especially that based on the images they would know better now where to stand during ongoing X-ray. The only interaction with the virtual scene that was provided was the head-movement. Participants could look freely from one point of view (POV) by using an HMD.

Guerra [12] focuses on the impact of image-based 360° VR on outdoor tourism and heritage sites. He states work that utilizes immersive technology and let users explore several locations in Portugal. This work involves pre-captured 360° panoramic images from distinct points near touristic sites. Argyriou et al. [1] transports similar concepts to AR and 360° videos. These videos are used for cultural heritage education. Within their implementation, they describe their content creation pipeline which consists of capturing videos with a simple 360° camera and scanning objects with laser scanner equipment. As for the video, they import it in a Unity environment and map it to an inverted sphere. The point of view that users can take is placed in the middle of the sphere. After developing the application with Unity they build it for a cardboard VR HMD.

Beside the content creation the actual guidance of users through a virtual demo is a challenge. Jan et al. [15] propose an implementation of an embodied tour guide that helps users exploring the scene. However, implementing virtual guides requires extensive knowledge in programming choice-driven interaction. Other work mentions that human mediators [18] are an established alternative, even though the mutual communication while using immersive technology is constrained.

Identified relating works mostly mention technical aspects and differ in the utilized hardware. Work that focuses on semantic and video-specific aspects, such as the integration of actors in the video material during the authoring process or a conceptual view for demonstrating virtual rooms was not found during our research.

3   360°-Video Virtual Reality Room Demo Concept

In this section we describe a concept for presenting an existing room, like a laboratory, in a virtual 360° demo setting.

We use our demo concept to provide virtual tours through real existing rooms. The users are able to move freely to predefined positions through the room and access marked objects in the room. For guiding the users through the virtual demo, we use UI elements that are leaned on common objects from the real world, such as street signs (signpost) as a metaphor for changing the position to the posted element (Fig. 1 left). Furthermore, we integrate real actors that are captured during the recording of the video to help guiding laymen users through the demo. The actors are part of each video of the actual objects in the room that should be presented. They introduce the objects to the user (e.g. they use them, point on different sub-parts, turn on machines etc.), but the actors are also utilized to welcome users in the virtual room (Fig. 1 right).

Fig. 1. Left: Signpost at the start point. Right: Welcome scene, translated in German language.

Each predefined position in the virtual world reflects one point of view (POV) from which the 360° videos are shot in the real laboratory. We distinguish between three classes of user positions in the demo: (1) *Starting points*, (2) *navigation points* and (3) *object points*. The starting point is the entry point for the user into the virtual demo. This point is utilized to give users an overview of the room, to orient them in the virtual environment and to briefly explain the navigation to them in a quick tutorial.

The only purpose of navigation points is to serve users as another POV, so that they might be able to see objects in the room that were covered from the POV of the starting point. From both starting and navigation points, users can select highlighted objects to jump to another POV that is recorded from a position close to the object of interest. The provided video presents its functionality or provides further information concerning the object. The user is now at an object point. Additional images, texts and voice-overs are placed at these points. These additional assets are only visible when users stand at object points. They are hidden from navigation points so that the overall view on the room remains obstructed. This incorporates a common visualization technique, which is providing overview and detailed views separate and provide these details on demand.

We distinguish between three modes within our laboratory demo concept. The user mode allows users to move freely in any order through the virtual laboratory points. We refer to a second mode as the story mode, in which the points can only be accessed in a predefined order. This mode ensures that users see the objects in a semantically correct order – which can be helpful when objects semantically build upon another (e.g. a femtosecond laser in a laser laboratory might be introduced before the machine is introduced that reads the samples that the laser produces). Depending on the use case, the authors of the demo can activate one or the other in order to guide them through the set of objects. The third mode is an author mode, which offers immersed users the possibility to partly self-adjust and customize the environment, such as choose highlights for objects of interest in the virtual room. This concept ensures that domain experts themselves participate in the authoring process, in particular where this domain specific know ledge is needed: When the objects of interest are chosen and visually delimited from other objects in the room.

4   Prototype Implementation

This section introduces our prototype implementation. Our prototype was built with Unity and is a virtual, partly self-adjustable tour through an optics and photonics (laser) laboratory of the local university. At first, we conducted an interview with the leading professor of the laboratory and his research associates. Upon their ideas we created a linear story line and a script for the demo (in particular for the story mode). On a second appointment in the room laboratory we recorded 360° videos from several points – one for each identified object of interest and a start point. From the view of the start point we decided whether additional navigation point were needed in order to reach each object. We used the Vuze 3D 360° VR camera[1].

We used one start point and one navigation point in this demo, because the view to one object of interest was obstructed from the start point. Four object points were used. Each point was realized as a distinct Unity scene within the prototype. Three laboratory experts acted in the recordings of the start, navigation and object points. At the start point they introduced themselves, welcomed the user and then walked to several objects of interest within the rooms. At the object points they demonstrated the functionality of the object. In the example of the laser, the professor took on necessary safety equipment, started the laser and then disassembled the laser so that the inside machinery could be seen by the users. In the navigation points the actors only idled within the laboratory at the object points to which they went in the start point in order to maintain the cinematic continuity of the demo. Figures 2 and 3 show two example scenes from the prototype, where additional information are given in textual form and actors introduce hardware within the laboratory.

The video material was imported into the various Unity scenes and projected from the inside onto a sphere whose normals were inverted. In fact, there are two spheres in each scene, one rendered for each separate eye, to preserve the stereoscopic 3D effect. An Oculus Go mobile VR HMD was used together with

---

[1] https://vuze.camera/buy/vuze-camera/ (accessed July 12, 2019).

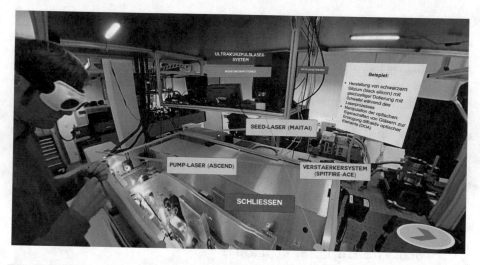

Fig. 2. POV from an object point. A femtosecond laser is partly disassembled to provide users a view insight the laser apparatus which in the real room can only be performed under high security precautions. Additional information is translated into German for the prototype.

its controller for this prototype. To address the VR hardware from within Unity we utilized the Virtual Reality Toolkit[2] (VRTK).

5   Evaluation

Besides implementing our demo concept as a proof-of-concept, we conducted a user study to evaluate the resulting demo. It involved participants in an in-the-wild experiment that aimed at the acceptance and usability of the laboratory demo. The participants of the study used the prototype in free exploration guided by the experimenter which ensured that all functionality was discovered and extensively used.

The user study involved 19 unpaid, voluntary participants (14 male, aged between 13 and 61 with Ø 28.52 and SD 14.97 years). Minor participants were only involved in the study with permission and the presence of their parents. Participants were recruited from an open house day event which they were guests at. The event took place in the local university. Participants were asked to indicate their level of experience with VR hardware from 0 (no experience) to 3 (high experience). These indications ranged from 0 to 1 with Ø 0.57 and SD 0.49, so that all the participants had none or little experience. The experimenter introduced the technology to the participants before usage. No further training was provided to them. Participants could ask questions during the demo which were answered by the experimenter. The closure of the demo was determined

---

[2] https://vrtoolkit.readme.io/ (accessed July 12, 2019).

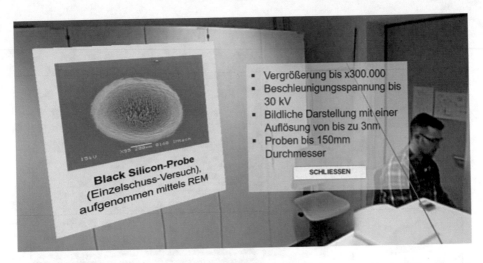

Fig. 3. POV from an object point. Additional information about a black sillicon sample are given in textual form and illustrated by a picture that was integrated in the room demo.

by the participants themselves at the time they mentioned they were finished. After the demo was completed in free exploration, the experimenters asked the participants to fill out a brief questionnaire.

The questionnaire contained 2 demographic questions and 5 specific questions which were translated into German as the native language of the participants: (Q1) How did you find the demo? (Q2) How did you find that the medium of VR was used for demonstrating the laboratory (opposed to the possibility of a tour through the real room in the university)? (Q3) How did you find the interaction with the virtual objects? (Q4) Do you think that using Virtual Reality has given you a better understanding of the content shown? (Q5) How much fun did you have using Virtual Reality in the demo? These questions were answered within a separate 7-point semantic differential scale, where high values submit positive and low values submit negative connoted ratings.

The *short*-version of the established AttrakDiff[3] [13] questionnaire was utilized additionally to get more detailed feedback on the acceptance of the demo relating to the hedonic quality, practical quality and the general attractiveness of the implementations. One participant did not fill out the AttrakDiff related items.

Analysis of the Demo Study. The overall ratings of the participants of the demo study for Q1–Q5 were: *Q1* Ø 5.42 and SD 0.65; *Q2* Ø 5.66 and SD 0.56; *Q3* Ø 4.95 and SD 1.09; *Q4* Ø 4.57 and SD 1.04; *Q5* Ø 5.8 and SD 0.39. Figure 4 left illustrates these ratings.

---

[3] http://attrakdiff.de/index-en.html (June 17, 2019).

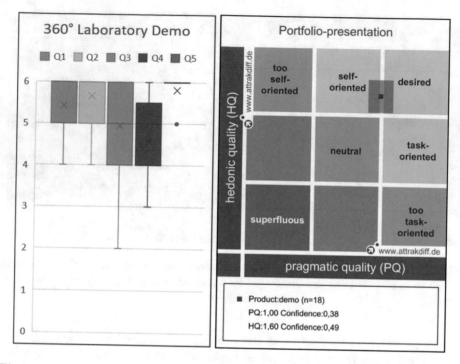

Fig. 4. Descriptive statistics for the demo study. Left: Box-plots of the five individual questions. Middle: Overall placement and confidence of the prototype within the portfolio presentation (AttrakDiff).

With the hypothetical neutral rating value of 3 points we conducted a Wilcoxon Signed-Rank test to draw conclusions on the significance of differences between negative (0 to 2) and positive (4 to 6) values by comparing the medians with the common null hypothesis H_0: The median of the user samples is identical with the neutral value of 3. The alternative hypothesis H_{alt} was formulated as follows: There exists a significant difference between positive and negative ratings. All ratings of Q1–Q5 were compared group-wise against the neutral value. The test indicated a significant difference by using the threshold $p \leq 0.05$ with $p \leq 0.00001$ for Q1, Q2, and Q5 and Q3 with $p = 0.00014$ and Q4 with $p = 0.0003$. Therefore H_0 was rejected for every Q and H_{alt} was accepted.

The ten ratings of the AttrakDiff questionnaire were analyzed on their hedonic and pragmatic qualities and the attractiveness. The results are shown in Fig. 4 right and middle. The overall rating (right) places the demo between the *desired* and the *self-oriented* area, with a confidence area that crosses both of these sectors. The description of word-pairs (right) illustrates the mean ratings of the participants for each item. No mean value is on the negative side of the neutral value.

Discussion of the Results. The significance against the neutral value and the positive Ø-value for each of the questions Q1–Q5 indicate that the participants accepted the 360° demo of the laser laboratory. The descriptive statistics in Fig. 4 and the unanimously positive or neutral ratings in the AttrakDiff questionnaire strengthen this assumption.

In Fig. 5, we can observe that two questions relating to the practical quality (PQ) fall between 0 and 1 and therefore are lower than the other values. This phenomenon is also reflected in the shift of the portfolio presentation (4 right) towards *self-oriented*. Presumably, a wish for a clearer structure of the demo and more predictability was expressed by the participants. This assumption is also supported by the illustration of the mean values for the three categories practical, hedonic quality and attractiveness (6). The mean value of the practical quality is lower than the hedonic quality and the attractiveness (Fig. 6).

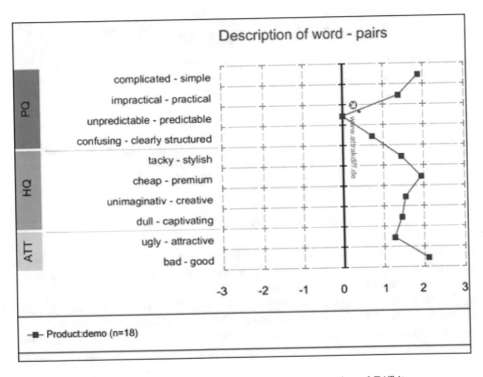

Fig. 5. Overview of the single ratings of word pair AttrakDiff items.

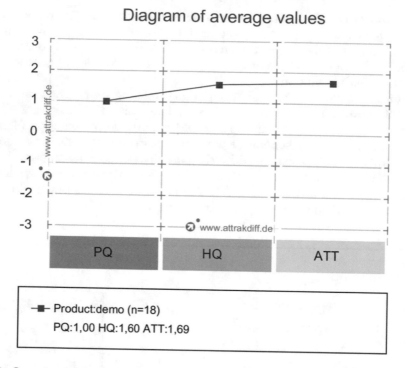

Fig. 6. Overview of the average values concerning the three categories of the AttrakD-iff questionnaire: Pragmatic quality (PQ), hedonic quality (HQ) and attractiveness (ATT).

6   Conclusion and Future Work

In this work we proposed a 360° VR demo concept for introducing existing rooms, like laboratories, to laymen. In a study we indicated that this concept was accepted well by the participants.

Potential future work could explore more comprehensive authoring environments for 360° VR demo applications. These authoring environments could enable domain experts themselves to create these demo, without a tedious or even costly communication with VR-experts. For authoring the entire VR demo, future work must provide experts with a toolkit that enables them to (1) actually shoot the required videos themselves and (2) integrate them in a VR environment together with additional assets (e.g. texts, images).

Future work also offers possibilities for integrating audio in these demos. Audio overlays for the 360° videos can help to increase an immersive experience for users in the demo. But they could also be used to provide additional information during the demo, so that written text can be reduced and the integration actors would play an even more important role. So audio could be regarded in future work in both the integration in the demo and the authoring procedure.

Acknowledgements. The work is supported by the Federal Ministry of Education and Research of Germany in the project Innovative Hochschule (funding number: 03IHS071).

References

1. Argyriou, L., Economou, D., Bouki, V.: 360-degree interactive video application for cultural heritage education. In: 3rd Annual International Conference of the Immersive Learning Research Network. Verlag der Technischen Universität Graz (2017)
2. Bruno, F., Bruno, S., De Sensi, G., Luchi, M.L., Mancuso, S., Muzzupappa, M.: From 3D reconstruction to virtual reality: a complete methodology for digital archaeological exhibition. J. Cult. Heritage **11**(1), 42–49 (2010)
3. Calongne, C., Hiles, J.: Blended realities: a virtual tour of education in second life. In: TCC, pp. 70–90. TCCHawaii (2007)
4. Clark, B.R.: Creating entrepreneurial universities: organizational pathways of transformation. Issues in Higher Education. ERIC (1998)
5. Davies, A.G., Crohn, N.J., Treadgold, L.A.: Can virtual reality really be used within the lecture theatre? BMJ Simul. Technol. Enhanced Learn. (2018). https://doi.org/10.1136/bmjstel-2017-000295
6. De Sa, A.G., Zachmann, G.: Virtual reality as a tool for verification of assembly and maintenance processes. Comput. Graph. **23**(3), 389–403 (1999)
7. Dörner, R., Kallmann, M., Huang, Y.: Content creation and authoring challenges for virtual environments: from user interfaces to autonomous virtual characters. In: Brunnett, G., Coquillart, S., van Liere, R., Welch, G., Váša, L. (eds.) Virtual Realities. LNCS, vol. 8844, pp. 187–212. Springer, Cham (2015). https://doi.org/10.1007/978-3-319-17043-5_11
8. Etzkowitz, H., Leydesdorff, L.: The dynamics of innovation: from national systems and mode 2 to a triple helix of university-industry-government relations. Res. Policy **29**(2), 109–123 (2000)
9. Freina, L., Ott, M.: A literature review on immersive virtual reality in education: state of the art and perspectives. In: The International Scientific Conference eLearning and Software for Education, vol. 1, p. 133. "Carol I" National Defence University (2015)
10. Gerken, K., Frechenhäuser, S., Dörner, R., Luderschmidt, J.: Authoring support for post-WIMP applications. In: Kotzé, P., Marsden, G., Lindgaard, G., Wesson, J., Winckler, M. (eds.) INTERACT 2013. LNCS, vol. 8119, pp. 744–761. Springer, Heidelberg (2013). https://doi.org/10.1007/978-3-642-40477-1_51
11. Green, M., Jacob, R.: Siggraph'90 workshop report: software architectures and metaphors for non-wimp user interfaces. ACM SIGGRAPH Comput. Graph. **25**(3), 229–235 (1991)
12. Guerra, J.P., Pinto, M.M., Beato, C.: Virtual reality-shows a new vision for tourism and heritage. Eur. Sci. J. ESJ **11**(9), 49–54 (2015)
13. Hassenzahl, M., Platz, A., Burmester, M., Lehner, K.: Hedonic and ergonomic quality aspects determine a software's appeal. In: Proceedings of the SIGCHI Conference on Human Factors in Computing Systems, pp. 201–208. ACM (2000)
14. Horst, R., Dörner, R.: Opportunities for virtual and mixed reality knowledge demonstration. In: 2018 IEEE International Symposium on Mixed and Augmented Reality (ISMAR-Adjunct), pp. 381–385. IEEE (2018)

442   R. Horst et al.

15. Jan, D., Roque, A., Leuski, A., Morie, J., Traum, D.: A virtual tour guide for virtual worlds. In: Ruttkay, Z., Kipp, M., Nijholt, A., Vilhjálmsson, H.H. (eds.) IVA 2009. LNCS (LNAI), vol. 5773, pp. 372–378. Springer, Heidelberg (2009). https://doi.org/10.1007/978-3-642-04380-2_40
16. Kerttula, M., Salmela, M., Heikkinen, M.: Virtual reality prototyping-a framework for the development of electronics and telecommunication products. In: RSP, p. 2. IEEE (1997)
17. Nebeling, M., Speicher, M.: The trouble with augmented reality/virtual reality authoring tools. In: 2018 IEEE International Symposium on Mixed and Augmented Reality Adjunct (ISMAR-Adjunct), pp. 333–337. IEEE (2018)
18. Roussou, M.: The components of engagement in virtual heritage environments. In: New Heritage, pp. 241–257. Routledge (2007)
19. Steed, A.: Some useful abstractions for re-usable virtual environment platforms. In: Software Engineering and Architectures for Realtime Interactive Systems-SEARIS (2008)
20. Van Kerrebroeck, H., Brengman, M., Willems, K.: When brands come to life: experimental research on the vividness effect of virtual reality in transformational marketing communications. Virtual Reality 21(4), 177–191 (2017)
21. Wingrave, C.A., LaViola, J.J.: Reflecting on the design and implementation issues of virtual environments. Presence 19(2), 179–195 (2010)
22. Wojciechowski, R., Walczak, K., White, M., Cellary, W.: Building virtual and augmented reality museum exhibitions. In: Proceedings of the Ninth International Conference on 3D Web Technology, pp. 135–144. ACM (2004)

A Computational System for Structural Visual Analysis of Labor Accident Data

Mateus Rodrigues[✉], Luciana Brito[✉], and Jose Gustavo S. Paiva[✉]

Federal University of Uberlandia, Uberlandia, Brazil
{mprodrigues,lubrito,gustavo}@ufu.br

Abstract. This paper presents a computational system that employs Information Visualization techniques to facilitate and enhance the analysis of labor accident data, a serious social problem. Our system uses associated geographical information to create interactive layouts to explore the underlying structure of the data. We present the results of applying our proposed system on data provided by the Brazilian Federal Labor Prosecution Office, demonstrating the potential of our strategy in revealing accident profiles, peculiar behaviors, and patterns associated with all levels of regional hierarchy, as well as in comparing the behavior of localities in the same/distinct regions, among other tasks. We believe that the proposed system provides effective and efficient means to help governments to evaluate current public policies and foment the creation of new ones to reduce these accidents and grant safety for employees, and also encourage citizen participation and transparency in governments.

Keywords: Labor accident · Governmental data · Information visualization

1 Introduction

Governmental data are information collected by official governmental agencies related to different sectors of the society in order to provide means for the administrative power to address the deficiencies of the country. These data are often large and contain a diversity of strategic information that can be used to validate previous knowledge, and to gain insights about specific areas [13], guiding public policies in reducing identified deficiencies.

A particular case of governmental data relates to labor accidents, which represent a serious social problem. Worldwide, approximately 374 million accidents are registered yearly, resulting in 2.78 million deaths, and generate an expenditure of 3.94% of the global GDP [5]. These accidents may severely impact a government budget, and result in losses for employers and physical/emotional damages to employees, impacting economy as a whole. In Brazil, detailed labor

This study was financed in part by the Coordenação de Aperfeiçoamento de Pessoal de Nível Superior - Brasil (CAPES) - Finance Code 001.

accidents information are collected by the Brazilian Federal Labor Prosecution Office (BFLPO) using a **Labor Accident Communication (LAC)**, which is a document that registers labor or route accidents, occupational diseases and/or death. These LACs are anonymised and provided in a public repository[1].

Governments can benefit from analyzing large data volumes to optimize expenditure and to improve interaction with the population [16]. Such analysis requires the development of mechanisms to effectively extract information and make sense from this data [2]. In this sense, Information Visualization approaches are suitable for data exploration, creating visual representations of data collections to enhance human perception [10] and thus information extraction. Although several visual strategies applied to governmental data can be found, little attention has been given to the analysis of labor accidents.

In this paper we propose a computational system that employs Information Visualization techniques for visual analysis of labor accident data. We use a set of visual strategies to communicate the underlying structure of those data, exploiting its heterogeneity and its associated hierarchical organization, among other aspects. We believe these visualizations allow the identification of behavior profiles related to accidents, localities or occupations, as well as correlations among several indices measured in diverse localities of the country, highlighting their similarities in different geographical hierarchy levels. The system provides a set of interactive tools to allow the user to explore these layouts, by navigating through the geographical localities' hierarchy, filtering/selecting subsets of the data, comparing different localities, among other tasks.

The main contribution of this work is a visual analysis system that enhances the analysis capabilities of experts from government departments, and can also be used by laymen. We also believe that such a system is useful to guide governors in ensuring safety to the employees, and to identify deficiencies that motivate the creation of new effective public policies. We evaluate our approach by performing a detailed analysis of LACs data provided by the BFLPO, demonstrating the potential of our approach with the analysis of several Brazilian localities.

The following sections present related work, our design considerations and the resulting system, a discussion about the results/limitations of our analysis and our conclusions.

2   Related Work

Visualization techniques have already been used to communicate diverse governmental data, however, the majority of them are more focused on simply informing, than on making exploration and analysis of the data feasible. Some of these undertakings include OpenData Albania [4] and Dataviva[2]. The first one presents several charts about many different measured indices in Albania, like education, economy, demographics, poverty, etc. Dataviva similarly presents different layouts covering specific governmental data from Brazil, which are employment,

---

[1] http://observatoriosst.mpt.mp.br.
[2] http://dataviva.info.

commerce, education and health. With the exception of a single visualization showing the amount of compensation benefits paid for workers in the USA, who had suffered crippling injuries to its limbs [3], the authors have no knowledge of any scientific project to visually analyze LA data.

Following a more analytical approach, in [14] a combination of a ThemeRiver layout with a map is used to monitor energy output from power plants in Germany, with the map serving as a filtering tool and the ThemeRiver as an analysis chart. This shows how simple but efficient coordination of layouts can result in useful analysis tools for governmental data.

In [8] data provided by the DataViva repository are displayed in scatterplot layouts using PCA and MDS techniques. The produced layouts allow the identification of groups of localities with similar behavior profiles, as well as localities with peculiar behaviors that diverge from what is expected by the measured indices. For instance, a PCA layout from international commerce of Brazilian mesoregions revealed groups with similar behavior among cities from different mesoregions, and also cities with significant peculiar behavior, such as the city of Uberaba. An MDS layout from higher education data also exhibited similar profiles for towns from different states, as well as several peculiar behaviors, demonstrating the potential of multidimensional projection techniques for the analysis of governmental data.

3   Data Preparation

We performed a set of pre-processing steps on the data obtained from the BFLPO. The original data is largely comprised of categorical variables detailing accident occurrences, such as day, type of lesion, occupation of the injured, among others. The BFLPO dataset only contains city and state of occurrence to identify the locality of an accident, so in order to better identify LACs' geographical distribution we decided to use the complete official Brazilian territorial division, as provided by the Brazilian Institute of Geography and Statistics[3], to the original dataset, along with a set of GeoJSON files[4]. The variables used to linked these data together is the name of the city and state, which are present in all the files. Some variables have a very high number of categories, so we grouped them into fewer, more general, categories. In order to summarize all the LACs for a given city, we decomposed categorical variables into n others, where n is the number of possible categories of the original variable. These new variables assume a value of 0 or 1 depending if that category is present or not. We then summed all the occurrences of each variable and normalized the data by dividing each sum by the total number of LACs in a given city.

4   Proposed System

Our proposed system comprises two distinct visualizations composed of two layouts each. The first visualization combines a scatterplot of a multidimensional

---

[3] https://www.ibge.gov.br/.
[4] https://github.com/fititnt/gis-dataset-brasil.

projection with a political map, while the second one combines a treemap with parallel sets. The system should be able to: (r1) identify work profiles; (r2) identify areas lacking attention; (r3) characterize localities, independent of its geographical position; (r4) characterize wide geographical areas. This section describes both visualizations in details, and the ideas behind their choosing.

4.1   Scatterplot + Map

Multidimensional projections map a n-dimensional dataset to a p-dimensional space, where $p \ll n$ and usually $p = 2$ for visualization purposes, whilst trying to highlight the relationship among data instances observed in the original space. Several multidimensional projection techniques exist in the literature, employing linear and/or non-linear strategies, considering global or local relationships, and also taking into account user manipulation. A detailed discussion of those techniques and its applications can be found in [11].

We employ a multidimensional projection aiming to identify groups of cities with similar behavior, as well as cities presenting deviant behavior, regarding LACs. These techniques were previously employed in analyzing governmental data [8], revealing interesting findings. We investigated three state of the art techniques: LSP [12], t-SNE [9] and LAMP [6]. LAMP resulted in a layout with better groups separation, and we decided to employ it in all the analysis.

A scatterplot layout is used to display the positioning of all cities, defined by the multidimensional projection. Each city is represented by a circle, and can be colored according to any categorical variable. The color of a city is associated with which is the most occurring category for that city. Users can also select a city or a group of cities and by hovering over this selection a tooltip appears displaying the name of the selected city(ies).

As the multidimensional projection does not take into account the geographical position of each city, we decided to coordinate the scatterplot with a geographical map to contextualize user exploration. The idea is, by showing where each city is located, to give insight about the distribution of cities with similar behavior in the country, as well as to help users in defining all the cities in a selection, in situations in which points occlusion occur. Thus, any selection on the scatterplot layout automatically highlights the corresponding cities on the map, enhancing the analysis and possibly improving the comprehension of several associated phenomena. Figure 1 shows the resulting visualization.

4.2   Treemap + Parallel Sets

Parallel Coordinates may fail to reveal relationships among variables when data is massively categorical, and identifying correlations among the axes will not be possible. We thus employed a derived layout called parallel sets [7], a flexible layout designed specifically for categorical data that allows the user to arrange the data in many different ways in order to produce meaningful visual patterns.

The first axis in our parallel sets layout is the locality, in order to better contextualize the analysis. The subsequent axes are initially arranged in a way

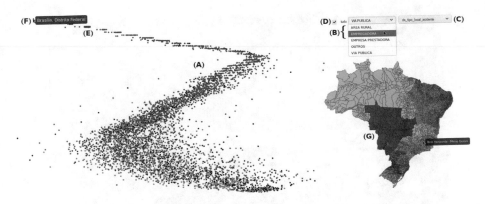

Fig. 1. (A) LAMP scatterplot. (B) Dropdown menu for instance coloring criteria. (C) Dropdown menu to select coloring variable. (D) Checkbox to toggle color of all points. (E) Points highlighted by user. (F) Tooltip showing a town name. (G) Selected cities highlighted in the map for geographical localization.

to provide a better overview of the observable patterns, but their position can be rearranged and the values in each can be sorted, in a way to obtain better associated visual patterns. This layout also benefits from hover functionalities showing tooltips to help the user to see the proportions of variable values in each axis, and highlight the relationship between categories in different variables.

In order to enhance the analysis with the parallel sets and better explore the BFLPO dataset's hierarchical aspect we employ a expandable treemap layout as a hierarchical navigation tool for the parallel sets layout. The localities currently displayed in the treemap are the same ones shown in the parallel sets.

In [15] a combination of a treemap with other non-proportional layouts is proposed, mainly due to the limitations imposed by the proportionality of a treemap, which prevents better comparison of parallel structures. We follow this idea of balancing the strengths and weaknesses of both types of layouts, but instead of embedding layouts inside treemap cells, we keep the layouts separate, but still contained in the same view, and fully integrated.

Each treemap cell shows the total LACs for a locality. Users may click on a cell to expand a specific locality, and perform the same exploration strategy for correspondent hierarchical sublevels. A small rectangle at the top of the treemap shows the full navigation path with the number of LACs in each hierarchical level, which can also be used to go back to previous levels. Hovering over a cell displays a tooltip with the name of the correspondent locality and the associated number of LACs. In addition, hovering over a cell also shows a preview of the subsequent hierarchy associated with that cell, if applicable. Figure 2 shows the layouts that compose this visualization.

The results of both visualizations can be combined to confirm patterns found in any of them, also providing a complementary exploration procedure. Both visualizations can also provide interesting ways to identify localities profiles, even if they are geographically distant.

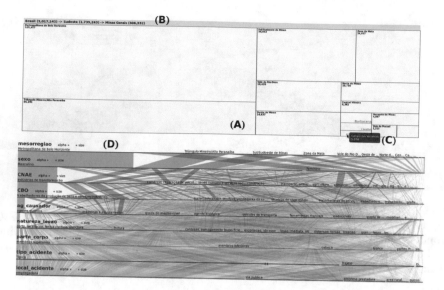

Fig. 2. (A) expandable treemap with Brazil's hierarchy. (B) hierarchy path with the amount of LACs in each hierarchy level. (C) Subsequent hierarchy tooltip with the name of the locality and the number of LACs. (D) parallel sets showing the locality selected in the treemap. Some axes were omitted for space.

5   Analysis Procedure

We performed several analysis using the proposed layouts. Using the Multidimensional Projection we first focused in analyzing the points distribution in the layout, identifying groups of cities, as well as isolated cities that may present anomalous behavior. We also investigated how the categorization produced by each measured variable - indicated by colors in the layouts - can be related to the labor accidents' behavior. We also used the coordinated geographical map to understand profiles that are independent of the cities' geographical location. We also relate these findings to the parallel sets layout. Our objective is, from a produced group of cities in the projection, explore the correspondent parallel sets layout to investigate how each measured variable helps to characterize this group, as well as to identify correlations among the associated variables, among other tasks. Finally, we freely explore the parallel sets to also investigate the role of each measured variable in characterizing groups of cities, or in distinguishing different groups, as well as if/how they correlate to each other. In each analysis we highlight elements in the proposed layouts that contributed to reveal each pattern, and to lead to a judicious decision making.

6   Results

Our goal is to identify, in localities, behavior profiles associated with LACs. Figure 1 shows the scatterplot produced by LAMP and associated map regarding all Brazilian localities, in which one notices a "Z" shape formation, with small groups present at the top. This configuration seems to reflect cities' size and economic development. In general, capitals, big cities, and regional centers are located at the top, in more coherent groups, while rural and smaller localities are located mostly in the bottom. Figure 3A shows the cities with the majority of accidents occurring in rural areas, colored in blue. Additionally, the Sul and Sudeste regions' cities are homogeneously distributed over the layout, reflecting the economic development diversity of cities from these regions, while cities from the Nordeste region, which is one of the poorest, are mostly positioned at the bottom of the layout, as shown in Fig. 3B. One notices that rural and small cities' position greatly overlap with the Nordeste cities.

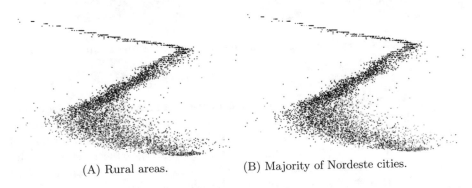

(A) Rural areas.   (B) Majority of Nordeste cities.

Fig. 3. Both rural areas and the majority of Nordeste cities are at the bottom of the layout, and largely overlap. (Color figure online)

When coloring the cities according to economic activity, one may notice that several capitals/big cities concentrate the majority of LACs in "human health and social services". This group is comprised of 127 cities, with 14 out of 27 capitals, including all capital cities from Sudeste and Sul region, 3 from the Centro-Oeste region, among them the Federal capital city Brasília, and 4 from Nordeste region. Each of these cities reported on average 3000 accidents related to this economic activity. Most of the remaining cities concentrate the majority of LACs in two economic activities: "transformation industries" (2021 cities) and "commerce and repair of vehicles" (708 cities). In this case, on average 450 "transformation industries" accidents and 600 "commerce and repair of vehicles" accidents were reported. These two analysis show how the kind of economic activities and related accidents are different in rich/big cities than in the rest of the country, independent of which region they belong to.

Figure 4 shows a complementary analysis using both visualizations. When coloring the scatterplot according to causer agent, "machines and equipment" is the largest causer agent for the majority of the cities. The parallel sets layout sheds more light on this observation, showing that 4 of the 5 regions have "machines and equipment" as causer agent with the largest number of LACs registered, except for the Norte Region, even though this causer agent is also top listed there. Those analysis fulfill *r1*.

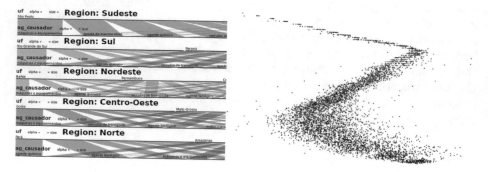

Fig. 4. All regions except one report "machines and equipment" as main causer of LAs.

Combining both layouts eases the identification of areas that may lack attention, fulfilling *r2*. For example, the scatterplot shows only a few cities in Brazil in which the accidents were mainly reported by syndicates or public authorities instead of by the employer, as required by law. Those cities are mainly in the Nordeste region, and the parallel sets show that this is the only region that have a noticeable number of accidents reported by syndicates, around 1.6%.

The farther away city in the scatterplot is Brasília (Capital of Brazil), close only to Santo André (metropolitan region of São Paulo). The parallel sets shows the similar behavior of these cities, and how they behave differently from the cities from the regions they belong to (Centro-Oeste and Sudeste, respectively, as show in Fig. 5). This analysis fulfills *r3*.

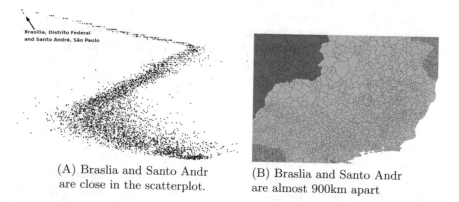

(A) Braslia and Santo Andr are close in the scatterplot.

(B) Braslia and Santo Andr are almost 900km apart

Fig. 5. Brasília and Santo André present several similarities, despite geographical distance

In Brasília 62% of LACs are of males, 10% less than the region average. As already highlighted by the scatterplot, "human health and social services" economic activity registered more accidents, but now other economic activities also registered a meaningful number of accidents. "Transformation industries" activities are responsible for only 6% of accidents, distant from the rest of the region, and the more balanced gender distribution in the economic activities suggests a better work force distribution. Women accidents are more prevalent in occupations related to Arts and Science, and Human Health, while men accidents are more prevalent in the production of goods and services. The occupation with the largest number of registered accidents is "service providers and sellers", reflecting how Brasília is the administrative center of Brazil, more focused in providing services, and with the highest concentration of public agencies.

Santo André shows several similarities to Brasília in its accidents profile. There is also a more equal gender distribution regarding labor accidents, with approximately 59% of men, 6% less male accidents than the region's average. A high percentage of accidents are associated with "human health and social services" economic activity (23%), but here the highest percentage is associated with "transformation industries" (27%). As occurred in Brasília, women accidents are concentrated in occupations related to Arts and Science and Health.

The Parallel sets also provided a good characterization of regions as a whole, fulfilling $r4$. Sul and Sudeste regions behave very similarly, both having the most equal distribution of male and female accidents, with 65% of males. They also have the same economic activities causing the majority of accidents, "transformation industries", "commerce and repair of vehicles", and "human health and services". All the other variables also present similar behavior, differing only in the distribution of accidents in the states. This is highlighted by the treemap presented in Fig. 6, which shows that the Sul region is considerably more homogeneous, presenting almost the same number of LACs in the three states, while Sudeste is largely dominated by São Paulo, with more than 60% of all accidents, while Espírito Santo only represents 4%.

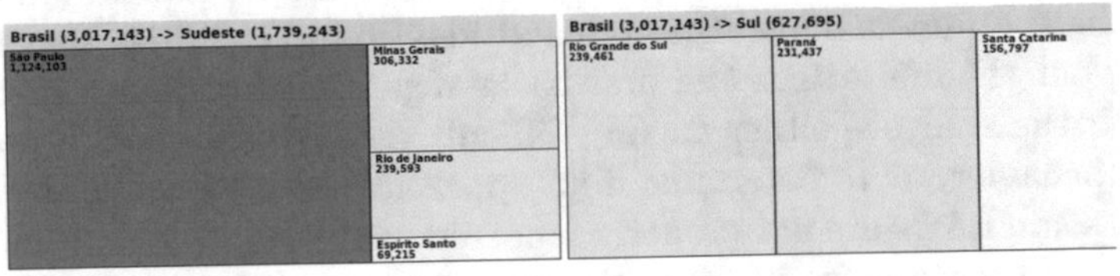

Fig. 6. Distribution of accidents is much more homogeneous in the Sul region, than the Sudeste region.

Both Nordeste and Centro-Oeste regions show a more significant number of accidents in the rural area, around 8%, and the percentage of male accidents is greater than 70%. They also present similar causer agents, mostly "machines and equipment", "chemical agent", "biological agent", and "vehicles".

The Norte region behaves significantly different from the others. More than 80% of LACs are of men, and economic activities reporting more accidents are completely different. Here, "human health and services" is very distant from the top, the main one, "transformation industries", is not so prevalent as in the other regions, and the second place, "construction", is not so high in the other regions, and the most reported causer agent is "chemical agent". The behavior of the Norte region seems to reflect the fact that it is the poorest region in Brazil, so we decided to perform a deeper investigation. When navigating in the states from this region one can confirm the poor industrialisation of the region. The economic activity of "transformation industries" is only the first due to the two principal states in the region, Pará and Amazonas, which together concentrate 70% of the accidents of the entire region. In the third state with most LACs, Rondônia, the number of LACs associated with "construction" is twice of the ones associated with "transformation industries". In all the other states the "transformation industries" percentages are negligible, and the LACs are mainly associated with rural activities, like fishing and agriculture, or transportation.

When exploring Pará and Amazonas it is possible to see that the LAcs associated with activities related to industry are reported mostly in their respective capitals, with the rest of the states presenting economic activities more similar to the rest of the region. Two mesoregions in Pará, Nordeste Paraense and Sudeste Paraense, are markedly characterized by accidents in pecuary and agriculture, showing that these capitals are outliers in this region. This can be noticed in the scatterplot, where both are at the top of "Z" shaped group, close to cities such as São Paulo, Rio de Janeiro and Goiânia.

7   Limitations

We were able to identify some limitations regarding the employed strategies, and regarding the data itself. The proportion of reported LACs is small when compared to the total amount of accidents that actually occur, specially in poorer regions, such as Norte. This is a serious problem that we partially address by shedding light on anomalous behaviors and identifying localities that may lack attention, but the limitations and drawbacks regarding the data collection process impair the analysis, either making difficult the identification of reasons for a specific behavior, or to determine if an apparent behavior really occurs. Furthermore, some LACs are not properly reported, resulting in loss of information that may be important for the analysis. In this sense, the system might help in identifying places where the data collection could be improved.

Regarding our proposed method, the use of a treemap to navigate in the parallel sets is useful to contextualize the analysis, and is intuitive, but it does not allow the comparison of localities from the same level but in different branches, such as mesoregions from different states. The BFLPO data is massively categorical, and in order to employ the point-placement techniques, it was necessary to transform this data into numerical values. Thus, our procedure became strongly dependent on these procedures, that may often result in information loss. However, we believe the combination of these procedures with traditional point-placement techniques already produced satisfactory results in terms of revealing useful patterns for analysis.

8   Conclusions and Future Work

In this work we presented a computational system to perform visual analysis of labor accidents data, using a set of visual strategies to communicate the underlying structure of these data. We explored the data's heterogeneity and its associated hierarchical organization.

We were able to identify profiles associated with individual cities, and behavior patterns associated with the whole country. Combining the observed patterns in both approaches we were able to find similarities among geographically distant localities, patterns related to the cities' size, the most frequent LA types in Brazil, and to characterize those LAs in terms of occupation type, gender differences, causer agent, among other aspects.

We also identified relationships among cities that would not be easy to identify if each city was analyzed only considering cities located in the same or close localities, as well as considering just tabular data, and we were also capable of finding relationships in the region level, which we believe would be hard to do otherwise. We also believe that the proposed visualizations provide complementary capabilities that allow the simultaneous analysis of different data aspects, for example the scatterplot depicts only cities, and the insights over higher hierarchical levels are gathered by the shape formed by the points' position and the colors, while the treemap and parallel sets visualization allows the characterization of entire regions, in all hierarchical levels.

We believe our system is capable of easily communicating the LA occurrence situation in the country to the population, which may foment popular participation in the government administration, allowing the inspection of the country's current situation and the demand of more effective public policies.

It would be interesting to analyze the structure of LA occurrences aspects over time, in order to explore the temporal evolution of the observed patterns. We have already developed a temporal visual LA analysis tool [1], and we intend to combine both strategies to perform such analysis. We also intend to perform a user experiment with specialists from the BFLPO, which are domain experts and may significantly benefit from the information provided by our tool, positively impacting in the decision making process.

References

1. Brito, L., Rodrigues, M., Paiva, J.G.S.: A computational system for temporal visual analysis of labour accident data. In: 23rd International Conference on Information Visualisation, pp. 88–93 (2019)
2. Graves, A., Hendler, J.: Visualization tools for open government data. In: Proceedings of the 14th Annual International Conference on Digital Government Research, dg.o 2013, pp. 136–145. ACM, New York (2013)

3. Groeger, L., Grabell, M., Cotts, C.: Workers' comp benefits: How much is a limb worth? (2015). https://projects.propublica.org/graphics/workers-compensation-benefits-by-limb
4. Hoxha, J., Brahaj, A., Vrandečić, D.: Open.data.al: increasing the utilization of government data in Albania. In: Proceedings of the 7th International Conference on Semantic Systems, I-Semantics 2011, pp. 237–240. ACM, New York (2011)
5. ILO: Safety and health at work (2019). http://www.ilo.org/global/topics/safety-and-health-at-work/lang-en/index.htm
6. Joia, P., Coimbra, D., Cuminato, J., Paulovich, F., Nonato, L.: Local affine multi-dimensional projection. IEEE Trans. Vis. Comput. Graph. **17**, 2563–2571 (2011)
7. Kosara, R., Bendix, F., Hauser, H.: Parallel sets: interactive exploration and visual analysis of categorical data. IEEE Trans. Vis. Comput. Graph. **12**(4), 558–568 (2006)
8. Lima, C.M., Paiva, J.G.: Análise de dados do dataviva utilizando técnicas de projeção multidimensional. In: Proceedings of the 13th Simpósio Brasileiro de Sistemas de Informação (2017)
9. van der Maaten, L., Hinton, G.: Visualizing data using t-SNE. J. Mach. Learn. Res. **9**, 2579–2605 (2008)
10. Munzner, T.: Visualization Analysis and Design. AK Peters Visualization Series. A K Peters/CRC Press, Boca Raton (2014)
11. Nonato, L.G., Aupetit, M.: Multidimensional projection for visual analytics: linking techniques with distortions, tasks, and layout enrichment. IEEE Trans. Vis. Comput. Graph. **25**(8), 1 (2018)
12. Paulovich, F.V., Nonato, L.G., Minghim, R., Levkowitz, H.: Least square projection: a fast high-precision multidimensional projection technique and its application to document mapping. IEEE Trans. Vis. Comput. Graph. **14**(3), 564–575 (2008)
13. Radl, W., Skopek, J., Komendera, A., Jäger, S., Mödritscher, F.: And data for all: on the validity and usefulness of open government data. In: Proceedings of the 13th International Conference on Knowledge Management and Knowledge Technologies, i-Know 2013, pp. 29:1–29:4. ACM, New York (2013)
14. Rodrigues, N., et al.: Visualization of time series data with spatial context: communicating the energy production of power plants. In: Proceedings of the 10th International Symposium on Visual Information Communication and Interaction, VINCI 2017, pp. 37–44. ACM, New York (2017)
15. Wittenburg, K., Turchi, T.: Treemaps and the visual comparison of hierarchical multi-attribute data. In: Proceedings of the International Working Conference on Advanced Visual Interfaces, AVI 2016, pp. 64–67. ACM, New York (2016)
16. Ying, Y., Xialing, T., Wei, T.: Study on governmental cultural resources purchase management based on public information behavior big data. In: Proceedings of the 8th International Conference on E-Education, E-Business, E-Management and E-Learning, IC4E 2017, pp. 72–75. ACM, New York (2017)

Fast Contextual View Generation in 3D Medical Images Using a 3D Widget User Interface and Super-Ellipsoids

Ken Lagos and Tim McInerney[✉]

Department of Computer Science, Ryerson University,
Toronto, ON M5B 2K3, Canada
tmcinern@ryerson.ca

Abstract. This paper presents a 3D widget user interface (UI), super-ellipsoid shape primitives and a customized volume rendering algorithm that together create an effective system for generating contextual views in 3D medical images. The widget UI supports the fast and precise positioning of a super-ellipsoid "paint blob". The paint blob can be deposited and automatically blended with previously deposited blobs to form an arbitrarily complex-shaped region of interest (ROI) enclosing target image features. The rendering of these "focus" regions can be controlled separately from the surrounding contextual region, allowing medical experts to examine and measure image features relative to the surrounding structures, regardless of the level of occlusion. The system's core algorithms execute in parallel on graphics processing units, resulting in real-time interaction and high-quality visualizations. The focus plus context visualization system is validated via a user study and a series of experiments.

Keywords: Visualization · 3D medical images · User interface

1 Introduction

Direct Volume Rendering (DVR) controlled by Transfer Functions (TFs) is a standard algorithm for generating visualizations in 3D medical images, especially for CT scans. Despite the extensive amount of research in TF design [1], quickly defining a single TF that generates a desired contextual view of a spatially localized focus region or target anatomical structure remains a non-trivial task. This may be due to the fact that TF specification is primarily a mapping of ranges/characteristics of voxel intensity values to color and opacity. Additional mechanisms (e.g. 2D TFs) provide more control to the user over the visualization output but often at the cost of more complex user interfaces that are still primarily indirect in nature. Fast, simple *direct* selection of a spatial sub-volume can complement a TF specification process by supporting separate and more easily defined TFs for this "focus" region and for the context region surrounding it.

However, designing interactive techniques enabling a user to quickly generate and easily modify a contextual view by directly selecting a focus ROI or selecting a specific target structure in a volume rendered image is a challenging human-computer interaction (HCI) task. Such a technique needs to augment TF specification by supporting

G. Bebis et al. (Eds.): ISVC 2019, LNCS 11845, pp. 455–468, 2019.
https://doi.org/10.1007/978-3-030-33723-0_37

the selection of objects adjacent to other objects that have been mapped by the TF to similar opacity and color values. Furthermore, desired ROIs may vary from regularly shaped regions, such as rectangular blocks or spheres, to arbitrarily complex, curving shaped objects/features, or to elaborate branching objects such as vasculature. In addition, the TF specification may result in a volume rendering in which a target ROI contains several visually disconnected objects or an ROI that is visually occluded by parts of other structures. Another important requirement of interactive ROI selection techniques to support the fast modification of the ROI as a user is exploring the volume from new viewpoints. Finally, the interaction issues are inherently tied to issues of the user's depth perception of the target ROI as well as the design of appropriate supporting visual cues, including interface signifiers to indicate affordance and help bridge the gulf of execution of the UI during ROI selection.

This paper presents an interactive view generation and ROI selection technique that is based on the manipulation and rendering of mathematically-compact and blend-able convex shape primitives known as super-ellipsoids (Fig. 1). Specifically, a user interface (UI) design that uses a mouse and 3D widgets for manipulating the super-ellipsoids is presented[1]. The main hypothesis is that the combination of a mouse, the 3D widget UI, blend-able super-ellipsoids and a standard TF interface is an efficient and flexible technique for quickly creating contextual views of spatially localized regions. Super-ellipsoids, referred to as "blobs", are defined using implicit functions and can be seamlessly and tightly blended to form volumetric "paint" that envelopes regions and image features in the volume image. Inside a selected ROI defined by the blobs, a special TF may be applied that controls color and opacity separately from the surrounding structures. Note that this work does not compare higher degree of freedom (DOF) input devices to our mouse-widget approach for 3D volume view generation. In our experience, for desktop systems, higher DOF input devices suffer from precision, muscle fatigue, comfort and occlusion problems.

This paper presents work that improves and significantly expands on previous work [2]. In [2] a more restrictive spherical paint blob and blob manipulation UI that utilized a (data iso-) surface painting metaphor (referred to in this paper as a *surface brush*) was employed. In this new work we instead use 3D widget handles to manipulate a super-ellipsoid blob, referred to as the *blob tool* (Fig. 2). The widget handles act as intuitive signifiers that allow users (from any scene viewpoint) to flexibly and accurately position, orient, resize and deposit blobs that envelope a target ROI anywhere in the volume. Another major contribution is the addition of a *blob region-grow tool*. The same widget UI and blob provides an intuitive, convenient mechanism for interactively constraining and steering a GPU region growing segmentation algorithm in real time. These combined capabilities, unified under a single widget UI, support the highly-efficient selection and modification of complex-shaped volumetric regions, individual objects, parts of an object, or objects with complex geometry and topology - such as artery networks - allowing for fast and flexible volume exploration in 3D images ranging from relatively clean CT scans to moderately noisy images such as MR scans.

---

[1] Several videos of the tools comprising the technique can be viewed at https://www.youtube.com/watch?v=NsgipyU1lfQ&list=PLtEweT4itM8Ef2D9HLQDAKu6G1Ou1Q3Yr&index=1.

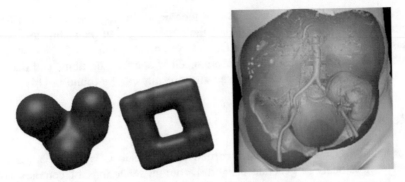

Fig. 1. Left – examples of super-ellipsoid blob blending. Right – blended blobs defining a region of interest. The interior region has separate TF controls from the exterior.

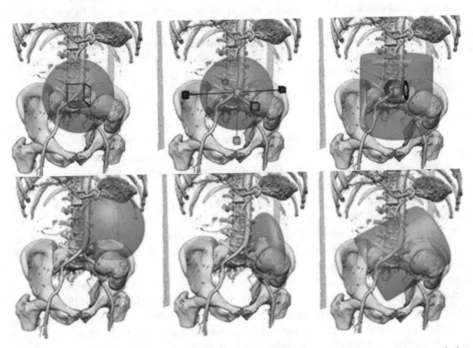

Fig. 2. Super-ellipsoid blob tool and its widget handles. Upper row, left to right: translation handle, resize handle, and rotation handle. Lower: effect of widget actions.

In addition, a new *open-view* capability can be activated for both tools to support real-time examination and measurement of occluded structures with respect to surrounding structures. Finally, the results of a user study comparing the 3D widget-based blob tool UI, the previously developed surface brush style UI and a standard cylinder "screen-space paintbrush" UI for defining a ROI are presented. Several experiments

458 K. Lagos and T. McInerney

demonstrating the use of our visualization technique for creating different views are also performed in order to further validate the effectiveness of the technique. Note that this paper will primarily focus on the UI and system functionality. Details of the blob and blob blending mathematical formulation, GPU shader algorithms and data structures, as well as tables detailing the user study results can be found in [14].

2 Related Work

A large amount of research has been carried out to create UI's and TF's that enable medical professionals to generate insightful volume renderings of complex volume images. In general, many of the 1D TF's and 2D TF's developed do not utilize global or local spatial information. However, how much spatial information is needed is perhaps task dependent [1]. Focus plus context visualizations attempt to visually combine a user-selected local spatial region of primary interest (the focus) with the surrounding information—or context—into a single display. One of the most common focus plus context techniques is to make occluding objects semi-transparent thereby revealing hidden objects [3]. For un-segmented volume data, the opacity of a sample point along a ray can be controlled by a function of shading intensity, gradient magnitude, distance to the viewer, and previously accumulated opacity [4]. In general, the use of transparency is limited – it does not provide a strong visual cue of the depth of the hidden objects and it can be visually confusing if there are multiple overlapping semi-transparent layers. The use of a distance function as part of the overall TF specification does use spatial information [5]. However, the distance-functions are typically radial in nature and do necessarily provide much local and shaped spatial control. Several researchers have developed techniques to generate focus plus context views where the focus region is more explicitly defined with a convex-shaped 3D "lens" [2, 3, 6–9]. The lens geometry is often a cylinder, sphere or cone or some other compactly defined mathematical function. Similar to some of the work presented in this paper, Bruckner and Gröller [10] uses a 3D volumetric painting approach with a 3D Gaussian lens. Lenses realized with super-ellipsoids have also been used by other researchers, albeit often in more restricted ways than in our work. Luo et al. [8] uses a super-ellipsoid distance function to define their focal probe region. Within this region, a different rendering style may be used than in the surrounding context. Radeva et al. [11] also uses a super-ellipsoid "lens". In our work the lens can also act as a tool tip to deposit multiple super-ellipsoid paint blobs that are smoothly blended to define a complex–shaped paint region. Another issue with a convex lens approach is the target region/object may be occluded (i.e. hidden) by other objects. Luo et al. [8] incorporates a view-dependent cone region to cutaway occluding voxels in front of the focal probe. We use a similar approach but the shape of the auxiliary lens is not restricted to a cone but rather is configurable and is designed to provide depth cues by orienting the cut surfaces of the occluding objects toward the viewer such that the relative position and depth of an object is easier to perceive (Sect. 3.3).

2.1 Selecting a Complex-Shaped ROI as a Focus Region

Interactive selection of *complex-shaped* 3D ROI selection techniques can be categorized in several ways. One categorization is data dependent techniques versus data independent techniques. A data independent technique specifies a ROI spatially (i.e. geometrically). A data dependent technique uses data attributes, such as voxel intensity or voxel gradient magnitude, to label voxels as part of the same structure. Data independent techniques are purely geometric and are primarily based on user interactive spatial specification of a ROI. The advantage of these techniques is that they can be applied to any volume, regardless of noise. However, they place emphasis on the user to navigate to an ROI and define an envelope and their effectiveness hinges upon the UI design. Techniques for interactive geometric specification of a ROI can also be categorized based on the underlying interaction metaphor used. Tracing, painting, sculpting, and deforming are among the most common metaphors used [2].

Data dependent selection (i.e. segmentation) techniques are a heavily researched field and advanced segmentation algorithms are often required to select structures in noisy images. Nevertheless, simpler highly-parallel GPU-based segmentation algorithms, such as voxel region growing [12, 13], can be used with great effect in volume rendered images such as CT and MR scans to quickly define a ROI and generate a contextual view for previewing and examining of a target region. These techniques may be sufficiently accurate to perform a visual analysis and measurement of hidden structures by supporting fast selection and removal of occluding structures. Region growing algorithms are susceptible to noise and are prone to leaking into neighboring structures and therefore benefit from interactive control of the overall growing/shrinking process. Some implementations allow for rough interactive control over the *localized* growing/shrinking of the selected voxels [12]. The volume visualization package LiveVolume [13] supports fast GPU region growing to select complex connected voxel regions. The UI is simple and effective – an initial point is selected, and the user uses the mouse to control the growing/shrinking of this region in 3D by moving the cursor away from, or towards this initial point. Chen et al. [12] support fast GPU region growing for segmentation using a UI where the user sketches curves on the screen to initiate the region growing. Localized region shrinking is supported by sketching additional curves to indicate regions to stop and reverse growth.

3 Implementation

This section provides an overview of the implementation and interface of the system. The super-ellipsoid blobs are defined using implicit functions and the functions are evaluated at each voxel location in a special 3D grid of voxels referred to as the *blob grid*. The blob grid has dimensions matching that of the input volume. The implementation allows users to place a large number of blobs, if desired, in real time. To ensure quick lookups into the grid, the blob grid is stored in GPU memory. A disadvantage of our implementation is that it requires a large amount of GPU memory but results in overall higher performance by avoiding expensive calculations in the volume ray cast shader program. Specifically, this gain in performance is achieved by computing the blob grid values in a separate rendering phase using a special, highly-efficient GPU vertex shader program. As the user deposits a new blob, it is blended with the existing blob grid field values computed from previously deposited blobs - there is no need to re-compute the grid field values for all blobs. Consequently, during the volume rendering phase, at each step along the ray these grid values can then be efficiently accessed from the volume rendering fragment shader program. In addition to the blob grid, two other grids are required to support the system functionality. The dimensions of both of these grids also match the input volume grid dimensions. A *region grow grid* is used to record voxels selected by the region grow tool. The *accumulation grid* is used to combine the voxel selections of the individual blob tool or region grow tool selections. The volume rendering algorithm blends the values from the input volume and the various grids to form the final image.

3.1 Blob Tool

Widget handles are designed to suggest their function (i.e. translate, rotate, scale) and operation as well as provide an additional visual depth cue for the blob (Fig. 2). Handles appear via a key press. When a handle is selected, it is then hidden to allow the user to clearly see the effects of their mouse movements on the tool tip blob. When the user releases the left mouse button, the handles reappear. GUI sliders can be used to change the shape and opacity of the blob. As the blob is manipulated, voxels inside are highlighted to provide visual feedback of the selection region. If a user is satisfied with the selection, they can deposit the blob (i.e. blend it with any previously applied paint blobs) via a key or GUI button. The user can instantly undo applied blobs in the order of last applied to first.

3.2 Blob Region-Grow Tool

As mentioned, a GPU-based region grow algorithm is a fast segmentation technique for selecting a complex-shaped connected structures. However, region grow algorithms are noise sensitive and are prone to "leaking" into neighboring regions with similar voxel intensity ranges to that of the target. Therefore, interactively controlling the region grow process prevents a user from wasting time manually correcting the region grow output by removing the leaked regions. In addition, the ability to interactively update the region growing allows users to generate new views "on the fly".

In our work, we use the widget UI to interactively constrain and "steer" 3D region growing. This *blob region-grow tool* (Fig. 3) can be applied directly to the volume image to select connected voxels, for example an artery "tree", or alternatively can be applied to connected voxels within a previous ROI selected by the blob tool - allowing the user to select ROIs even within a moderately noisy volume image.

The constrained region grow is implemented on the GPU following the algorithm in [12]. The user initiates region growing by first using the translation widget handles to place the tool tip blob around an anatomical structure they wish to select (Fig. 3 left). The user then moves the mouse along the surface of this structure and a small green circular region is highlighted, indicating a valid seed voxel is within the bounds of the blob. If the circular region is colored red, this indicates the seed voxel is outside the blob.

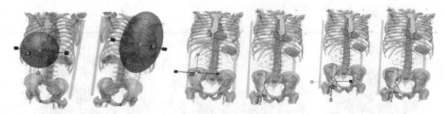

Fig. 3. Examples showing the blob region-grow tool selecting connected structures. 1, 2: the region growing algorithm is spatially-constrained by the super-ellipsoid blob. 3–6: The grown region can be dynamically resized/reshaped in real-time by using the widget handles to adjust the blob size/shape (rectangular blob not rendered). (Color figure online)

A valid seed point is then selected with a mouse click. The region grow process is then activated and all valid connected voxels within the blob boundary are selected, essentially instantaneously. Valid voxels are voxels that are visible in the scene and not already selected. The blob tip can then be interactively resized, reshaped or rotated using the widget handles and the selected region will automatically grow and/or shrink, in real-time, to stay within the blob (Fig. 3, 3–6). This includes one-sided control over resizing using one of the six resize handles. Other target regions can be dynamically added by reinitiating the region grow tool and selecting new seed voxels. The user can also use a key or GUI button to instantly undo any selected ROI. By having the region growing controlled by the same 3D widget UI as the blob tool, the user can precisely select regions of connected voxels that might be otherwise difficult and/or time-consuming to isolate using only a pure geometric blob tool - the tools are complementary.

3.3   Open-View

In situations where the 3D blob tool itself is occluded or the target object is occluded, the user may activate an *Open-View* mode to automatically remove the occluding objects without losing the surrounding context. The open-view capability is implemented with an (invisible) auxiliary "lens" with one lens endpoint fixed to the view-point and the other endpoint attached to the blob tool tip (Fig. 4). As the user manipulates the blob tool or rotates the scene, the open-view lens automatically cuts away any occluding visible voxels between the viewpoint and the tool tip blob. The shape of the Open-View lens is defined by a shaft region and an adjustable super-ellipsoid cap (Fig. 5). The cap can be translated, scaled, rotated and tapered using a similar widget interface as the blob tool. GUI sliders are also available to adjust the shape of the cap – which in turn automatically adjusts the shape of the shaft to match. A separate rounded or tapered cap creates an effective perceptual depth cue of the cutaway region by orienting the cut surfaces towards the viewer. Combining the open-view capability with the widget blob tool UI allows the user to quickly create specialized view dependent cutaway regions such that the contextual view is enhanced with effective depth cues provided by the surface of the cutaway region (Fig. 4).

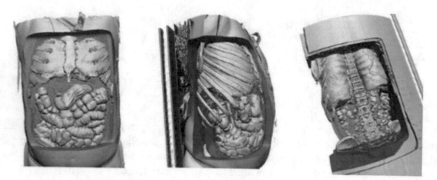

Fig. 4. Using *open-view* to create a cutaway region to reveal a user's earlier blob tool selection of the lungs and intestines. These structures can then be viewed relative to skin and bone.

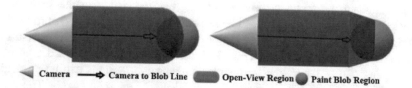

Fig. 5. An open-view lens" representation for spherical and tapered cubical cap shapes. The cap shapes are designed to orient cut surfaces toward the user, regardless of the length of the shaft.

4 Results and Validation

A user study was performed in an effort to quantitatively evaluate the UI efficiency and accuracy, as well as qualitatively evaluate the ease of use, flexibility, and rendering control of the super-ellipsoid based technique and its associated widget UI for selecting and visualizing a wide range of target ROIs and anatomical structures.

4.1 User Study Results

The user study was divided into four parts. Each part required participants to select a previously highlighted target object. Sixteen people participated in the study. The participants were asked to select several regions of interest with four different paint-based selection tools and then fill out a questionnaire. Efficiency, accuracy and user tool preference were recorded (See [14] for details of measurements). Participants consisted of 14 males and 2 females aged between 18–30 years old. Participant's average mouse usage per week was approximately 28 h, with an average of 11 h a week for video games and 2.4 h for 3D modeling software. The user study experiments were performed on a Windows 10 desktop computer with a mouse and keyboard. The computer was equipped with Nvidia 1080 GTX graphic card to ensure the system ran at a smooth 60 fps on a 1920 × 1080 native resolution monitor. The four paint tools used in the study were the blob tool, region-grow blob tool, a surface brush and a screen brush.

The UI of the surface brush and UI of the screen brush are briefly described below. Although the surface brush was implemented in a separate system, the system was updated to use matching super-ellipsoid blobs and matching volume rendering parameters. The surface brush employs an adjacent GUI panel to control brush size, orientation, and shape. The surface brush has two painting modes, a camera view-plane sliding mode and data iso-surface sliding mode. In both cases the blob orientation is automatically defined from the plane/iso-surface orientation. As the user moves the mouse the brush automatically adheres to and slides along the plane/surface. The screen brush is a screen space painting technique similar to 2D painting applications. A circular outline depicts the brush bounds and the brush is resized using a separate GUI slider. Users can paint on a volume rendered image by dragging the mouse along the screen to paint strokes. The brush also paints in depth and selects voxels based on the camera's perspective projection. The depth is set to the far side of the volume. An eraser is also supported. Therefore, to select a target object, users rotate the scene with the mouse to find a screen view such that the target object is visually separated from the surrounding objects. After painting and erasing the object from this viewpoint, the users then repeat this process from new viewpoints until the object has been selected.

The study used two CT scans and was comprised of four different target anatomical structures (Fig. 6). Each structure was specifically selected to tease out the strengths and weaknesses of each UI. In the hands of an experienced user, the selection tools used in the study can be used to quickly isolate a complex-shaped ROI consisting of multiple anatomical structures. However, in this study the participants are naïve users. Consequently, an ROI consisting of single, clearly defined anatomical structures were chosen as the targets, highlighted in yellow and with the remaining visible voxels de-emphasized by coloring them gray (Fig. 6). If the user correctly selects these voxels, they are instantly painted green. Incorrectly selected voxels (i.e. voxels inside the blob boundary but outside the target) were instantly painted red.

Both efficiency and accuracy were measured. The purely geometric tools (blob tool, surface brush, screen brush) were first compared to each other. In terms of efficiency almost all selection tasks were completed in well under two minutes. When comparing the tools to each other the results were mixed, with the screen brush on average the most efficient. However, the blob tool was consistently the most accurate selection technique for all trials. The widget region-grow tool was then introduced and compared to the other tools. As this technique selects connected voxels within a preset intensity range, it is slightly less accurate than the geometric tools. However, it is easily the most efficient technique for selecting a single connected structure, like those in the study. Details of the efficiency and accuracy results can be found in [14].

After the trials for each tool were completed, participants were asked to fill out a questionnaire to evaluate their level of satisfaction with the tool using a 7-point Likert scale. Users were also asked to pick their favorite tool before and after the introduction of the region grow tool. Before the introduction of the region-grow tool participants generally favored the screen brush as it provided a simple and familiar interface for the selection tasks. The blob tool was the second favorite as users with gaming or 3D modeling experience were familiar with the handle-based controls. Participants

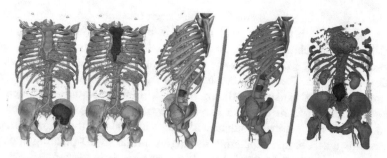

Fig. 6. A series of anatomical structures used in the user study. From left to right: kidney, sternum, single vertebra, double vertebra and aneurysm. (Color figure online)

overwhelmingly favored the blob region grow tool once it was introduced. The intuitive widget interface combined with the region-grow functionality allowed users to quickly and accurately select a single target object. As mentioned, because the participants were naïve users, single-object targets were used in the study for clarity and simplicity. This experimental setup may have introduced some bias towards a tool specifically designed for this task. The least favorite technique was the surface brush, most likely due to having the brush size and shape controls on a separate GUI panel, which several participants found frustrating for some target object selection tasks. This result was not unexpected. Although the surface brush is a more direct manipulation technique for positioning and automatic orientation, the cost of this capability is the difficulty of integrating blob resizing, depth control and blob orientation fine tuning into the interface.

4.2 Experiments

Additional experiments were performed by the authors to demonstrate the capabilities and flexibility of the system and UI for creating contextual, spatially localized views of a wide range of target structures. All experiments were performed in less than 5 min and a brief description of the selection process is provided for each.

Aneurysm. The region of interest for this CT dataset (down-sampled to $256 \times 256 \times 144$) was the aneurysm and connecting arteries (Fig. 7). An aneurysm is an excessive localized enlargement of an artery cause by a weakening of the artery wall. An initial voxel visibility intensity range was set to display bones and arteries via the TF. A region-grow tool was then used to initially select the aneurysm itself. At this point, the aneurysm volume can be measured, if desired. The widget handles were then used to resize the super-ellipsoid blob to instantly grow the region into the connecting arteries and the selected voxels were added to the accumulation grid. The minimum voxel visibility range was then lowered to render surrounding skin, muscles, and bones. A rectangular open-view lens was activated to create a view that allows users to clearly see the aneurysm's position in relation to various surrounding structures. The open-view lens also allows the user to view the aneurysm from any angle and quickly gain additional insight.

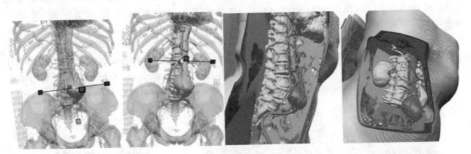

Fig. 7. Aneurysm selection experiment. From left to right: 1. Minimum and maximum visibility set to view aneurysm and surrounding structures. 2. Aneurysm selected with region-grow tool and tool adjusted to grow into connecting arteries. 3, 4. Selected voxels added to the accumulation grid and open-view lens activated to create various contextual views by changing the viewing angle and visibility settings.

Kidney. This experiment was conducted on a $256 \times 256 \times 296$ (down-sampled) CT scan and showcases how a user can create various contextual views of a kidney transplant (Fig. 8). Initially, the hip bone was selected using the blob tool and the selected voxels were added to the accumulation grid. The kidney and connecting arteries and vertebrae were then selected using a region-grow tool and were also added to the accumulation grid. A cubical blob tool was used and interactively adjusted (along with TF visibility settings) to create several contextual views. The kidney transplant position can be analyzed.

Fig. 8. Kidney transplant experiment. Initially a blob tool was used to select the hip bone. Left to right: 1. Region-grow tool used to select the connected arteries and the kidney. 2–4: Blob tool to create contextual views by changing the viewing angle and visibility settings.

Brain Tumor. This experiment uses a (down-sampled) $288 \times 288 \times 22$ MRI scan and demonstrates how the system can be used with nosier volume images to create effective views (Fig. 9). In this case, the object of interest is a tumor inside the brain. The tumor has a very high intensity value. To select the tumor, the minimum voxel visibility range was set to a high value and the region grow tool was used to select and add the tumor to the accumulation grid. To create cross sections in the brain, a rectangular blob tool was used with its minimum voxel visibility range set to the maximum value. Since voxels within the accumulation grid are not affected by the visibility settings of the blob tool, it allows users to interactively create cross sections by translating, rotating, or resizing the tool. This allows users to quickly ascertain and measure the tumor's position relative to other objects within the dataset.

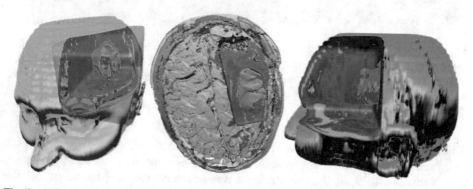

Fig. 9. MRI brain tumor selection experiment. Left: Set initial minimum and maximum visibility settings to view brain tumor without losing any detail. Select tumor with blob region grow tool and add to accumulation grid. Middle, Right: Use rectangular blob tool and set TF such that voxels are invisible. Tumor position and extent can now be measured from various angles.

Pulmonary Stent. This experiment was conducted on a $512 \times 512 \times 308$ CT scan and demonstrates how the system can be used to select a stent and inspect its position within the artery. Starting from the top left of Fig. 10, the voxel visibility range was adjusted to view the lungs, but unfortunately, the stent wasn't clearly visible until the voxel intensity range was reset to a higher value. As the surrounding area was clean, the blob tool was used to select the stent and the selected voxels were added to the accumulation grid. The voxel visibility range was then lowered to view the stent's position around the heart and top of the lungs. To get a clearer view, a blob was placed around the area of the stent and all outside voxels were removed. This allowed the user to zoom in and create an enlarged view of the stent and its surrounding objects for inspection. Voxels of lower intensity were then brought back, and an open view lens was added to show cross-sectional views of the stent within the artery. These two techniques allow the user to inspect the stent's position relative to other objects and to potentially verify correct placement.

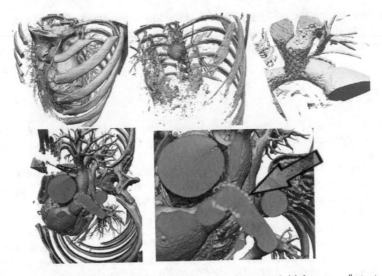

Fig. 10. Pulmonary stent experiment. From top left: 1. Create initial scene of stent and lung region using TF. 2, 3. Increase minimum visible voxel intensity via TF to isolate the stent and use the blob tool to select the stent and add it to accumulation grid. Bottom 4, 5. Add open-view lens to create contextual views. The arrow indicates the stent cross-section.

5   Conclusion

The goal of simply and efficiently exploring and selecting regions of any shape or level of occlusion, in order to examine and focus on specific structures and their spatial relationship to surrounding structures, can be difficult to achieve using only a TF approach. Fast and flexible interactive volume navigation and ROI selection tools can potentially augment TFs to realize this goal. However, the problem is shifted to one of designing an effective tool and UI. This paper presented one design and compared it to two other common selection tools with well-known UIs. Virtual surface paintbrush style UIs are well-known technique for easily selecting and removing outer region "layers" of voxels belonging to a specific tissue type, such as skin [2]. However, due to the nature of the painting style they mimic, they may not be optimal for enveloping (i.e. selecting for highlighting or removing) structures with varying thickness. They also cannot be easily used in noisy images. A 3D widget-based UI, on the other hand, is more "volume-oriented" and amenable to highly accurate envelopment but may require more user interaction to position and manipulate. However, unlike the surface brush it can be applied to noisy datasets. Finally, the standard screen-space paintbrush UI is familiar, highly intuitive and often more efficient for selecting some 3D objects. However, for fast modification of the ROI to support volume exploration and iterative generation of contextual views, the 3D widget UI is more flexible than both the surface and screen brush UIs. In addition, and more importantly, the widget UI provides a convenient and flexible control mechanism for steering a 3D region growing segmentation technique, adding powerful selection capabilities. The mixed results of the user study indicate that it may be beneficial to incorporate the best features of the surface and screen brush tools into the widget UI.

References

1. Ljung, P., Kruger, J.H., Groller, E., Hadwiger, M., Hansen, C.D., Ynnerman, A.: State of the art in transfer functions for direct volume rendering. Comput. Graph. Forum **35**, 669–691 (2016)
2. Faynshteyn, L., McInerney, T.: Context-preserving volumetric data set exploration using a 3D painting metaphor. In: Bebis, G., et al. (eds.) ISVC 2012. LNCS, vol. 7431, pp. 336–347. Springer, Heidelberg (2012). https://doi.org/10.1007/978-3-642-33179-4_33
3. Kriger, J., Schneider, J., Westermann, R.: ClearView: an interactive context preserving hotspot visualization technique. IEEE Trans. Vis. Comput. Graph. **12**(5), 941–948 (2006)
4. Bruckner, S., Grimm, S., Kanitsar, A., Gröller, M.E.: Illustrative context-preserving exploration of volume data. IEEE Trans. Vis. Comput. Graph. **12**(6), 1559–1569 (2006)
5. Tappenbeck, A., Preim, B., Dicken, V.: Distance-based transfer function design: specification methods and applications. In: Simulation and Visualization (2006)
6. Zhou, J., Döring, A., Tönnies, K.: Distance based enhancement for focal region based volume rendering. In: Tolxdorff, T., Braun, J., Handels, H., Horsch, A., Meinzer, H.P. (eds.) Bildverarbeitung für die Medizin 2004. Springer, Berlin (2004). https://doi.org/10.1007/978-3-642-18536-6_41
7. Monclus, E., Diaz, J., Navazo, I., Vazquez, P.P.: The virtual magic lantern: an interaction metaphor for enhanced medical data inspection. In: The 16th ACM Symposium on Virtual Reality Software and Technology, Kyoto, Japan (2009)
8. Luo, Y., Iglesias Guitián, J.A., Gobbetti, E., Marton, F.: Context preserving focal probes for exploration of volumetric medical datasets. In: Magnenat-Thalmann, N. (ed.) 3DPH 2009. LNCS, vol. 5903, pp. 187–198. Springer, Heidelberg (2009). https://doi.org/10.1007/978-3-642-10470-1_16
9. Ropinski, T., Steinicke, F., Hinrichs, K.: Tentative results in focus-based medical volume visualization. In: Butz, A., Fisher, B., Krüger, A., Olivier, P. (eds.) SG 2005. LNCS, vol. 3638, pp. 218–221. Springer, Heidelberg (2005). https://doi.org/10.1007/11536482_19
10. Bruckner, S., Gröller, M.: Volumeshop: an interactive system for direct volume illustration. In: 16th IEEE Conference on Visualization (VIS 2005), Baltimore, MD (2005)
11. Radeva, N., Levy, L., Hahn, J.: Generalized temoral focus + context framework for improved medical data exploration. J. Digit. Imaging **27**, 207–219 (2014)
12. Chen, H., Samavati, F., Sousa, M.: GPU-based point radiation for interactive volume sculpting and segmentation. Vis. Comput. **24**(7), 689–698 (2008)
13. LiveVolume. www.livevolume.com. Accessed 01 June 2017
14. Lagos, K.: Fast contextual view generation and region of interest selection in 3D medical images via superellipsoid manipulation, blending and constrained region growing. Master's thesis, Department of Computer Science, Ryerson University, Toronto, ON, Canada (2019)

A Virtual Reality Framework for Training Incident First Responders and Digital Forensic Investigators

Umit Karabiyik[✉], Christos Mousas, Daniel Sirota, Takahide Iwai,
and Mesut Akdere

Purdue University, West Lafayette, IN 47907, USA
{umit,cmousas,dsirota,tiwai,makdere}@purdue.edu

Abstract. This paper presents the basic functionalities of a virtual reality framework developed for training first responders and digital forensic investigators. The framework is divided into two modules: training and evaluation. The framework provides a variety of functionalities and behaviors that can be assigned to virtual objects and allows training and evaluation of crime scenes to be easily customized. During the training module, an individual can be trained to perform various procedures, pipelines, and task execution sequences. After the training is completed, the individual can then be immersed in and interact with a virtual reality crime scene by collecting as much evidence as possible. This process allows the system to evaluate the trainee's performance and the training process in general. In the evaluation process, the developed framework captures several types of information regarding the individual's performance, including missing evidence, the task execution sequence, and the task completion time. The collected data can then be provided to the trainee or supervisor for evaluation. A simple customizable scoring method was also developed and incorporated into the developed framework to provide immediate performance feedback to the trainee.

Keywords: Virtual reality · Training · Digital forensics · First responders · Task evaluation

1 Introduction

Digital forensics incident response and investigations are performed by individuals who receive ongoing training in their technical domains. The required training typically has the following characteristics: (i) lengthy, due to the significant changes in technology and the proliferation of digital devices; (ii) costly, because of the use of commercial products [19]; and (iii) provides less creativity where radical solutions may be needed. Training for digital forensics incident response and investigations has, traditionally, been conducted through simple presentations and on-site visits as investigators are required to travel to specific facilities to get proper training. However, due to the democratization of virtual reality

© Springer Nature Switzerland AG 2019
G. Bebis et al. (Eds.): ISVC 2019, LNCS 11845, pp. 469–480, 2019.
https://doi.org/10.1007/978-3-030-33723-0_38

technology, it is possible to transfer real-world training to virtual environments while providing an effective and immersive training experience. Thus, this paper presents a flexible virtual reality framework that provides a number of functionalities to allow realistic simulated experiences to incident first responders and digital forensics investigators. It should be noted that the developed proof-of-concept framework allows the use of various consumer-grade virtual reality headsets (e.g., Oculus Rift, HTC Vive, Samsung Odyssey, etc.) and hence lends itself well to standardized distribution for scaling up.

The developed framework is divided into two modules, which are the training and evaluation modules. The training module delivers simple scenarios that provide information about practical and cognitive tasks related to the training process, which is a learning-by-doing experience. The training is designed based on the best practices published by United States Secret Service [36] and National Institute of Justice [24]. The framework's evaluation module allows the trainee to navigate within the virtual environment, as well as perform different types of interactions with objects and tasks located within it to collect the necessary evidence. Through this immersive experience, in both the training and evaluation module of the framework, the trainee is taught the necessary practical and cognitive knowledge and skills required to process a real-life crime scene. Additionally, because the trainee performs all tasks within a virtual environment, we can include additional features that can later be used to evaluate its performance and provide feedback. To demonstrate the potential of the developed framework, we present a simple training and evaluation scenario.

The developed framework allows the logical integration of multiple features without requiring an experienced virtual reality developer to have knowledge of programming or other graphics- and virtual reality-related complex tasks. The framework is generalized to allow the addition of new functionalities and routines with minimal implementation effort. We believe that such a framework may provide insights to future researchers and developers who wish to create virtual reality training frameworks for various training domains and purposes. We also believe that the developed framework can be deployed in such a way that other training scenarios can be developed in addition to those related to incident first responds and digital forensics investigations.

2   Literature Review

In the current literature, there is variety of virtual reality applications proposed for various forensic science problems [6,17,25]. These applications focus on physical evidence that does not imply or support the existence of related digital evidence, hence they do not contribute to the digital forensics discipline. However, significant amount of physical evidence can be used to lead digital forensics investigations. Due to the lack of virtual reality training systems for digital forensics, we shift our focus in this section to discuss the literature review for virtual reality systems in general.

Virtual reality systems utilized for training purposes can be considered powerful learning tools [16]. With the use of virtual reality systems, it is possible to integrate technologies and allow users to interact with virtual reality scenarios in a multi-sensory manner, including physical interaction and tactile sensations [3,4,29]. Some studies have indicated that virtual reality environment in training experiences provides unique benefits compared to traditional monolithic training approaches. For example, such systems provide a learning-by-doing teaching approach [13,18,29]. Moreover, various types of cues, such as visual, auditory, or haptic, that are also available in the real world can also be provided, making the whole experience provided in virtual environments look realistic. Such cues are responsible for facilitating the learning task, as well as providing the ability to simulate learning modules in a flexible manner that allows adaptation to individual needs and training goals [13,18]. Virtual reality systems have been used to provide not only practical training, including medical training [12,15,39], driving [5,20], dance [7,9,21], painting [23,38], and safety [14,32], but also cognitive training, such as motor learning [27,33] and attention enhancement [11,31]. In the rest of this section, we present different virtual reality training applications that have been developed.

Virtual reality applications have been developed for training purposes in different domains. Training children to walk cross streets safely has been an interesting topic in the broader community, and based on the reported results of previous studies [26,34], utilizing virtual reality for road crossing training is quite effective. Driving simulations developed to teach safe driving skills have also been used extensively. In addition to the logical advantages that such a virtual reality driving training process provide, it has been found [2,22] that such training processes are quite appealing to the exposed individuals. Other virtual reality training applications deal with evacuation training processes in highly emergent conditions, and most of them, similar to the one that is presented in this paper, target professional practitioners. Virtual reality has been used for firefighter training [1,8,35], as well as evacuation and escape from different types of emergency situations [28,37]. It can be said that the advantage of virtual reality training in the abovementioned scenarios is that it enables people to practice skills in a safe environment that they will later need to perform under highly pressured and hazardous situations.

Virtual reality applications provide training, but they should also have a way to evaluate whether the individual has met the learning objectives. In previous studies, it was found that knowledge gained during virtual reality training can indeed transfer to evaluations conducted in the real-world or virtual reality [10,26,30]. Moreover, results obtained from previous studies [10,30] indicate that virtual reality training in highly immersive environments enhances learners' retention of knowledge gained during the training. Based on the abovementioned findings, we were inspired to develop a virtual reality framework to train incident first responders and digital forensics investigators. We believe it is possible that knowledge gained from virtual training can be efficiently transferred to real-world environments. To the best of our knowledge, no previous virtual reality applications or frameworks for training incident first responders and digital forensic investigators have been developed. Therefore, the effort made to identify different functionalities and incorporate them into a single framework in which the crime scene and the training process may be easily adapted can be considered as the main contribution of this paper.

3 Functionalities of the Framework

This framework is implemented via the Unity3D games engine. Several standalone functionalities that we implemented can be easily attached to the necessary training parts/object. Unity3D provides the flexibility of easily reusing scripts, which makes it ideal for such a framework since it allows a developer to change the training process and the crime scene scenario and simply attach the necessary scripts to the new components added in the three-dimensional (3D) scene. The next section describes the basic functionalities that a developer can choose from when implementing a new training and evaluation process.

3.1 Interaction Modules

Several different individual interaction modules and functionalities were implemented in the developed framework. Each of the interactive modules and functionalities works independently, and a developer can simply pick which module or functionality to include in the training and evaluation process. The developed modules and functionalities are presented below.

Navigation: Various navigation mechanisms were implemented. Specifically, a user can choose to either navigate using a standard gamepad, keyboard, or virtual reality controllers or perform natural locomotion. To do so, the user needs to pick one of the provided navigation mechanisms from the inspector window of Unity3D.

Object Interaction: The trainee has the ability to interact with objects that are located within the crime scene. To do so, a simple script was implemented that assigns different properties to the objects. Specifically, this script helps the developer to specify which objects are interactive. Objects that are assigned to be interactive can be grasped, moved, and rotated by the trainee to inspect them further. For the interactive objects, additional functionalities can be specified by the developer, such as turning on/off, copying clipboard data, or removing a part of a device (e.g. battery).

Repository: A digital repository was also implemented. This repository keeps track of evidence collected by the individual trainee and provides instant visual feedback to the trainee when needed. The repository simply represents the inventory list of collected evidence from the crime scene in real life investigations.

Tools: Several tools were implemented that can be useful during an investigation process. These tools are quite common and used almost always by investigators:

- **Tags:** When collecting objects from a crime scene, the investigator is required to tag the collected evidence by writing down necessary information on notes and assigning the notes to the collected evidence.
- **Bags:** Before placing the collected evidence into the repository, the investigator is required to put the object into a bag. This is an important procedure that an investigator must follow. The investigator should insert the associated tag on the bag.
- **Notebook:** A notebook is provided to the trainee to write notes during the investigation process. This helps the investigators remember small details if he or she needs to revisit the crime scene again.
- **Stickers:** The provided stickers are quite useful to the investigators since they can write down information about particular objects and areas of the crime scene and mark the visited areas.
- **Ruler:** A virtual ruler is provided so the investigator can measure the dimensions of not only the objects but also the crime scene itself. The ruler also allows the investigator to not only describe the object but also record the dimensions and the exact position it was found within the crime scene.
- **Flashlight:** A virtual flashlight is included to allow the investigator to explore dimly lit areas of the crime scene, which enhances the realism of the investigation process since not all crime scenes are well lit.
- **Camera:** The use of a camera when exploring crime scenes is a must since an investigator needs to collect not only the necessary evidence but also additional information about the crime scene. Record of the scene in pictures is indispensible for a successful investigation. Thus, a virtual camera is also included. Using this camera, the trainee can collect additional evidence. The captured pictures are placed in a separate 'pictures' repository, to which the investigator has access throughout the training and evaluation process to determine whether a particular image has already been taken.

3.2 Data Acquisition

Data acquisition is quite important in the trainee evaluation process. For this reason, different data that provide useful information about the evaluation process are collected during the runtime of the evaluation module:

- **Task execution sequence:** There are various sequences in which a task can be executed; however, in most cases, only one sequence can be considered correct. It may be noted that for various objects and types of evidence, the investigator needs to follow a specific sequence of actions to ensure safe and reasonable execution of the task. The developed framework provides the ability to store the sequence of actions used to collect each individual piece of evidence/object that the investigator decides to interact with, and the system stores the executed sequence. This approach was taken for three reasons.

First, the system can easily and automatically determine whether the task was performed in the right sequence. Second, the system can use this information to assess the investigator's performance. Third, the execution sequence of a task (especially the wrong one) can be provided as feedback to the investigator, and thus, the investigator can learn from his or her mistakes. Figure 1 depicts how the training tasks are executed by the trainee for a sample scenario where smartphone is found in turned off state. Green boxes represent correct tasks that an investigator is expected to follow where the red arrow and yellow boxes represent wrong direction and relatively correct tasks which might cause destruction or alteration of an evidence. Each box is assigned a score value that the trainee would gain if they perform that specific task before the conclusion of the process.

- **Missing evidence:** Each crime scene that is set up has predefined pieces of evidence that should be found and collected by the trainee. Once the trainee concludes that the investigation is complete and decides to exit the evaluation module of the framework, the system automatically determines whether there are any missing pieces of evidence and provides a percentage score of missing evidence to the trainee.

- **Task completion time:** This is the time that an individual investigator needs to finish the evaluation process. Although the task completion speed might not be directly related to the effectiveness of the training, when combined with the abovementioned data, it can provide information to the trainee about how detailed the investigation was. In most cases, rushing through an investigation may increase the risk of making mistakes hence causing the missing/destroying/altering evidentiary data.

3.3   Evaluation Method

In order to develop an evaluation method for our training, we developed a scoring system based on the best practices published in [24, 36] for investigators. When the training scenarios are developed, each task that an investigator should perform is assigned a score depending on how significant that specific task is compared to the other. In addition, we assigned penalties (usually significantly deducting possible points for a task) when the trainee performs a wrong action (see red/yellow items in Fig. 1). This is also decided based on the significance of a specific mistake. The possible mistakes we took into account are common mistakes that new investigators might possibly do.

As each training is designed not only to measure perfect actions of the trainee but also measure some partial scores for the action taken following any previous mistakes or wrong actions. As illustrated in Fig. 1, the trainee is expected to keep the device turned off to preserve the current state of the device. Following this action, some correct actions are still taken hence partial scores (e.g., 5 out of 15 for the first task) are given. In case of a serious mistakes are being made, no points will be given to the trainee.

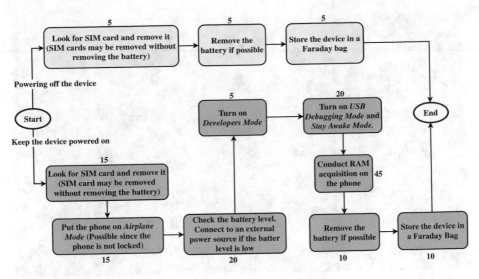

Fig. 1. Example diagram for the tasks given in a scenario where powered on smartphone is found. (Color figure online)

4   Training and Evaluation Modules

This section describes the two basic modules of the developed virtual reality framework. Each module is developed similar to the real life scenarios that we identified from the current digital forensics best practices publications.

4.1   Training Module

The training module of the developed framework affords the trainee the ability to, first, learn how to use the developed system and, second, gain both the practical and cognitive knowledge required. During the training process, the trainee is asked to interact with the embedded objects, which can be potential evidence in a crime scene. During this process, on-screen textual instructions are given to the trainee. These instructions follow specific guidelines provided by the developer of the training simulation and can be easily altered based on the individual needs and scenario. The trainee is then responsible for following the instructions and executing the necessary tasks. An example of the training module is depicted in Fig. 2. Once the training process is complete and the trainee feels confident about the knowledge he or she has gained, it can then switch to the evaluation module. Note that the trainee is allowed to perform each of the training tasks more than once in case it is required.

4.2   Evaluation Module

The evaluation module allows the trainee to test his or her newly acquired knowledge. In this case, a virtual reality crime scene is provided. The crime scene

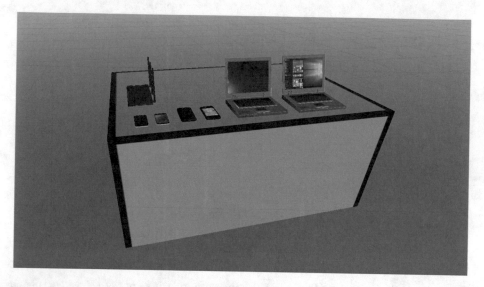

Fig. 2. Example of a training scene in which the trainee learns how to interact with the digital evidence and follow the task sequence.

includes various pieces of evidence that must be collected. During the evaluation module, the system records the pertaining data. No additional feedback is provided. Upon entering the virtual reality crime scene, the trainee is responsible for performing the necessary actions, collecting the necessary evidence, and report the results. We decided not to include time restrictions in the evaluation modules for two main reasons. First, the investigation process might take a long time and second, we did not want to put unnecessary pressure on the trainee. However, since the framework is responsible for collecting different types of data to assess the trainee's performance, completion time data can be used to understand how detailed the investigation process was.

For the purpose of this paper, a simple crime scene was developed, which is presented in Fig. 3. In this crime scene, the investigator should collect digital evidence (i.e., copy hard-drive data and browser history) and virtual devices (e.g., smartphones, laptops, and computers). The trainee is responsible for exiting the evaluation scene once he or she believes the process is complete. Next, the system provides a performance report to the trainee and the supervisor based on the developed scoring system, as well as additional feedback about mistakes made during the investigation process. Based on this feedback, the trainee might be asked to complete an additional training and evaluation process to ensure that the necessary knowledge is gained.

Fig. 3. The virtual crime scene (top) developed for this paper, and close-ups (bottom) of the digital evidence that should be collected.

5   Conclusions and Future Work

In this paper, we described the basic functionalities of virtual reality framework that is developed to train incident first responders and digital forensics investigators. The current version of the framework provides most of the necessary functionalities for training first responders and digital forensics investigators; however, various issues need to be addressed in future work. Specifically, in our future work, we are planning to extend the functionalities that should be included in such a framework. To do so, we are planning to consult with police officers and digital forensic investigators. We are planning to disseminate surveys and conduct in-depth interviews regarding possible digital forensic scenarios and functionalities that should be included to make this framework a useful tool for experimentation and training.

Additionally, in the current version of this framework, the individual developer needs to manually specify each piece of evidence and where it should be placed within the virtual environment. As a result, we are relying on our knowledge that the developed crime scenes provide effective training. For this reason, in the future extension of this framework, we are planning to develop a stochastic optimization algorithm that optimizes the difficulty of the crime scene by considering the location, as well as the number and types of pieces of evidence that needs to be collected. Such an extension will allow potential individuals to train at the same virtual crime scene repeatedly while experiencing new variations and different levels of difficulty.

Finally, in addition to the further development of this framework, we are also planning to conduct a number of user studies to investigate the potential of virtual reality training for incident first responders and digital forensics investigators. Such studies will help us further understand whether the proposed training framework can be used to substitute current training methods (i.e., slides and written notes) and increase training effectiveness and enhance trainee experience in the simulation.

References

1. Backlund, P., Engstrom, H., Hammar, C., Johannesson, M., Lebram, M.: Sidh-a game based firefighter training simulation. In: 2007 11th International Conference Information Visualization (IV 2007), pp. 899–907. IEEE (2007)
2. Backlund, P., Engstrom, H., Johannesson, M., Lebram, M.: Games and traffic safety-an experimental study in a game-based simulation environment. In: 2007 11th International Conference Information Visualization (IV 2007), pp. 908–916. IEEE (2007)
3. Basdogan, C., De, S., Kim, J., Muniyandi, M., Kim, H., Srinivasan, M.A.: Haptics in minimally invasive surgical simulation and training. IEEE Comput. Graph. Appl. 24(2), 56–64 (2004)
4. Baxter, B., Scheib, V., Lin, M.C., Manocha, D.: DAB: interactive haptic painting with 3D virtual brushes. In: Proceedings of the 28th Annual Conference on Computer Graphics and Interactive Techniques, pp. 461–468. ACM (2001)
5. Bayarri, S., Fernandez, M., Perez, M.: Virtual reality for driving simulation. Commun. ACM 39(5), 72–76 (1996)
6. Buck, U., Naether, S., Räss, B., Jackowski, C., Thali, M.J.: Accident or homicide-virtual crime scene reconstruction using 3D methods. Forensic Sci. Int. 225(1–3), 75–84 (2013)
7. Cai, Z.F., Liu, D.J., Zhang, A.Y.: Scheme study of automobile driving training simulator based on virtual reality. Acta Simulata Systematica Sinica 6 (2002)
8. Cha, M., Han, S., Lee, J., Choi, B.: A virtual reality based fire training simulator integrated with fire dynamics data. Fire Saf. J. 50, 12–24 (2012)
9. Chan, J.C., Leung, H., Tang, J.K., Komura, T.: A virtual reality dance training system using motion capture technology. IEEE Trans. Learn. Technol. 4(2), 187–195 (2010)
10. Chittaro, L., Buttussi, F.: Assessing knowledge retention of an immersive serious game vs. a traditional education method in aviation safety. IEEE Trans. Vis. Comput. Graph. 21(4), 529–538 (2015)
11. Cho, B.H., et al.: The effect of virtual reality cognitive training for attention enhancement. CyberPsychology Behav. 5(2), 129–137 (2002)
12. Colt, H.G., Crawford, S.W., Galbraith III, O.: Virtual reality bronchoscopy simulation: a revolution in procedural training. Chest 120(4), 1333–1339 (2001)
13. Derossis, A., Bothwell, J., Sigman, H., Fried, G.: The effect of practice on performance in a laparoscopic simulator. Surg. Endosc. 12(9), 1117–1120 (1998)
14. Filigenzi, M.T., Orr, T.J., Ruff, T.M.: Virtual reality for mine safety training. Appl. Occup. Environ. Hyg. 15(6), 465–469 (2000)

15. Gallagher, A.G., Cates, C.U.: Virtual reality training for the operating room and cardiac catheterisation laboratory. Lancet **364**(9444), 1538–1540 (2004)
16. Gavish, N., et al.: Evaluating virtual reality and augmented reality training for industrial maintenance and assembly tasks. Interact. Learn. Environ. **23**(6), 778–798 (2015)
17. Gee, A.P., Escamilla-Ambrosio, P.J., Webb, M., Mayol-Cuevas, W., Calway, A.: Augmented crime scenes: virtual annotation of physical environments for forensic investigation. In: Proceedings of the 2nd ACM Workshop on Multimedia in Forensics, Security and Intelligence, pp. 105–110. ACM (2010)
18. Gosselin, F., Ferlay, F., Bouchigny, S., Mégard, C., Taha, F.: Design of a multimodal VR platform for the training of surgery skills. In: Kappers, A.M.L., van Erp, J.B.F., Bergmann Tiest, W.M., van der Helm, F.C.T. (eds.) EuroHaptics 2010. LNCS, vol. 6192, pp. 109–116. Springer, Heidelberg (2010). https://doi.org/10.1007/978-3-642-14075-4_16
19. Hibshi, H., Vidas, T., Cranor, L.: Usability of forensics tools: a user study. In: 2011 Sixth International Conference on IT Security Incident Management and IT Forensics, pp. 81–91. IEEE (2011)
20. Ktena, S.I., Abbott, W., Faisal, A.A.: A virtual reality platform for safe evaluation and training of natural gaze-based wheelchair driving. In: 2015 7th International IEEE/EMBS Conference on Neural Engineering (NER), pp. 236–239. IEEE (2015)
21. Kyan, M., et al.: An approach to ballet dance training through ms kinect and visualization in a cave virtual reality environment. ACM Trans. Intell. Syst. Technol. (TIST) **6**(2), 23 (2015)
22. Lang, Y., Wei, L., Xu, F., Zhao, Y., Yu, L.F.: Synthesizing personalized training programs for improving driving habits via virtual reality. In: 2018 IEEE Conference on Virtual Reality and 3D User Interfaces (VR), pp. 297–304. IEEE (2018)
23. Lee, G.A., et al.: Virtual reality content-based training for spray painting tasks in the shipbuilding industry. ETRI J. **32**(5), 695–703 (2010)
24. Lothridge, K., Ftzpatrick, F.: Crime scene investigation: a guide for law enforcement (2013). https://www.nist.gov/sites/default/files/documents/forensics/Crime-Scene-Investigation.pdf
25. Ma, M., Zheng, H., Lallie, H.: Virtual reality and 3D animation in forensic visualization. J. Forensic Sci. **55**(5), 1227–1231 (2010)
26. McComas, J., MacKay, M., Pivik, J.: Effectiveness of virtual reality for teaching pedestrian safety. CyberPsychology Behav. **5**(3), 185–190 (2002)
27. Mirelman, A., Maidan, I., Herman, T., Deutsch, J.E., Giladi, N., Hausdorff, J.M.: Virtual reality for gait training: can it induce motor learning to enhance complex walking and reduce fall risk in patients with Parkinson's disease? J. Gerontol. Ser. A **66**(2), 234–240 (2011)
28. Mól, A.C.A., Jorge, C.A.F., Couto, P.M.: Using a game engine for VR simulations in evacuation planning. IEEE Comput. Graph. Appl. **28**(3), 6–12 (2008)
29. Nishino, H., Murayama, K., Kagawa, T., Utsumiya, K.: A Japanese calligraphy trainer based on skill acquisition through haptization. In: 2010 24th IEEE International Conference on Advanced Information Networking and Applications, pp. 1225–1232. IEEE (2010)
30. Padgett, L.S., Strickland, D., Coles, C.D.: Case study: using a virtual reality computer game to teach fire safety skills to children diagnosed with fetal alcohol syndrome. J. Pediatr. Psychol. **31**(1), 65–70 (2005)
31. Rizzo, A.A., et al.: The virtual classroom: a virtual reality environment for the assessment and rehabilitation of attention deficits. CyberPsychology Behav. **3**(3), 483–499 (2000)

32. Sacks, R., Perlman, A., Barak, R.: Construction safety training using immersive virtual reality. Constr. Manag. Econ. **31**(9), 1005–1017 (2013)
33. dos Santos Mendes, F.A., et al.: Motor learning, retention and transfer after virtual-reality-based training in Parkinson's disease-effect of motor and cognitive demands of games: a longitudinal, controlled clinical study. Physiotherapy **98**(3), 217–223 (2012)
34. Schwebel, D.C., Gaines, J., Severson, J.: Validation of virtual reality as a tool to understand and prevent child pedestrian injury. Accid. Anal. Prev. **40**(4), 1394–1400 (2008)
35. Tate, D.L., Sibert, L., King, T.: Virtual environments for shipboard firefighting training. In: Proceedings of IEEE 1997 Annual International Symposium on Virtual Reality, pp. 61–68. IEEE (1997)
36. U.S. Secret Service: Best practices for seizing electronic evidence (2015). https://www.cwagweb.org/wp-content/uploads/2018/05/BestPracticesforSeizing ElectronicEvidence.pdf
37. Xi, M., Smith, S.P.: Simulating cooperative fire evacuation training in a virtual environment using gaming technology. In: 2014 IEEE Virtual Reality (VR), pp. 139–140. IEEE (2014)
38. Yang, U., Lee, G.A., Shin, S., Hwang, S., Son, W.: Virtual reality based paint spray training system. In: 2007 IEEE Virtual Reality Conference, pp. 289–290. IEEE (2007)
39. Ziegler, R., Mueller, W., Fischer, G., Goebel, M.: A virtual reality medical training system. In: Ayache, N. (ed.) CVRMed 1995. LNCS, vol. 905, pp. 282–286. Springer, Heidelberg (1995). https://doi.org/10.1007/978-3-540-49197-2_36

Tactical Rings: A Visualization Technique for Analyzing Tactical Patterns in Tennis

Shiraj Pokharel[✉] and Ying Zhu

Department of Computer Science and Creative Media Industries Institute,
Georgia State University, Atlanta, GA 30303, USA
spokharel3@student.gsu.edu, yzhu@gsu.edu

Abstract. Sports data visualization can be a useful tool for analyzing or presenting sports data. In this paper, we present a new technique to visualize and analyze shot-by-shot tactical patterns in tennis. Previous work in tennis data analysis and visualization focus more on high-level statistics and overviews such as heat-maps but did not handle data analytics at micro-level. Our visualization technique can reveal patterns and imbalances in a tennis match that lead to a deeper understanding of the game. We demonstrate the application and benefits of our visualization technique with case studies.

Keywords: Visualization systems · Visual analytics · Visual data mining and knowledge discovery

1 Introduction

Many professional sports games are played at a hectic pace in a seemingly chaotic environment. As a result, non-expert viewers often miss the tactical patterns used by the players and therefore miss the opportunity to enjoy the games on a deeper level. It is not easy to describe such tactical patterns in words. As more detailed datasets become available, we can conduct data analysis to reveal the dynamics of the match. Sports data visualization and visual analytics can help reveal tactical patterns that are not otherwise obvious to the viewers.

Current tennis analytics focuses primarily on high-level statistics (such as serve percentage and number of unforced errors). Although very useful, the high-level statistics often fail to reveal the complexity and the dynamic nature of tennis matches. The visual analysis of a tennis match mostly uses heatmaps or ball trajectory tracing charts. There are many shortcomings to these approaches. For example, a heatmap blends all the shots without showing the sequence of the shots, which is important for understanding tactical patterns. A ball trajectory tracing chart shows the shot sequence and the placement of the balls. However, by plotting many overlapping ball trajectories in one chart, it often creates clutter and is difficult to interpret.

© Springer Nature Switzerland AG 2019
G. Bebis et al. (Eds.): ISVC 2019, LNCS 11845, pp. 481–491, 2019.
https://doi.org/10.1007/978-3-030-33723-0_39

We address the above problems by introducing a new visualization technique – Tactical Rings. Tactical Rings are designed to visualize tactical patterns in tennis. Each point in tennis is a sequence of shots, and specific combinations of shots become tactical patterns due to their effectiveness. Most of the points in tennis contain one or more tactical patterns. Expert tennis players practice various tactical patterns and use them in their games to gain advantages. Some players are well known for their favorite patterns. Tennis players, coaches, and analysts often study tactical patterns of a player to analyze his/her game. However, tactical patterns are not always easy to spot, especially to non-expert viewers.

Tactical rings are circles that can be recursively subdivided, leading to a set of concentric circles based on shot length. Each tactical ring contains tennis points of a certain rally length. Each cell in a tactical ring represents a unique shot pattern. An entire tennis match can be visualized by placing each point in a cell of tactical rings.

Tactical rings have several benefits. It makes efficient use of space. It can accommodate tennis points of any rally length and any combination since they can be recursively divided. The sequence of shots is visualized without creating a clutter of overlapping lines.

In this paper, we demonstrate the application of tactical rings with case studies that focus on the first four shots, which is the primary space for tactical patterns.

2   Related Works

There has been a rich set of research literature on sports data visualization and analytics, including some prior work on tennis visual analytics. A data visualization that shows the progression and tactical statistics of a tennis match was proposed in [1]. Models for visual analytics of performance anxiety and confidence in tennis were proposed in [2] and [3]. Visual analytics of tennis shot patterns with fractal tables was presented in [4].

Other researchers [5–10] have done important work on statistical modeling of tennis matches. A tennis match visualization system that shows the score, point outcomes, point lengths, service information, and match videos for tennis enthusiasts and coaching staff to gain insights into match performance was proposed in [11]. Liqun and Banks [12] proposed a technique to visualize the overall structure of the match as well as the fine details using a 2D display of translucent layers derived from Tree-Maps. Burch and Weiskopf [13] introduced techniques to visually encode the dynamics of a tennis match by using hierarchical and layered icicle representations. They place the time axis vertically as multiple aligned scales to indicate the duration of games and points. They also used color-coding to visualize additional attributes. An approach to analyze the similarity between players, which could be used for prediction and recommendation, was proposed in [14]. Probabilistic graphical models to study player behavior, which could be used to find factors such as location and speed of the incoming shot, has been developed in [15].

Previous work in tennis data analysis and visualization mainly focus on the point level data or higher. They have not explored micro-level match data like tactical shot patterns, which is the focus of our work.

Data analysis and visualization work has been done for other sports. For example, a visualization of table-tennis matches that includes time-oriented, statistical, and tactical analyses has been proposed in [16]. Working with domain experts to present a visual analytics system for soccer data, allowing users to track the spatio-temporal changes in formation and understand how and why such changes occur is proposed in [17]. A system to analyze high-frequency position-based soccer data at various levels of detail for analysis of movement features and game events is presented in [18].

3   Data

Our work is based on the tennis match data from Tennis Abstract [19], an open source project that provides both high-level and micro-level data of more than 5000 professional tennis matches. The micro-level data includes shot-by-shot descriptions, such as the shot types, the shot directions, the return depth, error types, and many other technical features.

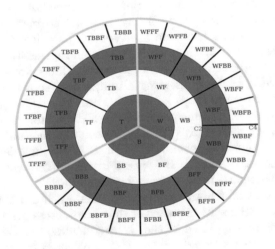

Fig. 1. A Tactical Ring with four-shot space

4   Method

4.1   Tactical Rings

Tactical Rings are circles that can be recursively expanded by shot length, leading to the creation of a set of concentric circles. The innermost ring represents one-shot points (i.e., aces), the second ring represents two-shot points (i.e., a service followed by a return), the third ring represents three-shot points, and so on. Each ring is further divided into multiple segments, which are called cells. Each cell contains points with a particular shot combination, such as "wide-service - backhand return - forehand - backhand". A tactical pattern is a short combination of shots, usually 2 to 4 shots. Therefore, in our visualization, the points are visually sorted by tactical patterns.

Due to limited space and also because the majority of the points in professional tennis matches fall within the four-shot space (about 70% according to ATP [20]), the visualizations in this paper only include the first four shots. However, our visualization technique can accommodate longer rallies by adding more rings.

Figure 1 shows how Tactical Rings are organized. The innermost ring C1 is the one-shot space (service aces) and is evenly divided by service directions: Wide (W), Body (B), and down the T (T).

The next ring C2 is the two-shot space (service and return). Like C1, the C2 ring is also divided into three service directions. Each service direction segment is further divided into two segments: forehand return and backhand return. Therefore, the C2 ring is divided into six cells, each representing a unique two-shot sequence.

The C2 ring is followed by the C3 ring (the three-shot space). The C3 ring inherits the six segments from the C2 ring, but each segment is further divided into two smaller segments based on the type of the third shot: forehand and backhand. Therefore, the C3 ring has 12 cells, each representing a unique three-shot sequence. The process continues in the C4 ring (four-shot space). Therefore, C4 ring has 24 cells, each representing a unique four-shot sequence. In Fig. 1, the shot sequence for each cell is labeled in green letters: W (serving wide), B (serving to the body), T (serving down the T), F (forehand), and B (Backhand). For example, the cell marked as WBFF represents the shot pattern: wide-serve-backhand return-forehand-forehand. If letter B is the first letter on the left, it means serving to the body. If B appears in the subsequent letter, it means backhand shot. Therefore, there is no ambiguity.

Points in a tennis match are displayed as dots. Each dot is placed in a particular cell based on the shot sequence of that point. Aces are placed in the C1 ring, two-shot points are placed in the C2 ring, and so on. For example, for a point in which player A serves down the T (T), player B returns with forehand (F), player A hits a forehand shot (F), and player B hits a forehand shot (F), this point will be placed in the cell marked as TFFF. To avoid crowdedness, if too many dots are placed in one cell, we aggregate multiple dots into bigger dots. Additional information, such as the outcome of the point and the type of error, can be encoded in the color and shape of the dots.

We choose to use a ring layout because it is the most natural and spatially efficient layout for this data visualization. It can expand and shrink naturally and evenly in all directions. Longer points are placed on the outer rings because they have more patterns. For example, to visualize the five-shot points, we simply add a bigger C5 ring outside of the C4 ring. The bigger circumference of the C5 ring would naturally accommodate the larger number of cells (48) for the five-shot space. In comparison, a table-based data visualization would need to be extended either vertically or horizontally.

The visualization is implemented in Javascript library D3 [21].

4.2   Visual Analytics

Using Tactical Rings, we can conduct three types of analysis: static analysis, dynamic analysis, and comparative analysis. In static analyses, we can study a player's shot pattern distribution and ask questions such as the following.

- Does this player have an advantage when he/she serves in a certain direction?
- Does this player have favorite tactical patterns?
- Does this player have an advantage in short points or long points?
- Does this player make more errors in certain shot patterns (e.g., backhand rallies, lateral movement)?

In dynamic analyses, we can use Tactical Rings to study how a player uses different tactical patterns at different stages of the match. Here are some examples.

- Does this player change tactics as the match progresses (e.g., as the player is getting tired)?
- Does this player have favorite tactical patterns at critical moments (e.g., game points, breakpoints, must-win points)?

In comparative analyses, we can use Tactical Rings to visually compare the strengths and weaknesses as well as the styles of multiple players. Tactical Rings can visualize the tactical imbalances between two players. For example, we can study the strengths and weaknesses of two players by using color to differentiate the points won by each player or the errors made by each player in Tactical Rings. We can highlight the cells with long forehand rallies or backhand rallies to see who has a better forehand or backhand. Which player tends to win long points?

5   Case Studies

In this section, we use several case studies to demonstrate the application and usefulness of Tactical Rings. We use the three matches played by Rafael Nadal and Roger Federer at Wimbledon (grass court) from 2006 to 2008 [19] and the five matches between them in the French Open (clay court) from 2005 to 2011 [19].

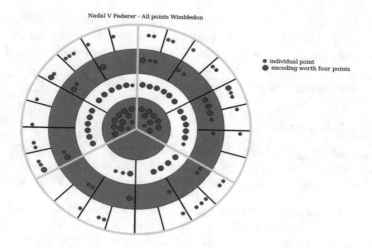

Fig. 2. All points Wimbledon (grass court)

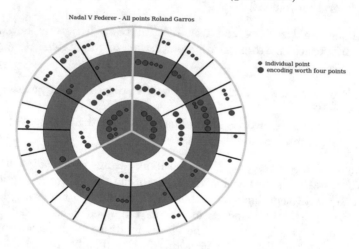

Fig. 3. All points Roland Garros (clay court)

5.1 Cumulative Match Analysis for Grass and Clay

Figure 2 shows the match data (first four shots) from Wimbledon. Figure 3 shows the match data (first four shots) from Roland Garros (the French Open). We can see that at Wimbledon, more points are played in the one or two-shot spaces. However, at Roland Garros, the points are more evenly distributed. There are far more aces at Wimbledon (grass) than at Roland Garros (clay). It also shows that points tend to end quicker on grass courts than on clay courts. In the one-shot space (i.e., aces or serve faults), we see serving to the body produces no ace. At Wimbledon, there are more aces serving to the T than serving wide, while at Roland Garros, there are aces serving wide than serving to the T.

The two-shot space has the most points than any other shot pattern, indicating the effectiveness of the players' serves and returns (i.e., either a return error or a return winner). In the two-shot space, the forehand and backhand returns are almost balanced. However, in the three and four-shot spaces, we see an imbalance – the majority of the points have a backhand return of serve, and this pattern exists for both grass and clay surfaces.

5.2   Point Outcome Analysis

Figures 4 and 5 show the unforced errors in the Tactical Rings. Unforced error is one of the most important metrics of a player's quality of play. From Fig. 4, we see that the vast majority of the unforced errors happen in the three-shot space, and somewhat surprisingly, very few two-shot and four-shot points end in unforced error. Besides, Federer made more unforced errors than Nadal in the three-shot points, and he made more unforced errors in the WBF and TFF patterns. Note that in both patterns, the points end with a forehand shot. A plausible explanation is that both players played aggressively in the third shots (thus leading to unforced errors), and Federer was more aggressive than Nadal on the grass court, particularly using his forehand. It seems that Federer had two favorite tactical patterns on grass: WBF and TFF. In the WBF pattern, Federer served wide to Nadal's backhand and then played aggressively with his forehand shot. In the TFF pattern, Federer served to the T (Nadal's forehand) and then played aggressively with his forehand.

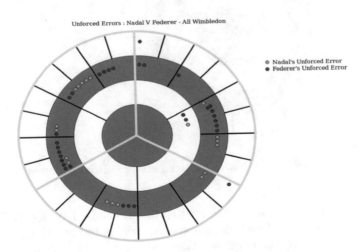

Fig. 4. Federer v Nadal: unforced errors at Wimbledon

It seems that both players were not very aggressive in their returns (hence the few unforced errors in returns), perhaps because the serves are fast on the grass court.

From Fig. 5, we see that most of the unforced errors are in the two-shot and three-shot points, and very few four-shot points end in unforced error. Both players played aggressively in their third shots, particularly with forehand shots. Again, Federer made more unforced errors than Nadal did, indicating that he was the more aggressive player. Compared with Wimbledon, both players were more aggressive in their service returns on the clay court, hence the higher number of unforced errors in their second shots. Federer still favored the WBF pattern on the clay court, but did not use the TFF pattern very often.

Nadal made many unforced errors in the WB and WBF patterns at Roland Garros but not at Wimbledon. This seems to indicate that Nadal returned Federer's wide serves more aggressively with his backhand on the clay court. Nadal also used WBF pattern more aggressively on the clay court, serving to Federer's backhand and then playing aggressively with his forehand.

From the data visualization, the imbalance of unforced errors between the two players is evident. The difference between Wimbledon and Roland Garros in the two-shot space is intriguing. The many unforced errors in the three-shot WBF pattern also raise interesting questions.

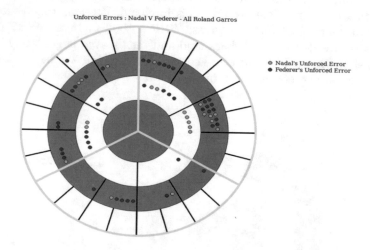

Fig. 5. Federer v Nadal: unforced errors at Roland Garros

Here we assume that most unforced errors are caused by aggressive play. Other factors may also cause unforced errors, such as fatigue, timing, or wind. However, for top-level players like Federer and Nadal playing in grand slam finals, we believe overly aggressive play is still the primary factor for unforced errors, especially within the first four shots. Our data visualizations are meant to reveal interesting patterns and raise questions for further investigation, not necessarily to give definitive answers. The true causes of these unforced errors may need to be investigated via detailed video analysis.

5.3   Very High Anxiety Points Outcome Analysis

Figures 6 and 7 show the very high anxiety points won by Federer and Nadal in Tactical Rings. Very high anxiety points [2,3] are critical points (e.g., deuce points) whose outcome may lead the game to either direction.

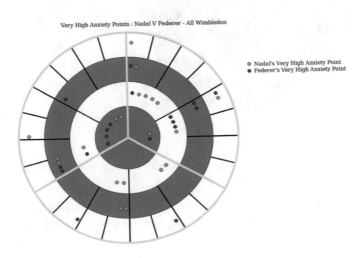

Fig. 6. Federer v Nadal: very high anxiety points at Wimbledon

In Fig. 6, we see that Federer won four aces by serving to the T, and only one ace by serving wide. In Fig. 7, he won three aces by serving to the T and two aces by serving wide. It seems that serving to the T is advantages for Federer at high anxiety points. On the other hand, there is no clear pattern for Nadal on both grass courts and clay courts. However, Nadal won far more high anxiety points in service return (two-shot space) than Federer did. The data seems to show that Nadal was a better returner at critical moments, while Federer was a better server at critical moments. Nadal returned Federer's wide serves particularly well at high anxiety moments.

From Fig. 6, we see that, on grass, Federer won more points serving to the T but had no advantage serving wide or to the body. On grass, Federer and Nadal are almost evenly matched in the three and four-shot spaces at critical moments.

From Fig. 7, we see that, on clay, Federer did better in the three-shot space serving wide, while Nadal did better in the three-shot space serving down the T. There are very few points in the four-shot space. No one has an advantage there.

Overall, our data visualizations suggest that Federer should serve more to the T on the grass court at critical moments. On grass, at critical moments, Federer should serve either wide or to the T, but not to the body. On the other hand, perhaps Nadal should serve more to the T on the clay court at critical moments.

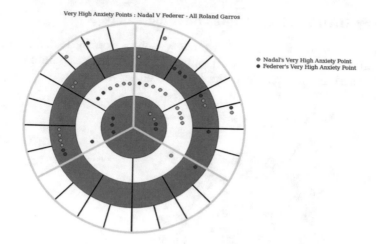

Fig. 7. Federer v Nadal: very high anxiety points at Roland Garros

The above analysis shows that Tactical Rings can be used to identify tactical imbalances in tennis games, which may help inform players' strategical decision-making.

6   Conclusions

In this paper, we described Tactical Rings, a novel method to visually analyze the shot patterns of tennis matches. Compared with the conventional tennis match analysis and visualization techniques, our method provides a new way to analyze tennis tactics on a shot-by-shot basis. Through the case studies, we have shown that our visualizations can reveal interesting patterns and dynamic imbalances that are not otherwise obvious. Tactical Rings is an analytics tool not only useful to fans and tennis enthusiasts but also to players, coaches, and analysts who are always looking for ways to improve and gain small advantages in a highly competitive sport. In the future, we plan to expand this technique to other aspects of tennis matches and other sports when such detailed datasets are available.

References

1. He, X., Zhu, Y.: TennisMatchViz: a tennis match visualization. In: Proceedings of International Conference on Visualization and Data Analysis (VDA) (2016)
2. Pokharel, S., Zhu, Y.: Analysis and visualization of sports performance anxiety in tennis matches. In: Bebis, G., et al. (eds.) ISVC 2018. LNCS, vol. 11241, pp. 407–419. Springer, Cham (2018). https://doi.org/10.1007/978-3-030-03801-4_36
3. Pokharel, S., Zhu, Y.: Micro-level data analysis and visualization of the interrelation between confidence and athletic performance. In: Proceedings of the 2nd International Conference on Computer Science and Software Engineering (CSSE) (2019)

4. Pokharel, S., Zhu, Y., Puri, S.: Micro-level analysis and visualization of tennis shot patterns with fractal tables. In: IEEE 43rd Annual Computer Software and Applications Conference (COMPSAC) (2019)
5. Madurska, M.: A set-by-set analysis method for predicting the outcome of professional singles tennis matches. Master's thesis, Imperial College London (2012)
6. O'Malley, A.J.: Probability formulas and statistical analysis in tennis. J. Quant. Anal. Sports 4, 1–23 (2008)
7. Newton, P., Keller, J.: Probability of winning at tennis I. Stud. Appl. Math. Theory Data Stud. Appl. Math. 114, 241–269 (2005)
8. Riddle, L.: Probability models for tennis scoring systems. J. Roy. Stat. Soc.: Ser. C (Appl. Stat.) 37, 63–75 (1988)
9. Jackson, D., Mosurski, K.: Heavy defeats in tennis: psychological momentum or random effect? Chance 10, 27–34 (1997)
10. MacPhee, I., Rougier, J., Pollard, G.: Server advantage in tennis matches. J. Appl. Probab. 41, 1182–1186 (2004)
11. Polk, T., Yang, J., Hu, Y., Zhao, Y.: TenniVis: visualization for tennis match analysis. IEEE Trans. Vis. Comput. Graph. 20, 2339–2348 (2014)
12. Liqun, J., Banks, D.G.: TennisViewer: a browser for competition trees. IEEE Comput. Graph. Appl. 17, 63–65 (1997)
13. Burch, M., Weiskopf, D.: Tennis plots: game, set, and match. In: Dwyer, T., Purchase, H., Delaney, A. (eds.) Diagrams 2014. LNCS (LNAI), vol. 8578, pp. 38–44. Springer, Heidelberg (2014). https://doi.org/10.1007/978-3-662-44043-8_5
14. Wei, X., Lucey, P., Morgan, S., Carr, P., Reid, M., Sridharan, S.: Predicting serves in tennis using style priors. In: Proceedings of the 21st ACM SIGKDD International Conference on Knowledge Discovery and Data Mining, pp. 2207–2215 (2015)
15. Wei, X., Lucey, P., Morgan, S., Sridharan, S.: Forecasting the next shot location in tennis using fine-grained spatiotemporal tracking data. IEEE Trans. Knowl. Data Eng. 28, 2988–2997 (2016)
16. Wu, Y., et al.: iTTVis: interactive visualization of table tennis data. IEEE Trans. Vis. Comput. Graph. 24, 709–718 (2018)
17. Wu, Y., et al.: ForVizor: visualizing spatio-temporal team formations in soccer. IEEE Trans. Vis. Comput. Graph. 25, 65–75 (2019)
18. Janetzko, H., Sacha, D., Stein, M., Schreck, T., Keim, D.A., Deussen, O.: Feature-driven visual analytics of soccer data. In: Proceedings of the IEEE Symposium on Visual Analytics Science and Technology (VAST), pp. 13–22 (2014)
19. Tennis Match Charting Project. https://github.com/JeffSackmann/tennis_MatchChartingProject. Accessed 15 July 2019
20. ATP Stats. https://www.atpworldtour.com/en/stats. Accessed 15 July 2019
21. Design Driven Documents. https://d3js.org/. Accessed 15 July 2019

Cross-Media Sentiment Analysis in Brazilian Blogs

Greice P. Dal Molin, Henrique D. P. Santos, Isabel H. Manssour,
Renata Vieira, and Soraia R. Musse(✉)

School of Technology, Graduate Program of Computer Science,
Pontifical Catholic University of Rio Grande do Sul, Porto Alegre, Brazil
soraia.musse@pucrs.br

Abstract. The use of social media is becoming highly present in our lives. It is through images, texts, and videos that human beings try to communicate in social networks and expose their opinions in the face of everyday events. Due to the increased volume of data transmitted over the Internet, it becomes difficult to do a human analysis of this content. For this reason, it is necessary to automate the task of classifying feelings' polarity. Although the area of classification of feelings in images and texts is well developed and applied in social network context, the classification of feelings from images together with texts is still under development. A challenge is to build algorithms and methods that can infer feelings just like humans perceive it. Firstly, we present Cross-media Brazilian Blog corpus, the dataset we built based on BlogSet-BR, which goal is to have a data ground truth (based on subjects opinions) concerning feeling perceived in texts and images, when analyzed separately as well as when presented together. Therefore, we tested some available technologies to detect sentiment polarities in texts and images and compare with the ground truth. In addition, we pursue a research specifically on the contradiction posts, i.e. when image is positive and text is negative from the same blog. Results indicate that subjectivity affects emotional judgments because there are variances between cultures.

Keywords: Cross-media blogset · Analysis of feelings in text · Analysis of feelings in images · Corpus · Contradiction between domains

1 Introduction

Images convey emotion to people much more easily than writing [21]. Based on that, we use a lot of images on social networks to express feelings, nowadays. As emotions are perceived by each individual differently, subjectivity plays an intrinsic role in the process of recognition of emotions. This is believed to be one of the major challenges in investigations for indexing emotions in images [15]. Even with limitations, analyzing emotion in images has applicability in many areas, such as industry, economics, advertising and health, because the

G. Bebis et al. (Eds.): ISVC 2019, LNCS 11845, pp. 492–503, 2019.
https://doi.org/10.1007/978-3-030-33723-0_40

image is much more than an object that has a location or action. The main goal of this paper is to apply pattern recognition techniques to provide sentiment classification in posts that contain texts in Portuguese language and images. Firstly, we built our dataset called Cross-media Brazilian Blog (from now on named CBB) that contains 880 blogs, based on BlogSet-BR, chosen because we want to work with the Portuguese language and also because it is considered the largest corpus with authoring information for Brazilian Portuguese, according to Santos et al. [14]. To provide the ground truth, we tested 880 blogs separately, providing feelings analysis for images and texts, and then together, having the blog sentiment. We used Figure Eight[1] for the annotation process where participants specified texts and images polarity. In addition, some available technologies have been used to classify the blogs and compare with ground truth. To perform sentiment classification of images, one classifier and two neural networks were applied in the corpus: SentiBank [3], DeepSentiBank [5] and VGG-T4SA as proposed in [19], respectively. Those methods are recent and focused on images in blogs. For textual prediction, we use the Linguistic Inquiry and Word Count method (LIWC) [2], Opinion Lexicon (OpLexicon) and sentiment lexicon (SentiLex) working with words in Portuguese. In our analysis, We found out some contradictory posts, where images and texts have different polarities and were classified as contradictory by subjects. We pursue a research to try to explain such classification and how those findings could be incorporated in existent technologies. We can summarize the contribution of this work as follows:

- Creation of a corpus of Cross-media Brazilian Blogs (from now on named as CBB) including texts and images of posts created by users;
- Classification of emotions in images and texts separated and together in the blog by subjects using Figure Eight;
- Obtained results when testing available technologies in our CBB dataset comparing results with obtained ground truth, and
- Discussion about contradictory posts aiming to find metrics that can be used to improve the automatic results.

The remaining of this paper is organized as follows: Sect. 2 presents some of the works present in literature and Sect. 3 describes the Corpus we create as well as the proposed methodology. Results are detailed and discussed in Sect. 4, while Sect. 6 addresses final comments and future work.

2   Related Work

This section presents the papers that served as the basis for this article. The two domains of study are images and text in the areas of analysis of feelings and contradictions. Recently, Peng et al. [12] define concepts, methodologies and present challenges in blogs classifications, indicating that the contradiction between domains is a complex and challenging subject. Regarding images analysis, Joshi et al. [10] refer to classification of feeling in images by involving a high

[1] https://figure-eight.com.

level of abstraction and subjectivity in the process of human recognition, encompassing tasks of visual recognition, such as objects, scenes, actions and events. This indicates that for supervised learning, millions of labeled and highly diversified images are required to cover the most diverse domains. Vadicamo et al. [19] propose a visual feeling classifier that uses a large set of contents generated and not labeled by the user. They compared studies and assessments for visual feeling analysis. In addition, authors found that texts containing many noises, making them poorly correlated with the image.

You et al. [22] compare the tweets with the images posted together and try to find out the emotion of the tweet by using these two features. They propose a CNN architecture for the analysis of feelings in images using Flickr and videos. They consider social networking a source of information about people's lives because users love to post their experiences and share their opinions on a wide range of subjects. The authors use a framework to classify resources using the work of LeCun [11] and Ciresan [6] among others. Peng et al. [12] describe an overview of cross-media query and outcome. Authors present concepts, methodologies, challenges and issues that are still open based on the analysis of 100 references in the subject. They construct a new dataset called XMedia that contains text, image, video, audio, and 3D model for public use so that new researchers can focus on creating algorithms that aid in cross-media retrieval. Borth et al. [3] describes an image-feelings classifier that uses the psychological model of emotions called the Plutchik's Wheel of Emotions. Initially, they work with the process of data mining, using the 24 emotions of Plutchik's theory to find images in the tweet and label them. Then text analysis and lexical-based feeling analysis tools are applied to detect the polarized (positive, neutral or negative) feeling of the created labels. Next, a classifier SVM is trained using emotion labeled in the worked images of the previous steps. Finally, the authors describe an overview of the model through visualization applications of the negative, neutral and positive feelings detected in images, as well as the labels of created emotions. In the research of Chen et al. [5] a method of classification of visual feeling based on deep neural networks (CNN) is proposed. They consider visual feelings the pairs of nouns and adjectives, called ANPs, that are detected in the tags of the images on the web. They also inform that these tags can be used as statistical clues to detect the emotion indicated in the image. Thousands of Flickr images were used for training, validation and testing of the concept classifier. The model is trained in the Framework Caffe and uses ImageNet network in order to treat the bias that exist in the images and to avoid overfitting. This model is called DeepSentiBank. Significant improvement in both accuracy and performance is proposed in relation to the SentiBank 1.1 classification model.

There are few published works in the area of contradiction analysis. Harabagiu et al. [9] contribution is to indicate a method for recognizing contradictions using a structure that combines negation processing and removal. It uses WordNet [8] mining for derivation of antonyms, and addresses the problem of classification to recognize textual alignment relationships. Marneffe et al. [7] seeks to define contradiction for Natural Language Processing (NLP) tasks and to typify contradictions along their degree of complexity. Singh [17] brings the concepts of humor, irony and satire. It indicates that there are differences and similarities between them. It deals with irony conceptually and defines three main types in the literature. In this work, we intend to contribute with a contradiction analysis including the image classification as perceived by people. In Sect. 3, we present the proposed work model.

3   Our Methodology

In this section we present the methodology developed in this work organized in basically three steps: firstly, we describe the corpus CBB, then we present the tested technologies and finally we investigate some contradiction aspects.

3.1   Data Collection

BlogSet-BR [14] is a collection of 7.4 million blog posts on the Blogspot platform generated by Brazilian users, and includes information about posts, user ids, date, among others information. In the context of this work, we use only the text and the associated image for each post. At the beginning, we have selected 5,649 blogs that have still with their available links, containing texts and images. Then, we applied two technologies to provide a polarity detection of each text and image separately from all blogs, they are: LIWC dictionary [2][2] and the VGG-T4SA model [16], respectively. These both technologies are presented in Sects. 3.2 and 3.3. Since our idea was to manually annotate the new corpus with Brazilian posts, we selected 1,000 from the 5,649 posts, which match the following rules.

- The image should contain polarity negative or positive, as computed by VGG, and present a polarity probability greater than 40%; and
- With respect to the text, it must contain more than 10 words and less than 500 words, and at least two words with polarity positive or negative must exist, according to LIWC.

Annotation Process. For the annotation process we used Figure Eight[3], a crowdsourcing platform for performing high volume and repetitive tasks, being a widely distributed workforce. In our case, we generate 1000 questions to be evaluated in order to cover the 1000 selected blogs. The evaluation process uses majority voting that can exclude responses based on the created test units. In Figure Eight, the images are randomly presented to the annotators, who review the images (3 annotators per image) in order to determine the feeling of presented images. The same happens for the texts. Although our definition takes into account only polarity, in Figure Eight the images and texts can be classified as positive, negative or neutral, as follows:

---

[2] http://143.107.183.175:21380/portlex/index.php/en/projetos/liwc

[3] https://figure-eight.com.

- Positive means that some aspects of the image/text reveal a positive mood, such as praise, recommendations or a favorable comparison.
- Neutral means that the image is only informative in nature and provides no indication as the mood of the image/text.
- Negative means that some aspects of the image/text reveal a negative climate, such as criticism, insults or a negative comparison.

The result was the creation of a corpus called CBB[4] with 880 annotated posts. The remaining 120 posts (from 1000) were not completed annotated (we have feedback of image or text sentiment, but not the both data, so it was not possible to use them). Using Figure Eight, 880 texts and 880 images were manually classified as positive, neutral and negative, as shown in Fig. 1 where the images polarization can be seen on the left and texts polarization in the center. In addition to the previous analysis, we also investigated the discrepancy or variation of the feelings classified between text and image of a same post. The objective was to classify the emotion of the post when there is divergence between the two domains. Indeed, Fig. 1 on the right shows the total number of posts in which image and text have the same polarity, that is, a total of 422 posts representing less than 50% of CBB total. In fact, it indicates that many posts have different polarities, if analyzed separately.

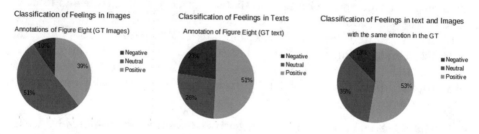

Fig. 1. On the left and on the center: Percentage of positive, neutral and negative polarity images and texts indicated in the GT through the annotations in Figure Eight (from 880 blogs). On the right: texts and images in the same post indicating the same polarity (from 422 blogs).

In a second step we proceeded with a Figure Eight analysis again, this time however the subjects have access to the complete blog (text and image simultaneously) and should answer firstly if the post represents a contradiction among the feelings observed in texts and images. If answer is yes, subjects should answer which one is the predominant feeling according to their perception (positive, neutral or negative). Obtained results regarding such questions are: 29 posts from 880 were considered contradictory and from them 11 were positive, 8 neutral and 10 negative as the predominant feeling.

Next sections present some technologies we have used to test CBB dataset in order to compare with the Ground Truth (GT), as answered by subjects using Figure Eight.

---

[4] https://github.com/nlp-pucrs/cross-media-sa.

3.2 Emotion Analysis in Texts

The technologies used in this study were chosen for two reasons: *(i)* Since the posts are written in Portuguese, it was necessary to choose lexicons that have the polarity classification in words of the Portuguese language; *(ii)* A few sentiment lexicons for the Portuguese language were detected, and the LIWC, SentiLex and OpLexicon are commonly cited in the text-sense analysis studies. They are following briefly described:

- The OpLexicon (Opinion Lexicon) [18] method, considered the largest word base, is a lexicon of feelings for the Portuguese language, composed of 32191 lines with 4 variables. Currently, Oplexicon[5] is in version 3.0 that has been reviewed by linguists regarding the polarity of some adjectives.
- The SentiLex (Sentiment Lexicon) [4] method is a lexicon of feelings for Portuguese that is composed by approximately 6,000 adjectives and 25,000 flexed forms. The SentiLex[6] was constructed from a corpus composed of commentaries on political subjects in newspapers. It contains, in addition to the classes of words, the polarity associated with each item, being positive, negative or neutral.
- The dictionary LIWC (Linguistic Inquiry and Word Count)[7] consists of a dictionary of words that allows to extract linguistic and psychological characteristics in the texts. The LIWC [2] method is a well-evaluated resource for analyzing feelings in texts.

In order to obtain the polarity of a certain text, we defined the simple algorithm as follows:

- Firstly, we have the 880 texts defined in the 880 blogs present in CBB;
- A preprocessing step is done in the text, removing stopwords, which may be considered irrelevant to the result set when constructing the model. An example is the following text: "I do not like the party, and also would not vote again on that ruler!", Resulting in "not like party I would not vote again on that ruler."
- The file is loaded with one of the lexical dictionaries as previously mentioned;
- A comparison is made between the relevant words in the text and the lexical dictionary to identify the polarity of the word. The quantification of positive, negative and neutral words are performed;
- A dataframe is created with the blog id, the preprocessed text, the number of words analyzed, and the number of polarized words, along with the polarity of the processed sentence; and
- A csv file is generated for later analysis.

---

[5] http://ontolp.inf.pucrs.br/Recursos/downloads-OpLexicon.php.
[6] http://xldb.fc.ul.pt/wiki/SentiLex-PT01.
[7] http://143.107.183.175:21380/portlex/index.php/en/projetos/liwc.

3.3   Emotion Analysis in Images

To perform the sentiment classification in the images of the corpus, three methods were applied in the corpus, SentiBank [3], DeepSentiBank [5] and VGG-T4SA [16]. Some briefly descriptions are presented as follows:

- SentiBank is an emotion classifier build using ontology of visual feeling. According to the context of the ontologies, it can be used to map the domain of the application and also to inform the degree of intensity of the emotion, being represented by a numerical value. SentiBank is based on a psychological model of emotions known as the Wheel of Emotions of Plutchik [13] and indicates accuracy of around 70% in its tests.
- DeepSentiBank is an improvement of the SentiBank method [5]. DeepSentiBank still outperforms SentiBank 1.5R by 8.9%.
- VGG-T4SA [16] is a convolutional neural network (CNN) that provides feeling analysis in twitters, hence the name VGG-T4SA. Given an image, the VGG network produces probabilities of the different classes to which an image may belong. For example, in relation specifically to the present research, the VGG network may indicate that a specific image may present a 80% confidence chance that exhibits a positive emotion, 10% chance to present negative emotions as well as 10% of a neutral emotion.

4   Results when Evaluating Our Corpus CBB

4.1   Image Analysis

We classified all 880 images from Corpus CBB using the classifier SentiBank and neural networks DeepSentiBank and VGG-T4SA. We confronted obtained classifications with the Ground Truth that we represent here as (GT Images), as answered by subjects using Figure Eight. Table 1 presents results.

Table 1. Comparing the results of the SentiBank, DeepSentiBank and VGG Network classification with the GT, resulting in predictions of around 39.20%, 40.56% and 32.84% (considering neutral) and 67.68% (without considering neutrals) accuracy in each network, respectively

Polarity	SentiBank and GT	DeepSentiBank and GT	VGG and GT
Positive	150	222	231
Neutral	174	92	0
Negative	21	43	58
Total	345	357	289
% hit	**39.20**	**40.56**	**32.84–67.68**

These values correspond to the number of correctly classified images when compared to GT. As you can see, we obtained low accuracy with the tested methods. Many aspects can be evaluated in a future work to discuss the obtained accuracy. Perhaps one consideration is that real, spontaneous blogs can use images that are not clearly positive or negative when compared to training data sets, and may complement primarily - or intentionally oppose the texts that accompany blogs.

4.2   Text Analysis

As done with the images, we processed the 880 texts present in the blogs. shows obtained results using OpLexicon as (Lexicon 1), SentiLex (Lexicon 2) and LIWC (Lexicon 3) (Table 2).

Table 2. Comparing the results of the classification of lexicons OpLexicon, Sentilex, LIWC with GT, resulting in predictions around 44.65%, 45.45%, 43.29% accuracy in each lexicon respectively.

Polarity	OpLexicon and GT	SentiLex and GT	LIWC and GT
Positive	234	225	202
Neutral	117	103	154
Negative	42	72	25
Total	393/880	400/880	381/880
% hit	**44.65**	**45.45**	**43.29**

As in the images, the results obtained in comparison with the Ground Truth that we represent here as (GT Text) were not accurate. Once again, the same considerations made for images can be made for the texts, that is, texts in blogs tested with lexicon present little precision in our Brazilian blog and should be better investigated to understand the real reasons. We suspect that other factors such as culture, contradictions, language variations may contribute to such results.

5   Contradictions in the Texts

One possible explanation for small accuracy in the blogs is the language and the culture, e.g. the usage of contradiction and irony. Such idea of contradiction can affect the images chosen by the user as well can affect the text. In Sect. 3.1 we showed that 422 posts were classified separately as having the same sentiment (Fig. 1). On the other hand, only 29 were clearly contradictory in subjects opinions. It can indicate that when people see separately the images and texts and when they see together the resulting perception regarding the blog sentiment is different. It happens because if one image is positive in a separated context, the subject can perceive it differently due to the text, and vice-versa. In order to investigate this aspect, we studied the contradiction itself in texts. Harabagiu [9] defines contradiction as the incompatibility between two different texts. These incompatibilities can be presented in various ways, such as: denial, antonyms or contrasts - semantic and pragmatic information. According to Marneffe [7], the types of contradiction are divided into two categories, one being easy to detect and one more complex. The easy category describes as relevant the following aspects: firstly, the context polarity which is used to determine whether antonyms create a contradiction; secondly, denial terms or phrases that can change the polarity of the sentence; and finally numeric information which incompatibility may indicate the existence of a contradiction. The category called complex contains types of contradiction that are not easy to detect, because the syntactic structure makes it difficult to guarantee structural difference in the text, making it complex to infer contradiction. The so-called easy category was chosen by the authors because the detection of Antonym and Negation are examples of features that are easily automated through the computer since, there is no need to understand the entire sentence.

For our research we will use adverbs with all their divisions, so we will include the negation classification quoted in the easy category within the grammar class adverbs because we would have redundant information when separating them. Torres [1] says that punctuation indicates in writing the pauses that should be observed by the speaker or reader. The use of the exclamation point (!) fits this definition because it can increase the magnitude of the intensity without changing the semantic orientation. The use of the semicolon (;) normally replaces the coordinating conjunctions. So the score was also a class for analysis. In the GT, 29 posts were detected as contradictory. In order to study these aspect in CBB, we proceed with a quantification of words of certain grammar classes as the literature presents as actives in sentences with contradiction. Vargas [20] and Marneffe [7] discussed the most significant grammatical classes for contradiction analysis are adverbs, antonym, conjunctions and punctuation.

To check the occurrence of such classes on blogs, we check the number of words in the CBB dataset posts for a given class and normalize them using the total number of words in the post. We then accumulate all posts in the same category (contradictory or not). Then we calculate the arithmetic mean of each class according to the category, and finally normalize this value to the average number of words in these posts, finding the percentage of words per class in a given category. In Fig. 2 oth contradictory and non-contradictory posts have a subjectivity value of around 50%, indicating that CBB, in general, has no incisive opinion or informational texts. The x-axis represents subjectivity percentage, while the y-axis indicates the number of posts corresponding to the percentages of subjectivity.

In order to show that the contradiction can be one of the reasons for bad accuracy in polarity blogs in comparison with GT, we show one example as indicated in Fig. 3. In this blog, we obtained opposed classified sentiments in the image and text. However, for the subjects when analyzing the complete blog,

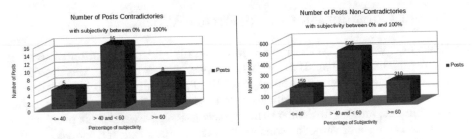

Fig. 2. On the left the number of contradictory posts and on the right the number of non-contradictory posts. Both indicate that CBB generally does not have opinion or informational texts in an incisive manner.

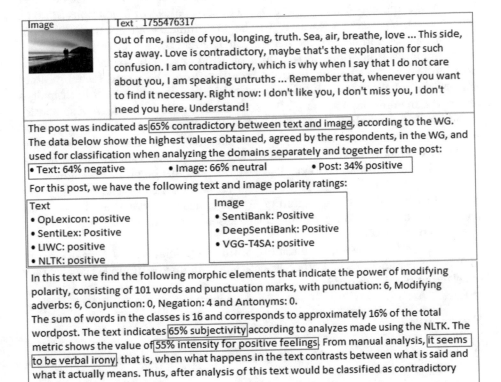

Fig. 3. Contradictory post with positive emotion.

it was not a contradictory blog, indicating that when seeing the image and text together, the blog was understood in a coherent and not contradictory way. In this blogs, we computed the grammar classes as previously described and we consider that it could be classified as having a contradictory text.

6 Final Considerations and Future Work

In this work, we describe the motivations, details and construction process of the Cross-media Brazilian Blog (CBB) corpus, whose creation was based on social network. It contains a Ground Truth (GT) of feelings with information in Portuguese. We analyze the classification of the feelings of the two domains, being text and image, and we investigate the contradictions between their predictions. We propose the use of three lexicons with text manipulation techniques and use three proposals of classification of feelings in images. The results obtained when analyzing the predictions in images are the comparison of the three networks separately which are very divergent in relation to the GT, since it indicates an approximate precision of 39.20%, 40.56% and 32.84% or 67.68% for the classifier 1, network 2 and network 3, respectively. For the analysis of predictions in texts, the lexicons, compared separately to the GT, indicate an accuracy of about 44.65%, 45.45% and 43.29% for the lexicon 1, 2 and 3, respectively.

The approach informed in the work of Joshi et al. [10] seems to show that possible reasons for the low accuracy resulting from the tested techniques are cultural, social and personal differences in the exposure of posts in both images and texts. In addition, Joshi et al. [10] comments on the importance of semantics in addressing aesthetics, which is a subjective theme, and also on emotional judgments because semantics vary across cultures. In the case of this work, the networks used for image classification were created for use in social environments, but not in the Brazilian context. The lexicons, despite being in Portuguese, do not deal with slang used in social networks and do not extend to languages adopted by individuals of a certain group. It is believed that these factors may have contributed to a low accuracy in this research and may present a potential new area of research.

As for the future work, we intend to train a Artificial Neural Network to try to detect contradictions and other aspects that can maybe improve the accuracy in selecting blogs polarity.

References

1. de Almeida Tôrres, A.: Moderna gramática expositiva da língua portuguesa. Editôra Fundo de Cultura (1963)
2. Balage Filho, P.P., Pardo, T.A.S., Aluísio, S.M.: An evaluation of the Brazilian Portuguese LIWC dictionary for sentiment analysis. In: Proceedings of the 9th Brazilian Symposium in Information and Human Language Technology (2013)
3. Borth, D., Chen, T., Ji, R., Chang, S.F.: Sentibank: large-scale ontology and classifiers for detecting sentiment and emotions in visual content. In: Proceedings of the 21st ACM International Conference on Multimedia, pp. 459–460. ACM (2013)
4. Carvalho, P., Silva, M.J.: Sentilex-pt: principais características epotencialidades. Oslo Stud. Lang. 7(1) (2015)
5. Chen, T., Borth, D., Darrell, T., Chang, S.F.: Deepsentibank: visual sentiment concept classification with deep convolutional neural networks. arXiv preprint arXiv:1410.8586 (2014)

6. Cireşan, D.C., Meier, U., Gambardella, L.M., Schmidhuber, J.: Deep, big, simple neural nets for handwritten digit recognition. Neural Comput. **22**(12), 3207–3220 (2010)
7. De Marneffe, M.C., Rafferty, A.N., Manning, C.D.: Finding contradictions in text. In: Proceedings of ACL 2008: HLT, pp. 1039–1047 (2008)
8. Fellbaum, C.: Wordnet. In: Poli, R., Healy, M., Kameas, A. (eds.) Theory and Applications of Ontology: Computer Applications, pp. 231–243. Springer, Dordrecht (2010). https://doi.org/10.1007/978-90-481-8847-5_10
9. Harabagiu, S., Hickl, A., Lacatusu, F.: Negation, contrast and contradiction in text processing. In: AAAI, vol. 6, pp. 755–762 (2006)
10. Joshi, D., et al.: Aesthetics and emotions in images. IEEE Signal Process. Mag. **28**(5), 94–115 (2011)
11. LeCun, Y., et al.: Backpropagation applied to handwritten zip code recognition. Neural Comput. **1**(4), 541–551 (1989)
12. Peng, Y., Huang, X., Zhao, Y.: An overview of cross-media retrieval: concepts, methodologies, benchmarks and challenges. IEEE Trans. Circ. Syst. Video Technol. **28**(9), 2372–2385 (2017)
13. Plutchik, R.: Emotion. A psychoevolutionary synthesis (1980)
14. dos Santos, H.D.P., Woloszyn, V., Vieira, R.: BlogSet-BR: a Brazilian Portuguese blog corpus. In: Calzolari, N., et al. (eds.) Proceedings of the Eleventh International Conference on Language Resources and Evaluation (LREC 2018). European Language Resources Association (ELRA), Paris, France, May 2018
15. Schmidt, S., Stock, W.G.: Collective indexing of emotions in images. A study in emotional information retrieval. J. Assoc. Inf. Sci. Technol. **60**(5), 863–876 (2009)
16. Simonyan, K., Zisserman, A.: Very deep convolutional networks for large-scale image recognition. arXiv preprint arXiv:1409.1556 (2014)
17. Singh, R.K.: Humour, irony and satire in literature. Int. J. Engl. Lit. (IJEL) **3**(4), 65–72 (2012)
18. Souza, M., Vieira, R.: Sentiment analysis on Twitter data for portuguese language. In: Caseli, H., Villavicencio, A., Teixeira, A., Perdigão, F. (eds.) PROPOR 2012. LNCS (LNAI), vol. 7243, pp. 241–247. Springer, Heidelberg (2012). https://doi.org/10.1007/978-3-642-28885-2_28
19. Vadicamo, L., et al.: Cross-media learning for image sentiment analysis in the wild. In: The IEEE International Conference on Computer Vision (ICCV), October 2017
20. Vargas, D.S.: Detecting contrastive sentences for sentiment analysis (2016)
21. Xu, C., Cetintas, S., Lee, K.C., Li, L.J.: Visual sentiment prediction with deep convolutional neural networks. arXiv preprint arXiv:1411.5731 (2014)
22. You, Q., Luo, J., Jin, H., Yang, J.: Robust image sentiment analysis using progressively trained and domain transferred deep networks. In: AAAI, pp. 381–388 (2015)

Diagnosing Huntington's Disease Through Gait Dynamics

Juliana Paula Felix[1]([⊠]) [iD], Flávio Henrique Teles Vieira[2],
Ricardo Augusto Pereira Franco[2], Ronaldo Martins da Costa[1],
and Rogerio Lopes Salvini[1]

[1] Instituto de Informática, Universidade Federal de Goiás, Goiânia, GO, Brazil
{julianafelix,ronaldocosta,rogeriosalvini}@inf.ufg.br
[2] Escola de Engenharia Elétrica, Mecânica e de Computação,
Universidade Federal de Goiás, Goiânia, GO, Brazil
flavio_vieira@ufg.br, ricardofranco3@gmail.com

Abstract. This study proposes an automatic method for identifying Huntington's disease using features extracted from gait signals derived from force-sensitive resistors. Features were extracted using metrics of fluctuation magnitude and fluctuation dynamics, obtained from a detrended Fluctuation Analysis (DFA). In the classification, five machine learning algorithms (Support Vector Machines (SVM), K-Nearest Neighbor (KNN), Naive Bayes (NB), Linear Discriminant Analysis (LDA) and Decision Tree (DT)) were compared by the leave-one-out cross-validation method. Our experiments showed that SVM and DT provided the best results, achieving an average accuracy of 100.0%, representing an improvement compared to other results in the literature, and proving the effectiveness of the proposed method.

Keywords: Automatic diagnosis · Huntington's disease · Machine learning · Gait dynamics

1 Introduction

Huntington's Disease (HD) is a genetic disorder that causes the progressive breakdown of nerve cells in the brain. Today, there are approximately 30,000 symptomatic Americans and more than 200,000 at-risk of inheriting the disease [3]. The symptoms are similar to those of other neurodegenerative diseases, such as Parkinson's Disease or Amyotrophic Lateral Sclerosis (ALS), which includes: personality changes, mood swings and depression, forgetfulness and impaired judgment, slurred speech, difficulty in swallowing, involuntary movements and unsteady gait [3].

An unsteady gait leads to altered gait rhythm and gait dynamics. In this sense, an analysis of temporal gait parameters has a high potential of presenting an automatic non-invasive method based on gait dynamics for the classification of neurodegenerative diseases [4,28]. There are many previous studies in

G. Bebis et al. (Eds.): ISVC 2019, LNCS 11845, pp. 504–515, 2019.
https://doi.org/10.1007/978-3-030-33723-0_41

the literature that have analyzed gait signals from subjects with different neurodegenerative diseases and compared them with healthy subjects [7, 15–20, 28]. Moreover, much progress has been made when it comes to the use of machine learning techniques applied to the classification of Huntington's Disease through analysis of gait patterns [5, 8, 12, 28].

Some studies have previously shown that patients that suffer from some neurological disease present increased fluctuation magnitude, as well as an altered fluctuation dynamics, including those related to the fractal organization [13, 15, 16]. In this sense, we wanted to investigate the effect of using measures of fluctuation magnitude and fluctuation dynamics, such as the coefficient of variation (CV) and detrended fluctuation analysis (DFA) [17, 18], alone, on automatic diagnosis of Huntington's disease.

In this work, we propose an automatic method for the diagnosis of Huntington's Disease using the information from gait dynamics, and we evaluate the performance of five well-known classifiers [6, 22] (Support Vector Machines (SVM), K-Nearest Neighbors (KNN), Naive Bayes (NB), Linear Discriminant Analysis (LDA) and Decision Tree (DT)) in accurately classifying gait signals from an unknown subject under consideration as being from a subject suffering with Huntington's Disease or being from a healthy subject. The novelty of our approach consists of using metrics of fluctuation dynamics and fluctuation magnitude to obtain a simple feature vector of size two that serves as input for these classifiers. We evaluate the performance of our method using three statistical measurements: sensitivity, specificity, and accuracy. Our results show that the method proposed is effective, being able to correctly identify all data, therefore achieving an average accuracy of 100.0% when either SVM or DT is used.

The remainder of this paper is structured as follows. Section 2 describes the proposed method, including the dataset description, preprocessing, feature extraction techniques and classification details. Our results are presented in Sect. 3, and a comparison of our results with other methods found in the literature is presented in Sect. 4. Finally, Sect. 5 concludes our work.

2   Proposed Method

We propose a complete method for identifying Huntington's Disease using gait dynamics. The proposed system receives a time series signal extracted from the gait. Some preprocessing of the signal is performed, and features are then extracted. These features are then fed to the classifier, which outputs the diagnosis, that is, if the signal belongs to a subject with Huntington's Disease or not. The outline of the proposed method is shown in Fig. 1, and an explanation of each step follows.

2.1   Dataset Description

In this work, we used a publicly available database on Gait Dynamics in Neuro-Degenerative Disease. The database was provided by Hausdorff et al. [15, 16] and

Fig. 1. Outline of the proposed method.

is available online on the web page of *Physionet* [14]. It consists of a collection of different gait cycle parameters collected using force-sensitive resistors placed in the subject's shoe. Each subject was requested to walk for 5 min at their usual pace along a 77 m hallway. In total, there are 20 (6 males/11 females) records from patients with Huntington's disease (HD) and 16 (2 males/14 females) records from healthy control subjects (CO).

The database also provides some information on the subjects that participated in the experiments, including age, height (m), weight (kg), gender, and the mean gait speed (m/s). The latter was determined by dividing the total distance walked by a subject by the duration of the walk time. Although additional time was required for subjects to turn around at the end of the hallway during data acquisition, the values reported by Hausdorff et al. [15] for mean gait speed of control subjects is similar to previously reported normal values [1]. This information has been summarized in Table 1, where μ stands for the mean and SE stands for the standard error of the mean, calculated as $\sigma/\sqrt{n}$, where σ is the standard deviation and n is the total number of observations.

Table 1. Statistical data from Huntington's Disease and control subjects.

Group	Age (years)		Height (m)		Weight (kg)		Gait Speed (m/s)	
	μ	SE	μ	SE	μ	SE	μ	SE
Huntington's (HD)	47	3	1.83	0.02	72.1	3.7	1.15	0.08
Control (CO)	39	4	1.83	0.02	66.8	2.7	1.35	0.04

From each foot (left/right), three time series were obtained from the force-sensitive resistors placed in each participant's shoe, corresponding to different phases of the gait, namely: stride interval (the time elapsed between the first contact of two consecutive footsteps of the same foot), swing interval (time during which the foot is in the air), and stance interval (the phase during which the foot remains in contact with the ground). Moreover, the database also provides the double support interval (time during which both feet are in contact with the ground), which was derived from the signals from both sensors. Figure 2 shows an example of the left and right stance interval time series derived from a subject with HD (Fig. 2a) and the corresponding ones derived from a healthy subject (Fig. 2b).

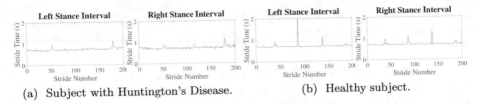

(a) Subject with Huntington's Disease.   (b) Healthy subject.

Fig. 2. An example of time series of stance intervals derived from the left and right foot from participants with Huntington's Disease (a) and from a healthy participant (b).

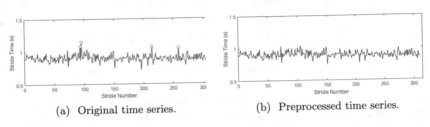

(a) Original time series.   (b) Preprocessed time series.

Fig. 3. Sample right stride interval time series from a subject suffering with Huntington's Disease.

2.2 Data Preprocessing

The creators of the database mentioned some start-up effects associated with the moment the participants of the experiment began to walk on the hallway [15,16]. In order to remove these effects, the first 20 s of the recorded data from each one of the subjects were removed. Moreover, some turn-around were occasionally needed so that the subject could continue walking. For each subject, we identified these noise observations by applying a median filter, i.e., data points that were 3 standard deviations greater than or less than the median value were replaced by the median value of the corresponding time series. Figure 3 shows the result of the application of this process on the right stride interval series of subject number 1 with HD. The red dots present in Fig. 3a were identified as being outliers when the median filter was applied. These points were replaced for the median value of the series, resulting in the preprocessed time series presented in Fig. 3b.

2.3 Feature Extraction

Studies have shown that measures of fluctuation magnitude (stride-to-stride variability), such as the coefficient of variation, as well as metrics of fluctuation dynamics, such as the fractal scaling index α have great potential of differentiating healthy subjects from those suffering from some types of neurodegenerative diseases, including Huntington's Disease [11,15,16]. In this study, we were interested in verifying the effectiveness of these two features alone – CV and α – in performing a binary classification between a subject with Huntington's Disease and a control subject. Next, we explain how each of these features was obtained.

Coefficient of Variation (CV). The mean (μ) and standard deviation (σ) of each time series from each subject was calculated. Then, the coefficient of variation (CV), a measure of the magnitude of stride-to-stride variability and gait unsteadiness, was determined by calculating $100 \times (\sigma/\mu)$.

Fractal Scaling Index (α). In order to calculate the fractal scaling index of a time series, we first need to perform a Detrended Fluctuation Analysis (DFA) on it. The DFA method, first proposed in [23], is a modified random-walk analysis that has proven useful in revealing the extent of long-range correlations in time series. Briefly, the time series to be analyzed (with N samples) is first integrated. The next step consists of dividing the integrated time series into windows of equal length, n – that is, each window considers n strides. In each window, a least squares line is fit to the data (representing the trend in that window). The y coordinate of the straight line segments is denoted by $y_n(k)$. In each window, we detrend the integrated time series $y(k)$, by subtracting the local trend, $y_n(k)$. The root-mean-square fluctuation of this integrated and detrended time series is then calculated by

$$F(n) = \sqrt{\frac{1}{N} \sum_{k=1}^{N} [y(k) - y_n(k)]^2}. \tag{1}$$

This process of detrending followed by fluctuation measurement is repeated over a range of different window sizes n, and a log-log graph of $F(n)$ against n is constructed. Finally, the scaling exponent α is calculated as the slope of a straight line fit to the log-log graph of n against $F(n)$ using least-squares. In this study, the region of $10 \leq n \leq 20$ was used, for this range has been shown to provide a statistically robust estimate of stride time correlation properties despite the length of data [16,24].

Thus, each time series was finally represented by two numerical values, namely, the coefficient of variation (CV) and its fractal scale index α, creating a feature vector of size two to be fed to each classifier.

2.4   Classification and Performance Evaluation

In this work, we compared Support Vector Machine (SVM) [27], K-Nearest Neighbors (KNN) [21], Naive Bayes (NB) [26], Linear Discriminant Analysis (LDA) [10] and Decision Trees (DT) [25] algorithms on Huntington's disease diagnosis when metrics of fluctuation magnitude and fluctuation dynamics extracted from gait signals were used as input to these classic classifiers.

A linear kernel was used for SVM, and Euclidean distance was used as metric for K-Nearest Neighbors, expressed by Eq. 2,

$$d(S,T) = \sqrt{\sum_{i=1}^{n}(S_i - T_i)^2} \tag{2}$$

where $d(S,T)$ is the distance between input feature vectors S and T.

To validate the performance of the proposed method, we performed a leave-one-out cross-validation (LOOCV) method [9] over the database, i.e., one subject was left out at a time and used for testing, and other remaining subjects were used as training data. The performance of our model was evaluated by three statistical measurements: *Sensitivity*, *Specificity* and *Accuracy*, which were defined according to [2, 29] and are presented below,

$$\text{Sensitivity:} \frac{TP}{TP + FN} \times 100, \tag{3}$$

$$\text{Specificity:} \frac{TN}{TN + FP} \times 100, \tag{4}$$

$$\text{Accuracy:} \frac{TP + TN}{TP + TN + FN + FP} \times 100, \tag{5}$$

where TP is the number of True Positives values, TN is the number of True Negatives values, FP is the number of False Positives values, and FN is the number of False Negatives values. In our work, the *sensitivity* measures the percentage of subjects who were correctly identified as having HD, the *specificity* measures the percentage of healthy people who were correctly identified as not having HD, and the *accuracy* measures the proportion of correct results among the total number of cases examined. The reported classification accuracies represent the average accuracies on the test sets.

Experimentation code to perform classification and metrics evaluation was developed using MATLAB R2017a using Statistics and Machine Learning Toolbox.

3 Results

In Table 2, we present the average classification accuracies, along with its standard error of the mean (SE), obtained when features different combinations of gait signals of the left (Table 2a) and right (Table 2b) foot were used. The results show that, when using parameters derived from the left stride, left swing and left stance interval, overall classification accuracies of 94.4%, 83.3%, and 94.4% were obtained, respectively. On the other hand, the highest average accuracy when right stride and right swing parameters were used turned out to be 97.2%

Table 2. Classification Accuracies when features were extracted from all the seven possible combinations of gait signals from each foot.

Classifier	Stride		Swing		Stance		Stride swing		Stride stance		Swing stance		Stride swing stance	
	μ (%)	SE (%)	μ (%)	SE (%)	μ (%)	SE (%)	μ (%)	SE (%)	μ (%)	SE (%)	μ (%)	SE (%)	μ (%)	SE (%)
(a) Left foot														
SVM	91.7	4.7	83.3	6.3	91.7	4.7	91.7	4.7	91.7	4.7	86.1	5.8	88.9	5.3
KNN	94.4	3.9	77.8	7.0	80.6	6.7	88.9	5.3	91.7	4.7	86.1	5.8	88.9	5.3
NB	86.1	5.8	83.3	6.3	86.1	5.8	91.7	4.7	83.3	6.3	88.9	5.3	86.1	5.8
LDA	83.3	6.3	80.6	6.7	83.3	6.3	80.6	6.7	83.3	6.3	77.8	7.0	80.6	6.7
DT	88.9	5.3	77.8	7.0	94.4	3.9	86.1	5.8	83.3	6.3	94.4	3.9	80.6	6.7
(b) Right foot														
SVM	94.4	3.9	88.9	5.3	100.0	0.0	94.4	3.9	97.2	2.8	97.2	2.8	97.2	2.8
KNN	94.4	3.9	88.9	5.3	97.2	2.8	94.4	3.9	97.2	2.8	94.4	3.9	94.4	3.9
NB	86.1	5.8	91.7	4.7	91.7	4.7	91.7	4.7	91.7	4.7	91.7	4.7	91.7	4.7
LDA	80.6	6.7	83.3	6.3	80.6	6.7	83.3	6.3	80.6	6.7	80.6	6.7	80.6	6.7
DT	97.2	2.8	86.1	5.8	100.0	0.0	97.2	2.8	97.2	2.8	100.0	0.0	97.2	2.8

and 91.7%, respectively, while right stance parameters produced an average of 100.0% accuracy.

In order to analyze if the concatenation of features extracted from more than one phase of the gait from the same foot could improve the results, four other cases were considered and are presented in Table 2: stride and swing interval, stride and stance interval, swing and stance interval, and finally, stride, swing and stance interval. We can observe, however, that combining features from different time series does not necessarily imply an improvement. Figure 4 presents bar graphs for each foot, grouped per classifier, showing the classifier accuracies along with its confidence intervals. Confidence interval was based on 5% of significance.

Table 3 shows our results when double support interval parameters were considered. The best overall accuracy achieved was 94.4% when either KNN, NB or DT was used as a classifier. When observing all gait variables presented in Tables 2 and 3, the right stance interval is the one that stands out, for it produced the highest average accuracy for both SVM, KNN and DT (100.0%, 97.2%, and 100.0%, respectively). Linear Discriminant Analysis' highest accuracy was 83.3%, and it was obtained when left stride or left stance (or the concatenation of features derived from both) signals were used, while NB's highest accuracy obtained was 94.4% when features extracted from the double support signal was taken as input to the classifier.

For further evaluation, a confusion matrix was constructed considering the case where each classifier achieves its highest average accuracy. Figure 5 presents the confusion matrix for each classifier. It is possible to observe that SVM and DT have appropriately identified all subjects from each class. KNN has mistaken

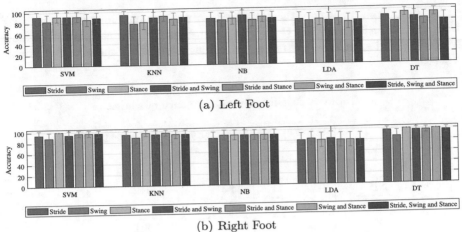

(a) Left Foot

(b) Right Foot

Fig. 4. Bar graph of classifier accuracies with confidence interval.

Table 3. Average classification accuracy of double support interval parameters.

Classifier	Double support	
	μ (%)	SE (%)
SVM	80.6	6.7
KNN	94.4	3.9
NB	94.4	3.9
LDA	58.3	8.3
DT	94.4	3.9

only one subject as being healthy while, in fact, it should be classified as HD. NB confused exactly one HD subject as being from CO, and vice-versa. LDA presented greater confusion, being able to classify accurately almost all of the control subjects but wrongly classifying 5 HD subjects as being healthy.

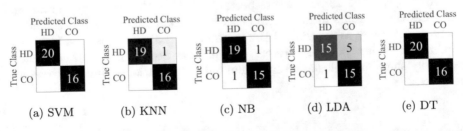

Fig. 5. Classifier confusion matrices.

Finally, Table 4 presents the classification performance measures, extracted from the confusion matrices (Fig. 5) of each classifier. We can note that both sensitivity and specificity present equal values when the same classifier is considered.

Table 4. Classification performance measures.

Classifier	Accuracy (%)	Sensitivity (%)	Specificity (%)
SVM	100.0	100.0	100.0
KNN	97.2	97.5	97.5
NB	94.4	94.4	94.4
LDA	83.3	84.4	84.4
DT	100.0	100.0	100.0

4   Comparison

In this section, we compare our method to other approaches found in the literature that also uses the *Physionet* database [14–16]. Zeng and Wang [28] used the Radial Basis Function (RBF) classifier to perform a binary classifier to distinguish from HD and CO. In their approach, all data points from the left and right swing interval, and left and right stance interval from each subject were used as input to the classifier, and they have achieved 83.3% of accuracy. Gupta et al. [12] used the mutual information criterion to select the 500 most essential features which were used to construct a decision tree classifier, leading to an accuracy of 88.5%. Another approach, from Baratin et al. [5], used Discrete Wavelet Transform, extracting two features from each of the seven levels of decomposition performed, and then feeding it to an SVM, resulting on the improvement of accuracy to 86.1%. Daliri [7], on the other hand, used an SVM classifier fed with 12 features obtained as result after performing a genetic algorithm during the feature selection phase, obtaining 90.3% of accuracy. These results have been summarized in Table 5.

Although [5,7,12,28] achieved respectable classification accuracy, our method surpasses these results in four of the classifiers analyzed, as well as equals the result of Zeng and Wang when LDA is used, all that while using a small feature vector of size two. Furthermore, the features used in our method demand relatively simplified calculation and minimal computational time and required resources.

Table 5. Comparison of the accuracy between this work and previous works using the same dataset.

Feature selection method	# of features	Classifier	Accuracy
Deterministic learning theory [28]	*	RBF	83.3%
Mutual information criterion [12]	500	DT	88.5%
Discrete wavelet transform (7 levels) [5]	14[a]	SVM	86.1%
Genetic algorithm [7]	12	SVM	90.3%
Our approach	2	LDA	83.3%
	2	NB	94.4%
	2	KNN	97.2%
	2	**SVM**	**100.0%**
	2	**DT**	**100.0%**

*Concatenation of all data points from left swing interval, right swing interval, left stance interval and right stance interval.
[a]Two from each level.

5   Conclusions

In this paper, we presented a novel classification approach that analyzes gait patterns in order to identify subjects with Huntington's Disease from healthy subjects. We evaluated and compared the performance of our method using five different classifiers fed with features extracted from times series from different phases of the gait. The highest accuracy was obtained by SVM and Decision Tree when features were extracted from the right stance interval, resulting in an average accuracy of 100.0%. The KNN classifier also achieved a high accuracy of 97.2% when features from the same time series were considered. The best accuracy of NB and LDA were 94.4% and 83.3%, respectively, however using features derived from other phases of the gait. Our method represents an improvement on previously reported results, which was 90.3% [7].

The results presented in this paper showed that there was no apparent improvement of the mean accuracy of the five classifiers when their feature vector was composed of the concatenation of features extracted from more than one time series. Moreover, we observed that the average accuracy obtained by SVM, KNN, NB, LDA and DT were, in general, higher when the features were extracted from the right foot rather than from the left. Although this difference of accuracy might be related to the sensors used in the experiment, which sometimes requires calibration, it is still unknown the effect of the disease on gait asymmetry [14]. Therefore, these results might help future studies understand and analyze how gait asymmetry is related to Huntington's Disease.

Therefore, in addition to improving the classification accuracy for the diagnosis of HD, our approach also provides a reduction on the number of features required to feed the classifier, thereby providing a simple but efficient method. We conclude that the metrics used in our approach may be promising for the research area of identifying Huntington's Disease through gait dynamics, and

514   J. Paula Felix et al.

future research work may be carried out so as to analyze the potential of such metrics in other neurodegenerative diseases, as well as in larger HD databases with the purpose of validating these results.

References

1. Alexander, N.B.: Gait disorders in older adults. J. Am. Geriatr. Soc. **44**(4), 434–451 (1996). https://doi.org/10.1111/j.1532-5415.1996.tb06417.x
2. Altman, D.G., Bland, J.M.: Diagnostic tests. 1: sensitivity and specificity. BMJ: Br. Med. J. **308**(6943), 1552 (1994). https://doi.org/10.1136/bmj.308.6943.1552
3. America, H.D.S.: Overview of Huntington's disease. https://hdsa.org/what-is-hd/overview-of-huntingtons-disease/
4. Aziz, W., Arif, M.: Complexity analysis of stride interval time series by threshold dependent symbolic entropy. Eur. J. Appl. Physiol. **98**(1), 30–40 (2006). https://doi.org/10.1007/s00421-006-0226-5
5. Baratin, E., Sugavaneswaran, L., Umapathy, K., Ioana, C., Krishnan, S.: Wavelet-based characterization of gait signal for neurological abnormalities. Gait Posture **41**(2), 634–639 (2015). https://doi.org/10.1016/j.gaitpost.2015.01.012
6. Bishop, C.M.: Pattern Recognition and Machine Learning. Information Science and Statistics. Springer, New York (2006)
7. Daliri, M.R.: Automated diagnosis of Alzheimer disease using the scale-invariant feature transforms in magnetic resonance images. J. Med. Syst. **36**(2), 995–1000 (2012). https://doi.org/10.1007/s10916-011-9738-6
8. Daliri, M.R.: Automatic diagnosis of neuro-degenerative diseases using gait dynamics. Measurement **45**(7), 1729–1734 (2012). https://doi.org/10.1016/j.measurement.2012.04.013
9. Duda, R.O., Hart, P.E., Stork, D.G.: Pattern Classification, 2nd edn. Wiley-Interscience, Hoboken (2000)
10. Foody, G.M., Mathur, A.: A relative evaluation of multiclass image classification by support vector machines. IEEE Trans. Geosci. Remote Sens. **42**(6), 1335–1343 (2004). https://doi.org/10.1109/TGRS.2004.827257
11. Goldfarb, B., Simon, S.: Gait patterns in patients with amyotrophic lateral sclerosis. Arch. Phys. Med. Rehabil. **65**(2), 61–65 (1984)
12. Gupta, K., Khajuria, A., Chatterjee, N., Joshi, P., Joshi, D.: Rule based classification of neurodegenerative diseases using data driven gait features. Health Technol. 1–14 (2018). https://doi.org/10.1007/s12553-018-0274-y
13. Hausdorff, J.M., Cudkowicz, M.E., Firtion, R., Wei, J.Y., Goldberger, A.L.: Gait variability and basal ganglia disorders: stride-to-stride variations of gait cycle timing in Parkinson's disease and Huntington's disease. Mov. Disord. **13**(3), 428–437 (1998). https://doi.org/10.1002/mds.870130310
14. Hausdorff, J.M., Lertratanakul, A., Cudkowicz, M.E., Peterson, A.L., Kaliton, D., Goldberger, A.L.: Gait dynamics in neuro-degenerative disease data base. https://doi.org/10.13026/C27G6C. https://physionet.org/physiobank/database/gaitndd/
15. Hausdorff, J.M., Lertratanakul, A., Cudkowicz, M.E., Peterson, A.L., Kaliton, D., Goldberger, A.L.: Dynamic markers of altered gait rhythm in amyotrophic lateral sclerosis. J. Appl. Physiol. **88**(6), 2045–2053 (2000). https://doi.org/10.1152/jappl.2000.88.6.2045
16. Hausdorff, J.M., et al.: Altered fractal dynamics of gait: reduced stride-interval correlations with aging and Huntington's disease. J. Appl. Physiol. **82**(1), 262–269 (1997). https://doi.org/10.1152/jappl.1997.82.1.262

17. Hausdorff, J.M., Peng, C., Ladin, Z., Wei, J.Y., Goldberger, A.L.: Is walking a random walk? Evidence for long-range correlations in stride interval of human gait. J. Appl. Physiol. **78**(1), 349–358 (1995). https://doi.org/10.1152/jappl.1995. 78.1.349

18. Hausdorff, J.M., Purdon, P.L., Peng, C., Ladin, Z., Wei, J.Y., Goldberger, A.L.: Fractal dynamics of human gait: stability of long-range correlations in stride interval fluctuations. J. Appl. Physiol. **80**(5), 1448–1457 (1996). https://doi.org/10. 1152/jappl.1996.80.5.1448

19. Joshi, D., Khajuria, A., Joshi, P.: An automatic non-invasive method for Parkinson's disease classification. Comput. Methods Programs Biomed. **145**, 135–145 (2017). https://doi.org/10.1016/j.cmpb.2017.04.007

20. Keloth, S.M., Arjunan, S.P., Kumar, D.: Computing the variations in the self-similar properties of the various gait intervals in Parkinson disease patients. In: 2017 39th Annual International Conference of the IEEE Engineering in Medicine and Biology Society (EMBC), Seogwipo, South Korea, pp. 2434–2437. IEEE, July 2017. https://doi.org/10.1109/EMBC.2017.8037348

21. Kim, J., Kim, B.S., Savarese, S.: Comparing image classification methods: k-nearest neighbor and support vector machines. Ann Arbor **1001**, 48109–2122 (2012)

22. Mitchell, T.M.: Machine Learning, 1st edn. McGraw-Hill Inc., New York (1997)

23. Peng, C.K., Buldyrev, S.V., Havlin, S., Simons, M., Stanley, H.E., Goldberger, A.L.: Mosaic organization of DNA nucleotides. Phys. Rev. E **49**(2), 1685 (1994). https://doi.org/10.1103/PhysRevE.49.1685

24. Peng, C.K., Buldyrev, S., Goldberger, A., Havlin, S., Simons, M., Stanley, H.: Finite-size effects on long-range correlations: implications for analyzing dna sequences. Phys. Rev. E **47**(5), 3730 (1993). https://doi.org/10.1103/physreve.47. 3730

25. Quinlan, J.R.: Induction of decision trees. Mach. Learn. **1**(1), 81–106 (1986)

26. Rish, I., et al.: An empirical study of the naive Bayes classifier. In: IJCAI 2001 Workshop on Empirical Methods in Artificial Intelligence, vol. 3, pp. 41–46 (2001)

27. Steinwart, I., Christmann, A.: Support Vector Machines. Springer, New York (2008). https://doi.org/10.1007/978-0-387-77242-4

28. Zeng, W., Wang, C.: Classification of neurodegenerative diseases using gait dynamics via deterministic learning. Inf. Sci. **317**, 246–258 (2015). https://doi.org/10. 1016/j.ins.2015.04.047

29. Zhou, X., Obuchowski, N., McClish, D.: Statistical Methods in Diagnostic Medicine. New York, NY (2002). https://doi.org/10.1002/9780470906514

On the Potential for Facial Attractiveness as a Soft Biometric

Moneera Alnamnakani$^{(\boxtimes)}$, Sasan Mahmoodi$^{(\boxtimes)}$, and Mark Nixon$^{(\boxtimes)}$

Southampton University, Southampton, UK
{mhalal7, sm3, msn}@soton.ac.uk

Abstract. This paper describes the first study on whether human facial attractiveness can be used as a soft biometric feature. By using comparative soft biometrics, with ranking and classification, we show that attractiveness does have the capability to be used within a recognition framework using crowd-sourcing, by using groups from the LFW dataset. In this initial study, the Elo rating system is employed to rank subjects' facial attractiveness based on the comparative descriptions. We will show how facial attractiveness attributes can be exploited for identification purposes and can be described in the same way and can add to performance of comparative soft biometrics attributes. Attractiveness does not appear to be as powerful as gender for recognition. It does however increase recognition capability and it is interesting that a perceptual characteristic can improve performance in this way.

Keywords: Comparative soft biometrics · Face recognition · Facial attractiveness · Facial attributes · Ranking

1 Introduction

Society requires human identification for business as usual, and for security. Biometrics is the science of recognizing individuals based on physical features and attributes; these attributes are chosen from human characteristics that use unique data to perform identification. Soft biometrics are attracting a lot of interest with the spread of surveillance systems, and have been developed to augment the performance achieved with 'hard biometrics' [1–3].

Soft biometrics for identification relate to behavioral and physical attributes that can be semantically defined and are describable by other people [4]. Such traits can be used for recognition, which can be extracted in the form of descriptors, labels and measurements [5]. It relies on individual characteristics, which must often be used to identity persons at a distance and under adverse visual surveillance conditions [3, 6]. There are two kinds of soft biometrics for identification: comparative and categorical. 'Comparative' means a person's attributes are classified in comparison with those of another person [7]. For an annotator to judge a figure comparatively to another figure is more natural than using absolute relations 'categorical' [3].

Developments in closed-circuit television (CCTV) networks, which have expanded in recent decades world-wide, have enlarged the reliance on – and capacity of – surveillance data for identification. There remains considerable uncertainty, however,

© Springer Nature Switzerland AG 2019
G. Bebis et al. (Eds.): ISVC 2019, LNCS 11845, pp. 516–528, 2019.
https://doi.org/10.1007/978-3-030-33723-0_42

in the available data. This is a major challenge encountered by law enforcement organizations in criminal investigations. This challenge has motivated research in soft biometrics for identification, including the face [2, 3, 5, 8], body [9, 10], and clothing [11]. These studies have investigated the sources of attributes that permit human identification. Of these, the human face appears the most potent for recognition at short distances [6].

A feature of soft biometrics is that information is required to be clear, unforgettable, and describable for identification, to allow search of a dataset during eyewitness statements and identification. A key characteristic distinguishing unforgettable faces from less memorable ones is beauty or 'attractiveness', as many experimenters have noted [12]. This suggests that it is prudent to study facial attractiveness as a soft biometric. In Fig. 1 (as found in our study), one can differentiate the two faces by attractiveness, in the same way as by gender. The question then is whether attractiveness is a generic description that can be used to aid identification within a larger pool of subjects.

Fig. 1. Illustrating attractiveness as a face description.

Although numerous studies have investigated the impact of facial features on performance in recognition, no previous work has considered facial attractiveness as a soft biometric. Our contribution in this work is to investigate whether facial attractiveness can be considered a comparative soft biometric attribute and thus to contribute to face recognition. This paper appears to be the first to propose the use of attractiveness, to investigate the effects of facial attractiveness on facial recognition, and to investigate the accuracy of face recognition when attractiveness is included.

1.1 Importance of Facial Attractiveness

The attractiveness of a face plays a significant role in many daily and public activities. Evaluating or codifying facial attractiveness is, however, a very challenging concept, and has been debated by philosophers, artists, and scientists for many years [13]. The attractiveness of a face can apparently be easily decoded by the human brain, and can be hard to develop automated methods to measure it. Though attractiveness can be recognized instantly, it is still challenging to articulate how this can be achieved or even described [14].

Several studies have tried to use computational methods in order to analyze and evaluate facial attractiveness [13]. Although the study of facial attractiveness by a computational framework is still relatively new, it has potential for significant impact. Attractiveness has been the subject of significant consideration in the field, with the most common concentration being on integrating techniques from image processing, computer vision and machine learning. Multiple events highlight the capabilities and effectiveness of information inferred from facial attractiveness for recognizing people [14, 15].

In this work, a new set of proposed semantic facial attractiveness attributes is introduced, along with their comparative labels. We have discussed the background related to the problem. The remainder of the paper is organized as follows. Section 2 defines the new semantic facial attractiveness attributes and descriptive labels for annotation. Section 3 involves the crowdsourcing of comparative labels using the LFW dataset. Subsequently, it presents and defines the Elo rating system to compare features, for inferring relative measurements in the future. In Sect. 4, the attractiveness attribute is analyzed via the correlation attributes and via feature selections. In Sect. 5, the performance of the attractiveness attribute is evaluated, through the responses received for a sample of different subjects. Finally, the conclusions and suggestions for future work are put forward in Sect. 6.

2 Attribute and Label Derivation

Recent psychological studies have shown that the human perception of facial attractiveness is largely constituted by variations between different individuals, for both male and female observers [16]. Moreover, findings have shown that estimations of beauty are dependent on the physiognomy of the face, and persons in all places use related criteria in their decisions. A strong relationship between beauty and specific features is presented in [17], which characterized neonate, mature and expressive attributes, such as a small nose, high forehead, prominent cheekbones or arched eyebrows. They concluded that the attractiveness ought not to be considered a poetic, inexpressible feature lying only in the eye of the beholder [14, 18].

Research shows that general attributes such as facial symmetry, averageness, and secondary sex characteristics are attractive in both men's and women's faces, and across cultures [14, 19, 20]. Nevertheless, the published studies have not yet reached a consensus on these hypotheses or rules [15]. To consider facial attractiveness features as soft biometric identifier, people should find them easy to remember and describe. Based on previous works on soft biometrics, a human identification technique is presented in [8] using comparative facial soft biometrics – creating a set of soft biometric attributes, which cover the most important facial components. In our study, we propose a list of 15 attributes similar to those used in a previous study. Seven more attributes are also added here as these might putatively relate to and describe facial attractiveness.

2.1 Label Comparisons of Facial Features

Naturally, people describe humans using estimations of physical attributes and labels. Comparative labels characterize the grade of comparisons of relative features. This study will use comparative labels associated with the attributes, defined based on a 4-point bipolar scale following a consistent format: "More A", "Same", "Less A/or More B" corresponding to label values 1, 0, and −1, respectively with −2 for

"Cannot See" [8]. We need to measure the strengths fairly, because by establishing numerical value scores we can form an ordered list for each trait, and use this result to rank subjects. We have used attributes (listed in Table 1) of the most dependably understood facial attractive 'scales'. For each feature, an appropriate group of comparative labels is defined to describe these attributes.

Table 1. Soft facial attractiveness biometrics attributes and possible associated response labels.

	Soft traits	Comparative labels			
		1	0	−1	−2
1	Age	More old	Same	More young	Cannot see
2	Attractiveness	Less Attractive	Same	More attractive	Cannot see
3	Cheek shape	More flat	Same	More prominent	Cannot see
4	Chin length	More long	Same	More short	Cannot see
5	Eyebrow length	More long	Same	More short	Cannot see
6	Eyebrow thickness	More thick	Same	More thin	Cannot see
7	Eyes size	More large	Same	More small	Cannot see
8	Face length	More long	Same	More short	Cannot see
9	Face width	More wide	Same	More narrow	Cannot see
10	Facial hair	Less facial hair	Same	More facial hair	Cannot see
11	Forehead hair	Less forehead hair	Same	More forehead hair	Cannot see
12	Gender	More masculine	Same	More feminine	Cannot see
13	Jaw size	More narrow	Same	More wide	Cannot see
14	Lip thickness	More thick	Same	More thin	Cannot see
15	Nose length	More long	Same	More short	Cannot see
16	Nose width	More wide	Same	More narrow	Cannot see
17	Nose-mouth distance	More Short	Same	More Long	Cannot see
18	Proportions	More average	Same	Less average	Cannot see
19	Figure (Shape)	More fat	Same	More thin	Cannot see
20	Skin color	More dark	Same	More light	Cannot see
21	Skin smoothness	Less smooth	Same	More smooth	Cannot see
22	Symmetry	Less symmetrical	Same	More symmetrical	Cannot see

3 Deriving Facial Attractiveness Labels

3.1 Facial Attractiveness Dataset

We use the Labelled Faces in the Wild (LFW) dataset [21], which displays a large variety of the subjects. The LFW dataset is a popular database for studying uncon-strained recognition and has been chosen since it reflects the environment of surveil-lance situations. Such variations more accurately reflect the challenges of image recognition in the real world. The aim here is to assess the general usage of attrac-tiveness and collect physically unconstrained data to more accurately model normal human observations and explanation given to others, compared to additional limiting annotation jobs, as seen in [4].

In this study, we investigate the facial attractiveness of humans via comparative soft biometrics using subjects. A subset of subjects has been chosen within the dataset, in the total of 100 subjects, and four samples for each subject as the initial test for results in our study. In other words, these samples were used as justification for testing and computing the accuracy.

3.2   Crowdsourcing of Facial Attractiveness

Crowdsourcing is a relatively novel and effective method of collecting labels from human annotators for a dataset, and it is increasingly changing how datasets are created and deployed. A well-designed crowdsourcing job can be directed at a huge collection of high-quality comparative annotations and permits the collection of data from annotators from diverse national, linguistic and cultural backgrounds. This creates original ground-truth information and produces the chance to eliminate social anno-tation bias. Nowadays, with platform facilities, it is possible to assign annotation jobs to hundreds or more of computer-literate employees and produce verifiable outcomes in a matter of hours [22].

To construct and run the crowdsourced annotation job for this study, we used the Figure-Eight platform to gather labels. A worldwide network of contributors is con-nected to that platform; therefore, the questions must be clear and definitive. In addi-tion, the platform offers control tools and widespread data analysis, and allows customers to agree to take a range of answers whilst refusing non-honest responses. Each labeler compared chosen attributes between two faces, using the labels in Table 1. An example of our crowdsourced comparison via the Figure-Eight platform is pre-sented in Fig. 2.

Fig. 2. Example question from our Figure-Eight job.

For the chosen comparative labels, the annotation procedure required a user to compare one subject on the left, with another subject on the right. The style of each question is fundamentally a psychometric technique. Within the platform, test questions are designed and presented to the labelers to allow us to quantify the accuracy of the contributor and reduce the number of false answers. The crowdsourcing task was repeated to make sure that, by involving as many labelers as possible within our limited time frame, the responses could be regarded as strongly and confidently as possible. A total of 8,378 labelers, provided a total of 184,316 labels for the 400 subject images.

3.3 Ranking by Relative Attractiveness Attributes

All comparisons provided a label value as mentioned in Sect. 2. The value of the label is used to calculate the comparative strength of the subjects' attributes, based on the various ranking systems. This will represent the difference in the feature between two subjects where complete or absolute measurements of the attributes cannot be detected due to the inexactness of verbal or written descriptions. Subsequently, to evaluate the labels and performance of facial attractiveness, it is necessary to rate or "rank" the subjects according to the powers or levels of their attributes. Various ranking algorithms such as the Elo ranking system can be applied for this purpose [3].

Elo is a well-known score-based rating system for rating the players of chess matches based on their estimated and real scores. Such a rating system could be used to rank subjects in a soft biometrics framework, including facial attractiveness as a comparative attribute. Its effectiveness for comparative soft biometrics has previously been confirmed and demonstrated in [3], where it was used to create biometric signatures and to determine the comparative rates of the features from comparative labels.

4 Facial Attractiveness for Recognition

To express a thorough understanding of the collaboration and association between facial attractiveness and other facial soft biometrics attributes, an advance analysis may be needed to investigate how these attributes combine for purposes of identification.

4.1 Correlation Analysis

To discover any dependences or relations between the attractiveness and the other 20 facial attributes, correlation was calculated for all the pairs of attributes. The analysis was performed with the relative scores for the features [15]. The correlation is performed using the Pearson's correlation coefficient, r which can be calculated as:

$$r = \frac{\sigma_{XY}}{\sigma_X \sigma_Y} = \frac{\sum_{i=1}^{n}(x_i - \bar{x})(y_i - \bar{y})}{\sqrt{\sum_{i=1}^{n}(x_i - \bar{x})^2}\sqrt{\sum_{i=1}^{n}(y_i - \bar{y})^2}} \tag{1}$$

Where X and Y are two variables representing the label values of two different semantic traits used to describe an individual. Specifically, X_i and Y_i are two labels of the ith annotation describing the same subject. Thus, r is calculated by dividing the covariance of X and Y, represented as σ_{XY}, by the product of σ_X and σ_Y the standard deviations of X and Y correspondingly. The correlation matrix is calculated by using Eq. (1) is illustrated in Fig. 3.

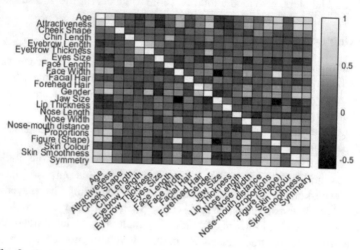

Fig. 3. Correlation between attractiveness and the other 21 facial attributes.

To represent the correlation coefficient between two labels, the resulting value of r lies between 1 and -1. A value $r = 0$ means there is no linear correlation between labels. The nearer r is to 1 the more it reproduces a total higher positive linear correlation between labels. The nearer r is to -1 the more it reflects a total higher negative linear correlation between labels. From this figure, it is evident that there is a strong correlation between attractiveness and figure, proportions, smoother face skin, and symmetry (shapeliness). This supports what was previously discussed in Sect. 2, about traits associated with facial attractiveness in most studies. In addition, we can determine some important positive linear correlations between attractiveness on one side, and two of global soft biometrics traits (age and gender) on the other [4, 9].

It can be seen from Fig. 4 that the results agree with our original intuition. For example, there is a positive linear correlation between attractiveness and between symmetry, smoother face skin and age; which means youngest people with smoother skin and more symmetry faces are very likely to be rated attractive, or vice versa, as shown in Fig. 4. The correlations and exploration of features' significance resulted in a better comprehension of the contribution of each attribute to identification and recognition, and may lead to improved or expanded predictability of other attributes. It is noted that supplementary investigations of correlations between couples of attributes, including attractiveness, could supply valuable information within a future study.

Fig. 4. The top images represent the subjects ranked top by attractiveness, while the bottom images show the lowest-ranked

4.2 Discriminative Power of Attractiveness

The estimation of an attribute's importance is significant for recognizing its strength as a semantic descriptor and to discover its contribution to human identification and recognition.

Mutual Information (MI): was used to evaluate the significance of the attractiveness attribute [23]. MI (typically written as $I(X, Y)$) is a quantity that measures how much a random variable, X, is related to another random variable, Y, (or vice versa). The MI is calculated as follows:

$$MI = I(X, Y) = \sum_{x \in X} \sum_{y \in Y} p(x, y) ln\left(\frac{p(x, y)}{p(x)p(y)}\right) \tag{2}$$

In the context of the facial attributes in a soft biometric framework, X represents the attribute relative rates and Y represents the subjects' labels, resulting in a computation of the MI of these two traits. While $p(x, y)$ is the joint probability distribution function for the random variables X and Y respectively, where $p(x)$ and $p(y)$ are the marginal probability distribution functions respectively.

In this study, MI was used to determine the discriminative power of the attractiveness attributes. MI was applied to the comparative rating data of each attribute, as shown in Fig. 5. It was computed for each of the 22 attributes discussed in Sect. 2, according to Eq. (2).

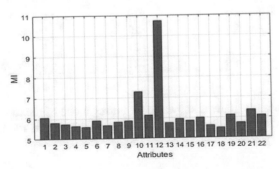

Fig. 5. Mutual information (MI) for each 22 attribute.

We can see that MI method rated attractiveness together with skin color as having modest discriminative power. Interestingly, some attributes such as gender, facial hair, skin smoothness, figure and symmetry were rated with high discriminative power. The results also show that proportions, eyebrow length and nose-mouth distance have the lowest discriminatory power compared with the other attributes. MI scoring methods enforce ranking for each trait independently. We can consider the attractiveness attribute to a discriminative attribute of the human face.

Sequential Floating Forward Selection (SFFS) Algorithm: is a familiar and widely-used trait subset selection method. It does not implement scoring for each feature individually, in contrast with the MI scoring method. Basically, SFFS is a bottom-up search technique which attains new attributes by starting with an empty set, then, at each repetition retaining the next best informative feature to the subset of selection. At each iteration, we form a soft biometric verification system, and change the specific set of features used, selecting the following attribute depending on the already selected features. After each forward step insertion of the best feature, SFFS implements backward rejection steps of the worst feature, as long as the new subset (after the elimination) increases the previous performance of a subset. This is done until the highest likely performance is achieved [24].

This analysis leads to practical understanding of how appropriate and significant attractiveness is to human face identification. By employing the SFFS algorithm, the attractiveness is listed within the top attributes by SFFS ordering of the soft biometrics attributes. Table 2 provides different trait ordering lists obtained by feature selection method.

Table 2. Ordered list of comparative facial soft traits inferred using SFFS methods.

Ordering	SFFS	Ordering	SFFS
1	Gender	12	Figure (Shape)
2	Facial hair	13	Nose-mouth distance
3	Age	14	Chin length
4	Attractiveness	15	Skin color
5	Forehead hair	16	Face width
6	Eyebrow thickness	17	Symmetry
7	Nose length	18	Eyebrow length
8	Skin smoothness	19	Eyes size
9	Lip thickness	20	Proportions
10	Jaw size	21	Face length
11	Nose width	22	Cheek shape

The attractiveness attribute is shown to be amongst one of the top traits by SFFS. It is the most potent feature in the SFFS ordering in contrast to its modest rating by MI.

5 Performance of Attractiveness

This section produces the analysis and experimental study into the capabilities of soft biometrics using attractiveness attributes for recognition. The identification of the unidentified subject was achieved by computing the sum of Euclidean distance between each subject in the probe set and all subjects in the gallery sets, resulting in a distance matrix. We can use the Euclidean distance to calculate the recognition accuracies with a Leave-one-out cross-validation (LOOCV) strategy by using a k-nearest neighbors (k-NN) classifier. Figure 6 shows the accuracy by using all of the attributes in this study, which is 71.5%. In comparison, a recognition rate of 57.21% is reported in [8] by using 24 comparative attributes. It is also noted that our dataset contains 100 subjects with four images per subject in total 400 subjects.

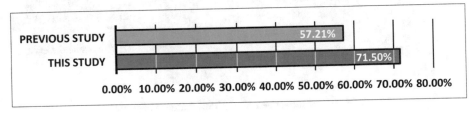

Fig. 6. Comparison the accuracy with previous study.

The Cumulative match characteristic (CMC) curve summarizes the identification accuracy, by the k-NN method, which scores the presence of the correct subjects. The CMC curves showed good identification performance using 22 soft facial traits in this study. In terms of verification, to measure the effect of the attractiveness. Using all attributes, recognition is still good (see Fig. 7) and the system performance increases once the attractiveness attribute is used as a trait in the recognition process.

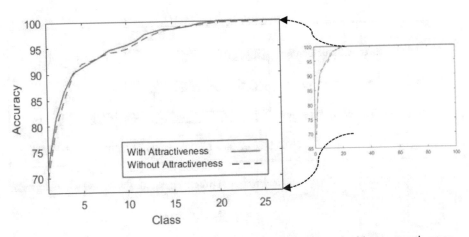

Fig. 7. Recognition via CMC performance on this study with and without attractiveness.

5.1   Abilities of Attractiveness

Figure 8, shows the histograms of inter- and intra-class variations Manhattan distances with attractiveness, and without attractiveness. As shown in Fig. 8, attractiveness attribute improves the results since the proportion of false positives is reduced when attractiveness attribute is included with these study attributes.

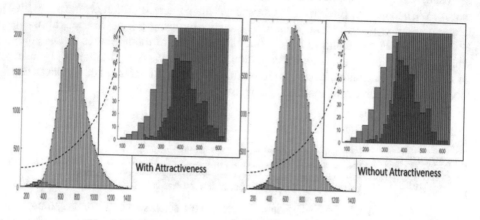

Fig. 8. Effect of attractiveness with all features of this study.

Attractiveness is used to complement the soft traits in subject recognition. Figure 9 shows that the performance of the recognition system significantly improves when attractiveness is added to this study traits in comparison with the case where attractiveness has not been included in the set of the traits. We can establish the rate of accuracy with the attractiveness attribute in light of the investigation introduced in this section; the identification rate is improved when introducing attractiveness information or by up to 1.8% when introducing the whole set of soft biometrics attributes and the rate is improved 3.3% when introducing gender information, as depicted in Fig. 9.

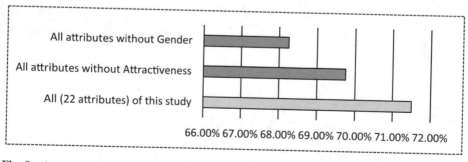

Fig. 9. Accuracy of 21 attributes with and without attractiveness, also with and without gender.

6 Conclusions and Future Work

This paper highlights the potential for facial attractiveness as a soft biometric tool. It presents an initial study of comparative facial attractiveness as a novel attribute for person description in a soft biometric framework for the purpose of recognition. To the best of our knowledge, this study is the first to use facial attractiveness in soft biometrics and the results of analyzing attractiveness through the designated attributes and suggests that there is advantage when facial attractiveness is used as a soft biometric.

One of our immediate future work is to use the whole LFW database. Humans can recognize the gender of a person, through some features. Our work on the correlations between attractiveness attributes can be used to improve gender recognition. It has not been known yet whether facial attractiveness is correlated to body attractiveness. This therefore gives an appropriate avenue for future research. This approach does not permit for collection of reliable features and also allows the estimation of the probability of facial attractiveness attributes from existing body attributes and vice versa. It will also be prudent to consider inclusion of automated approaches that assess attractiveness by computer vision. In this way, we intend to capitalize on and develop further this new approach.

References

1. Gonzalez-Sosa, E., Fierrez, J., Vera-Rodriguez, R., Alonso-Fernandez, F.: Facial soft biometrics for recognition in the wild: recent works, annotation, and COTS evaluation. IEEE TIFS 13(8), 2001–2014 (2018)
2. Zhang, H., Beveridge, J.R., Draper, B.A., Phillips, P.J.: On the effectiveness of soft biometrics for increasing face verification rates. CVIU 137, 50–62 (2015)
3. Reid, D., Nixon, M., Stevenage, S.: Soft biometrics; human identification using comparative descriptions. IEEE TPAMI 36(6), 1216–1228 (2013)
4. Tome, P., Fierrez, J., Vera-Rodriguez, R., Nixon, M.: Soft biometrics and their application in person recognition at a distance. IEEE TIFS 9(3), 464–475 (2014)
5. Arigbabu, O., Ahmad, S., Adnan, W., Yussof, S.: Recent advances in facial soft biometrics. Vis. Comput. 31(5), 513–525 (2014)
6. Nixon, M., Correia, P., Nasrollahi, K., Moeslund, T., Hadid, A., Tistarelli, M.: On soft biometrics. Pattern Recogn. Lett. 68, 218–230 (2015)
7. Parikh, D., Grauman, K.: Relative attributes. In: IEEE ICCV, pp. 503–510 (2011)
8. Almudhahka, N., Nixon, M., Hare, J.: Semantic face signatures: recognizing and retrieving faces by verbal descriptions. IEEE TIFS 13(3), 706–716 (2018)
9. Samangooei, S., Guo, B., Nixon, M.: The use of semantic human description as a soft biometric. In: Proceedings of the BTAS, pp. 1–7 (2008)
10. Martinho-Corbishley, D., Nixon, M., Carter, J.N.: Super-fine attributes with crowd prototyping. IEEE TPAMI 41(6), 1486–1500 (2018)
11. Jaha, E., Nixon, M.: From clothing to identity: manual and automatic soft biometrics. IEEE TIFS 11(10), 2377–2390 (2016)
12. Shepherd, J., Ellis, H.: The effect of attractiveness on recognition memory for faces. Am. J. Psychol. 86(3), 627 (1973)
13. Kagian, A., Dror, G., Leyvand, T., Cohen-Or, D., Ruppin, E.: A humanlike predictor of facial attractiveness. In: NIPS, pp. 1–8 (2007)

14. Liu, S., Fan, Y., Samal, A., Guo, Z.: Advances in computational facial attractiveness methods. Multimed. Tools Appl. **75**(23), 16633–16663 (2016)
15. Chen, F., Zhang, D.: A benchmark for geometric facial beauty study. In: Zhang, D., Sonka, M. (eds.) ICMB 2010. LNCS, vol. 6165, pp. 21–32. Springer, Heidelberg (2010). https://doi.org/10.1007/978-3-642-13923-9_3
16. Thornhill, R., Gangestad, S.: Facial attractiveness. Trends Cognit. Sci. **3**(12), 452–460 (1999)
17. Cunningham, M.: Measuring the physical in physical attractiveness: quasi-experiments on the sociobiology of female facial beauty. J. Pers. Soc. Psychol. **50**(5), 925–935 (1986)
18. Eisenthal, Y., Dror, G., Ruppin, E.: Facial attractiveness: beauty and the machine. Neural Comput. **18**, 119–142 (2006)
19. Xie, D., Liang, L., Jin, L., Xu, J., Li, M.: SCUT-FBP: a benchmark dataset for facial beauty perception. In: Proceedings of the IEEE SMC, pp. 1821–1826 (2015)
20. Rhodes, G.: The evolutionary psychology of facial beauty. Annu. Rev. Psychol. **57**, 199–226 (2006)
21. Huang, G., Ramesh, M., Berg, T., Learned-Miller, E.: Labeled faces in the wild: a database for studying face recognition in unconstrained environments. Technical report 07-49, University of Massachusetts Amherst (2007)
22. Welinder, P., Perona, P.: Online crowdsourcing: rating annotators and obtaining cost-effective labels. In: Proceedings of the IEEE CVPR Workshops, pp. 25–32 (2010)
23. Guo, B., Nixon, M.: Gait feature subset selection by mutual information. IEEE TSMC A **39**(1), 36–46 (2009)
24. Pudil, P., Novovičová, J., Kittler, J.: Floating search methods in feature selection. Pattern Recogn. Lett. **15**(11), 1119–1125 (1994)

A Modified Viola-Jones Detector
for Low-Cost Localization of Car Plates

Victor H. M. Amorim, Bruno M. Carvalho[✉][iD], and Antônio C. G. Thomé

Department of Informatics and Applied Mathematics, Federal University of Rio
Grande do Norte, Natal, RN, Brazil
victorhugomacedoamorim@gmail.com,
{bruno,thome}@dimap.ufrn.br

Abstract. Over the last decade there has been a large increase of the
worldwide car fleet, which implies on a larger volume of vehicles in situations that require the intervention of humans or efficient computer
systems, such as in traffic surveillance and control, stolen car detection
and access control to restricted areas. Those are usually dealt with by
using Automatized License Plate Recognition (ALPR) based systems.
This technology is used to identify vehicles on images and video, usually
by identifying the license plate number. In general, ALPR based systems
are composed by three sequential stages: license plate location, character
segmentation and character recognition. There exists a great number of
methods developed of each of those stages, using well known digital image
processing and machine learning algorithms. On this study we use the
Viola-Jones cascade detector along with a pre-processing step in order to
perform the license plate location step on the two current models of the
Brazilian license plates. The results of several detector configurations are
compared and discussed. The results point to an efficient and accurate
detector.

Keywords: Automatized License Plate Recognition · Plate detection ·
Viola-Jones detector

1 Introduction

According to a 2018 study [13] the Brazilian circulating fleet of cars, trucks
and buses was composed of roughly 30 million vehicles in 2009. By the end of
2017 the same fleet had grown to over 43 million vehicles, which represents a
44% increase. Given this huge number os vehicles, problems like traffic control
and surveilance, stolen car detection and access control to restricted areas have
become harder to solve without an automatized tool. The automatized vehicle
recognition is core to systems projected with this objective in mind.

Since the license plate is the most discriminant feature when analyzing vehicles, the vehicle recognition task based on finding and identifying the license
plate is labeled as Automatized License Plate Recognition (ALPR). An ALPR

© Springer Nature Switzerland AG 2019
G. Bebis et al. (Eds.): ISVC 2019, LNCS 11845, pp. 529–540, 2019.
https://doi.org/10.1007/978-3-030-33723-0_43

system is usually composed of three stages: license plate location, character segmentation and character recognition. There exists a big number of approaches developed over the last decades for each of those stages. However, they are mostly limited to their home country license plates and also are greatly impacted by the existence of many plate models and by image or video capture conditions.

The license plate location can be described as a stage where the image regions that contain license plates are located. By finding these regions, the next stage has a much smaller and characteristic region to work with. It is also considered the most critical stage on this type of ALPR system, since the license plate characters can only be segmented and recognized by the next stages if the location provides the region containing the complete license plate number.

In the current Brazilian vehicle licensing system there are two types of plates based on shape: car plates and bike plates. As for further variations, there are many license plate colors considering both plate and character color. There are also irregular plates, which are mostly distinguished by the use of typesets other than the standard. In addition, some Brazilian states have begun licensing vehicles with the new Mercosur plate model, which has the same shapes as the old model but different color patterns and letter-number formatting.

Several authors have proposed using the Viola-Jones [14] cascade as a means to detect the license plate on a image. One of the reported main issues with this approach is the apparent large number of false positives detected by the cascade. On this paper we present an approach composed by the Viola-Jones detector and a pre-processing stage to the images analyzed by it. The pre-processing stage eliminates the color pattern problem, making any plate of the same shape to look similar. It also reduces the effects of some bad plate conditions such as physical deformation, partially erased characters and weaker lighting problems while also reducing the false positive ratio when compared to a Viola-Jones detector trained with no pre-processing stage.

2   Related Work

According to Peg et al. [10], the majority of plate detection methods can be classified into two categories, rule-based heuristic methods and machine learning based methods. Other approaches, such as the ones proposed by [5,6,8] make use of morphological operations in the plate location stage.

Several works, such as the ones proposed by [1,3,4,9,18,22] make use of border detection techniques to perform the plate localization, since the rectangular outer border as well as the characters borders allows for a robust detection. Usually, methods of this type are robust in the presence of changes in illumination or plate inclination but are susceptible to the presence of noise. Thus, they are usually coupled with a blurring step.

The machine learning based methods consider the object locallization problem as a pattern recognition problem. They perform a training step, using a large number of samples to extract object features that are used by classifiers. The features are grouped in descriptors that are learned by the classifiers. The main task on these methods is then the determination of the descriptors and classifiers to be used. Of course, the amount of samples of the training set and their variability is directly tied to the accuracy and generalization capability of the trained classifier.

Several researchers have used the original Viola-Jones detector [14] for plate localization. In several works is mentioned that the original Viola-Jones detector generates a large number of false positives when applied to the plate localization. Thus, several works, such as [2,10,16,17,19-21] propose changes to it in order to make it more accurate. Some of these changes include the addition of new types of features [10,18] to the original feature set, alternative feature selection methods, alternative training algorithms [20] and changes to the internal classifier cascade structure.

More specifically, the work of [21] proposes a framework that utilizes two Viola-Jones detectors in parallel, that employ the extended feature set proposed by [7]. Both detectors are trained with the same positive samples but with different negative samples. In the pre-processing phase, they perform an image size reduction, followed by a histogram equalization and Gaussian blurring.

On a different approach, Peng et al. [10] adds new types of features to the Viola-Jones detector, the line segment features. The idea is to reduce the number of Haar-like features in the final detector through the early elimination of background regions using these new features, thus, reducing the detector's training and processing time. The line segment features are computed from the vertical line segments of the processed region. These are obtained during the pre-processing phase, by performing a histogram equalization, border detection and using the Hough Transform.

Finally, we mention the short survey of Reji and Dharun [12], that references and comments on the results of 17 different works.

3   The Proposed Method

The proposed method was developed with the objective of detecting Brazilian license plates regardless of their model, while maintaining a low cost. The proposed approach is divided into two stages: the pre-processing of the image and the location of the plates by a Viola-Jones cascade detector on the resulting image representation. The Brazilian plates, both the old and the new Mercosur models, have a 3:1 aspect ratio, similar character displacement and font size. The base resolution of the detector is set as 60×20.

As mentioned above, the usage of the original Viola-Jones detector to the detection of license plates results in many false positives. Since the plate regions have many lighter to darker color transitions, which is key to the detector internal calculations, most of the problems must be related to the similar geometric patterns on other objects and the existance of many plate patterns. Considering this, a pre-processing stage was conceived to both reduce the possibility of confusion with other object patterns and reduce the plate variations. Another

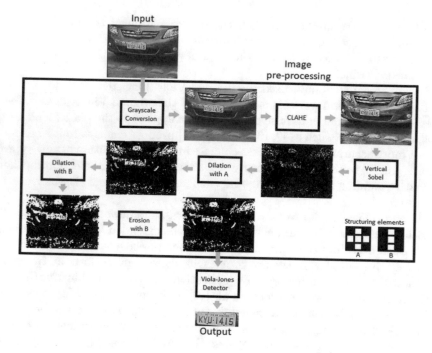

Fig. 1. Stages of the proposed license plate localization method.

objective of this first stage is to reduce the influence of problems such as physical deformation on the plate, partially erased characters and uneven lighting problems.

The original Viola-Jones detector works internally with grayscale images and fixed size regions that are scalable during the detection. When dealing with old model red-white plates, we have one pattern where the characters have higher intensities than the background. This is the opposite of the most common old model gray-black plates and Mercosur model plates, where the character has a lower intensities than the background.

As the red-white old model plates have a different pattern than the gray-black old model plates or the Mercosur model plates, it is necessary to make them have a similar pattern so the detector can detect any of them without having to learn multiple patterns, which would lead to bigger and likely less accurate detectors. Both red-white and gray-black old model plates and any Mercosur model plates have borders which are represented by lighter to darker color transitions. Since their character displacement, font and plate sizes are all similar, the borders should have approximately the same positions on all of them. As the plate region is rich with vertical borders, a border detection algorithm should be a valid option as a means to create a shared pattern between the plate models. Horizontal borders are avoided to reduce the number of similar patterns with other objects. Also, by changing the representation to a binary image, the aforementioned problems have a lessened influence.

However, the contrast on the plate region must be high enough so that the border detection can correctly detect the vertical borders with a high threshold, intended to erase most of the image. After some experimentation, the Contrast Limited Adaptive Histogram Equalization [11] was chosen specially because of its reduced susceptibility to lighting peaks.

After the contrast enhancement by CLAHE, the vertical borders are detected by the Sobel operator. It is the lowest cost operator amongst the border detectors, but it does a good job on finding the vertical edges needed to create the plate pattern that is different from other object patterns.

Since most of the vertical borders and edges detected by the Sobel operator are thin, it should be harder for the training algorithm to find favorable thresholds for the internal classifiers as the majority of the plate region is now empty. As the operator is applied to the whole image, many false positives could be found since it is likely to be sparse. Thus, a enhancement step is added as a final step in order to try to create better patterns.

To use morphological operations such as dilation and erosion, a structuring element must be used. The one defined as A is a cross-shaped matrix of ones, while the one defined as B is just a one column shaped matrix. By using A, we hope to connect the borders by enlarging them in four directions. By using B we hope to connect vertical border fragments that were likely part of a same border.

After some experimentation, the best alternative to the enhancement was chosen as two dilations followed by an erosion. The second best alternative was the one composed by one dilation followed by one erosion and was also considered on the results. To summarize, the pre-processing is composed by the following steps:

1. Grayscale conversion;
2. Contrast Limited Adaptive Histogram Equalization (CLAHE);
3. Vertical border detection by Sobel operator;
4. Morphological dilation with A structuring element;
5. Morphological dilation followed by erosion with B structuring element.

When all the pre-processing steps are done, the image is searched by the Viola-Jones detector standard multi-scale sliding window procedure. The detector is trained with images which underwent the same pre-processing steps.

4   Results

To obtain the results with the proposed method, two sets of experiments were made. On the first, 5 Viola-Jones detectors were trained on a 1st training set, each using the training images processed on a different pre-processing stage. After establishing which one had the best results, 2 more detectors were trained using the same pre-processing as the selected detector, but trained on 2nd training set, extended from the first one. This two part approach was made to reduce the time spent on training the Viola-Jones detectors, which can take from hours to days.

4.1   Training Sets

To build this first training set, both positive and negative samples are needed. A total of 838 old model plates were manually cropped from car images on different positions and lighting conditions, therefore composing the positive set. The car images used were part of a private database used on a commercial system called Kapta. The database is composed by low resolution (320×240) vehicle images captured automatically by the use of magnetic presence sensors on many different capture conditions.

A total of 2,461 images were obtained from web sources to compose the negative samples of this training set. Two public databases were included in this set: the Calltech background dataset, containing 900 grayscale background images and the Google "thing" dataset, containing 520 color images of assorted things. Both were obtained from the University of Oxford Visual Geometry Group web page [15]. The remaining images were obtained by the use of a web search engine and by modifying images from the Kapta set not used on the positive samples. The modifications were plates covered by black rectangles and images cropped enough to remove part of the license plate number. The 2nd training set was an extension to the first, adding to a total of 3,497 positive samples and 13,616 negative samples.

4.2   Test Sets

For testing, two test sets were assembled. The first one used 1,803 images of the Kapta database, whose plate regions were manually selected. Those images contained one license plate each. The second contained 123 manually collected images that contained the Mercosur license plates. On this second set, a 320×240 sub-window was put on the car that contained the Mercosur license plate, to crop the image, so it would have the same size than the Kapta database images.

4.3   Analysis Criteria

To evaluate the accuracy of the trained detectors we used the IoU (Intersection over Union) metric to decide which of the detected regions were good enough to be considered as acceptable detections. By doing so, the threshold of 0.6 was set to split the good and bad detections. Along with the accuracy, we also use the number of undetected plates and the false positive ratio. A false positive is considered a detected region that does not intersect the license plate region of an image. When dealing with multiple detected regions that intersect the the license plate region, only the one with highest IoU value is considered to be a possible good detection and the remaining are treated as false positives. The false positive ratio is the average number of false positives per image.

The IoU metric gives the spatial precision of one detection by measuring how much one region found by the detector overlaps the plate region. However, the detector can detect multiple plates on a single image or even no plates at all.

The following S metric is defined as a means to score the whole detection quality on a image. It can be calculated by the Eq. 1.

$$S = \left(\frac{1}{tn} \sum_{i=1}^{tn} \max_{j=1}^{gn} IoU(t_i, g_j) \right) e^{\frac{min(0, tn-gn)}{k}} \tag{1}$$

In Eq. 1, the S value associated with an image is the IoU value or its average, when the image contains more than one license plate, penalized by the exceeding number of detected regions (gn) in relation to the number of plates (tn). The max function returns the IoU value of the best detected region (g_j), defined as the region which scored the highest IoU value with the analyzed plate region (t_i). The penalty is weighted by an empirically defined constant k, which defines the severity of having false positives. As the defined test sets contain images with one plate only, that Equation is simplified by removing the averaging of the IoU value.

4.4 Experiments

We first analyze the 5 detectors of the first set. The RAW detector was trained with the original color images, while the AEQ detector was trained with the images resulting of the second step of the pre-processing: CLAHE application post grayscale conversion. The SOBEL detector was trained with images resulting of the third step of the pre-processing: vertical border detection using Sobel operator. The MOR1 and MOR2 detectors both enhance the borders found by the third step. The first uses a dilation followed by a erosion, both with the structuring element A (3×3 cross shaped). The second starts by a dilation with the structuring element A, followed a by a dilation and a erosion with the structuring element B (3×3 central column shaped).

The training of the detectors was made by the use of the opencv_traincascade application on OpenCV 3.3. Both training and testing were executed on the same machine, a PC equipped with a core i5 3330 processor with 8GB of memory. For parameters, the base resolution of the detector was set to the previously defined 60×20 and a scale factor of 1.1. The maximum false alarm rate of 25% and minimum detection rate of 99,5% were used, and we also used twice number of positive samples for the negative samples per level on training. Those 5 detectors use the base Haar features set. The k value used to calculate the S value was empirically defined to 15.

Table 1 summarizes the results of these 5 detectors on the 1,803 old model plates test images. The accuracy is given by IoU threshold of 0.6 on the best detection of the respective image. Undetected is the number of undetected plates. FPR stands for false positive ratio. The following two columns contain the average S value to the images and its respective standard deviation (σ). It also contains the data obtained with the second set of detectors, which will be explained soon.

Table 1. Accuracy of detectors by using IoU ≥ 0.6 as detection threshold, number of undetected plates, false positive ratio, average detection score and its standard deviation on old model plates

Detector	Accuracy	Undetected	FPR	$\overline{S}$	$\sigma(S)$
RAW	69.38%	06.21%	1.0388	0.6036	0.2321
AEQ	67.11%	11.87%	0.4038	0.6069	0.2657
SOBEL	89.24%	06.21%	0.3045	0.7376	0.2130
MOR1	89.35%	05.88%	0.1547	0.7458	0.2091
MOR2	93.34%	01.83%	0.5141	0.7553	0.1452
MOR2b	92.62%	06.54%	0.0144	0.7646	0.2143
MOR2b-ALL	94.51%	02.38%	0.3233	0.7560	0.1464

The MOR2 detector, while not exhibiting the best results, considering false positive ratio, still has a higher average image score than the other preceding 4 detectors. As the S value is penalized by false positives, it means the regions detected by the MOR2 detector must be more precise even if it has a lower number of undetected plates. Its accuracy considering the best detection is also the highest between the 5 first detectors. With that in mind, the MOR2 pre-processing has been proven effective by improving accuracy, reducing the undetected number and more precise regions.

The second set of detectors is composed by detectors MOR2b and MOR2b-ALL, both trained on the second training set. Their training parameters are the same as the other 5 detectors, with the exception of MOR2b-ALL which uses the extended Haar feature set proposed by Lienhart et al. [7]. They both have the same pre-processing steps as the MOR2 detector, since it was selected as the best amongst the initial 5. By training those detectors, we have the objective of trying to decrease the false positive ratio of the MOR2 detector by having a bigger training set.

From the results of Table 1, it can be seen that even though the MOR2b-ALL detector seems the best in terms of accuracy, the MOR2b detector can be considered in some situations the best because of its incredibly low false positive ratio. It is more strict than the other detectors, greatly reducing the false positive ratio at the cost of less detected regions. That also leads to a increase on the average S value.

In addition, as it can be seen on Fig. 2, the old model test set has images of varying quality in relation to the plate visibility and associated noise. By the obtained results it can also be said that the pre-processing successfully decreases the influence of problems such as physical deformation, partially erased characters and weaker lighting conditions. The Table 2 summarizes the results obtained on the Mercosur model plates test set.

Table 2. Accuracy of detectors by using IoU $\geq$ 0.6 as detection threshold, number of undetected plates, false positive ratio, average detection score and its standard deviation on Mercosur model plates

Detector	Accuracy	Undetected	FPR	$\overline{S}$	$\sigma(S)$
RAW	60.98%	13.82%	0.8943	0.5245	0.2754
AEQ	56.91%	26.83%	0.3415	0.5049	0.3464
SOBEL	58.54%	33.33%	0.1220	0.5024	0.3725
MOR1	57.72%	39.84%	0.0488	0.4964	0.4140
MOR2	66.67%	21.95%	0.1463	0.5909	0.3473
MOR2b	52.03%	47.15%	0.0163	0.4375	0.4186
MOR2b-ALL	71.54%	24.39%	0.1382	0.5917	0.3539

Although the MOR2b detector works well with both plate models considering the low false positive ratio, its undetected number of plates is very high. So the MOR2b-ALL detector can be seen as better fit to the task of detecting both plate models, since it achieves greater average image detection score and higher accuracy compared to the MOR2 detector. Both plate models are very similar in appearance so the MOR2b-ALL training has made a better job by selecting features amongst the extended set which are more common between the models. The Table 3 lists the average time spent per image on each of the trained models, in seconds, followed by its standard deviation.

Table 3. Average time spent by the detectors (in seconds) on test images including pre-processing, in seconds

Detector	RAW	AEQ	SOBEL	MOR1	MOR2	MOR2b	MOR2b-ALL
$\overline{T}$	0.0059	0.0127	0.0115	0.0126	0.0128	0.0130	0.0129
$\sigma(T)$	0.0005	0.0004	0.0001	0.0002	0.0002	0.0002	0.0002

All detectors aside from RAW have spent similar average time on the images, including the whole pre-processing steps cost. The CLAHE step used to enhance image contrast is considered the highest cost step on the proposed method. The following steps have low cost considering the low resolution images and morphological operations on binary images. While considering cost-benefit, the proposed method has doubled the time spent per image but increased the accuracy by over 25% on the old models and 10% on the Mercosur model, while greatly decreasing the false positive ratio. Further experimentation would be required to attain better results on the Mercosur plates while keeping the old model results. Some of the detection results by the detectors RAW, MOR2, MOR2b and MOR2b-ALL can be seen on Fig. 2.

Fig. 2. Detection results of detectors on some of the test images with green rectangle being the ground truth and the red rectangles being the detections; first row containing old model good quality image, second row containing old model average quality image, third row containing old model low quality image, fourth and fifth row containing Mercosur model images. (Color figure online)

5 Conclusion

We proposed a new metric for evaluating the task of localizing license plates on images. We also proposed a simple and efficient method to perform license plate location on Brazilian license plates that uses the well known Viola-Jones cascade detector. The addition of the pre-processing step made it possible to improve the accuracy and reduce the false positive ratio of the detector, while keeping a low computational cost, our main objective, since tis is intended to work on an embedded system. It also leaves room for improvement such as the use of different contrast enhancement options and even changes on the internal structure of the detector. Further experimentation is needed to improve detection rate on

Mercosur model plates, and incorporate low-cost algorithms for performing the segmentation and classification of the plate's characters. We plan to do that and compare with the results of several approaches available in the literature [12] using our proposed measure, in order to validate it under a more general setting. Finally, we plan to investigate variations of the detection metric used, by incorporating penalties for missed characters on plates' detected areas, to better encode the quality of the results of this task.

Acknowledgment. The authors would like to thank the financial support provided by the Coordenação de Aperfeiçoamento de Pessoal de Nível Superior – Brasil (CAPES) – Finance Code 001, during the development of this work.

References

1. Bai, H., Zhu, J., Liu, C.: A fast license plate extraction method on complex background. In: Proceedings of the 2003 IEEE International Conference on Intelligent Transportation Systems, vol. 2, pp. 985–987, October 2003. https://doi.org/10.1109/ITSC.2003.1252633
2. Greati, V., Ribeiro, V., Silva, I., Martins, A.: A Brazilian license plate recognition method for applications in smart cities. In: 4th IEEE International Conference on Smart Cities, pp. 43–48, August 2017. https://doi.org/10.1109/S3C.2017.8501395
3. Heo, G., Kim, M., Jung, I., Lee, D., Oh, I.: Extraction of car license plate regions using line grouping and edge density methods. In: 2007 International Symposium on Information Technology Convergence, ISITC 2007, pp. 37–42, November 2007. https://doi.org/10.1109/ISITC.2007.79
4. Hongliang, B., Changping, L.: A hybrid license plate extraction method based on edge statistics and morphology. In: Proceedings of the 17th International Conference on Pattern Recognition, ICPR 2004, August 2004, vol. 2, pp. 831–834 (2004). https://doi.org/10.1109/ICPR.2004.1334387
5. Hsieh, J.W., Yu, S.H., Chen, Y.S.: Morphology-based license plate detection from complex scenes. In: Object Recognition Supported by User Interaction for Service Robots, vol. 3, pp. 176–179, August 2002. https://doi.org/10.1109/ICPR.2002.1047823
6. Lensky, A.A., Jo, K., Gubarev, V.V.: Vehicle license plate detection using local fractal dimension and morphological analysis. In: 2006 International Forum on Strategic Technology, pp. 47–50, October 2006. https://doi.org/10.1109/IFOST.2006.312243
7. Lienhart, R., Maydt, J.: An extended set of haar-like features for rapid object detection. In: Proceedings of International Conference on Image Processing, vol. 1, p. I-900, September 2002. https://doi.org/10.1109/ICIP.2002.1038171
8. Martin, F., García, M., Alba, J.L.: New methods for automatic reading of vlp's (vehicle license plates). In: Proceedings of the SPPRA (2002)
9. Nguyen, C., Ardabilian, M., Chen, L.: Real-time license plate localization based on a new scale and rotation invariant texture descriptor. In: 2008 11th International IEEE Conference on Intelligent Transportation Systems, pp. 956–961, October 2008. https://doi.org/10.1109/ITSC.2008.4732691

10. Peng, Y., Xu, M., Jin, J.S., Luo, S., Zhao, G.: Cascade-based license plate localization with line segment features and haar-like features. In: 2011 Sixth International Conference on Image and Graphics, pp. 1023–1028, August 2011. https://doi.org/10.1109/ICIG.2011.154

11. Pizer, S.M., et al.: Adaptive histogram equalization and its variations. Comput. Vision Graph. Image Process. **39**(3), 355–368 (1987). https://doi.org/10.1016/S0734-189X(87)80186-X

12. Reji, P., Dharun, V.: License plate localization: a review. Int. J. Eng. Trends Technol. (IJETT) **10**(13), 604–615 (2014)

13. Sindipeças: Report on current fleet 2018, March 2018. https://www.sindipecas.org.br/sindinews/Economia/2018/R_Frota_Circulante_2018.pdf

14. Viola, P., Jones, M.: Rapid object detection using a boosted cascade of simple features. In: Proceedings of the 2001 IEEE Computer Society Conference on Computer Vision and Pattern Recognition, CVPR 2001. vol. 1, pp. I, December 2001. https://doi.org/10.1109/CVPR.2001.990517

15. Visual Geometry Group: Data - department of engineering science, university of oxford. http://www.robots.ox.ac.uk/vgg/data3.html (2017). Accessed 31 Oct 2017

16. Wang, S., Lee, H.: A cascade framework for a real-time statistical plate recognition system. IEEE Trans. Inf. Forensics Secur. **2**(2), 267–282 (2007). https://doi.org/10.1109/TIFS.2007.897251

17. Wu, Q., Zhang, H., Jia, W., He, X., Yang, J., Hintz, T.: Car plate detection using cascaded tree-style learner based on hybrid object features. In: 2006 IEEE International Conference on Video and Signal Based Surveillance, p. 15, November 2006. https://doi.org/10.1109/AVSS.2006.30

18. Zhang, H., Jia, W., He, X., Wu, Q.: A fast algorithm for license plate detection in various conditions. In: 2006 IEEE International Conference on Systems, Man and Cybernetics, vol. 3, pp. 2420–2425, October 2006. https://doi.org/10.1109/ICSMC.2006.385226

19. Zhang, H., Jia, W., He, X., Wu, Q.: Learning-based license plate detection using global and local features. In: 18th International Conference on Pattern Recognition (ICPR 2006), vol. 2, pp. 1102–1105, August 2006. https://doi.org/10.1109/ICPR.2006.758

20. Zhang, X., et al.: License plate-location using AdaBoost algorithm. In: The 2010 IEEE International Conference on Information and Automation, pp. 2456–2461, June 2010. https://doi.org/10.1109/ICINFA.2010.5512276

21. Zhao, Y., Gu, J., Liu, C., Han, S., Gao, Y., Hu, Q.: License plate location based on Haar-like cascade classifiers and edges. In: 2010 Second WRI Global Congress on Intelligent Systems, vol. 3, pp. 102–105, December 2010. https://doi.org/10.1109/GCIS.2010.55

22. Zheng, D., Zhao, Y., Wang, J.: An efficient method of license plate location. Pattern Recogn. Lett. **26**(15), 2431–2438 (2005). https://doi.org/10.1016/j.patrec.2005.04.014. http://www.sciencedirect.com/science/article/pii/S0167865505001406

Evaluating Fiber Detection Models Using Neural Networks

Silvia Miramontes[1,2]([✉]), Daniela M. Ushizima[1,2]([✉]),
and Dilworth Y. Parkinson[2]([✉])

[1] University of California, Berkeley, CA, USA
[2] Lawrence Berkeley National Laboratory, Berkeley, CA, USA
{mirasilvia,dushizima,dyparkinson}@lbl.gov

Abstract. Ceramic matrix composites are resistant materials that withstand high temperatures, but quality control of such composites depends on microtomography image analysis to enable the spatial analysis of fibers, matrix cracks detection, among others. While there are several approaches for fiber detection from microtomography, materials scientists lack computational schemes to validate the accuracy of different fiber detection models. This paper proposes a set of statistical methods to analyse images of CMC in 3D and visualize respective fiber beds, including a lossless data reduction algorithm. The main contribution is our method based on a convolutional neural network that enables evaluation of results from automated fiber detection models, particularly when compared with human curated datasets. We build all the algorithms using free tools to allow full reproducibility of the experiments, and illustrate our results using algorithms designed to probe sample content from gigabyte-size image volumes with minimalistic computational infrastructure.

Keywords: Computer vision · Materials science · CNN

1 Introduction

Shape and structural properties of dense materials can be imaged using X-rays from synchrotron radiation as part of metrology processes to infer the function and resilience of new compounds, such as ceramic matrix composites (CMCs) [2,4]. CMCs have evolved from an increasing demand for lighter materials that withstand higher temperature and are damage-tolerant. They have applications in the construction of industrial turbines, and jet engines; for example, GE Aviation has been developing the next-generation of CMC components to build turbine blades [5]. CMCs manufacturing relies on combining silicon carbide fibers to a matrix to reinforce the composite; the quality of the resulting material depends on stress tests imaged using microtomography (microCT), such as the spatial distribution of fibers, matrix, fiber pullouts, matrix cracks, among others.

Both data and computer codes will be available upon acceptance of this paper.

This is a U.S. government work and not under copyright protection in the U.S.;
foreign copyright protection may apply 2019
G. Bebis et al. (Eds.): ISVC 2019, LNCS 11845, pp. 541–552, 2019.
https://doi.org/10.1007/978-3-030-33723-0_44

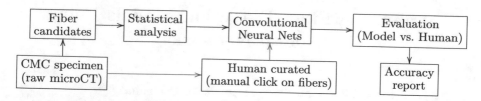

Fig. 1. Scheme to investigate experiments reporting on fiber detections and evaluation of results (fiber candidates) when compared with fibers specified by human expert.

While the frequency in which microCT data is collected increases, as well as its resolution, transforming this expanding data from experiments into scientific discovery continues to demand new analytical tasks with higher accuracy and scalability. Materials scientists often struggle in understanding their microCT content due to the gigabyte file sizes inherent to the experimental procedure. What is needed is a set of tools for quick assessment of the specimen with the microCT volume, and other derivatives from the microCT digital file such as fiber detections, overall fiber cross-sectional area, and fiber morphology.

One of our contributions is the implementation of a pipeline that enables statistical analysis of CMC data and respective 3D fiber bed given the segmentation of a fiber detection algorithm. Additionally, we provide classification of fibers using a convolutional neural network (CNN), which detects areas corresponding to a fiber cross-section profile from other material phases; we also demonstrate how to probe for fiber continuity when analysing the results of fiber detection algorithms for datasets that do not fully fit in memory.

For full reproducibility of our results, we use `skimage` and 3D image publicly available, as well as their respective ground-truth as in [11]. The fiber detection model we evaluate comes from a semi-automated method developed over years by Larson et. al [8–10]. Their method uses Hough Transform, mathematical morphology, and statistical filters implemented using Matlab. While the previous work lacks details for the re-implementation of the fiber detection model, the online dataset at [11] provides valuable results of fiber detections for several stacks. Thus, another contribution is the design of fully automated reports based on Jupyter Notebooks [7] that evaluate fiber detection models using a CNN, and compare the authors results with curated data by a human expert. We also designed algorithms to probe specimens from gigabyte-size microCT with minimalistic computational infrastructure, such as running these experiments in standard laptops. The pipeline to achieve this evaluation is displayed in Fig. 1.

2   Materials

In order to investigate the microstructure evolution during matrix impregnation and curing in unidirectional fiber beds, materials scientists use X-ray microCT images, such as those publicly available at [11]. Image acquisition took place at Beamline 8.3.2 at the Advanced Light Source (ALS) at Lawrence Berkeley

National Laboratory using 17 keV light (20–30% transmission) with a PCO edge camera and 10X lens, with field of view of about $1.7 \times 1.7 \times 1.4\,\mathrm{mm}^3$ [8,10]. All the data used in these publications can be downloaded from The Materials Facility, an online free service [3] that offers a simple way to publish, discover, and access materials datasets by allowing: (a) Identification of collections with persistent identifiers (e.g. DOI); (b) Description of datasets with appropriate metadata, and provenance; (c) Curation of dataset metadata and data composition; and (d) Verification of dataset contents over time. Together, these capabilities help preserve critical experimental data in a state that increases transparency, reproducibility, and encourages reuse.

From the Materials Facility, we select the images from fiber-reinforced CMC, also fully described in Larson et al. [8,11]. Their work investigated new manufacturing processes for curing preceramic polymer using impregnation of polymer resins, here allylhydridopolycarbosilane (silicon carbide preceramic polymer), into unidirectional fiber beds to reinforce CMCs. In order to inspect the quality of specimens following different specifications, they imaged test samples with width of approximately 1.5 mm, permeated by several fibers coated with boron nitride. Each fiber presents $6.4 \pm 0.9\ \mu m$ average radius, with diameter ranging from 13 to 20 pixels in the micrographs. After curation, the fiber bed porosity was 0.32–0.39 with about 5,000 to 6,200 fibers per stack.

Larson et al. [8] designed important methods to describe fiber rearrangement and void formation through critical stages of the CMC processing cycle, however their reports lack valuable information about the segmentation algorithm and validation, which can highly influence conclusions regarding microstructural heterogeneity, and resilience of the material.

The training and experiments conducted in our methods below are performed on the images of a single fiber-reinforced CMC sample. From the data available at [11], we illustrate our algorithms using two image stacks. The first stack contains 2,160 image cross-sections from raw microCT data, which we will refer to as "raw image stack"[1]. The second stack contains 1,000 image cross-sections of the segmented results by [8], which we will denote as the "ground truth stack". Fibers in these material experiments should be mostly continuous throughout the stack, i.e., fiber breaks are not expected. Notice that the ground truth stack is shorter than the raw image stack, as [8] seems to only include the segmentation results for image slices in the range [159–1158]. Thus, in our experiments we assure that the image slices from the raw image stack correspond to the same slices as in those available in the ground truth stack.

3   Methods

3.1   MicroCT Image Analysis and Visualization

This section describes a set of tools for the microstructure assessment of a specimen using the raw microCT stack, e.g., detection of specimen within microCT

---

[1] Filename: "rec20160318_191511_232p3_2cm_cont_4097im_1500ms_ML17keV_6h5" as available in the Materials Facility website [3].

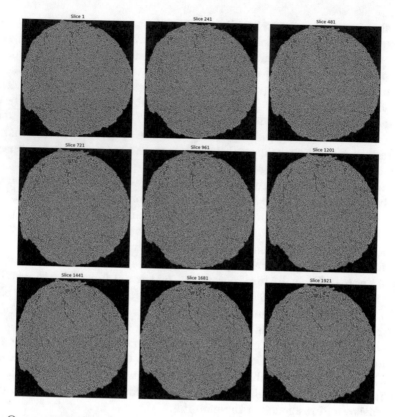

Fig. 2. Our new routines for quick stack overview: automated masking of specimen core and montage with slices across sample.

as illustrated in Fig. 2. Also, we create routines to estimate spatial properties from fiber segmentation results such as: (a) number of fiber detections per slice: list the number of connected components in each image of the stack; (b) fiber cross-sectional area: sum of pixels in each connected component; (c) fiber eccentricity: the ratio of the focal distance (distance between ellipse focal points) over the major axis length. Values are in the interval $[0, 1)$, with 0 indicating a circle; (d) fiber solidity: the ratio between pixels in the region to the convex hull.

In order to extract the region properties, we apply methods on image processing using `scipy` and `skimage` libraries that include non-linear filters, such as median, mathematical morphology and binarizations. We followed a stereological approach in which each cross-section is processed individually. In addition, we also integrate information from slices, such as for determining the frequency of events as illustrated in Sect. 4.

Lossless Data Reduction Algorithm: During tomographic experiments, cylindrical sample holders often surround CMC specimens, however the microCT of such containers show relatively homogeneous area, with low intensity variation, particularly for the volume projection over the z-axis. This realization motivates the use of binary classification to first segment the image into two groups of voxels, sample vs. cylinder and interstitial space.

Fig. 3. Maximum projection of stack across z-axis for microCT core detection and lossless data reduction: high intensity indicates dense material.

By combining IsoData [14] with the maximum projection (Fig. 3) across axis z of the raw microCT images, we are able to: (a) improve result of image enhancements as it removes background volume and respective artifacts; (b) reduce the stack volume without specimen data loss; (c) automatically detect specimens within a cylindrical metal container; (d) eliminate irrelevant interstitial space, which is often confused with other texturally homogeneous regions; (e) work with microCT stacks in [11] containing unidirectional fibers, aligned to z-axis.

The maximum projection of the stack guides our lossless volume reduction (65.91%) before further microCT analysis that follows throughout this paper.

3.2   Setting up Inputs for CNN

Before our automated method evaluates the segmented results in [11] through classification, we create two datasets intended for the training and testing of the CNN model. Each of these datasets contains image crops enclosing fibers and void spaces, here corresponding to the fiber matrix as illustrated in Fig. 4. The first dataset establishes the baseline used for the training of the CNN, which we will denote as the *Baseline Dataset*. The images for this dataset come from the manual labeling of a human expert. Expertise includes the ability to identify the composition of CMC phases and placement of fibers within a specimen. The second dataset, denoted as the *Segmented Crops Dataset*, will be used for the

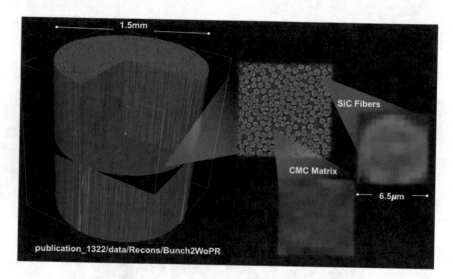

Fig. 4. From global view to local analysis of fiber patterns with CNN: volume rendering with TomViz [6], local analysis with `skimage`, and CNN with `keras`.

testing of our model. This set of images are derived from the segmentation results available at [11], which may or may not have inaccurate fiber detections.

The experiments outlined below are all conducted on a single stack from [11] as illustrated in Fig. 4. Our proposed pipeline utilizes the `skimage` package for image manipulation, such as cropping, rigid body transformation, and the `keras` package for the construction of the CNN. The workflow for the creation of image crops is explained in the next paragraphs.

Below, we summarize the data generation process for each dataset through the usage of the developed methods denoted as `auto_crop` and `manual_crop`. The first method is employed in the creation of fiber crops derived from the manual clicks for the *Baseline Dataset*. The second method automatically creates crops of void spaces and fibers, each of which respectively belong to the *Baseline and Segemented Crops Datasets*.

The Baseline Dataset: Since the physical experiments conducted in [8] are known to cause visual distortions, we perform the crops on the image located around half-way of the specimen z-axis, here, image cross-section #1,000. On this image, we manually label all present fibers with a macro designed in Fiji [13] software, where all the selections are done at the center of the fiber, and each selection is saved as (x, y) coordinates in a csv file. In `manual_crop`, these coordinates are later extracted to crop the fibers from the raw image cross section. The desired size of the crops was obtained by approximating the window size to the fiber area. This process represents our manual segmentation approach to identify all the fibers located in the image cross section (#1,000), to ultimately compare our labeling with the segmentations in [11]. From this approach, we obtained a total of 5,637 image crops containing fibers. The 3,177 image crops containing void spaces corresponding to this image cross section are created with the auto_crop method. Thus, adding both fiber and void spaces crops, the *Baseline Dataset* results in 8,814 10 × 10 pixel size image crops.

The Segmented Crops Dataset: With the given appropriate parameters, auto_crop crops both fibers and void spaces according to the segmentations in [11]. With the ground truth image cross-sections given by the authors, and raw microCT data, we label the already segmented image to measure the region properties. This enables the extraction of the salient regions resulting from the semi-automated method presented in [8], which facilitates the cropping of fibers and void spaces. The 5,806,836 generated crops are normalized and stored in the user's directory of choice.

Void Spaces Crops: To achieve this, we utilize the ground truth images from [11] to highlight the voids by segmenting the areas that do not correspond to the pixel intensities of fibers. Once segmented, we erode to shrink the bright fiber regions and enhance the dark regions within the void spaces. This results in a labeled image, which allows for the measurement of potential void regions. Lastly, to match the dimensions of our *Baseline Dataset*, we use the outputted regions to crop a 10 × 10 pixel sized image. Once cropped, the image is then normalized and stored. A total of 3,388,983 void crops were generated, all of which were added to the *Segmented Crops Dataset*.

3.3   LeNet-5 Based CNN for Fiber Detection

With the intention to validate the image crops resulting from the segmentation in [11], we classified such crops using a variant of a CNN LeNet-5 [12]. There are three main advantages of using a CNN here: (a) automated feature extraction from microCT cross-sections, (b) high performance on images with relatively simple features, and (c) previous experiments using similar classifiers [1]. The architecture of our model differs from LeNet-5 on the input size, and the number of classes on the output layer. In our case, our inputs are 16 × 16 sized images, and target a binary classification problem: "fiber" or "non-fiber". The CNN consists of seven layers, three of them are convolutional layers, two are average pooling layers, and the last two are fully connected layers. Below we give details on the activation functions applied in each layer.

The hyperbolic tangent activation function (1) is used in every layer before output. *tanh* ranges from [−1,1], which serves to our advantage because the negative inputs x will be penalized as strongly negative and zero inputs will be mapped near zero.

$$f(x) = tanh(x) = \frac{2}{1 + e^{-2x}} - 1 \tag{1}$$

The "softmax" function (2) is applied to the outputs of the second to last fully-connected layer. These are later converted to probability distributions for the potential outcomes of the one-hot-encoded binary labels (1, 0) or ("fiber", "non-fiber"). In the equation below, the y vector represents the output elements from the second to last fully-connected layer, which are passed into the "softmax" function. On the far left, we have the calculated probabilities corresponding to 3 images for either class "fiber" and "non-fiber".

$$y \begin{bmatrix} 2.0 \\ 1.0 \\ 4.0 \end{bmatrix} \rightarrow S(y_i) = \frac{e^{y_i}}{\sum_j e^{y_j}} \rightarrow \begin{array}{l} p = 0.5, 0.5 \\ p = 0.4, 0.6 \\ p = 0.1, 0.9 \end{array} \tag{2}$$

The loss function (3) is employed on the model is categorical cross entropy. This function assures that the robustness of the model increases at the end of each epoch, by measuring the inconsistency between the predicted values and the actual labels. Below, the double sum is over observations ranging from i to N, and categories c, which in our case $C = 2$. The first term $1_{y_i \in C_c}$ represents the indicator function of the ith observation in the c category. As seen in the softmax equation, the neural network outputs a vector with C categories or two columns. Given that this is a binary classification problem, the network outputs one single probability $\hat{y}_i$, with the other being the output. We summarize the CNN architecture in Table 1.

$$-\frac{1}{N} \sum_{i=1}^{N} \sum_{c=1}^{C} 1_{y_i \in C_c} \log p_{model} [y_i \in C_c] \tag{3}$$

Table 1. Summary of the CNN model designed to identify fiber patterns.

Layer	Feature map	Size	Kernel size	Strides	Activation
Input image	1	16 × 16	N/A	N/A	N/A
1. Convolution	6	12 × 12	5 × 5	1	tanh
2. Average pooling	6	6 × 6	2 × 2	2	tanh
3. Convolution	16	2 × 2	5 × 5	1	tanh
4. Average pooling	16	1 × 1	2 × 2	2	tanh
5. Convolution	120	1 × 1	5 × 5	1	tanh
6. FC	N/A	84	N/A	N/A	tanh
Output FC	N/A	2	N/A	N/A	softmax

4   Results

We created tools to build reports and dashboards for statistical analysis and visualization of fundamental properties of microCT and results from fiber segmentation models. First, our routines can detect the dense specimen as in Fig. 2 by using our proposed maximum projection method using the raw microCT.

Another advantage of this method is to enable lossless data reduction to 65.91% of the original volume. Second, we use the fiber segmentation results publicly available in [11] to illustrate both the need to evaluate the accuracy of fiber detection models and how our routines solved the problem qualitatively (Figs. 5 and 6) and quantitatively (Table 2).

Figure 5 shows a large variation of fiber cross sectional area that goes beyond the reported 13 to 20 pixels for diameter as in [8] – if their statement was accurate, then we should find high concentration of fibers between 452 and 1,017 pixels for area, but instead the result of their method leads to peak of detected fibers with area between 200 and 500, including likely invalid area cross-section, i.e., less than 100 pixels. In addition to the analyses on a random slice, our new python routines for 3D analysis (Fig. 6) show the size and shape of detected fibers. Eccentricity around 0.35 indicates fibers tend to be circular instead of elliptical, and a solidity around 0.95 indicates that fibers tend to be concave, which apparently agrees with expected results. However, the fiber counts across stack clearly indicate problems with the segmentation since fiber breaks are not expected in this experiment, therefore count oscillations from 6,272 to 6,444, particularly abrupt ones, indicate errors by the segmentation algorithm.

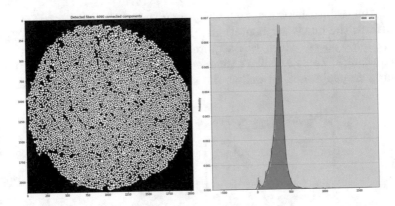

Fig. 5. Fiber segmentation (left) and fiber area counts for slice #159 (right).

We train the CNN with the *baseline dataset* (8,814 image crops), which include 3,177 void and 5,637 fiber crops. Before input, we rescale all images to 16 × 16 pixels to meet the input size requirements of the constructed CNN. We then randomize (following a hypergeometric distribution) all images and labels to avoid any bias during the network's learning. From the randomized images, 70% of these are used for training, and the remaining 30% for validation purposes resulting in an accuracy of 96.56% and a loss of 0.0894 on the validation data. The entire data generation process yielded a total of 5,806,836 fiber crops in 1.34 h and 3,388,983 void crops in 2.56 h. Figure 7 displays the learning performance of our model on 11 epochs.

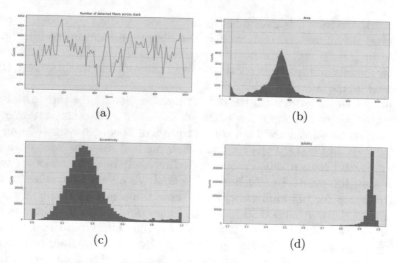

Fig. 6. Spatial analysis of fiber segmentation results: fundamental views from whole stack: (a) fiber count, (b) cross-sectional area, (c) eccentricity, (d) solidity.

With the trained network, we classify a subset of the generated image crops derived from the image segmentations in [11]. The subset contains 10% of the available 1,000 slices, which was acquired by extracting the image crops from every tenth slice. Table 2 displays the metrics for the classification on 10% of the segmented crops dataset, as well as the augmented (rotated at 90°) version.

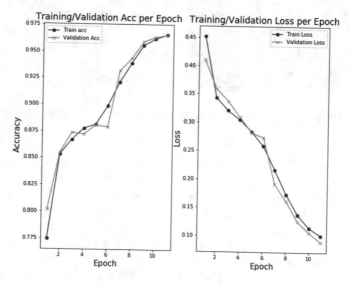

Fig. 7. LeNet Performance for the training and validation of the baseline dataset.

Table 2. Classification results and augmentation by rotation of the segmented crops dataset.

Crops	Accuracy	Precision	Specificity	Sensitivity
Segmented	0.9375 ± 0.0034	0.9788 ± 0.0048	0.9659 ± 0.0072	0.9209 ± 0.0041
Augmented	0.9523 ± 0.0059	0.9497 ± 0.0091	0.9117 ± 0.0145	0.9767 ± 0.0023

Classification of the segmented crops (fiber detection model) resulted in an average accuracy of 93.75%. After testing the CNN's behavior on the rotated images, the model yields an average accuracy of 95.23%. However, with a sensitivity rate averaging to 92%, and a specificity rate averaging to 96% on the segmented crops, there is an indication that the segmentation model in [8] hardly mislabeled non-fibers as fibers, however it misses a few true fibers.

5 Conclusion and Discussion

One of the main steps in CMC analysis is the detection of fibers, and recent models present different levels of inaccuracy. This paper proposed a systematic framework for comparative analysis between manual fiber detection and automated fiber segmentation methods. We analyzed qualitatively and quantitatively the results of a fiber detection method [8] that has been used for years in research applied to CMC manufacturing. Since only the results of the fiber detection were available, we used those as input to our routines and showed the value of our proposed tools in evaluating such fiber detection models. Our routines emphasized the large variation of fiber cross sectional area that goes beyond the expected fiber diameters specified by the manufacturer. Also, we organized a workflow for quickly pointed out fiber count oscillations across the stack, a clear indication of errors in the segmentation model since fiber breaks were not expected in the CMC experiment. Our routines also identified that their method has no fiber tracking as most of fibers lack continuity in z-axis.

This preliminary investigation led to python-based tools that build automated reports from microCT images using standard computational resources, which is a much needed tool set for material scientists as they can be generalized to other 3D datasets. The performance of the CNN model shows encouraging results and might serve as a method to probe the segmentations made by other scientists, as well as a tool to eliminate false negative from fiber detection models that contribute to the lack of fiber continuity within a microCT stack. Future models should account for the wider variability of fibers, e.g. radius, and fiber coating variations; these are often found in CMC fibers, but not necessarily present in the training set since we use random partitioning, and still have to explore the remaining image stacks available in [11]. Different CNN architectures as well as other augmentation protocols to increase number of samples during CNN training will soon be incorporated to increase the models robustness to fibers of various sizes and under different deformations.

Acknowledgments. This research is funded in part by the Gordon and Betty Moore Foundation through Grant GBMF3834 and by the Alfred P. Sloan Foundation through Grant 2013-10-27 to the University of California, Berkeley. Algorithmic work is partially supported by the Office of Science of the US Department of Energy (DOE) under Contract No. DE-AC02-05CH11231, Advanced Scientific Computing Research (ASCR) Early Career Award. Any opinions, findings, and conclusions or recommendations expressed in this material are those of the authors and they do not necessarily reflect the views of DOE or the University of California.

References

1. Araujo, F.H., et al.: Reverse image search for scientific data within and beyond the visible spectrum. Expert Syst. Appl. **109**, 35–48 (2018)
2. Bale, H.A., et al.: Real-time quantitative imaging of failure events in materials under load at temperatures above 1,600 c. Nat. Mater. **12**, 40–46 (2012)
3. Blaiszik, B., Chard, K., Pruyne, J., Ananthakrishnan, R., Tuecke, S., Foster, I.: The materials data facility: data services to advance materials science research. J. Mater. **68**(8), 2045–2052 (2016)
4. Cox, B.N., et al.: Stochastic virtual test systems for ceramic matrix composites. Annu. Rev. Mater. Res. **44**, 479–529 (2014)
5. Gardiner, G.: The next generation of ceramic matrix composites (2017). https://www.compositesworld.comblog/post/the-next-generation-of-ceramic-matrix-composites
6. Hanwell, M.D., et al.: OpenChemistry/tomviz: Tomviz 1.3.0 Release Candidate 2, April 2018
7. Kluyver, T., et al.: Jupyter notebooks-a publishing format for reproducible computational workflows. In: Positioning and Power in Academic Publishing: Players, Agents and Agendas, p. 87 (2016)
8. Larson, N., Cuellar, C., Zok, F.: X-ray computed tomography of microstructure evolution during matrix impregnation and curing in 2 unidirectional fiber beds. Compos. A Appl. Sci. Manuf. **117**, 243–259 (2019)
9. Larson, N., Zok, F.: Insights from in-situ x-ray computed tomography during axial impregnation of unidirectional fiber beds. Compos. A Appl. Sci. Manuf. **107**, 124–134 (2018)
10. Larson, N., Zok, F.: In-situ 3D visualization of composite microstructure during polymer-to-ceramic conversion. Acta Mater. **144**, 579–589 (2018)
11. Larson, N.M., Zok, F.W.: Ex-situ XCT dataset for x-ray computed tomography of microstructure evolution during matrix impregnation and curing in unidirectional fiber beds. https://doi.org/10.18126/M2QM0Z (2019)
12. LeCun, Y., Bottou, L., Bengio, Y., Haffner, P.: Gradient-based learning applied to document recognition. Proc. IEEE **86**(11), 2278–2324 (1998)
13. Rasband, W.: ImageJ, U. S. National Institutes of Health, Bethesda, Maryland, USA (1997–2018). https://imagej.nih.gov/ij/
14. Ridler, T., Calvard, S.: Picture thresholding using an iterative selection method. IEEE Trans. Syst. Man Cybern. B Cybern. **8**(8), 630–632 (1978)

RISEC: Rotational Invariant Segmentation of Elongated Cells in SEM Images with Inhomogeneous Illumination

Ali Memariani[1]([✉]), Bradley T. Endres[2], Eugénie Bassères[3], Kevin W. Garey[3], and Ioannis A. Kakadiaris[1]

[1] Department of Computer Science, Computational Biomedicine Lab,
University of Houston, Houston, TX, USA
{amemaria,ikakadia}@central.uh.edu
[2] Clement J. Zablocki VA Medical Center, Milwaukee, WI, USA
bradley.endres@va.gov
[3] Department of Pharmacy Practice and Translational Research,
University of Houston, Houston, TX, USA
{ebassere,kgarey}@central.uh.edu

Abstract. Detection of *Clostridioides difficile* cells in scanning electron microscopy images is a challenging task due to the challenges of cell rotation and inhomogeneous illumination. Currently, orientation-invariance in deep ConvNets is achieved by data augmentation. However, training with all possible orientations increases computational complexity. Furthermore, conventional illumination-invariance models include pre-processing illumination normalization steps. However, illumination normalization algorithms remove important texture information which is critical for the analysis of SEM images. In this paper, RISEC (Rotational Invariant Segmentation of Elongated Cells in SEM images with Inhomogeneous Illumination) is proposed to address the challenges of cell rotation and inhomogeneous illumination. First, a generative adversarial network segments the candidate cell regions proposals, addressing the inhomogeneous illumination. Then, the region proposals are passed to two capsule layers where a rotation-invariant shape representation is learned for every cell type via dynamic routing. Our experiments indicate that RISEC outperforms the state of the art models (e.g., CapsNet, and U-net) by at least 11% improving the dice score.

Keywords: Instance segmentation · Orientation-invariance · Illumination · Convolutional capsules · Generative adversarial networks

1 Introduction

Clostridioides difficile infection (CDI) is a significant cause of death in the USA [1]. Computing cell information such as deformation, length, and count, in the scanning electron microscopy (SEM) images, is essential for quantification of

© Springer Nature Switzerland AG 2019
G. Bebis et al. (Eds.): ISVC 2019, LNCS 11845, pp. 553–563, 2019.
https://doi.org/10.1007/978-3-030-33723-0_45

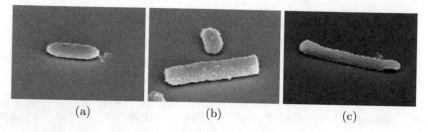

(a)   (b)   (c)

Fig. 1. Depiction of CDI cells in SEM images with inhomogeneous illumination in various rotations: (a) shadows on a spore, (b) bright areas around a vegetative cell, and (c) shadows on a vegetative cell.

the effects of the CDI treatment [2]. Therefore, segmentation of CDI cells is an important task. However, SEM images are inhomogeneously illuminated. Moreover, elongated CDI cells are in various orientations which is a major drawback for deep ConvNets, making the segmentation more challenging. Deep neural networks are able to segment a variety of objects (e.g., cars, pedestrians, animals) that do not tend to change their vertical or horizontal poses. A primitive solution to address rotation invariance is to acquire images of rotated objects and train a deeper network with larger tensor volumes. However, training such networks considering all possible orientations of the same objects, dramatically increases the computational complexity. Deep models in biomedical image analysis (e.g., Fully convolutional networks [5,11], and U-net [8]) have not considered the segmentation of elongated objects with orientation invariance.

Rotation changes the order of the input feature. Sending appropriate features to the next layer in the network is called feature routing. Recently, CapsNet [9,10] and Harmonic network [12] proposed feature routing models with rotation invariance. However, feature routing is hindered by the image resolution. Computing the appropriate features needs an extra loop inside each epoch. Image resolution increases the number of capsules in each layer and thus the number of part-whole connection between layers. Furthermore, every capsule is connected to all the capsules in the next layer. Therefore, increasing image resolution increases the computations between capsule until routing convergence.

Moreover, SEM images suffer from inhomogeneous illumination. Figure 1 depicts samples of cells with inhomogeneous illumination in various orientations. Conventional illumination normalization algorithms could reduce this effect. However, illumination normalization removes the texture of the image which is essential in segmenting the cells from the background [3] in SEM images. Recently, adversarial networks have gained more attention to model the effect of illumination as an adversarial attack [4,7]. Adversarial loss improves the segmentation output to be similar to the ground truth without increasing the complexity of the network during deployment.

In this work, a region proposal network is proposed to extract potential cell areas and apply feature routing only on such regions. Specifically, this paper

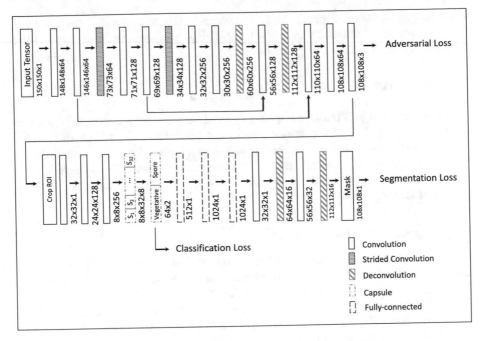

Fig. 2. Depiction of RISEC pipeline. First, the adversarial segmenter network separates the potential cell areas. Then, regions of interest are passed through two layers of convolution. The resulting volume is reshaped to form capsules, representing local shape properties of the cells. The capsules in the primary layer are fully connected to the capsules in the secondary layer, performing dynamic feature routing. The secondary capsule layer learns two shape representation for vegetative cells and spores. Finally, the representation is passed to a decoder to provide the segmentation.

presents RISEC, an algorithm for Segmentation of Elongated Cells with Inhomogeneous Illumination and Orientation Invariance. Our contributions are:

(i) An adversarial training to segment the potential cell regions, simplifying the shape of the object for parametric shape representation (Sect. 2.1), and
(ii) Dynamic feature routing applied on simplified shapes in the region proposals to learn a parametric shape representation of cells (Sect. 2.2).

The learned representation is passed to a decoder to segment instances of two cell types (i.e. vegetative and spore) in various orientations based on their shape. The segmentation masks provided by RISEC could be used to quantify shape information of cells such as the length of the major axis to quantify the efficacy of the treatments. Such quantifiable measurements provide a unique opportunity for clinical research where the treatments are developing (specifically CDI infection) to compare the efficacy of the treatments. The rest of the paper is organized as follows: Sect. 2 presents the RISEC's pipeline. Section 3 illustrates the experimental results comparing the segmentation performance of RISEC with the state-of-the-art provided by U-net and CapsNet. Finally, Sect. 4 draws the conclusions. The results indicate that RISEC outperforms the state-of-the-art by at least 11% improving the dice score.

2   Methods

RISEC consists of two parts: a region proposal network and a segmentation network. The region proposal network selects the potential cell regions and models the inhomogeneous illumination as an adversarial variation. The segmentation network learns a shape representation via dynamic routing [9] and predicts the cell type and the corresponding segmentation mask. Figure 2 depicts the architecture of the pipeline.

2.1   Region Proposal Network

The region proposal network (RPN) is similar to U-net with an adversarial loss. The adversarial loss models the illumination as an adversarial attack and gives feedback to RPN to improve the segmentation.

The RPN consists of six convolutional units: the first three units include a 3×3 convolution layer, a ReLU layer and a 2×2 max pooling layer with a stride of two, downsampling the image. The next three units include an upsampling of the features followed by a 2×2 deconvolution. RPN loss function is the cross-entropy loss combined with an adversarial loss:

$$L_S = \mathbf{w_c} * L_C\Big(\mathcal{S}(\mathbf{I}), \mathbf{G}\Big) + L_C\Big(\mathcal{D}\big(\mathcal{S}(\mathbf{I})\big), 1\Big), \tag{1}$$

where $L_C\big(\mathcal{S}(\mathbf{I}), \mathbf{G}\big)$ denotes a cross-entropy term between the predicted labels $\mathbf{S}$ corresponding to the image $\mathbf{I}$ and the ground truth $\mathbf{G}$. Since cell areas are smaller than the background portion of the image, the segmenter cross-entropy loss is weighted by $\mathbf{w_c}$. The minority class has a higher weight in the loss function. The second term $L_C\big(\mathcal{D}(\mathcal{S}(\mathbf{I})), 1\big)$ is the adversarial loss term, computed by the discriminator. The label map of image $\mathbf{I}$ generated by the RPN is denoted by $\mathcal{S}(\mathbf{I})$ and $\mathcal{D}$ denotes the discriminator network [7]. The adversarial loss penalizes the RPN to produce label maps similar to the ground truth, reducing the effect of the illumination. The discriminator is a conventional ConvNet classifier trained on the ground truth and predicted segmentation provided by the RPN. The discriminator improves the generated labels by sending feedback to the generator if the RPN labels are significantly different from the ground truth. It does not increase the complexity of the network since it is used only during training. It consists of five convolutional layers with valid padding, followed by ReLU activations and average pooling. Furthermore, two fully connected layers are placed at the end of the discriminator. The discriminator $\mathcal{D}$ computes the cross-entropy of the ground truth label maps $\mathbf{G}$ and 1, and the cross-entropy of the generated label maps $\mathcal{S}(\mathbf{I})$ and 0, minimizing the following loss function:

$$L_D = L_C\Big(\mathcal{D}(G), 1\Big) + L_C\Big(\mathcal{D}(\mathcal{S}(\mathbf{I})), 0\Big). \tag{2}$$

During the training, the discriminator improves the RPN, penalizing the candidate regions that do not look like manually label areas (e.g., with misclassified shadows on top and bright areas around the cell). Therefore, the adversarial training reduces the effect of the inhomogeneous illumination. A fixed window size is defined that can contain the largest cell in our dataset. The RPN provides a primary segmentation of images of any size larger than the window size. The primary segmentation is then filtered to select the candidate regions where the sum of the pixel probabilities is above a threshold t_c. Non-max suppression is applied to reduce the number of candidate regions.

2.2 Dynamic Routing for Rotational Invariant Segmentation

ConvNets are sensitive to object transformation such as rotation since they change the order of the low level features [9]. Feature routing is the process to put such features to the appropriate order. Max-pooling is a primitive feature routing to overcome translation. However, max-pooling hinders the equivariance property of the network. Therefore, local information about object shape and pose are lost throughout the network, resulting in the ConvNet to be sensitive to the transformation of the object.

To accomplish rotation invariance, dynamic feature routing [9] is applied to put the rotated parts (features) together to create the shape of an object. If part i belongs to object j then i and j are coupled together with a coupling coefficient c_{ij} close to one where $c_{ij} \in [0, 1]$. A two-layer capsule architecture is used in which the first layer capsules represent the local pose information and the second layer capsules represent the overall shape and orientation of a cell based on the overall agreement between the local pose information. First, two layers of convolution are applied to a candidate region. Then, the primary capsule layer is formed by reshaping the output of the convolution volume so that every bloc (e.g., $8 \times 8 \times 1$) in the convolution volume represent a 64×1 capsule vector s_i. The length of the vector $\mathbf{v_i}$ is then squashed to $[0, 1]$:

$$\mathbf{v_i} = \frac{\|\mathbf{s_i}\|^2}{1 + \|\mathbf{s_i}\|^2} \cdot \frac{\mathbf{s_i}}{\|\mathbf{s_i}\|} \ . \tag{3}$$

Next, the likelihood $\mathbf{v_{j|i}}$ of capsule j in the second capsule layer, representing a vegetative cell or a spore, is estimated as:

$$\mathbf{v_{j|i}} = \mathbf{W_{ij}} . \mathbf{v_i} \ , \tag{4}$$

where the weight matrix $\mathbf{W_{ij}}$ is learned during training. Then, the weighted sum of inputs i over capsule j is computed as:

$$\mathbf{s_j} = \sum_i c_{ij} . \mathbf{v_{j|i}} \ , \tag{5}$$

where c_{ij} is the coupling coefficient, acting as a prior, for the likelihood $\mathbf{v_{j|i}}$.

The coupling coefficient c_{ij} is defined as the softmax of b_{ij}, where b_{ij} is computed as the cumulative sum of agreements between capsules over routing iterations. In every routing iteration, the agreement a_{ij} is added to the log prior b_{ij} until convergence. The agreement a_{ij} between two capsules is defined as the scalar product of the squashed mean v_j and the likelihood $\mathbf{v_{j|i}}$:

$$a_{ij} = \mathbf{v_j} . \mathbf{v_{j|i}} . \tag{6}$$

Alternatively, a clustering algorithm could be applied over each capsule layer and define the proximity of a capsule vector to the mean of the cluster as the agreement [10]. Algorithm 1 depicts the training steps of RISEC.

Algorithm 1. Depiction of RISEC Training

Input   : Augmented training images, Segmentation ground truth, and class labels
Output: Trained network
1 **begin**
2   **for** *number of pretraining iterations* **do**
3   Select a batch of labels $\mathbf{G}$
4   Train the discriminator with the cross-entropy loss $L_C(\mathcal{D}(\mathbf{G}), 1)$
5   **end**
6   **for** *number of adversarial iterations* **do**
7   Select a batch of training images and their labels $\{\mathbf{I}, \mathbf{G}\}$
8   Predict the segmentation $\mathcal{S}(\mathbf{I})$. Compute the segmentation cross-entropy loss $L_C(\mathcal{S}(\mathbf{I}), \mathbf{G})$
9   Compute the adversarial loss $L_C(\mathcal{D}(\mathcal{S}(\mathbf{I})), 0)$
10   Given the labels $\mathbf{G}$, compute the discriminator cross-entropy loss $L_C(\mathcal{D}(\mathbf{G}), 1)$
11   Compute $L_\mathcal{D}$ and backpropagate the gradients through the discriminator and the segmenter.
12   Compute $L_\mathcal{S}$ and backpropagate the gradients through segmenter.
13   **end**
14   For all i in the first capsule layer and j in the second capsule layer: Set $b_{ij} = 0$
15   **for** *number of dynamic routing iterations* **do**
16   Compute $c_{ij} = softmax(b_{ij})$
17   Compute $\mathbf{v_i}$ (Eq. 3) and $\mathbf{v_{j|i}}$ for every (i, j) (Eq. 4)
18   Compute $\mathbf{s_j}$ (Eq. 5) and $\mathbf{v_j}$ (Eq. 3)
19   Compute the agreement a_{ij} between capsules (i, j) (Eq. 6)
20   Update $b_{ij} \leftarrow b_{ij} + a_{ij}$
21   Compute the loss L_R (Eq. 7) and backpropagate the gradients to update the tensor $\mathbf{W_{ij}}$
22   **end**
23 **end**

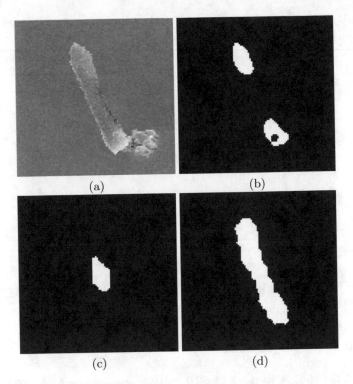

(a)   (b)

(c)   (d)

Fig. 3. Effect of inhomogeneous illumination is depicted. (a) Shadows and bright spots have divided a cell into different parts. (b) U-net detected a vegetative cell as two spores since different parts of the cell are inhomogeneously illuminated. (c) CapsNet is able to detect the rotation of the cell but fails to segment the entire cell. (d) RISEC has inferred that inhomogeneously illuminated parts are likely to belong to a single vegetative cell based on their shape and orientation. The detected boundaries could be improved.

A decoder is added to the output of the second capsule layer to compute the segmentation mask by increasing the resolution of the feature map using two deconvolution steps. Finally, the routing loss function,

$$L_R = L_M + L_C(\mathbf{I}, \mathbf{G}), \tag{7}$$

consists of two terms: classification loss L_M and $L_C(\mathbf{I}, \mathbf{G})$ cross-entropy loss of the segmentation. The classification loss L_M enforces that the output vector of capsule representing class k has a large length if and only if an object of class k is present:

$$L_M = \sum_k t_k.max(0, m^+ - \|\mathbf{v_k}\|)^2 + \lambda(1 - t_k)max(0, \|\mathbf{v_k}\| - m^-)^2 \tag{8}$$

where $t_k = 1$ indicates the presence of object of class k and m^+, m^+, and λ denote the hyperparameters of the model. The lambda parameter prevents the initial learning from shrinking the activity vector for the absent classes.

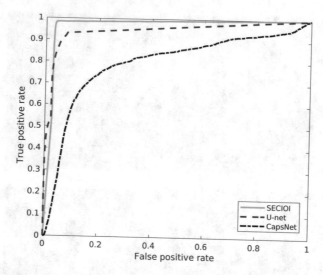

Fig. 4. The ROC curve indicates that RISEC outperforms U-net [8] and CapsNet [9] in segmenting the cells.

3   Experimental Results

Dataset: UH-Cdiff1 a dataset of CDI cell images acquired via SEM imaging with pixel dimensions 411×711 and 10,000x magnification with two CDI cell types [6], is applied to train and validate RISEC, with two classes of vegetative cell and spore. A training set of synthesized images is created by synthesizing background images of size 150×150. Then, cells were randomly selected and placed into the center of the image. The cells were slightly warped to generate variant images. A dataset of 12,000 samples is divided into a training set with 1,000 images (5,000 samples of each cell type) and a validation set with 2,000 images (1,000 samples for each cell type). The same training set is applied to train RISEC, and our baselines, U-net, and CapsNet. The validation set is not seen by the network during the training and includes cells in various random orientations.

Implementation Details: The RPN segmenter loss is weighted with $\mathbf{w_c} = [0.1, 0.9]$ to penalize the misclassification of the minority cell regions. The implementation of RPN follows the architecture used in SoLiD [7]. A window size of 108×108 is applied to filter the result of the RPN. In case, the sum over the candidate area was more than 150 pixels the region is proposed to the capsule layer for classification. To compute the routing loss $m^+ = 0.9$, $m^+ = 0.1$, and $\lambda = 0.5$ are used as the hyperparameters values. The routing weight matrix W_{ij} is initialized with a normal distribution $\mathcal{N}(0, 0.01)$ and overall agreements b_{ij} between capsules (i, j) are initialized as zero. The segmentation method is implemented in TensorFlow 1.5.0. Adam optimization is applied to learn the

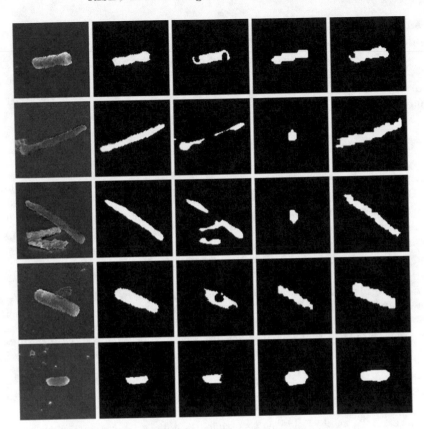

Fig. 5. Qualitative depiction of RISEC segmentation results compared to the results from U-net, and CapsNet. From left to right: Original image, ground truth, U-net, CapsNet, RISEC. Inhomogeneous illumination results in partial segmentation of objects.

routing parameters (i.e., output vectors $\mathbf{v}$, coupling coefficients c_{ij}, and weights W_{ij}) by minimizing the loss function on a NVIDIA GeForce GTX GPU with 12 GB capacity.

Table 1. Comparative results between the segmentation performance of RISEC and the state-of-the-art in biomedical instance segmentation by U-net and CapsNet.

Method	Dice (Vegetative)	Dice (Spore)	Dice (Total)	AUC
CapsNet [9]	0.56	0.68	0.62	0.80
U-net [8]	**0.86**	0.60	0.73	0.94
RISEC	0.78	**0.83**	**0.81**	**0.97**

Results: Table 1 summarizes the segmentation performance of RISEC with the results of U-net and CapsNet. Figure 4 depicts the ROC curve of RISEC with CapsNet and U-net. The dice scores were computed to measure the segmentation performance. Figure 5 depicts sample results of the segmentation. U-net produces accurate boundaries but is highly sensitive to illumination and artifacts in the image.

4   Conclusion

This paper proposed RISEC, a deep pipeline for segmentation of two classes of CDI cells (i.e. vegetative and spore) in SEM images. RISEC learns a shape representation of the cell for each class and outperforms the state of the art in cell segmentation in SEM images with debris and inhomogeneous illuminated cells in various orientations. In addition, post-processing steps could be applied to improve the boundaries detected by RISEC.

Acknowledgments. This work was supported in part by NIH/NIAID 1UO1 AI-24290-01 and by the Hugh Roy and Lillie Cranz Cullen Endowment Fund. At the time of data collection. Dr. Endres was a postdoctoral fellow at the University of Houston. All statements of facts, opinion or conclusions contained herein are those of the authors and should not be construed as representing official views or policies of the sponsors.

References

1. Endres, B.T., et al.: Epidemic Clostridioides difficile ribotype 027 lineages: comparisons of Texas versus worldwide strains. In: Open Forum Infectious Diseases, vol. 6, no. 2, pp. 1–13. Oxford University Press, New York (2019)
2. Endres, B.T., et al.: A novel method for imaging the pharmacological effects of antibiotic treatment on clostridium difficile. Anaerobe **40**, 10–14 (2016)
3. Han, H., Shan, S., Chen, X., Gao, W.: A comparative study on illumination preprocessing in face recognition. Pattern Recognit. **46**(6), 1691–1699 (2013)
4. Ko, M., Kim, D., Kim, M., Kim, K.: Illumination-insensitive skin depth estimation from a light-field camera based on cgans toward haptic palpation. Electronics **7**(11), 336 (2018)
5. Long, J., Shelhamer, E., Darrell, T.: Fully convolutional networks for semantic segmentation. In: Proceedings Computer Vision and Pattern Recognition, pp. 3431–3440, Boston(2015)
6. Memariani, A., Nikou, C., Endres, B., Bassères, E., Garey, K., Kakadiaris, I.A.: DETCIC: detection of elongated touching cells with inhomogeneous illumination using a stack of conditional random fields. In: Proceedings International Joint Conference on Computer Vision, Imaging and Computer Graphics Theory and Applications, pp. 574–580 (2018)
7. Memariani, A., Kakadiaris, I.A.: SoLiD: segmentation of clostridioides difficile cells in the presence of inhomogeneous illumination using a deep adversarial network. In: International Workshop on Machine Learning in Medical Imaging, pp. 285–293, September 2018

8. Ronneberger, O., Fischer, P., Brox, T.: U-net: convolutional networks for biomedical image segmentation. In: Proceedings of Medical Image Computing and Computer-Assisted Intervention, pp. 234–241, Munich (2015)
9. Sabour, S., Frosst, N., Hinton, G.E.: Dynamic routing between capsules. In: Advances in Neural Information Processing Systems, pp. 3856–3866, Long Beach, December 2017
10. Sabour, S., Frosst, N., Hinton, G.E.: Matrix capsules with EM routing. In: Proceedings of International Conference on Learning Representations, Vancouver, Canada, May 2018
11. Shen, D., Wu, G., Suk, H.I.: Deep learning in medical image analysis. Annu. Rev. Biomed. Eng. **19**, 221–248 (2017)
12. Worrall, D.E., Garbin, S.J., Turmukhambetov, D., Brostow, G.J.: Harmonic networks: deep translation and rotation equivariance. In: Proceedings IEEE Conference on Computer Vision and Pattern Recognition, pp. 5028–5037, Honolulu (2017)

Performance Evaluation of WebGL and WebVR Apps in VR Environments

Renato M. Toasa[1]($\boxtimes$) (iD), Paúl Francisco Baldeón Egas[1]($\boxtimes$) (iD),
Miguel Alfredo Gaibor Saltos[1]($\boxtimes$) (iD), Mateo A. Perreño[2]($\boxtimes$),
and Washington X. Quevedo[3]($\boxtimes$) (iD)

[1] Universidad Tecnológica Israel, Quito, Ecuador
{rtoasa,pbaldeon,canciller}@uisrael.edu.ec
[2] Universidad Politécnica Salesiana, Quito, Ecuador
mparrenoa@est.ups.edu.ec
[3] Universidad de las Fuerzas Armadas ESPE, Sangolqui, Ecuador
wjquevedo@espe.edu.ec

Abstract. This paper presents an evaluation of devices and browsers performance when executing web applications in WebGL and WebVR. For this purpose, the measurement of several computational resources is performed to determine which technology optimizes hardware resources when working with this type of technologies. For the purpose of this study, an application has been developed in Unity 3D that provides the exact values that the computational resources consume. In this context objects and particle systems are used to give a stress behavior on hardware entities. As a result, it was determined that WebGL and WebVR have similar performances in executions on a PC while for WebVR mobile devices it has a remarkable performance compared to WebGL.

Keywords: Virtual reality · WebGL · WebVR

1 Introduction

In the last years, applications in virtual reality (VR) are experiencing a very big revolution, as these increasingly resemble the real world and allow the user to interact with several elements in an artificial 3D environment [1]. In virtual reality a widely used term is spatial immersion, which is defined as the perception of being physically present in a non-physical world [2]. VR applications were initially executed on specialized platforms, new technologies such as WebGL (Web-based Graphics Library) and WebVR (Bringing Virtual Reality to the Web) have been developed, which allow the execution of VR applications on several browsers and devices.

When mentioning a 3D browser, one of the first thoughts of the user is "A Dom (document object model) to the web page"; although it is possible to produce web versions of classic 3D games in the browser, 3D is more powerful and with a wide field of development. The web is not a one-way communication, it allows not only the dissemination of information but also allows collaboration and communication like no other medium. This particularity of the web has made possible the creation of applications that are not possible in autonomous mode [3]. 3D web content is just another

© Springer Nature Switzerland AG 2019
G. Bebis et al. (Eds.): ISVC 2019, LNCS 11845, pp. 564–575, 2019.
https://doi.org/10.1007/978-3-030-33723-0_46

form of this growing set of diverse applications [4]. One of many technologies that bring 3D graphics on web is WebGL. WebGL for VR applications is WebVR that brings a VR experience attached in a webpage.

WebGL is a software library related to graphics which is designed to integrate extended JavaScript programming language with OpenGL (Open Graphics Library) to generate accelerated 3D graphics within any supported web browser. WebGL allows the user to incorporate to the Web a 3D graphic without complements, implemented directly in the browser. The main providers of browsers are Apple (Safari), Google (Chrome), Microsoft (Edge) and Mozilla (Firefox). These providers are members of the WebGL Working Group. WebGL is also widely used in the fields of visualization, 3D modeling and has been implemented on desktop, tablets and smart phones. [5]. Several works have determined that the potential use of WebGL is 3D modeling. For example, the Tinkercad project which allows users to draw Tinkercad 3D models within a web browser and send them to any 3D printer. Also, WebGL has been applied to the visualization of complex data that requires 3D presentation. One of these projects is described in [6], which proposes a new and innovative use of WebGL in medical applications using 3D images for better interpretation of medical examinations. Another field of study that has benefited from this technology is Geospatial. Data sets were introduced and WebGL was used to visualize the result of environmental models in 3D [7].

WebVR is an Internet-based virtual reality web technology which provides support for virtual reality devices, such as virtual reality glasses e.g. Oculus Rift or HTC Vive. WebVR allows developers to translate screen position and motion information into a 3D scene [8]. This has numerous interesting applications, from virtual product tours and interactive training applications to immersive games. Some of the browsers that support this specification are Chrome for Android, Chromium, Firefox, Microsoft Edge, Oculus Browser and Safari. [9]. WebVR affects frame rates considerably when using high quality effects such as shadows, soft lighting and image clarity. It is also a great improvement over Three.js Implementation (it is a light library written in Java-Script to create and display computer animated graphics in 3D in a Web browser). It is natively supported in mobile browsers [10].

Today, developers and researchers are exploring the use of multisensorial input and output devices to work with WebVR applications [11]. Based on this, a system was built to help firefighters simulate emergency rescues for VR technology accidents [12]. A project for "Immersive and Collaborative Data Visualization" was presented in 2014 with the aim of maximizing intrinsic human pattern recognition skills through the use of emerging technologies associated with immersive RV [13]. In this context it is planned to test WebGL and WebVR technologies in Virtual Reality environments to show the advantages and disadvantages of each technology running them as web applications on remote servers.

Now with the penetration of mobile devices in much of the world's population and the rapid adoption of virtual reality applications, it is imperative to determine the most optimal use of web technologies that can be run in virtual reality environments on mobile devices. As already seen WebGL and WebVR are highly used to display 3D graphics on the web and thanks to virtual reality browsers, this content can be consumed in virtual environments and interact with Game Objects. The main aim of this article is to compare the performance of each technology on different devices to determine the best option when developing web applications that run in virtual reality environments.

The rest of the document is organized as follows: Sect. 2 presents a formal description of the problem being studied, Sect. 3 details the structure of the evaluation, Sect. 4 shows the evaluation carried out with different case studies, then Sect. 5 mentions the results obtained and the discussion of these, finally the conclusions and future work are mentioned in Sect. 6.

2 Problem Definition

According to several studies found in literature, the evaluation of performance is a determining factor for the success or failure of a system computer applications. Web and mobile devices have taken over several business processes being used as strategic tools for business success, regardless of the area in which they are located [14]. The use of these applications is not a luxury but a necessity that large companies have to manage their strategic, operational and support processes [15]. However, despite all the technological advances, there are still certain challenges that need to be addressed and solved, for example, browser complements, use of computational resources from the browser, efficient 3D visualization and compatibility with mobile devices [16].

A critical factor in the development of WebGL and WebVR applications is to determine the level of support and performance offered by different technologies (for example: devices, operating systems and browsers) when running these types of applications, as they consume large computing resources (RAM, CPU, GPU). This is a big problem for developers since it is not easily defined which browser or device is adequate to evaluate and validate their applications; depending on the purpose of these, some will run better in one browser or device than on another. As far as browsers are concerned, the best known are: Chrome, Firefox, Safari; as far as the devices are concerned, the ones that are currently setting the trend are: Oculus Rift, GearVR and smartphones [17].

Another problem that arises in this type of applications is related to the management of computational resources that are used, because in some cases resources are wasted by running a simple application on a computer with great features or on the contrary running a complex application on a mobile device that has limited resources to run these applications. In this study, it is proposed to evaluate the different technologies that work with WebGL and WebVR in order to determine which type of application to use and in which technology.

In the following sections, different case studies will be mentioned in which several scenarios are considered, shaped by the different technologies described in the previous image. In addition, different computational resources are evaluated in order to identify the ideal scenario to work with these technologies.

3 Evaluation Structure

The structure of the evaluation process is detailed in Fig. 1, which has 4 consequential stages. The process begins with a methodological stage in which the way of evaluating, the case studies and the variables to be measured will be defined. For the Configuration stage, the entities that will intervene in the entire evaluation process are specified, as well as the indicators of each test. Next in the Test stage, the way in which the data coming from the entities defined in the Configuration stage is obtained and processed will be explained. Finally, the Results stage shows a comparative analysis based on the data obtained in the Test stage. It ends with conclusions about the use of WebGL and WebVR technologies for specific purposes detailed in each one. Next, a detailed explanation of each evaluation stage is made.

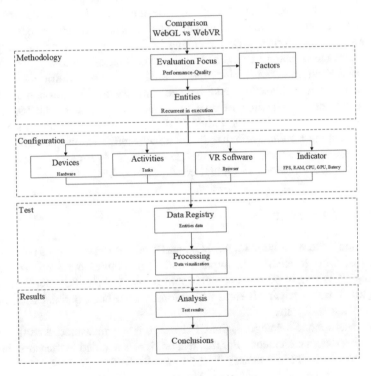

Fig. 1. Structure of evaluation process

In stage *(i) Methodology*, the way in which it will be evaluated is specified, in this case, a focus will be made on performance and quality, principles on which the usability of the system and the user experience are based [18]. In order to use this approach, it is necessary to define the factors that will intervene in the evaluation of the technologies and that will eventually become indicators of the experiment. The block entities specify the instances that will intervene in the experiment such as devices, activities, VR software and indicators.

Next, in stage *(ii) Configuration* the blocks are specified: Devices, Activities, VR Software and Indicators. In the device's block the hardware to be used is established, considering the most commonly used VR devices in the market and the current trend as a standard in the development of virtual reality [19]. They are divided into 2 groups: PC-Based and Mobile. In PC-Based, HTC VIVE and Oculus Rift devices are used; on mobile devices GearVR and a smartphone are used. In the Activities block, tasks are specified to saturate the system by increasing instances in the environment and their interaction between themselves. Two types of activities have been selected, the first activity is to drop boxes from the top to the ground in order for the system to calculate the collisions between the boxes, and with more instances, the stress level will rise. The second activity consists in instances of a particle system which saturates the system, while more particles and interactions between them are given. For the VR Software block, browsers that run in virtual reality will be used because the applications are hosted on web servers and their access will be through a URL inside virtual environments. In the indicator block the variables to be measured are: frames per second (FPS), RAM consumption in MB, percentage of CPU usage, percentage of GPU use and the percentage of battery consumed in the execution of the test.

In stage *(iii) Test*, the Data Registry blocks are in charge of acquiring and saving the data of each test in a classified and labeled form, while the processing block is responsible for the visualization of data by means of graphs. In the last stage *(iv) Results*, the graphs obtained in the previous stage are interpreted through of trend of values and grouping results, to finalize in the conclusions section to detail the average values of the measurements in each test that determine the best performance of WebGL and WebVR in many devices and initial conditions established.

4 Evaluation Design

The evaluation of technologies for WebGL and WebVR depends on several essential factors: CPU, GPU & RAM consumption and FPS (Frames per second) [22] at the runtime app. These are important computational resources that allow applications to be optimal [20]. For this paper different technologies have been defined for evaluation, using particles and objects.

For the smartphone's category, the CPU usage is not measured directly, due to it requiring other external elements. For this reason, it was decided to measure the battery level. Tests are designed in 2 phases: WebGL and WebVR with stress level variants in each execution of the same application. The variants of each run are: device, browser and activities (see Fig. 2).

In the devices section, consider desktop (PC needed to run the application) and mobile devices like: HTC VIVE & Oculus Rift and GearVR & Smartphone respectively. The activities contemplate the use of particle systems and game objects according to the saturation level of the test. In the particle system is considered a flamethrower system with 1000 particles and a lifetime of 10 s. In the object system, the use of 10 Unity cube Objects with simple textures for every 10% saturation level was developed.

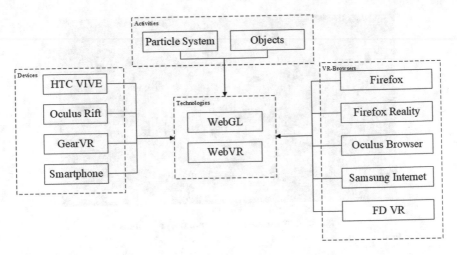

Fig. 2. Variants for evaluation

For the test purposes in the browser's component, the most used software and only those that run in VR environments were selected for each device. On the PC-based devices, Firefox used in HTC VIVE & Oculus Rift; Firefox Reality & Oculus Browser used in GearVR, and for smartphones Android & iOS, FD VR and VR Browser were selected respectively. For the development of application test the IDE Unity were used and to achieve the least impact on the factors that we want to measure the app only uses gameobjects and native resources (cubes, particle systems and lights) [21]. The target platform has been configured as WebGL, and for WebVR has been used with the WebVR unitypackage powered by Mozilla.

For both WebGL and WebVR executions, the app consists of an interface that allows the user to select the type of test between the particle and object options, as well as a slider that sets the level of stress that will be applied to the test (from 0% to 100%). In addition, it has a Start Test button that allows user to begin with the test. The Reset button allows the user to delete all the objects that are part of the test and enables the Start Test button to perform a new test. Finally, there is an indicator of computational device resources such as: FPS, CPU, RAM, VRAM (Video Random Access Memory), GPU. As shown in Fig. 3

The execution of each test allows the user to collect the data according to the following table. Through the combination of devices, technologies, activities and browsers, 28 tests are determined and each of them considers 5 cases of measurement: 20%, 40%, 60%, 80% and 100% corresponding to the level of stress applied in each activity. This methodology is determined by the devices target to the measure in which they are PC-based and mobile (see Table 1).

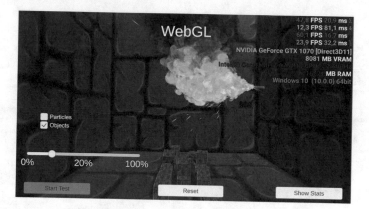

Fig. 3. Consumption of computing resources

Table 1. Data for evaluation

Devices	Browser	Activities	Technologies
-HTC VIVE -Oculus Rift	-Firefox	-Particles -Objects	-WebGL -WebVR
-GearVR	-Firefox Reality -Oculus Browser -Samsung Internet		
-Smartphone (iOS y Android)	-Full Dive VR -VR Browser		

5   Results and Discussion

The results obtained through the different case studies detailed in the previous chapter, provide information on the performance of the different VR technologies used. To simplify the 28 tests carried out in total, a compilation is presented in each category. The VR App is published on a webserver and its necessary to access through a link. The duration of each test is unique due to the loading and representation time of each browser.

5.1   PC

In this category an Alienware 17 R4 computer has been used with the following specifications: Intel Core i7-6700HQ @ 2.60 GHz Processor, 16 GB of RAM and a Nvidia GeForce-GTX 1070 graphics card with 8 GB of memory. For the first result, HTC VIVE headset (as a virtual reality device) and the Firefox browser have been used, running the test application in an online server, as shown in Fig. 4. It can be seen that the performance in FPS in the WebVR application is slightly higher as is the consumption of CPU and GPU resources, which indicates that, faced with a greater consumption of resources, there is no significant difference in performance in the FPS number.

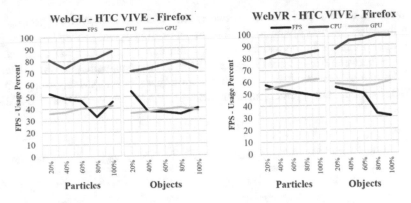

Fig. 4. HTC VIVE test results

For memory consumption VRAM is 512 MB for both technologies, but differs in 256 MB RAM for WebGL and 64 MB for WebVR.

The following result has been used with the Oculus Rift and Firefox browser, as can be seen in Fig. 5. The graphics behave similarly to the execution in the HTC VIVE headset which entails the same description. There are no relevant differences between the performance in FPS compared to the computational and graphic cost caused in the use of WebVR. For VRAM consumption it is the same for the two 512 MB technologies, but differs in 256 MB RAM for WebGL and 64 MB for WebVR.

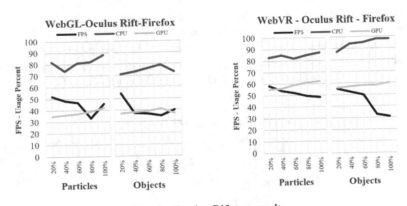

Fig. 5. Oculus Rift test results

5.2 Mobile

This section considers the use of a smartphone Samsung Galaxy S7 Edge with Android 8.0 OS and the following features: Exynos 8890 Octa 2.3 Ghz processor, 4 GB of RAM, Mali-T880 GPU and 3600mAh battery. In the first result, the GearVR glasses were used with the Oculus Browser, as can be seen in Fig. 6. The graphs have an improvement in FPS performance between the WebGL and WebVR technologies, giving the latter the best option for the execution of 3D content in web browsers inside virtual environments. In the battery section, a similar consumption has been recorded that ranges between 6%–8% for the execution of all the tests, which does not determine a competitive advantage between both technologies. For RAM consumption it is 512 MB for both, but it differs in 256 MB of VRAM for WebGL and 64 MB for WebVR.

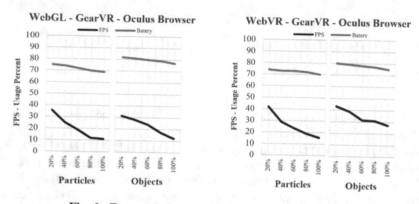

Fig. 6. Test results in GearVR running in OculusBrowser

In the second result we have used the Firefox Reality browser designed precisely to run remote applications in WebVR inside virtual environments. It should be mentioned that the application in WebGL was not executed by the browser, therefore there are no results as shown in Fig. 7. WebVR shows a lower performance than that achieved in the Oculus Browser, which indicates that the browser performs the remote application optimally. The consumption of RAM is 512 MB and for VRAM is 64 MB.

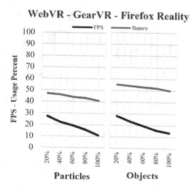

Fig. 7. Test results in GearVR running on Firefox Reality

In the third result, the Cardboard glasses were used in conjunction with the FullDive VR navigator, resulting in lower performance in FPS performance even with WebVR, as shown in Fig. 8. This determines that the best execution in the testing context has been performed in the Oculus Browser with the GearVR glasses. For the battery level, a similar value of consumption is observed in the execution of the tests of around 7% and 9%, which differs intimately in comparison to the energy consumed in the tests carried out with the GearVR glasses. For RAM consumption it is 512 MB for both technologies, but it differs in VRAM, 256 MB for WebGL and 64 MB for WebVR.

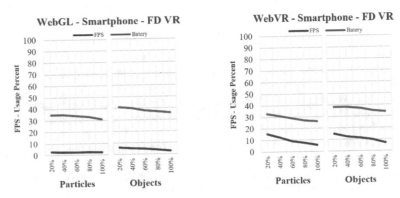

Fig. 8. Test results in Gear VR running on Firefox Reality

For iOS smartphones, no results have been registered because no existing browser has managed to run the remote application in either WebGL or WebVR.

6   Conclusions

The main objective of this work is to evaluate the performance of the devices and applications mentioned, for this purpose 28 experiments have been developed with the same test approach, in which the measurement of indicators such as: FPS, RAM, VRAM, CPU, GPU and battery have been recorded. The results vary slightly in resource consumption for PC platforms, and a marked difference in FPS performance for mobile devices (GearVR and Smartphones) can be seen.

Based on the tests carried out, we affirm that: WebVR technology performs efficiently on the mobile system due to lower VRAM memory consumption and a higher level of stable SPF compared to the same execution in a WebGL environment. Whereas WebGL performs stably but not more efficiently than WebVR based on the results obtained in the tests performed in this work.

From the mobile approach GearVR was identified as the technology that performs best executing the test. WebVR had the best performance in FPS on average, which determines an efficient consumption of computing resources in mobile devices, whose purpose is the efficiency in the execution of software.

From the PC point of view for HTC VIVE and Oculus Rift similar results have been seen in FPS performance on average. A slight difference in computational resource consumption between WebGL and WebVR determines that the use of these technolo-gies will depend on the application approach you plan to develop.

Finally, it is important to mention that the proposed evaluation was made by the need of the research group, to determine which devices and technologies are optimal for the development of applications in WebGL and WebVR. Future work is intended to evaluate the performance of the battery of the different devices, focused on factors that affect their proper functioning.

References

1. Maisto, M., Pacchierotti, C., Chinello, F., Salvietti, G., De Luca, A., Prattichizzo, D.: Evaluation of wearable haptic systems for the fingers in augmented reality applications. IEEE Trans. Haptics 10(4), 511–522 (2017)
2. Slater, M., Wilbur, S.: A framework for immersive virtual environments (FIVE): Speculations on the role of presence in virtual environments. Presence Teleoperators Virtual Environ. 6, 603–616 (1997)
3. Carrozzino, M., Bruno, N., Bergamasco, M.: Designing interaction metaphors for Web3D cultural dissemination. J. Cult. Herit. 14(2), 146–155 (2013)
4. Leung, C., Salga, A.: Enabling WebGL. In: Proceedings of the 19th International Conference on World Wide Web - WWW 2010, p. 1369 (2010)
5. Chen, B., Xu, Z.: A framework for browser-based Multiplayer Online Games using WebGL and WebSocket. In: 2011 International Conference on Multimedia Technology, pp. 471–474 (2011)
6. Mobeen, M.M., Feng, L.: High-performance volume rendering on the ubiquitous WebGL platform. In: 2012 IEEE 14th International Conference on High Performance Computing and Communication and 2012 IEEE 9th International Conference on Embedded Software and Systems, p. 381 (2012)
7. Tinkercad-Team, Tinkercad|Create 3D digital designs with online CAD. https://www.tinkercad.com/. Accessed: 19 Jul 2019
8. Congote, J., Segura, A., Kabongo, L., Moreno, A., Posada, J., Ruiz, O.: Interactive visualization of volumetric data with WebGL in real-time. In: Proceedings of the 16th International Conference on 3D Web Technology - Web3D 2011, p. 137 (2011)
9. Kopeć, A., Bała, J., Pięta, A.: WebGL based visualisation and analysis of stratigraphic data for the purposes of the mining industry. Procedia Comput. Sci. 51, 2869–2877 (2015)
10. Lv, Z., Yin, T., Han, Y., Chen, Y., Chen, G.: WebVR-web virtual reality engine based on P2P network (2011)
11. Fominykh, M., Prasolova-Førland, E., Morozov, M., Smorkalov, A., Molka-Danielsen, J.: Increasing immersiveness into a 3D virtual world: motion-tracking and natural navigation in vAcademia. IERI Procedia 7, 35–41 (2014)
12. Neelakantam, S., Pant, T.: Introduction to VR and WebVR. In: Learning Web-based Virtual Reality, pp. 1–4. Apress, Berkeley (2017)
13. Letic, M., Nenadic, K., Nikolic, L.: Real-time map projection in virtual reality using WebVR. In: 2018 41st International Convention on Information and Communication Technology, Electronics and Microelectronics (MIPRO), pp. 1439–1443 (2018)

14. Butcher, P.W.S., Roberts, J.C., Ritsos, P.D.: Immersive Analytics with WebVR and Google Cardboard. In: Posters of IEEE VIS, pp. 30–32 (2016)
15. Lee, V.W., et al.: Debunking the 100X GPU vs. CPU myth. ACM SIGARCH Comput. Archit. News **38**(3), 451 (2010)
16. Smith, S.P., Trenholme, D.: Rapid prototyping a virtual fire drill environment using computer game technology. Fire Saf. J. **44**(4), 559–569 (2009)
17. Donalek, C., et al.: Immersive and collaborative data visualization using virtual reality platforms, October 2014
18. Vermeeren, A.P.O.S., Law, E.L.-C., Roto, V., Obrist, M., Hoonhout, J., Väänänen-Vainio-Mattila, K.: User experience evaluation methods. In: Proceedings of the 6th Nordic Conference on Human-Computer Interaction Extending Boundaries - NordiCHI 2010, p. 521 (2010)
19. Gonçalves, Y.A., Boas, V.: Overview of Virtual Reality Technologies. In: Interactive Multimedia Conference, pp. 20–26 (2013)
20. Asano, S., Maruyama, T., Yamaguchi, Y.: Performance comparison of FPGA, GPU and CPU in image processing, In: 2009 International Conference on Field Programmable Logic and Applications, pp. 126–131 (2009)
21. Yang, K., Jie, J., Haihui, S.: Study on the virtual natural landscape walkthrough by using Unity 3D. In: 2011 IEEE International Symposium on VR Innovation, pp. 235–238 (2011)
22. Lugrin, J.L., Cavazza, M., Charles, F., Le Renard, M., Freeman, J., Lessiter, J.: Immersive FPS games: user experience and performance. In Proceedings of the 2013 ACM International Workshop on Immersive Media Experiences, October 2013, pp. 7–12. ACM (2013)

IFOC: Intensity Fitting on Overlapping Cover for Image Segmentation

Xue Shi[✉] and Chunming Li

University of Electronic Science and Technology of China (UESTC), Chengdu, China
xueshi00@mail.com

Abstract. Region-based image segmentation methods often require a global statistical description of the image intensities in the entire foreground and background, which however is in general not available for real world images due to the complicated intensity variation within the regions of interest. In this paper, we propose a foreground-background segmentation algorithm for images with intensity inhomogeneity in a level set framework, which exploits simple distribution of local image intensities. We assume that the intensities of the foreground and background within a small enough neighborhood are separable and can be well approximated by two constants. We call such a neighborhood an intensity separable neighborhood (ISN). Given a set of overlapping ISNs that form a cover of the entire image domain or a region of interest, we formulate image segmentation as a problem of seeking for an optimal level set function that represents the foreground and background with its positive and negative sign, and a pair of constants that approximate the local foreground and background intensities within the ISNs. This formulation is a significant extension and improvement of our previous work. The main contributions in this paper include: (1) We eliminate an intrinsic drawback in our previous work that the fitting functions are not well defined for points far away from the zero level set, which causes unstable performance of segmentation; (2) The new algorithm is more efficient than our previous algorithm due to the sparse placement of the ISNs.

Keywords: Level set · Overlapping neighborhoods · Image segmentation · Intensity inhomogeneity

1 Introduction

Image segmentation is a well-studied area which plays an increasingly important role in quantitatively analyzing the information in medical imaging applications. In recently years, segmentation algorithms in level set framework have attracted much attention. Comparing with other segmentation methods [7], level

C. Li—This work is supported by NSFC (Grant numbers G0561671135, G0591630311, M0501020111531005). The authors thank the anonymous reviewers for their valuable comments.

G. Bebis et al. (Eds.): ISVC 2019, LNCS 11845, pp. 576–585, 2019.
https://doi.org/10.1007/978-3-030-33723-0_47

set method can achieve sub-pixel accuracy of the object boundaries, and automatically handled topological changes, and incorporate various prior knowledge.

Yang *et al.* [11] embed a Markov random field (MRF) energy function to the conventional level set energy function to enhance the robustness against noise, they explored algebraic multigrid (AMG) and sparse field method (SFM) to increase the time step and reduce the computational domain. Wu *et al.* [10] demonstrated that the unique global minimized value of the energy function is within the interval $[-1,1]$ of any image, so they proposed a level set formulation with a strict convex energy function. Swierczynski *et al.* [9] developed a mathematical formulation to jointly segment and register based on a level set formulation.

In [6], Ngo *et al.* proposed level set method combining with deep learning for the automated segmentation of the left ventricle. Combination of these methods brings together the advantages of both approaches, requiring small training sets and producing precise segmentation results. However, this method do not use in images with intensity inhomogeneities.

In real-world images, intensity inhomogeneity is common, which arising from the imperfections of imaging acquisition processing and unavoidably leads to many difficulties and challenge in image processing and computer vision. So far numerous level set algorithms have been proposed to segment images with intensity inhomogeneity.

In [12], inhomogeneous objects are modeled as Gaussian distributions of different means and variances, where the original image is mapped to another domain using a sliding window to defined a maximum likelihood energy function. A level set method based on local approximation of Taylor expansion proposed by Min *et al.* [5] to solve the nonconvex optimization problem in the context of intensity inhomogeneity. In this method, the local statistical information and the variation degree information of intensity inhomogeneity are combined into the proposed model. This method can segment intensity inhomogeneity regions, unlike other linear approximation method. However, high computational cost occurred because of the complicated local information in the formulation.

In this paper, we propose a novel foreground-background segmentation algorithm for images with intensity inhomogeneity in a level set framework. Our method is based on a number of overlapping neighborhoods that form a cover of the image domain. The basic idea is to introduce a Intensity Fitting on Overlapping Cover (IFOC) model in a variational formulation, so that the segmentation result can be achieved by seeking for an optimal level set function. Moreover, it is not sensitive to initialization in the new proposed method. Compared with the previous work [1,3], we demonstrate that our segmentation method is competitive and presents better results both in terms of effectiveness and efficiency.

2   Intensity Fitting on Overlapping Cover

In [2], Li *et al.* proposed a local binary fitting (LBF) model for image segmentation based on images with intensity inhomogeneity. The LBF model is based on

578 X. Shi and C. Li

the assumption that the image intensities on the two sides of the object boundary can be locally approximated by two constants. More specifically, Li *et al.* consider the neighborhood $\mathcal{O}_y$ for every point y in the image domain Ω. If $\mathcal{O}_y$ is divided by the object boundary into two parts, then the image intensities within the two parts can be approximated by two constants $f_1(\mathbf{y})$ and $f_2(\mathbf{y})$. Therefore, they define the following local binary fitting energy

$$E_y(\phi, f_1, f_2) = \lambda_1 \int K(\mathbf{x} - \mathbf{y})|I(\mathbf{x}) - f_1(\mathbf{y})|^2 H(\phi(\mathbf{x}))d\mathbf{x}$$

$$+\lambda_2 \int K(\mathbf{x} - \mathbf{y})|I(\mathbf{x}) - f_2(\mathbf{y})|^2 (1 - H(\phi(\mathbf{x})))d\mathbf{x} \qquad (1)$$

where ϕ is the level set function. H is the Heaviside function. Thus, image segmentation is formulated as a problem of seeking for optional level set function ϕ and the fitting functions $f_1(\mathbf{y})$ and $f_2(\mathbf{y})$, such that the local binary fitting energy $E_y(\phi, f_1, f_2)$ is minimized for every neighborhood $\mathcal{O}_y$ for all $\mathbf{y}$ in Ω. This can be achieved by minimizing the integration of the LBF energy $E_y(\phi, f_1, f_2)$ with respect to the neighborhood center $\mathbf{y}$ over the entire image domain Ω. Therefore, a global energy $F(\phi, f_1, f_2)$ is defined as

$$F(\phi, f_1, f_2) = \int E_y(\phi, f_1(\mathbf{y}), f_2(\mathbf{y}))d\mathbf{y} \qquad (2)$$

The choice of the kernel function K is flexible. In this paper, it is defined by

$$K(\mathbf{u}) = \begin{cases} a, \, for \, |\mathbf{u}| \leq r \\ 0, \, otherwise \end{cases} \qquad (3)$$

where a is a positive constant such that $\int K(\mathbf{u}) = 1$, and r is the radius of the neighborhood $\mathcal{O}_{u,r}$. This kernel function K is a truncated uniform function.

Let ϕ be a level set function defined on the image domain Ω. We define

$$\Omega_+ = \{\mathbf{x} : \phi(\mathbf{x}) > 0\}$$
$$\Omega_- = \{\mathbf{x} : \phi(\mathbf{x}) < 0\} \qquad (4)$$

We consider an image with a foreground and a background, denoted by Ω_f and Ω_b, respectively. Our goal is to find a level set function ϕ such that the regions Ω_+ and Ω_- match the foreground Ω_f and background Ω_b, respectively. To achieve this goal, we formulate our method as following.

For a point $u \in \Omega$, we consider the image intensities $I(\mathbf{x})$ in a neighborhood

$$\mathcal{O}_{u,r} = \{\mathbf{x} : |\mathbf{x} - u| < r\} \qquad (5)$$

which includes a part of foreground and background. We assume that the intensities $\Omega_f \cap \mathcal{O}_{u,r}$ and $\Omega_b \cap \mathcal{O}_{u,r}$ are separable and can be well approximated by the constants $f_1(u)$ and $f_2(u)$, respectively. We call such a neighborhood an intensity separable neighborhood (ISN), and u is the ISN center.

Due to the intensity inhomogeneity in the image, it does not make sense to approximate the intensities in Ω_b and Ω_f by two global constants c_1 and c_2, respectively. However, the local intensities $I(\mathbf{x})$ for $\mathbf{x}$ in $\mathcal{O}_{u,r} \cap \Omega_f$ and $\mathcal{O}_{u,r} \cap \Omega_b$ can be well approximated by the constants, denoted by $f_1(u)$ and $f_2(u)$, respectively.

The ISN center can be placed in different ways. In this paper, the ISN centers are only placed near the zero level set of the level set function, such that the ISN is always divided by the zero level set into two parts. Thus, $f_1(u)$ and $f_2(u)$ are defined as the constants that approximate the image intensities in the two parts of the ISN divided by the zero level set. Note that, in RSF model in [3], the fitting functions $f_1(u)$ and $f_2(u)$ are not well defined for u far away from the zero level set, which does not pass through the ISN centered at u. Therefore, the fitting functions f_1 and f_2 are not well defined at such location. This is a theoretical drawback of RSF model, which in fact cause some undesirable segmentation results as shown in Figs. 3 and 4, due to the not-well-defined fitting functions f_1 and f_2 in RSF model. In this paper, we eliminate this drawback by placing the ISN centers only near the zero level set, such that the ISN is always divided by the zero level set into two parts, as shown in Fig. 1.

Given a set of ISNs with centers at u_k, $k = 1, \cdots, N$, which form an overlapping cover of the entire image domain or a region of interest, both denoted by Ω. For each ISN centered at $u_k \in \Omega$, we define the following local intensity fitting energy:

$$
\begin{aligned}
E_{u_k}&(\phi, f_1(u_k), f_2(u_k)) \\
&= \lambda_1 \int_{\Omega_+} K(\mathbf{x} - u_k)|I(x) - f_1(u_k)|^2 dx \\
&\quad + \lambda_2 \int_{\Omega_-} K(\mathbf{x} - u_k)|I(x) - f_2(u_k)|^2 dx
\end{aligned}
\tag{6}
$$

It can be seen that the above defined local intensity fitting energy E_{u_k} is minimized when the zero level set of ϕ matches the interface between the foreground Ω_f and background Ω_b, as in the case shown in Fig. 1(b), and the constants $f_1(u_k)$ and $f_2(u_k)$ best approximate the image intensities $I(x)$ in $\Omega_+ \cap \mathcal{O}_{u_k,r}$ and $\Omega_- \cap \mathcal{O}_{u_k,r}$, respectively.

$$
E(\phi, f_1, f_2) = \sum_{k=1}^{N} E_{u_k}(\phi, f_1(u_k), f_2(u_k))
\tag{7}
$$

In level set methods [8], a contour $\phi \subset \Omega$ is represented by the zero level set of a Lipschitz function $\phi : \Omega \to R$, which is called a level set function. In this paper, we let the level set function ϕ take positive and negative values outside and inside the contour $\mathcal{C}$, respectively. Let H be the Heaviside function, then the energy functional $E_{u_k}(\phi, f_1(u_k), f_2(u_k))$ can be expressed as

$$E_{u_k}(\phi, f_1(u_k), f_2(u_k))$$

$$= \sum_{i=1}^{2} \lambda_i \int K_\sigma(\mathbf{x} - u_k)|I(\mathbf{x}) - f_i(u_k)|^2 M_i(\phi(\mathbf{x}))d\mathbf{x}$$

$$+ \nu \int |\nabla H(\phi(\mathbf{x}))|d\mathbf{x} \tag{8}$$

where $M_1(\phi) = H(\phi)$ and $M_2(\phi) = 1 - H(\phi)$. Thus, the energy E in (7) can be written as following,

$$E(\phi, f_1, f_2) = \sum_{k=1}^{N} E_{u_k}(\phi, f_1, f_2) \tag{9}$$

thus,

$$E(\phi, f_1, f_2)$$

$$= \sum_{i=1}^{2} \sum_{k=1}^{N} \lambda_i \left(\int K_\sigma(\mathbf{x} - u_k)|I(\mathbf{x}) - f_i(u_k)|^2 M_i(\phi(\mathbf{x})))d\mathbf{x} \right.$$

$$+ \nu \int |\nabla H(\phi(\mathbf{x}))|d\mathbf{x} \tag{10}$$

where the last term $\int |\nabla H(\phi()\mathbf{x})|d\mathbf{x}$ computes the length of the zero level contour of ϕ. The length of the zero level contour can be equivalently expressed as the integral $\int \delta(\phi)|\nabla \phi|d\mathbf{x}$ with the Dirac delta function ϕ.

To preserve the regularity of the level set function ϕ, which is necessary for accurate computation and stable level set evolution, we introduce a level set regularization term in our variation level set formulation. As proposed in Li's article [4], we define the level set regularization term as

$$\mathcal{P}(\phi) = \int \frac{1}{2}(|\nabla \phi(\mathbf{x})| - 1)^2 d\mathbf{x} \tag{11}$$

which characterizes the deviation of the function ϕ from a signed distance function. Therefore, we propose to minimize the energy functional

$$\mathcal{F}(\phi, f_1, f_2) = E(\phi, f_1, f_2) + \mu \mathcal{P}(\phi) \tag{12}$$

where μ is a positive constant.

We minimize the energy functional $\mathcal{F}(\phi, f_1, f_2)$ with respect to ϕ using the standard gradient descent method by solving the *gradient flow equation* as follows:

$$\frac{\partial \phi}{\partial t} = - \delta(\phi)(\lambda_1 e_1 - \lambda_2 e_2) + \nu \delta(\phi)\text{div}(\frac{\nabla \phi}{|\nabla \phi|})$$

$$+ \mu(\nabla^2 \phi - \text{div}(\frac{\nabla \phi}{|\nabla \phi|})) \tag{13}$$

where δ is the Dirac delta function. In numerical implementation, the Dirac delta function is replaced by a smooth approximation as in [3], e_1 and e_2 are the functions

$$e_i(\mathbf{x}) = \sum_{k=1}^{N} \int K_\sigma(\mathbf{x} - u_k)|I(\mathbf{x}) - f_i(u_k)|^2 d\mathbf{x}, \quad i = 1, 2 \tag{14}$$

where f_1 and f_2 are given by follows,

$$f_1(\mathbf{x}) = \frac{\int K_\sigma(\mathbf{x} - u_k)I(\mathbf{x})H(\phi(\mathbf{x}))d\mathbf{x}}{\int K_\sigma(\mathbf{x} - u_k)H(\phi(\mathbf{x}))d\mathbf{x}} \tag{15}$$

$$f_2(\mathbf{x}) = \frac{\int K_\sigma(\mathbf{x} - u_k)I(\mathbf{x})(1 - H(\phi(\mathbf{x})))d\mathbf{x}}{\int K_\sigma(\mathbf{x} - u_k)(1 - H(\phi(\mathbf{x})))d\mathbf{x}} \tag{16}$$

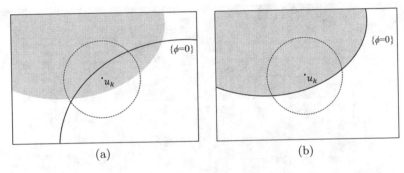

(a)   (b)

Fig. 1. Two situations of the location of the zero level set (solid dark line) and the foreground (shaded region) and background (white region). (a) The zero level set does not match the interface between foreground and background. (b) The zero level set match the interface between foreground and background.

3   Experiment Results

Our method has been validated on the real vessel images and the data set for the Medical Image Computing and Computer Assisted Intervention (MICCAI) 2009 grand challenge on cardiac segmentation, respectively. Contour accuracies in terms of Dice Similarity Coefficient (DSC) are used to quantitatively evaluate the accuracy of our method. DSC is defined as

$$DSC = \frac{2 \times |R_1 \cap R_2|}{|R_1| + |R_2|} \tag{17}$$

where $|\cdot|$ is the area of a region, R_1 is the region obtained from a segmentation algorithm, and R_2 is a reference region. In the following experimental results, we use a segmented region of a segmentation algorithm as the reference region R_2 to compute its similarity with other segmentation results. It can be easily seen that a higher value of DSC indicates a better performance. The parameters in this paper are set as follows: σ is set to 5.0 , ϵ is set to 1.0 , μ is set to 1.0. Others, λ_1, λ_2, ν, and the time step $\triangle t$ are set to 1.0, 1.5, 0.004, 0.1, respectively.

The proposed IFOC algorithm has been tested on the number of images of different modalities. In this section, we show some examples mainly of medical images. For examples, Fig. 2 shows the segmentation results of IFOC on 8 test images: the real image of a T-shaped object suffers from non-uniform illumination; the synthetic image, two X-ray images of vessels are typical images with intensity inhomogeneity, and the second row are cardiac different modality images (including CT and MR). The final segmentation results in Fig. 2 show that the proposed IFOC method can achieve desirable results for all images with intensity inhomogeneities.

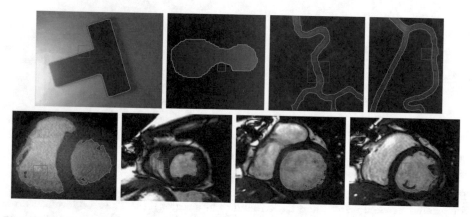

Fig. 2. Performs of our new method for different images. The initial contours (green contours) and final segmentation results (red contours) are shown in every image. (Color figure online)

With the DSC metric, we can quantitatively evaluate the performance of our method with different initializations. We applied IFOC to X-ray vessel image (Fig. 3) and cardiac magnetic resonance (MR) image (Fig. 4) with 20 different initializations of the contour. Figures 3 and 4 demonstrate the robustness of proposed method IFOC to initialization. In Fig. 3, we show three of the 20 initial contours (green contours) and corresponding results (red contours). For comparison, we also applied RSF model in [3] to these images with the same initializations. It can be seen that despite the significant difference in the locations of initial contours, the proposed method precisely produces the same results, all accurately capturing the object boundaries, while the RSF model is sensitive to initialization. In this paper, we are not able to quantitatively evaluate the

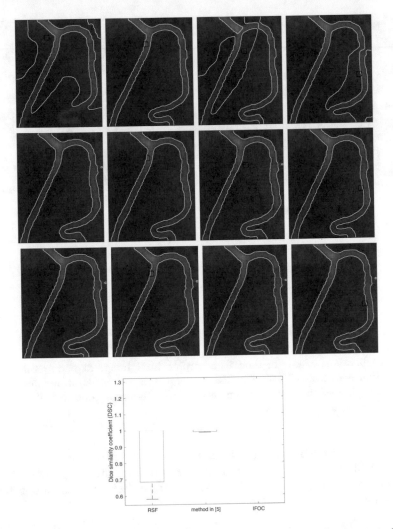

Fig. 3. Robustness of our method to contour initializations is demonstrated by its results for a X-ray vessel image with different initial contours comparing with RSF model. Row 1: Segmentation result of RSF model; Row 2: Segmentation result of our new method; Row 3: Comparison of two methods in term of accuracy measured with DSC.(Color figure online)

segmentation accuracy without ground truth obtained by manual segmentation. By comparing the IFOC with the RSF [3], we observed that the results of two methods are similar if the initial contours are placed appropriately. However, we found that the proposed IFOC algorithm is significantly less sensitive to contour initialization than RSF model. This can be quantitatively verified by computing the DSC between the segmentation results for 19 initializations with the 20th initialization as a reference. The boxplots in Figs. 3 and 4 show that the 19 DSC

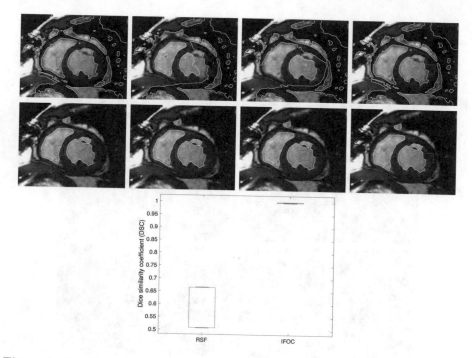

Fig. 4. Applications of our method to a cardiac MRI image at end-systole. Row 1: Segmentation result of RSF model; Row 2: Segmentation result of our new method; Row 3: Variation of the segmentation results from different contour initialization in terms of Dice similarity coefficient.

values of IFOC segmentation results are all very close to 1, while the 19 DSC values of RSF segmentation results significantly vary in a considerable large range. This experiment quantitatively demonstrate that IFOC is more robust to initialization.

4   Conclusions

In this paper, we introduce a novel region-based image segmentation method in a level set framework, which is not only effective and efficient when segment images with intensity inhomogeneity, but also has ideal performance in different initializations. The new algorithm IFOC reduce the dependence on initialization, significantly improve the robustness. Due to the sparse placement of the ISNs, our new algorithm is efficient than our previous work and eliminate an intrinsic drawback in our previous work. Experimental results have demonstrated the advantages of our new method over other methods in terms of accuracy, efficiency, and robustness.

References

1. Li, C., Huang, R., Ding, Z., Gatenby, J., Metaxas, D., Gore, J.: A level set method for image segmentation in the presence of intensity inhomogeneities with application to MRI. IEEE Trans. Image Process. **20**(7), 2007 (2011)
2. Li, C., Kao, C., Gore, J., Ding, Z.: Implicit active contours driven by local binary fitting energy. In: Proceedings of IEEE Conference on Computer Vision and Pattern Recognition (CVPR), pp. 1–7. IEEE Computer Society, Washington (2007)
3. Li, C., Kao, C., Gore, J., Ding, Z.: Minimization of region-scalable fitting energy for image segmentation. IEEE Trans. Image Process. **17**(10), 1940 (2008)
4. Li, C., Xu, C., Gui, C., Fox, M.: Level set evolution without re-initialization: a new variational formulation. In: IEEE Computer Society Conference on Computer Vision and Pattern Recognition, CVPR 2005, vol. 1, pp. 430–436. IEEE (2005)
5. Min, H., Jia, W., Zhao, Y., Zuo, W., Ling, H., Luo, Y.: Late: a level set method based on local approximation of Taylor expansion for segmenting intensity inhomogeneous images. IEEE Trans. Image Process. **27**(10), 5016–5031 (2018)
6. Ngo, T.A., Lu, Z., Carneiro, G.: Combining deep learning and level set for the automated segmentation of the left ventricle of the heart from cardiac cine magnetic resonance. Med. Image Anal. **35**, 159–171 (2017)
7. Oktay, O., et al.: Anatomically constrained neural networks (ACNNS): application to cardiac image enhancement and segmentation. IEEE Trans. Med. Imaging **37**(2), 384–395 (2018)
8. Osher, S., Sethian, J.: Fronts propagating with curvature-dependent speed: algorithms based on Hamilton-Jacobi formulations. J. Comput. Phys. **79**(1), 12–49 (1988)
9. Swierczynski, P., Papież, B., Schnabel, J., Macdonald, C.: A level-set approach to joint image segmentation and registration with application to CT lung imaging. Comput. Med. Imaging Graph. **65**, 58–68 (2018)
10. Wu, Y., He, C.: A convex variational level set model for image segmentation. Sign. Process. **106**, 123–133 (2015)
11. Yang, X., Gao, X., Tao, D., Li, X., Li, J.: An efficient MRF embedded level set method for image segmentation. IEEE Trans. Image Process. **24**(1), 9–21 (2015)
12. Zhang, K., Zhang, L., Lam, K., Zhang, D.: A level set approach to image segmentation with intensity inhomogeneity. IEEE Trans. Cybern. **46**(2), 546–557 (2016)

Author Index

Printed in the United States
By Bookmasters